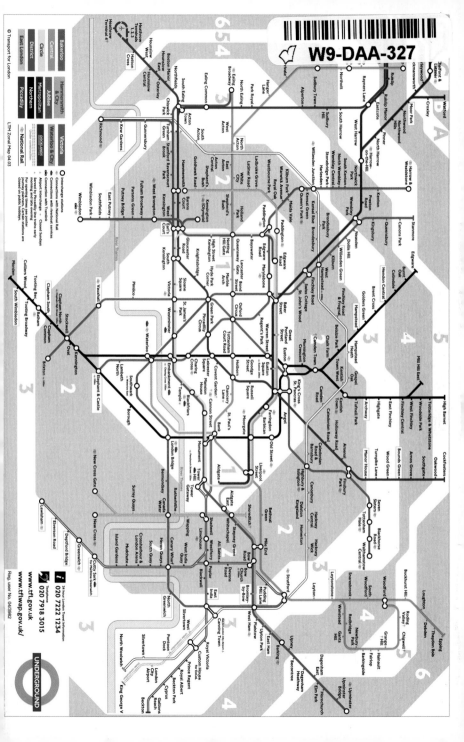

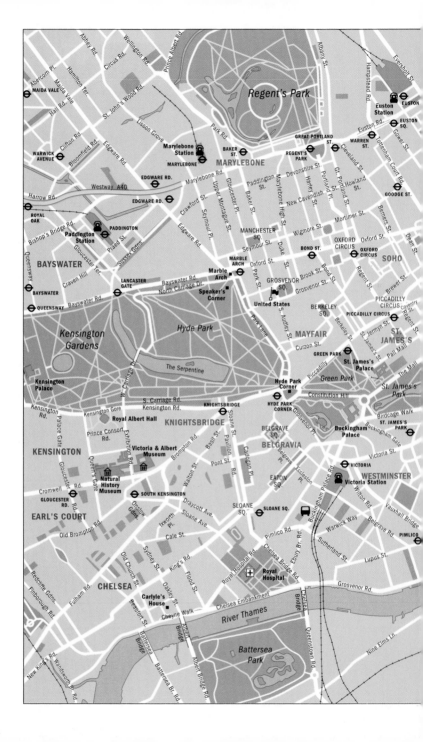

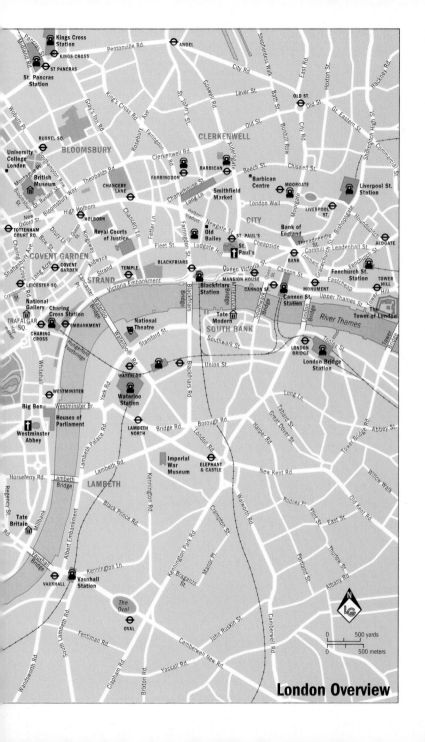

London Overview

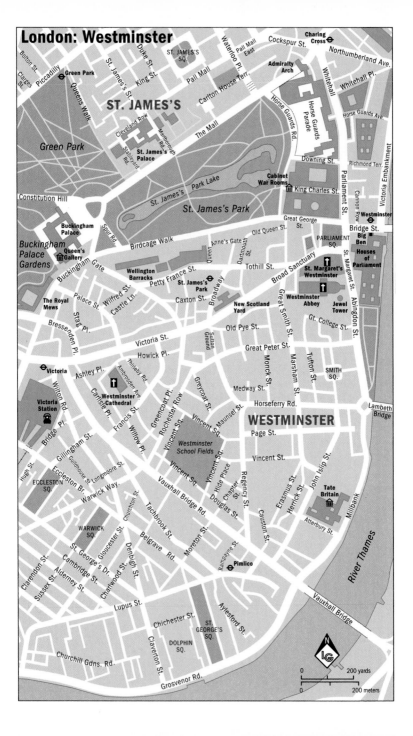

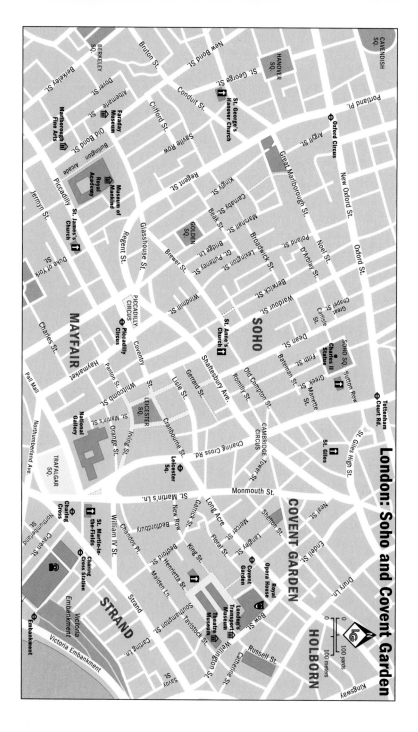
London: Soho and Covent Garden

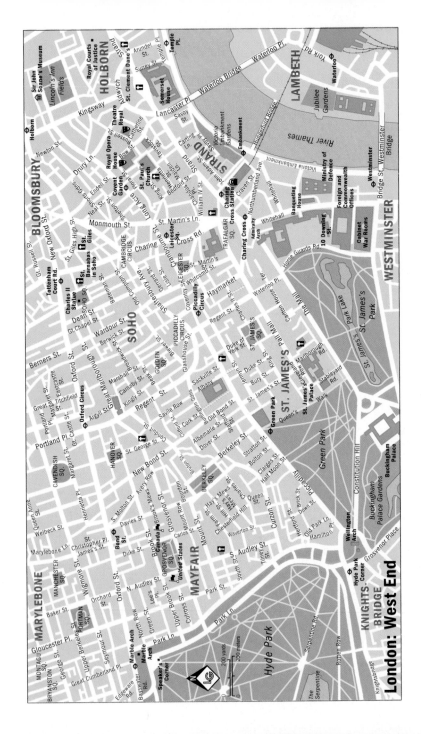

London: West End

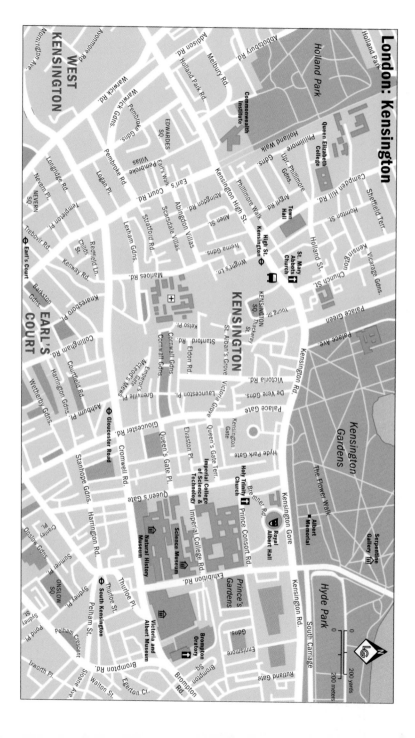

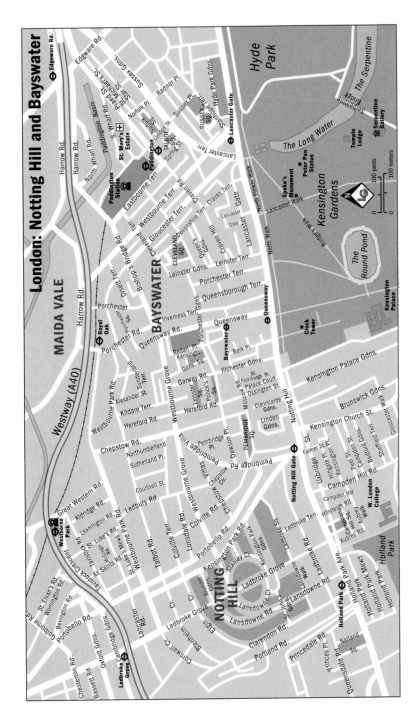

London: Notting Hill and Bayswater

LET'S GO

■ THE RESOURCE FOR THE INDEPENDENT TRAVELER

"The guides are aimed not only at young budget travelers but at the indepedent traveler; a sort of streetwise cookbook for traveling alone."

—*The New York Times*

"Unbeatable; good sight-seeing advice; up-to-date info on restaurants, hotels, and inns; a commitment to money-saving travel; and a wry style that brightens nearly every page."

—*The Washington Post*

"Lighthearted and sophisticated, informative and fun to read. [Let's Go] helps the novice traveler navigate like a knowledgeable old hand."

—*Atlanta Journal-Constitution*

"A world-wise traveling companion—always ready with friendly advice and helpful hints, all sprinkled with a bit of wit."

—*The Philadelphia Inquirer*

■ THE BEST TRAVEL BARGAINS IN YOUR PRICE RANGE

"All the dirt, dirt cheap."

—*People*

"Anything you need to know about budget traveling is detailed in this book."

—*The Chicago Sun-Times*

"Let's Go follows the creed that you don't have to toss your life's savings to the wind to travel—unless you want to."

—*The Salt Lake Tribune*

■ REAL ADVICE FOR REAL EXPERIENCES

"The writers seem to have experienced every rooster-packed bus and lunar-surfaced mattress about which they write."

—*The New York Times*

"A guide should tell you what to expect from a destination. Here Let's Go shines."

—*The Chicago Tribune*

"[Let's Go's] devoted updaters really walk the walk (and thumb the ride, and trek the trail). Learn how to fish, haggle, find work—anywhere."

—*Food & Wine*

LET'S GO PUBLICATIONS

TRAVEL GUIDES

Alaska 1st edition **NEW TITLE**
Australia 2004
Austria & Switzerland 2004
Brazil 1st edition **NEW TITLE**
Britain & Ireland 2004
California 2004
Central America 8th edition
Chile 1st edition
China 4th edition
Costa Rica 1st edition
Eastern Europe 2004
Egypt 2nd edition
Europe 2004
France 2004
Germany 2004
Greece 2004
Hawaii 2004
India & Nepal 8th edition
Ireland 2004
Israel 4th edition
Italy 2004
Japan 1st edition **NEW TITLE**
Mexico 20th edition
Middle East 4th edition
New Zealand 6th edition
Pacific Northwest 1st edition **NEW TITLE**
Peru, Ecuador & Bolivia 3rd edition
Puerto Rico 1st edition **NEW TITLE**
South Africa 5th edition
Southeast Asia 8th edition
Southwest USA 3rd edition
Spain & Portugal 2004
Thailand 1st edition
Turkey 5th edition
USA 2004
Western Europe 2004

CITY GUIDES

Amsterdam 3rd edition
Barcelona 3rd edition
Boston 4th edition
London 2004
New York City 2004
Paris 2004
Rome 12th edition
San Francisco 4th edition
Washington, D.C. 13th edition

MAP GUIDES

Amsterdam
Berlin
Boston
Chicago
Dublin
Florence
Hong Kong
London
Los Angeles
Madrid
New Orleans
New York City
Paris
Prague
Rome
San Francisco
Seattle
Sydney
Venice
Washington, D.C.

COMING SOON:
Road Trip USA

LONDON

2004

ANDREW NOBLE SODROSKI EDITOR
MIRANDA LASH ASSOCIATE EDITOR

RESEARCHER-WRITERS
NICOLE CLIFFE
SHELLEY CHEUNG
TIFFANY HSIEH

JENNIFER O'BRIEN MANAGING EDITOR
CHRISTINE PETERSON MAP EDITOR

ST. MARTIN'S PRESS ⚓ NEW YORK

HELPING LET'S GO If you want to share your discoveries, suggestions, or corrections, please drop us a line. We read every piece of correspondence, whether a postcard, a 10-page email, or a coconut. **Address mail to:**

> **Let's Go: London**
> **67 Mount Auburn Street**
> **Cambridge, MA 02138**
> **USA**

Visit Let's Go at **http://www.letsgo.com,** or send email to:

> **feedback@letsgo.com**
> **Subject: "Let's Go: London"**

In addition to the invaluable travel advice our readers share with us, many are kind enough to offer their services as researchers or editors. Unfortunately, our charter enables us to employ only currently enrolled Harvard students.

ABOUT LET'S GO

GUIDES FOR THE INDEPENDENT TRAVELER

Budget travel is more than a vacation. At *Let's Go*, we see every trip as the chance of a lifetime. If your dream is to grab a knapsack and a machete and forge through the jungles of Brazil, we can take you there. Or, if you'd rather enjoy the Riviera sun at a beachside cafe, we'll set you a table. If you know what you're doing, you can have any experience you want—whether it's camping among lions or sampling Tuscan desserts—without maxing out your credit card. We'll show you just how far your coins can go, and prove that the greatest limitation on your adventure is not your wallet, but your imagination. That said, we understand that you may want the occasional indulgence after a week of hostels and kebab stands, so we've added "Big Splurges" to let you know which establishments are worth those extra euros, as well as price ranges to help you quickly determine whether an accommodation or restaurant will break the bank. While we may have diversified, our emphasis will always be on finding the best values for your budget, giving you all the info you need to spend six days in London or six months in Tasmania.

BEYOND THE TOURIST EXPERIENCE

We write for travelers who know there's more to a vacation than riding double-deckers with tourists. Our researchers give you the heads-up on both world-renowned and lesser-known attractions, on the best local eats and the hottest nightclub beats. In our travels, we talk to everybody; we provide a snapshot of real life in the places you visit with our sidebars on topics like regional cuisine, local festivals, and hot political issues. We've opened our pages to respected writers and scholars to show you their take on a given destination, and turned to lifelong residents to learn the little things that make their city worth calling home. And we've even given you Alternatives to Tourism—ideas for how to give back to local communities through responsible travel and volunteering.

OVER FORTY YEARS OF WISDOM

When we started, way back in 1960, Let's Go consisted of a small group of well-traveled friends who compiled their budget travel tips into a 20-page packet for students on charter flights to Europe. Since then, we've expanded to suit all kinds of travelers, now publishing guides to six continents, including our newest guides: *Let's Go: Japan* and *Let's Go: Brazil*. Our guides are still annually researched and written entirely by students on shoe-string budgets, adventurous travelers who know that train strikes, stolen luggage, food poisoning, and marriage proposals are all part of a day's work. Even as you read this, work on next year's editions is well underway. Whether you're reading one of our new titles, like *Let's Go: Puerto Rico* or *Let's Go Adventure Guide: Alaska*, or our original best-seller, *Let's Go: Europe*, you'll find the same spirit of adventure that has made *Let's Go* the guide of choice for travelers the world over since 1960.

GETTING IN TOUCH

The best discoveries are often those you make yourself; on the road, when you find something worth sharing, please drop us a line. We're Let's Go Publications, 67 Mt. Auburn St., Cambridge, MA 02138, USA (feedback@letsgo.com).

For more info, visit our website: www.letsgo.com.

①②③④⑤

PRICE RANGES >>LONDON

Our researchers list establishments in order of value from best to worst; our favorites are denoted by the Let's Go thumbs-up (☑). Since the best value is not always the cheapest price, we have incorporated a system of price ranges for quick reference. Our price ranges are based on a rough expectation of what you will spend. For **accommodations,** we base our price range off the cheapest price for which a single traveler can stay for one night. For **restaurants** and other dining establishments, we estimate the average amount that you will spend in that restaurant. The table below tells you what you will *typically* find in London at the corresponding price range; keep in mind that a particularly expensive ice cream stand may still only be marked a ❷, depending on what you will spend.

ACCOMMODATIONS	RANGE	WHAT YOU'RE *LIKELY* TO FIND
❶	under £20	Most dorm rooms, such as HI or other hostels or university dorm rooms. Expect bunk beds and a communal bath; you may have to provide or rent towels and sheets.
❷	£21-34	Upper-end hostels or small hotels. You may have a private bathroom, or there may be a sink in your room and communal shower in the hall.
❸	£35-49	A small room with a private bath. Should have decent amenities, such as phone and TV. Breakfast will probably be included in the price of the room.
❹	£50-74	Similar to 3, but may have more amenities or be in a more touristed area.
❺	above £75	Large hotels or upscale chains. If it's a 5 and it doesn't have the perks you want, you've paid too much.
FOOD	RANGE	WHAT YOU'RE *LIKELY* TO FIND
❶	under £5	Mostly street-corner stands, pizza places, or snack bars. Besides pub sandwiches, rarely a sit-down meal.
❷	£5-8	Sandwiches, pub grub, fish&chips, and cheap ethnic eateries. You may have the option of sitting down or getting take-out.
❸	£9-12	Mid-priced entrees. Fancier gastro-pubs and higher-quality ethnic food. Tip'll bump you up a couple dollars, since you'll probably have a waiter or waitress.
❹	£13-16	A somewhat fancy restaurant with a decent wine list or the very best gastro-pubs. Few restaurants in this range have a dress code, but most look down on t-shirt and jeans.
❺	above £16	Elegant setting and a long wine list. Trousers and dress shirts are usually expected. Don't order PB&J.

CONTENTS

■ discover london 1

▢ once in london 23

▢ life & times 45

◎ sights 61

▥ museums & galleries 119

▢ food & drink 143

▢ pubs 171

▨ nightlife 183

♫ entertainment 199

▢ shopping 223

▮ accommodations 245

◪ daytripping 271

◪ planning your trip 293

⦚ alternatives to tourism 313

⅀ service directory 329

⅂ index 337

⦚ map appendix 353

HOW TO USE THIS BOOK

PRICE RANGES AND RANKINGS. All listings are ordered by ranking in each neighborhood—with the best listings of each neighborhood listed first. Our absolute favorites in all chapters are denoted by the Let's Go thumbs-up (🕮). Since the best value does not always mean the cheapest price, we have incorporated a system of price ranges into the guide. The table below lists how prices fall within each bracket.

LONDON:	❶	❷	❸	❹	❺
FOOD	under £5	£5-8	£9-12	£13-16	£17+
ACCOMMODATIONS	under £20	£20-34	£35-49	£50-74	£75+

WHEN TO USE IT

TWO MONTHS BEFORE. Our book is filled with practical information to help you before you go. **Planning Your Trip** (p. 293) has advice about passports, plane tickets, insurance, and more. The **Accommodations** chapter (p. 245) can help you with booking a room from home.

ONE MONTH BEFORE. Take care of travel insurance and write down a list of emergency numbers and hotlines to take with you. Make a list of packing essentials and shop for anything you're missing. Make any necessary reservations, and talk to your bank and credit card company about getting cash in London.

TWO WEEKS BEFORE. Start thinking about your ideal trip. **Discover London** (p. 1) lists the city's top delights and also includes our new **Walking Tours** (complete with maps), Let's Go Picks (the best and quirkiest that London has to offer), and the scoop on each of the city's neighborhoods. It also includes itineraries for seeing **London In One Week (Or Less),** and our list of the top 25 reasons to visit London.

ON THE ROAD. Once in London (p. 23) will be your best friend once you've arrived, with all the practical information you'll need, plus tips on acting like a true Londoner. You'll find interviews with some of the London's most famous icons in **The Local Story.** You'll hear from a London DJ, a West End star and, yes, we actually got a Queen's Guard to speak to us. When you reach London, you'll spend most of your time in the following chapters: **Sights, Museums, Food & Drink, Nightlife, Entertainment,** and **Shopping.** Don't miss our **Hidden Deal** and **Big Splurge** sidebars, which point you to some of the best ways to save (and to spend) your pounds—from cheap CDs to Indian massages. When you feel like venturing outside the city, the **Daytripping** chapter will help: it provides a list of options for one-day and overnight trips away from London from elegant Hampton Court to charming Cambridge. The **Service Directory** contains a list of vital local services from where to find transport information, to how to contact your Embassy. Finally, remember to put down this guide once in a while and go exploring on your own; you'll be glad you did.

RESEARCHER-WRITERS

Nicole Cliffe *Bloomsbury, The City of London, Holborn, Westminster, East London, West London, Richmond.*

Born in Kingston, Ontario, Nicole has had a lifetime to fall in love with the Queen. She spent her childhood watching Inspector Morse re-runs, which served her well in London—her fake English accent wasn't quite as good as Morse's, but she managed to pass for a Londoner for the entire summer. Nicole's mastery of London's pub culture and her sharp writing made her a force to be reckoned with, from the ancient alleys of Holborn to the bars and clubs of SoHo.

Shelley Cheung *Bayswater, Chelsea, Clerkenwell, Hyde Park, Marylebone & Regent's Park, Notting Hill, The West End, North London.*

Shelley travelled from Chelsea, MA, to Chelsea, London, and barely noticed the difference. Her quirky fashion sense has revitalized our Shopping section. She witnessed the arrival of the latest Harry Potter offering in a frenzied Clerkenwell, was nearly run over (again and again and again!) in The West End, searched fruitlessly for Hugh Grant in Notting Hill, and braved insectoid foes in the wilds of North London.

Tiffany Hsieh *Kensington & Earl's Court, Knightsbridge & Belgravia, The South Bank, The West End, North London, South London.*

By day, Tiffany was a compulsive shopper with a keen eye for design, just as at home in the Victoria & Albert Museum as in the sleek boutiques of the West End. In the evening, her love of art cinema came to the fore. At night (and into the morning!), she was a dedicated clubber with her finger on the pulse of London's fast-changing nightlife. She fell in love the South London club scene immediately, and spent her summer shuttling between the arty South Bank and booty-shaking Brixton.

CONTRIBUTING WRITERS

Jeremy Faro is a student at Cambridge Univesrity.

Haneen Rabie conducts research in London on International Fund Management.

Charlotte Douglas, Editor, Britain & Ireland.

Chloe Schama, Associate Editor, Britain & Ireland.

Jennifer Cronin, Researcher-Writer, Britain & Ireland (Oxford, Stratford-Upon-Avon).

Joshua Rosaler, Researcher-Writer, Britain & Ireland (Canterbury, Cambridge, Salisbury and Stonehenge, Windsor and Eton).

Matthew Sussman, Researcher-Writer, Britain & Ireland (Bath).

ACKNOWLEDGMENTS

LET'S GO

Andrew Thanks: Nicole, Tiffany, and Shelley—sexy, stylish, and the best RWs an editor could ask for. Jenn O'Brien, for her tireless help and amazing edits, despite everything. I couldn't have done it without you. Christine Peterson, for putting up with my grand schemes and then making them happen—you've been more patient than I deserve. Miranda, for edits, advice, and friendship. Sarah Robinson, tribune of the people, for standing up for the city guides. Thomas and Jeff, for all their patience, help, and EDM. Ariel Fox, for being the mother I never had. Except for my own mother. Whom I also thank, even though she didn't edit my copy; my dad didn't either, so thanks for nuthin'. Suzanne, for putting up with me and putting up the cash. All the podmates.

Barb, for reminding me that it can get worse. Pat, for coffee, cigars, and a 14-inch St. Francis. Frances, for tempting me with tales from abroad. Andrei Tarkovsky, Werner Herzog, Fritz Lang, and Andrzej Wajda. G.M. Hopkins and Matthew Arnold. AMDG.

Miranda Thanks: Many thanks to Andrew, to our mapper Christine and to our wonderful RWs. Scrobins, for smiles and scorpion bowls. All my love to Cristina, who brightened my days with her silliness and charm. I was so happy to have you. Thanks to Becky for keeping an eye out for me. A million thanks over to my Mom and Dad for their love and support. And thanks to Danny, who was always there for me with friendship and affection. You put up with my ranting and gave me an extra boost when I needed it most. Texas here I come!

Christine Thanks: Thanks to Nicole, Tiffany, and Shelley for their dazzling color-coordinated corrections. Andrew and Miranda, you're awesome editors. And Mapland, you rock!

Editor Andrew Sodroski
Associate Editor Miranda Lash
Managing Editor Jennifer O'Brien
Map Editor Christine Peterson
Photographers D. Jonathan Dawid, Luke Marion
Typesetter Thomas Bechtold

Publishing Director
Julie A. Stephens
Editor-in-Chief
Jeffrey Dubner
Production Manager
Dusty Lewis
Cartography Manager
Nathaniel Brooks
Design Manager
Caleb Beyers
Editorial Managers
Lauren Bonner, Ariel Fox,
Matthew K. Hudson, Emma Nothmann,
Joanna Shawn Brigid O'Leary,
Sarah Robinson
Financial Manager
Suzanne Siu
Marketing & Publicity Managers
Megan Brumagim, Nitin Shah
Personnel Manager
Jesse Reid Andrews
Researcher Manager
Jennifer O'Brien
Web Manager
Jesse Tov
Web Content Director
Abigail Burger
Production Associates
T.Michael Bechtold, Jeffrey Hoffman Yip
IT Directors
Travis Good, E. Peyton Sherwood
Financial Assistant
R. Kirkie Maswoswe
Associate Web Manager
Robert Dubbin
Office Coordinators
Abigail Burger, Angelina L. Fryer,
Liz Glynn

Director of Advertising Sales
Daniel Ramsey
Senior Advertising Associates
Sara Barnett, Daniella Boston
Advertising Artwork Editor
Julia Davidson

President
Abhishek Gupta
General Manager
Robert B. Rombauer
Assistant General Manager
Anne E. Chisholm

Discover London

London offers the visitor a bewildering array of choices: Leonardo at the National or Hirst at Tate Modern; tea at Brown's or chilling in the Fridge; Rossini at the Royal Opera or Les Mis at the Palace; Bond Street couture or Covent Garden cutting-edge—you could spend your entire stay just deciding what to do and what to leave out. This chapter is designed to help put some method into the madness of visiting London.

London is often described as more a conglomeration of villages than a unified city. While this understates the civic pride Londoners take in their city as a whole, it is true that locals are strongly attached to their neighborhoods—in part because each area's heritage and traditions are still alive and evolving, from the City's 2000-year-old association with trade to Notting Hill's West Indian Carnival. Thanks to the feisty independence and diversity of each area, the London "buzz" is continually on the move—every few years a previously disregarded neighborhood explodes into cultural prominence. In the 60s Soho and Chelsea swung the world; the late 80s saw grunge rule the roost from Camden; and in the 90s the East End sprung Damien Hirst and the Britpack artists on the world. More recently, South London has come to prominence with the cultural rebirth of the South Bank and the thumping nightlife of a recharged Brixton.

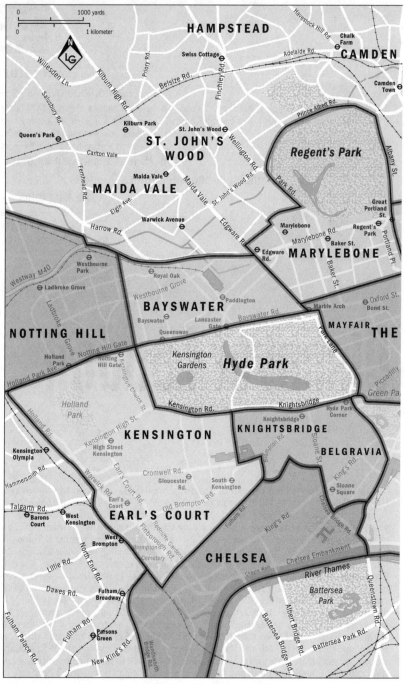

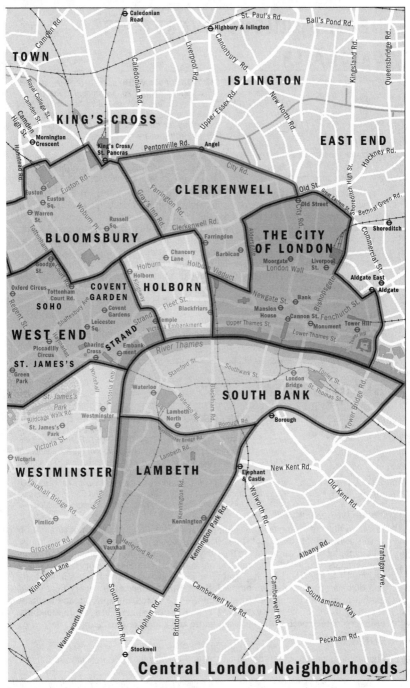

Central London Neighborhoods

NEIGHBORHOOD OVERVIEWS

ICAL OVERVIEWS

BAYSWATER

SEE MAP, p. 361

🗊 **BAYSWATER QUICKFIND: Food & Drink,** p. 148; **Pubs,** p. 173; **Entertainment,** p. 207; **Shopping,** p. 226; **Accommodations,** p. 252. **TRANSPORTATION:** Bayswater falls into two halves, with most shops and restaurants in the west and accommodations in the east. **Tube:** Bayswater and Queensway for the west; Paddington and Lancaster Gate for the east. Note that there are two separate Paddington Tube stations: the Hammersmith & City line runs from tracks in the Paddington train station; the other lines run from a station underground.
Buses: Plenty of routes converge at Paddington from the West End and Knightsbridge The #12 and #94 run along Hyde Park from Marble Arch.

Bayswater has neither the fashionable status of Notting Hill, nor the respectability of Marylebone, despite a sterling position neighboring Hyde Park. This was once London's most stylish neighborhood, until the Paddington canal and the railway turned it into a transportation hub. Today, while the area could hardly be considered seedy, it is not one of London's more glamorous neighborhoods. But this all works to the traveler's advantage. Because of lower property prices, Bayswater has the densest conglomeration of convenient budget beds anywhere in London. Another result of Bayswater's low cost of living is great ethnic diversity—it can rightly claim to be the original London home of curries and kebabs. The wide array of cheap ethnic restaurants is perfectly placed for the hordes of travelers staying nearby.

DON'T MISS...

Food & Drink: Wonderful Greek food at Aphrodite Taverna; La Bottega del Gelato—so many flavors, so little time.

Shopping: Whiteleys, the biggest shopping center in central London.

BLOOMSBURY

SEE MAP, p. 362

🗊 **BLOOMSBURY QUICKFIND: Sights,** p. 74; **Museums & Galleries,** p. 125; **Food & Drink,** p. 148; **Pubs,** p. 173; **Entertainment,** p. 207; **Shopping,** p. 226; **Accommodations,** p. 254. **TRANSPORTATION:** Though fairly large, Bloomsbury is a pleasant district to walk around. **Tube:** A plethora of stations make Bloomsbury easy to get to from all over London: King's Cross is the system's biggest interchange, while Goodge St. and Russell Sq. are most central for the sights. **Buses:** Run mostly north-south, either between Warren St. and Tottenham Court Rd. stations (along Gower St. heading south, along Tottenham Court Rd. heading north), or between Euston and Holborn along Southampton Pl.

Home to dozens of universities, colleges, and specialist hospitals, not to mention both the British Museum and the British Library, Bloomsbury is London's undisputed intellectual powerhouse. In the early 20th century, the quiet squares and Georgian terraces resounded to the intellectual musings of the Bloomsbury Group, which included T.S. Eliot, E.M. Forster, and Virginia Woolf; today, they house student halls and dozens of affordable accommodations. Bloomsbury offers everything you'd expect in an area dominated by students—bookstores, cheap food, and brilliant shopping. Don't come here expecting a campus atmosphere; instead, Bloomsbury offers a sedate appeal, with fine architecture and some great restaurants.

DON'T MISS...

Sights: The splendor of the British Library and the dignity of St. Pancras Old Church, oases of quiet in the bustle of King's Cross.

4

Museums: Revisit childhood at the delightful Pollock's Toy Museum; revisit everything else at the recently revamped British Museum, worthy devourer of entire vacations.

Food & Drink: Great food cheap at Diwana Bhel Poori House, a paradise for vegetarians; great food even cheaper at ICCo.

Accommodations: The Generator, "the only place to stay in London"; the Jenkins Hotel, the best of the excellent B&Bs that Bloomsbury has to offer.

CHELSEA

⚐ CHELSEA QUICKFIND: Sights, p. 76; **Museums & Galleries,** p. 126; **Food & Drink,** p. 150; **Entertainment,** p. 208; **Shopping,** p. 227. **TRANSPORTATION:** In a borough where even the poorest resident drives a BMW, public transportation is a low priority—be prepared to walk. **Tube:** Sloane Sq., on Chelsea's eastern boundary, is the lone stop. **Buses:** Most run from Sloane Sq. down the King's Rd. on their way from Knightsbridge or Victoria.

SEE MAP, p. 363

Chelsea has the cachet of Knightsbridge and Kensington without their stuffiness. In the 19th century, Cheyne Walk and surrounding streets hummed to the discussions of Edgar Allan Poe, George Eliot, Dante Gabriel Rossetti, Oscar Wilde, J.M.W. Turner, John Singer Sargent, and James MacNeill Whistler. The tone was a bit different in the 1960s and 1970s, when King's Rd. was the launching point for miniskirts and punk rock. Stifled by a surfeit of wealth, today's Chelsea has little stomach for radicalism. You'll find nothing more shocking than electric-blue frocks on the King's Rd., and local luminaries now include Hugh Grant, Liz Hurley, Britt Ekland, and a string of B-list celebrities and trust-fund kids known collectively as "Sloane Rangers." Nonetheless, Chelsea still manages to retain a little of that old-time glamour, helped along by the presence of numerous modeling agencies around Sloane Sq.

DON'T MISS...

Sights: The National Army Museum, educational and entertaining both for army buffs and the rest of us.

Entertainment: All that jazz at the 606 Club.

Food & Drink: Late, lazy breakfast at the Chelsea Bun.

Shopping: The glamorous vintage collection at Speinberg & Tolkien.

THE CITY OF LONDON

⚐ THE CITY OF LONDON QUICKFIND: Sights, p. 78; **Museums & Galleries,** p. 126; **Food & Drink,** p. 150; **Pubs,** p. 174; **Entertainment,** p. 208. **TRANSPORTATION:** Public transportation in the City is geared toward getting office workers around; within the compact City, walking is easiest. **Rail:** Cannon St., Liverpool St., and Blackfriars, along with London Bridge across the river, provide service to commuters. **Tube:** Of the numerous Tube stations, Bank and St. Paul's are within easy reach of most sights; Tower Hill is useful for destinations farther east. **Buses:** Dozens of routes pass through the City: those from the West End and Holborn arrive along Ludgate Hill and Holborn Viaduct, while Liverpool St. station is the terminus for buses arriving from north London.

SEE MAP, p. 364

The City is where London began—indeed, for most of its history, the City *was* London. The City's past sits uneasily with its present: to most Londoners the most important financial center in Europe is an outlying irrelevance. A quarter of a million people work here during the day, but by night the City's population shrinks to a measly 8000, most of whom live in the 1970s towers of the luxury **Barbican Centre**. Not surprisingly, not much happens here outside office hours. The majority of restaurants and pubs are aimed squarely at the millions of tourists who outnumber the pigeons at **St. Paul's Cathedral** and who storm the **Tower of London**—London's two most famous sights, which look glorious seen from the water at **Tower Bridge** or from the air at the top of the **Monument.** For a less crowded, equally breathtaking view of the City, try standing on the **Millennium Bridge** facing St. Paul's at dusk. If you're a fan of Christopher Wren, the City is the place for you, with 24 of his churches squeezed between temples of commerce.

DON'T MISS...

Sights: London at your feet from the top of the Monument; Elizabeth II's baubles and superb Beefeater tours at the Tower of London.

Museums & Galleries: 1970 years of history at the fabulous Museum of London.

Food & Drink: The best of a new breed of Indian restaurants, Café Spice Namaste; hidden veggie delights at The Place Below.

Entertainment: Top plays and musical acts in the hard-to-navigate Barbican Centre.

CLERKENWELL

SEE MAP, p. 365

🄵 **CLERKENWELL QUICKFIND: Sights,** p. 82; **Museums & Galleries,** p. 128; **Food & Drink,** p. 151; **Pubs,** p. 174; **Nightlife,** p. 185; **Entertainment,** p. 210; **Accommodations,** p. 259. **TRANSPORTATION:** *Walking is the best way to get around Clerkenwell.* **Tube:** *Everything is in walking distance of Farringdon, while southern and eastern parts can be reached from Barbican.*

Under the vamped-up guise of "Cityside"—a reference to its position on the boundaries of the City of London—Clerkenwell was the success story of the late 1990s. If it's no longer cutting-edge cool, that's a bonus: less attitude, more fun. With stylish restaurants, new-age bars, popular club venues, and a pub at every corner, this quiet neighborhood wakes up when the lights dim. Behind the industrial facade and the bustling nightlife, Clerkenwell harbors deep historical roots, and it is this coexistence of modernity and history that defines its character.

DON'T MISS...

Sights: The ancient, beautiful church of St. Bartholomew the Great; St. John's Gate, the heart of Clerkenwell.

Pubs: Some of London's best pub grub, from a full English breakfast at Fox & Anchor to a Mediterranean lunch at The Eagle; specialty ales at The Jerusalam Tavern.

Nightlife: Dancing like there's no tomorrow at fabu megaclub Fabric; leisurely lounging at Fluid.

HOLBORN

SEE MAP, p. 365

🄵 **HOLBORN QUICKFIND: Sights,** p. 84; **Museums & Galleries,** p. 128; **Food & Drink,** p. 152; **Pubs,** p. 175; **Nightlife,** p. 187; **Entertainment,** p. 210; **Shopping,** p. 229. **TRANSPORTATION:** *Holborn is easily walkable—compact and easy to navigate.* **Tube:** *Holborn, Farringdon, Chancery Ln. (closed Su), and Temple (closed Su).* **Buses:** *Dozens run up and down Fleet St., linking Holborn to the City and the West End.*

London's second-oldest area, Holborn was the first part of the city settled by Saxons—"Aldwych," on the western edge of Holborn, is Anglo-Saxon for "old port." A center of medieval monasticism, today Holborn is associated with two unholy professions: law and journalism. If you thought lawyers had it good at home, wait until you see the **Inns of Court,** colleges-*cum*-clubs for barristers that have been growing in wealth and power for centuries. East of the Inns, **Fleet Street** remains synonymous with the British press even though the newspapers have since moved on. After hours, the nightlife is restricted to Holborn's many historic pubs, some once frequented by Sam Johnson and Samuel Pepys.

DON'T MISS...

Sights: St. Etheldreda's, a gem to rival the wares of Hatton Garden; the labyrinthine gardens and halls of the Temple.

Museums & Galleries: Genius run wild at the eclectic museum of Sir John Soane; silver parrots and gold snuffboxes at the Gilbert Collection Galleries.

Pubs: Ye Olde Mitre, probably the best pub in London; take part in a fourth century of ale appreciation at Ye Olde Cheshire Cheese; fine pub grub at The Old Bank of England.

KENSINGTON & EARL'S COURT

⊠ KENSINGTON & EARL'S COURT QUICKFIND: Sights, p. 88; **Museums & Galleries,** p. 130; **Food & Drink,** p. 153; **Pubs,** p. 176; **Entertainment,** p. 210; **Shopping,** p. 229; **Accommodations,** p. 259. **TRANSPORTATION:** One of central London's larger neighborhoods, you'll need public transport to get around here. **Tube:** Stations are helpfully named: High St. Kensington for the High St., South Kensington for the South Ken museums, and Earl's Court for Earl's Court. **Buses:** Numerous buses ply the High St. before climbing up Kensington Church St. to Notting Hill; to get to South Kensington take #49 or 70.

SEE MAP, pp. 366-367

Until recently the stomping ground of Princess Diana, Kensington is characterized by two major divisions: the posh consumer mecca of **Kensington High Street** in the west and the awe-inspiring museums and colleges of **South Kensington's** "Albertopolis" in the east—no prizes for guessing which was Di's favorite. The presence of 2000 French schoolkids at the local *lycée* gives parts of South Kensington a distinctly continental feel, with a corresponding number of good, cheap restaurants. Both High St. and South Ken have a smattering of budget accommodations, but neither can compare with "Kangaroo Valley" in **Earl's Court** to the southwest. In the 1960s and 70s, South Kensington was the sole preserve of Aussie backpackers and gays. Today others have caught on to its combination of cheap accommodations with good transport links to central London.

DON'T MISS...

Sights: Great, gilded Albert reigning over his South Kensington legacies; the Royal Dress Collection in Kensington Palace, Diana's former home.

Museums & Galleries: South Kensington's imperial triumvirate: the Victoria & Albert tops most people's lists, but those with kids shouldn't ignore the Natural History and Science Museums nearby.

Food & Drink: Complex and contemplative Indian cuisine at Zaika; tea at the Palace in the Orangery.

Shopping: Oxford St. variety without Oxford St. crowds on Kensington High St.; sophisticated adornments at the British Hatter.

KNIGHTSBRIDGE & BELGRAVIA

⊠ KNIGHTSBRIDGE & BELGRAVIA QUICKFIND: Sights, p. 90; **Food & Drink,** p. 154; **Pubs,** p. 176; **Shopping,** p. 230; **Accommodations,** p. 262. **TRANSPORTATION:** Knightsbridge and Belgravia are both easy and pleasant to walk around. **Tube:** Knightsbridge station is near all the shops; most of the hotels in Belgravia are accessible from Victoria, while the north end, near the park, sits on top of Hyde Park Corner. **Buses:** Numerous routes converge on Knightsbridge from Piccadilly, Oxford St., Kensington, and Chelsea, but all manage to bypass Belgravia.

SEE MAP, p. 368

For two centuries London's most coveted districts, Knightsbridge and Belgravia are naturally both smug and wildly expensive. The location comes at such a price that even millionaire penthouse owners have had to sell their property to foreign embassies and consulates, the only people who can afford the land anymore. Not surprisingly, the primary draw for tourists is the windowshopping. **Knightsbridge**

challenges the West End's shopping stranglehold: like the locals, famed department stores Harrods and Harvey Nichols exude an air of superiority. **Belgravia,** which occupies the region east of Sloane St., is an expanse of grand 19th-century mansions occupied by aforementioned millionaires and embassies.

DON'T MISS...

Sights: Apsley House, with a 26 ft. silver centerpiece; the Wellington Arch, which offers a rare glimpse into Buckingham Palace gardens.

Shopping: Harrods—you have to see it to believe it; Harvey Nichols, Diana's favorite department store and still the most fashionable; designer collections on Sloane St. and designer clothes for much, much less at Pandora and The Exchange.

MARYLEBONE & REGENT'S PARK

SEE MAP, p. 369

⛳ MARYLEBONE & REGENT'S PARK QUICKFIND: Sights, *p. 92;* **Museums & Galleries,** *p. 132;* **Food & Drink,** *p. 155;* **Entertainment,** *p. 211;* **Accommodations,** *p. 262.. TRANSPORTATION: The main problem getting around Marylebone is crossing the vast and boring expanse in the middle.* **Tube:** *Baker St. is convenient for Marylebone's northern sights; Bond St. covers the south. Confusingly, there are two entirely separate Edgware Rd. stations; fortunately, they're not far apart.* **Buses:** *The best way of getting across Marylebone. 10 bus routes link north and south via Baker St. (going south) and Gloucester Pl. (heading north), while seven more ply Edgware Rd.*

Marylebone is defined by its borders. To the east, beautiful **Portland Place** is an architectural wonder. To the west, culturally eclectic **Edgware Road** boasts many Middle Eastern eateries, shops, and markets. To the south, the West End's **Oxford Street** is a shopaholic's paradise. Rounding out the northern border of Marylebone, **Regent's Park** is a giant and popular expanse of greenery surrounded by elegant Regency terraces. More than London's biggest football practice-ground, the park is home to a panoply of sights including the golden dome of the London Central Mosque, while nearby, Marylebone Rd. and Baker St. trap tourists with Madame Tussaud's and the Planetarium. Yet Marylebone's center is not entirely hollow: Marylebone High St. drives a wedge of trendy shops, cafes, and restaurants on its way from Marylebone Rd. to Oxford St.

DON'T MISS...

Sights: A slow, leisurely walk through Regent's Park, London's loveliest open space.

Museums: The Wallace Collection, combining one of the world's finest private art collections with Britain's biggest array of armor.

Food & Drink: Mandalay, a charming culinary experience; fun and delicious Persian food at Patogh.

NOTTING HILL

SEE MAP, p. 361

⛳ NOTTING HILL QUICKFIND: Sights, *p. 94;* **Food & Drink,** *p. 156;* **Pubs,** *p. 177;* **Nightlife,** *p. 187;* **Entertainment,** *p. 211;* **Shopping,** *p. 231.. TRANSPORTATION: Getting to Notting Hill is easy; getting around is another matter.* **Tube:** *Notting Hill Gate serves the south, while Ladbroke Grove deposits you close by Portobello Rd.* **Buses:** *#52 runs from Ladbroke Grove down to the Gate and Kensington Park Rd. From the West End, #12 and 94 will get you to Notting Hill Gate, while a plethora of buses make the trip up from High St. Kensington.*

For decades one of London's most vibrant, ethnically mixed neighborhoods, Notting Hill has become a victim of its own boho-chic trendiness (helped on by a certain movie). In some spots, the mix of bohemians, immigrants, and blue-collar workers that sustained its vitality is being displaced by an influx of yuppies, which explains some of the lofty prices. The northern portion of **Portobello Road** around the Westway, where the tenements and local markets lie, still retains much of its original character, but venture too far off Portobello Rd., and you'll be find a quiet neighborhood of indistinguishable two-family homes. Every year during the final week in August, the whole neighborhood explodes with Caribbean color and sound during the **Notting Hill Carnival;** originally started by West Indian immigrants as a local street party, it has become a giant summer festival annually attended by over two million people.

DON'T MISS...

Food & Drink: Yummy, affordable pastries at Lisboa; greasy, delicious fish and chips at George's.

Nightlife: Groove to the market in The Market.

Shopping: The bustling sights and sounds of Portobello Market on a Sunday; your choice of caffeinated concoctions at Tea and Coffee Plant.

THE SOUTH BANK

🚩 *THE SOUTH BANK QUICKFIND: Sights, p. 95; Museums & Galleries, p. 132; Food & Drink, p. 157; Pubs, p. 177; Entertainment, p. 212; Accommodations, p. 263. TRANSPORTATION: Poorly served by public transportation, most South Bank attractions are best reached by walking along the river. Tube: The closest station to the South Bank Centre is across the river at Embankment; take the Hungerford foot bridge. Use Waterloo for inland attractions, Bankside for Southwark, and London Bridge for Borough and Butlers Wharf.*

SEE MAP, pp. 370-371

Close to the City, but exempt from its party-squelching laws, the South Bank has long been London's entertainment center. In Shakespeare's time it was renowned for its theaters, cock-fighting, bull-baiting, and gentlemanly diversions of less reputable forms. Dominated by wharves and warehouses in the 19th century, the devastation of WWII forced the South Bank to rebuild—an opportunity for the neighborhood to reassert its fun-loving heritage. Now, the **"Millennium Mile"** stretches from the twirling London Eye in the west to the swank restaurants of Butlers Wharf in the east, passing by the cultural powerhouses of the Festival Hall, Hayward Gallery, National Theatre, National Film Theatre, Tate Modern, and Shakespeare's Globe Theatre, as well as the quirky riverside shops and eateries of Gabriel's Wharf and the OXO Tower.

DON'T MISS...

Sights: London—all of it, as seen from the top of the London Eye; the Queen's Walk, with the Thames on one side and artistic distractions on the other.

Museums & Galleries: Tate Modern, the world's largest modern art museum; award-winning, cutting-edge style at the Design Museum; shocking and provocative Britart exhibits at the new Saatchi Gallery; medical horrors of the past in the Old Operating Theatre and Herb Garret.

Food & Drink: A trio of affordable lunches with beautiful river views at the People's Palace, Tate Modern, and Cantina del Ponte; top Turkish treats at Tas.

Entertainment: Top drama at the National Theatre, the Old Vic, and the Globe; classical, jazz, and world music at the South Bank Centre; celluloid variety at the National Film Theater and literally enormous cinematic experiences at the BFI IMAX Theatre.

from the road

Road Hazards

Drivers—I thought I had seen the worst of them in Boston. Then I came to London. After becoming intimately acquainted (as in missed by mere centimeters) with more than a few vehicles that I had not even seen coming, I learned to be more careful, or at least less reckless. Crossing the streets is not a matter to be taken lightly, and is a skill that requires careful honing. Let's take a closer look at some of the vehicles that can cause damage:

Cars: They tend to be small and cute in London. But they're not so cute or small when they're rushing at you at neck-breaking speeds. Do not expect drivers to stop or even slow down when they see you attempting to cross the street; expect them to speed up.

Cabs: The same size as cars, but more dangerous because cab drivers, seasoned Londoners that they are, have no mercy.

Police cars: Do not let your guard down. They are still cars, and therefore not an exception to the rule. Yours truly was almost run down by a cruiser—twice.

THE WEST END

SEE MAP, p. 356

THE WEST END QUICKIND: **Sights**, p. 98; **Museums & Galleries**, p. 134; **Food & Drink**, p. 158; **Pubs**, p. 178; **Nightlife**, p. 188; **Entertainment**, p. 213; **Shopping**, p. 233; **Accommodations**, p. 263. *TRANSPORTATION:* At the hub of London's transportation network, the West End is also surprisingly easy to walk. **Tube:** The Tube is best for getting in and out of the West End; it's not worth it for travelling one or two stops within the area. **Buses:** The best way to get around. Many routes head from Trafalgar Sq. to the Strand, Piccadilly, and Charing Cross Rd.; more bus lines converge at Oxford Circus, from where they run south down Regent St. to Piccadilly Circus, west up Oxford St. to Marble Arch, and east to Tottenham Court Rd. Trafalgar Sq. is also the departure point for most of the **Night Bus** network.

Whether it's shopping, eating, theatergoing, or clubbing, the West End is London's popular (and populist) heartland, with a wider variety of activities than any other neighborhood in the city. This ill-defined district between royal Westminster and the financial powerhouse of the City was first settled by nobles wanting to be close to both; over time, the area became a patchwork of distinct communities. Wealthy Londoners still live in mansions in prestigious **Mayfair** and socialize in neighboring **St. James's** gentlemen's clubs. On the other side of Piccadilly Circus, young Londoners party in very different clubs—in **Soho**, London's nightlife nexus, and around the very gay Old Compton St. **Oxford Street**, which forms Mayfair's northern boundary, has been London's premier shopping street for over 150 years—on the weekend before Christmas, there's barely room to stand. The more fashion-conscious head to the boutiques of **Covent Garden**, southwest of Soho, along with crowds of tourists who just hang out in Inigo Jones's Piazza. South of Covent Garden, the **Strand** provides glimpses of London's past and theaters and touristy restaurants on its way to majestic, pigeon-infested **Trafalgar Square**, a reminder of Britain's greater days.

DON'T MISS...

Sights: Soak in the atmosphere: smug St. James's; Oxford St. overload on Saturday; sunny Covent Garden Piazza; slinky Soho by night.

Museums & Galleries: Tubes and trams at London's Transport Museum, fun for all ages.

Food & Drink: Top-notch Thai dishes at Busaba Eathai; monorail-delivered fusion sushi at Itsu; a truly bazaar experience at Mô's Moroccan tea-room; the Piazza cafes of St. Christopher's Place.

Shopping: Funky clothes and shoes galore on Floral St. and Neal St., Covent Garden; top DJs' favorite record stores in Soho; window-shopping at the *couture* boutiques on Bond St.; Selfridges, London's favorite department store.

Nightlife: Chilling on the couches at Freud and Detroit; the labyrinthine Heaven, Britain's most famous gay nightclub.

Entertainment: Blockbusters, classic films, and sing-a-long *Sound of Music* in and around Leicester Sq.; jazz legends at Ronnie Scott's; the funniest funny-men around at the Comedy Store.

WESTMINSTER

⧉ WESTMINSTER QUICKFIND:
Sights, p. 104; **Museums & Galleries,** p. 136; **Food & Drink,** p. 162; **Pubs,** p. 179; **Entertainment,** p. 216; **Accommodations,** p. 264. . **TRANS-PORTATION:** *Getting here is not a problem. Victoria, to the west, doubles as a mainline train sta-*

SEE MAP, p. 372

tion and the nearby London terminus for most long-distance **coach** *services.* **Tube:** *Westminster deposits you near most sights; use St. James's Park for Buckingham Palace; use Pimlico for accomodations and Tate Britain.* **Buses:** *Numerous buses swirl around Parliament Sq. before being catapulted up Whitehall to Trafalagar Sq., down Victoria St. to Victoria, along the Embankment to Pimlico, and across the river into Lambeth.*

Westminster, with its postcard-friendly spires and lush parks, often feels like the heart of the old British Empire. It is, after all, home to both the Houses of Parliament and the Queen herself. But away from the towering elegance of Nelson's Column in Trafalgar Square, the bureaucracy of Whitehall, and the Gothic grandeur of the Abbey, Westminster is a surprisingly down-to-earth district—hundreds of thousands of office workers make Victoria London's busiest Tube station. **Pimlico,** south of Victoria, is a quiet residential district with some of London's best B&Bs. With some notable exceptions, this is not the neighborhood for shoppers, clubbers, or foodies; still, with its proximity to Soho, the West End, Knightsbridge, and Chelsea, Westminster makes a great home base for any visit—and its sights are unbeatable.

DON'T MISS...

Sights: Nelson scowling from his pedestal above bustling Trafalgar Square; two duelling visions—the Gothic splendor of Westminster Abbey, and the neo-Byzantine grandeur of Westminster Cathedral; the Changing of the Guard at Buckingham Palace.

Museums & Galleries: The incomparable array of fine art at the National Gallery; the claustrophobic, secretive corridors and chambers of the Cabinet War Rooms.

Motorcycles: They come from hell. You hear them before you see them—which gives you exactly 3.72 seconds to get out of the way.

Bicycles: Not as damaging as motorcycles, but more elusive. They tend to ignore protocol, sometimes even pretending to be a pedestrian on the sidewalk. Beware.

Rickshaws: Rare, but around nonetheless. And they're at least as harmful as a bicycle. Don't be caught unprepared.

Buses: Like cars, only bigger.

Double-decker buses: There's nothing more like death knocking on the door than seeing a double-decker round a corner right at you at full speed. One may think that big vehicles should move slower—they do not.

Tips for staying alive:

1. Get to know the crosswalk. They're almost always far away from the location you want to cross the street. Jaywalk at your own risk.

2. Get to know the green man. He is your friend. Note, however, that the flashing green man is not your friend.

3. Look both ways. Sure the instructions on the ground may say "look left," but why risk it?

4. Follow the crowd. Being a rebel is useless when dead.

5. Run. It does nothing for your self-esteem or your suave image, but then again, neither does death.

—Shelley Cheung

🖊 LET'S GO PICKS

Best place to be beheaded: Tower Hill, outside the **Tower of London** (p. 70), long the site of public beheadings.

Best headless dead guy: **Jeremy Bentham** (p. 74), UCL's founder, whose preserved corpse is still on display—the head is wax.

Best talking moose head: **Strawberry Moons** (p. 188), a hot, fun danceclub that also features a "Time Machine."

Best place to be trampled to death: The left side of a Tube escalator during rush hour.

Best place to be beaten with an umbrella: The left side of a Tube escalator during rush hour.

Best place to buy an umbrella: Strike back with a quality fightin' brollie from **James Smith & Sons** (p. 227).

Best route to a heart attack: "Full English breakfast, please." Rinse. Repeat.

Best place to blow £1000: **Sloane Street** (p. 230), home to every posh chain imaginable.

Best place to get Blow for £1000: The drug dealers around **King's Cross** (p. 107).

Best meal for under £4: An 11" pizza from **ICCo.** (p. 149).

Best Pub: Ye Olde Mitre (p. 175), in Holborn.

Accommodations: Pimlico's best B&Bs provide red-carpet treatment at down-to-earth prices.

NORTH LONDON

🄵 *NORTH LONDON QUICKFIND: Sights, p. 107; Museums & Galleries, p. 137; Food & Drink, p. 163; Pubs, p. 180; Nightlife, p. 192; Entertainment, p. 216; Shopping, p. 240; Accommodations, p. 265. . TRANSPORTATION: Most individual neighborhoods are walkable, once you are there. Tube: Long distances make this the way to get around. Note that north of Euston you are in Zone 2, while Highgate and Golders Green are in Zone 3. Buses: Essential for getting to some out-of-the-way locations. Take advantage of the bus and local-area maps in Tube stations and at bus stops to help you find your way.*

Green and prosperous, North London's inner suburbs are some of London's older outlying communities. **Hampstead** and **Highgate** were pleasant country retreats for centuries before urban sprawl engulfed them, and both still retain a distinct village atmosphere. Of the two, Hampstead is busier and more urbane, with a long line of intellectual associations from John Keats to Sigmund Freud. Closer to the center, **Camden Town** and **Islington** were grimy, working-class areas for most of the 19th and 20th centuries, but in the 1980s their stock shot up and both are now populated with wealthy liberals. Tony Blair lived in Islington before making the move to Downing St. During the weekend in Camden Town, though, you'd be hard-pressed to notice the yuppification: the gigantic street market is more popular than ever, attracting what looks like half the under-25 population of Europe every Sunday. In Islington the prosperity is more apparent: Upper St. has become one of London's top eating destinations, with over 100 restaurants within walking distance of Angel Tube. **Maida Vale** and **St. John's Wood** are wealthy northern extensions of Marylebone and Bayswater; particularly picturesque is **Little Venice,** at the confluence of three canals, while the most famous sight in these parts is the fairly unremarkable pedestrian crossing at **Abbey Road.**

DON'T MISS...

Sights: The wild and tangled Hampstead Heath; Kenwood House, a picture-perfect country mansion with a great art collection; the hidden pastures of the Hill Garden; fragrant memorials at the Golder's Green Crematorium.

Food & Drink: Rolled-up goodness at La Creperie de Hampstead; understated excellence at Bloom's; Carmelli's challah; superb *kebaps* at Gallipoli.

Pubs: The delights of an enormous, no-frills hot salt beef sandwich at the Wenlock Arms.

Shopping: Total weekend madness at Camden market; a near museum of clubbing culture at Cybercity.

Nightlife: Offbeat fun at Electric Ballroom; gay cabaret at the Black Cap; Funky dance madness at WKD.

Entertainment: Top-notch acts at Jazz Cafe; Tricycle's offbeat picks and flicks.

SOUTH LONDON

🏠 *SOUTH LONDON QUICKIND: Sights, p. 111; Museums & Galleries, p. 138; Food & Drink, p. 166; Nightlife, p. 194; Entertainment, p. 212; Shopping, p. 241. TRANSPORTA-TION: This area is largely bypassed by the* **Tube;** *overland* **rail** *makes up the difference, with service from Victoria, Waterloo, and London Bridge.* **Buses:** *From Brixton, the P4 will take you to all the Dulwich sights.*

Few divides are harder to bridge than that which separates South from North London. With a few exceptions (notably the South Bank), North Londoners regard everything south of the Thames as inherently disreputable, and South Londoners view their northern neighbors as insufferably pretentious. The truth is that South London's relatively recent development lacks a historical center to match that of the north, and so can easily appear as a mess of Victorian railway suburbs. Yet this anonymity hides some of London's most dynamic neighborhoods. From a tourist perspective, two South London areas stand out: **Brixton** today is largely black, after a wave of West Indian immigrants during the 1940s and 1950s that led to race riots in the 1980s and 1995. Despite long being associated with drug-soaked poverty, Brixton is home to some thumping nightlife: clubs are often open until 10am. Neighboring **Dulwich** couldn't be more different, a quiet and prosperous hilly village filled with golf greens and country clubs.

DON'T MISS...

Museums: The Imperial War Museum, offering a surprisingly sensitive and balanced view of conflicts since 1914; Dulwich Picture Gallery, a fantastic collection of Old Masters in one of the first purpose-designed galleries in the world.

Food & Drink: Fresh-squeezed juices and smoothies in the quirky Café Bar and Juice Bar; top vegetarian food and fish in an atmospheric church crypt at Bug.

Nightlife: Grooving in the jam-packed Tongue&Groove; serious trance action at the Fridge; the world heavyweight champion of clubbing, the Ministry of Sound.

Entertainment: Headline rock, pop, and world acts at the famous Brixton Academy.

EAST LONDON

🏠 *EAST LONDON QUICKFIND: Sights, p. 112; Museums & Galleries, p. 139; Food & Drink, p. 167; Pubs, p. 181; Nightlife, p. 196; Entertainment, p. 219; Shopping, p. 242. TRANSPORTATION: Much of East London is surprisingly central; you're unlikely to get beyond Zone 2.* **Tube:**

Best view/stairs ratio: Monument (p. 78), in The City, which provides an amazing view, plus a certificate of achievement for getting to the top.

Best place to ponder the meaning of life inside a fake pharmacy: Damien Hirst's art installation at **Tate Modern** (p. 123).

Best place to ponder the meaning of boogie inside a fake pharmacy: Damien Hirst-designed nightclub **Pharmacy** (p. 187).

Best Chinese pagoda: The 10-story fantasy pagoda at **Kew Gardens** (p. 116), complete with dragons.

Best Chinese fish lips: Mr. Kong (p. 161) in Soho—they come with goose web.

Best Chinese china: The **Percival David Foundation** (p. 125), with over 1700 ceramics.

Best Italian manor that's lost its way: Chiswick House (p. 116), an improbable Italian estate in the middle of West London.

Best place to buy a hookah: Edgware Road (p. 92), in "Marlebanon."

Best place to buy a hooker: The alleys around **King's Cross** (p. 107).

Best James Bond villain named for a London architect: Goldfinger, named for the architect who ruined Ian Fleming's view with Two Willow Rd. (p. 109).

The East End is well served by the Underground. Old St. is best for Hoxton/Shoreditch while Aldgate East and Liverpool St. are nearest Whitechapel sights. Farther east, the Tube swings away and the DLR takes over: these driverless trains (travelcards valid) will take you all the way down to Greenwich. Buses: Useful for getting from the City to the East End, but for distances farther east, the Tube and DLR are quicker.

At Aldgate, the fabulous wealth of the City abruptly gives way to the historically impoverished **East End.** The divide is centuries-old: since both prevailing winds and the river current conspired to waft the pollution of the crowded City eastward, the rich fled to West London and the poor were grounded in the east. Cheap land together with proximity to the docks made the East End a natural site for immigration. Older residents still remember when this was a predominantly Jewish neighborhood, but today it's solidly Bangladeshi. **Brick Lane,** famed for its market and its restaurants, is now at the center of a new influx: independent artists and designers colonizing one of the last affordable areas in central London. East of Whitechapel, the East End remains poor until **Docklands.** Since the late 1980s, this vast man-made archipelago has been busy building itself up from an abandoned port into a mini-metropolis. Unfortunately, the construction has decimated the area's traditional communities and bulldozed much of its history—there's not much reason to get off the elevated DLR trains as they shuffle south toward **Greenwich.** Once the favorite residence of Elizabeth I, Greenwich is far removed from East London's present: steeped in history, it's a beautiful district with a wealth of sights.

DON'T MISS...

Sights: The Sunday market crawl—check out Spitalfields and Brick Ln., then hop on the DLR to see what Greenwich's three separate markets have to offer.

Museums & Galleries: The history of English Domestic Interiors—from china to chintz—at the Geffrye Museum; promising newcomers and established talents at the spectacular Whitechapel Art Gallery.

Food & Drink: Cruise the bagel and balti joints along Brick Ln.

Nightlife: Dive into the Shoho (see p. 113) scene with a drink in Cargo's candlelit lounge, then head to nearby Herbal or 333 to mix with the Beautiful People.

WEST LONDON

◪ WEST LONDON QUICKFIND: Sights, *p. 115; **Food & Drink,** p. 168; **Entertainment,** p. 220; **Shopping,** p. 243; **Accommodations,** p. 266. **TRANSPORTATION:** West London is huge, but most sights are easy to get to. If you've got the time, a **river boat** is the most relaxing way of getting to Kew. **Tube:** The District Line goes to most sights. **Buses:** Invaluable for getting to some of the more obscure sights and also an efficient way of getting between West London neighborhoods.*

West London stretches for miles along the Thames before petering out in the hills and vales of the Thames valley. The river changes tack so often and so sharply that it makes no sense to talk about the north or south bank, and communities have developed almost in isolation from their neighbors. **Shepherd's Bush,** one of these relatively autonomous districts, distinguishes itself with a number of well-known concert and theater venues, while **Hammersmith** bridges the gap between the shopping malls around the Tube station and the pleasant parks and pubs along the Thames. Historically, the western reaches of the Thames were fashionable spots for country retreats, and the river still winds through the grounds of stately homes and former palaces.

DON'T MISS...

Sights: The lush gardens and lavish furnishings of Chiswick House; the even lusher Kew Gardens, recently named a UN World Heritage site.

Food & Drink: All things French at Maison Blanc; vegetarian delights at the Gate.

Entertainment: Being part of a live studio audience at BBC Television Centre; sampling international art flicks at Riverside Studios.

TOP 25 REASONS TO VISIT LONDON

25. Somerset House. This elegant manor is home to three top museums: The Gilbert Collection of Decorative Arts, The Hermitage Rooms, and the world-famous Courtaud Institute Galleries. See p. 129.

24. St. Paul's. Christopher Wren's masterpiece, the towering dome of St. Paul's dominates The City of London; inside are the tombs of such greats as John Donne and the Duke of Wellington. See p. 68.

23. Richmond Park. Europe's largest urban park, Richmond is home to spectacular countryside and over 800 deer—and it's accessible by Tube. See p. 273.

22. Fabric. As big and bold as a nightclub can get, Fabric's three dancefloors can (and often do) hold up to 2000 dedicated clubbers. See p. 186.

21. The view from the Monument. From atop Christopher Wren's memorial to the Great Fire of 1666, you can see everything—and they even give you a certificate of achievement just for climbing up. See p. 78.

20. The Wenlock Arms. One of London's very best pubs, with traditional decor, a great selection of ales, and a hot-salt-beef sandwich that will blow your mind. See p. 180.

19. Café Zagora. This is what London's multiculturalism is all about—a Moroccan-Lebanese restaurant staffed by Poles in Hogarth's old neighborhood. The decor is elegant, the food remarkable, and the service impeccable. See p. 168.

18. Portobello Road Markets. Everything you've never wanted or needed, all in one place. Portobello Rd. has to be seen to be believed—come on a Saturday morning for the full effect of hundreds of thousands of people combing through everything from used clothes to antique china. See p. 231.

17. Houses of Parliament. Neo-Gothicism's greatest architectural triumph, the Houses of Parliament bear their history and traditions with grace and stunning beauty. See p. 64.

16. The Temple. Once the seat of the Knights Templar, this complex of buildings is hidden among Holborn's alleyways. The Temple boasts London's first Gothic church, an original Norman doorway, and innumerable gardens and squares. The Temple is an oasis of ancient calm and architectural beauty. See p. 84.

15. Zaika. The best Indian restaurant in the world, Zaika wows with its innovative, intelligent colors and flavors. The service is excellent, and the decor is hip but comfortable. One bite, and you'll be hooked on "British" food forever. See p. 153.

14. The London Eye. The largest observational wheel in the world, the London Eye offers 360-degree views of all of London. Time your visit right, and you can look down on the Houses of Parliament and Buckingham Palace glowing in the sunset. See p. 95.

13. St. Etheldreda's. One of few medieval buildings left in London, St. Etheldreda's is also among the most beautiful churches in the entire city. Built in the mid-1200s, the church has survived Reformation, the Great Fire, and the Blitz to awe us with its enormous windows and soaring nave. See p. 86.

12. The British Museum. Imagine every museum you've ever been to, then multiply by ten. The British Museum has over 50,000 items, from the Rosetta Stone and endless mummies to African fetish dolls and tribal costumes. See p. 119.

11. Shakespeare's Globe Theatre. You can take a tour to see behind-the-scenes, but for the full Globe experience, attend one of the many performances. You can see the excellent, innovative productions from the hard wooden benches, or commune with Elizabethan peasantry as a groundling. See p. 213.

10. Ye Olde Mitre. Hands-down our favorite pub in London, Ye Olde Mitre was built in 1546 by the Bishop of Ely. Its two dark rooms are incredibly cozy, the staff is friendly, and the bitters are excellent. See p. 175.

9. The Tower of London. Arrive early in the morning to beat the crowds, and you'll be treated to one of London's most evocative sights. Home to a long and bloody past and a resplendent present—the Yeomen of the Guard and the Crown Jewels are guaranteed to impress. See p. 70.

8. The British Library Galleries. A stunning collection of books and manuscripts is on display in the new British Library building. Highlights include a Magna Carta, Joyce's handwritten *Finnegan's Wake*, and original handwritten Beatles lyrics. See p. 125.

7. Oxford Street. London's shopping mecca, Oxford St. is always packed—on Saturdays, you can barely move. It's all worth it, though, with every major chain, countless bargain stalls, and tons of one-off boutiques offering the most stylish clothes and accessories you'll find anywhere in the world. See p. 233.

6. Brixton nightlife. Brixton is home to London's most exciting new club scene—not bad for a former slum. Clubs like Tongue&Groove and the Fridge are both hip and welcoming, filled with energetic, stylish young dancers. What's more, many Brixton clubs and bars stay open all night so you can party until dawn. See p. 194.

5. The Victoria & Albert Museum. The largest museum of decorative arts in the world, the V&A is home to a 500-year-old Iranian carpet, a pair of 1990s latex hotpants, and just about everything in between. Raphael, Dürer, and Holbein share space with medieval vestments and samurai armor in this museum dedicated to displaying "the fine and applied arts of all countries, all styles, and all periods." See p. 123.

4. Tea at Brown's. The quintessential English tea, Tea at Brown's offers visitors the ultimate in luxury and old-fashioned elegance. Feast on cucumber sandwiches, scones, and clotted cream—for a few hours you can live like royalty. See p. 144.

3. Westminster Abbey. In its thousand years, this beautiful building has seen countless kings crowned, celebrated, and buried. The Abbey is the resting place of Britain's greatest men and women, from kings and queens to poets and scientists. Its architecture is astounding, a late-Gothic extravaganza that is sure to take your breath away. See p. 65.

2. The National Gallery. The National Gallery holds an incredible collection of art. The brand-new Sainsbury Wing is a treasure trove of medieval art, including the stunning *Wilton Diptych* and Botticelli's *Venus and Mars*. Other rooms house Manet, Van Gogh, Rubens, Rembrandt, and two of only 34 Vermeers in the world. No matter what your taste in art, you'll never want to leave. See p. 121.

1. The Tate Modern. London is home to the world's most active and innovative modern art community, and this is where it shows. Tate Modern displays art of every stripe, from sculpture to installations to claymation; all is carefully curated and guaranteed to be both refreshing and challenging. See p. 123.

LONDON IN ONE WEEK (OR LESS)
THREE DAYS

DAY 1: ROYAL WESTMINSTER

Begin your visit with our **Walking With Royalty** walking tour (p. 18). The tour takes you through all the major Westminster sights, from **Buckingham Palace** to **Westminster Bridge**, via the **National Gallery.** After dinner, have a pint with the politicians at **The Red Lion** pub (p. 179).

DAY 2: TOWER AND SOUTH BANK

Take our **Millennium Mile** walking tour (p. 20) to experience the full range of London's appeal—begin at the **Tower of London,** visit **Tate Modern,** and finish with a spectacular vista from the **London Eye.** Cap off the day with a pint at one of the South Bank's historic and beautiful **pubs** (p. 177), or head farther south to **Brixton** for some serious clubbing (p. 194).

DAY 3: THE WEST END

The West End offers enough amusements to fill an entire week, let alone one day. Spend the morning hitting the boutiques on **Oxford Street** (p. 233), but don't miss **Hamley's** (p. 234), the toy store of the gods. Take tea at **Brown's** (p. 144) and feel like an aristocrat for a few hours. In the evening, sample the jazz at **Ronnie Scott's** (p. 214) or head to **Strawberry Moons** (p. 188) for a night of booty-shaking.

FIVE DAYS

DAY 4: HOLBORN AND THE CITY

Begin your day at **St. Paul's Cathedral** (p. 68)—get there early to avoid the crowds, then head to the **Museum of London** (p. 126) to get the inside scoop on London's history. Next, visit Holborn and see the **Temple** (p. 84), once the seat of the Knights Templar, or watch a trial at the **Royal Courts of Justice** (p. 87). A short walk will take you to **St Etheldreda's** (p. 86), a stunning medieval church, and of **Ye Olde Mitre** (p. 175), our favorite London pub. The nearby **Bleeding Heart Tavern** (p. 152) serves English classics with great skill.

DAY 5: KENSINGTON

Spend the morning in Albertopolis: visit the **Victoria & Albert Museum** (p. 123), **The Natural History Museum,** or **The Science Museum** (p. 130)—there's only time for one, as **Kensington High Street** beckons with its brilliant shopping (p. 229). Royals fans should visit **Kensington Palace** (p. 89), home of the Royal Dress Collection. The Palace is on the edge of **Hyde Park** (p. 73), which contains rolling hills, a pond, and even an art gallery. For dinner, head to **Zaika** (p. 153), which serves London's best Indian food.

SEVEN DAYS

DAY 6: GO WEST, YOUNG MAN

Take a daytrip to **Richmond** (p. 273). **Richmond Park** has enough rolling fields and woods to fill the day, but be sure to visit the **aristocratic manors** in the area, especially **Ham House,** with its stunning grounds and gardens. The manors have their own amazing gardens, but none can match the **Royal Botanical Gardens, Kew** (p. 116), whose glasshouses and gardens display flora from throughout the world. **Café Zagora** (p. 168) is on the way back to the city and offers Moroccan-Lebanese food in an amazing atmosphere.

DAY 7: PUBS, CLUBS, & MANUSCRIPTS

Spend in the morning in the **British Museum,** but don't linger too long or you may never leave. Walk up Gower St., past **University College London**—if you've the stomach for it, visit UCL founder **Jeremy Bentham,** whose embalmed corpse is still on display (p. 74). The **British Library Galleries** (p. 125) house a must-see collection of historical documents, from Magna Carta to the Beatles. At night, head to Clerkenwell for a **pub crawl** (p. 174), or to megaclub **Fabric** (p. 186) to dance the night away.

KIDS IN THE CITY

There's plenty in the capital to keep the little ones occupied. Of the major **sights,** a beefeater tour of the **Tower of London** (p. 70) is a must, as is posing with the Household Cavalry on **Horseguards Parade** (p. 105) and the bearskin-hatted Foot Guards outside **Buckingham Palace** (p. 63). Live animals are always a draw: **London Zoo** (p. 93) is fun, and don't neglect the Queen's horses in the **Royal Mews** (p. 106). While most major **museums** offer themed activity sheets to keep hands and eyes busy, some are naturally bigger hits than others. Robotic dinosaurs and an interactive human biology display make the **Natural History Museum** (p. 130) a firm favorite with children, while the hands-on galleries next door at the **Science Museum** (p. 131) are specifically tailored to different age groups. Budding engineers are sure to love the planes, tanks, and guns at the **Imperial War Museum** (p. 138) and the **Royal Airforce Museum** (p. 137), not to mention clambering all over the battleship **HMS Belfast** (p. 96) and Tubes at the **London's Transport Museum** (p. 134). Quiet kids might prefer the array of dolls and more sedate playthings at **Pollock's Toy Museum** (p. 125) and the **Museum of Childhood** (p. 140). If the weather's too nice to stay indoors, **Coram's Fields** (p. 75) is a park reserved solely for kids.

When it comes to **food,** don't despair. The **Lazy Daisy Café** (p. 157) is very popular with families and even offers kids a bin of toys. **Giraffe** (p. 155) is bright, fun, and has a kid-friendly menu, while **Tartuf's** pancake-like concoctions are cutlery-free (p. 163). Of the major chains, **Pizza Express** and **Yo!Sushi** (p. 147) are used to families. Note that pubs don't admit kids under 14 inside, though they're normally allowed in outside beer gardens. For **entertainment,** try the street performers of **Covent Garden** (p. 103) or, around Christmas time, a traditional **pantomime.** Older kids will love the spectacle at **Shakespeare's Globe Theatre** (p. 213), even if they don't catch every word, while musicals such as the **Lion King** (p. 202) were made with kids in mind.

A tour of Royal London has no rival—there is simply nothing that compares to a day in Westminster. By covering the circumference of St. James' Park, this walking tour covers the great traditions and monuments of British history, from Westminster Abbey, sight of royal coronations, to the artistic jewels of the National Gallery, to the seat of modern British politics: the imposing halls of Westminster.

To maximize your enjoyment of this tour, call stops 2 and 7 one month ahead.

Time: 7-9 hr.

Distance: 1.7 mi. (2.7km)

When To Go: Early morning

Start: Westminster Abbey

Finish: The Houses of Parliament

What To Bring: A snack & a picnic lunch

Call well ahead: Stops 2, 7.

1 WESTMINSTER ABBEY. Avoid the crowds by **arriving early** at medieval Westminster Abbey (p. 65). As a place for Royal coronations and burials since 1065, the Abbey immortalizes past monarchs in the impressive Royal Tombs. Along with the departed literati and musicians in the Poet's Corner, the Abbey also shelters the remains of Winston Churchill. The Abbey has been the sight of royal coronations from the Middle Ages to the present—the Abbey will hold Prince Charles's coronation, should he become King of England. Explore the monastery and gardens, but limit yourself to approximately 1hr. before heading to Buckingham Palace. Either make the 15min. walk there or take the Tube from Westminster to St. James's Park.

2 BUCKINGHAM PALACE. First occupied by Queen Victoria in 1832, the Palace (p. 63) continues to house the Royal family. During the months of August and September, the State Rooms, the Throne Room, the White Drawing room, the magnificent Galleries and the beautifully manicured Gardens are open for tours. *Call well ahead for tickets.*

The **Changing of the Guard** outside Buckingham Palace takes place at 11:20am, though to gain an unobstructed view aim to arrive by 10:30am. *The Changing of the Guard takes place daily Apr.-Oct., every other day Nov.-Mar., provided the Queen is in residence, it is not raining too hard, and there are no pressing state functions.*

After the Palace, take a stroll down the Mall, following the same annual route of the Queen on her way to open Parliament. To your right, **St. James's Park** (p. 106) offers a pleasant site for a snack. To your left is **St. James's Palace**. Approaching the end of the Mall pass thorugh Admiralty Arch and into...

3 TRAFALGAR SQUARE. Designed by John Nash, London's largest square today serves as a forum for public rallies and protest movements, not to mention controversial art. On December 31, the square hosts the City's largest New Year's Eve celebration (p. 104). All proceedings are soberly observed by statues of Lord Nelson (perched on his column), George IV, Charles I and George Washington. The eastern "Fourth Plinth" is reserved for rotating contemporary sculpture installations.

4 NATIONAL GALLERY. Don't miss the **National Gallery** (p. 121). Considering the thousands of works on display, it's hard to believe that this gallery was founded with only 38 pictures. Depending on your interests, spend anywhere from 1hr. to the remainder of the day savoring European masterpieces dating from the Middle Ages to the close of the 18th century. The Gallery, organized chronologically into four wings, contains gems from the Italian Renaissance, the Dutch and Spanish Golden Ages and French Impressionism, along with rotating exhibitions on single artists. To use your time most efficiently, design your own tour at the electronic stations (p. 121).

Hungry? The expensive restaurant atop the National Portrait Gallery offers spectacular views of the city. Tachbrook St. has a number of cheap establishments. Consider a having a picnic lunch at the feet of Trafalgar Square's bronze lions. After lunch, walk south along Whitehall, where you will pass a long stretch of imposing Ministry building facades (p. 105).

5 HORSEGUARDS. The Guards on the world's most popular postcard inspire giggles and distraction attempts from thousands of tourists per year. Because it's highly unlikely that any provocation will prompt a response, we saved you the trouble and interviewed one of the Queen's Life Guards (p. 62). Technically "the Queen's Guard" only refers to those at Buckingham Palace and St. James's Palace.

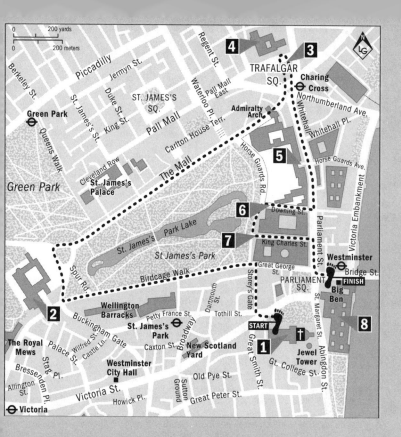

6 10 DOWNING STREET. Former residence of Churchill, Thatcher, and all the other British Prime Ministers, today 10 Downing St. is home to... Gordon Brown, Chancellor of the Exchequer. Tony Blair's family is too big for No. 10 so he's now in No. 11 (p. 105).

7 CABINET WAR ROOMS. From 1938 to 1944, Winston Churchill ran the British war effort from these converted coal cellars (p. 136). The 19 rooms on show have been perfectly restored to their wartime appearance, right down to the paperclips. Highlights include "Churchill's personal loo"—a small room containing the top-secret transatlantic hotline.

8 THE PALACE OF WESTMINSTER. Also known as **The Houses of Parliament** (p. 64) and the final stop of our walking tour. Containing both the House of Lords and the House of Commons, Westminster Palace has been at the heart of English governance since the 11th century. Crossing MPs can be spotted from the **New Palace Yard,** while the **Old Palace Yard** was formerly a site for executions. Look above to see famous **Clock Tower.** Big Ben, the 14-ton bell inside the clock, still chimes on the hour. To enter Parliament, either wait in line for the limited seats in the Stranger's Gallery, or pre-book a tour of the State Rooms. *Call ahead to arrange tours and find out what time debates are for the day.*

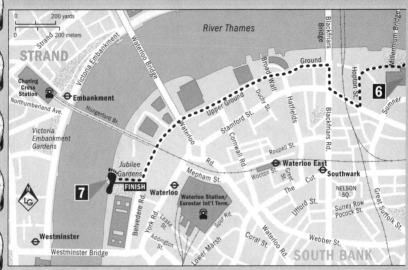

Once a rather seedy neighborhood, the South Bank is now home to London's densest concentration of cultural centers. The Tate Modern is just one of the South Bank's artistic powerhouses. Shakespeare's Globe Theatre had its first season in 1997, and each subsequent season brings bolder interpretations of Will's works. Concert halls in the area host every type of music, and

Distance: 2.5 mi. (4km)

When To Go: Start early morning

Start: Tower Hill Underground

Finish: Westminster Underground

Call Ahead: 5,7.

theatres present an unparalleled range of new works. Commercial Gabriel's Wharf thrives in the excitement of the area. Fantastic city views from Tate Modern, OXO Wharf and, of course, London Eye, in addition to the understated beauty of a walk along the Thames, are constant draws. Meanwhile, the highly acclaimed Jubilee Line Extension—which includes a revamped interior at London Bridge—has greatly facilitated transportation to the South Bank and helped to transform the area into the cultural powerhouse it was originally intended to be.

1 TOWER OF LONDON. Begin your trek to the Tower early to avoid the crowds. Tours given by the Yeomen Warders meet every 90min. near the entrance. Listen as they expertly recount tales of royal conspiracy, treason, and murder. See the **White Tower,** once both fortress and residence of kings. Shiver at the executioner's stone on the tower green and pay your respects at the Chapel of St. Peter ad Vinculum, holding the remains of 3 queens. First get the dirt on the gemstones at **Martin Tower,** then wait in line to see the **Crown Jewels.** The jewels include such glittering lovelies as the First Star of Africa, the largest cut diamond in the world (p. 70).

2 TOWER BRIDGE. An engineering wonder that puts its plainer sibling, the London Bridge, to shame. Marvel at its beauty, but skip the **Tower Bridge Experience.** Or better yet, call ahead to inquire what times the Tower drawbridge is lifted (p. 79).

3 DESIGN MUSEUM. On Butler's Wharf, let the Design Museum introduce you to the latest innovations in contemporary design, from marketing to movements in haute coture. See what's to come in the forward-looking Review Gallery or hone in on individual designers and products in the Temporary Gallery. From the DM, walk along the **Queen's Walk.** To your left you will find the **HMS Belfast,** which was launched upon Normandy, France on D-Day, 1938.

WALKING TOUR

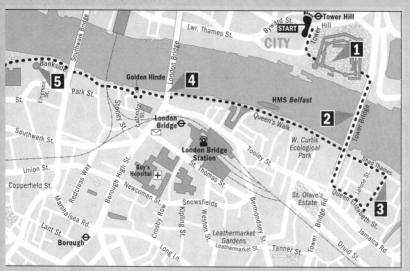

4 LONDON BRIDGE. See the fifth incarnation of a London classic, hopefully more sturdy than its predecessors. The 1832 Old London Bridge is now relocated in Lake Havasu City, Arizona. The **Golden Hinde** is docked on the other side of London Bridge, a full-size and functional replica of Sir Francis Drake's 16th-century war ship (p. 97).

5 SHAKESPEARE'S GLOBE THEATER. "I hope to see London once ere I die," says Shakespeare's Davy in *Henry IV, Part II*. In time, he may see it from the beautiful recreation of Will's most famous theater. Excellent exhibits reveal how Shakespearean actors dressed and the secrets of stage effects, and tell of the painstaking process of rebuilding of the theater almost 400 years after the original burned down (see p. 95). You might be able to catch a matinee performance if you time your visit right. *Call ahead for tour and show times.*

6 TATE MODERN. It's hard to imagine anything casting a shadow over Shakespeare's Globe Theatre, but the massive former Bankside Power Station does just that. One of the world's premier modern art museums, the Tate's arrangements promise a new conceptual spin on well-known favoritesand works by emerging British artists. Be sure to catch one of the informative docent tours and don't forget to ogle the rotating installation in the Turbine Room.

Having fulfilled your theatrical and artistic appetites, now may be a good time to have a quick bite to eat. **Café 7** and the **East Room** of the Tate Modern offer meals and snacks, respectively, not to mention fabulous views of the City (see p. 122).

As a cheaper alternative, check out the cafes, bars, and boutiques of colorful **Gabriel's Wharf.** If you missed the top floor of the Tate Modern, go to the public viewing gallery on the 8th floor of the **OXO Tower** Wharf (see p. 97).

Pass by the **South Bank Centre** on your way to the London Eye. Established as a primary cultural center in 1951, it now exhibits a range of music from Philharmonic extravaganzas to low-key jazz. You may even catch one of the free lunchtime or afternoon events (see p. 96). *Call ahead for dates and times.*

7 LONDON EYE. Once known as the Millennium Wheel; given its siblings—the misbehaving "Bridge" and bloated ego of "Dome"—it's no surprise that it shed its Millennium maiden name at the first possible chance (p. 95). The London Eye has now firmly established itself as one of London's top attractions, popular with locals and tourists alike. The Eye offers amazing 360° views from its glass pods. If you time it right, you can see all of London lit up in the sunset. *Book in advance to avoid the long queues.*

Once in London

This chapter is designed to help you navigate the quirks of London after your arrival—for pre-departure arrangements, see **Planning Your Trip** (p. 293).

GETTING INTO LONDON

THE AIRPORTS

HEATHROW

🖪 Location: *Near Hounslow, West London, 15 mi. from Central London.* **Contact:** ☎ *0870 000 0123; www.baa.co.uk/main/airports/heathrow.*

Heathrow is ugly, sprawling, crowded, and chaotic—just what you'd expect from the world's busiest international airport. Airlines and destinations are divvied up among its four terminals as listed below, with a few exceptions—if in doubt, check with the airline.

Terminal 1: Domestic flights and British Airways's European destinations, except for flights to Amsterdam, Athens, Basle, Moscow, and Paris.

Terminal 2: All non-British Airways flights to Europe with the exception of Air Malta and KLM; British Airways flights to Basle.

Terminal 3: Intercontinental flights, except British Airways, Qantas, and Sri Lankan Airlines; British Airways flights to Miami.

Terminal 4: British Airways's intercontinental flights (except Miami) and services to Amsterdam, Athens, Moscow, and Paris; Air Malta; KLM; Qantas; Sri Lankan Airlines; and any other flights that won't squeeze into terminals 1, 2, or 3.

TRANSPORTATION TO/FROM CENTRAL LONDON

UNDERGROUND. The cheapest and best way to get to London from Heathrow. Heathrow's two Tube stations form a loop on the end of the Piccadilly Line—trains stop first at **Heathrow Terminal 4** and then at **Heathrow Terminals 1, 2, 3** (both Zone 6) before swinging back towards central London. Note that stairs are an integral part of most Tube stations. (☎ *0845 330 9880; www.thetube.com. 50-70min. from central London, every 4-5min. £3.70, under-16s £1.50.)*

TRAIN. The **Heathrow Express** provides a speedy but expensive connection from Heathrow to Paddington station. An added bonus is check-in facilities at Paddington. Ticket counters at Heathrow even accept foreign currency. Wheelchair accessible. (☎ *0845 600 1515; www.heathrowexpress.co.uk. 15min., daily every 15min. 5:10am-11:40pm. Railpasses and Travelcards not valid. £14, return £25 (valid until 30 days after purchase); child £6/£11.50; £2 extra if bought on the train. Ask about day returns and group specials. AmEx/MC/V.)*

BUS. The **Airbus A2** crawls from Heathrow to King's Cross, stopping off at various points on the way. (☎ *0870 580 8080; www.nationalexpress.com. 1¼-1¾ hr.; every 20-45min. 5:45am-11pm Heathrow-King's Cross, 4am-8pm King's Cross-Heathrow. £10, return £15; ages 5-15 half price.)* **National Express** (which operates Airbus) also runs coaches between Heathrow and Victoria Coach Station. (*Contact and prices as above. 40-80min., approx. every 15-40min. 5:40am-9:35pm Heathrow-Victoria, 7:30am-11:30pm Victoria-Heathrow.)*

SHUTTLE. **Hotelink** runs shared shuttles from Heathrow to hotels in London. Book at least 48hr. ahead. (☎ *01293 532 244; www.hotelink.co.uk. Operates daily 4am-6pm Heathrow-London, 6am-10pm London-Heathrow. £15, return £25.)*

TAXI. With metered fares to central London unlikely to be under £50, and journey times never under 1 hr., you'd have to be rich *and* stupid to take a **licensed taxicab** from Heathrow to London by yourself. A **minicab** is slightly cheaper and just as slow. You can have a contact in London (hotel and hostel owners will often oblige) book a minicab to meet you; expect to pay £25-30 including waiting, parking, and tip.

GATWICK

🖪 Location: *Sussex, 30 mi. south of London.* **Contact:** ☎ *0870 000 2468; www.baa.co.uk/main/airports/gatwick.*

Though Gatwick is much farther from London, numerous swift and affordable train services often make it easier to get to than Heathrow. Transport facilities are concentrated in the **South Terminal;** a futuristic free monorail shuttle connects the South Terminal to the newer **North Terminal,** which has better shops and restaurants.

TRANSPORTATION TO/FROM CENTRAL LONDON

TRAIN. Three train companies run between Gatwick and London, and they all charge different prices and tickets are non-transferable between services. The **Gatwick Express** non-stop service to Victoria station would like you to think it's the only train to London, but the cheaper **Connex** commuter trains run the same route just as frequently and take just a few minutes longer. (*Gatwick Express:* ☎ *0845 850 1530; www.gatwickexpress.co.uk. 30-35min., Departs Gatwick 4:30am, 5am, then every 15min. until midnight. £11, return (good for 30 days after purchase) £21.50; ages 5-15 £5.50/£11. Connex:* ☎ *0870 603 0405; www.connex.co.uk. 35-45min., every 15-20min. 5am-midnight and every 30-60min. midnight-5am. £8.20, return £16.40; ages 5-15 £4.10/£8.20.)* Additionally,

Thameslink commuter trains head regularly to King's Cross, stopping in London Bridge and Blackfriars. Beware that Thameslink stations typically have lots of stairs. (☎ 0845 330 6333; www.thameslink.co.uk. 50min.; daily every 15-30min. £10, return £20.)

BUSES, SHUTTLES, & TAXIS. Gatwick's distance from London makes road services slow and unpredictable. National Express's **Airbus A5** takes 1½ hr. to travel to Victoria bus station. (Contact details and prices same as for Heathrow. Hourly 4:15am-9:15pm from Gatwick, 6am-11pm from Victoria.) The **Hotelink** shuttle offers a pick-up service from Gatwick to London hotels. (See Heathrow for details. Operates 5am-4pm daily. £20 per person, return £35.) You should never take a **licensed taxi** from Gatwick to London; the trip will take over an hour and cost at least £90. **Minicabs** are cheaper (£30-£40) but still leave you at the mercy of traffic; plus, you'll have to have a contact in London arrange for pickup. If you have heavy bags, take the train to Victoria and catch a taxi from there.

STANSTED

🏢 *Location:* Essex, 30 mi. north of London. *Contact:* ☎ 0870 000 0303; www.baa.co.uk/main/airports/stansted.

TRANSPORTATION TO/FROM CENTRAL LONDON

TRAINS. The train station is below the terminal building. The **Stansted Express** offers frequent service to Liverpool St. Station (☎ 08745 850 0150; www.stanstedexpress.co.uk. 45min.; M-Sa every 15-30min. 5:30am-midnight from Stansted, 4:30am-11:30pm from Liverpool St. £13, return £23.) **WAGN** runs a slower train along the same route for 20p more. (☎ 08457 48 49 50; www.wagn.co.uk. 1-1¼hr.; every hr. 7am-10:30pm.)

BUS. The **Airbus A6/A7** runs every 30min. to Victoria station, 24hr. The A6 goes via the West End, the A7 via The City. (Contact and prices same as for Heathrow. 1¼-1¾hr.)

LUTON

🏢 *Location:* Bedfordshire, 32 mi. north of London. *Contact:* ☎ 0158 240 5100; www.london-luton.co.uk.

Luton serves mostly charter flights and no-frills budget airlines.

TRANSPORTATION TO/FROM CENTRAL LONDON

The **Thameslink train** line that links Gatwick to King's Cross also continues north to Luton. (Contact as for Gatwick. 30-50min.; every 15-30min. M-Sa 3:20am-1am, Su less frequently 6am-11:15pm. Single £9.50, return £18.) **Green Line 757 buses** link Luton to the West End and Victoria. (☎ 0870 608 7261; www.greenline.co.uk. 1-1¾hr.; every 30min. 8am-8pm, hourly 8pm-midnight and 3am-8am. £8, return £13; ages 5-15 £4/£6.50.)

LONDON CITY AIRPORT

🏢 *Location:* Docklands, East London. *Contact:* ☎ 7646 0088; www.londoncityairport.com.

Built over the former Royal Docks, it was once the heart of London's trading empire. Today, the main export is pin-striped business men.

TRANSPORTATION TO/FROM CENTRAL LONDON

Every 10min., **shuttles** make the 30min. run to Liverpool St. via Canary Wharf, or the 5min. run to Canning Town. (To and from Liverpool St. via Canary Wharf: M-F 6:50am-9:20pm, Sa 6:50am-1:10pm, Su 11am-9:20pm; £3 to Canary Wharf, £6 to Liverpool St. To and from Canning Town: M-F 6am-10:30pm, Sa 6am-1pm, Su 10am-10:20pm; £2.50.) The **#69** bus also runs to Canning Town, while the **#474** stops at Silvertown rail station. (Both approx. every 10min., 6am-midnight, 70p.)

TRAIN STATIONS

London's nine mainline stations date from the Victorian era, when each railway company had its own London terminus. After being unified for most of the 20th century, the 1990s saw the railways broken up and privatized again. Corporate loyalty means that some station staff are unwilling to tell you about rival services. For impartial advice, call **National Rail Enquiries.** *(24hr.* ☎ *0845 748 4950)* All London termini are well served by bus and Tube services.

BUS STATIONS

Victoria Coach Station (Tube: Victoria), Buckingham Palace Rd., is the hub of Britain's long-distance bus network. **National Express** is the largest operator of intercity services. *(*☎*0870 580 8080; www.nationalexpress.com.)* International services are dominated by **Eurolines,** which offers regular links to all major European cities. *(*☎*1582 415 841; www.eurolines.co.uk.)* Much of the area around London is served by **Green Line** coaches, which leave from the Eccleston Bridge mall behind Victoria station. Purchase tickets from the driver. *(*☎*0870 608 7261; www.greenline.co.uk.)*

GETTING AROUND LONDON

Londoners love to complain, and they love nothing better than complaining about transportation—even the weather gets a better rap. Whether it's overcrowding on the Tube or British Rail delays, nothing is more deeply ingrained in the London psyche than the idea that its transport infrastructure is falling to pieces. For all this, London's transport system remains one of the world's best; there's hardly a spot in the city not served by frequent Tubes, buses, or trains. If occasionally there is a 20min. wait for a bus, or an overcrowded Tube, that's just part of the fun—and an opportunity to appreciate the fact that, when it comes to politeness under pressure (and avoiding bodily contact), Londoners are first-rate. Oddly, what shocks visitors the most about London transportation seems least important to locals: the expense. **Count on spending approximately £5 per day on public transportation.**

BY PUBLIC TRANSPORTATION

🔢 *Operated by Transport for London. 24hr. info, including route advice* ☎ *7222 1234; www.tfl.gov.uk. Current delays and route changes* ☎ *7222 1200.*

Local gripes aside, London's public transport is remarkably efficient—and it's getting better. London's Mayor, Ken Livingstone, is the man who first introduced Travelcards in the 1980s, and scarcely a week goes by without new talk about making travel in London easier and cheaper. New fares are generally introduced in January.

ZONES

The public-transport network is divided into a series of concentric zones; ticket prices depend on the zones passed through during a journey. To confuse matters, there are two different zoning systems. The **Tube, rail,** and **Docklands Light Railway (DLR)** network operates on a system of six zones, with Zone 1 being the most central. The **Buses** reduce this to four zones. Bus Zones 1, 2, and 3 are the same as for the Tube, and Tube Zones 4, 5, and 6 are bus Zone 4. **Almost everything of interest to visitors is found in Zones 1 and 2.**

TRAVEL PASSES

🔢 *All passes expire at 4:30am the morning after the printed expiration date.*

London's public transportation is the best way to get around the city, and you're almost bound to save money by investing in one of London's range of travel passes. Passes work on the Zone system (see above). Note that a Zone 1-4 pass will cover all bus routes in London, but Tube and other services only up to the Tube Zone 4 boundary. Passes can be purchased at Tube, DLR, and commuter rail stations. Avoid **ticket touts** hawking second-hand One-Day Travelcards, LT Cards, and Bus Passes; you might save a few pounds, but there's no guarantee the ticket will work. More importantly it's illegal—penalties are stiff, and the Tube has been cracking down on offenders.

To qualify for child fares, teenagers **aged 14-15** must display a **child-rate Photocard** when purchasing tickets and traveling on public transportation. To qualify for student fares, full-time students at London universities must obtain a **Student photocard**. These can be obtained free of charge from any Tube station on presentation of proof of age and a passport-sized photo.

DAY TRAVELCARDS. Valid for bus, Tube, DLR, and commuter rail services for one day. There are 2 types of Day Travelcards—**Peak** cards (valid from midnight); **Off-Peak** cards (valid from midnight Sa-Sun, but from 9:30am M-F). Both Peak and Off-Peak Travelcards are valid until 4:30am the morning after the printed expiration date. **Fare:** Zones 1-2 Peak £5.10, Off-Peak £4.10; Zones 1-4 £7/£4.50; Zones 1-6 £10.70/£5.10. **Child Fare (ages 5-15):** Peak, half the adult fare; Off-Peak Zones 1-6 £2.

LT CARDS. LT Cards are just like Peak Day Travelcards except they're not valid on the commuter rail. The only type available to adults is for all 6 zones, which means you're only likely to use one when heading to or from Heathrow, for which it's cheaper than a Peak Day Travelcard. **Fare:** Zones 1-6 £8. **Child Fare (ages 5-15):** £3.50.

CARNET. A book of 10 singles, for a Tube journey starting and finishing in Zone 1 only; cannot be used as extensions, nor can you purchase extensions for them. Each ticket must be validated at the station before you use it; failure to do so counts as fare evasion. Cheaper than buying individual singles, but unless you plan to do a lot of walking, a Travelcard is probably better. **Fare:** £11.50. **Child Fare (ages 5-15):** £5.

FAMILY TRAVELCARDS. For 1-2 adults and 1-4 children traveling together. When the only child is under 5, a child fare must be paid; otherwise under-5s go free. Each member must hold a Family Travelcard and must travel together. Validity as for Day Travelcards Off-Peak. **Fare:** Zones 1-2 £2.70, 1-4 £3, 1-6 £3.40, 2-6 £2.40. **Child Fare (ages 5-15):** 80p.

WEEKEND TRAVELCARDS. Valid 2 consecutive days Sa, Su and public holidays (e.g,, Easter Sunday and Easter Monday). **Fare:** Zones 1-2 £6.10, 1-4 £6.70, 1-6 £7.60, 2-6 £5.40. **Child Fare (ages 5-15):** Zones 1-6 £3.

SEASON TICKETS. Weekly, monthly, and annual Travelcards can be bought at any time and are valid for 7 days, 1 month, or 1 yr. respectively from the date of purchase. Matching **Photocard** required, free from Tube stations with an ID photo. **Rate:** Zone 1 only £16.50 weekly, £63.40 monthly; Zones 1-2 £19.60/£75.30. **Child Rate (ages 5-15):** Zone 1 only £6.80/£26.20; Zones 1-2 £8/£30.80.

BUS PASSES. Since Tube passes include access to the bus, buy a bus pass only if you won't be using the Tube. **One Day Bus Pass:** £2 all Zones. Child (ages 5-15) £1. **Weekly Bus Passes:** £8.50 all Zones. Child (ages 5-15) £4. Longer periods available.

YOUTH & STUDENT PASSES. those aged 16-17 and full-time students at a London university can buy weekly, monthly, and annual passes at 30% off the adult rate. A "16-17" or "Student" photocard is required (see below).

TICKET EXTENSIONS. If you travel beyond the validity of your pass, **you must purchase an excess fare at the start of your journey**—this will be just the single fare from the last point included in your pass to your destination. Failure to do so counts as fare evasion, £10 fine if caught.

SENIORS & DISABLED TRAVELERS

FREEDOM PASS. London residents aged over 60 (for women) or 65 (for men) and those who are registered as disabled, qualify for the free Freedom Pass, which offers unlimited travel on most services after 9am M-F and all day Sa-Su and holidays. A utility bill in your name or driver's license made out to a London address usually suffices as evidence of residency. To obtain the pass, contact the local council.

DISABLED ACCESS. Traveling by public transport in London with a disability is difficult, but measures are constantly being taken to improve facilities. The only fully wheelchair-accessible transportation system is the **Docklands Light Railway.** Only 40 of 275 Tube stations are stair-free; accessible stations are marked on Tube maps with a wheelchair icon. **Buses** are marginally better. Wheelchair-friendly "kneeling buses" are being introduced on many routes, while most newer buses incorporate features to make them easier to use for the elderly and disabled. Those qualifying as London residents (as above, a utility bill in your name or driver's license with a London address usually proves residency.) can take advantage of **Dial-a-Ride** and **Taxicard** schemes giving free or reduced-rate accessible shuttle-bus and taxi rides all over London; contact your local council for details. For information on accessibility on London transport, call ☎ 7941 4600.

THE UNDERGROUND

🚻 *24hr. ☎ 7222 1234; www.thetube.com. Free **Maps** of the Underground network are available at Tube stations and Transport for London info centers.*

Universally known as "the Tube," the Underground provides a fast and convenient way of getting around the capital. Within Zone 1, use the Tube only for longer journeys; adjacent stations are so close together that walking or taking a bus makes more sense. If you use the Tube frequently (and chances are you will), a **Travelcard** (see p. 27) will save you money.

NAVIGATING THE SYSTEM. Color-coding makes navigating the 12 lines a breeze. **Platforms** are labeled by line name and general direction. If traveling on one of the any lines that splits into two or more branches, check platform indicators or the front of the train. Unless you want to be run down by a commuter in full stride, **stand to the right** on escalators.

HOURS OF OPERATION. The Tube runs daily from approximately 5:30am to midnight, giving clubbers that extra incentive to party till dawn. The exact time of the first and last train from each station should be posted in the ticket hall; check if you think you'll be taking the Tube any time after 11:30pm. Trains run less frequently early mornings, late nights, and Sundays.

TICKETS. You can buy tickets from ticket counters or machines in all stations. Each station displays a chart showing how much a ticket costs to any other station in the network. Tickets must be bought at the start of a journey and are valid only for the day of purchase (including return tickets, but excluding carnets). **Keep your ticket for the entire journey;** it will be checked on the way out and may be checked at any time. There's a £10 **on-the-spot fine** for traveling without a valid ticket.

BUSES

🚻 *www.tfl.gov.uk/buses. For 24hr. travel info, use the Transport for London information line (☎ 7222 1234. **Bus maps** are available at most Tube stations and at Transport for London information centers.*

Only tourists use the Tube for short trips in central London—chances are you'll spend half as long walking underground as it would take to get to your destination. If it's only a couple of Tube stops, or if it involves more than one change, a bus will likely get you there faster. Excellent signage makes the bus system easy to use even for those with no local knowledge. Most stops display a map of local routes and nearby stops together with a key to help you find the bus and stop you need faster than you can say "mind the gap." Most stops also have their name posted; if you're not sure where to get off, ask the driver or conductor to tell you.

Buses run approximately 5:30am to midnight; a reduced network of **Night Buses** (see below) fills in the gap. During the day, double-deckers generally run every 10-15min., while single-decker hoppers should come every 5-8min, though it's not uncommon to wait 30min. only for three buses to show up in a row.

BUS STOPS. Officially bus stops come in two varieties, regular and request: supposedly buses must stop at regular stops (red logo on white background), but only pull up at request stops (white on red) if someone rings the bell, or someone at the bus stop indicates to the driver with an outstretched arm. In reality, it's safest to ring/indicate at all stops. On the older open-platform "Routemaster" buses, you're free to hop on and off whenever you like. **Never try to board or alight from a moving bus.**

BUS TICKETS. On newer buses, show your pass or buy a ticket from the driver as you board: state your destination or just say the price. Older buses still use conductors, who make the rounds between stops to collect fares. Despite the "exact change" warnings posted on buses, drivers and conductors usually give change, though a £5 note will elicit grumbles and anything larger risks refusal. Keep your ticket until you get off the bus, or you face a £5 **on-the-spot fine.** For **Prices,** see **"Fares Please!"** p. 30.

NIGHT BUSES. When honest folk are in bed, London's army of Night Buses comes out to ferry party-goers home. Night Bus route numbers are prefixed with an N; they typically operate the same route as their daytime equivalents, but occasionally start and finish at different points. Many routes start from Trafalgar Sq. Most Night Buses operate every 30min. or 60min. midnight to 5:30am.

DOCKLANDS LIGHT RAILWAY

🔳 *Customer service ☎ 7363 9700 (open 8:30am-5:30pm M-F). Docklands travel hotline ☎ 7918 4000 (24hr.). www.tfl.gov.uk/dlr. The DLR operates M-F 5:15am-12:30am, Sa and holidays 6am-12:30am, and Su 7:30am-11:30pm.*

The toy-like driverless cabs of this elevated railway provide a vital link in the transport network of East London. Obvious physical differences aside, the network is basically an extension of the Tube, with the same tickets and pricing structure;

FARES PLEASE!
Tube and DLR fares

Ticket prices on the London Underground depend on two factors: how many zones traveled (p. 27), and whether you traveled through Zone 1 or not.

For journeys **including Zone 1,** prices are as follows (ages 5-15 given in parentheses):

Zone 1 only: £1.60 (60p)
1-2: £2 (80p)
1-3: £2.30 (£1)
1-4: £2.80 (£1.20)
1-5: £3.40 (£1.40)
1-6: £3.70 (£1.50)

The **Carnet** offers 10 tickets for travel in Zone 1 for £11.50. Unlike other Tube tickets, Carnet tickets are valid for a year, not just on the day of purchase.

Outside Zone 1, prices are:

any 1 zone: £1 (40p)
2 zones: £1.30 (£60)
3 zones: £1.70 (80p)
4 zones: £2.10 (£1)
5 zones: £2.30 (£1)

BUS FARES

Trips **including Zone 1** cost £1; journeys wholly **outside Zone 1** cost 70p. Before 10pm, ages 5-15 pay 40p regardless of zones traveled; after 10pm they pay the adult fare.

NIGHT-BUS FARES

Night buses cost £1 for journeys **including Zone 1,** and 70p **outside Zone 1.** Note that One Day and Family Travelcards, LT cards, and Bus Passes are valid only for journeys starting before 4:30am of the following day.

All the above ticket prices are valid until at least January 2004.

within the validity of a given ticket, you can transfer from Tube to DLR at no charge. Those combining Greenwich and Docklands in one day should enquire about **Rail and Sail** tickets (see p. 114).

SUBURBAN RAILWAYS

🚆 *Schedule and fare information* ☎ *0845 748 4950 (24hr.) and at www.railtrack.co.uk.*

In the suburbs, London's commuter rail network is almost as extensive as the Tube. In much of South and East London, it's the only option. Services are run by a range of companies: **Thameslink** heads north-south from Clerkenwell and The City of London; **Silverlink** runs east-west from Docklands to Richmond via Islington and Hampstead; and **WAGN** trains run from Liverpool St. to Hackney to name a few. Trains can dramatically cut journey times thanks to direct crosstown links—Silverlink takes 25min. from Hampstead to Kew, versus an hour by Tube. Trains run less frequently than the Tube—generally every 20-30min.—but service often continues later into the night. For journeys combining rail travel with Tube and DLR, you can buy a single ticket valid for the entire trip. Travelcards are also valid on most suburban rail services, though not on intercity lines that happen to make a few local stops.

COMMUTER BOATS

🚆 *www.tfl.gov.uk/river. For 24hr. travel info, use the Transport for London (TfL) information line* ☎ *7222 1234.* **Maps** *available at piers and TfL Travel Information Centres.*

London's most important transport artery for most of its history, for the last century the Thames has been little used except for pleasure cruises. Nevertheless, a small number of regularly scheduled commuter boats are once more plying the river. There are three routes in operation: **Chelsea Harbour to Embankment via Cadogan** (near Tate Britain), operated by Riverside Launches (☎ *7352 5888; M-F rush hours only; £4, return £8);* **Savoy to Masthouse Terrace via Canary Wharf** run by Thames Clippers (☎ *7977 6892. M-F 6:20am-7:30pm and occasionally through the weekend; fares from £1.80, children half fare);* and **Hilton Docklands to Canary Wharf,** also by Thames Clippers (*daily 6:30am-8:30pm; £1.80, return £3.40; ages 5-15 90p/£1.70).* See the TfL website for detailed timetables of departure times for all boats. Note that holders of a valid **Travelcard** receive one-third off most boat fares.

BY TAXI

LICENSED TAXICABS

🚖 **Charges:** *First 390yd./1¼min. £2, then £1.80 per mi. or 40p per min. until fare reaches £12.40, then 20p per 124yd./½min., more on Sa-Su, public holidays, and M-F 8pm-6am; 40p per additional passenger, 10p per item of luggage,* **Pick-up** *minimum £2 extra. The meter is running upon arrival and can be up to £3.80 extra. See p. 334 for* ☎ *numbers.* **Lost Property:** *200 Baker St. (☎ 7918 2000). Tube: Baker St. Open M-F 9am-4pm.*

"Black cabs" are very expensive: driving a London taxi is skilled work. Your driver has studied for years to pass a rigorous exam called "The Knowledge" to prove he knows the name of every street in central London and how to get there by the shortest possible route. When considering the expense, remember that all is relative—four people in a cab can save money on the Tube fare over shorter distances.

Black cabs are specially designed for London's narrow streets and can turn on a sixpence—don't be afraid to hail one on the other side of the road. Available cabs are indicated by the blue "for hire" light by the driver and the orange "taxi" sign on the roof; frantic waving and a loud cry of "TAXI!" should do the trick. Taxis are obliged to take passengers anywhere in central London, even just one block, but longer journeys (excluding Heathrow airport) are at their discretion—it's best to negotiate a fare in advance if you're going outside the

ENGLISH	AMERICAN
aubergine	eggplant
bangers and mash	pork sausage and mashed potato
bank holiday	public holiday
bap	soft bun
barmy	insane, erratic; hot weather
bathroom	room containing a bathtub
bird (slang)	girl
biro	ballpoint pen
bit of alright (slang)	attractive (of girls)
biscuit	cookie or cracker
bloke	guy
bobby (slang)	police officer
bonnet	car hood
brilliant (exclamation)	awesome
(car) boot	car trunk
braces	suspenders
bum bag	fanny pack
busker	street musician
caravan	trailer, mobile home
car park	parking lot
cheeky	mischievous
cheers	thanks
chemist	pharmacy
chips	french fries
chuffed	happy
coach	inter-city bus
courgette	zucchini
crisps	potato chips
dicey, dodgy	sketchy
the dog's bollocks (slang)	the best
dosh, dough (slang)	money
durex	(common brand of) condom

city. In any case, a **10% tip** is expected. It's possible to order a licensed cab by phone (see **The Service Directory,** p. 329, for numbers), but most people book cheaper minicabs (see below).

MINICABS

*For listings of minicab services, see the **Service Directory,** p. 329.*

Anyone with a car and a driving license can set themselves up as a "minicab" company—while only licensed cabs can ply the streets for hire, there are no regulations concerning pre-arranged pickups. As a result, competition is fierce and prices are lower than licensed cabs—but unless you know a reliable company, ordering a minicab is something of a crapshoot, though there's rarely any danger involved (not counting the often hair-raising driving). However, be especially careful with the dodgy drivers that turn up outside nightclubs at closing time. Note down a number before you go out and call from the club, or arrange to be picked-up in advance. Always agree on a price with the driver before getting in; some firms now have standardized price lists.

BY CAR

*For listings of car-rental firms in London, see the **Service Directory,** p. 329.*

You'd be crazy to drive in central London—unless you have a secret parking spot, leave it to professionals. Various thoroughfares are off-limits to private vehicles during the week, on-street parking is almost non-existent, and off-street parking hideously expensive. Not to mention the labyrinthine one-way streets and psychotic van drivers. Cars are only really useful for trips to the outer suburbs and for daytrips, though extensive rail and bus networks can get you most everywhere without a car.

The driving age in the UK is 17, though almost no one will rent out cars to those under 23. It may be cheapest to organize car rental before you leave from one of the major international companies, most of which offer online booking.

BY FOOT

Too few visitors to London see any more of the city than the brief sprint from Tube station to sight and back—a pity as London is a great walking city. You can best appreciate London's various neighborhoods by spending some time walking around. Wherever you go, keep a lookout for the **blue plaques** that adorn the former residences of the great, the good, and the honorably obscure. Since London does not have a neat grid system, a good map is key to successful walking. An essential first purchase for travelers in London is the pocket-sized ▓**London A-Z**. (Geographer's A-Z Map Company, £5.95.), available at most newsstands. Every Londoner owns one, and if you combine it with the maps in this book, you'll never (well, rarely) go wrong.

As in any big city, it's best to use caution when on foot. While London enjoys a remarkably low level of violent crime, **theft** is an increasing problem; be on the alert for pickpockets by day, and move in groups at night. Stick to busy, well-lit thoroughfares, especially in unfamiliar areas, and stay away from open spaces after dark. For more information, see **Crime,** p. 41. A far bigger menace to most foreigners than crime, though, is the fact that Britons drive on the left—remember to **look right when crossing the road** and be very cautious—traffic is fast and unforgiving. Always use crosswalks and **never jaywalk.**

BY BIKE

◪ *For a listing of bicycle and scooter rental shops in London, see the* **Service Directory,** *p. 329.*

Biking in London is not for the faint of heart. A strong motorists' lobby fights against any proposal to give an inch of the crowded streets over to cycle lanes, while bus drivers take delight in scaring the living daylights out of bikers who seek refuge in bus lanes. Always wear a helmet when riding; you'll probably want a face mask, too.

Aside from a brief period in the 1960s, **motor scooters** have never been as fashionable in London as they are in Europe—maybe it's the weather. Undeniably fun and fast, they're also dangerous and unstable, especially in the wet. Expect no mercy from London drivers, either. A driving license is sufficient to drive a 50cc moped; for 100cc you need to have taken Compulsory Basic Training (a government-approved course in handling 2-wheelers); over 500cc you need a special motorcycle licence.

London Bicycle Tour Company, 1a Gabriel's Wharf, 56 Upper Ground (☎ 7928 6838; www.londonbicycle.com). Tube: Blackfriars or Waterloo. Organizes bicycle tours of the city. Also rents bikes and roller skates. Open Apr.-Oct. daily 10am-6pm; call ahead Nov.-Mar.

London Cycling Campaign, 30 Great Guildford St. #228 (☎ 7928 7220; www.lcc.org.uk), ceaselessly works to improve the cyclists' lot in London. They also sell a series of maps detailing cycle routes in London and organize group rides. Open M-F 10am-5pm.

ENGLISH	AMERICAN
ensuite	with bathroom
fag (slang)	cigarette
fanny (obsolete)	vagina
first floor	second floor
fortnight	two weeks
full stop	period (punctuation)
gob (vulgar)	mouth
grotty	grungy
high street	main street
to hire	to rent
holiday	vacation
hoover	vacuum cleaner,
ice lolly	popsicle
interval	intermission
jumper	sweater
knob (vulg.)	penis, awkward person
to knock up	to knock on someone's door
lavatory, loo	restroom
lay-by	roadside turnout
leader (press)	editorial
legless (slang)	drunk
to let	to rent (property)
lift	elevator
lorry	truck
mad	crazy
mate	pal
motorway	highway
mobile phone	cellphone
naff (slang)	shabby, in poor taste
pants	underpants; bad (slang)
petrol	gasoline
phone box, call box	telephone booth
take the piss, take the mickey (slang)	make fun
pissed	drunk

ENGLISH	AMERICAN
Paki (derog.)	racial slur for Pakistani or any South Asian.
plaster	generic Band-Aid
poof (vulgar)	gay person
prat (vulgar)	unpleasant person
prawn	shrimp
pudding	dessert
public school	prestigious private school
punter	average person, customer
quid (slang)	pound (money)
to queue (up), queue	to stand in line, a line
quay (pron. "key")	river bank
return ticket	round-trip ticket
to ring (up)	to telephone
roundabout	rotary intersection
rubber	eraser
to sack, give the sack	to fire someone
self-catering	with kitchen
serviette	napkin
single ticket	one-way ticket
snog (slang)	kiss
slag (vulgar)	bitch
sod it (vulgar)	forget it
sultanas	a type of raisin
suspenders	garters
subway	underpass
swish	swanky
ta (slang)	thanks
ta-ta (slang)	goodbye
thick (slang)	stupid
toilet	restroom
torch	flashlight
Tory	supporter of Conservative Party
tosser (vulgar)	see wanker
trousers	pants

34

EMBASSIES & CONSULATES

CONSULAR SERVICES IN LONDON

Australia: Australia House, Strand (☎ 7379 4334 or 7887 5776; www.australia.org.uk). Tube: Temple. Open M-F 9am-5pm; **consular** services 9:30am-3:30pm. In an **emergency,** dial ☎ 0500 890 165 toll-free to contact the Foreign Affairs Dept.'s Consulate Officer in Canberra.

Canada: MacDonald House, 1 Grosvenor Sq. (☎ 7258 6600; www.dfait-maeci.gc.ca/london). Tube: Bond St. or Charing Cross. Open M-F 9am-5pm.

Ireland: 17 Grosvenor Pl. (☎ 7235 2171). Tube: Hyde Park Corner. **Consular** services at Montpelier House, 106 Brompton Rd. (☎ 7225 7700). Tube: Knightsbridge. Open M-F 9:30am-4:30pm.

New Zealand: New Zealand House, 80 Haymarket (☎ 7930 8422; www.nzembassy.com). Tube: Piccadilly Circus. **Consular** section open M-F 10am-5pm.

South Africa: South Africa House, Trafalgar Sq. (☎ 7451 7299; www.southafricahouse.com). Tube: Charing Cross. **Consular** services at 15 Whitehall (☎ 7925 8901). Open M-F 9am-5pm.

United States: 24 Grosvenor Sq. (☎ 7499 9000; www.usembassy.org.uk). Tube: Bond St. or Marble Arch. Open M-F 8:30am-5:30pm. Phones answered 8am-10pm.

KEEPING IN TOUCH

BY MAIL

🛈 *Royal Mail* ☎ *0845 774 0740; www.royalmail.co.uk. See the leaflet* **All you need to know,** *available at Post Offices, for details of all domestic and international rates.*

The Royal Mail's official monopoly on stamped mail ran out in April 2001, but competitors are nowhere to be found. Britain's post is perhaps the best in the world. Mail a letter at 5pm and it will arrive by 10am the next day almost anywhere in the UK.

SENDING MAIL WITHIN THE UK

Collection times are posted on each postbox; the last weekday collection from most boxes is at around 3-4pm, with late collections in some post offices at 7-8pm. **First Class** mail is delivered the next day (except Sunday), while **Second Class** takes up to three days. For letters under 60g

(2oz), you can insure yourself against rises in postage rates by buying "non-value indicator" stamps, which display only "1st" or "2nd" (class) rather than the purchase price. *(1st class 28p up to 60g, 2nd class 20p. 750g weight limit on all 2nd class mail.)*

SENDING MAIL ABROAD

The Royal Mail divides the outside world into three price bands: Europe, World Zone 1, and World Zone 2. World Zone 1 includes North and South America, the Middle East, Africa, South and Southeast Asia. World Zone 2 is everything else. **Customs labels** are required for packets and parcels being sent outside the EU.

AIRMAIL. Letters should get to their destination country within 2 days for Western Europe, 3 for Eastern Europe, and 4 for everywhere else; the ultimate delivery time is dependent on the receiving mail system. All airmail should bear an "airmail" sticker (available at post offices) or have "PAR AVION—AIR MAIL" clearly marked in the upper-left-hand corner. **Rates:** to Europe up to 20g 38p, 20-40g 53p; to World Zones 1 and 2 42p for postcards, up to 10g 47p, 10-20g 68p.

SURFACE MAIL. surface mail is best for parcels: it's not available for letters within Europe, nor is it much cheaper than airmail for letters to the rest of the world. Delivery times are 2 weeks to Western Europe, 4 to Eastern Europe, and 8 weeks elsewhere. **Rates:** Letters to World Zone 1/2: up to 20g 37p, 20-60g 61p. Small Packet and Printed Matter to anywhere: up to 100g 60p, rising in stages to £2 for 450g (about 1 lb.).

RECEIVING MAIL IN LONDON

London enjoys two morning deliveries per day M-F, and one Sa. To ensure speedy delivery, make sure mail bears the full **post code,** consisting of the 2-5 initial characters of the postal district (e.g. W1 in the West End, or WC2 for Holborn), followed by a space and then a number and two more letters that define the street.

POSTE RESTANTE. If you don't have a mailing address in London, you can still receive mail via Poste Restante (General Delivery). Up to five items will be held free of charge for a limited time at most larger London post offices. To find the address of a participating post office, call the Post Office counter service at ☎ 084 5722 3344. Mail to Poste Restante should be addressed as follows:

ENGLISH	AMERICAN
vest	undershirt
waistcoat	men's vest
wanker (vulgar)	see tosser
way out	exit
WC	restroom
wellies, Wellington boots	waterproof boots
wicked (slang)	cool
yob (slang)	uncultured person
Yorkshire pudding	eggy pastry served with roast beef
zed	the letter Z

WRITTEN	PRONOUNCED
Berkeley	BAHK-lee
Berkshire	BAHK-sher
Birmingham	BERM-ing-um
Cholmondely	CHUM-lee
Derby	DAR-bee
Dulwich	DULL-ich
Edinburgh	ED-in-bur-ra
Featherstonehaw	FAN-shaw
Gloucester	GLOS-ter
Greenwich	GREN-ich
Grosvenor	GRO-vna
gaol	JAIL
Islington	IHZ-ling-tun
Leicester	LES-ter
Marylebone	MAR-lee-bun
Magdalen	MAUD-lin
quay	KEY
Norwich	NOR-ich
Salisbury	SAULS-bree
Southwark	SUTH-uk
Thames	TEMS
Worcester	WOO-ster

POSTE RESTANTE,
[Post office name],
[Post office street address],
LONDON [Post office postcode],
UNITED KINGDOM
Hold for: [Name of Recipient].

FORWARDING MAIL. Call the Royal Mail helpline (☎ 084 5774 0740) for a redirection form to have mail automatically forwarded, or ask at a post office. The Royal Mail will not forward mail from hotels, hostels, or colleges. *(Domestic redirection £6.45 for 1 month, £32.40 per year; international £12.90/64.80.)* A riskier but free method for forwarding mail within the UK is to ask someone at your old address to scribble your new address over the old one on any letters that arrive, and pop them back in the post; if the letter is unopened, no extra postage is required. This is not guaranteed to work, as the letter may be returned to sender.

TELEPHONES

Over 50% of Britons own a mobile phone, and in London the percentage is even higher. At the same time, an explosion of low-cost calling cards is making calling abroad from land lines ever cheaper. If you plan to stay in London for a prolonged period, consider buying a mobile phone with free incoming calls. Mobile phones in London cost around £65, and they often run on prepaid minutes that are easily purchased at a variety of locations. For more info about obtaining a mobile phone abroad, try these sites: www.vodafone.com, www.orange.co.uk, www.roadpost.com, www.t-mobile.com, and www.planetomni.com.

LONDON PHONE NUMBERS

London's phone code is 020; within this area all numbers are 8 digits long. **Note that all telephone numbers given in this book are in area code 020 unless otherwise specified.** *For other common codes and useful numbers, see the **Phone Facts" sidebar.*

London's phone codes have changed four times in the last 16 years, so you may encounter some out-of-date numbers while in London. Here's the low-down on how to convert from the old numbers to the new ones: starting in the late 1980s, London had two phone codes, 071 and 081; in the 90s this was changed to 0171 and 0181. To convert these old 7-digit numbers to the new 8-digit number, just prefix 7 (if it was an 0171 number) or 8 (for 0181) to the start of the old number.

ESSENTIAL
INFORMATION

PHONE FACTS

USEFUL NUMBERS

Directory Enquiries: ☎ 152 (UK), ☎ 192 (international). Both free from payphones, 50p from a land line.

Operator: ☎ 100. Free.

Reverse-charge (collect): ☎ 155. Expensive (but not for you).

Talking Pages: ☎ 0800 600 900. Say what you need and where, and they'll find it. Free.

COUNTRY CODES

For an international line, dial ☎ 00 plus:

Australia: 61
Canada: 1
France: 33
Ireland: 353
Italy: 39
New Zealand: 64
South Africa: 27
USA: 1

Drop any leading zero from the local area code.

OTHER UK CODES

Aside from 020, there are a few other UK phone codes you should watch out for:

0800 and **0808** numbers are free.

0845 numbers are charged at the local rate.

0870 numbers are charged at the national (long-distance) rate.

Numbers starting with **09** are premium rate, charging £1-£1.50 per min. or more.

Numbers starting with **07** are mobile phones, costing around 30p per minute to call from a land line (more from a payphone).

CALLING HOME FROM LONDON

To call abroad from a UK phone, dial the **international access code** (00), the **country code**, the **area code** less any leading zero, and finally the **local number**. Thus to call the Dublin number (01) 234 5678, dial 00-353-1-2345678, where 353 is the Ireland country code. A number of country codes are given in **Phone Facts**, see p. 36. Most international calls are cheaper M-F 6pm-8am and Sa-Su; calls to Australia and New Zealand are cheaper 2:30-7:30pm and midnight-7am.

PAYPHONES & REVERSE-CHARGE (COLLECT) CALLS. Payphones are an expensive way to phone abroad. Still, that's nothing compared to the coronary implications of a **reverse-charge** international call—save them for people you really don't like. *(Reverse-charge operator ☎ 155.)*

PREPAID CALLING CARDS. Probably the cheapest way to call long-distance, prepaid calling cards are sold in newsagents and post offices. Be sure to check **rates** and **connection charges** before you buy. If you're planning to make one long call, go for the card with the cheapest rate; for lots of short calls, look for a low connection charge.

BILLED CALLING CARDS. Convenient, especially if someone else is paying the bill, these calling cards must be set up in your home country before you leave: contact your telephone provider. In the USA, AT&T, Sprint, and MCI all offer their own versions. From the UK, simply dial the free access number and your account code: you'll then either be able to make a direct-dial call home, or reach an operator who'll make the connection for you. Once a month, the bill will be sent home—make sure someone's around to pay it! The disadvantage of these cards is that rates are not always low, and they're only good for calling their home country—you can make calls to other countries, but you'll be charged the rate for calling home *plus* the rate from home to the other country.

CALLING WITHIN THE UK

To make a local call, simply dial the number without the area code. For a long-distance call, you must first dial the 3- to 5-digit area code, including the initial zero. In foreign publications and some websites, the zero is sometimes omitted when the number is quoted with the UK country code (e.g. a London number may be given as + 44 20 rather than 020). Call rates vary depending on the distance, the time of day, and the telephone company used. Rates are highest M-F from 9am until 6 or 7pm, somewhat lower on weekday evenings, and lowest on weekends.

BT PAYPHONES. The majority of payphones are operated by BT (formerly British Telecom), recognizable by the red-and-blue piper logo. While newer phones typically accept phonecards, coins, and credit cards, some older payphones only accept **BT phonecards** (now almost entirely phased out) and the newer **Phonecard Plus.** This is essentially a combination BT phonecard and calling card—you can either stick it in a payphone, or call the access number from any land phone. They're tricky, though—payphone calls cost more than calling-card ones. *(Phonecard Plus available from most newsagents and kiosks. Cards available in £3-20 denominations.)*

If you're paying by cash, the minimum deposit is 20p. The **dial tone** is a continuous purring sound; a repeated double-purr means the line is **ringing.** For the rest of the call, the display ticks off in 1p increments; a series of beeps warn you to insert more money when your time is up. Once you hang up, your remaining phonecard credit is rounded down to the nearest 10p, or unused coins are returned. Payphones do *not* give change—if you use 22p from a 50p coin, the remaining 28p is gone once you put the receiver down. If you want to make another call, transfer remaining credit by pushing the "follow-on call" button—hang up and you'll lose the money. Note that **freephone (☎0800 and 0808)** and **emergency** calls (☎999) can be made free from any phone without inserting a card or coins.

One final word of warning: the party who initiates the call always pays, even when calling a cell phone—this means that you're charged a cell-phone rate (sometimes as high as 30p/minute) when you call someone's cell phone. This, in addition to the connection charge and the fact that you pay for ring-time means that calling cell phones can be quite expensive. One solution when calling friends: call the cell phone and quickly ask them to call you back, as payphones accept incoming calls.

OTHER PAYPHONES. Other companies besides BT operate payphones in central London. To use these, you'll either need the company's special phonecard, or you can often use cash or a credit card. More common are private payphones, often installed in hostels and pubs. Since the owner can set his own rates on these money-gobbling devices, you'll probably save money by heading outside.

EMAIL & THE INTERNET

Although more people are getting connected at home and on the move, the number of cybercafes is burgeoning—scarcely a major street in London is without a dedicated Internet shop, or at least a regular cafe with a couple of terminals. *Let's Go* lists when Internet facilities are available in accommodations, while cybercafes are listed in the Service Directory (p. 329). One innovation is the BT Multi.phone, a souped-up payphone that also offers impressively fast Internet access via a touch screen and keyboard. Multi.phones are very expensive (from 50p for 5min.), and can be found in Tube stations, hotels, museums and a few hostels.

MONEY

⚐ *For pre-departure info, including exchange rates, see* **Planning Your Trip,** *p. 297.*

A trip to London can easily break the bank, but it doesn't have to. Always be on the lookout for discounts, especially if you're a student, under 26, or an "OAP" (Old Age Pensioner; women over 60 and men over 65)—it pays to ask about discounts at *every* shop. Discount rates for students and seniors are often posted as **concessions** or **"consc."** on price lists. **Families** should note that children under 5 travel for free on public transportation, while those aged 5-17 get reduced rates (also see **Family Travelcards,** p. 27 and **Youth and Student passes,** p. 28). Child rates at sights and museums normally apply to those under 16; children under 5 are often free.

EXCHANGING MONEY

BANKS & BUREAUX DE CHANGE

Contrary to what you might expect, the best exchange rates are usually found at **banks,** not specialist **bureaux de change** (though on weekends and after 4:30pm M-F, you won't have any choice); look for a spread of no more than 10% between the "buy" and "sell" rates. It's almost always cheaper to exchange large amounts at the same time rather than a succession of small quantities. Beware of "commission-free" deals—if you have to change a small amount, they're the best option, but for larger sums what you gain in commission you give away in poor rates.

TRAVELER'S CHECKS

🔁 *For information on buying traveler's checks, see **Planning Your Trip**, p. 297.*

Banks often give better rates than the issuing institutions for foreign-denominated **Traveler's Checks,** but you may have to pay a service fee or commission; *bureaux de change* usually have worse rates *and* charge commission. Sterling-denominated checks can be exchanged commission-free at issuing institutions and affiliated banks—ask your issuer for a list of affiliates. In department stores and some hotels, you may be able to pay directly in traveler's checks; if your checks are foreign-denominated, however, exchange rates are almost guaranteed to be worse than those you'll find on the street.

ATM, DEBIT & CREDIT CARDS

🔁 *Cards accepted by establishments are detailed in listings as follows: V for Visa, MC for Mastercard, AmEx for American Express. Discover and Diners Club are rarely accepted, and are not listed.*

Pay with a credit or debit card whenever possible—you'll get a much better exchange rate than for cash or travelers checks. If you use a credit card, **interest charges** can offset any gains if you don't pay off the full balance at the end of the month. (Make sure there's someone at home to pay it if you'll be away, or arrange for it to be debited automatically from your bank account. Another option is to set up web payment; contact your credit card issuer.) Credit cards also offer some level of **purchase protection**—invaluable if that new gadget stops working when you get home. Most ATM and debit cards will work in London ATMs, and most shops, restaurants, and sights accept plastic. You should always carry some cash, though, as there's often a £5-10 minimum purchase for payment in plastic; small establishments, market stalls, and takeaways are often cash only.

CREDIT CARDS. Where accepted, credit cards often offer superior exchange rates—up to 5% better than the retail rate used by banks and other currency exchange establishments. Credit cards may also offer services such as insurance or emergency help, and are sometimes required to reserve hotel rooms or rental cars. **MasterCard** and **Visa** are most welcomed; **American Express** cards are rarely accepted, **Diners Club** and **Discover** almost never. Credit cards are also useful for **cash advances,** which allow you to withdraw local currency from associated banks and ATMs abroad (see p. 40). If you intend to use your credit card extensively in London, alert your card issuer before leaving; otherwise, they could block your card for "suspicious activity." If you will also be making cash advances through cash machines in London, you will need to ask your card issuer for a 4-digit PIN.

ATMS. If you have an **ATM card,** chances are it will be able to withdraw money from UK ATMs; other ATM functions (including checking your balance, transferring funds, etc.) may not be accessible depending on what kind of ATM card you have. British machines only accept **4-digit PINs,** so if yours is longer, check with your bank to see if the first four digits will work in the UK or if you need a new code. UK cash machines do not have letters on the keypad, so be sure to memorize your PIN in numerical form. You'll get the same wholesale exchange rates as credit cards, but beware that many banks levy fees for withdrawing money abroad—up to US$5 per transaction. For details of a **common scam** to steal cash cards and PINs, see p. 41. **Be sure to note your bank's phone number before you leave.**

DEBIT CARDS. Debit cards are as convenient as credit cards but withdraw money directly from your bank account. A debit card can be used wherever its associated credit card company (usually Mastercard or Visa) is accepted. Debit cards often also function as ATM cards. The two major international money networks are **Cirrus** (to locate ATMs US ☎800-424-7787; www.mastercard.com) and **Visa/PLUS** (to locate ATMs US ☎800-843-7587; www.visa.com). ATMs of major British banks (including Barclays, HSBC, Lloyds TSB, National Westminster, Royal Bank of Scotland) usually accept both networks.

CASH ADVANCES. In an emergency, you can also withdraw money from most cash machines and bank tellers with a credit card, up to your cash advance limit. (To use a machine, you'll need to set up a 4-digit PIN with your card issuer before you leave.) There are often high transaction fees associated with foreign cash advances (up to US$10 plus 2-3%), plus cash advances are normally charged at higher interest rates than purchases, with no grace period for payment until interest kicks in, either.

US STATE DEPARTMENT (US CITIZENS ONLY). In dire emergencies only, the US State Department will forward money instantly to the nearest consular office, which will then disburse it according to instructions for a US$15 fee. To use this service, contact the Overseas Citizens Service division of the US State Department (☎001-202-647-5225; nights, Sundays, and holidays ☎001-202-647-4000).

SALES TAX

The prices of most items sold in Britain include a 17.5% **Value-Added Tax (VAT).** Books, medicine, food (in stores), and children's clothes are VAT-free, and tobacco, alcohol, and certain luxury items are taxed at a higher rate. If you live outside the EU, you may be able to claim some VAT back through the **Retail Export Scheme.** This only applies to articles that are being exported out of the EU; meals and lodging do not qualify. Only larger stores in heavily-touristed areas normally participate in the scheme, and there is often a £50-100 minimum purchase. If the store participates, you will need to request a VAT refund form from the shopkeeper. Upon leaving the country, take this form and the goods to the Tax-Free Refund desk at the airport, where officers will ensure the items are being exported and stamp your forms; this process can take up to an hour. After going through passport control, mail the form back to the shop, which will then eventually send you a refund (less an administrative fee) by check or credit it to your credit card. This scheme only applies to purchases made within three months of departure.

TIPPING & BARGAINING

Tips in restaurants are often included in the bill (sometimes as a service charge); if gratuity is not included, you should tip your server about 15%. Taxi drivers should receive a 10-15% tip, and bellhops and chambermaids usually expect somewhere between £1-3. Never tip bartenders, even in pubs. If you're at an outdoor market, bargaining is sometimes acceptable. The only other places where you should haggle are the electronics shops along **Tottenham Court Road** (p. 207).

HEALTH & SAFETY

MEDICAL CARE

🖪 In an **Emergency,** dial ☎**999** free from any phone. For a list of Accident and Emergency rooms in London, see the **Service Directory,** p. 333.

Medical care in the UK is either part of the government-run National Health Service or is privately administered: often the same doctors and hospitals do both NHS and private work. **EU** citizens, citizens of many **Commonwealth** countries and full-time **students** at British universities are eligible for free treatment on the NHS. Many **US health insurance** plans (but not Medicare) will cover emergency treatment abroad in private clinics, but you may be asked to pay up front and then apply for a reimbursement to your insurer. If you're unsure whether you have medical coverage in the UK, it's best to play it safe and buy **travel insurance** (see p. 300) before you leave.

CHEMISTS (PHARMACIES). For minor ailments (light burns, blisters, coughs, and sneezes), you can try going to a chemist. **Boots** is the biggest chain. You'll find a trained pharmacist behind the prescription drugs counter. They'll either recommend medication, or advise you to see a doctor if they think it's serious. Note that chemists are rarely open late or on Sundays. Most hospitals have 24hr. pharmacies, but may only serve patients with prescriptions.

MEDICAL EMERGENCIES. In a life-threatening situation, call ☎999 from any phone to request an ambulance. For less acute situations, most London hospitals run 24hr. **Accident and Emergency** (A&E) or **Casualty** wards. A list of A&E departments in London can be found in the **Service Directory** on p. 332. If your condition isn't judged serious, be prepared to wait for hours, especially on F-Sa nights.

CRIME

🔊 In case of *Emergency,* dial ☎*999* free from any phone.

If you're a victim of a crime, **report it to the police**—not only will it help future travelers, it's normally required if you intend to make an insurance claim afterwards.

VIOLENT CRIME. London is as safe a big city as you're likely to find. By American and even most European standards, violent crime is rare, and police rarely carry anything more deadly than a truncheon. Nevertheless, while crime levels are low, they're not zero, and those unfamiliar with London will inevitably be at higher risk than locals. While most of London's dodgier neighborhoods—Hackney, Tottenham, and parts of South and East London—are far off the tourist trail, you should take extra care after dark around **King's Cross,** the **East End,** and **Brixton.** Finally, never venture alone into **parks** after dark, and **never admit you're traveling alone.**

THEFT. When it comes to theft (especially **pickpocketing** or **bag snatching**), London's track record is worse than many major cities. Don't put a **wallet** in your back pocket, and don't keep all your valuables (money, important documents) in one place. Make **photocopies** of all your important cards and documents; keep the photocopies in a safe place, and leave one copy with someone at home. If you carry a **handbag,** buy a sturdy one with a secure clasp and wear it crosswise with the clasp against you. Use a money belt and keep a small cash reserve (say £40) somewhere safe, like in a sock.

ATM SCAMS. One common ruse at **ATMs** is for someone to claim you've dropped something. You look down, and sure enough there's a £10 note on the floor—by the time you've picked it up, an accomplice standing behind you—who's already memorized your PIN—has made off with the card and has probably withdrawn your daily limit from a nearby cash machine before you've even realized what's happened. **Ignore everything except the cash machine when you're withdrawing money.**

TERRORISM. The risk of injury from terrorism in London is minute—you're far more likely to be run over. Vigilance is still called for—if you see an abandoned bag or package in a public space, Tube, or bus, *always* alert the nearest police officer or member of staff. More information on international and domestic terrorism and the UK's response is available from the Foreign and Commonwealth Office (☎7270 1500; www.fco.gov.uk), the Prime Minister's office website (www.pm.gov.uk), and the Metropolitan Police (☎7230 1212; www.met.police.uk).

The most important thing for travelers is to gather as much information as possible before leaving and to **keep in contact** while overseas. The US Department of State website (www.state.gov) is a good place to research the current situation anywhere you plan to travel. Depending on the circumstances at the time of your trip, you may want to register with your home embassy or consulate when you arrive. **Travel advisories** (below) lists offices to contact and websites to visit to get the most updated list of advisories for travelers.

TRAVEL ADVISORIES. The following government offices provide travel information and advisories by telephone, by fax, or via the web:

Australian Department of Foreign Affairs and Trade: ☎ 1300 555 135; faxback service 02 6261 1299; www.dfat.gov.au.

Canadian Department of Foreign Affairs and International Trade (DFAIT): In Canada and the US call ☎ 800-267-6788, elsewhere 613-944-6788; www.dfait-maeci.gc.ca. Ask for their free booklet, *Bon Voyage...But.*

New Zealand Ministry of Foreign Affairs: ☎ 04 494 8500; fax 494 8506; www.mft.govt.nz/trav.html.

United Kingdom Foreign and Commonwealth Office: ☎ 7008 0232; fax 7008 0155; www.fco.gov.uk.

United States Department of State: ☎ 202-647-5225 or 202-647-4000, toll-free 888-407-4747; faxback service 202-647-3000; http://travel.state.gov. For their booklet *A Safe Trip Abroad,* call ☎ 202-512-1800.

RACISM. London has traditionally prided itself on being an exceptionally tolerant city, but the great increase in immigration since the 1950s has taken its toll. While overall London is color-blind, in **South London,** tensions are worst between black immigrants and poor whites; there's also friction within the black community between West Indians and Africans. In **East London,** South Asians are on the receiving end. These trouble spots aside, races mix in London to a greater extent than in most cities: among second-generation immigrants, there's little cultural distinction.

DRUGS & ALCOHOL

The legal **drinking age** in the UK is a complicated beast. Technically, it's legal for anyone to drink alcohol in private, but there are many regulations regarding who can buy or sell it. To buy alcohol in a **shop,** you have to be at least 18; it's illegal to buy alcohol on behalf of an underage person. Eighteen is also the normal drinking age in **bars** and **pubs,** but you can drink in a pub at 16 with food, or even at 14 in a **restaurant.** Enforcement is lax—you need to look *really* young before anyone will demand ID—but punishments are severe. **Smoking** is simpler—you have to be 16 or older.

Drugs are dealt with harshly. **Ecstasy, cocaine, heroine, amphetamines,** and practically all other drugs are illegal. Possession is subject to strict penalties; you may also be subjected to a blood test, and you could be jailed or deported if convicted. Be especially wary in nightclubs—people have died of poisoning after taking impure ecstasy tablets, and many people have bought something no more mind-enhancing than aspirin. If you need to take a drug for **medical reasons,** check that it is legal in the UK, and always carry a prescription or note from you doctor. **Cannabis** has been recently downgraded to a Class C drug, meaning that carrying a small amount of marijuana is no longer an arrestable offense; possession of larger amounts risks your being treated as a dealer, for which penalties are far stiffer.

THE MEDIA

PRINT MEDIA

NEWSPAPERS

Although circulation has been dropping in the UK for the last 40 years, newspapers still wield enough power to make and break governments. Best-selling *The Sun* claims that its surprise switch from Conservative to Labour handed Tony Blair the 1997 election; indeed, in the 1992 election Labour had seemed set for victory until the right-wing press turned the tide. But *The Sun* is merely the most popular—and most sensational—of the mass-market **tabloids** that dominate the British newspaper market. The *Daily Mail* tries to bridge the intellectual gap between the tabloids and the unmanageable pages of **broadsheets.** *The Times* has gone downmarket under the ownership of Rupert Murdoch (who also owns *The Sun*); arch-rival *The Daily Telegraph* retains a more aloof tone. Both are unmistakably right-wing, as is the *Financial Times.* Leaning to the left are *The Independent* and *The Guardian.* Daily papers usually share their name with an overgrown **Sunday** double; *The Guardian* and *The Sun* are exceptions: their Sunday equivalents are *The Observer* and *The News of the World*, respectively. London's best **local daily,** the tabloid-format but marginally more intelligent *Evening Standard* is published in several editions throughout the day. The *Standard* was joined in 1999 by the daily *Metro*, available free in Tube stations M-F (though they're usually all gone by 9am).

MAGAZINES

News magazines are generally published weekly and provide a more in-depth examination of issues than the papers—with a strong political slant. *The Economist* is the most respected and apolitical of the bunch; political hacks get their kicks from the New Labour *New Statesman* and the Tory *Spectator*. For a less reverent approach, *Private Eye* walks a fine line between hilarity and libel.

Lifestyle magazines are the biggest sellers. The UK editions of women's mags such as *Cosmopolitan* tend to be more forthright than their US counterparts, while men's equivalents *FHM* and *Loaded* leave little to the imagination. Pure **style** magazines range from the ad-laden pages of British *Vogue* to the object-oriented Starck recommendations of *i-D* and *Wallpaper*. **Music** mags such as *Melody Maker* and *New Musical Express* carry details of gigs, and **clubbing** reviews *Mixmag* and *Jockey Slut* give the biz on hot nightspots. Still, the Londoner's bible is *Time Out* (W), worth every penny of its £2.20 cover price.

BROADCAST MEDIA

Whether on radio or TV, British broadcasting has a strong national identity. While there's no denying the influence from across the Atlantic, it's largely limited to pop music and the occasional show—national resilience is illustrated by the fact that America's top-rated sit-com, *Seinfeld*, bombed in Britain. In fact, the most popular British programs are about as far from showbiz glamour as possible: the number one soap, *Eastenders*, follows the working-class lives of people in East London; ridiculously long-running radio rival *The Archers* does the same for struggling farmers. As for comedy, the renowned British sense of humor has resulted in some of the world's funniest and least-exportable. Lately, British television has had a wide worldwide impact—*Survivor, Who Wants to be a Millionaire,* and *The Weakest Link* were all British, and reality TV continues to dominate.

RADIO

The national radio market is dominated by the **BBC's** public offerings, though "the Beeb" or "Auntie" as it's affectionately (or sarcastically) known also has at least one local station available everywhere in the country. It's largely thanks to the BBC that commercial pop and phone-in shows have not yet achieved total domination of the airwaves. **BBC Radio 4** offers insightful news and analysis, while **Radio 3** is Britain's cultural herald, with challenging classical music, literary readings, and radio plays. For a listing of radio stations available in London, see **On the Air.**

TELEVISION

British television's self-image as the best in the world is buckling under the same commercial pressures found in the rest of the Western world, but there's still a large variety of shows to be found on the telly's five broadcast channels. This is largely because every television-set owner in Britain is required to purchase an annual "TV licence," the proceeds of which go directly to the BBC—in return, the BBC is not allowed to run advertisements. (Although it's publicly funded, the BBC is independent of the Government.) This guarantees money for serious programming, alongside an obligation to satisfy the people who foot the bill—which includes the lower-income groups that advertisers normally scorn. The publicly-funded **BBC 1** remains more popular than its commercial rivals, and its presence results in an unavoidable upwards pressure on its main commercial rival **ITV.** The BBC's "cultural" channel, **BBC 2,** has a commercial counterpart in **Channel 4;** both mix in-depth news, documentaries, and ground breaking dramas with test-runs of comedies which, if successful, often transfer to their more populist siblings. Finally, **Channel 5,** launched in the late 1990s, has yet to carve itself a British following.

Life & Times

LONDON THROUGH THE AGES

ROMANS TO NORMANS (AD 43-1042)

LONDON BRIDGE, TAKE I. In AD 43, **Aulus Plautius** landed in Kent with 40,000 battle-hardened Romans and marched north until he found his way barred by the Thames. Pausing here to await the Emperor Claudius, Aulus busied his troops with the building of a bridge. Situated at the lowest navigable point on the river, and soon the center of an excellent network of Roman roads, the crossing naturally became a focal point for trade. Merchants set up on the north bank of the river: London—or rather, Londinium—was born. By the end of the second century London could boast a forum four times the size of Trafalgar Square and a population of 45,000 drawn from all over the Empire.

A NEW BEGINNING. In the mid-fifth century, Angles and Saxons overran southern Britain and began ethnically cleansing their new home of its Celtic inhabitants. In 604, on a mission from Rome, **St. Augustine** converted the local king and consecrated the first Bishop of London, **Mellitus.** In the same year, work started on the first **St. Paul's Cathedral.** The City of London's higgledy-piggledy street plan can also be traced to this

in recent news

Experimenting 'Softly, softly' with Drugs

Along with its vibrant night-life, the Brixton and Lambeth areas have been just as well-known for drugs and crime: rampant mugging and rampant sale of cannabis. The "softly, softly" experiment, instituted in July 2001 by former police commander Brian Paddick, was a desperate effort to control the latter. Since then, people caught with small amounts of cannabis in the borough have been let off with a formal warning, instead of being arrested. And since police have taken this approach to cannabis in the Lambeth area, Brixton has cleaned up its act dramatically: from 2001 to 2002, Lambeth experienced London's highest reduction in robberies, falling by an astounding 50%.

As the pilot scheme continued, Home Secretary David Blunkett announced in July 2002 that cannabis would be reclassified from a Class B (which includes barbiturates and speed) to a Class C drug; he also announced that the Lambeth experiment would be extended throughout London. As of July 2003, cannabis will be officially a Class C drug. This re-classification also intends to allow police to refocus their attention on

era: turning the orderly Roman city inside-out, the new inhabitants built their houses on the solid surface of the old Roman roads.

LONDON BRIDGE, TAKE II. London's prosperity brought unwelcome attention: 9th-century **Vikings** made the transition from raiders to conquerors. In 871, the Danes occupied London; it took **Alfred the Great** 15 years to retake it. Even so, Danes still controlled half of England (the "Danelaw"), and intermittent war continued for over a century. In 1013, London came under Danish rule once more when **King Æthelred the Unready** (an Old English pun—his name means "Well-advised the ill-advised") fled to Normandy. This time London was reconquered with the help of a 19-year-old Norwegian, Olaf, who hitched ropes between his fleet and the bridge supports and rowed away. The supports gave way, the Danes fell into the Thames, and the song "London Bridge is Falling Down" was born. Even so, when Æthelred died in 1016 the kingdom passed (peacefully) to a Dane, **Canute,** who made London the capital of an empire encompassing England, Denmark, and Norway.

THE MIDDLE AGES (1042-1485)

CONQUEST. Canute's successors held on to England until 1042, when Æthelred's son **St. Edward the Confessor** became king. London owes its status as a capital to Edward, who wanted to live near his favorite new church, the West Minster; **Westminster** has been home to the English government ever since. Edward's death in 1066 set the scene for the most famous battle in English history. **William of Normandy** claimed that Edward (who grew up in Normandy and was half-Norman) had promised him the throne; **Harold,** Earl of Wessex, disagreed. The difference was resolved on October 14th, at Hastings. By sunset Harold was dead, and William had a new kingdom. The Norman monarchs tried to awe their new capital into submission with the construction of the **Tower of London** (see p. 70) and the now-vanished Baynard's and Montfichet castles.

INCORPORATION. Desperate for money to finance their wars, Norman kings made numerous concessions to London. London was incorporated in 1191, granting the city a measure of self-governance and independence from the crown: the first Mayor, **Henry FitzAilwyn,** was elected in 1193. His present-day successor, the Lord Mayor, still presides over the 680 acres of the City of London; even today, the Queen may not enter the City without the mayor's permission.

A CENTURY OF HORRORS. The 14th century was a time of calamity. In 1348, plague arrived, borne by rats carried on ships from Europe. The resulting **Black Death** claimed the lives of 30,000 people—perhaps half the city's total population; thousands more died in later outbreaks in 1361, 1369, and 1375. In 1381 came the **Peasants' Revolt.** Incensed by a new poll tax, 60,000 men marched on London, destroyed the Savoy palace, and burned legal records in the **The Temple** (see p. 84).

After the peasants occupied the Tower, the 14-year-old **Richard II** agreed to meet their leader **Wat Tyler** at Smithfield. During a heated discussion, the Mayor of London killed Tyler with a dagger; Richard rode calmly forward and informed the peasants that he would grant all their demands if only they would return peacefully to their homes. Incredibly, the crowd believed him. As soon as he was safe, Richard had the ringleaders executed and withdrew his promises of better conditions.

A THORNY PROBLEM. The year 1387 saw the birth of the future **Henry V,** England's first ruler since the Conquest to speak English as his first language. While Henry V proved to be one of England's most capable kings, his son **Henry VI** led England into the quagmire known as the **Wars of the Roses.** As told by Shakespeare, in **Middle Temple Garden** (see p. 85) the warring parties plucked the red and white roses that would serve as their emblems. Tired of Henry's dithering, London's merchants gave full backing to the financially astute **Edward IV,** whose shared interest in business led them to overlook his equally shared interest in their wives. Under Edward's patronage, in 1476 **William Caxton** set up a printing press in Westminster; after his death, his aptly named assistant Wyknyn de Worde moved the presses to **Fleet Street** (see p. 87), which remained at the heart of the British printing industry until the 1980s.

THE FLOWER OF CITIES (1485-1685)

THE TUDOR AGE. In the next century, London's population would quadruple to 200,000, mostly through immigration from rural areas hit hard by agricultural changes and by **Henry VIII's** dissolu-

Class A drugs, which include heroin, cocaine, and ecstasy.

Despite the significant drop in the Lambeth crime rate, the "softly, softly" experiment has come under fire from both Brixtonians and local MPs, who argue that it has made drug trafficking a socially acceptable activity. Even though Paddick has said that the more lenient policy has not led to an increase in the amount of drug tourism in the area, and though a 2002 poll showed that 83% of the Lambeth population supported the reclassifcation, local residents have complained of pushers harassing shoppers and tourists to purchase their illicit substances, especially at night.

The Brixton experiment comes on the heels of studies conducted in 2001 by the National Centre for Social Research. These studies indicated that drug use is rife among children in the UK: the drug of choice is cannabis, which over a third of 15- 16-year-olds have used. The same year, the Department of Health revealed that a third of those being treated for drug abuse were under 25. In an effort to combat drug abuse by young people, the Home Office is launching a new campaign of drug education that new approach centers around 'Frank,' a discreet source of information and advice for those concerned about drugs. It remains to be seen whiether people will turn to 'Frank' for help.

tion of the monasteries in 1536. Many of the new arrivals found employment on Henry's numerous building projects, including palaces at **Hampton Court** (see p. 271), **Whitehall** (p. 105), and **St. James's** (p. 100); others on the equally luxurious houses that soon lined the Strand between the City and Westminster. The sumptuousness of the court can be seen in the portraits of Henry's court artist, the German **Hans Holbein.**

Henry's only son, **Edward VI,** reigned only six years before dying in 1553 at the age of 15. He was succeeded by his Catholic sister **Mary I,** who earned her nickname "Bloody Mary" for her campaign against the Anglican church established by her father—though in reality, Henry VIII and Elizabeth both led far bloodier religious persecutions.

ELIZABETH'S LONDON. Elizabeth I, daughter of Henry VIII and Anne Boleyn, inherited none of her father's marital woes—indeed, her refusal to marry earned her the title "The Virgin Queen." Under Elizabeth's reign, explorers Sir Francis Drake and Walter Raleigh expanded the horizons of England's world, and dramatists such as **William Shakespeare, Christopher Marlowe,** and **Ben Jonson** expanded its literary horizons. At first, plays were performed in the courtyards of London inns, with audiences packed into the galleries. The city authorities soon sent the actors packing over the river to Southwark, where **James Burbage** had constructed London's first custom-built playhouse, The Theatre, later renamed **The Globe** (see p. 95).

A SCOTTISH KING. Elizabeth's refusal to take a husband led to her cousin James VI of Scotland inheriting the throne as **James I.** If London had loved Elizabeth, it only tolerated James. Closing himself up in Whitehall, James replied to the people's desire to see his face with the retort "then I will pull down my breeches and they shall also see my arse." Nevertheless, James was not wholly uncaring of the fate of Londoners: he gave his backing to an ambitious project to supply London with fresh drinking water via hollowed-out wooden pipes from a new reservoir in Clerkenwell. Such improvements were all the more necessary as London continued its unchecked expansion: the city was increasingly spilling beyond the city walls and into the future **West End**—which was preferred since prevailing winds carried the stench and pollution of the growing metropolis eastward.

WAR & REGICIDE. James's autocratic tendencies meant that his passing, in 1625, was little mourned. Affairs got no better under his son, **Charles I.** Beset by military defeat abroad and religious dissent at home, Charles's skirmishes with Parliament degenerated into the **Civil War** in 1642. London's support for Parliament sealed the king's fate: without the city's money and manpower, his chance of victory was slim. After a stand-off between the king's army and the London militia at Turnham Green at the outset of the war, Charles never threatened London again; when next he returned to his former capital it was as a captive of **Oliver Cromwell.** The king was tried for treason in Westminster Hall, spent his last night in **St. James's Palace** (p. 100), and was executed on the lawn of Banqueting House on January 25, 1649.

Though Cromwell's firm hand restored the health of the new Puritan-dominated **Commonwealth,** Parliament proved to be as repressive and unpopular as the King it replaced. Not content with outlawing theater and most other forms of entertainment, it went as far as to ban music in churches and even, in 1652, to abolish Christmas, which Cromwell accused of being a Catholic superstition.

A TUMULTUOUS DECADE. The Commonwealth didn't last long. In 1660, **Charles II** returned from exile in Holland to a rapturous welcome. Among those accompanying him on his return was **Samuel Pepys** (PEEPS), whose diary of 1660s London provides an invaluable account of this tumultuous time. The happy-go-lucky atmosphere of the Restoration's early years died in the **Great Plague** of 1665, in which 100,000 Londoners perished. Worse disaster was to follow: early in the morning of September 2, 1666, fire broke out in a bakery on Pudding Ln.. When the **Great Fire** was finally extinguished, 80% of London lay in ruins, including 80 churches, 13,000 homes, St. Paul's, the Guildhall, and virtually every other building of note save the Tower.

In the face of this devastating double blow, **Christopher Wren** submitted a daring plan to rebuild London on a rational basis, with wide boulevards and sweeping vistas. His grand scheme floundered in the face of opposition from existing landowners, and in the end Wren had to settle for the commission to rebuild **St. Paul's Cathedral** (see p. 68) and 51 lesser churches. The fire itself was commemorated by Wren's simple **Monument** (see p. 78), a 202 ft. high column situated 202 ft. from the spot where the fire broke out.

As London rebuilt, some former refugees discovered that they preferred life beyond the city limits. In the latter part of the century speculators threw up numerous handsome squares and terraces in the West End; **Downing Street** (see p. 105) was the brainchild of George Downing, a Massachusetts native, early Harvard graduate, and—appropriately enough—consummate political fixer.

THE ENLIGHTENED CITY (1685-1783)

A GLORIOUS REVOLUTION. Under the leadership of the Dutch **William and Mary**, London gradually supplanted Amsterdam as the linchpin of international trade, an achievement greatly aided by the founding of the **Bank of England** (see p. 81) on the model of the Bank of Amsterdam in 1694. Other future financial behemoths had less obvious beginnings: **Lloyd's of London** (see p. 82) the world's oldest insurance market, started out as Edward Lloyd's coffee shop, where captains congregated to exchange shipping gossip.

PARLIAMENT SUPREME. On the accession of William, Parliament fixed the line of succession to ensure that no Catholic would ever sit on the throne again. The upshot was that in 1714 the crown passed to a German prince who spoke no English: **George I,** formerly the Elector of Hanover. By this time, however, most of the business of government was handled by the man who invented for himself the role of Prime Minister, **Robert Walpole.** During Walpole's 20 years at the top, writers such as **Jonathan Swift, Alexander Pope,** and **Henry Fielding** wrote articles criticizing Walpole, while **John Gay's** wildly popular *Beggar's Opera* (1728) simultaneously satirized government corruption and the current fad for Italian operas. Walpole and the King were far more comfortable with the music of **George Frederick Handel,** who had followed

A Night To Remember

Americans do it on July 4th, Canadians on July 1st, and the French on July 14th. The British, however, wait until cold, damp November 5th to let off their fireworks. That's the date of **Guy Fawkes Night,** which commemorates the failure of a plot to blow up the opening of Parliament (and with it King James I) in 1605.

Determined to rid England of its increasingly repressive Protestant government, the Catholic Guy Fawkes and his co-conspirators came within hours of success. The plot was averted only after one of their number wrote an anonymous letter to his brother-in-law, Lord Monteagle, warning him to stay away. Suspicions aroused, and a search of the premises led to the discovery of Fawkes setting the fuses on 36 barrels of gunpowder packed into a cellar beneath Parliament.

The anniversary of the plot soon became an annual event marked by bonfires, rabid anti-Catholicism and the burning of an effigy of Guy Fawkes or the local Catholic priest. The years have mellowed the holiday's anti-Catholic overtones, and this last tradition has fallen by the wayside, but the night is still one of celebration with bonfires, fireworks, mulled wine, and the traditional verse:

"Remember, remember the fifth of November, gunpowder, treason, and plot.

I see no reason why gunpowder treason should ever be forgot."

George I from Hanover. Handel is best remembered for his English-language oratorios such as the *Messiah* (1741), and his later music is recognized as quintessentially English—something his royal master never achieved.

JOHNSON'S LONDON. When **George III** came to the throne in 1760, Britain had its first English-speaking king in 70 years. Although George is best remembered for losing America and going mad, between these two calamities the capable hands of **Pitt the Younger** (only 24 when he became Prime Minister in 1783) restored Britain to robust financial health. Meanwhile, London added an intellectual sheen to its mercantile character. The **British Museum** opened its doors in 1759, and the city eagerly followed the well-publicized doings of **Samuel Johnson,** famed wit and author of the charmingly idiosyncratic *Dictionary* (1755). Together with his good friend, the painter **Sir Joshua Reynolds,** Johnson founded **The Club** in 1764, an exclusive institution whose members included historian **Edward Gibbon,** economist **Adam Smith,** and writer **James Boswell,** whose *Life of Johnson* provides an unforgettable portrait of the great man and his age. Reynolds was also the prime mover behind the 1768 foundation of the **Royal Academy of Arts** (see p. 133), whose early members included **Thomas Gainsborough.**

A MODERN CITY. In the latter part of the 18th century, London began to take on many of the characteristics of the present-day city. As the focus of life shifted westwards, **Oxford Street** became the capital's main shopping artery, tempting customers with new-fangled ideas such as window displays and fixed prices. And in 1750, London Bridge—until then the sole crossing over the Thames—acquired a neighbor, **Westminster Bridge,** which in 1802 inspired poet **William Wordsworth's** tribute to the beauty of the sleeping city, *Composed upon Westminster Bridge.*

With the trappings of a modern city, London also acquired modern problems, not least among them a massive increase in crime. Much of this could be attributed to the widening gulf between rich and poor, but there was another cause: cheap liquor. **Gin,** invented in Holland in the 17th century, was so cheap and plentiful that by the 1730s consumption had risen to an average of two pints per week for every man, woman, and child in the city—memorably illustrated in **William Hogarth's** allegorical prints, which oppose *Gin Lane* with the cheerful *Beer Street.* In 1751 Parliament passed the Gin Act, imposing government regulation of the sale of alcohol; as a result, mortality rates dropped dramatically. In the same year magistrate and novelist **Henry Fielding,** together with his brother John, established the **Bow Street Runners,** a band of volunteer "thieftakers" which evolved into the Metropolitan Police. Even so, crime was still prevalent enough that in the 1770s the Prime Minister, the Lord Mayor, and even the Prince of Wales were all robbed in broad daylight.

FROM REGENCY TO EMPIRE (1783-1901)

THE HAPPY PRINCE. There could be no mistaking the Prince of Wales (the future George IV) for his staid father. From the moment he turned 21 in 1783, the Prince announced himself through flamboyant opposition to his father's ministers and an utter disregard for convention. When, after overcoming an earlier bout in 1788 (subject of the play and film, *The Madness of King George III*), the King descended into permanent insanity in 1811, the heir to the throne assumed power as the **Prince Regent.**

Unpopular as a wastrel ruler concerned more with his appearance than the state of the country, the Regent's obsession with self-aggrandizement nevertheless brought important benefits to London. Inspired by the changes wrought by Napoleon in Paris, he dreamt of creating a grand processional way leading from Marylebone Park to his residence at Carlton House. **John Nash** was the architect chosen to transform this vision into reality: the result was some of London's best-loved architecture, from the grand **Nash Terraces** surrounding the renamed and remodeled **Regent's Park** (see p. 92), to the great sweep of **Regent's Street** leading up to **Piccadilly Circus** (see p. 100), from where the Haymarket would complete the journey to Carlton House. Alas, all this work was in vain: when the Prince Regent finally became **George IV** in 1820 (five years before the completion of Piccadilly Circus), he abruptly ordered Carlton House demolished, and commissioned Nash to remodel **Buckingham Palace** (see p. 63) for his future residence.

It was the age of the dandy and the aesthete. Fashion was changed forever when **Beau Brummel,** the king's confidant and self-appointed arbiter of taste, did away with gold braid and lace, and made black the new pink. **Romanticism** announced itself in the works of **Lord Byron** and **John Keats;** the London these men occupied can still be seen in the masterful landscapes of **John Constable** and **J.M.W. Turner.**

UNDERGROUND, OVERGROUND.

If the Regency gave London a new face, the Victorian age supplied the skeleton. By the time the 18-year-old **Queen Victoria** ascended to the throne in 1837, London was already at the heart of the largest Empire the world had ever seen, and the city's population increased by almost another million for every decade of Victoria's 64-year reign. Just as the expansion was driven by the new factories of steam-powered manufacturing, so it was made possible by steam-powered transportation. London's first **railway** opened in 1836, connecting London Bridge to the then-distant suburb of Greenwich; by 1876 there were 10 railway companies connecting London to the rest of Britain, each with its own terminal and tracks. Pressure on the capital's roads was relieved with the inauguration of the **Metropolitan Line,** the world's first underground railway, in 1863. Together with horse-drawn trams, the railways made commuting possible for the first time: once-rural villages such as Islington and Hampstead were rapidly engulfed by the voracious city.

Victorian architects reacted to the rush of modernization with a return to the distant past. **Neo-Gothic** architecture was all the rage, as can be seen in **Charles Barry's** enormous, ornate **Houses of Parliament** (see p. 64). A similar sensibility motivated painter-poet **Dante Gabriel Rossetti,** who founded the influential **Pre-Raphaelite Brotherhood** and unleashed on the unsuspecting public a wave of stylized medieval pastiche and dark-lipped maidens. The general anti-modern feeling of the age was best captured by designer and poet **William Morris,** who founded the **Arts and Crafts** movement in the belief that the Industrial Revolution had destroyed notions of taste and craftsmanship.

THE SATANIC CITY.

Many Victorian artistic movements were deeply influenced by the work of visionary poet and artist **William Blake,** who as early as 1804 had written

KEY DATES

AD 43 Romans bridge the Thames at Londinium

60 Boudicca's rebellion

604 St. Augustine in London

871 Vikings occupy London

1066 Norman Conquest

1176-1209 Construction of Old London Bridge

1189 Incorporation of the city

1269 Westminster Abbey rebuilt and reconsecrated

1348 Black Death kills 30,000—half the city

1381 Peasants' Revolt

1455-1485 Wars of the Roses

1485-1603 Tudor dynasty

1599 Globe Theatre opens

1603-1649 and **1660-1688** House of Stuart

1605 Gunpowder Plot against James I and Parliament fails

1649 Charles I beheaded and Commonwealth declared

1666 Great Fire destroys city

1675-1710 Rebuilding of St. Paul's Cathedral under Wren

1688-9 Glorious Revolution

1714 House of Hanover takes power with George I

1759 British Museum opens

1837-1901 Queen Victoria

1858 The Great Stink

1863 Metropolitan line opens, the first underground railway

1888 Jack the Ripper

1915 German bombs bring WWI to London

1940 The Blitz devastates the City and the East End

1953 Elizabeth II crowned

1960-1968 London swings

2000 Ken Livingstone, first democratic Mayor of London

of the "dark satanic mills" spawned by the Industrial Revolution. Working and living conditions for the majority of the capital's inhabitants were appalling, with health-care and sanitation almost non-existent. **Child labor** was unregulated until 1886, **cholera** raged unchecked until the **Great Stink** of 1858 forced Parliament to reform the city's sewers, and air pollution was such that in 1879 the capital was shrouded in smog for the entire winter. A more human tragedy struck in 1888, when police searched in vain for serial killer **Jack the Ripper.**

This was the London that inspired **Charles Dickens** to write such urban master-pieces as *Oliver Twist* (1837-1839), and saw **Karl Marx** lead the proto-communist First International, founded in London in 1864. Even so, it was not until the last third of the century that significant progress was made: in 1867, the **Reform Bill** extended the vote to most of London's working men and 1870 saw the **Education Act** provide schooling for all. Organized labor also made headway: in 1889, Marx's daughter Eleanor led gas workers in a strike which won recognition for the 8-hour day, while in 1893 the working classes found a political voice with the estab-lishment of the **Independent Labour Party.**

THE 20TH CENTURY

THE APEX OF POWER. Although **Edward VII** did not succeed his mother until 1901, Victorian morality had already begun to crumble during the "naughty nineties," when two Irish-born adopted Londoners, taboo-breaking **George Ber-nard Shaw** and flamboyant **Oscar Wilde,** thrilled theatergoers and shocked the authorities. **Emmeline Pankhurst** started the Woman's Social and Political Union to win the vote for women, a struggle that lasted until 1928. The stunts pulled off by her and her **suffragettes** were meat and drink to the new **tabloid press,** which had been born with the launching of the *Daily Mail* in 1903 and rapidly became London's main source of news.

The changes wrought on London by steam in the previous century were com-pleted by the advance of **electricity** and **petroleum** power in the new; already by the outbreak of the First World War in 1914, London was recognizably the same city it is today. Red double-decker buses and clean, electrically powered Under-ground trains delivered Londoners to new department stores such as **Selfridges** (opened 1909) and **Harrods,** which moved to its present site in 1905. Londoners could entertain themselves at one of 30 West End theaters or any of 250 **cine-mas,** and from 1905 they could call their friends from the brand new **telephone boxes** mushrooming all over town.

THE LOSS OF INNOCENCE. Londoners greeted the outset of **World War I** in 1914 with jubilant confidence, and recruiting stations were besieged by eager young men. The horror of modern warfare was soon brought home, when in 1915 the first German **air raid** on London killed 39. As the boom brought on by the wartime econ-omy came to an end, London began to feel the pain: unemployment rose and in 1926 the 10-day **General Strike** brought the nation to a standstill amid fears of revolution. In the end, though, the main beneficiary of the strike was **radio;** the paralyzing of Fleet St. during the strike made the nation dependent on the new **BBC** for news.

ACTION & REACTION. While **George Orwell** took the conscious decision to share in the people's plight—his experiences living with the East End poor are chron-icled in *Down and Out in Paris and London*—others chose to argue from positions of comfort. Such were the members of the intellectual circle known as the **Bloomsbury Group.** So-called because it met in Bloomsbury, the group was less a school of thought than a group of extremely talented friends. Those asso-ciated with the group included novelists **Virginia Woolf** and **E.M. Forster,** and economist **John Maynard Keynes;** the fringes of the group were populated with

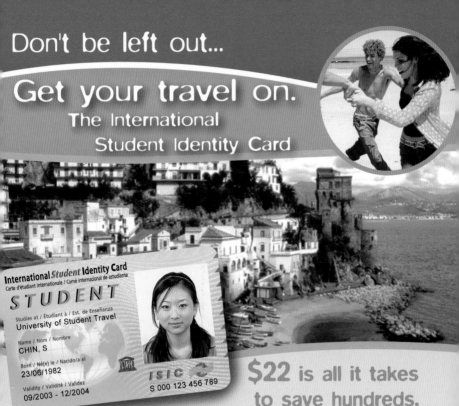

enough already...
Get a room.

Book your next hotel with the people who know what you want.

no-less extraordinary intellects, including philosopher **Bertrand Russell,** writer **Aldous Huxley,** and poet **T.S. Eliot.**

LONDON DEFIANT. London's first showdown with Fascism took place in 1936 at the **Battle of Cable Street,** when a local crowd attacked a deliberately provocative march through the Jewish East End by **Oswald Mosley's** Black-shirts. When **World War II** broke out in 1939, London was ill-prepared: the thousands of gas-masks issued in expectation of German chemical attacks were useless against the incendiary devices of **The Blitz.** Starting on September 7th, 1940, London suffered 57 days of consecutive bombing; regular raids continued until 1941. In 1944, a new rain of death started with the advent of V-1 and V-2 missiles.

By the end of the war, London had suffered destruction on a scale unseen since the Great Fire. If the all-night vigils of volunteer firefighters had saved St. Paul's, the same could not be said for the House of Commons, Buckingham Palace, or most of the East End. Over 130,000 houses had been damaged beyond repair, and a third of the City of London flattened.

REDIRECTION & REDEVELOPMENT. Home to thousands of European exiles and American troops during the war, London transformed itself from hidebound Capital of Empire to cosmopolitan city of the world. **Carnaby Street** and the **King's Road** became the twin foci of a London peopled by hipsters and bohemians. Local boys the **Rolling Stones** battled for supremacy with the **Beatles,** who set up in **Abbey Road** in 1964, and **The Who** chronicled the fights between scooter-riding "mods" and quiff-toting "rockers." Somewhat belatedly, in 1966 *Time* magazine announced that London "swings, it is the scene."

Swinging London died with the oil shocks of the 1970s. Unemployment rose as conflict between unions and the government resulted in the three-day week in 1974 and the **winter of discontent** five years later. A nation in crisis sought refuge in the strong leadership promised by the "Iron Lady" **Margaret Thatcher,** who was elected Prime Minister in 1979. A polarizing figure in British politics even today, Thatcher's program of economic liberalization combined with a return to "Victorian values" in everyday life brought her into direct conflict with the overwhelmingly Labour-dominated **Greater London Council** and its charismatic leader "Red" **Ken Livingstone.** Thatcher's solution was to abolish the GLC, depriving London of its sole unified administrative structure and devolving power to the 33 boroughs.

Ethnic London

While ethnic "ghettos" are rare in London, most communities have a neighborhood focus, where members can find the sights, smells, and sounds (if not the sunshine) of their former homeland.

(South) **Asians,** London's largest ethnic group, are also the most fragmented. Sikhs from **Punjab** congregate in Ealing, the **East End** is the center of the **Bengali** community, and **Pakistanis** prefer **Walthamstow.**

London's **Black** population is divided into two main groups: those of **Caribbean** origin, whose cultural focus is in **Brixton,** and 160,000 **Africans,** mostly West African in origin, who tend to settle in **West London.**

Though few of London's ethnic **Chinese** still live there, they still pack **Soho's** Chinatown on weekends to shop and eat—though today they're often outnumbered by tourists.

From oil-rich Saudis to Lebanese refugees, **Arabs** come together over kebabs and strong coffee on **Edgware Rd.**

Many other ethnic groups are harder to spot. The majority of the strong **Jewish** community lead secular lives, though you'll still see plenty of shtreimels in **Golders Green.** A large number of **Cypriot Greeks** gather in numerous *tavernas* around **Camden Town.** London's largest foreign-born community is also its least visible— you won't find any **Irish** neighborhoods, but there's good *craic* in any number of Irish pubs around the city.

The Mother of Parliaments

Britons regard the reverence Americans accord their constitution with bemusement—after all, they've managed quite nicely without one for centuries. Instead, British democracy rests on a foundation of tradition, legislation, and common sense that has evolved since the barons forced King John to sign the Magna Carta in 1215.

Britons take immense pride in this **"unwritten constitution,"** whose flexibility allowed for a virtually bloodless transition from agrarian monarchy to industrial democracy over the last 350 years. In a dramatic example of its ongoing evolution, 1999 saw over 700 hereditary peers barred from voting in the House of Lords—instead, only government-appointed **life peers**, whose titles are not inherited, will be allowed to sit in the Lords.

Although the once-equitable division of power between the **Crown,** the **Lords,** and the **Commons** formed the model for the US system of President, Senate, and House, since the 17th century the Commons has been in the ascendancy.

Tradition now demands that the **Prime Minister** and the **Cabinet** be Members of Parliament (MPs), while the power of the Lords to initiate and modify legislation has been steadily diminished, and the monarchy reduced to a rubber stamp.

No less controversial was her other major contribution to London, the redevelopment of **Docklands.** London's docks had refused to containerize in the 1960s, and shipping simply moved to the containerized port downriver at Tilbury. By 1981, for the first time in almost 2000 years, not a single dock was in operation. Thatcher's response was to make the enormous area—as large as Manhattan—into an "enterprise zone," a study in market forces free from normal planning restrictions. Home to London's first new transport system in a century (the futuristic, driverless **Docklands Light Railway**), a new airport, and Britain's tallest building (the 800ft. **Canary Wharf**), Docklands is seen today as a spectacular success, with a near-doubling in population since the scheme's inception in 1981.

INTO THE FUTURE. On March 31, 1990, a peaceful protest by 100,000 against a highly unpopular new tax degenerated into an orgy of destruction. The **Poll Tax Riots** sealed the fate of an increasingly out-of-touch Mrs. Thatcher and led to her replacement with the lackluster **John Major.** Real change, though, would have to wait for 1997 and the election of another charismatic reformer, **Tony Blair.** Having rid the "New" Labour Party of most of its socialist baggage, Blair's overriding obsession, it would seem, is with continuous re-election. Eagerly embracing the cultural mini-Renaissance painfully known as **Cool Britannia,** the new government poured millions into a misconceived plan to make London the "Capital of the Millennium." In the event, the much-vaunted "river of fire" merely fizzled, and thousands of VIP guests had to wait for hours outside the **Millennium Dome.**

Other projects have had more success. Gilbert Scott's 1930s Bankside power station reopened in 2000 as the world's largest modern art museum, **Tate Modern** (see p. 123); if **Norman Foster's** reputation suffered when his **Millennium Bridge,** was closed for safety reasons after just three days, it recovered with his ambitious reworking of the **Great Court** (see p. 120), of the British Museum.

On the political front, London regained a unified voice with the election of maverick Ken Livingstone as its first-ever directly **elected mayor** in 2000. Relationships with Westminster soured even before Ken took office, during a bitter primary campaign in which Tony Blair tried to prevent the highly popular Livingstone from winning the Labour Party nomination. Undaunted, Ken stood as an independent and won by a landslide.

THE LIVING CITY
THE CITY TODAY

SIZE

London is a city of 7 million people— down from its pre-war peak of almost 9 million, but still the largest city in Europe, especially if you include the further 3 million living just outside the boundaries of **Greater London** (so called to distinguish it from the historic square mile of the City of London). Even so, London's enormous size—over 30 miles wide east-west, covering some 650 square miles—has less to do with its population that with the English aversion to apartments: the majority of homes are single-family houses, each with its own patch of garden. Add to this an aversion to city-wide planning and a strong sense of community, and you're left with a sprawling, messy metropolis of proudly distinct neighborhoods— which somehow manages to be the most vibrant, exciting city in the world.

ETHNIC COMPOSITION

Today, one in three Londoners belongs to an ethnic minority, a figure that will rise to 40% in five years. London's origins as a trading center and port mean that it has always been home to a number of small foreign communities. The first large-scale immigration occurred in the 17th century, as religious wars sent Protestants from all over Europe seeking refuge in England: 1685 saw the arrival of 30,000 French **Huguenots.** A new wave of persecutions in the 19th century brought 20,000 Russian and Polish **Jews,** many of whom were cheated into believing they had arrived in America, while the rise of fascism in the 1930s saw their numbers swelled by fleeing Germans and Austrians. After WWII, Communism sent hundreds of thousands of Central and Eastern Europeans of all creeds spilling into England, including 250,000 Polish refugees. The post-war collapse of the British Empire brought a new type of immigrant: rather than fleeing persecution, these were people who had been brought up in the British system and had been taught to think of Britain as their "mother country"—or at least a source of economic opportunity unheard of at home. If the 250,000 **Irish** and 60,000 **Chinese** in London tended towards the latter, the former was true for many of London's 300,000 **West Indians** and 500,000 **Asians** (in Britain, "Asian" always refers to someone of Indian, Pakistani, or Bangladeshi origin). More recently, political upheaval in Britain's former colonies has sent a new wave of refugees to London, including some 160,000 **West Africans.**

Although **general elections** to the Commons must be held at least every 5 years, between elections the government has almost unlimited power. Britain's electoral system means the Prime Minister almost always commands an absolute majority of votes in the Commons, while judges have no power to strike down new laws. As a result, despite the weekly theatrics of **Question Time,** when opposition MPs grill the Prime Minister on his performance, the only real check on government power is the court of public opinion.

Today, however, Britain's traditional constitution is under threat: already legislation passed by the European Union supersedes British law, while since 2000, British judges have been able to strike down legislation deemed incompatible with the European Convention on Human Rights. While some see this as a long-needed change to prevent abuses of power, others regard the transfer of power to an unelected international body with trepidation.

CONTEMPORARY CULTURE

MUSIC

The central role London has played on the world music scene since the 1960s needs no introduction. The **Beatles** may have started in Liverpool, but they hotfooted it down to London as soon as possible, where the **Rolling Stones** soon joined battle over the hearts and minds of teenagers everywhere. The scooter-riding **Mod** movement abhorred American-influenced rock'n'roll, preferring introspective ballads by **The Kinks** and **The Who,** who soon expanded into "Rock Operas" such as *Quadrophenia* (1973). This new genre of musical theater had been pioneered five years earlier, when composer **Andrew Lloyd Webber** and lyricist **Tim Rice** wrote *Joseph and the Amazing Technicolor Dreamcoat* for a high-school production. Despite such revolutionary beginnings, the duo soon descended into polished populism: Lloyd Webber went on to write such crowd-pleasers as *Starlight Express* and *Phantom of the Opera,* and Rice's collaboration with Disney on films such as *Aladdin* and *The Lion King* has won him three Oscars. Just when it seemed that London music had reached an artistic dead end, it roared back to life in the hands of the **Sex Pistols,** created by Malcolm McLaren to drum up publicity for his King's Rd. boutique, "Sex."

In the late 1980s the focus of British music swung north to Manchester, before landing back down with a bump in the mid-1990s as groups like **Blur** and **Pulp** fought it out with Manchester-boys-come-south **Oasis.** Meanwhile, musical standards reached a new low with the carefully crafted appeal of the **Spice Girls.** Another nineties phenomenon was the explosive growth of electronic music, born of the rave craze that started in Britain in the late 1980s: bands like **Prodigy, Portishead, Massive Attack,** and the **Chemical Brothers** provide the high-octane power for serious dancing in the capital's mega-clubs.

LITERATURE

A nomination for the annual **Booker Prize,** Britain's most prestigious award for literature, brings instant best-seller status, even though recent winners such as Margaret Atwood's *The Blind Assassin* (2000) or Arundhati Roy's *The God of Small Things* (1997) are anything but easy novels. London's home-grown literature tends to continue the tradition of satire and dry humor started by Jonathan Swift and Samuel Johnson in the 18th century. **Julian Barnes's** *Letters from London* (1995)—a collection of *New Yorker* pieces about life in the capital—provides outsiders with an insider perspective. **Dorris Lessing's** *London Observed* (1993) chronicles London through the eyes of an outsider-turned-insider, and **Martin Amis's** murder mystery *London Fields* (1991) turns the city inside-out. More recently, fictional diaries have been all the rage: **Helen Fielding** charts the trials and tribulations of being young, single, and insecure in the wildly popular *Bridget Jones's Diary* (1999) and its sequel, *The Edge of Reason* (2001), while **Sue Townsend**—whose *Secret Diary of Adrian Mole, aged 13 3/4* was a hit with teenagers in 1989—has followed her hapless protagonist to premature middle age with *Adrian Mole: the Cappuccino Years* (2000). But, a couple of years into the millennium the hapless protagonist has given way to mischievous witch—**J.K. Rowling's** Harry Potter, who has smashed every children's book sales record known to man.

ART

If there's one thing the varied strands of contemporary London art have in common, it's an uncanny ability to unnerve. London's earliest proponents of the stomach-churning school were figurative: the late **Francis Bacon** (1909-1992), who ghoulishly reworked Velazquez's portrait of Innocent X in his *Screaming Popes* series; and **Lucien Freud** (b. 1922), Sigmund's grandson, whose oddly unrealistic "realist" nudes continue to break new ground in portraiture. In the 1960s, the eyestrain inducing abstractions of "Op-Art" created by **Bridget Riley** (b. 1931) sent aspirin sales soaring. After going underground in the 1980s, the London art scene reexploded on the national consciousness in 1995 when **Damien Hirst** won Britain's most prestigious artistic accolade, the **Turner Prize.** Other recent works to have provoked a storm include brothers **Jake** and **Dinos Chapman's** sculptures of toy figures engaged in highly unnatural activities and **Rachel Whiteread's** *House*, a concrete cast of the inside of a London townhouse. With the turn of the century it seems that shock art may have had its day. A sober piece by video artist **Steve MacQueen** beat **Tracey Emin's** unmade bed (complete with used condoms) to the 1999 Turner, and the 2000 prize went to **Wolfgang Tillmans**, a German-born but London-based photographer, over **Glenn Brown's** reproduction of a sci-fi bookjacket.

FILM

The British film industry began as an extension of the stage. British films of the 1910s-20s tended to be technologically crude; many were nothing more than recordings of stage plays, often with the same sets and actors. American companies moved in during the mid-20s, and home production withered.

Alexander Korda spearheaded a minor resurgence in the 1930s. Korda founded London Films and turned it into one of the finest film studios in the world. London Films produced a slew of great films, including *Things to Come, The Scarlet Pimpernel*, and **The Private Life of Henry VIII,** a brilliant and successful film that made Charles Laughton a star. A post-WWII boom saw British studios expand, only to slump in the 1960s with the rise of television. While the major studios shrivelled, independent production expanded with the aid of American expats like John Houston and Stanley Kubrick. A lack of government support has left the industry high and dry since the early 80s-the best it's been able to manage in recent years is **Trainspotting.**

SPORT

Londoners have always been sports mad. Medieval Londoner William FitzStephen described **football** (soccer) games being played in the 12th century, and football is still the capital's prime diversion. From August until May, thousands turn out every weekend to see top London teams **Arsenal** (or "Gun-

in recent news

THE MEN WHO WOULD BE KING

Poor Prince Charles. His sappy phone conversations with long-time companion Camilla Parker-Bowles are overheard by a giggling nation. The Queen's glowing good health is making it increasingly obvious that he may never, ever become King. And the polls indicate that no one wants him to, anyway.

Poor Prince William. He stumbles through his first year at university, proves himself a dismal cook, and his own uncle sneaks film crews on campus to record his struggles. Then, just when he wants to relax and enjoy himself, a "Comedy Terrorist" dressed as Osama Bin Laden (in a pink gown) crashes his 21st birthday party. It's little wonder he's thought of emigrating.

Poor Prince Harry. Every week, tabloids publish pictures of him falling off his horse in yet another polo match. He admits to smoking pot and gets dragged off to a rehab centre to listen to horror stories. And, of course, he's as about as likely to inherit the crown as he is to replace his brother as the "sexy one."

Really, if it weren't for the tens of millions of pounds, the slew of castles, the Royal Yacht, the Royal Train, and the fawning yes-men, you'd almost feel sorry for them.

ners"), **Chelsea, West Ham,** and **Tottenham Hotspur** ("Spurs" for short). Football is very much a lads game—beer and rude songs are essential parts of the ritual—but violence is more publicized than prevalent; you'll often see fathers and their young sons (dressed, naturally, in full team "strip" and matching scarf) cheering on their team from the terraces.

Rugby, similar to American football but without the body armor, is the other main winter sport, though it's far less popular in London than in the North. Divided into two slightly-differing species, Rugby Union and Rugby League, Union rules the roost in London: **Wasps, Harlequins,** and **Saracens** are the top London teams. More than football, though, Rugby is a game of international rivalries: even those with no team affiliation follow the ups and downs of England at the international matches at **Twickenham.**

In spring, when the rugby fields are little more than expanses of mud, attention turns to **cricket.** A game, according to one anonymous commenter, "which the English have invented in order to give themselves some conception of eternity," cricket is the ideal way to spend long summer days: play starts at 11am and typically run until dusk, with breaks for lunch and tea; matches last one to five days. **Middlesex** and **Surrey** are the main London sides; their grounds, at **Lords** and the **Oval** respectively, are also used to host international **Test Matches,** in which England traditionally loses abysmally. Anything else would be "just not cricket," as they say.

Ironically, the sport which gives London the most international attention is the one Londoners care the least about. Although it has a long and distinguished history in the city (Henry VIII was a keen player in his youth), **tennis**—seen as a snob's game—is something most Londoners tune into during **Wimbledon** fortnight, then promptly tune out again. More democratic is the **London Marathon,** held every April, which sees over 30,000 runners complete the grueling 26-mile course from Greenwich, in south-east London, to the final stretch just outside Buckingham Palace.

Recently, electronic dance music (EDM) has found its way into mainstream media as background music for luxury sports sedan commercials, action movies, and radio DJ prattle. However, the proper place to appreciate EDM is not in the privacy and comfort of home, but in the sweaty, frenzied, shared environment of the dance floor. In EDM, loops of synthesized and sampled sounds mix with the occasional vocal or live instrumental embellishment, and rhythm takes precedence over melody and harmony. Repetitive loops, a near-religious adherence to 4/4 time with 16-bar phrasing, the general form of most tracks (intro, drop, groove, break, drop, groove, out), and the interplay between expectation and reward all contribute to the music's trance-like intensity.

The two major categories of beats used in EDM are "four on the floor" and "breakbeat." A "four on the floor" beat emphasizes each beat with a kick drum. Offbeats may be accented by a cymbal or hi-hat, and backbeats may be accented with a snare or a synth hand-clap; this kind of beat grew out of disco and 80s synth-pop. In contrast, "breakbeats" are more irregular and may have a rock-and-roll-like snare emphasis on the backbeat with a funky, skipping kick drum underneath, or a chopped-up and filtered snare sample looped in weirdly syncopated patterns. The name "breakbeat," in fact, derives from the fact that the breakbeats were originally made by early rap producers by sampling naked drum beats in old funk and R&B records; the drum breaks from "Funky Drummer" by James Brown and "Amen, My Brother" by the Winstons are heavily represented in EDM, as well as in hip hop and pop. Finally, an acid line is a rhythmically complex, repetitive, sibilant loop generated by a synthesizer, which could be described, perhaps, as an updated wah-wah disco rhythm guitar sound or the sound that a broken washing machine makes during the spin cycle.

"House" music is probably the most frequently encountered flavor of EDM at night clubs, and its origins in disco and early-80s synth-pop are obvious. It is characterized, musically, by a moderate tempo, thumping four on the floor beat, simple harmonic changes, catchy instrumental or vocal meolodies, and bouncy bass lines. House is often described as having *soul*, being *funky* or *sensual*, or *bumpin'.* Yet "techno" contends with house for popularity and seniority on the club scene. The word "techno" is often used by EDM outsiders to describe all of EDM. But to insiders, techno describes a style of music that is characterized by a driving four on the floor beat within a slightly higher tempo range than house. Vocals, if there are any, are likely to be warped beyond recognition. A mechanical, harsh, and synthetic feel is afforded by the extensive use of synthesized sounds, acid lines, and heavily processed samples. Some techno tracks can be described as tweaky, thumping collections of ordered beeps, whistles, and noises.

"Trance" lies somewhere between house and techno—and also someplace completely different. Musically, it is characterized by a driving four on the floor beat played against a bouncy, offbeat bass line, simple harmonic melodies, some vocals, synth strings, and complex rhythmic layering. "Hardcore" takes the four on the floor beat and turns the tempo way up; it's not for the faint of heart or unsound of mind. "Gabba" is on the more threatening, industrial side—techno multiplied by ten zillion— while happy hardcore sounds like a blinking, whirling, fluorescent, plastic carousel gone terribly awry.

"Breakbeat" or "breaks" covers several styles that share the common characteristic of using, ahem, breakbeats at 90-140 beats per minute (BPM). Breaks carried the innovations in production technology and style brought by early 80s rap to a house and techno audience. A spirit of competitive swagger drives b-boys to battle each other for dance floor supremacy. The sub-style is accessible to many EDM newcomers in part because of the commercial success of breaks artists such as the Crystal Method and the Prodigy, but also because of its links to rap and hip hop, both of which occupy a dominant position in the commercial record industry. "Drum and Bass" and "Jungle" are terms that describe a family of fast breakbeat electronic music, though there is considerable controversy over which is the better term, or the extent to which they overlap. Tracks range from 160-190 BPM and reference many other musical styles. It is aggressive music that is, at times, angry, mischievous, or sinister, but always high-energy.

James Lozada graduated from Harvard in 1998 and has been a Drum and Bass DJ for the past eight years. He is now pursuing a M.D. in Syracuse.

Sights

The sights in London are unbeatable—you're guaranteed to find far too many sights of interest than you have time for, no matter how long your stay. If you're looking for traces of London's Roman past, the City of London is the place to be. Medieval buildings are rare in London, but the few that remain are remarkable. The Tower of London gets the most attention, but don't miss The Temple and St. Etheldreda's, both in Holborn, and the medieval churches of Clerkenwell. There's no shortage of Renaissance buildings, since practically the entire city was rebuilt after the Great Fire of 1666. Architect Christopher Wren built dozens of churches throughout London after the fire—the highest concentration can be found in the City of London, alongside his masterpiece St. Paul's. If you're a Royals buff, Westminster can't be beat—let our **Walking with Royalty** walking tour (p. 18) guide you through Royal London, from Westminster Abbey to Buckingham Palace. For the best of modern London, take our **Millennium Mile** walking tour (p. 20), which takes you from the Tower of London, past London bridge and Shakespeare's Globe Theatre, to the Tate Modern and the London Eye. If it all gets to be too much, try leaving Central London for a day—the grand manors of West London and the maritime past of East London are just a Tube ride away.

ORGANIZED TOURS

Although it may sound hackneyed, a good city tour has its advantages: it offers a quick overview of London's major sights and historic neighborhoods, and while few venture off the beaten path, sightseeing from the top of a bus will give you a better sense of Lon-

the local story

Queen's Life Guard

Corporal of Horse Simon Knowles, in his 18th year at The Queen's Guard.

Q: What sort of training did you undergo?

A: In addition to a year of basic military camp, which involves mainly training on tanks and armored cars, I was also trained as a gunner and radio operator. Then I joined the service regiment at 18 years of age.

Q: So it's not all glamour?

A: Not at all, that's a common misconception. After armored training, we go through mounted training on horseback in Windsor for 6 months where we learn the tools of horseback riding, beginning with bareback training. The final month is spent in London training in full state uniform.

Q: Do the horses ever act up?

A: Yes, but it's natural. During the Queen's Jubilee Parade, with 3 million people lining the Mall, to expect any animal to be fully relaxed is absurd. The horses rely on the rider. If the guard is riding the horses confidently and strongly, the horse will settle down.

don's geography than point-to-point excursions by Tube. However, don't make the mistake of thinking a city tour will give you time to see everything properly—just because your tour has stops at every important sight, it doesn't follow that you'll be able to see it all in a day. Instead, treat a tour as a helpful starting point in trying to plan the rest of your stay.

BUS TOURS

The classic London tour is on an open-top double-decker bus—and in good weather, it's undoubtedly the best way to get an overview of the city. However, if you're booking in advance, you might prefer to insure against rain and choose a bus with a roof upstairs, since you'll see little from street level. Most operators run hop-on, hop-off services, but be sure to check schedules and how long tickets are valid before purchasing. Tickets are often sold at hotels and by agencies all over London, but be careful—travelers have reported overpaying for tickets and being misled about concessionary (concs.) and child fares by untrustworthy middlemen. In any case, you can usually buy tickets on the bus.

The Big Bus Company, 48 Buckingham Palace Rd. (☎ 7233 9533; www.bigbus.co.uk). Tube: Victoria. Choice of live commentary in English or recorded in 8 languages. 3 routes, with buses every 5-15min. 1hr. walking tours and mini Thames cruise included. Also books fast-track entry tickets to many attractions. Tickets valid 24hr. from first use. £17, children £8.

London Duck Tours, County Hall (☎ 7928 3132; www.frogtours.com). Tube: Waterloo or Westminster. Duck Tours operates a fleet of amphibious vehicles that follow a 70min. non-stop road tour with a splash into the Thames for a 30min. cruise. Tours depart County Hall, opposite the London Eye. £16.50, concessions £13, children £11, family £49.

Original London Sightseeing Tour (☎ 8877 1722; www.theoriginaltour.com). 4 different routes, with buses every 20min. Also books fast-track entry tickets to many attractions. Tickets valid 24hr. £15, under-16 £7.50; online booking £1 off.

WALKING TOURS

For a more in-depth account, try a walking tour led by a knowledgeable guide. Tours usually focus on a specific aspect of a neighborhood's past, often taking in parts of London most visitors never see. Prebooking is rarely required—though an umbrella is a good idea!

Original London Walks (☎ 7624 3978; recorded info 7624 9255; www.walks.com). The oldest and biggest walking-tour company. Weekly program (12-

16 walks per day), from "The Beatles Magical Mystery Tour" to nighttime "Jack the Ripper's Haunts" and guided visits to larger museums. Most walks last 2hr. £5, concessions £4, under-16 free.

Streets of London (☎07812 501 418; www.thestreetsoflondon.com). 2hr. tours (2-4 walks per day) concentrating on the City of London and Clerkenwell. £5, concessions £4.

ALTERNATIVE TOURS

BY BIKE. Organized bicycle tours let you cover plenty of ground while still taking you to places double-decker buses can't go. The **London Bicycle Tour Company** has been operating bike tours for eight years. The pace is leisurely, and tours are designed to keep contact with road traffic to a minimum; prices include bike hire, helmet, and comprehensive insurance. The *Royal West* tour takes you along the South Bank, Chelsea, Kensington, and the West End, while the *East Tour* encompasses the City, Docklands, and the East End. The shorter Middle London tour takes in The City and Covent Garden. *(Tours start from the LBTC store, 1a Gabriel's Wharf. ☎ 7928 6838; www.londonbicycle.com. Tube: Waterloo or Southwark. Royal West Su 2pm; East Sa 2pm. Both 9 mi., 3½hr. Middle London M-F 6 mi., 3hr. Book in advance. £15.)*

BY BOAT. A trip on the Thames provides an alternative, and in some ways more authentic overview of London—for centuries, the river was London's main highway. Pick up the *River Thames Boat Service Guide* at Tube stations for comprehensive details of all London's different river services; for commuter services, see p. 31, for trips upriver to Hampton Court, see p. 271, and for services to Greenwich, see p. 113. **Catamaran Cruises** operates a non-stop sightseeing cruise with recorded commentary, leaving year-round from Waterloo Pier and from Embankment Pier. *(☎7987 1185; www.bateauxlondon.com. £7.50, concessions £5.80, children £5.50.)*

MAJOR ATTRACTIONS

BUCKINGHAM PALACE

⊓ LOCATION: *At the end of the Mall, between **Westminster, Belgravia**, and **Mayfair**. WESTMINSTER QUICKFIND: Sights, p. 104; Museums & Galleries, p. 136; Food & Drink, p. 162; Pubs, p. 179. CONTACT: ☎7839 1377; www.royal.gov.uk. TUBE: St. James's Park, Victoria, Green Park, or Hyde Park Corner.*

Originally built for the Dukes of Buckingham, Buckingham House was acquired by George III in 1762, and converted into full-scale pal-

Q: Your uniforms look pretty heavy. Are they comfortable?

A: They're not comfortable at all. They were designed way back in Queen Victoria's time, and the leather trousers and boots are very solid. The uniform weighs about 3 stone [approx. 45lbs.] in all.

Q: How do you overcome the itches, sneezes, and bees?

A: Inherent discipline is instilled in every British soldier during training. We know not to move a muscle while on parade no matter what the provocation or distraction—unless, of course, it is a security matter. But our helmets are akin to wearing a boiling kettle on your head, so to relieve the pressure sometimes we use the back of our sword blade to ease the back of the helmet forward.

Q: How do you make the time pass while on duty?

A: The days are long. At Whitehall the shift system is derived on inspection in Barracks. Smarter men work on horseback in the boxes in shifts from 10am-4pm; less smart men work on foot from 7am-8pm. Some guys count the number of buses that drive past. Unofficially, there are lots of pretty girls around here, and we are allowed to move our eyeballs.

Q: What has been your funniest distraction attempt?

A: One day a taxi pulled up, and out hopped 4 playboy bunnies, who then posed for a photo shoot right in front of us. You could call that a distraction if you like.

ace by George IV, who commissioned John Nash to expand the existing building. Neither George IV nor his successor William IV ever lived in the Palace, with good reason: when the newly crowned Victoria finally took possession in 1837, she discovered a host of costly structural problems, including faulty drains. Nash's structure was soon found to be too small for her rapidly growing family; a solution was found by closing off the three-sided courtyard, concealing the best architecture with Edward Blore's uninspiring facade.

THE STATE ROOMS. The Palace opens to visitors every August and September while the Royals are off sunning themselves; advance booking is recommended. Don't look for any insights into the Queen's personal life—the State Rooms are used only for formal occasions, such as entertaining visiting heads of state; they are also the most sumptuous in the Palace. Look for the secret door concealed in one of the **White Drawing Room's** mirrors, through which the Royals enter the state apartments. In addition to chromatically labeled drawing rooms, you also see the **Throne Room,** whose unusual plaster frieze treats the War of the Roses in classical style—Tudor costumes give the game away. The **Galleries** display many of the finest pieces in the Royal Collection, including works by Rembrandt, Rubens, Vermeer, Van Dyck, and Canaletto, as well as Gobelins tapestries. Liz has graciously allowed commoners into the **Gardens**—keep off the grass! *(Enter on Buckingham Palace Rd. Tickets available from ☎ 7766 7300; www.royal.gov.uk; or (from late July) the Ticket Office, Green Park. Open daily early Aug.-Sept. 9:30am-4:30pm. £12, concessions £10, under 17 £6, under-5s free, family £30.)*

CHANGING OF THE GUARD. The Palace is protected by a detachment of Foot Guards in full dress uniform, bearskin hats and all. "Changing of the Guard" refers not to replacing the sentries, but to the exchanging of guard duty between different Guards regiments. When they meet at the central gates of the palace, the officers of the regiments then touch hands, symbolically exchanging keys, *et voilà,* the guard is officially changed. To witness the spectacle, show up well before 11:30am and stand directly in front of the palace, or use the steps of the Victoria Memorial as a vantage point. For a less-crowded close-up of the guards, watch along the routes of the troops prior to their arrival at the palace (10:40-11:25am) between the Victoria Memorial and St. James's Palace or along Birdcage Walk. *(Daily Apr.-Oct., every other day Nov.-Mar., provided the Queen is in residence, it's not raining too hard, and there are no pressing state functions. Free.)*

THE HOUSES OF PARLIAMENT

🏴 LOCATION: *Parliament Sq, in* **Westminster.** *Enter at St. Stephen's Gate, between Old and New Palace Yards.* **WESTMINSTER QUICKFIND:** *Sights, p. 98; Museums & Galleries, p. 136; Food & Drink, p. 162; Pubs, p. 179.* **CONTACT:** *Commons Info Office ☎ 7219 4272; www.parliament.uk. Lords Info Office ☎ 7219 3107; www.lords.uk.* **TUBE:** *Westminster.* **DEBATES:** *Both houses are open to all while Parliament is in session (Oct.-July. M-W); afternoon waits can be over 2hr. M-Th after 6pm and F are least busy, but there may be an early adjournment. Ask the security guards when they expect the queue to move most quickly. Tickets required for Prime Minister's Question Time (W 3-3:30pm); for tickets write to your MP; non-residents contact your embassy.* **Commons** *usually in session M-W 2:30-10:30pm, Th 11:30am-7:30pm, F 9:30am-3pm.* **Lords** *usually sits M-W from 2:30pm, Th 3pm, occasionally F 11:30am; closing times vary.* **TOURS: British residents:** *Tours held year-round M-W 9:30am-noon and F 2:30-5:30pm; contact your MP to book.* **Overseas visitors:** *Oct.-July, tours only F 3:30-5:30pm. Non-residents must apply in writing at least 4 weeks ahead to: Parliamentary Education Unit, Norman Shaw Building, SW1A 2TT (☎ 7219 4600; edunit@parliament.uk).* **Summer tours:** *Open to all Aug.-Sept. M-Sa 9:15am-4:30pm. Reserve through Firstcall (☎ 0870 906 3773). £7, concessions £3.50.*

The Palace of Westminster, as the building in which Parliament (the House of Lords and House of Commons) sits is officially known, has been at the heart of English governance since the 11th century, when Edward the Confessor established his court here. William the Conqueror found the site to his liking, and under the Normans the palace was greatly extended, most notably with the addition of Westminster Hall in 1097. The massive fire of 1834 wiped out all that remained of the Norman Palace, with the exception of Westminster Hall (see below). The rebuilding started in 1835 under the joint command of classicist Charles Barry and Gothic champion Augustus Pugin, and the resulting clash of temperaments created a masterful combination of both styles of architecture. Access to the Palace has been restricted since a bomb killed an MP in 1979. Few visitors are able to take part in one of the immensely popular tours, but don't despair; debates are open to all while the Houses are in session.

BIG BEN & VICTORIA TOWER. Refer to the **Clock Tower** by its more popular nickname in the presence of Parliamentary administrators, and prepare to be corrected—"Big Ben" strictly refers only to a 14-ton bell, and not even the one in the clock tower (the authentic Ben is inside). Ben was named after the robustly proportioned Sir Benjamin Hall, who served as Commissioner of Works when the bell was cast and hung in 1858. At 98.5m, the southern **Victoria Tower** is 2m taller than its northern brother. Designed to hold the parliamentary archives, the tower holds copies of every Act of Parliament passed since 1497. A flag flown from the top indicates that Parliament is in session.

WESTMINSTER HALL. Behind the scowling statue of Oliver Cromwell squats this low, unadorned chamber, the sole survivor of the 1834 fire. The Hall's relatively modest facade stuns from within with a magnificent hammerbeam roof, constructed in 1394 and considered the finest timber roof ever made. Originally the setting for medieval feasts, it was converted into law courts when Henry VIII decamped to Whitehall; famous defendants have included Saint Thomas More and Charles I. Today it's used for public ceremonies, the lying-in-state of monarchs, and occasional exhibitions.

DEBATING CHAMBERS. Visitors to the debating chambers must first pass through **St. Stephen's Hall,** which stands on the site of St. Stephen's Chapel. Formerly the king's private chapel, in 1550 St. Stephen's became the meeting place of the House of Commons. The Commons have since moved on, but four brass markers still show where the Speaker's Chair used to stand. At the end of the hall, the octagonal **Central Lobby** marks the separation of the two houses, with the Commons to the north and the Lords to the south. Access to the **House of Lords** is via the Peers' Lobby, which smug MPs have bedecked with scenes of Charles I's downfall. The ostentatious chamber itself is dominated by the sovereign's Throne of State under a gilt canopy—only when the throne is occupied can the Commons and the Lords gather together. The Lord Chancellor presides over the Peers from the **Woolsack,** a red cushion the size of a VW Beetle. Next to him rests the almost 6 ft. **Mace,** which is brought in to open the House each morning. In contrast with the Lords, the restrained **House of Commons** has simple green-backed benches under a plain wooden roof. This is not entirely due to the difference in class—the Commons was destroyed by bombs in 1941, and rebuilding took place during a time of post-war austerity. The Speaker sits at the center-rear of the chamber, with the government MPs to his right and the opposition to his left. However, with room for only 437 out of 635 MPs, things can get hectic when all are present. The front benches are reserved for government ministers and their opposition "shadows"; the Prime Minister and the Leader of the Opposition face off across their dispatch boxes.

WESTMINSTER ABBEY

⚑ LOCATION: *Parliament Sq., in* **Westminster.** *Access Old Monastery, Cloister, and Garden from Dean's Yard, behind the Abbey.* **WESTMINSTER QUICKFIND:** *Sights, p. 104; Museums & Galleries, p. 136; Food & Drink, p. 162; Pubs, p. 179.* **CONTACT:** *Abbey ☎7222 5152; Chapter House ☎7222 5897; www.westminster-abbey.org.* **TUBE:** *Westminster or St. James's Park.* **OPEN: Abbey:** *M-Tu and Th-F 9:30am-3:45pm, W 9:30am-7pm, Sa 9:30am-1:45pm, Su open for services only.* **Museum:** *Daily 10:30am-4pm.* **Chapter House:** *Daily Apr.-Oct. 9:30am-4:45pm, Nov.-Mar. 10am-4pm.* **Cloisters:** *Daily 8am-6pm. Garden Apr.-Sept. Tu-Th 10am-6pm, Oct.-Mar. 10am-4pm.* **AUDIOGUIDES:** *Available M-F 9:30am-3pm, Sa 9:30am-1pm. £2.* **TOURS:** *90min. guided tours M-*

F 10, 11am, 2, 3pm; Sa 10, 11am; Apr.-Oct. also M-F 10:30am and 2:30pm. £3, including Old Monastery. **ADMISSION: Abbey and Museum:** £6, concessions and ages 11-15 £4, under-11s free, family (2 adults and 2 children) £12. Services free. **Chapter House:** £1, concessions 80p. **Cloisters & Garden:** Free. No photography.

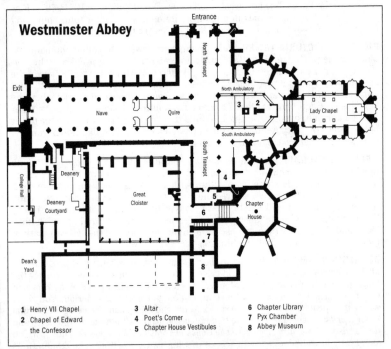

Westminster Abbey

Entrance

North Transept

Exit

Nave

Quire

North Ambulatory

3

3 2

South Ambulatory

South Transept

Lady Chapel 1

College Hall

Deanery

Deanery Courtyard

Great Cloister

Dean's Yard

4

5

6

7

8

Chapter House

1 Henry VII Chapel
2 Chapel of Edward the Confessor
3 Altar
4 Poet's Corner
5 Chapter House Vestibules
6 Chapter Library
7 Pyx Chamber
8 Abbey Museum

On December 28, 1065, Saint Edward the Confessor, last Saxon King of England, was buried in his still-unfinished Abbey church of the West Monastery; almost exactly a year later, on Christmas day, the Abbey saw the coronation of William the Conqueror, who had swiftly completed the Norman invasion of England. Thus even before it was completed, the Abbey's twin traditions as the figurative birthplace and literal resting place of royalty had been established. Almost nothing remains of St. Edward's Abbey: Henry III's 13th-century Gothic reworking created most of the grand structure you see today. Later monarchs continued to add to the Abbey, but the biggest change was constitutional rather than physical: in 1540, Henry VIII dissolved the monasteries, expelling the monks and stripping them of their wealth. Fortunately, Henry's respect for his royal forebears outweighed his vindictiveness against the Pope, and so uniquely among the great monastic centers of England, Westminster escaped destruction and desecration; Henry also decided not to make the Abbey into an Anglican cathedral. Instead, the Abbey became a "Royal Peculiar," under the direct control of the crown. With this ambiguous status, the Abbey has become more than anything the center of ceremony for the nation. Every ruler since 1066 has been crowned here, and many married here. Alternatively sprawling and disjointed, the Abbey's hodge-podge of statues, tombs, and plaques carries a symbolic connection to the changing empire itself.

INSIDE THE ABBEY

Due to the Abbey's status as a tourist mecca, visitors are obliged to follow a set route, entering through the **Great North Door** and immediately into a strange assortment of monuments to 18th- and 19th-century politicians. Victorian Prime Ministers

Disraeli and Gladstone could not stand each other in life, but in death their figures stand close together. Following the trail around, the **ambulatory** leads past a string of side chapels to the left, to a side cove where **Elizabeth I** shares a gilded tomb with her Catholic half-sister and rival **Bloody Mary.** You'll come out into the splendid gothic **Henry VII Chapel**—the fan vaulting on the ceiling creates an unexpected sense of openness, a rarity in the Abbey's crowded passages. On the ground are the stalls of the Knights of the Order of Bath; look at the plaques on the back of the stalls to see the owner or check out the calligraphy register at the end of the chapel that lists recent inductees (now, many foreign presidents). At the end, **Henry VII** lies in front of the **Royal Airforce Chapel,** on the spot where Oliver Cromwell lay for three years before the monarchy was restored and he was removed and hanged posthumously. Along the south side of the chapel the ornate tomb of **Mary, Queen of Scots** distracts visitors from the plainer graves of Charles II, William III, Mary II, and Queen Anne.

At the far end of the Shrine stands the **Coronation Chair,** built for Edward I; the shelf below the seat was made to house the Scottish Stone of Scone, which Edward brought south in 1296—the Stone was finally returned to Scotland in 1996, but will be returned for future coronations. Behind the coronation chair is the **Chapel of St. Edward the Confessor,** the Abbey's founder, whose tomb is surrounded by those of the monarchs from Henry III (d. 1272) to Henry V (d. 1422).

The south transept holds the Abbey's most famous and popular attraction: **Poet's Corner.** Its first member was buried here for reasons nothing to do with literary repute—**Chaucer** had a job in the Abbey administration. Plaques at his feet commemorate both poets and prose writers, as does the stained-glass window above. Most of the artists with plaques are not buried here, including **Shakespeare** (buried in Stratford). Nor do you need to be a writer to be honored here—**Handel** is feted with three separate monuments. Joining these poetic ranks are noted actors such as Laurence Olivier and Sir Henry Irving. At the very center of the Abbey, a few stairs lead up to the **Sanctuary,** where coronations take place. Cordons prevent you from climbing up to admire the 13th-century Cosmati mosaic floor.

The trail leads outside into the cloisters and gardens (see below). Visitors re-enter into the **nave,** the largest uninterrupted space in the Abbey and the part used for daily services. Every hour, on the hour, vistors are invited to join with the clergy here for a brief prayer. At the western end is the **Tomb of the Unknown Warrior,** surrounded by poppies and bearing the remains of an unidentified WWI soldier from the trenches of Flanders, with an oration poured from molten bullets. Hanging from a column by the tomb is the **US Congressional Medal of Honor,** laid on the grave in 1921 by General Pershing. Just beyond the tomb is the simple grave of a well-known hero, **Winston Churchill.** Stretching eastwards, the North Aisle starts with memorials to 20th-century Prime Ministers. Isaac Newton's massive monument, set into the left-hand Quire screen, presides over a tide of physicists around his grave in the nave itself, while adjacent in the aisle biologists cluster around would-be pastor Charles Darwin. Just beyond, in the shadow of the Quire, is the resting place of the Abbey's organists, including John Blow and William Purcell—its remit has been extended to include the likes of Edward Elgar, Vaughan Williams, and Benjamin Britten. As you exit look behind you to see the 10 statues of 20th-century martyrs, including Martin Luther King, Jr.

OLD MONASTERY, CLOISTERS & GARDENS

Formerly a major monastery, the Abbey complex still stretches far beyond the church itself; on the grounds are the buildings of Westminster School, founded in 1560 by Elizabeth I. Note that all the sights below are accessible through Dean's Yard without going through the Abbey. The **Great Cloisters** hold yet more tombs and commemorative plaques; a passageway running off the southeastern corner leads to the idyllic **Little Cloister,** from where another passage leads to the 900-year-old **College Gardens,** which are kept in immaculate condition by the dedicated groundskeeper. A door off the east cloister leads to the octagonal **Chapter House,** the original meeting place of the House of Commons, whose 13th-century tiled floor is the best-preserved in Europe. In 1395, the Abbey succeeded in throwing the MPs out; the faded but still exquisite frescoes of the Book of Revelations around the walls date from this period. Next door, the lackluster **Abbey Museum** is housed in the Norman undercroft. The self-proclaimed highlight of the collection is the array of **funeral effigies,** from the unhealthy-looking wooden models of the 14th century to fully-dressed 17th-century wax versions.

ST. PAUL'S CATHEDRAL

◪ LOCATION: *St. Paul's Churchyard,* **The City of London.** *THE CITY OF LONDON QUICKFIND: Sights, p. 94; Museums & Galleries, p. 126; Food & Drink, p. 150; Pubs, p. 174.* **CONTACT:** ☏ *7246 8348; www.stpauls.co.uk.* **TUBE:** *St. Paul's or Mansion House.* **OPEN:** *M-Sa 8:30am-4:30pm, last admission 4pm; open for worship daily 7:15am-6pm; dome open M-Sa 9:30am-4pm.* **AUDIOGUIDE:** *available 10am-3:30pm; £3.50, concessions £3.* **TOURS:** *90min. M-F 11, 11:30am, 1:30, 2pm. £2.50, concessions £2, children £1.* **EVENSONG:** *The cathedral choir sings evensong M-Sa at 5pm. Arrive at 4:50pm to be admitted to seats in the Quire. 45min., free.* **ADMISSION:** *£6, concessions £5, children £3; worshippers free.*

St. Paul's continues to dominate its surroundings even as modern usurpers sneak up around it. Christopher Wren's masterpiece is the fifth cathedral to occupy the site; the original was built in AD 604 shortly after St. Augustine's mission to the Anglo-Saxons. Incredibly, Wren's is not the largest of the five: the fourth, "Old St. Paul's," begun in 1087, bore Europe's tallest spire, a third as high again as the current 111m dome. By 1666, when the Great Fire swept it away, Old St. Paul's was already ripe for replacement. Even so, only in 1668 did the authorities abandon hope of restoring the old building and invite Wren to design a new cathedral. Church and architect were at loggerheads from the start: when the bishops rejected his third design, Wren simply ignored them and, with Charles II's approval, started building. Sneakily, Wren had persuaded the king to let him make "necessary alterations" as work progressed, and the building that emerged from the scaffolding in 1708 bore a closer resemblance to Wren's second "Great Model" design. Child of one fire, the cathedral only just survived another: on December 29, 1940, St. Paul's was again in flames. Fifty-one German firebombs landed on the cathedral, all put out by the volunteer St. Paul's Fire Watch.

INTERIOR. The entrance leads to the north aisle of the **nave,** the largest space in the cathedral with seats for 2500 worshippers; here, the enormous memorial to the **Duke of Wellington** completely fills one of the arches. Note that, unlike medieval churches, no one is actually buried in the cathedral floor—the graves are all downstairs in the crypt. The second-tallest freestanding **dome** in Europe (after St. Peter's in the Vatican) seems even larger from inside, its height exaggerated by the false perspective of the paintings on the inner surface. An ongoing restoration project will obstruct portions of the dome until mid-2005, but the **Galleries** will remain open (see below). The north transept functions as the **baptistry,** with William Holman Hunt's third version of *The Light of the World* hanging opposite the font; the south transept holds the **Nelson Memorial.** The stalls in the **Quire** narrowly escaped a bomb, but the old altar did not. It was replaced with the current marble **High Altar,** above which looms the ceiling mosaic of *Christ Seated in Majesty.* The altar itself bears a dedication to the Commonwealth dead of both World Wars, while immediately behind it is the **American Memorial Chapel,** in honor of the 28,000 US soldiers based in Britain who died during WWII. The north quire aisle holds Henry Moore's *Mother and Child,* perhaps the church's best piece of sculpture. The south quire aisle contains one of the few monuments to survive from Old St. Paul's: a swaddled tomb effigy of **John Donne** (Dean of the Cathedral 1621-31).

SCALING THE HEIGHTS. St. Paul's dome is built in three parts: an inner brick dome, visible from the inside of the cathedral; an outer timber structure; and between the two, a brick cone that carries the weight of the lantern on top. The first stop is the narrow **Whispering Gallery,** reached by 259 shallow steps or (for those in

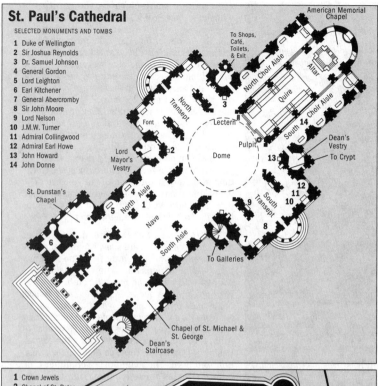

St. Paul's Cathedral

SELECTED MONUMENTS AND TOMBS

1 Duke of Wellington
2 Sir Joshua Reynolds
3 Dr. Samuel Johnson
4 General Gordon
5 Lord Leighton
6 Earl Kitchener
7 General Abercromby
8 Sir John Moore
9 Lord Nelson
10 J.M.W. Turner
11 Admiral Collingwood
12 Admiral Earl Howe
13 John Howard
14 John Donne

American Memorial Chapel

To Shops, Café, Toilets, & Exit

North Choir Aisle

Altar

Quire

South Choir Aisle

North Transept

Font

Lectern

Pulpit

Dome

Dean's Vestry

To Crypt

Lord Mayor's Vestry

St. Dunstan's Chapel

North Aisle

Nave

South Aisle

South Transept

To Galleries

Chapel of St. Michael & St. George

Dean's Staircase

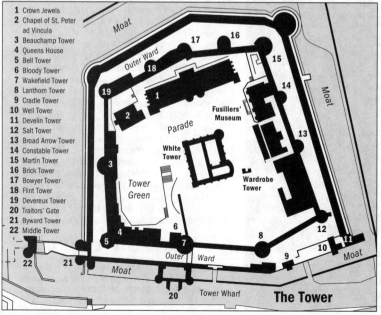

1 Crown Jewels
2 Chapel of St. Peter ad Vincula
3 Beauchamp Tower
4 Queens House
5 Bell Tower
6 Bloody Tower
7 Wakefield Tower
8 Lanthorn Tower
9 Cradle Tower
10 Well Tower
11 Develin Tower
12 Salt Tower
13 Broad Arrow Tower
14 Constable Tower
15 Martin Tower
16 Brick Tower
17 Bowyer Tower
18 Flint Tower
19 Devereux Tower
20 Traitors' Gate
21 Byward Tower
22 Middle Tower

Moat

Outer Ward

Fusiliers' Museum

Parade

White Tower

Wardrobe Tower

Tower Green

Outer Ward

Moat

Traitors' Gate

Tower Wharf

Moat

The Tower

Ravens Misbehavin'

No one's quite sure how, why, or when ravens took to living in the Tower, but these large black birds have become an integral part of London folklore. According to legend, when the ravens leave, the Tower will crumble and the monarchy will fall. To prevent such calamitous occurrences, Charles II ordered that ravens be kept at the Tower, if not exactly under lock and key, then at least under a very close watch; even today the incumbents have their wings clipped.

There's little reason for the birds to wander far, though—they rival the Beefeaters in popularity and are treated suitably regally, being fed each day on 6oz. of raw meat and blood-soaked biscuits. Even so, some birds seem to prefer life outside; Grog escaped to the Rose and Punchbowl pub in 1981.

Naturally, with all the tourist attention they get, the ravens have to be on best behavior all the time; cantankerous fowl have been given the sack. George was dismissed in 1986 after becoming obsessed with eating TV aerials. The dispatch read "On Saturday 13 Sept 1986, Raven George, enlisted 1975, was posted to the Welsh Mountain Zoo. Conduct unsatisfactory, services therefore no longer required."

need only) a small elevator, though it's not wheelchair accessible. Circling the base of the inner dome, the gallery is a perfect resounding chamber: whisper into the wall, and your friend on the other side should be able to hear you—or, they could if everyone else weren't trying the same thing. Instead, admire the scenes from the life of St. Paul painted on the canopy. From here, the stout of heart and leg can climb another 119 steps (this time steep and winding) to the **Stone Gallery,** outside the cathedral at the base of the outer dome. The heavy stone balustrade, not to mention taller modern buildings, result in an underwhelming view, so take a deep breath and persevere up the final 152 dizzying steps to the **Golden Gallery** at the base of the lantern. The view from the top almost makes it all worth it, though a better vista can be had for fewer steps from the top of the Monument (see p. 78).

PLUMBING THE DEPTHS. The sheer number of memorials in St. Paul's **crypt** makes the free "Key to the Crypt" brochure from the information desk indispensable. The crypt is packed wall-to-wall with plaques and tombs of great Britons (and the occasional foreigner). **Nelson** commands pride of place, with radiating galleries festooned with monuments to other military heroes, from Epstein's bust of **T.E. Lawrence** (of Arabia) to a plaque commemorating the casualties of the Gulf War. **Florence Nightingale** is also honored here. The neighboring chamber contains **Wellington's** massive tomb, its stark simplicity in contrast to the ornate monument upstairs. The rear of the crypt, now the chapel of the "most excellent Order of the British Empire," bears the graves of artists, including **Sir William Blake, J.M.W. Turner,** and **Henry Moore,** crowded around the black slab concealing the body of **Sir Christopher Wren.** Inscribed on the wall above is his famous epitaph: *Lector, si monumentum requiris circumspice* ("Reader, if you seek his monument, look around"). Also in the crypt are models of St. Paul's various incarnations and the **treasury,** with a glittering collection of plate, cups, and robes, including the Bishop of London's Jubilee cope, a silk robe with 73 churches and St. Paul's Cathedral embroidered upon it in gold silk. A memorial to the late **Queen Mother** has been added to the new Golden Jubilee Display.

THE TOWER OF LONDON

◪ LOCATION: *Tower Hill, next to Tower Bridge, in the **The City of London,** within easy reach of the **The South Bank** and the **East End. THE CITY OF LONDON QUICKFIND:** Sights p. 78; Museums & Galleries p. 126; Food & Drink* *p. 150; Pubs, p. 174.* **CONTACT:** ☎ 7709 0765; www.hrp.org.uk. **TUBE:** *Tower Hill or* **DLR:** *Tower Gateway.* **OPEN:** *Mar.-Oct. M-Sa 9am-6pm, Su 10am-6pm; buildings close at 5:45pm, with last ticket sold at 5pm and last entry at 5:30pm; Nov.-Feb. all closing times 1hr. earlier, and on M opens at 10am.* **TOURS:** *Yeoman Warder Tours: Meet near entrance. 1hr., every 90min. M-Sa 9:30am-2:30pm, Su 10am-2:30pm.* **AUDIOGUIDES:** *£3.* **ADMISSION:** *£12, concessions £9, ages 5-15 £7.80, under-5s free, family (5 people, including 1-2 adults) £36. Tickets also sold at Tube stations; buy them in advance, as queues at the door are horrendous.*

The Tower of London, one of the most deservedly popular attractions in the city, has served as palace, prison, and living museum for over 900 years. William the Conqueror's wooden palisade of 1067 was replaced in 1078 by a stone structure that over the next 20 years would grow into the White Tower. Richard the Lionheart began the construction of additional defenses in 1189, and further work by Henry III and Edward I brought the Tower close to its present condition. The whole castle used to be surrounded by a broad moat, but cholera epidemics led to its draining in 1843; it's since sprouted a tennis court for the Yeomen Warders. These "Beefeaters"—whose nickname may be a reference to their daily allowance of meat in former times—still guard the fortress, dressed in their distinctive blue everyday uniforms or red ceremonial uniforms. To be eligible for Beefeaterhood, a candidate must have at least 22 years of service in the armed forces, as well as a strong appetite for flash photography. All this history and tradition notwithstanding, with 2.5 million visitors a year, the Tower can sometimes feel like a medieval theme park. To make the most of your visit, buy tickets in advance and arrive as early as possible—before the school buses unload. If you show up at 9am on a M-Th morning, you'll have the run of the place; show up at noon on a Saturday, and you'll be standing in line for hours. Happily for visitors, the fortress is divided into seven more-or-less self-contained areas, which can be visited in any order. An enjoyable and popular way to get a feel for the Tower is to join one of the ◪**Yeoman Warders' Tours** (see above), which will fill you in on the history and legends associated with the Tower. Keep the kids away from the famous **ravens**—they bite!

WESTERN ENTRANCE & WATER LANE. Historically, the main overland entrance to the Tower was over a double system of drawbridges via mini-fortress where the ticket offices now stand. **Lion Tower,** of which only the foundations remain, was the first line of defense, followed by **Middle Tower,** where today tickets are collected and bags searched. After passing over the moat, you enter the **Outer Ward** through **Byward Tower.** The password, required for entry after hours, has been changed daily since 1327. Just beyond Byward Tower, the massive **Bell Tower** dates from 1190; the curfew bell has been rung nightly for over 500 years. The stretch of the Outer Ward along the Thames is **Water Lane,** which until the 16th century was adjacent to the river. The partially submerged **Traitor's Gate** was built by Edward I but is now associated with the most famous prisoner to pass through it, Saint Thomas Becket.

MEDIEVAL PALACE. In this sequence of rooms, archaeologists have attempted to recreate the look and feel of the Tower during the reign of Edward I (1275-1279). The tour starts at **St. Thomas's Tower,** a half-timbered set of rooms above Traitor's Gate. The rooms start out bare and are progressively reconstructed to 13th-century appearance. A small but extraordinary collection of 13th-century objects ends the tour and makes it all worthwhile.

WALL WALK. The Wall Walk runs along the eastern wall constructed by Henry III in the mid-13th century. The wall is entered via **Salt Tower,** whose long service as a prison is witnessed by the fascinating inscriptions scratched out by bored inmates, including religious messages from Catholic martyrs and extraordinarily elaborate astrological tables carved by a convicted sorcerer. Unsurprisingly, the tower is allegedly haunted—dogs refuse to enter it. At the end of the walk is **Martin Tower.** In 1671, the self-styled "Colonel" Thomas Blood nearly pulled off the heist of the millennium. Blood befriended the warden of the Martin Tower, where the crown jewels were then kept, and visited him at night with some "friends." They subdued the guard and stuffed their trousers with booty, only to be caught at the nearby docks. Charles II was so taken with Blood's bravado that he awarded the colonel a privileged spot in his court. The Martin Tower is now home to a fascinating collection of retired crowns, *sans* gemstones (which have been recycled into the current models) along with paste models of some of the more famous jewels, including the fist-sized Cullinan diamond, the largest ever found, at 3106 carats.

CROWN JEWELS. Be sure to visit Martin Tower before seeing the crown jewels—Jewel House has almost no documentation, and the jewels are much more interesting once you know the story behind them. The queue at the Jewel House (formerly Waterloo Barracks) is a miracle of crowd management. Tourists file past room after room of rope barriers while video projections show larger-than-life depictions of the jewels in action. Finally, visitors are ushered into the vault, past two-foot thick steel doors, and onto moving walkways that whisk them past the crowns and ensure that no awestruck gazers hold up the queue. Most of the items on display come from the spectacular Coronation regalia; with the exception of the Coronation Spoon, everything dates from after 1660, since Cromwell melted down the original booty. While the eye is naturally drawn to the **Imperial State Crown,** home to the Stuart Sapphire along with 16 other sapphires, 2876 diamonds, 273 pearls, 11 emeralds, and five rubies, don't miss the **Sceptre with the Cross,** topped with the First Star of Africa, the largest quality cut diamond in the world. Look for the **Queen Mother's Crown,** which contains the Koh-I-Noor diamond; legend claims the diamond will bring luck only to women.

WHITE TOWER. Originally a royal residence, the Conqueror's original castle has also served as a wardrobe, storehouse, records office, mint, armory, and prison. Visitors are given the option of long or short routes; unless you have trouble with spiral staircases or are particularly pressed for time, take the long version, which starts with the first-floor █**Chapel of St. John the Evangelist.** Remarkable for its quietly stunning simplicity, this 11th-century Norman chapel is one of the oldest and most beautiful spaces in the Tower. The spacious hall next door was most likely the royal **bedchamber,** with numerous garderobes (medieval toilets) set into the walls. The larger room next door would have been his **Great Hall.** Today it houses a collection of armor and weapons from the Royal collection: don't miss Henry VIII's corset, without which he couldn't fit into his tournament armor, and the miniature suits of armor designed for young nobles. The visit passes through endless displays of swords, cannons, and muskets on the second floor, before dropping down two levels to meet up with the start of the short route. This trails through a set of historic misrepresentations, starting with the **Spanish Armory**—torture instruments that were displayed in the 17th century as being captured from the Spanish Armada (1588), but were actually from the Tower's own armory. Finally, you exit via the basement past a display telling how the Victorians "restored" the Tower to their ideal of a medieval fortress, demolishing many of its historic buildings along the way.

TOWER GREEN. The grassy western side of the Inner Ward, site of the Tower's most famous executions, is surrounded by a suite of houses that have been home to Tower officials for centuries. The Tudor **Queen's House** (which will become the King's House when Charles ascends the throne) is now occupied by the Governor of the Tower. Nearby, the **Beauchamp Tower** was usually reserved for high-class "guests," many of whom carved intricate inscriptions into the walls during their detention. On the north of Tower Green is the **Chapel Royal of St. Peter ad Vinculum.** Originally just another City church, by the 13th century it found itself well within the Tower walls. Three queens of England—Anne Boleyn, Catherine Howard, and Lady Jane Grey—are buried here, as well as Catholic martyrs Saint Thomas More and John Fisher. *(Open only by Yeoman tours or after 4:30pm.)* Across the green is **Bloody Tower,** the site where Richard III allegedly imprisoned and murdered his young nephews, including Edward V, the 12-year-old rightful heir to the throne. In 1674, the bones of two children were unearthed beneath a nearby staircase and subsequently interred in Westminster Abbey. Inside, the tower has been restored to its appearance in the early 17th century, when it housed erstwhile adventurer and treason suspect Sir Walter Raleigh.

OUTSIDE THE TOWER. The Tower's jurisdiction extends beyond its walls into the surrounding area, known as the **Liberty of the Tower. Tower Hill** was the traditional site for public beheadings. The last execution was that of 80-year-old Lord Lovat, leader of the Jacobite rebellion, in 1747. *(In Trinity Gardens next to Tower Hill Tube station.)* Between the Tower and the Thames, the **Wharf** offers a view of Tower Bridge and Southwark. Ceremonial salutes are fired from the river bank here on Royal birthdays and during state visits.

CEREMONY OF THE KEYS. As the oldest continuously occupied castle in Europe, the Tower has a wealth of traditions. One of the most popular is the Ceremony of the Keys. This nightly locking-up ritual has been performed every night without fail for over 700 years. At precisely 9:53pm, the Chief Warder locks the outer gates of the Tower before presenting the keys to the Governor amid much marching and salutation. *(For tickets, write 6 weeks in advance with the full name of those attending, a choice of at least 3 dates, and a stamped addressed envelope or international response coupon to: Ceremony of the Keys, Waterloo Block, HM Tower of London, EC3N 4AB. Free.)*

HYDE PARK & KENSINGTON GARDENS

◪ LOCATION: *Framed by Kensington Rd., Knightsbridge, Park Ln., and Bayswater Rd.; bordered by* **Knightsbridge, Kensington, Bayswater, Marylebone,** *and* **Mayfair. CONTACT:** ☎*7298 2100.* **TUBE:** *Queensway, Lancaster Gate, Marble Arch, Hyde Park Corner, or High St. Kensington.* **OPEN:** *Hyde Park daily 5am-midnight, Kensington Gdns. dawn-dusk.* **ACCESSIBILITY:** *"Liberty Drive" rides for seniors and the disabled.* ☎*077 6749 8096.* **ACTIVITIES & EVENTS:** *A full program of music, performance, and children's activities takes place during the summer; see park noticeboards for details.* **ADMISSION:** *Free.*

Surrounded by London's wealthiest neighborhoods, Hyde Park has served as the model for city parks around the world, including Central Park in New York and Paris's Bois de Boulogne. Henry VIII stole the land from Westminster Abbey in 1536, and the park remained a royal hunting ground until James I opened it to the public in 1637—the first royal park to

NO **WORK** ALL **PLAY**

ROYAL ASCOT

One of the best occasions for Londoners to strut their stuff is the **Royal Ascot.** Founded by Queen Anne in 1711, today it stages 25 days of racing throughout the year. Most famous is the lavish four-day Royal Meeting, held in the third week of June.

The Royal Enclosure is synonymous with a strict dress code, namely hats—from tiny, streamlined pill-boxes to elaborate feathered affairs. Ladies must wear formal day dresses or trouser suits, and hats that cover the crown of the head; men must don a black or gray morning suit and a top hat. Shorts or sneakers will result in ejection from the Enclosure. To enter this exclusive area, you must apply in advance and be sponsored by existing Royal Enclosure badge holders who have attended the Royal Meeting on at least four occasions.

Fortunately, the enclosures for the general public have much less complicated rules of entrance. The Grandstand and Silver Ring areas, for instance, do not require ladies to wear hats, but simply encourage that everyone look as smart as possible.

Grandstand and Paddock tickets are £52; those in the Silver Ring are £16. Book well ahead. Trains run to Ascot from London Waterloo station (☎08457 484 950; www.southwesttrains.co.uk).

be so opened. It's still the largest public space in central London. **Kensington Gardens,** contiguous with Hyde Park and originally part of it, was created in the late 17th century when William and Mary set up in Kensington Palace.

THE SERPENTINE. Officially known as the Long Water West of the Serpentine Bridge, the 41-acre Serpentine was created in 1730. From the number of people who pay to row and swim here, you'd think it was the fountain of youth. South of Long Water, some way from the lake itself, the **Serpentine Gallery** displays contemporary art (open daily 10am-6pm, free). *(**Boating:** ☎7262 1330. Open Apr.-Aug. daily 10am-5pm (6pm in fine weather). £3.50 per person for 30min., £5 per hr.; children £1/£2. Deposit may be required. Cash only. **Swimming:** At the Lido, south shore. ☎7706 3422. Open June-early Sept. daily 10am-5:30pm. £3, seniors £2, children 60p, family £6.50.)*

MARBLE ARCH. Looking rather displaced by itself, Marble Arch was never meant to be a stand-alone monument. Designed by Nash in 1828 as the front entrance to Buckingham Palace, extensions to the Palace soon rendered it useless, so it was moved to the present site as an entrance into Hyde Park. Then new roads cut the arch off, leaving it stranded forlornly on a traffic roundabout. The arch stands close to the former site of the Tyburn gallows, London's main execution site until 1783. *(Near the intersection of Park Ln., Oxford St., Edgware Rd., and Bayswater Rd. Tube: Marble Arch.)*

OTHER PARK SIGHTS. Running south of the Serpentine, the dirt horse track **Rotten Row** stretches out westwards from Hyde Park Corner. The name is a corruption of *Route du Roi* or "King's Road," as this was the royal route from Kensington Palace to Whitehall; it was the first English thoroughfare lit at night to deter crime. At the southern end of Hyde Park clusters a group of statues: **Diana fountain** (the goddess, not the princess); the "family of man"; a likeness of **Lord Byron;** and a fig-leafed **Achilles** dedicated to Wellington. At the northeastern corner of the park, near Marble Arch, you can see free speech in action as proselytizers, politicos, and flat-out crazies dispense the fruits of their knowledge to bemused tourists at **Speaker's Corner** on Sundays.

SIGHTS BY NEIGHBORHOOD

BLOOMSBURY

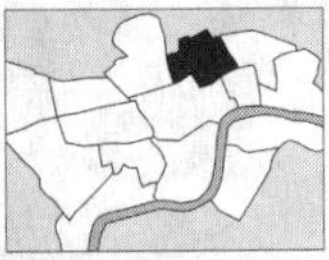

SEE MAP, p. 362

***BLOOMSBURY QUICKFIND: Museums & Galleries,** p. 125; **Food & Drink,** p. 148; **Pubs,** p. 173; **Entertainment,** p. 207; **Shopping,** p. 226; **Accommodations,** p. 254.*

First settled in the 18th century, Bloomsbury acquired its intellectual character in the 19th century as the home of both the British Museum and University College, London's first university. This reputation was bolstered in the early 20th century as Gordon Sq. rang with the philosophizing and womanizing of the Bloomsbury Group. Though few besides students and tourists sleep here nowadays, the high concentration of academic and artistic institutions maintains the cerebral atmosphere.

ACADEMIA

***TUBE:** Warren St., Goodge St., and Tottenham Court Rd. stations serve the northern, central, and southern ends of Gower St., respectively. **BUSES:** Numerous buses run north-south down Gower St., returning along Tottenham Court Rd.*

The strip of land along **Gower Street** and immediately to its east is London's academic heartland. The well-kept streets of this district are lined with world-renowned institutions such as University College, London (UCL; see below) and the Royal Academy of Dramatic Art (RADA; see p. 207). On the other side of UCL from Gower St., **Gordon Square** was home to much of the Bloomsbury Group, while farther down Gower St. handsome **Bedford Square** is the only Bloomsbury square to retain all its original Georgian buildings.

UNIVERSITY COLLEGE LONDON. Established in 1828 to provide an education to those excluded from Oxford and Cambridge, UCL was the first in Britain to admit Catholics and Jews and, later, the first to allow women to sit for degrees. The college founder, **Jeremy Bentham**, has himself sat in the South Cloister since 1850—embalmed, dressed, and sitting congenially in a simple glass enclosure. The doctor was unable to preserve his head, so a wax model was used: the official line is that the original is kept in the college vaults, but student lore holds that it was stolen by rascals from rival King's College. *(Main entrance on Gower St. South Cloister entrance through the courtyard. Gates to the quadrangle close at midnight; access to Jeremy Bentham ends at 6pm. Free.)*

SENATE HOUSE. The sight of UCL's massive central administrative building would quash the spirits of any student radical—it rises out of the ground like a cement monolith. Appropriately enough for such a Stalinist construct, during WWII it housed the BBC propaganda unit. George Orwell, who was employed at this so-called "Ministry of Information," used his experience there as the model for the Ministry of Truth in *1984*. *(At the southern end of Malet St. Tube: Goodge Str. or Russell Sq. Closed to the public.)*

ST. PANCRAS & EUSTON ROAD

⌘ TUBE: King's Cross St. Pancras unless otherwise specified.

The opening of the British Library in 1998 has rejuvenated this neighborhood, which was barely considered part of Bloomsbury until recently; still, signs of its gritty past are everywhere. **Travelers should be on their guard while walking alone near King's Cross Station, especially after dark.**

BRITISH LIBRARY. Castigated during its long construction by traditionalists for being too modern and by modernists for being too traditional, since its 1998 opening the new British Library building continues to impress visitors and regulars alike with its stunning interior. The heart of the library is underground, with 12 million books on 200 mi. of shelving; the above-ground brick building is home to the cavernous reading rooms, and an engrossing museum (see p. 125). Displayed in a glass cube toward the rear of the building, the 65,000 volumes of the **King's Library** were collected by George III and bequeathed to the nation by his less bookish son, George IV, in 1823. *(96 Euston Rd. ☎ 7412 7332; www.bl.uk. All public spaces (including exhibition galleries) open M and W-F 9:30am-6pm, Tu 9:30am-8pm, Sa 9:30am-5pm, Su 11am-5pm. Audioguides £3.50, concessions £2.50. **TOURS:** Tours of public areas M, W, F, Sa 3pm, and Sa 10:30am; £5, concessions £3.50. Tours including one of the reading rooms Tu 6:30pm, Su and Bank Holidays 11:30am and 3pm; £6, students and concessions £4.50. Reservations recommended for all tours. Library free.)*

ST. PANCRAS STATION. If asked, most visitors would assume that the low, modern concourse on one side of the Midland Rd. and Euston Rd. intersection was a railway station, and the soaring Gothic spires on the other the British Library. In fact, the Victorian extravaganza is the facade of St. Pancras Station, whose massive 1868 trainshed was once the largest undivided indoor area in the world. Current construction means that views of the exterior occasionally will be obstructed by scaffolding. *(Euston Rd.)*

OTHER BLOOMSBURY SIGHTS

CORAM'S FIELDS. One of the most delightful spots in all of London, these seven acres of old Foundling Hospital grounds have been preserved as a spectacular (and free) children's park. Kids of all ages will love the petting zoo and paddling pond, not to mention the special under-5 toilets; under-12s will relish the hi-tech playgrounds. *(93 Guilford St. ☎ 7833 0198. Open daily 9am-dusk. No adults admitted without children. Free.)*

ST. GEORGE'S BLOOMSBURY. Time, the Blitz, and general disrepair have taken their toll on the facade of this 1730 Hawkmoor church, but the interior is in perfect condition, with an unusual flat ceiling undecorated except for a central plaster rose.

Westminster Cathedral

Buckingham Palace

Changing of the Guard

Anthony Trollope was baptized before the gilded mahogany altar, which was also the setting of Dickens's *Bloomsbury Christening.* The church's most unusual feature is its stepped spire, based on the ancient Mausoleum of Halikarnassos (much of the original is now in the British Museum) and topped by a statue of George I. A massive and much-needed restoration of the exterior is ongoing, with the goal of restoring the portico to its former splendor. *(Bloomsbury Way. ☎ 7405 3044. Tube: Russell Square. Open M-Sa 9:30am-5:30pm, but hours will vary greatly as restoration continues; call to confirm for the day of your visit.)*

NEARBY MUSEUMS & GALLERIES
Major Collections: British Museum, p. 119.

Other Permanent Collections: British Library Galleries, p. 125; Percival David Foundation of Chinese Art, p. 125; Pollock's Toy Museum, p. 125.

Exhibition Spaces: Brunei Gallery, p. 126.

CHELSEA

SEE MAP, p. 363

CHELSEA QUICKFIND:
Museums & Galleries, p. 126; *Food & Drink,* p. 150; *Entertainment,* p. 208; *Shopping,* p. 227. . *TRANSPORTATION:* The only **Tube** station in Chelsea is Sloane Sq.; from here **buses** #11, 19, 22, 211, and 319 serve King's Rd.

As wealthy as neighboring Belgravia and Kensington, Chelsea boasts a riverside location and a strong artistic heritage. Henry VIII's right-hand man (and later victim) Saint Thomas More was the first big-name resident in the 16th century, but it was in the 19th century that the neighborhood acquired its reputation as an artistic hothouse. **Cheyne** (CHAIN-ee) **Walk** was home to J.M.W. Turner, George Eliot, Dante Gabriel Rossetti, and more recently Mick Jagger (at no. 48). Oscar Wilde, John Singer Sargent, and James McNeill Whistler lived on **Tite Street,** while Mark Twain, Henry James, and T.S. Eliot were also Chelsea residents at various times. The latest artist-in-residence is none other than Damien Hirst, who recently purchased a large houseboat moored near Cheyne Walk.

THE ROYAL HOSPITAL
Location: Two entrance gates on Royal Hospital Rd. *Contact:* ☎ 7881 5204. *Museum, Great Hall, and Chapel:* Open M-Sa 10am-noon and 2-4pm, Su 2-4pm. (Museum closed on Su Oct.-Mar.) *Grounds:* Open Nov.-Mar. M-Sa 10am-4:30pm, Su 2-4:30pm; Apr. closes 7:30pm; Sept. 7pm; summer 8:30pm. *Admission:* Free.

The majestic environs of the Royal Hospital are home to the **Chelsea Pensioners,** who totter around the grounds as they have done since 1692, dressed in blue on normal days and scarlet on ceremonial occasions. Charles II established the place as a retirement home for army veterans ("hospital" meaning a place of shelter), and the entrance criteria have barely changed since: 20 years of distinguished service or a disability incurred while in service. Given that a soldier can only move in if he (there are no shes) has no dependents, most are eager for a conversation about their military glory days if you'll oblige them. The Hospital remains a military institution, with pensioners arranged in companies under the command of a retired officer; until 1805, pensioners remained armed and carried out guard duties. Today they run the post office and museum. The graceful layout is a hallmark of Christopher Wren's design, and the beautifully smooth lawns are broken only by the gilded statue of Charles II in the central **Figure Court.** From this central court, doors lead to the **chapel** and **Great Hall,** where pensioners dine surrounded by captured enemy standards and an engraved list of every battle fought by the British. Off the west court, a small **museum** details the history and everyday life of the hospital and pensioners, along with a room of glittering medals, all bequeathed by their former owners.

RANELAGH GARDENS. Accessible through the hospital grounds, these gardens were opened to the public in 1724 and soon became a fashionable spot, with meals served in the enormous Rotunda. When the Hospital re-acquired the land in 1805, the Rotunda was demolished; now the gardens are a quiet oasis free of high society—except during the week of the **Chelsea Flower Show,** May 25-28 in 2004, when the braying masses of the Royal Horticultural Society descend *en masse. (www.rhs.org.uk. Tickets to the show must be purchased well in advance. Gardens open May-Aug. M-Sa 10am-12:45pm and 2-8:30pm, Su 2-8:30pm; Nov.-Mar. closes 4:30pm, Apr. 7:30pm, Sept. 7pm, Oct. 5pm.)*

OTHER CHELSEA SIGHTS

SLOANE SQUARE AND KING'S ROAD. Sloane Square takes its name from British Museum founder Sir Hans Sloane (1660-1753), who spearheaded the neighborhood's transformation from sleepy backwater to fashionable suburb. Until 1829, **King's Road,** stretching southwest from Sloane Sq., served as a private royal route from Hampton Court to Whitehall. In the 1960s Mary Quant launched the miniskirt on an unsuspecting world from King's Rd; two decades later punk rock's most famous spokesmen, the Sex Pistols, were started as a publicity stunt for Malcom McLaren's boutique at the **World's End,** 430 King's Rd. (see p. 228).

CHELSEA PHYSIC GARDEN. Founded in 1673 to provide medicinal herbs, the Physic Garden remains a carefully ordered living repository of useful, rare, or just plain interesting plants, ranging from opium poppies to leeks. It has also played an important historic role, serving as the staging post from which tea was introduced to India and cotton to America. It is a colorful, quiet place for wandering, picnics, and teas. Tea served from 2:30-4:45pm. *(66 Royal Hospital Rd. Entrance on Swan Walk. ☎ 7352 5646; www.chelseaphysicgarden.co.uk. Open early Apr.-Oct. W noon-5pm, Su 2-6pm; M-F noon-5pm during Chelsea Flower Show (May 25-28 in 2004) and Chelsea Festival (mid-June). £5, students and under 16 £3.)*

CHELSEA OLD CHURCH. This Saxon church had to be restored after WWII; fortunately, the bombs spared the southern chapel, where Saint Thomas More worshipped in the 16th century. Henry VIII is reported to have married Jane Seymour here before the official wedding took place. Just down the street is **Crosby Hall,** a 15th-century hall that was More's residence in Bishopsgate before being moved, stone by stone, to its present position in 1910. *(2 Old Church St. www.domini.org/chelsea-old-church. Open Tu-F 2-5pm and for services Su 8am, 11am, 12:15pm, 6pm.)*

CARLYLE'S HOUSE. In his time, the "Sage of Chelsea" Thomas Carlyle was the most famous writer and historian in England—at his death in 1881, admirers purchased his house and preserved it as a national monument. The house and garden in which he entertained Dickens, Tennyson, George Eliot, and Ruskin are more or less as they were during his lifetime. *(24 Cheyne Row. ☎ 7352 7087. Open Apr.-Oct. W-F 2-5pm, Sa-Su 11am-5pm, last admission 4:30pm. £3.70, under 16 £1.80.)*

NEARBY MUSEUMS & GALLERIES

Permanent Collections: National Army Museum, see p. 126.

THE CITY OF LONDON

SEE MAP, p. 364

⚑ THE CITY OF LONDON QUICKFIND: Museums & Galleries, p. 126; **Food & Drink**, p. 150; **Pubs**, p. 174; **Entertainment**, p. 208. For **St. Paul's Cathedral**, see Major Attractions p. 68. For **The Tower of London**, see Major Attractions p. 70. The **City of London Information Centre**, St. Paul's Churchyard (☎ 7332 1456); Tube: St. Paul's. Open Apr.-Sept. daily 9:30am-5pm; Oct.-Mar. M-F 9:30am-5pm, Sa 9:30am-12:30pm. Offers leaflets and maps, sells tickets to sights and shows, and gives info on traditional municipal events. One of the largest is the **Lord Mayor's Show**, held each year on the second Sa of Nov.

The City of London (usually shortened to "the City") is the oldest part of London—as its name suggests, for most of its 2000 years this *was* London, all other districts being merely outlying villages. Today, archaeology is pulling that history out of the ground, and the ancient roots of the City are becoming ever more visible. Roman gold glimmers in the City's museums; the ruins of a Roman temple lie in the shadow of a modern office block; and above it all rise the dome of **St. Paul's** (p. 68) and the battlements of the **Tower of London** (p. 70). The 39 surviving churches and street names recalling the local population or trades once practiced there—Lombard St., Jewry, Bread St., Poultry, even Love Ln.—are almost the only reminders of the time when this was the beating heart of London. If sightseeing in the City, make the most of the morning and lunchtime—you'll have trouble finding anything open after 6pm. Churches can be especially troublesome—their actual hours can vary considerably from those listed, depending on whether and when the vester decides to show up. Fortunately, the City packs enough into its small area that alternative sights are never far off.

👁 MONUMENT

⚑ Location: Monument St. **Contact:** ☎ 7626 2717. **Tube:** Monument. **Open:** Daily 9:30am-5pm; last admission 4:40pm. **Admission:** £2, children £1.

The only non-ecclesiastical Wren building in the City, this plain Doric pillar topped with a gilded, flaming urn is a lasting reminder of the Great Fire. Erected in 1677, the 202 ft.-tall column stands exactly that distance from the bakery on Pudding Ln. where fire first broke out. As the inscription on the outside says, the fire "rushed devastating through every quarter with astonishing swiftness and worse." In 1681, a small addition was made: "but Popish frenzy, which wrought such horrors, is not yet quenched." This bit of rabid anti-Catholicism was removed in 1830. The column offers an expansive view of London that beats even that from atop St. Paul's. The 311 steps may seem daunting, but the experience is well worth it—as is the commemorative certificate you receive on the way out. The Monument and the **Tower Bridge Experience** (see below) offer joint admission for £5.50, concessions £3.50.

👁 ALL HALLOWS-BY-THE-TOWER

⚑ Location: Byward St. **Contact:** ☎ 7481 2928. **Tube:** Tower Hill. **Open:** Church M-F 9am-5:45pm, Sa-Su 10am-5pm; crypt M-Sa 11am-4pm, Su 1-4pm.

Nearly hidden by City redevelopment projects, All Hallows bears its longevity with pride. Near the church bookshop stands a Saxon arch dating from AD 675, and the undercroft museum is home to a surprisingly diverse and fascinating collection, well worth a look. Samuel Pepys witnessed the spread of the Great Fire from its tower, while American associations include John Quincy Adams (married here) and William Penn (baptized here in 1644). The spectacular Lady Chapel is home to a magnificent altarpiece dating from 1500 and has been restored to look much as it did when it was built in 1489. The stark cement arches and barred windows of the nave, rebuilt after the Blitz, give this small church a mysterious and impressive dignity.

TOWER BRIDGE

⚑ Location: *Entrance to the Tower Bridge Experience is through the west side (upriver) of the North Tower.* **Contact:** ☎ *7940 3985, lifting schedule* ☎ *7378 7700; www.towerbridge.org.uk.* **Tube:** *Tower Hill or London Bridge.* **Open:** *Daily 9:30am-6pm; last entry 5pm.* **Admission:** *£4.50, concessions £3.*

When TV and movie directors want to say "London," nine times out of ten they settle for a shot of Tower Bridge, which helps explain why tourists often mistake it for its plainer sibling, London Bridge. A marvel of engineering, the steam-powered lifting mechanism remained in use from 1894 until 1973, when electric motors took over. Though clippers no longer sail into London very often, there's still enough large river traffic for the bridge to be lifted around 900 times per year—call to find out the schedule, or check the signs posted at each entrance. For a deeper understanding of the history and technology behind the bridge, the **Tower Bridge Experience** combines scenic walkways with videos to present a history of the bridge replete with bells and whistles. If you're a fan of cheesy animatronics and oversized machinery, don't miss the Engine Room. The Tower Bridge Experience and the **Monument** (see above) offer combined admission for £5.50, concessions £3.50.

GUILDHALL YARD

⚑ Location: *Off Gresham St.* **Tube:** *St. Paul's, Moorgate, or Bank.*

Since the founding of the Corporation in 1193, the City has been governed from this site, the centerpiece of which is the Guildhall itself. As the name suggests, this is where the representatives of the City's 102 guilds, from the Fletchers (arrow-makers) to the Information Technologists, meet under the aegis of the Lord Mayor. Excavations in the 1990s revealed the remains of a Roman amphitheater below the Yard; its ruins are on display in the Guildhall Art Gallery (see p. 127).

Wrenovations

On the morning of September 2, 1666, fire broke out in a bakery on Pudding Ln. By the time it had burned itself out, 3 days later, most of the City was a smoldering ruin, including the medieval Old St. Paul's and all but 11 of the City's 87 churches.

Christopher Wren, who had already proposed replacing the dilapidated cathedral, submitted a masterplan for the reconstruction of the entire City on rational lines. Expense and time ruled out this ambitious plan (which influenced later proposals for Washington, D.C. and Paris), but Wren was commissioned with rebuilding both St. Paul's and 51 new churches to replace those lost.

Of these, 23 have survived, along with the towers of 6 more. Often constrained by tiny or oddly shaped plots of land, no 2 are alike in style. They range from perpendicular Gothic to daring domes. Seemingly on every city street corner, it's easy to ignore them altogether and impossible to see them all in a day. If you're pressed for time, don't miss St. Bride's (p. 79), St. Mary-le-Bow (p. 88), St. Stephen Walbrook (p. 88), and, of course, St. Paul's Cathedral (p. 67).

GUILDHALL. The vast Gothic hall dates from 1440, though after repeated remodeling in the 17th and 18th centuries—not to mention almost complete reconstruction following the Great Fire and the Blitz—little of the original remains. The stained-glass windows bear the names of all Mayors and Lord Mayors of the Corporation, past and present—the builders foresaw the City's longevity, as there's room for about 700 more. On either side of the wooden Minstrel's Gallery are 9 ft. statues of Apocalyptic giants Gog and Magog. The hall has seen numerous trials, including those of Lady Jane Grey and Archbishop Cranmer; these days it hosts banquets and, every third Thursday of the month, public meetings of the **Court of Common Council,** presided over by the Lord Mayor, bedecked in traditional robes and followed by a sword-wielding entourage. These meetings are open to the public, and begin at 1pm—no cameras and no wandering around the hall. *(Enter the Guildhall through the low, modern annex. Occasional tours offered—call ☎ 7606 3030, ext. 1463 for information; other inquiries ☎ 7606 3030. Open May-Sept. daily 10am-5pm; Oct.-Apr. closed Su. Last admission 4:30pm. Free.)*

OTHER GUILDHALL YARD SIGHTS. To the right of the Guildhall is the brand-new **Guildhall Art Gallery** (see p. 127), built with the express purpose of being a permanent companion to the Guildhall—the architects claim it has a "design life of centuries." The **Guildhall Library,** in the 1970s annex and accessed via Aldermanbury, specializes in the history of London and is open to all. It houses the **Guildhall Clock Museum** (p. 127) as well. *(Entrance on Aldermanbury. ☎ 7332 1839. Library open to the public M-Sa 9:30am-5pm. Free.)*

THE BARBICAN

🖪 *Location: Between London Wall, Beech St., Aldersgate, and Moorgate. **Tube:** Barbican or Moorgate.*

After WWII, the Corporation of London decided to redevelop this bomb-flattened 35-acre plot in the north of the City (the site of the ancient Roman barbican—"fort") as a textbook piece of integrated development. Construction took 20 years, starting only in 1962, and the result bears all the hallmarks of its time: 40-story tower blocks and masses of grey concrete, linked by an intricate system of overhead walkways and open spaces. The industrial dreariness is mitigated somewhat by the incorporation of lakes and gardens into the overall design. Notoriously difficult to navigate, the Barbican is currently undergoing a multi-million-pound renovation, which plans to simplify the layout and improve its status and accessibility as an entertainment venue. Construction is scheduled to carry over into 2004 and will result in the interruption of many Barbican events—be sure to call before making any visits.

BARBICAN CENTRE. Smack in the center of the Barbican is, logically enough, the Barbican Centre, a powerhouse of the arts. Described at its 1982 opening as "the City's gift to the nation," the complex incorporates a concert hall, two theaters, a cinema, three art galleries, and numerous cafeterias, bars, and restaurants—if you can find them. The **Lakeside Terrace** is a large piazza with picnic tables, sculpture, and sunken fountains flowing over waterfalls into a giant rectangular lake, opposite the 16th-century church of St. Giles Cripplegate. Skip the pricey bistros by the water, and bring a picnic lunch. Most surreal is the level-3 **Conservatory,** a literal concrete jungle—tropical plants burst forth on multiple levels amid ventilation ducts and pipes from the center below. *(Main entrance on Silk St. From Tube: Moorgate or Barbican, follow the yellow painted lines. ☎ 7638 8891; www.barbican.org.uk. Open M-Sa 9am-11pm, Su 10:30am-11pm.)*

OTHER BARBICAN SIGHTS. Just behind St. Giles is a well-preserved section of **London Wall,** the city wall built by the Romans and maintained into the Middle Ages. Next to the Barbican Centre, overlooking the lake, is the distinctive and distinguished **Guildhall School of Music**—on hot days you can often hear students practicing. At the complex's southwestern corner is the **Museum of London** (see p. 126).

ST. MARY-LE-BOW

⚐ Location: *Cheapside, by Bow Ln. Access to the crypt via stairs in the courtyard.* **Contact:** *☎ 7246 5139.* **Tube:** *St. Paul's or Mansion House.* **Open:** *M-F 7:30am-6pm.* **Concerts:** *Occasional Th 1:05pm, free.*

Another Wren creation, St. Mary's is most famous for its Great Bell, which from 1334 to 1874 rang the City curfew at 9pm and the reveille at 5:45am. In order to be a "real" Cockney, you must have been born within earshot of the bells. The bells toll "I do not know" according to *Oranges and Lemons,* and help make up for the church's gaudy modern interior. The church had to be rebuilt almost completely after the Blitz, but the 11th-century **crypt,** whose "bows" (arches) gave the church its epithet, survived. Since the 12th century, it has hosted the ecclesiastical Court of Arches, where the Archbishop of Canterbury swears in bishops. Today, the court shares space with **The Place Below** restaurant (see p. 151).

Lloyd's of London

BANK OF ENGLAND

⚐ Location: *Threadneedle St.* **Tube:** *Bank.*

Government financial difficulties led to the founding of the "Old Lady of Threadneedle St." in 1694, as a way of raising money without raising taxes—the bank's creditors supplied ₤1.2 million, and the national debt was born. The 8 ft. thick, windowless outer wall, enclosing four acres, is the only remnant of Sir John Soane's 1788 building; above it rises the current 1925 edifice. Top-hatted guards in pink tailsuits will direct those who wander into the main entrance to the **Bank of England Museum,** around the corner on St. Bartholomew Ln. (see p. 127).

Guildhall, City of London

LOWER THAMES STREET

⚐ Location: *Just north of the Thames between London Bridge and the Tower.* **Tube:** *Monument.*

So busy that it must be crossed by overhead walkways, Lower Thames St. passes a number of interesting sights. It starts at **London Bridge,** more interesting for its history than its current bland incarnation. Close to the spot of the original Roman bridge, the first stone bridge across the Thames stood here from 1176 until 1832—and would have survived until today had not 18th-century "improvements" fatally weakened the structure. Its replacement lasted until 1973, when a wealthy American bought it for ₤1.03 million and shipped it to Arizona. A few steps up Lower Thames from the bridge, St. Magnus-the-Martyr proudly displays a chunk of wood from a Roman jetty. According to T.S. Eliot, its walls "hold inexplicable splendor of Ionian white and gold." (☎ 7626 4481. Open Tu-F 10am-4pm, Su 10am-1pm.)

Stock Exchange

OTHER CITY SIGHTS

TEMPLE OF MITHRAS. Dwelling incongruously in the shadow of the Temple Court building are the remains of this late 2nd-century Roman temple devoted to Mithras, an Eastern god popular among the legions. The foundations, floor, and 2 ft. of wall were discovered during construction work in 1954 and shifted up 18 ft. to current street level. The evocative ruins have been well preserved, complete with nubs of former columns. The **Museum of London** (see p. 126) displays artifacts unearthed during the excavation. *(Just off Queen Victoria St. Tube: Mansion House or Bank.)*

ST. STEPHEN WALBROOK. On the site of a 7th-century Saxon church, St. Stephen (built 1672-79) was Wren's personal favorite and arguably finest church. The unexpected simplicity and openness of the interior perfectly complements Henry Moore's stark freeform altar. An honorary phone, donated by British Telecom, commemorates current rector Chad Varah, who founded the Samaritans—a hotline that advises the suicidal and severely depressed—here in 1953. *(39 Walbrook. ☎ 7283 4444. Tube: Bank or Cannon St. Open M-Th 9am-4pm; F 12:30pm for 1hr. organ concert.)*

ST. MARY WOOLNOTH. The only City church untouched by the Blitz, St. Mary's confirms the talent of Wren's pupil Nicholas Hawksmoor. The lack of lower windows arises from the lack of open space around the site at the time of its building (1716-1727); even so, the domed design results in a light, airy feel. The remarkable altarpiece is a standout. *(Junction of King William and Lombard Sts. ☎ 7626 9701. Open M-F 9:30am-4:30pm.)*

OTHER LOCAL SIGHTS. The most famous modern structure in the City is **Lloyd's of London,** built by Richard Rogers in 1986 for the organization that grew from a 17th-century coffeehouse to the largest insurance market in the world. With towering metal ducts, lifts, and chutes on the outside, it wears its heart (or at least its internal organs) on its sleeve. *(Leadenhall St. Tube: Bank.)* Only the tower remains of Wren's **St. Dunstan-in-the-East,** sister church to **All Hallows-By-The-Tower** (see p. 78). The unusual design, with a pointed spire supported on hollow buttresses, is reminiscent of the Warrant Model Wren submitted for St. Paul's Cathedral. The blitzed, mossy ruins have been converted into a stunning garden that makes a surprisingly peaceful picnic spot. *(St. Dunstans Hill. Tube: Monument or Tower Hill.)* When rebuilding **St. Margaret Lothbury** in 1689, Wren was obliged to follow the lines of the former church, despite its north wall being shorter than its south; the result is a roof that's noticeably off-kilter. Like most of the furnishings, the sumptuous carved-wood screen was saved from other, now-demolished, City churches. *(Lothbury. ☎ 7606 8330; www.stml.org.uk. Tube: Bank. Open M-F 8am-4:30pm; occasional concerts Th 1:10pm.)*

NEARBY MUSEUMS & GALLERIES

Permanent Collections: Museum of London, p. 126; Guildhall Art Gallery, p. 127; Guildhall Clock Museum, p. 127.

CLERKENWELL

SEE MAP, p. 365

⚑ CLERKENWELL QUICKFIND: Museums & Galleries, p. 128; **Food & Drink,** p. 151; **Pubs,** p. 174; **Nightlife,** p. 185; **Entertainment,** p. 210; **Accommodations,** p. 259. **TRANSPORTATION:** All sights are closest to Tube: Farringdon unless otherwise stated.

Clerkenwell may be the new Soho in terms of trendy bars and nightclubs, but much history can be found here. From the 12th century until Henry VIII's break with Rome, Clerkenwell was dominated by the great monasteries. After a brief period of aristocratic fashion in the early 17th century, Clerkenwell descended first to an artisans' quarter, and then to the notorious slum detailed in Charles Dicken's *Oliver Twist*. In the late 20th century this progression reversed, with artists taking advantage of cheap rents in the 1980s and propelling Clerkenwell to the height of loft-living trendiness in the 1990s. Today, it's less chic but definitely more fun.

CLERKENWELL GREEN

Not very green at all—actually just a wider-than-normal street—Clerkenwell Green boasts venerable historical associations. Wat Tyler rallied the Peasants' Revolt here in 1381, while Lenin published the Bolshevik newspaper *Iskra* from no. 37a The Green's oldest building (1737), it now houses the **Marx Memorial Library.** (☎ 7253 1485. Open M-Th 1-2pm, book in advance for large groups.) In opposition to these revolutionary tendencies, the 1782 **Old Sessions House** was formerly the courthouse for the county of Middlesex—note the Middlesex arms on the portico. Reputedly haunted, it's now the enigmatic London Masonic Centre. (Closed to the public.) These days, the Green hosts gatherings of a less political sort when the work day ends and the area's young professionals spill into pubs.

CLERKENWELL VISITOR CENTRE. The friendly staff of this family-run info center and gift shop cheerfully embraces those smart enough to visit. It offers a wealth of information and leaflets on the area, including a historic guide (£1) to the **Clerkenwell Historic Trail,** which tours sights both fascinating and deservedly obscure. (Tip: skip everything north of Bowling Green Ln.) The shop sells fun novelty wares of local artisans, as well as organic ice cream for £1.30. (53 Clerkenwell Close, by St. James' Church. ☎ 7281 6311. Open M-Sa 11am-6pm.)

ST. JOHN'S SQUARE

Bisected by the busy Clerkenwell Rd., St. John's Sq. occupies the site of the 12th-century **Priory of St. John,** former seat of the Knights Hospitallers. The Hospitallers (in full, the Order of the Hospital of St. John of Jerusalem) were founded in 1113 during the First Crusade to simultaneously tend the sick and fight heathens. What remains of their London seat is now in the hands of the British Order of St. John. Unaffiliated with the original order—which still exists, based in the Vatican—this Protestant organization was founded in 1887 to provide first-aid service to the public.

ST. JOHN'S GATE. Originally the main entrance to the priory, this 16th-century gateway now arches grandly over the entrance to St. John's Sq. The small ground-floor museum mixes artifacts relating to the original priory and Knights Hospitallers with hi-tech displays detailing the order's modern-day exploits in bringing band-aids to the masses. Join a tour to see the upstairs council chamber and the priory church (see below) which is otherwise closed to the public. (St. John's Ln. ☎ 7324 4070; www.sja.org.uk/history. Open M-F 10am-5pm, Sa 10am-4pm. Tours Tu and F-Sa 11am and 2:30pm; £5, concessions £3.50. Exhibition free; donation requested.)

PRIORY OF ST. JOHN. On the other side of Clerkenwell Rd. from the gate, cobblestones in St. John's Sq. mark the position of the original Norman church; the current building, which dates to the 16th century, lies at the end of a pleasant cloister garden. Two panels of the 1480 Weston Triptych stand on their original altar, but the real treasure of the church is the crypt, a survival from the original 12th-century priory and one of London's few remaining pieces of Norman architecture. (Open only for tours of St. John's Gate, see above.)

THE CHARTERHOUSE

🔲 **Location:** On the north side of Charterhouse Sq. **Contact:** ☎ 7251 5002. **Tube:** Barbican. **Open:** Only for 1½hr. tours May-Aug. W 2:15pm. Book months in advance. Free; donation requested.

A forbidding wall and arched gateway separate Charterhouse Sq. from the Charterhouse itself. The Charterhouse was founded in the 14th century as a Carthusian monastery. In 1611 **Thomas Sutton** bought the property and established a foundation for the education of 40 boys and the care of 80 impoverished old men. Charterhouse School rapidly established itself as one of the most prestigious (and expensive) schools in England, but in 1872 moved to Surrey, leaving the complex to the (still penniless) pensioners. The weekly tour guides you through the grounds and into some of the buildings, including the Duke of Norfolk's Great Hall and the chapel with Thomas Sutton's ornate tomb. If you miss the tour, you can admire the **main gate,** the same wooden door to which Henry VIII nailed the severed hands of the last Catholic monks. The small **garden** to the right of the gate, just visible through some thick foliage, occupies the site of the original 14th-century monastic chapel, with the low tomb of monastery founder Sir Walter de Manney.

ST. BARTHOLOMEW THE GREAT

Location: *Little Britain, off West Smithfield.* **Contact:** ☎ *7606 5171.* **Tube:** *Barbican.* **Open:** *Tu-F 8:30am-5pm, Sa 10:30am-1:30pm, Su 8:30am-1pm and 2:30-8pm. Free; recommended donation £3.*

Enter through a 13th-century arch, cunningly disguised as a Tudor house, to reach this gem of a Norman church. The peaceful, elevated courtyard provides a closer view. The current neck-stretching nave was just the chancel of the original 12th-century church, which formerly reached all the way to the street. Hogarth was baptized in the 15th-century font, and at one time Benjamin Franklin worked at a printers' in the Lady Chapel. The tomb near the central altar belongs to **Rahere,** who in 1123 founded both the church and the neighboring **St. Bartholomew's Hospital.** The hospital, just across Little Britain, was reconstructed in the 18th century and is one of London's largest as well as its oldest. Within the hospital walls are the 16th-century church of **St. Bartholomew the Less** and a small **museum** on the hospital history (see p. 128).

NEARBY MUSEUMS & GALLERIES

Permanent Collections: Museum of St. Bartholomew's Hospital, p. 128.

HOLBORN

SEE MAP, p. 365

HOLBORN QUICKFIND: Museums & Galleries, *p. 128;* **Food & Drink,** *p. 152;* **Pubs,** *p. 175;* **Nightlife,** *p. 187;* **Entertainment,** *p. 210;* **Shopping,** *p. 229..*

Holborn native Sam Johnson once advised, "You must not be content with seeing Holborn's great streets and squares but must survey the innumerable little lanes and courts." The great delights of Holborn are now, as ever, to be found in the unexpected: jewel-like gardens hidden by sprawling offices, extraordinary historic facades dropped haphazardly between modern establishments, the lanes and ancient buildings jumbled around **The Temple.** Those who leave the confines of High Holborn and Fleet Streets will find themselves richly rewarded as well, with the gothic splendor of Ely Place's **St. Etheldreda's** and the astonishing riches of **Somerset House.**

▧ THE TEMPLE

Location: *Between Strand/Fleet St., Essex St., Victoria Embankment, and Temple Ave./Bouvier St.; turn south from Fleet St. down Middle Temple Ln., across from the Royal Courts of Justice.* **Tube:** *Temple or Blackfriars.* **Admission:** *Free.*

The Temple is a complex of buildings that derives its name from the crusading Order of the Knights Templar, who embraced this site as their English seat in 1185. Today, the Temple houses legal and parliamentary offices. South of Fleet St., this intricate compound encompasses the inns of the Middle Temple to the west and the Inner Temple to the east, separated by Middle Temple Ln.—there was once also an Outer Temple, but it has long since gone. The **Inner Temple** was virtually leveled by bombs in the Blitz; fortunately, the gabled Tudor **Inner Temple Gateway,** between 16 and 17 Fleet St., survived. The Temple is full of surprises—including **Elm Court,** tucked behind the church, a tiny yet exquisite garden ringed by massive stone structures.

TEMPLE CHURCH. Temple Church is the finest surviving medieval round church and London's first Gothic church, completed in 1185 on the model of Jerusalem's Church of the Holy Sepulchre. Stained-glass windows, towering ceilings, an original Norman doorway, and 10 armored effigies complete the impressive interior. Adjoining the round church is a rectangular Gothic choir, built in 1240, with an altar screen by Wren (1682). The church hosts frequent recitals and musical services, including weekly organ recitals. *(☎ 7353 3470. Open W-Th 11am-4pm, Sa 10am-2:30pm, Su 12:45-2:15pm. Organ recitals W 1:15-1:45pm; no services Aug.-Sept.)*

MIDDLE TEMPLE. The Middle Temple largely escaped the destruction of World War II and retains fine examples of 16th- and 17th-century buildings. In **Middle Temple Hall** (closed to the public), Elizabeth I saw Shakespeare act in the premiere of *Twelfth Night* on Groundhog Day, 1601. More Shakespearean legend is attached to **Middle Temple Garden**—according to his *Henry VI,* the red and white flowers that served as emblems throughout the War of the Roses were plucked here. *(Middle Temple Garden open May-Sept. M-F noon-3pm.)*

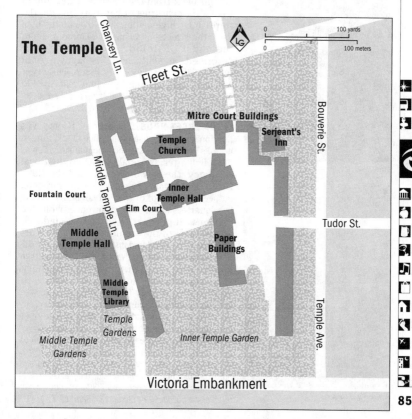

Tower Bridge

Hyde Park

University of London

ELY PLACE

⚑ Location: *From the Tube, walk east along High Holborn onto Charterhouse St., then make an immediate left through the gates.* **Tube:** *Chancery Ln.*

Step through the gates separating Ely Place from Holborn Circus, and you're no longer in London. In the 13th century, the Bishop of Ely built a palace here, later appropriated by Henry VIII. Though the palace is long gone, by a constitutional quirk the street remains outside the jurisdiction of local government (and police). Next to Ely Place, **Hatton Garden** (actually a street) is the center of Britain's gem trade, with dozens of diamond merchants proving that all that glitters is not gold.

⛪ ST. ETHELDREDA'S. The mid-13th-century church of St. Etheldreda is the last remaining vestige of the Bishop of Ely's palace and the sole surviving complete edifice of its age in London. St. Etheldreda's is now the only pre-Reformation Catholic church in the city, bought back from the Church of England in 1870 after centuries of captivity. Inside, the surprisingly high ceiling swallows up the bustle of the streets, creating an island of calm in the midst of Holborn Circus. The self-described "ancient rector" is happy to hold forth on the history of Ely Place. The crypt houses a cafe serving light lunches. (☎ 7405 1061. Church open daily 7:30am-7pm. Cafe open M-F noon-2:30pm. Free.)

⛪ SOMERSET HOUSE. Somerset House was London's first purpose-built office block, though it looks just like the aristocratic mansions it was modelled after. Originally home to the Royal Academy, the Royal Society, and the Navy Board, the elegant Neoclassical courtyard long induced a shiver of distaste in Londoners as the headquarters of the Inland Revenue. While the taxman still presides over the west and east wings, most of the building houses three art museums, the **Courtauld Institute Galleries,** the **Gilbert Collection of Decorative Art,** and **The Hermitage Rooms** (see p. 129). On sunny days, they face some competition from the spectacular view afforded by the **River Terrace** and its attractive but pricey outdoor cafe. From December to January, the central **Fountain Courtyard** is iced over to make an open-air rink, while Thursday evenings from mid-June to mid-July bring classical music concerts.(*Strand, just east of Waterloo Bridge.* ☎ 7845 4600, events ☎ 7845 4670; www.somersethouse.org.uk. Tube: Charing Cross or Temple. Open daily 10am-6pm. Courtyard open daily 7:30am-11pm. 45min. tours of the building Sa 1:30 and 3:45pm. £2.75.)

ROYAL COURTS OF JUSTICE

🔒 Location: *At the point where the Strand becomes Fleet St.; rear entrance on Carey St.* **Contact:** ☎ *7936 6000.* **Tube:** *Temple or Chancery Ln.* **Open:** *M-F 9am-4:30pm; cases are heard 10am-1pm and 2-3:30pm. Be prepared to go through a metal detector security checkpoint when you enter. Cameras are not permitted inside the building.* **Admission:** *Free.*

This massive neo-Gothic structure, designed in 1874 by G.E. Street, holds its own amongst the distinguished facades of Fleet St. Inside are 88 courtrooms, chambers for judges and court staff, and cells for defendants. On slow court days, the real star here is the architecture—exterior views from Carey St. are spectacular, and the breathtaking Great Hall features Europe's largest mosaic floor. Skip the uninspired display of legal costume and the insipid video tour (at the top of the stairs at the rear of the Great Hall); instead, watch the real thing: the back bench of every courtroom is open to the public during trials, unless the courtroom door says "In Chambers." The noticeboards beside the Enquiry Desk in the Great Hall display a list of cases being tried, or ask the Press Association office if there's anything particularly lurid that day.

FLEET STREET

🔒 Location: *Fleet St. is the continuation of the Strand between Temple Bar and Ludgate Circus. Note that Fleet St. is numbered up one side and down the other.* **Tube:** *Temple.*

Named for the river (now underground) that flows from Hampstead to the Thames, Fleet St. became synonymous with the London press in the 19th century, when it housed all of the major dailies. Though "Fleet Street" is still used to describe London-based newspapers, the famous facades, such as the *Daily Telegraph*'s startling Greek and Egyptian Revival building and the *Daily Express*'s Art Deco manse of chrome and black glass no longer hum to the sound of the presses: after a standoff with the printers in 1986, Rupert Murdoch moved all his papers (including *The Times*) to Wapping, Docklands, initiating a mass exodus. Today, Fleet St. is home to some extraordinary churches sandwiched between coffee shops and photocopying stores—Fleet Street's last nod to the printing process.

ST. CLEMENT DANES. Legend places this church over the tomb of Harold Hare-foot, a Danish warlord who settled here in the 9th century; its fame with Londoners derives from its opening role in the famous nursery rhyme (*Oranges and Lemons say the bells of St. Clement's*—and they still do, daily, at 9am, noon, 3, and 6pm). In 1719, Gibbs replaced Wren's tower with a slimmer spire, and in 1941, the interior was gutted by firebombs. Restored inside to white-and-gold splendor, it's now the official church of the Royal Air Force. The church houses the RAF regimental standards and a moving tribute to the American airmen who died in WWII (left of the inner doors). The quiet, simple crypt houses an eerie collection of 17th-century funerary monuments. **Take care exiting** since traffic drives right through the cobblestoned square. *(At the eastern junction of Aldwych and Strand. ☎ 7242 8282. Tube: Temple. Open M-F 9am-4pm, Sa-Su 9:30am-3:30pm.).*

GRAY'S INN. With an appropriately colored facade on Gray's Inn Rd., Gray's Inn does not inspire joy from the outside—Dickens dubbed it "that stronghold of melancholy"—but inside, it's actually quite pleasant. Though the **Hall** (on the left as you pass through the Gray's Inn Rd. entrance) is closed to the public, its small chapel, with original 16th-century stained glass, is open weekdays. Francis Bacon maintained chambers here and purportedly designed the **gardens,** the largest and loveliest of any Inn. *(Between Theobald's Rd., Jockey's Fields, High Holborn, and Gray's Inn Rd.; the entrances along Gray's Inn Rd. are not marked—look for the "Private Road" signs. Tube: Chancery Ln. or Holborn. Chapel open M-F 9am-6pm. Gardens open M-F noon-2:30pm.)*

ST. BRIDE'S CHURCH. The unusual spire of Wren's 1675 church is the most imitated piece of architecture in the world: perhaps taking his cue from the church's name, a local baker used it as the model for the first multi-tiered wedding cake. Dubbed "the printers' cathedral" in 1531, when Wyken de Worde set up his press here, it has long been closely associated with nearby newspapermen. More literary associations include Pepys, baptized here, and Milton, who lived in the churchyard, which is today a popular lunchtime destination. The crypt, closed in 1853 following a cholera epidemic, reopened in 1952 as a museum; eclectic displays include the baker's wife's wedding dress, party dress, and bonnet, as well as the remains of a Roman pavement and ditch. (*St. Bride's Ave., just off Fleet St.* ☎ 7427 0133; www.stbrides.com. Tube: Blackfriars. Open daily 8am-4:45pm. Free lunchtime concerts. Free.)

ST. DUNSTAN-IN-THE-WEST. An early-Victorian neo-Gothic church crammed between Fleet St. facades, St. Dunstan is most notable for its 17th-century clock, whose bells are struck every 15min. by a pair of hammer-wielding muscle-men representing the mythical giants Gog and Magog. The statue of Elizabeth I adorning the porch was saved from the 16th-century Lud Gate that stood nearby. The church today is a model of ecumenical worship—seven separate and lavish chapels house seven different faiths. While inside, note the elaborate wooden altar screen of the Eastern Orthodox chapel and take a peek at the plaque in memory of "The Honest Solicitor," that rarest inhabitant of Fleet St. (*Fleet St., just north of the Temple. Tube: Temple or Chancery Ln. Free.*)

LINCOLN'S INN

🖪 *Location:* Between Lincoln's Inn Fields and Chancery Ln. *Tube:* Chancery Ln. or Holborn. *Open:* Chapel M-F noon-2:30pm. *Admission:* Free.

Just to the east of **Lincoln's Inn Fields,** home to Sir John Soane's Museum and the Royal College of Surgeons (see p. 128), sprawl the grounds of Lincoln's Inn. John Donne, St. Thomas More, Walpole, Gladstone, and Disraeli are only a few of the Inn's illustrious former occupants. Since most of the Inn's buildings are closed to the public, its draw lies in superb architecture and serene grounds. The main gates into the Inn from the Fields deposit you in **New Square,** an open square of houses appearing much as it did when built in the 1690s. Adjacent to the Fields, the neo-Tudor **New Hall** and **Library** (closed to the public) stand among manicured gardens. On the other side of the gardens are the **Old Buildings,** including the 15th-century **Old Hall** (closed to the public). The **Chapel,** whose foundation stone was laid in 1620 by John Donne, sits above a unique open undercroft—once a popular spot for abandoning babies, who would be brought up in the Inn under the surname Lincoln.

NEARBY MUSEUMS & GALLERIES

Permanent Collections: 🖾 Sir John Soane's Museum, p. 128; Hunterian Museum, p. 128.

Other Collections: Somerset House p. 129, containing 🖾 The Courtauld Institute, Hermitage Rooms Gilbert Collection.

KENSINGTON & EARL'S COURT

SEE MAP, pp. 366-367

🖪 *KENSINGTON & EARL'S COURT QUICKFIND: Museums & Galleries,* p. 130; *Food & Drink,* p. 153; *Pubs,* p. 176; *Entertainment,* p. 210; *Shopping,* p. 229; *Accommodations,* p. 259.

Nobody took much notice of Kensington before 1689, when the newly crowned William III and Mary II decided to move into Kensington Palace and high society followed. In 1851, the Great Exhibition brought in enough money to finance the museums and colleges of South Kensington, converting it from a quiet residential suburb to a powerhouse of the arts and sciences; South Kensington remains quiet and intellectual, while the North and West are distinctly posh. Blending into Kensington's southwestern corner, **Earl's Court** is a grimier district that never shook off its reputation as "Kangaroo Valley," earned in the 1960s and 1970s for its popularity with Australian expats.

KENSINGTON PALACE

🚩 *Location: Western edge of Kensington Gardens; enter through the park. Contact: ☎ 7937 9561; www.hrp.org.uk. Tube: High St. Kensington or Queensway. Open: Mar.-Oct. daily 10am-6pm, Nov.-Feb. 10am-5pm; last admission 30min. before closing. Admission: £10.50, concs £8, ages 5-15 £7, family (2 adults and 3 children) £31.*

In 1689, William and Mary commissioned Christopher Wren to remodel Nottingham House into a palace. Kensington remained a principal royal residence until George III decamped to Kew in 1760, but it is still in use—Princess Diana was the most famous recent inhabitant. The palace tour includes the Hanoverian **State Apartments,** with *trompe l'oeil* by William Kent, but they are rather underwhelming. More impressive is the **Royal Ceremonial Dress Collection,** a magnificent spread of beautifully tailored, expensively embroidered garments and accessories, including "The Queen's Hats and Handbags" (through April 2004) and a number of Diana's evening gowns. Nothing is labeled, so you must submit to the audio tour. Those who love gowns, royals, or both, will be in heaven; others should skip it and instead wander through the palace **grounds,** set apart from the rest of Kensington Gardens and free. The gardens encompass Vanbrugh's grand 1704 **Orangery,** built for Queen Anne's dinner parties and now a popular setting for **afternoon teas** (see p. 144).

"ALBERTOPOLIS"

🚩 *Location: Roughly bounded by Hyde Park to the north, Exhibition Rd. to the east, Cromwell Rd. to the south, and Queen's Gate to the west. Tube: South Kensington or High St. Kensington unless stated otherwise.*

Not to be outdone by self-congratulatory exhibitions of French arts and industry in Paris, Prince Albert, Queen Victoria's husband, proposed to hold a bigger and better "Exhibition of All Nations" in London. The Great Exhibition opened on May 1, 1851, in Hyde Park, housed in the Crystal Palace—a gigantic iron-and-glass structure 1,848 ft. long, 408 ft. wide, and tall enough to enclose mature trees. By the time the exhibition was dismantled a year later, six million people had passed through it—as many as saw the Millennium Dome in 2000—and the organizers were left with a profit of £200,000. At Albert's suggestion, the money was used to buy 86 acres of land in South Kensington and found institutions promoting British arts and sciences. Even he would be surprised at how his dream has blossomed; today on this land stand not only the quartet of the **Royal Albert Hall,** the **Victoria & Albert Museum** (p. 123), the **Science Museum** (p. 131), and the **Natural History Museum** (p. 130), but also the **Royal College of Music,** the **Royal College of Art,** and the **Imperial College of Science and Technology,** all world-beating institutions in their fields.

ALBERT MEMORIAL. Nightmarish or fairy-tale, depending on your opinion of Victorian High Gothic, George Gilbert Scott's canopy recently saw sunlight again after a 10-year, £11.2m restoration project. At Albert's blindingly gilded feet, friezes represent the Four Industries, the Four Sciences, and the Four Continents, themes chosen more for their symmetry than their relation to reality. (☎ *7495 0916. Kensington Gore, on the edge of Kensington Gardens, just north of Royal Albert Hall. Tours Su 2 and 3pm; 45min. £3.50, concessions £3.)*

ROYAL ALBERT HALL. In contrast to the ornate Albert Memorial across the street, the classical Royal Albert Hall is one of the more restrained pieces of Victorian architecture, though there's nothing restrained about its size. Intended as an all-purpose venue, guests at the 1871 opening immediately noticed one shortcoming of the elliptical design—a booming echo that made it next to useless for musical concerts. Acoustic scientists solved this problem in 1968, installing dozens of discs suspended in a haphazard fashion from the dome. The hall has hosted Britain's first full-length indoor marathon, the first public display of electric lighting, and the world premiere of *Hiawatha.* It

St. Paul's Cathedral

Chinatown Gate

Tower of London

remains a versatile venue holding everything from boxing to rock concerts, but it's best known as the seat of the **Proms** classical-music concerts (see p. 210). Cirque du Soleil will hold their acrobatic spectacle *Dralion* here, opening January 9, 2004. *(☎ 7589 8212; www.royalalberthall.com. Kensington Gore, just south of Kensington Gardens and the Albert Memorial. Box office at Door 12, open daily 9am-9pm.)*

OTHER KENSINGTON SIGHTS

LEIGHTON HOUSE. The home of painter Lord Fredric Leighton (1830-1896) is a perfect example of all that is endearing and ridiculous in Victorian tastes. Inspired by his trips to the Middle East, Leighton's home combines oriental pastiche, neoclassicism, and English homeliness. The centerpiece is the Arab Hall, a Moorish extravaganza of tilework and mosaic complete with fountain and carpets—the walls bear one of Europe's best collections of medieval Arabian tile. The other rooms contain works by Leighton and his contemporaries, including Millais and Edward Burne-Jones. *(12 Holland Park Rd. ☎ 7602 3316; www.rbkc.gov.uk/ leightonhousemuseum. Tube: High St. Kensington. Open M and W-Su 11am-5:30pm. 50min. tours W-Th 2:30pm, £3. 50min. audio guide, £3. Adults £3, concessions £1, families £6.)*

NEARBY MUSEUMS & GALLERIES
Major Collections: Victoria & Albert Museum, p. 123.
Other Permanent Collections: ▨ Natural History Museum, p. 130; ▨ Science Museum, p. 131.
Exhibition Spaces: Serpentine Gallery, p. 131.

KNIGHTSBRIDGE & BELGRAVIA

⚐ KNIGHTSBRIDGE & BELGRAVIA QUICKFIND: *Food & Drink,* p. 154; *Pubs,* p. 176; *Shopping,* p. 230; *Accommodations,* p. 262..*

SEE MAP, p. 368

Currently home to London's most expensive stores, it's hard to imagine that in the 18th century **Knightsbridge** was a racy district known for its taverns and highwaymen, both taking advantage of the area's position just outside The City's jurisdiction. Gentrification has merely pushed the highway robbery indoors—just take a look at the price tags in Harrods and Harvey Nichols, partners in crime.

Squeezed between Knightsbridge, Chelsea, and Westminster, the wedge-shaped district of **Belgravia,** like Mayfair and Kensington before it, was catapulted to respectability by the presence of royalty. When George IV decided to make Buckingham Palace his official residence in the 1820s, developers were quick to build suitably grand buildings for aristocratic hangers-on nearby. **Belgrave Square,** the setting for *My Fair Lady,* is the most impressive of the set-pieces, now so expensive that the aristocracy has had to sell out to foreign governments. The primary reason most travelers come here is to get their passports replaced.

APSLEY HOUSE

🖪 *Location: Hyde Park Corner. Contact:* ☎ *7499 5676; www.apsleyhouse.org.uk. **Tube:** Hyde Park Corner. **Open:** Tu-Su 11am-5pm. **Admission:** £4.50, students £3, under-18s and seniors free.*

Named for Baron Apsley, the house later known as "No. 1, London" was bought in 1817 by the Duke of Wellington, whose heirs still occupy a modest suite of rooms on the top floor. The opulent house warrants a visit itself, but most come for Wellington's fine collection of art, much of which was given in gratitude by the crowned heads of Europe following the battle of Waterloo. Most of the old masters hang in the **Waterloo Gallery,** where the Duke held his annual Waterloo banquet around the stupendous silver centerpiece donated by the Portuguese government (now displayed in the dining room). X-ray analysis revealed that the famous Goya portrait of Wellington on horseback—the model for a thousand pub signs—was originally of Napoleon's brother Joseph Bonaparte. In the basement gallery are caricatures from Wellington's later political career—his nickname "the Iron Duke" comes not from his steadfastness in battle, but from the metal shutters he put up on his windows to protect himself from stone-throwing reformers.

WELLINGTON ARCH

🖪 *Location: Hyde Park Corner. Contact:* ☎ *7973 3494; www.english-heritage.org.uk. **Tube:** Hyde Park Corner. **Open:** Apr.-Sept. W-Su 10am-5:30 pm; Oct. 10am-5pm; Nov.-Mar. 10am-4pm. **Admission:** £2.50, concessions £2, children (ages 5-16) £1.50.*

Standing at the center of London's most infamous traffic intersection, the Wellington Arch was long ignored by tourists and Londoners alike. All that changed in April 2001, when the completion of a long restoration project revealed the interior to the public for the first time. Built in 1825, the "Green Park Arch" marked the western boundary of London. In 1838, it was dedicated to the Duke of Wellington, who lived across the street—and eight years later it was encumbered by a gigantic statue of the Duke. The government immediately ordered the statue's removal, but desisted when Wellington threatened to resign from the army. The statue was finally replaced in 1910 by the even bigger *Quadriga of Peace.* Inside the arch, exhibitions on the building's history and the changing nature of war memorials play second fiddle to the two viewing platforms.

BROMPTON ORATORY

🖪 *Location: Thurloe Pl., Brompton Rd. Contact:* ☎ *7808 0900. **Tube:** South Kensington or Knightsbridge. **Open:** Daily 6:30am-8pm, except during frequent short services. Solemn Mass Su 11am. **Admission:** Free.*

On entering this church, properly called the Oratory of St. Philip Neri, you are transported to a world of ornate Baroque flourishes and lofty domes. London's second-largest Catholic church, the Oratory was built from 1874-1884 and was deliberately designed with a nave wider than St. Paul's. One of the altars was considered by the KGB to be the best dead drop in London—until 1985, agents left microfilm and other documents behind a statue for other agents to retrieve. The church lives up to its reputation for music during its **Solemn Masses,** sung in Latin.

MARYLEBONE & REGENT'S PARK

SEE MAP, p. 369

▸ MARYLEBONE & REGENT'S PARK QUICKFIND: *Museums & Galleries,* p. 132; *Food & Drink,* p. 155; *Entertainment,* p. 211; *Accommodations,* p. 262.

Marylebone's most popular sights cluster along its northern edge. The inexplicably popular Madame Tussaud's and the lawns of Regent's Park can all be found close to **Baker Street** Tube. A few more attractions cling to the southern boundary near Oxford St.; the vast expanse in between may be devoid of textbook tourist attractions, but harbors some fine 18th-century architecture. Many of the Georgian houses have been home to famous residents including Elizabeth Barrett, John Milton, and John Stuart Mill. The area's most famous resident is undoubtedly the fictional Sherlock Holmes who called **221b Baker Street** home. 221 Baker St. is actually the headquarters of the Abbey National bank (there was never a 221b). Unsurprisingly, the Baker St. area has more than its share of Holmes-related tourist traps.

MADAME TUSSAUD'S & THE LONDON PLANETARIUM

▸ Location: *Marylebone Rd.* **Contact:** ☎ *0870 400 3000; www.madame-tussauds.com.* **Tube:** *Baker St.* **Open:** *M-F 10am-5:30pm, Sa-Su 9:30am-5:30pm. Planetarium shows start every 30min.* **Admission:** *All tickets sold at both Madame Tussaud's and the Planetarium and valid for both. Prices depend on day of the week, entrance time, and season. £17-20, under 16 £12.50-15, concessions £14-16. Advance booking (by phone or online) £1 extra; groups (10+) approx. £1.50 less per person.*

Together, Madame Tussaud's and the London Planetarium constitute London's third-largest tourist attraction, a fact that continues to amaze locals. Unless you enjoy spending hours waiting outside and paying exorbitant prices, make sure to book ahead, get together with at least nine fellow-sufferers to use the group entrance, or hit during off-peak hours (late afternoon). The Planetarium and Madame T's are internally connected and can be visited in either order—there are ticket offices in both buildings. Unless seeing a remarkably unrealistic wax figure of Hugh Grant is worth hours of your life and dozens of your pounds, our best advice is to avoid going in the first place.

MADAME TUSSAUD'S. The only place in the world where George Bush and Saddam Hussein can peacefully coexist in the same room, Madame Tussaud's takes gaudiness and tasteless ostentation to new levels. Appealing mostly to children and unknowing tourists, the novelty of the displays wears off quickly, but can still be guiltily entertaining. The would-be grand finale, the **Spirit of London** rides through a British history packed with ridiculous animatronics and hilariously cheesy voice-overs. If you've got money to burn and exceedingly low expectations, you just might be amused; otherwise, stay away.

THE LONDON PLANETARIUM. Those who remember 40min. informative displays with a live narrator will be shocked to find that today's show is a 20min. simulated rocket-ride through the universe, complete with travel through wormholes and narrow brushes with black holes. Clearly aimed to amuse kids (one recent show was based on Disney's *Treasure Planet*), entertainment-value is minimal for anyone over the age of twelve. Don't expect to learn anything earth-shattering either, as the show's educational content is limited to superficial descriptions of the planets. The inadequately air-conditioned waiting area, filled with a shoving, screeching mass of children, is an experience in itself.

▧ REGENT'S PARK

▸ Location: *500 acres of gardens stretching north from Marylebone Rd. to Camden Town.* **Contact:** ☎ *7486 7905; police* ☎ *7935 1259.* **Tube:** *Baker St., Regent's Park, Great Portland St., or Camden Town.* **Open:** *Daily 6am-dusk.* **Admission:** *Free.*

London's most attractive and most popular park, with a wide range of landscapes from soccer-scarred fields to Italian-style formal gardens. It's all very different from the plans John Nash had in mind when he set out to redevelop the hunting ground and farmlands of Marylebone Park in the early 1800s. Nash's vision was a secluded paradise of wealthy villas hidden among exclusive, private gardens; fortunately for us commonfolk, Parliament intervened in 1811 and opened the space to all.

The exclusive-sounding **Inner Circle** road separates the regal, flower-filled **Queen Mary's Gardens** from the park without. Within the gardens, the **Rose Garden** stands out, while one quadrant is now given over to the **Open-Air Theatre** (see p. 211). Arching around Inner Circle is the **Boating Lake,** though boaters are confined to the central portion. You can rent a rowboat for use on the main lake; children can enjoy themselves on pedalos in the tiny **Children's Boating Lake.** *(Open Apr.-Sept. M-F 10am-5pm, Sa-Su 9am-7pm. Rowboats £4 for 30min., £5.50 for 1hr.; under 14under 14 £2.50/£3.50; £5 deposit; under 16 with adult only. Pedalos £3 per 20min.; children must be 70cm (28in.) tall at hips.)* Of the 40 villas planned by Nash, eight were built, and of these only two remain. After decades of housing charities, hospitals, and learned societies, **The Holme** and **St. John's Lodge** have returned to their intended function as private residences for the unimaginably rich. On the northern edge of Inner Circle, the fine, formal **St. John's Lodge Gardens**—a blaze of lavender entered through an easy-to-miss gate near the Royal Parks office—look like something straight out of the *Secret Garden* and remain open to the public. Other buildings in the park include the large red-brick complex of **Regent's College,** to the south of Inner Circle, and neo-Georgian **Winfield House,** the residence of the US ambassador, set within the park's western edge.

LONDON ZOO

Location: *Main gate on Outer Circle, Regent's Park.* **Contact:** ☎ *7449 6576; www.londonzoo.com.* **Tube:** *Camden Town plus 12min. walk guided by signs, or short ride on bus #274 from Camden Town station. Or, a 15min. walk through Regent's Park.* **Open:** *Apr.-Oct. daily 10am-5:30pm, last admission 4:30pm; Nov.-Mar. daily 10am-4:30pm.* **Admission:** *£12, concessions £10.20, ages 3-16 £9, family of 4 £38.*

London Zoo has come a long way since first opening in 1826—the earliest buildings are now considered too small to house animals, and instead test parents with an array of stuffed toys. Today, thousands of little critters from around the world run around freely, their keepers trying frantically to keep up, as the animals look on with indifference from their enclosures. Gibbons swing around a jungle gym of bars and rope and lions eye the domestic animals of the petting farm from a very English-looking patch of savannah. Everyone's favorite is the **Penguin Pool,** where penguins waddle around on sleek structures designed by avant-garde firm Tecton in 1934. If the cool, white architecture and clean lines are straight out of the Bauhaus, the spiral slide is pure Fisher Price. Pick up a *Daily Events* leaflet to catch all the special displays and keeper talks.

PORTLAND PLACE

Tube: *Oxford Circus.*

Perhaps the handsomest street in London, Portland Pl. was first laid out by Robert and James Adam in the 18th century. Of the original buildings, only that at no. 46 survives; the attraction of today's Portland Pl. lies in the great variety of architectural styles found here. The street is a natural home for the **Royal Institute of British Architects** (RIBA), whose 1932 home is the most imposing building on Portland Pl.—particularly at night, when the facade is lit an eerie blue. Parts of the building are open to the public, including three exhibition galleries, an impressive architecture bookshop, and a small cafe/restaurant. *(66 Portland Pl. ☎ 7580 5533. Open M-F 9:30am-6pm, Sa 10am-5pm. Free.)* Guarding the entrance to Portland Pl. from Regent St., the curved facade of **Broadcasting Center** is instantly recognizable to all Britons as the symbol of the BBC. Today, Broadcasting House remains the BBC's

the BIG $plurge

TWO VIEWS FOR TWO

Forget the fancy restaurant dinners and walks on the beach. For a different kind of romantic evening, reserve a "Cupid's Capsule" just for two on the **London Eye**, and whisk your significant other 135m into the air. What could be more charming than cuddling up in your private glass pod as you slowly ascend to the top of the Eye and revel in the spectacular 360-degree birds-eye views?

After returning to the ground, follow up the evening of sightseeing with a leisurely **champagne cruise** on the Silver Bonito boat, which departs from the pier at the Eye. St. Paul's, the Houses of Parliament, the Tower of London, the Globe Theatre, and the Tate Modern are all visible from the boat, which also offers live commentary, sun-deck seating and covers in case of rain. On a clear night, you can watch the sun set... twice.

The **London Eye and River Cruise Experience**, £50. Package guarantees fast-track entry (no long lines!) to the London Eye, followed by a 45-minute champagne cruise, souvenir guidebook and single-use flash camera. Book on ba-londoneye.com, ☎870 443 9185, or in person in County Hall ticket office.

main center for radio production. On the facade is Eric Gill's sculpture of Shakespeare's Arial, together with the BBC motto, "Nation shall speak peace unto nation."

ALL SOULS LANGHAM PLACE. John Nash's plan to connect Regent St. and Portland Pl. in one straight shot was thrown off by the Langham family, who refused to let him build across their land. Forced to make an ungainly kink in his road at Langham Pl., Nash designed All Souls to fit into the bend. The combination of circular design and classical columns is still grand today; it accomplished his aim of creating a church that looked the same from both sides of the bend. A bust of Nash stands outside the entrance hall, to the right of the door.

OTHER MARYLEBONE SIGHTS

EDGWARE ROAD. To the west, Edgware Rd. is the center of London's large Lebanese community, though it's popular with Middle Easterners of all nationalities. Lined with countless restaurants, shops, and grocery markets, Edgware Rd. is full of affordable, hidden gems. From Marble Arch to where it meets Marylebone Rd., middle-aged men converse in Arabic over strong coffee and hookahs, and veiled women swish in and out of English businesses signposted in Arabic. *(Tube: Marble Arch or Edgware Rd.)*

NEARBY MUSEUMS & GALLERIES

Permanent Collections: ◧ Wallace Collection, p. 132; Sherlock Holmes Museum, p. 132.

NOTTING HILL

SEE MAP, p. 361

🏴 NOTTING HILL QUICKFIND: *Food & Drink*, p. 156; *Pubs*, p. 177; *Nightlife*, p. 187; *Entertainment*, p. 211; *Shopping*, p. 231

Notting Hill's best bits are on the outside. At the south, **Notting Hill Gate** is a relatively nondescript road of 1950s facades, but offers a good range of shops and bars. To the north, **Portobello Road** houses a strong West Indian community, characterized by the reggae-heavy record stores and market stalls selling Caribbean foods. Intersecting Portobello Rd. north of the Westway, **Golborne Road** has its own colorful street scene, with Moroccan and Portuguese shops and cafes. Fans of modernist architect Erno Goldfinger (see **Two Willow Road**, p. 109) will love the forbidding high-rise **Trellick Tower** at the end of Golborne Rd. If you plan to visit Notting Hill, try to do so on Friday or Saturday, when the world-famous **Portobello Market** (see p. 231) is held. It spreads from Golborne Rd. all the way down Portobello Rd. and the surrounding streets, almost to Notting Hill Gate itself.

THE SOUTH BANK

🔢 THE SOUTH BANK QUICKFIND: Museums & Galleries, p. 132; **Food & Drink,** p. 157; **Pubs,** p. 177; **Entertainment,** p. 212; **Accommodations,** p. 263.

SEE MAP, pp. 370-371

During the Middle Ages, the South Bank was London's entertainment center. Banished from the strictly-regulated City, all manner of illicit attractions sprouted in "the Borough" at the southern end of London Bridge. After the Civil War, the South Bank's fortunes turned to the sea, as wharves groaned under the weight of cargoes from across the Empire. By the time shipping moved elsewhere in the late 1950s, the seeds of regeneration had been sown. From the 1951 Festival of Britain sprang the Royal Festival Hall, the nucleus of the future South Bank Centre and the heart of the new South Bank. The National Theatre followed 20 years later, and development has continued at such a pace that the South Bank is now once more the heart of the London art scene.

🖼 LONDON EYE

🔢 Location: Jubilee Gardens, between County Hall and the Festival Hall. **Contact:** ☎ 0870 444 5544; www.ba-londoneye.com. **Open:** Daily late May to mid-Sept. 9:30am-10pm; Apr. to late May and late Sept. 10:30am-8pm; Jan.-Mar. and Oct.-Dec. 10:30am-7pm. Ticket office open daily 8:30am-6:30pm. **Tickets:** Buy tickets from box office at the corner of County Hall before joining the queue at the Eye; advance booking recommended. £11, seniors and disabled guests £10, under 16 £5.50.

Also known as the Millennium Wheel, at 135m (430 ft.) the British Airways London Eye is the biggest observational wheel in the world, taller than St. Paul's Cathedral and visible from miles around. The Eye has established itself as one of London's top attractions with locals and tourists alike—the lines are millennium-long, but move quickly. The ellipsoid glass "pods" give uninterrupted views from the top of each 30min. revolution: on clear days you can see Windsor in the west, though eastward views are blocked by skyscrapers farther down the river. In-flight guides are available in County Hall (£2.50).

TATE MODERN & THE MILLENNIUM BRIDGE

🔢 Location: Queen's Walk, Bankside. **Tube:** Southwark, Blackfriars, or (across the bridge) St. Paul's.

Squarely opposite each other on Bankside are the biggest success and the most abject failure of London's millennial celebrations. **Tate Modern** (see p. 123), created from the shell of the former Bankside power station, is the runaway success of recent years, as visually arresting as its contents are thought-provoking. Built to link Tate to the City—with a grand walkway leading from the northern end right up to St. Paul's—the **Millennium Bridge** outdid even the Dome for underachievement. Not only was the bridge completed six months too late for the Y2K festivities, but it also closed down within days following a literally shaky debut. Now that it finally has its legs under it, however, the bridge is as practical as it is scenic.

SHAKESPEARE'S GLOBE THEATRE

🔢 Location: Bankside, close to Bankside pier. **Contact:** ☎ 7902 1500; www.shakespeares-globe.org. **Tube:** Southwark or London Bridge. **Open:** daily May-Sept. 9am-noon and 1-4pm (exhibition only), Oct.-Apr. 10am-5pm. **Tours:** Run daily May-Sept. 9am-noon and Oct.-Apr 10am-5pm, 10am-noon when there's a matinee. **Admission:** £8, concessions £6.50, ages 5-15 £5.50, family (2 adults and 3 children) £24; 50p reduction when no tour operates. **For info on performances, see** p. 213.

In the shadow of the Tate Modern, the half-timbered Globe rises just 200m from where it first stood. The original burned down in 1613 after a 14-year run as the Bard's preferred playhouse. Today's reconstruction had its first full season in

1997, and now stands as the cornerstone of the International Shakespeare Globe Centre. The informative exhibition inside covers both the story of the rebuilding of the Globe and the life and times of the original. Other amusements include a sound archive of famous performances and an interactive display where you get to trade lines with recorded Globe actors. Try to arrive in time for a tour of the theater itself. Tours are the only way to gain admission to the **Rose Theatre,** where both Shakespeare and Christopher Marlowe performed.

SOUTHWARK CATHEDRAL

◪ Location: *Montague Close.* **Contact:** *☎ 7367 6700; www.dswark.org.* **Tube:** *London Bridge.* **Open:** *Cathedral daily 8am-6pm; exhibition M-Sa 10am-6pm, Su 11am-5pm (last admission 30min. before closing).* **Audioguide:** *Cathedral tour £5, concessions £4, ages 5-15 £2.50.* **Photography:** *Camera permit £1.50; video permit £5.* **Admission:** *Cathedral free (£3.50 suggested donation); exhibition £3, concessions £2.50, under-11s £1.50, family (2 adults and 3 children, includes audioguide) £12.50.*

One of London's oldest gothic churches is its newest Anglican cathedral. The parish church of St. Saviour was promoted in 1905, even though Christians have worshipped here since 606. The cathedral is now the proud home of a brand-new **Visitor Centre,** housing "The Long View of London" exhibition. Three rooms house high-tech exhibits, including an "X-Ray wall" where you can search for hidden archeological treasures. Near the visitor centre, the **archeological gallery** is actually a small excavation by the cathedral wall, revealing a 1st-century Roman road along with Saxon, Norman, and 18th-century remains. The oldest complete part of the cathedral itself is the **Retrochoir,** separated from the main choir by a wonderfully carved 16th-century **rood screen** (though the statues are 20th-century). Next to the 13th-century **north transept,** the **Harvard chapel** commemorates John Harvard, baptized here in 1607.

HMS BELFAST

◪ Location: *At the end of Morgans Ln. off Tooley St., also accessible via the Queen's Walk.* **Contact:** *☎ 7940 6300; www.iwm.org.uk.* **Tube:** *London Bridge.* **Open:** *Mar.-Oct. daily 10am-6pm, Nov.-Feb. daily 10am-5pm. Last admission 45min. before closing.* **Admission:** *£6, concessions £4.40, under 16 free.*

This enormous cruiser was one of the most powerful ships in the world when launched in 1938. The Belfast led the landing at Normandy on D-Day and supported UN forces in Korea before graciously retiring in 1965. In 1971 she went on display and still holds her regal floating spot on the Thames. Today the 6-inch guns are trained on a motorway service station 11 miles away, ready to punish speeding drivers. Children will love clambering over the decks and aiming the 40mm anti-aircraft guns at dive-bombing seagulls. Inside, almost every room is on show, from the kitchens to the operations room, where waxworks and sound recordings recreate the sinking of the German battleship Scharnhorst in 1943. Steep staircases and ladders from deck to deck make exploring the boat a considerable physical challenge.

THE SOUTH BANK CENTRE

◪ Location: *On the riverbank between Hungerford and Waterloo Bridges; road access from Belvedere Rd. and Upper Ground.* **Tube:** *Waterloo or Embankment (take the Hungerford foot bridge across the river).* **See also:** *For Festival Hall, Purcell Room, Queen Elizabeth Hall, and National Film Theatre, p. 212; for Hayward Gallery, p. 133.*

Sprawling on either side of Waterloo Bridge along the Thames, this symphony of concrete is Britain's premier cultural center. Its nucleus is the **Royal Festival Hall,** a classic piece of white 1950s architecture. The gigantic lobby—whose stepped ceiling is actually the underside of the 2700-seat concert hall—often hosts free events, from photo exhibits to jazz concerts. Near the Festival Hall, the **Purcell Room** and **Queen Elizabeth Hall** cater to intimate audiences and smaller concerts, while just behind it the spiky ceiling of the **Hayward Gallery** shelters excellent shows of modern art. On the embankment beneath Waterloo Bridge, the **National Film Theatre** offers

London's most varied cinematic fare, while past the bridge looms the **National Theatre.** Despite the raw concrete exterior, the exceptional quality of productions is rarely in doubt. To find out how one of the world's largest, most modern theaters operates, join an hour-long backstage tour. (☎ 7452 3000; www.nationaltheatre.org.uk. Tours M-Sa 10:15am, 12:15pm and 5:15pm. £5, concessions £4.25.)

GABRIEL'S WHARF & OXO TOWER

🚩 **Location:** Between Upper Ground and the Thames. **Tube:** Blackfriars, Southwark, or Waterloo.

The most colorful new additions to the South Bank resulted from the unflagging efforts of the Coin Street Community Builders (CSCB), a non-profit development company which has sought to preserve the area as a model of integrated, affordable living. **Gabriel's Wharf** is a kitchy and craftsy market-like area just a block down from the Art Deco **OXO Tower**. Built by a company that once supplied instant beef-stock to the entire British Empire, the OXO Tower is famous for its clever subversion of rules prohibiting advertising on buildings (the windows spell out "OXO"). The Tower is now enveloped in the brick mass of the **OXO Tower Wharf,** another Coin Street development full of tiny boutiques and workshops run by some of London's most innovative young designers. A free public viewing gallery on the eighth floor allows for prime sightseeing.

OTHER SOUTH BANK SIGHTS

▧VINOPOLIS. This Dionysian Disneyland offers patrons an interactive (yes, that means samples) tour of the world's wine regions. France hogs the limelight, but there are also displays on less-well-known vinicultural centers, like India, China, and Israel. Bombay Sapphire gin cocktails are served in a futuristic blue bar. A truly extravagant production, the Vinopolis experience can be time-consuming—but with five generous tastings (from a choice of dozens) included in the price, by the end of the tour you'll be happy to abide. (1 Bank End, at the end of Clink St. ☎ 0870 4444 777; www.vinopolis.co.uk. Tube: London Bridge. Open M noon-9pm, Tu-Th and Su noon-6pm, F-Sa noon-9pm. Last admission 2hr. before closing. £12.50, seniors £11.50, ages 5-15 (fruit juice tastings) £5; book of 5 extra tasting vouchers £2.50.)

▧OLD OPERATING THEATRE & HERB GARRET. In the loft of a 19th-century church is the oldest surviving operating theater in the world. No doubt highly dramatic in the days before anesthesia, these days it occasionally features drama of a different sort, like experimental site-specific plays. A fearsome array of saws and knives substantiates the exhibition on surgical history, accompanied by vivid amputation illustrations. The neighboring **herb garret** was used by the hospital apothecary to prepare medicines (one cure for venereal disease starts "take 6 gallons of snails..."). The calming effect of fragrant herbs is destroyed by a display of frightful medical instruments, such as a trepanning drill, used to relieve headaches by boring a hole in the skull. (9a St. Thomas's St. ☎ 7955 4791; www.thegarret.org.uk. Tube: London Bridge. Open daily 10:30am-4:45pm. Closed annually Dec. 12-Jan. 5. £4, concessions £3, children £2.50, family £10.)

GOLDEN HINDE. This garishly colored boat is a full-sized replica of the 16th-century warship in which Sir Francis Drake became the first Englishman to circumnavigate the world. The replica has comprehensively outsailed the original since its launch in 1973, clocking up over 100,000 miles, rounding the globe twice, and starring in films from *Swashbuckler* to *Shogun*. Visitors are free to roam the deck and the sparsely-furnished rooms, but after ducking all the low ceilings in the gloomy innards of the ship, you'll be left wondering how Drake's crew managed it for a few months. (St. Mary Overie's Dock, Cathedral St. ☎ 7403 0123. Tube: London Bridge. Open daily 9am-5:30pm. £2.50, concessions £2.10, children £1.75, family £6.50.)

HAY'S GALLERIA & BUTLERS WHARF. Now paved-over, glass-topped, and lined with uninspiring chain stores and restaurants, **Hay's Galleria** was once Hay's Wharf, one of the busiest docks in London and frequented by clippers such as the Cutty Sark (see p. 114). Full of independent prints, some on loan from the Tate, the independent **Hay's Gal-**

lery presents more compelling browsing than the stores around it. *(London Bridge City, off Tooley St. ☎ 7940 7770. Tube: London Bridge.)* Just east of Tower Bridge, **Butlers Wharf** is still crisscrossed by overhead walkways originally intended for cargo transport. During the 1970s Butlers Wharf became home to London's largest artists' colonies. The party ended in 1980, when developers moved in: today the wharf is lined with restaurants taking advantage of the fantastic views, including ▓**Cantina del Ponte** (see p. 157).

LONDON AQUARIUM. As aquariums go, this is a small fish in a big sea. The main attractions are two three-story ocean tanks—one holds Atlantic fish, the other Pacific fish, including sharks. Children can pet rays and fish at the two petting tanks if they don't mind getting their arms wet all the way up to the shoulder. *(☎ 7967 8000; www.londonaquarium.co.uk. Open daily 10am-6pm, last admission 5pm. £8.75, concessions £6.50, under 14 £5.25, family (2 adults and 2 children) £25.)*

DALÍ UNIVERSE. "500 works of art," scream the posters. This tells you all you need to know about this "gallery": it's quantity over quality. Almost all the works in this collection are multiple-run prints, castings, or reproductions. You'll find a better set of Dalís for free in the Tate Modern (see p. 123), but if melting watches and lithographs are your thing, spend on. *(☎ 7620 2720; www.daliuniverse.com. Open daily 10am-5:30pm. £8.50, concessions £7.50, ages 10-14 £4.95, ages 3-9 £1, family (2 adults and 3 children) £22.)*

LONDON DUNGEON. The most effective instrument of torture here is the unbelievably long queue. The gloomy and slightly mildewy inside offers weak imitations of various London horrors, from the Great Fire to Jack the Ripper. In "Judgement Day," visitors are convicted, sentenced, and hauled off to be executed for being gullible enough to waste their money on this grisly franchise. If you must see it, arrive when it opens or buy tickets in advance. *(28-34 Tooley St. ☎ 0207 403 7224; www.thedungeons.com. Tube: London Bridge. Open daily mid-July to Sept. 10:30am-8pm (last admission); Apr. to mid-July and Sept.-Oct. 10:30am-5:30pm, Nov.-Mar. 10:30am-5pm. £12.95, concessions £11.25, children £8.25. Groups get 11th ticket free.)*

NEARBY MUSEUMS & GALLERIES
Major Collections: Tate Modern, p. 123.
Other Permanent Collections: Design Museum, p. 133; Clink Prison Museum, p. 133.
Exhibition Spaces: Hayward Gallery, p. 133; Bankside Gallery, p. 133; Saatchi Gallery, p. 133.

THE WEST END

OXFORD STREET & REGENT STREET

◪ *OXFORD STREET & REGENT STREET QUICKFIND: Museums & Galleries, p. 134; Food & Drink, p. 158; Pubs, p. 178; Nightlife, p. 188; Entertainment, p. 213; Shopping, p. 233; Accommodations, p. 263.*

SEE MAP, p. 356

OXFORD CIRCUS & ENVIRONS

◪ *Tube: Oxford Circus.*

Oscar Wilde famously quipped that **Oxford St.** is "all street and no Oxford"; there's precious little of beauty or historic interest on London's biggest commercial thoroughfare. Still, if you're intent on a photo-op with end-to-end double-decker buses, it's the place to be. **Regent St.** is more imposing, even though none of Nash's original Regency arcades have survived. For some reason, **Oxford Circus** is one of London's most visited landmarks, although it's actually an extremely busy junction where Regent St. and Oxford St. cross. At Christmas, the crowds are so crazy that the police are called in to control the crosswalks.

CARNABY STREET. In the 1960s, Carnaby St. was the center of Swinging London, a hotbed of sex, fashion, and youth culture. Since then, it's spent 30 years as a lurid tourist trap, with little more than postcards and Tube t-shirts. Now it's starting to look as though Carnaby could swing again, with an influx of trendy (if chain) boutiques providing an alternative to the mainstream selection of Regent St. During the early evenings a large after-five crowd of yuppies and shoppers lingers around Carnaby St. outside various pubs and bars.

THE STRAND

Tube: *Charing Cross.*

Simply known as "Strand," this busy road is perhaps the most ancient in London, predating the Romans. Originally a riverside track, shifting watercourses and Victorian engineering conspired to leave it high and dry; yet as the main thoroughfare between Westminster and the City, it remains as busy as ever. The only reminder of the many episcopal and aristocratic palaces that once made it London's top address are in street names nearby: Villiers St. recalls George Villiers, Duke of Buckingham, while Essex St. honors Elizabeth I's favorite, Robert Devereux, Earl of Essex.

CHARING CROSS. The tiered Gothic monument standing outside the Charing Cross station and Thistle Hotel was the last of the 14 crosses erected by Edward I in 1290 to mark the passage of his wife's funeral cortege. Though many will tell you that "Charing" is a corruption of *chère reine*, French for "dear Queen," the word actually comes from the Old English *ceiring*, meaning a bend in the river. The original was destroyed by Cromwell in 1647, and the current monument is a 19th-century replica. To complete the deception, it's not even in the right place—the original stood on the spot now occupied by Charles I's statue in Trafalgar Sq.

THE SAVOY. Considered the "fairest manor in all England," John of Gaunt's great Palace of Savoy was gleefully destroyed by rampaging peasants in 1381. Five hundred years later, the D'Oyly Carte Opera Company moved into the new **Savoy Theatre,** the first in the world to be lit entirely by electricity, followed soon after by the opening of the **Savoy Hotel.** Managed by César Ritz, it was every bit as decadent as the Palace that once stood on the site. Don't be afraid to wander into the Savoy's grand foyer, second only to the Ritz in popularity for afternoon tea (see p. 144). Be careful as you cross the Savoy **driveway**—this short, narrow road is the only street in the UK where people drive on the right. *(On the south side of the Strand.)*

the hidden deal

In The Red- Bus #14

If you balk at the cost of an organized tour, take a regular bus and save pounds. An all-day bus pass costs just £2. Yes, you'll miss the commentary but you can get on and off according to your own schedule. Plus, you'll be riding the *genuine* Double Deckers.

The #14 route:

South Kensington: Welcome to Albertopolis, arguably the greatest concentration and finest collaboration of museums in the world (see p. 130).

Knightsbridge: High-brow Harrods and Haughty Harvey Nick's (see **p. 230**).

Hyde Park Corner: The First Royal Park and bastion of free speech at Speaker's Corner on Sunday (see **p. 73**).

Piccadilly Circus: Eros, neon signs and plenty of tourists (see **p. 102**).

Leicester Square: In case you still haven't decided which West End show to see—or if you want to see another (see **p. 102** and **p. 215**)!

Tottenham Court Road: Shopping mecca which meets Oxford St. for the hard core shoppers (see **p. 226** and **p. 233**).

MAYFAIR & ST. JAMES'S

◪ *MAYFAIR & ST. JAMES'S QUICKFIND*: *Museums & Galleries*, p. 134; *Food & Drink*, p. 159; *Pubs*, p. 178; *Entertainment*, p. 213; *Shopping*, p. 235; *Accommodations*, p. 263.

The average tourist doesn't linger in Mayfair and St. James's—many would-be sights, such as St. James's Palace and the gentlemen's clubs, are strictly out-of-bounds to all but aristocrats. Meanwhile, haughty sales people and outrageous prices do their best to keep window shoppers on the streets. On the other hand, the combination of wealth and conservatism make the area one of the few in London to retain its historic atmosphere, and this, together with its parks and art galleries, makes Mayfair well worth a day's wander.

PICCADILLY

◪ *Tube*: Piccadilly Circus or Green Park. For details of **Piccadilly Circus,** see Soho, p. 102.

Frilly ruffs were big business in the 16th century—one tailor made enough money from manufacturing these "piccadills" to build himself a fancy mansion called Pickadill House. The name stuck, though the house and the tailoring industry are long gone. Piccadilly is no longer the preferred address of gentlemen, but as home to the Ritz, Fortnum and Mason, and the Royal Academy, it's still posh, with a capital P.

BURLINGTON HOUSE. Piccadilly's only aristocratic mansion to survive, Burlington House was built in 1665, though its current neo-Renaissance appearance dates from a remodeling in the 1870s. The Earls of Burlington have long since departed, but the house still has an aristocratic grandeur about it, thanks to its sheer size and peaceful open courtyard. Today, Burlington House is home to numerous regal societies, including the Royal Society of Chemistry, the Royal Astronomical Society, and the **Royal Academy of Art** (see p. 134).

19TH-CENTURY ARCADES. Around Piccadilly are a number of early covered passageways lined with glass-fronted boutiques, which served as the earliest malls—in the beginning of the 19th century. Today, the arcades make for a picturesque but anachronistic shopping experience. The oldest is the **Royal Opera Arcade,** between Pall Mall and Charles II St.; the most prestigious is the **Royal Arcade,** patronized by Queen Victoria and home of palace *chocolatiers* Charbonnel et Walker. The most famous, and longest, is the **Burlington Arcade,** next to Burlington House (see above) where top-hatted "beadles" enforce the original 1819 laws banning whistling, singing, and hurrying.

ST. JAMES'S CHURCH PICCADILLY. William Blake was baptized in this building, whose exterior is now darkened by the soot of London's dark, satanic mills. The grime belies the fact that the current structure is largely a post-war reconstruction of what Wren considered his best parish church; the original wooden flowers, garlands, and cherubs by master carver Grinling Gibbons escaped the Blitz. The churchyard is home to a tourist-oriented craft market. *(Enter at 197 Piccadilly or on Jermyn St.* ☎ *7734 4511. Church open daily 8am-7pm. Market Tu-Sa 10am-6pm.)*

ST. JAMES'S

◪ *Tube:* Piccadilly Circus or Green Park.

Ever since Henry VIII chose St. James's Palace to be the residence of the royal court—foreign ambassadors to Britain are still officially called "Ambassadors to the Court of St. James"—this has been London's most aristocratic address. Current occupants include Prince Charles; the late Queen Mum lived in neighboring Clarence House. Nearby **Pall Mall** is lined with exclusive **gentlemen's clubs,** steadfast bastions of wealth, tradition, and male privilege (most do not admit women); more can be found on **St. James's St.** For us commoners, this is an area to be seen primarily from the outside.

ST. JAMES'S PALACE. Built in 1536, St. James's is London's only remaining purpose-built palace (Buckingham Palace was a rough-and-ready conversion of a Duke's house). The massive gateway on St. James's St. is one of the few parts of the original palace to survive; outside, a pair of bearskin-hatted guards stomp and turn in perfect unison (see The Local Story, p. 62). As the official home of the Crown, royal proclamations are issued every Friday from the balcony in the interior Friary Court, which is also where the accession of a new monarch is first announced. Unless your name starts with HRH (or ends with Parker-Bowles), the only part of the Palace you're likely to get into is the **Chapel Royal,** open for Sunday services from October to Easter at 8:30 and 11:30am. From Easter to July, services are held in the Inigo Jones's **Queen's Chapel,** across Marlborough Rd. from the Palace, which was built in the 17th century expressly for the marriage of Prince Charles.

CARLTON HOUSE TERRACE & WATERLOO PLACE. Sweeping down from Piccadilly Circus, Regent St. comes to an abrupt halt at Waterloo Pl. with steps leading down to the Mall. Regent St. was built to be a triumphal route leading to the Prince Regent's residence at Carlton House, but by the time it was finished, the Prince (now George IV) had moved on to Buckingham Palace and had his old house pulled down. The aging royal architect, John Nash, was recommissioned to knock up something quickly on the site; the result was **Carlton House Terrace,** a pair of imposing classical buildings that dominate the northern side of the Mall. On **Waterloo Place,** between the two buildings, the Duke of Wellington is dwarfed by a vast column topped by his boss, the "Grand Old" Duke of York, who docked the pay of his men in order to pay for the monument.

OTHER MAYFAIR SIGHTS

SHEPHERD MARKET. This pedestrian area just north of Green Park occupies the site of the original **May Fair** that gave the neighborhood its name. A 17th-century version of Camden Market, the infamously raucous fair was closed down in 1706. Later in the century, one Edward Shepherd developed the area as a market (hence the name). Today the 18th-century buildings house tiny restaurants, shops, and pubs. *(Tube: Hyde Park Corner or Green Park.)*

BOND STREET & SAVILE ROW. The oldest and most prestigious shops, art dealers, and auction houses in the city are found on these streets. **Old Bond St.,** the Piccadilly end of the street, is dominated by art and jewelry dealers, including home-grown luxury megastore Asprey and Gerrard, which stocks essentials such as leather Scrabble boards with gold inlay. Versace and Ralph Lauren aside, most of the designer boutiques are found on **New Bond St.,** nearer Oxford St. *(Tube: Bond St. or Green Park. Note that Bond St. Tube is not on Bond St.; exit right onto Oxford St., then take the 2nd right onto New Bond St.)* **Savile Row,** running parallel to Bond St., is synonymous with elegant and expensive tailoring. The Beatles performed their last live gig on the roof of no. 3, during the filming of *Let It Be. (Tube: Piccadilly Circus.)*

GROSVENOR SQUARE. One of the largest squares in central London, Grosvenor Sq. has gradually evolved into a North American diplomatic enclave, alongside its more popular role as a beautiful picnic spot. John Adams lived at no. 9 while serving as the first US ambassador to England in 1785. A century and a half later, Eisenhower established his wartime headquarters at no. 20; memory of his stay persists in the area's nickname, "Eisenhowerplatz." The **US Embassy** faces the unassuming **Canadian High Commission** across the square. *(Tube: Bond St. or Marble Arch.)*

NEARBY MUSEUMS & GALLERIES

Exhibition Spaces: ▨ Royal Academy, p. 134; ▨ Institute of Contemporary Art, p. 134.

Commercial Galleries & Auctioneers: Annely Juda Fine Art, Bernard Jacobson, Christie's, Marlborough Fine Arts, Robert Sandelson, and Sotheby's, p. 135.

SOHO

▣ **SOHO QUICKFIND: Museums & Galleries,** p. 134; **Food & Drink,** p. 159; **Pubs,** p. 178; **Nightlife,** p. 189; **Entertainment,** p. 213; **Shopping,** p. 237; **Accommodations,** p. 263.

Soho has a history of welcoming all colors and creeds to its streets—early settlers included French Huguenots fleeing persecution in the 17th century. Today, a concentration of gay-owned restaurants and bars has turned **Old Compton Street** into the heart of gay London. Soho also has a rich literary past: William Blake and Daniel Defoe lived on **Broadwick Street,** and a blue plaque above Quo Vadis restaurant at **28 Dean Street** marks the two-room flat where Karl Marx lived with his wife, maid, and five children while writing *Das Kapital.*

PICCADILLY CIRCUS

🚇 Tube: *Piccadilly Circus.*

Four of the West End's major arteries (Piccadilly, Regent St., Shaftesbury Ave., and the Haymarket) merge and swirl around Piccadilly Circus. Tourist- and pigeon-ridden, the square is flanked by the music triumvirate of HMV, Virgin Megastore, and Tower Records London. In the middle of all the glitz and neon stands the **Statue of Eros.** Dedicated to the Victorian philanthropist Lord Shaftesbury, Eros originally pointed his bow and arrow down Shaftesbury Ave., but recent restoration work has put his aim significantly off.

LEICESTER SQUARE

🚇 Tube: *Leicester Sq. or Piccadilly Circus.*

Amusements at this entertainment hub range from London's largest cinemas to the **Swiss Centre** glockenspiel, whose renditions of anything from folk songs to Beethoven's *Moonlight Sonata* are enough to make even the tone-deaf cringe. *(Rings M-F at noon, 6, 7, and 8pm; Sa-Su noon, 2, 4, 5, 6, 7, and 8pm.)* After this you can get a henna tattoo, sit for a caricature, or humor the rants of innumerable street preachers. In the summer, a small funfair invades the square, adding to its hectic atmosphere.

CHINATOWN. It wasn't until the 1950s that immigrants from Hong Kong started moving *en masse* to these few blocks just north of Leicester Sq. Pedestrianized **Gerrard Street,** with scroll-worked dragon gates and pagoda-capped phone booths, is the self-proclaimed center of this tiny slice of Canton. Grittier **Lisle Street,** one block to the south, has more authenticity and less claustrophobia. Chinatown is most exciting during the Mid-Autumn Festival at the end of September, and the raucous Chinese New Year Festival in February; see Festivals p. 294. *(Between Leicester Sq., Shaftesbury Ave., and Charing Cross Rd.)*

OTHER SOHO SIGHTS

SOHO SQUARE. First laid out in 1681, Soho Sq. is a rather scruffy patch of green popular with picnickers and sunbathers; its removed location makes Soho Sq. more hospitable than its big brother, Leicester. If you're lucky, you might bump into Paul McCartney, whose business HQ is at no. 1 (MPL Communications)—crane your neck for a view of his first-floor office. Two monuments to Soho's cosmopolitan past border the square: London's only **French Protestant Church,** founded in 1550, and **St. Patrick's Catholic Church,** long the focal point of Soho's Irish and Italian communities. *(Tube: Tottenham Court Rd. Park open daily 10am-dusk.)*

ROYAL OPERA HOUSE. The Piazza's new boutique-lined colonnade is now the rear of the ROH's rehearsal studios and workshops. The public is free to wander the ornate lobby of the original 1858 theater and preview shows on the giant projector screen, except before performances; the enormous, glass-roofed **Floral Hall** is also open to the public. From Floral Hall, take the escalator to reach the sunny **terrace** overlooking the Piazza, where you can see the London Eye slowly turning in the distance and peek into the neighboring costume workshop. *(Enter on Bow St. or through the northeast of the Piazza. ☎7304 4000; www.royaloperahouse.org. 75min. backstage tours M-Sa 10:30am, 12:30pm, and 2:30pm; reservations essential. Open daily 10am-3:30pm. £8, concessions £7. For performances, see p. 245.)*

COVENT GARDEN

⚑ COVENT GARDEN QUICKFIND: Museums & Galleries, *p. 125;* **Food & Drink,** *p. 161;* **Nightlife,** *p. 190;* **Entertainment,** *p. 213;* **Shopping,** *p. 238;* **Accommodations,** *p. 263.* **TRANSPORTATION: Tube:** *Covent Garden unless stated otherwise.*

One of the few parts of London popular with locals and tourists alike, Covent Garden retains an insulated charm even as its shops become more mainstream. On the very spot where Samuel Pepys saw the first Punch and Judy show in England 350 years ago, street performers still entertain the hordes who flock here summer and winter, rain or shine. It's hard to imagine that for centuries this was London's main vegetable market; only in 1974 did the traders transfer to more spacious premises south of the river.

ST. PAUL'S. Not to be confused with St. Paul's Cathedral, this 1633 Inigo Jones church is now the sole remnant of the original square. Shortage of funds explains its simplicity: the Earl of Bedford instructed the architect to make it "not much better than a barn." Known as "the actors' church" for its long association with nearby theaters, the interior is festooned with plaques commemorating the achievements of Boris Karloff, Vivien Leigh, and Charlie Chaplin. Non-thespian associates include artist J.M.W. Turner, who was baptized here, and master carver Grinling Gibbons, buried in the church. To enter the church, you must first pass through the peaceful **churchyard,** whose award-winning gardens provide a welcome shelter from the bustle of the surrounding streets. *(On Covent Garden Piazza; enter via King St., Henrietta St., or Bedford St. ☎ 7836 5221; www.spcg.org. Open M-F 8:30am-4:30pm, Sunday at 11am for morning services.)*

THEATRE ROYAL, DRURY LANE. Charles II met Nell Gwynn here in 1655, and 8 years later the Theatre Royal was founded. Even though the current building dates from 1812, this is the oldest of London's surviving theaters. Join one of the actor-led backstage tours and you'll discover gems of Drury Ln. lore, like the corpse and dagger found bricked up in the theater wall in the 19th century. *(Entrance on Catherine St. ☎ 7850 8791; box office ☎ 0870 890 1109. Tours M-Tu and Th-F 2:15 and 4:45pm; W and Sa 10:15am and noon. £8.50, concessions £6.50.)*

SEVEN DIALS. This radial configuration of six streets is a rare surviving example of 16th-century town planning. Thomas Neale commissioned the central pillar in 1694, with one sundial facing each street; the seventh dial is the column itself. The original column was pulled down in 1773 to rid the area of the "undesirables" who congregated around it. A replica, erected in 1989, attracts all types, including those just trying to avoid the oncoming traffic. *(Intersection of Monmouth, Earlham, and Mercer St.)*

CLEOPATRA'S NEEDLE. By far the oldest monument in London, this Egyptian obelisk was first erected at Heliopolis in 1500 BC—making it some 1400 years older than Cleo herself. The Viceroy of Egypt presented it to Britain in 1819 in recognition of their help in booting Napoleon out of Africa, but it wasn't shipped out until 1877. The ship sank en route, but a salvage operation recovered the obelisk and it was finally re-erected in 1879. Underneath it is a Victorian time-capsule containing a railway guide, numerous Bibles, and pictures of the 20 prettiest British women of the day. The scars at the needle's base and on the (Victorian) sphinx to its right were left by the first-ever bombing raid on London, by German zeppelins in 1917. *(North bank of the Thames between Hungerford and Waterloo Bridges.)*

NEARBY MUSEUMS & GALLERIES

Permanent Collections: ◪ London's Transport Museum, p. 134; Theatre Museum, p. 134.
Exhibition Spaces: Photographers' Gallery, p. 135.

Trafalgar Square

Boating

Cabinet War Rooms

WESTMINSTER

⚑ WESTMINSTER QUICKFIND:
Museums & Galleries, p. 136;
Food & Drink, p. 162; **Pubs,** p.
179; **Entertainment,** p. 216;
Accommodations, p. 264. For
Buckingham Palace, see
Major Attractions, p. 63. For
SEE MAP, p. 372 **The Houses of Parliament,** see
Major Attractions, p. 64. For
Westminster Abbey, see Major Attractions, p. 65.

◧ TRAFALGAR SQUARE

⚑ Tube: Charing Cross or Leicester Sq.

John Nash first suggested laying out this square
in 1820, but it took almost 50 years for London's
largest traffic roundabout to take on its current
appearance: Nelson only arrived in 1843, the
bronze lions in 1867. If they don't look very
fierce, it's because sculptor Edmund Landseer's
model died during the sittings, forcing him to
work from a decomposing animal. Far scarier are
the legions of pigeons dive-bombing the square—
enough to make a Hitchcock fan quake.

Trafalgar Sq. traditionally has been a focus
for public rallies and protest movements, from
the Chartist rallies of 1848 to the anti-apartheid
vigils held outside South Africa House on the
square's east side, in the early '90s. More joyful
congregations gather here on **New Year's Eve** to
ring in midnight with the chimes of Big Ben.
Every December since the end of WWII, the
square has hosted a giant **Christmas Tree,**
donated by Norway as thanks for British assistance against the Nazis.

NELSON'S COLUMN. Not until the 1830s was
it proposed to dedicate the square to England's
1805 defeat of Napoleon's navy at Trafalgar—
considered to be the nation's greatest naval
victory. The fluted 51m granite column was
erected in 1839. Before the statue was hoisted
into place in 1843, dinner was served to 14
brave patriots on the column's summit. The
reliefs at the column's base were cast from
captured French and Spanish cannons and
commemorate Nelson's victories at Cape St.
Vincent, Copenhagen, the Nile, and Trafalgar.

OTHER STATUES. Nelson is not the only
national hero to watch over the square; to prove
that the English are not sore losers, **George Washington** keeps watch from a horse just in front of
the National Gallery (see p. 121). On leaving
England, Washington vowed never to set foot on
English soil again; and true to his word, the small
plot of soil underneath his statue was specially

brought over from the United States. The statue of **George IV** in the northeastern corner was originally intended to top Marble Arch (see p. 74). The eastern "Fourth Plinth" was empty until 1999—it has hosted changing displays of modern sculpture since. To the south of the square, a rare monument to **Charles I** stands on the site of the original Charing Cross (see below). The statue escaped Cromwell's wrath with the aid of one John Rivett, who bought it "for scrap" and did a roaring trade in souvenirs supposedly made from the figure. It was, in fact, hidden and later sold at a tidy profit to Charles II.

ST. MARTIN-IN-THE-FIELDS. James Gibbs's 1726 creation is instantly recognizable: the groundbreaking combination of a Classical portico and a Gothic spire made it the model for countless Georgian churches in Britain and America. George I was the church's first warden, and it's still the Queen's parish church; look for the royal box above and to the left of the altar. Handel and Mozart both performed here, and the church hosts frequent concerts (see p. 216). Outside the churchyard is a tourist-oriented **daily market.** The **crypt** is home to a surprisingly extensive and delicious **cafe,** bookshop, art gallery, and the popular **London Brass Rubbing Centre,** where you can create charcoal impressions of medieval brass plates. *(St. Martin's Ln., northeast corner of Trafalgar Sq.; crypt entrance on Duncannon St. ☎ 7766 1100; crypt ☎ 7930 9306; www.stmartin-in-the-fields.org. Tube: Leicester Sq. or Charing Cross. Market open daily 11am-7pm. Brass rubbing £2.90-15. Open M-Sa 10am-6pm, Su noon-6pm.)*

WHITEHALL

🚩 *Location: Between Trafalgar Sq. and Parliament Sq. **Tube:** Westminster, Embankment, or Charing Cross.*

A long stretch of imposing facades housing government ministries, "Whitehall" is synonymous with the British civil service. From 1532 until a devastating fire in 1698, it was the home of the monarchy and one of the grandest palaces in Europe, of which very little remains. Towards the northern end of Whitehall, before Trafalgar Sq., **Great Scotland Yard** marks the former HQ of the Metropolitan Police—although the front entrance (and commemorative plaque) is one block south, at 3-8 Whitehall Pl. Nearer Parliament Sq., where Whitehall changes name to Parliament St., steel gates mark the entrance to **Downing Street.** In 1735, no. 10 was made the official residence of the First Lord of the Treasury, a position that soon became permanently identified with the Prime Minister. The Chancellor of the Exchequer traditionally resides at no. 11, the Chief Whip at no. 12. Tony Blair's family, however, is too big for no. 10, so he's swapped with Gordon Brown next door. The street is closed off to visitors, but the intrepid can wait by the gate early in the morning to get a wave from Tony on his way to work. Outside the entrance to Downing St., in the middle of Whitehall, Edward Lutyen's **Cenotaph** (1919) stands a tall and proud commemoration to the dead of WWI.

HORSE GUARDS. Immediately recognizable from the crowds of giggling tourists snapping photos of (almost) motionless men in red, this 18th-century building is where the burnished cuirassiers of the Household Cavalry, in shining breastplates and plumed helmets, guard a shortcut to St. James's Park. While anyone can walk through, only those with a special ivory pass issued by the Queen may drive past the gates. The guard is changed M-F 11am, Sa 10am, with a dismount for inspection daily 4pm—a tradition which has continued for 200 years, broken only by WWII. Beyond the neoclassical building is the pebbly expanse of **Horse Guards Parade,** where the Queen ceremonially sizes up her troops during the Trooping of the Colour on the second Saturday in June.

PARLIAMENT SQUARE

🚩 *Tube: Westminster.*

Laid out in 1750, Parliament Square rapidly became the focal point for opposition to the government. Today, demonstrators are dissuaded by a continuous stream of heavy traffic—with no pedestrian crossings—but still make their voices heard via eye-catching placards that encourage drivers to honk their horns in protest. Those who make it across will find statues of Parliamentary greats (Lord Palmerstone) and forgotten heroes (Ian Smut). Standing opposite the **Houses of Parliament** (see **Sights** p. 64), Winston Churchill was famously given a turf mohawk during the May 2000 anti-capitalist demonstrations. South of the square rises **Westminster Abbey** (see **Sights** p. 65). A tip for all would-be anarchists: if crossing Parliament St. scares you, use the Westminster subway tunnels.

ST. MARGARET'S WESTMINSTER. Literally in Westminster Abbey's shadow, St. Margaret's was built for local residents by Abbey monks sick of having to share their own church with laymen, and has been beautifully restored in the past few years. Since 1614, it's been the official worshipping place of the House of Commons—the first few pews are cordoned off for the Speaker, Black Rod, and other dignitaries. The **Milton Window** (1888), above the North Aisle, shows the poet (married here in 1608) dictating *Paradise Lost* to his daughters. Lining the South Aisle, the extraordinary grey-hued 1966 **Piper Windows** replace those destroyed in WWII. The **West Window** commemorates Sir Walter Raleigh, executed across the street in 1618 and now lying in the chancel, neighboring the High Altar. *(Parliament Sq. ☎ 7222 6382. Tube: Westminster. Open M-F 9:30am-3:45pm, Sa 9:30am-1:45pm, Su 2-5pm. Free.)*

WESTMINSTER CATHEDRAL

🚩 *Location: Cathedral Piazza, off Victoria St. Contact: ☎ 7798 9055; www.westminstercathedral.org.uk. Tube: Victoria. Open: Daily 7am-7pm. Bell Tower: Open daily 9:30am-12:30pm and 1pm-5pm. £3, concessions £1.50, family £7. Admission: Free, suggested donation £2.*

Following Henry VIII's break with Rome, London's Catholic community remained without a cathedral for over three centuries until 1887, when the Church purchased a derelict prison as the site from which the new neo-Byzantine church was to rise. Construction began in 1895, but the architect's plan outran available funds; by 1903, when work stopped, the interior remained unfinished—a blessing in disguise. The three blackened brick domes contrast dramatically with the swirling marble of the lower walls and the magnificence of the side chapels. Eric Gill's **stations of the cross** (1918), were originally criticized for their diagrammatic designs that eschewed tradition; today they are among the Cathedral's most prized possessions. A lift—well worth the minimal fee—carries visitors up the striped 273 ft. **bell tower** for an all-encompassing view of Westminster, the river, and Kensington.

OTHER WESTMINSTER SIGHTS

ST. JAMES'S PARK & GREEN PARK. The lead-up to Buckingham Palace is flanked by two expanses of greenery. **St. James's Park,** acquired along with St. James's Palace by Henry VIII in 1531, owes its informal appearance to a re-landscaping by John Nash in 1827. In the middle of the space is the placid St. James's Park Lake where you can catch glimpses of the pelicans that call it home—the lake and the grassy area surrounding it is an official waterfowl preserve. Across the Mall, **Green Park** is the creation of Charles II; "Constitution Hill" refers not to the king's interest in political theory, but to his daily exercises. Sit on one of the lawn chairs scattered enticingly around both parks, and an attendant will magically materialize and demand money. *(The Mall. Open daily 5am-midnight. Lawn chairs available Apr.-Sept. 10am-6pm; June-Aug. 10am-10pm. £1.50 for 4hr.)*

THE ROYAL MEWS. Doubling as a museum and a working carriage house, the Mews's main attraction is the Queen's collection of coaches, from the "glass coach" used to carry Diana to her wedding to the four-ton **Gold State Coach,** which can occasionally be seen tooling around the streets very early in the morning, on practice runs for major events. The attendant guarding the coach is himself a goldmine of royal information, full of tips on when and where to catch glimpses of their Royal Highnesses. Children will enjoy a chance to get up close to the carriage horses themselves, each named personally by the Queen. Each horse has undergone years of training to withstand the distractions of crowds, street traffic, and fireworks. You can also see pictures of the Queen herself, in her more vigorous days, riding her black Burmese stallion at the Trooping of the Colour. Note that horses and carriages are liable to be absent without notice, and opening hours are subject to change. *(Buckingham Palace Rd. ☎ 7766 7302. Tube: St. James's Park or Victoria. Open Apr.-July and Sept. daily 11am-4pm, last admission 3:15pm; Aug.-Sept., 10am-5pm, last admission 4:15pm. £5, seniors £4, under 17 £2.50, family £12.50.)*

VICTORIA TOWER GARDENS. South of the Palace of Westminster and just west of the Thames, the magnificent backdrop makes the gardens a favorite spot for TV crews running political features. For similar reasons, it's a first-rate picnicking venue. Check out the superb cast of Rodin's *Burghers of Calais*, and the memorial to suffragette Emmeline Pankhurst, which stands just inside the front gate. On the opposite side from the Palace, a neo-Gothic gazebo commemorates the abolition of slavery on British territory in 1834. *(On Millbank. Tube: Westminster. Open daily until dusk.)*

ST. JOHN'S, SMITH SQUARE. Four assertive corner towers distinguish this unusual example of English Baroque. Dickens once described it as "some petrified monster on its back with its legs in the air." The church is nicknamed "Queen Anne's Footstool" after the story that when the architect, Thomas Archer, asked the impatient Queen's advice, she upended her footstool and told him "like that." The church stood ruined for years following a bomb hit in 1941, reopening as a concert hall in 1969. *(Smith Sq. ☎ 7222 1061; www.sjss.org.uk. For concert info, see p. 216. Tube: Westminster or St. James's Park.)*

NEARBY MUSEUMS & GALLERIES
Major Collections: National Gallery, p. 121.
Permanent Collections: Cabinet War Rooms, p. 136; Queen's Gallery, p. 137; National Portrait Gallery, p. 136.

NORTH LONDON

Nelson's Column

Docklands

OXO Tower

CAMDEN TOWN

An island of good, honest tawdriness in an increasingly affluent sea, Camden Town has thrown off attempts at gentrification thanks to **Camden Market**, now London's fourth-most-popular tourist attraction.

CAMDEN HIGH STREET & CAMDEN MARKET

🚇 *Tube: Camden Town or Chalk Farm. For more details, see p. 240.*

Thanks to its markets, Camden Town turns into a sea of people every weekend. The stores on **Camden High St.**, to the right as you get off the Tube, are most remarkable for their facades, with giant shoes, masks, and other brightly colored papier-mâché objects protruding dangerously from the storefronts. If you actually want to shop, come on a weekday, when the stores are open and the crowds are gone. Of the many cobblestoned markets off the High St. (primarily open on the weekends), the most visually appealing is **Camden Lock Market**, which is spread out over a series of buildings around an open courtyard facing the canal. You can find plenty of unique and artistic market wares among millions of useless "curios" at **Stables Market**. The tackier **Camden Market** and **Camden Canal Market**, filled with cheap trinkets and clubwear, are the most crowded and popular.

REGENT'S CANAL

🚇 *Location: The Camden Lock Market (Tube: Camden Town) is the best place to catch boats.*

Regent's Canal is part of the Grand Union Canal, which was the main artery for bringing goods to London from the north in the days before railways. The canal today has little practical use, but a boat ride along its length can be relaxing and scenic. The still-functioning Camden Lock sits where Camden High St. crosses the canal; grab a bite from one of the courtyard eateries in the Camden Lock Market and watch water buses being raised and lowered through the locks. Passenger boats leave from here and head west to where the post-industrial landscape gives way first to Victorian houses and then to Regent's Park. The canal actually passes through the middle of London Zoo on the way to Little Venice, though the banks are too high to afford a view of any wildlife. The **London Waterbus Company** leaves from the Camden Lock Market (see p. 241) and makes the 90min. trip to Little Venice, with a stop at the Zoo. (☎ 7482 2660. *Apr.-Oct. daily departures every hr. 10am-5pm; Nov.-Mar. Sa-Su every hour 11am-4pm. Single to Little Venice £4.80, children and seniors £3.10; return £6.20/£4. Single to Zoo, including admission, £12.70/£9.30.)*

NEARBY MUSEUMS & GALLERIES

Permanent Collections: The Jewish Museum, Camden, p. 138.

HAMPSTEAD & HIGHGATE

HAMPSTEAD VILLAGE

🚇 *Tube: Hampstead.*

KEATS HOUSE. In this house, the great Romantic poet John Keats produced some of his finest work, fell in love with Fanny Brawne—who lived in the second apartment of the house—and coughed up his first drops of consumptive blood, all between 1818 and 1820. Unfortunately, little of the original furnishing remains and the house as it stands is a sparse recreation of its 1820 appearance. Inside the house, copies of Keats's poems lie scattered about the well-kept rooms, together with Keats memorabilia and informative biographical displays. (*Keat's Grove.* ☎ 7435 2062; www.keatshouse.org.uk. *Open Apr.-Nov. Tu-Su noon-5pm; Nov.-Mar. Tu-Su noon-4pm. £3, concessions £1.50, under 16 free. Ticket valid for one year of unlimited visits.)*

FENTON HOUSE. Dating from 1686, this was one of the first houses built in Hampstead, and provides a glimpse into the world of a 17th-century merchant. The first two floors of the house are home to a delicate collection of china, porcelain, and needlework, as well as a remarkable collection of early keyboard and stringed instruments that continues on the upper floors. The intricate French garden provides a picturesque stroll and a prime relaxation spot. *(Hampstead Grove.* ☎ *7435 3471. Open Apr.-Oct. W-F 2-5pm, Sa-Su 11am-5pm; Mar. Sa-Su 2-5pm. Baroque Concerts May-Aug, every other Th; £14, students £12. Admission £4.60, children £2.30, family £11.50. Joint ticket with 2 Willow Rd. (see below) £6.40. Garden only £1.)*

TWO WILLOW ROAD. Looking like an unimposing 1950s-style mini-block, Two Willow Road was actually built in 1939 as the avant-garde home of architect Erno Goldfinger. Ian Fleming hated it so much, he named a James Bond villain after Goldfinger. The house is a masterpiece of modernist living, designed by Goldfinger down to the last teaspoon. With clothes still in their dry-cleaning plastic sheaves, everything looks as if the family had just popped out to raid Fort Knox. Family photos on the mantelpiece sit next to works of art by Max Ernst, Marchel Duchamp, and Goldfinger's wife, Ursula Blackwell. *(15min. walk from Tube: Hampstead.* ☎ *7435 6166. Open Apr.-Oct. Th-Sa 12-5pm. Timed ticket and 1hr. guided tours available at 12pm, 1pm, and 2pm. £4.50, children £2.25, family £11; joint ticket with Fenton House £6.40.)*

HAMPSTEAD HEATH

⚑ Tube: *Hampstead or Train: Hampstead Heath.* **Open:** *24hr.* **Be very careful after dark.**

Hampstead Heath is one of the last remaining traditional commons in England, open to all since at least 1312, thanks to the pluckiness of local residents, who, in the 19th century, successfully fought off attempts to develop it. Since Parliament declared in 1871 that the Heath should remain "forever open, un-enclosed, and un-built-upon"; it has since grown from 336 to 804 acres. Unlike so many other London parks, the Heath is not comprised of manicured gardens and paths, but wild, spontaneous growth tumbling over rolling pastures and forested groves. The dirt paths through the Heath are not well signed and are as random as the surrounding vegetation. Human sightings are rare beyond the occasional jogger and dog-walker. On public holidays in spring and summer, **funfairs** are held at South End Green and on the south side of Spaniards Rd.

⬛ HILL GARDEN. This secret garden hides so quietly in an annex of the Heath that most nearby neighbors don't know about it. There are a few paths down to the garden from North End Way, but you may have to poke through the forest a bit if you miss the signed path. You'll know you're there when you see the exquisite, raised *pergola* (Italian arched walkway). The flower-encrusted walkway passes over the former kitchen gardens of Lord Leverhulme's mansion. The walkway was built as a way to go from the mansion of Lord Leverhulme (founder of Lever Soap) to his pleasure gardens without walking through an ancient right-of-way that still passes under the pergola. At the end of the pergola, the reflecting pool and pleasure garden lie in wait. *(Open daily 8:30am to 1hr. before sunset.)*

⬛ KENWOOD HOUSE. This picture-perfect English country estate and its sprawling grounds occupy the northeast corner of Hampstead Heath. The most impressive entrance sits at the head of the pasture. Come up through the **Kenwood forest** to the south, past the estate's pond, and the grandiose cream-stuccoed facade is magnificently revealed. On summer nights the pasture becomes an amphitheater for concerts on a bandstand across the pond (see p. 216). The estate was owned by the Earl of Mansfield from its construction until 1922, when the Earl of Iveagh came and brought the real treasures—a spectacular collection of Old Master paintings (see p. 137) that is now on display in the beautifully restored rooms. *(Road access from Hampstead Ln. Walk from Hampstead or Highgate (both about 20min.) or take bus #210 from Tube: Archway or Golders Green (Zone 3).* ☎ *8348 1286. Grounds open Apr.-Oct. daily 8am-8:30pm, Oct.-Mar. daily 8am-4:45pm.)*

PARLIAMENT HILL. Legend claims that Guy Fawkes and his accomplices planned to watch their destruction of Parliament from the top of this hill in 1605 (see p. 49). The hike to the top yields a panorama stretching to Westminster and beyond. At the foot of the hill, a series of ponds marks the final gasp of the River Westbourne before it vanishes under concrete on its way to the Thames; the brave can swim for free in the dark waters of the sex-segregated **bathing ponds.** *(The southeastern part of the Heath. Rail: Gospel Oak or Hampstead Heath.)*

NEARBY MUSEUMS & GALLERIES

Permanent Collections: ▓ Iveagh Bequest, p. 137.

GOLDERS GREEN

🚇 *Tube: Golders Green (Zone 3).*

This little corner of North London is the center of Britain's Jewish community. **Golders Green Rd.** is the axis around which life revolves; turn right from the station, and a few blocks down Hebrew signs start to predominate. The main attraction of the area is Golders Hill Park—a western extension of Hampstead Heath—as well as the kosher restaurants along Golders Green Rd. (see p. 166).

GOLDERS GREEN CREMATORIUM. Though visiting a crematorium may seem a bit grim, the forbidding neo-Romanesque facade hides several acres of picturesque, beautifully maintained gardens. Paths wander through leafy groves, water gardens, and rose beds, providing a fitting and peaceful memorial sanctuary. Each flower serves as a living grave for an individual and bears the names of the departed who were sprinkled there. Britain's first crematorium is still its busiest; luminaries to have ended up here include T.S. Eliot, H.G. Wells, Peter Sellers, Bram Stoker, Anna Pavlova, and five prime ministers. Sigmund Freud's ashes, in his favorite Greek vase, are locked in the Ernest George Columbarium; ask an attendant to let you in on weekdays. *(From Tube: Golders Green (Zone 3), turn right out of the exit, then right onto Finchley Rd. and follow it under the bridge for 5min. before turning right on Hoope Ln. ☎ 8455 2374. Grounds open summer daily 9am-6pm, winter daily 9am-4pm; Chapel and Hall of Memory daily 9am-4pm. Free.)*

NEARBY MUSEUMS & GALLERIES

Permanent Collections: Royal Airforce Museum, p. 137.

ST. JOHN'S WOOD & MAIDA VALE

LORD'S CRICKET GROUND. The most famous cricket ground in the world, Lord's is home to the local Marylebone Cricket Club (MCC) and host to most of London's international matches. To see the **Lord's Museum,** home to the **Ashes Urn** (see *Dust to Dust...*, p. 206), attend a match or take a 100min. tour. Included in the tours are the MCC members' Long Room, the ground and stands, and the architecturally striking media center. On game days, tours after 10am skip the Long Room and media center, though visitors get a discount on game tickets as compensation (no tours during international Test matches). Games take place on most days in summer, and tickets are usually quite cheap; MCC games are £10 (students £4.50), but tickets to the rare international test matches are £45 and hard to get. *(Enter at Grace Gate, on St. John's Wood Rd. ☎ 7432 1066; www.lords.org.uk. Tube: St. John's Wood plus 10min. walk. Tours daily noon and 2pm, Apr.-Sept. also 10am. Tours £7, concessions £5, under 16 £4.50, family £19.)*

ABBEY ROAD. Abbey Rd. itself is a long, busy thoroughfare stretching from St. John's Wood to Kilburn, but most people are only interested in the famous **zebra crossing** at its start, where it merges with Grove End Rd. Much to the annoyance of local drivers, everyone wants a photo-op crossing the street before adding to the adulatory graffiti on the nearby street signs and walls. Next to the crossing, the **Abbey Road Studios** (3 Abbey Rd.), where the Beatles made most of their recordings, is closed to the public. *(Tube: St. John's Wood.)*

OTHER NORTH LONDON SIGHTS

ST. PANCRAS OLD CHURCH. The oldest parish in Britain, the first church on this site was reputedly founded by Roman legionaries in 314, although the present building dates from the 13th century—some of the original masonry is visible on the north wall of the nave. The church is now a rather desolate spot, hard to get into except for services; if you do get a peek, don't miss the 6th-century altar stone that once belonged to St. Augustine of Canterbury. The large and lovely **churchyard** belies its macabre history—one would hardly imagine that here Mary Godwin (author of *Frankenstein*) met Percy Bysshe Shelley in 1813 and insisted they make love on her mother's grave. Also in the churchyard is Sir John Soanes's lavish mausoleum and the **Hardy Tree:** designed by a young Thomas Hardy, it features hundreds of tightly clustered headstones which seem to spring from the roots of a weeping ash. *(St. Pancras Rd. www.stpancrasoldchurch.org.uk. ☎ 7424 0724. Prayer services M-F 9am; Mass Su-M 9:30am, Tu 7pm. Free.)*

SOUTH LONDON

🔁 *SOUTH LONDON QUICKFIND: Museums & Galleries, p. 138; Food & Drink, p. 166; Nightlife, p. 194; Entertainment, p. 219; Shopping, p. 241*

Initially, **Brixton** was just another South London railway suburb—actually a rather prosperous one, as Electric Ave. and Electric Ln. (the first streets in South London with electric lighting) testify. A poor, working-class area by the turn of the century, however, Brixton's greatest upheaval came after WWII. A steady stream of Caribbean immigrants starting in 1948 made Brixton the heart of London's West Indian community, and simmering racial tensions erupted with major riots in 1981, 1985, and 1995. Today, Brixton is a fashionable area for young artists and students, who have fueled the rise of Brixton's impressive club scene. During the day, though, their influence is mostly invisible: the neighborhood is still poor, and is infamous for having more drug-dealers than police. You can see the best of old Brixton early in the day, when **Brixton Market** is in full swing, and the best of new Brixton late at night, as young Brixtonians pile out of work and into the clubs and bars. *Tube: Brixton.*

A short bus or train ride from Brixton, **Dulwich** could hardly offer a greater contrast. South London's snobbiest suburb, Dulwich bumbled along as an unremarkable country village until 1605, when Elizabethan heartthrob Edward Alleyn (played by Ben Affleck in *Shakespeare in Love*) bought the local manor. His legacy lives on in the College of God's Gift, established according to his will for the education of 12 poor children. The original **Old College** buildings, including the chapel where Alleyn is buried, still stand close to Dulwich Picture Gallery (see p. 139), though **Dulwich College**, now with 1600 very wealthy pupils, has since moved south to a palatial 19th-century site on College Rd. The college still profits from its private stretch of College Rd., south of the Common: its **toll gate** is the last in London. *(Rail: North or West Dulwich.)*

BROCKWELL PARK & LIDO. This massive stretch of ill-maintained grass, perfect for joggers and unleashed dogs, is actually rather picturesque once you walk past the rampant graffiti at the entrance. Along with tennis courts, a dilapidated basketball court, and a BMX track, the park also has refreshment rooms at its summit, which provide lovely views of London landmarks. A vaguely Druidic central clearing lends a quaint charm to the place. *(Between Tulse Hill and Dulwich Rd.; from Tube: Brixton, turn left, bear left at the fork onto Effra Rd., then turn left again onto Brixton Water Ln., which has an unassuming entrance to the park on the right. Open daily 7:30am-dusk.)* The eastern edge of the park, off Dulwich Rd., holds the popular **Brockwell Lido,** a 1930s outdoor swimming pool often described as "London's beach." *(☎ 7274 3088. Open M-F 6:45am-10am and noon-7pm, Sa-Su noon-6pm.)*

NEARBY MUSEUMS & GALLERIES

Permanent Collections: Dulwich Picture Gallery, p. 139; Horniman Museum, p. 139.

EAST LONDON

🖪 *EAST LONDON QUICKFIND: Museums & Galleries, p. 139; Food & Drink, p. 167; Pubs, p. 181; Nightlife, p. 196; Entertainment, p. 219; Shopping, p. 242.*

WHITECHAPEL & THE EAST END

The boundary between the East End and City of London is as pronounced today as it was when Aldgate and Bishopsgate were actual gates in the wall separating the City from the poorer quarters to the east. The oldest part of the East End, **Whitechapel** is home of London's largest Bangladeshi community, as evidenced by the minaret of the **East London Mosque.** *(82-92 Whitechapel Rd. Tube: Aldgate East.)* Cheap rents have also drawn independent designers and artists. The best reason to visit the East End, though, is for its **markets** (see **Shopping,** p. 242), where shoppers from all over London look for saris on colorful Brick Ln., leather jackets on posh Petticoat Ln., and crafts in cultural Spitalfields.

CHRIST CHURCH SPITALFIELDS. Christ Church is Nicholas Hawksmoor's largest church, and considered by many to be his masterpiece. Alas, this 1729 building is in a sorry state; derelict since 1957, it is only now slowly being restored to its former glory. A £7million renovation project has been underway since 2001; the church will be closed to visitors until spring 2004. Call for opening hours. *(Commercial St., opposite Spitalfields market. ☎ 7247 0165. Tube: Liverpool St.)*

SPITALFIELDS MARKET. Originally one of London's main vegetable markets, Spitalfields was threatened with commercial development when the traders moved farther east to Leyton. Thanks to strong local opposition, one half of the enormous market hall was saved and now hosts a thriving array of clothes, crafts, antiques, and bric-a-brac along with food stalls and cafes, plus an organic food market on Fridays. *(Commercial St. ☎ 7377 1496. Tube: Liverpool St. For market details, see p. 242.)*

BRICK LANE. In Brick Ln., the epicenter of Bangladeshi Britain, even the signs are written in Bengali. Noted for its Sunday market, its hip boutiques, and its endless stretch of curry houses, Brick Ln. has become the hub of the East End's creative renaissance. The former **Truman Brewery,** covering 11 acres on both sides of Brick Ln., is now occupied by design and media consultants, sleek stores, and a cafe-bar-club trio that is one of East London's hottest nightspots (see p. 196). *Tube: Shoreditch (open only at rush hr.), Aldgate East, or Liverpool St.*

NEARBY MUSEUMS & GALLERIES

Permanent Collections: Museum of Childhood, p. 140.
Exhibition Spaces: Whitechapel Art Gallery, p. 140.

HOXTON & SHOREDITCH

◪ Tube: *From Tube: Old St., walk down Old St.; the center of the "Shoho scene" spreads either side of Old St. between the junction with Great Eastern St. and Kingsland Rd./Shoreditch High St.*

Only the occasional abandoned warehouse or graffitied storefront reveals the derelict roots of **"Shoho,"** now one of London's most fashionable districts. In the old days, struggling artists such as Damien Hirst and Tracey Emin saw potential in the neighborhood's dirt-cheap property and vacant industrial buildings, and Hoxton became the focus of an underground art scene that soon burst onto the world stage. Eventually, word got around that this was the cool place to be, bringing an influx of artists from all over the world, followed by graphic designers, web designers, and ultimately media execs. The real artists were forced farther out, but the region still clings to its hip, dingy past: stop by before lunchtime—when most people are still sleeping off the night before—to get the full "deserted slum" experience.

NEARBY MUSEUMS & GALLERIES

Permanent Collections: Geffrye Museum, p. 140.

Exhibition Spaces: Deluxe Gallery, p. 140.

Commercial Galleries: Victoria Miro, p. 141; White Cube^2, p. 141.

DOCKLANDS

Bristling with skyscrapers, scaffolding, and secretaries, Docklands provides a much-needed antidote to the "ye olde with a vengeance" attitude of its more tourist-oriented neighbors. Until the 1960s, this man-made archipelago was the commerical heart of the British Empire, until the switch to deep-water container ships robbed the docks of their usefulness in the 1960s. The area lay idle until the Conservative reforms of the 1980s. The London Docklands Development Corporation (LDDC) was founded to revitalize the region (as large as metropolitan Paris) in 1981. Since then, Docklands has become the largest commercial development in Europe—a mix of hi-tech office buildings and suburban-style housing, linked by the driverless trains of the Docklands Light Railway. Today, it rivals the City as the entrepreneurial heart of London.

CANARY WHARF. At 800 ft., the pyramid-topped tower of **One Canada Square,** commonly called Canary Wharf is Britain's tallest building. In the past two years it has been joined by a brace of almost equally tall companions—the most visible sign of Dockland's current boom. The real draw here, besides the architecture, are the vast **Canada Place** and **Cabot Square** malls under the tower, which contain over 120 different shops, restaurants, and banks. The dockside plaza is less thrilling—it's lined with upscale corporate restaurants and bars. *(Tube/DLR: Canary Wharf.)*

GREENWICH

◪ TRANSPORTATION: DLR: Cutty Sark unless stated otherwise. *The Greenwich Tourist Information Centre, Pepys House, 2 Cutty Sark Gdns. (☎0870 608 2000) offers all the usual services as well as a slick exhibition on local history. Walking tours around the center daily at 12:15pm and 2:15pm (£4, concessions £3, under 14 free.). Open daily 10am-5pm.*

Greenwich first found fame and fortune as the site of Elizabeth I's favorite palace, Placentia. Home of the Royal Navy until 1998, Greenwich's position as the "home of time" is intimately connected to its maritime heritage. The Royal Observatory, site of the Prime Meridian, was originally founded to produce accurate star-charts for navigation. This connection with timekeeping led to Greenwich being chosen as the site of Britain's most famous white elephant, the **Millennium Dome.** Situated some way from the historic sights in North Greenwich, it's soon to enter into a new incarnation as a 26,000-seat stadium. With several interesting (and largely free) sights and museums, Greenwich is a more than pleasant place to spend a day.

RIVER TRIPS. Many people choose to make the **boat** trip (1hr.) from Westminster; boats also run to the Thames Barrier (see p. 115). Travelcard holders get 33% off riverboat fares. **City Cruises** operates from Westminster Pier to Greenwich via the Tower of London. (☎ 7930 9033; www.citycruises.com. Mar.-Nov. daily. Schedule changes constantly; *call for schedules.* Adult return £6.30, all-day "rover" ticket £8.50; child £3.15/£4.25; family rover: 2 adults 3 children, £21.) **Thames River Service** boats also head from Westminster Pier to Greenwich, with some boats going to the Thames Barrier as well. (☎ 7930 4097. Apr.-Oct. daily every 30 min, 10am-5pm. June-Aug. until 7pm. Adult return £8, child £4, student £3.75, senior £6.50, family £21.50.) There is also a return service from Greenwich directly to the Thames Barrier. (Practical information same as above. Adult return £5.40, child £2.70, student £3.75, senior £4.40, family £14.20.)

ROYAL OBSERVATORY GREENWICH

🏛 *Location:* At the top of Greenwich Park, a steep climb from the National Maritime Museum; for an easier walk, take The Avenue from the top of King William Walk. *Contact:* ☎ 8312 6565; www.rog.nmm.ac.uk. *Open:* Daily 10am-5pm; last admission 4:30pm. *Admission:* Free.

The climb to the peak of Greenwich Park is not for the faint of heart, but the view proves to be well worth the trek. The peak is home to the rather dull **Royal Observatory.** Charles II founded this historic site in 1675, along with the post of Astronomer Royal, accelerating the quest to solve the problem of determining longitude. Even though longitude was eventually solved without reference to the stars, the connection lives on—the **Prime Meridian** is the axis along which the astronomers' telescopes swung. The meridian is marked by an LED strip in the courtyard that is endlessly flashing Observatory trivia; play the "now I'm east, now I'm west" game before ducking into **Flamstead House,** created by Wren "for the Observator's habitation and little for pomp." Next to the Meridian Building's telescope display, climb the **Observatory Dome,** cunningly disguised as a freakishly large onion, to see the 28-inch telescope, constructed in 1893. It's still the 7th-largest refracting 'scope in the world, though light pollution led to the abandoning of Greenwich as a scientific observatory in 1954.

CUTTY SARK

🏛 *Location:* King William Walk, by Greenwich Pier. *Contact:* ☎ 8858 2698; www.cuttysark.org.uk. *Open:* Daily 10am-5pm, last entry 4:30pm. *Admission:* £3.95, under 16 and concessions £3, families £10. 20% discount for groups.

The last of the great tea clippers, even landlubbers will appreciate the Cutty Sark's thoroughbred lines—she was the fastest ship of her time, making the round trip from China in only 120 days, laden with 1.3 million pounds of tea. Retired from the sea in 1938, the deck and cabins have been restored to their 19th-century prime (complete with animatronic sailors). The hold houses an exhibition on the ship's history and a fascinating collection of figureheads, from a set of cherubs by Grinling Gibbons to a stern figure of Abraham Lincoln. Close by "The Queen of Clippers," is the **Gypsy Moth,** the cozy 54 ft. craft in which 64-year-old Francis Chichester sailed solo around the globe in 1966. Though he didn't achieve his goal of matching the Cutty Sark, he set numerous solo-sailing speed records during his 226 days afloat and was knighted on his return.

ROYAL NAVAL COLLEGE

🏛 *Location:* King William Walk. *Contact:* ☎ 8269 4741; www.greenwichfoundation.org.uk. *Open:* Daily 12:30-5pm. *Admission:* Free.

On the site of Henry VIII's Palace of Placentia—where both he and Elizabeth I were born—the Royal Naval College was founded by William III in 1694 as the Royal Hospital for Seamen, a naval retirement home along the same lines as the army's Royal Hospital in Chelsea (see p. 76). However, the strict regime proved unpopular with former seamen, and in 1873 it was converted into the Royal Naval College. In 1998, the Navy packed its bags and the newly formed University of Greenwich blew in. Visitors are free to wander the expansive grounds of Christopher Wren's campus. Make sure to check out the extravagant **Painted Hall**, which took Sir James Thornhill 19 years to complete, and the simple **Chapel**, as well as the bizarre **Crown Jewels of the Millennium** exhibit. The fact that it's held in the university bar should alert you to the fact that the 140 crowns, from the Tsar's to the Shah's, might not be genuine articles.

OTHER GREENWICH SIGHTS

GREENWICH PARK. Another former royal hunting ground, Greenwich Park is still home to recreation as young people and families come out in droves to sunbathe, strike up football games, and toss a frisbee. Sights scattered around its hills include the remains of a 1st-century Roman settlement and Saxon tumuli (burial mounds). On the east side of the park is the **Queen Elizabeth Oak,** a rather grand title for a big dead log; for centuries before collapsing a few years ago, the tree marked the spot where Henry VIII frolicked with an 11-fingered Anne Boleyn. The garden in the southeast corner of the park combines English garden and fairy tale, complete with a deer park. The **Children's Boating Pool** gives children a chance to unleash pent-up seafaring energy accumulated in the nearby museums. *(Park open daily 7am-dusk.)*

THAMES BARRIER. Around the next bend in the Thames from Greenwich stands the world's largest movable flood barrier, the reason that London no longer enjoys the exciting high tides of yesteryear. Constructed during the 1970s and (over)hyped as "the eighth wonder of the world," the barrier spans 520m and consists of 10 separate movable steel gates. When raised, the main gates stand as high as a five-story building. *(Take the Thames River Services boat from Greenwich (see p. 114), or take bus #161 or a 45min. walk from Tube: North Greenwich (Zone 3). ☎8305 4188. Open M-F 10am-5pm, Sa-Su 10:30am-5:30pm. £3.40, concessions £2, families £7.50.)*

NEARBY MUSEUMS & GALLERIES

Permanent Collections: National Maritime Museum, p. 139.

WEST LONDON

🎒 **WEST LONDON QUICKFIND: Food & Drink,** *p. 168;* **Entertainment,** *p. 220;* **Shopping,** *p. 243;* **Accommodations,** *p. 266.* **TRANSPORTATION:** *Confusingly, Shepherd's Bush and Hammersmith (both Zone 2) each have two entirely separate Tube stations. In* **Shepherd's Bush,** *the Central Line station is at the west end of the Green, while the Hammersmith and City Line is far west of the Green on Uxbridge Rd. Tube: Goldhawk Rd. is also convenient. Both* **Hammersmith** *stations are close to each other, but the Piccadilly and District Lines are more convenient for the bus station.*

SHEPHERD'S BUSH & HAMMERSMITH

BBC TELEVISION CENTRE. This vast media complex, sprawling north of Shepherd's Bush, is ground zero for British entertainment. The BBC is always looking for people to be part of studio audiences (see p. 220); for a more in-depth experience, take a 90min. **backstage tour** of the center. *(Wood Ln. ☎8743 8000; www.bbc.co.uk. Tube: White City. Tours M-Sa 10:20am, 1, and 2:40pm. Minimum age 10. Booking required; no tickets sold at the door. £8, seniors £7, students and children £6.)*

FARTHER WEST

CHISWICK

🚇 TRANSPORTATION: *For sights, use Tube: Hammersmith then bus #190 or Tube: Turnham Green and bus #E3. The walk from Tube: Turnham Green can be confusing: walk south to Chiswick High Rd. Turn left, then right onto Chiswick Ln.; follow this until you hit Great West Rd., which is a major highway and cannot be crossed. Chiswick Ln. turns to the right, becoming Devonshire Grove—follow this until you come to the subway near the overpass. The subway is T-shaped—follow the signs for Chiswick House.*

CHISWICK HOUSE. Both Chiswick House and its gardens were created by Richard Boyle, 3rd Lord Burlington (1694-1753), the first of many Englishmen to try to recreate Italy's hills in his (very English) backyard. Based on Palladio's Villa La Rotonda in Rome, the house's cool, airy design, packed with Italian details, was hugely influential, kick-starting the English aristocracy's obsession with Palladian architecture and drawing criticism from Lord Burlington's more nationalistic contemporaries. The beautiful **gardens** were as innovative; laid out by William Kent, they were the first example of the naturalistic design that came to be known as the English style—which is ironic, given its Italian pretensions. *(Between the Great West Rd. and the Great Chertsey Rd. ☎ 0995 0508. House open Apr.-Sept. Su-F 10am-6pm, Sa 10am-2pm; Oct. daily 10am-5pm; Nov.-Mar. W-Su 10am-4pm. Gardens open daily 8am-dusk. House £3.50, concessions £3, children £2; gardens free. Frequently closes early for functions, call ahead.)*

ROYAL BOTANICAL GARDENS, KEW

🚇 Location: *Kew, on the south bank of the Thames. The main entrance and visitors center is at Victoria Gate, nearest the Tube.* **Contact:** *☎ 8332 5000, 24hr. recorded information ☎ 8332 5655; www.kew.org.* **Tube:** *Kew Gardens (Zone 3).* **Tours:** *Start at Victoria Gate visitors center. 1hr.* **walking tours** *daily 11am, 2pm; free. "Explorer" hop-on-hop-off* **shuttle** *makes 35min. rounds of the gardens; first shuttle departs Victoria Gate daily 11am, last 3:35pm. £3, children £1. "Discovery" 1hr.* **buggy tours** *for mobility impaired M-F 11am and 2pm; booking required, free.* **Open:** *Apr.-Aug. M-F 9:30am-6:30pm, Sa-Su 9:30am-7:30pm; Sept.-Oct. daily 9:30am-6pm; Nov.-Jan. daily 9:30am-4:15pm; Feb.-Mar. daily 9:30am-5:30pm. Last admission 30min. before closing. Glasshouses close 5:30pm Feb.-Oct., 3:45pm Nov.-Jan.* **Admission:** *£7.50, "late entry" (from 45min. before the glasshouses close) £5:50; concessions £5:50; under 16 free with adult.*

In the summer of 2003, the United Nations announced that the Royal Botanical Gardens is now a World Heritage Site—an honor shared by the Taj Mahal and the Great Wall of China, among others. Founded in 1759 by Princess Augusta as an addendum to Kew Palace, the Royal Botanical Gardens extends in a 300-acre swath along the Thames, and has maintained an admirably English placidity. No ordinary park, Kew is a leading center for botany thanks to its collection of thousands of flowers, fruits, trees, and vegetables from across the globe. It currently houses some 30,000 living species, and about seven million pressed varieties.

The three great **conservatories** and their smaller offshoots house a staggering variety of plants ill-suited to the English climate. The steamy Victorian **Palm House** is the least interesting of the three, but does boast Encephalartos Altensteinii, "The Oldest Pot Plant In The World," which is not at all what it sounds like. The **Princess of Wales Conservatory,** opened in 1987 by Diana but named for Augusta (the mother of George III), has a larger area under glass than any other, thanks to its innovative pyramid-like structure. The interior is divided into 10 different climate zones, from rainforest to desert, including one entirely devoted to orchids. The **Temperate House** is the largest ornamental glasshouse in the world, with an overwhelming display of flora—the room devoted to South African plants is among the most beautiful in the park. Less beautiful but more massive, the 20m-tall, 158-year-old Jubaea Chilensis is the world's largest indoor plant. The **Plants and People** exhibition, across the Pond from the Palm House, is a strikingly obvious examination of the uses of plants—did you know that pineapple can be eaten, or that wood can be used for making wooden toys? Outside the controlled environment of the houses, the gardens are home to a variety of flora from around the world. Created in 1910, the **Japanese Gateway and Garden** brings eastern flora to a collection that also includes local specialities such as the **Lilacs,** the **Azaleas,** and **Rhododendron Dell.** The gardens blaze most brightly during spring. Be sure to visit the **Rock Garden** and the **Rose Pergola** for the gardens' most impressive displays. Out-of-season visitors will not be disappointed—the **Woodland Glade** is renowned for displays of autumn color, while the **Winter Garden** flowers between November and February. Close to the Thames in the northern part of the gardens, **Kew Palace** (closed for renovations until 2006) is a modest red-brick affair originally built by a Dutch merchant in 1631. Behind the palace, 17th-century medicinal plants flourish in the stunning **Queen's Garden;** small placards label one that "procureth hair on beardlesse men" and those that cure back pain "caused by overmuch use of women." At the opposite end of the gardens, **Queen Charlotte's Cottage** is a faux-rustic building given by George III to his wife as a picnic site. Younger visitors will welcome the opportunity to **Be a Badger!**—a human-sized reconstruction of a badger's den, complete with tunnels, nests, and foodstores.

Museums & Galleries

Centuries as the capital of an empire upon which the sun never set, together with a decidedly English penchant for collecting, have endowed London with a spectacular set of museums. Art lovers, history buffs, and amateur ethnologists will not know which way to turn when they arrive. And there's even better news for museum lovers—after a decade which saw many museums shed their free admission to become some of the capital's most expensive attractions, admission to all major collections is now free indefinitely in celebration of the Queen's Golden Jubilee. However, note that almost all charge extra for temporary exhibitions—often so popular that tickets must be booked in advance.

MAJOR COLLECTIONS

BRITISH MUSEUM

🔢 *LOCATION: Great Russell St., **Bloomsbury**. BLOOMSBURY QUICKFIND: Sights, p. 74; Museums & Galleries, p. 125; Food & Drink, p. 148; Pubs, p. 173. CONTACT: ☎ 7323 8000; www.thebritishmuseum.ac.uk. TUBE: Tottenham Court Rd., Russell Square, or Holborn. AUDIOGUIDES: £2.50. TOURS: Start at Great Court info desk; free. **Highlights Tour** (90min.): M-Sa 10:30am and 1pm; Su 11am, 12:30, 1:30, 2:30, and 4pm. Advanced booking recommended. £7, concessions £4. **Focus tour** (60min.): M-W and Sa 3:15pm; Th-F 3:15, 5:30, and 7pm; Su 4:30pm. £5, concs £3. OPEN: Great Court Su-W 10am-5:30pm, Th-Sa 9am-9pm. Galleries daily 10am-5:30pm, selected galleries have extended hours Th-F. ADMISSION: Free; £2 suggested donation. Temporary exhibitions around £7, concessions £3.50.*

The funny thing about the British Museum is that there's almost nothing British in it. Founded in 1753 as the personal collection of Sir Hans Sloane, in 1824 work started on the current Neoclassical building, which took another 30 years to construct. With

50,000 items, the magnificent collection is somewhat undermined by a chaotic layout and poor labeling, especially in the less popular galleries, while staff shortages mean that even famous galleries are frequently and randomly closed to the public. If you've got your heart set on a particular exhibit, call ahead to check for closings. To avoid getting lost, take one of the free tours, or purchase the color map available at the entrance (£2).

GREAT COURT. Opened in December 2000, the arresting **Great Court** is the largest covered square in Europe. For the past 150 years used as the book stacks of the British Library, the courtyard is still dominated by the **Reading Room.** The blue chairs and desks, with ingenious fold-out lecterns, have shouldered the weight of research by Marx, Lenin, and Trotsky as well as almost every major British writer and intellectual.

WEST GALLERIES. From the main entrance, the large double doors to the left of the Reading Room lead to the Museum's most popular wing. The star of the **Egyptian sculpture** is the **Rosetta Stone,** whose trilingual inscriptions (in Greek, Heterotic, and Hieroglyphic) made the deciphering of ancient Egyptian possible. *(Room 4.)* Just as imposing are the monumental friezes and reliefs of the Assyrian, Hittite, and other ancient **Near-Eastern** civilizations. *(Rooms 6-10, ground floor; the southern end of room 4 leads into room 6.)* Most famous of the massive array of **Greek sculpture** on show are the **Elgin Marbles,** statues from the Parthenon that were carved under the direction of Athens's greatest sculptor, Phidias. *(Room 18.)* Equally impressive (and far less crowded) are the almost perfectly preserved **Bassae Friezes,** displaying scenes from the battle between Perseus and the Amazons. *(Room 16, upstairs from 17.)* Other Hellenic highlights include remnants of two of the seven Wonders of the Ancient World, the **Temple of Artemis** at Ephesus and the **Mausoleum of Halikarnassos.** *(Rooms 21-22.)* Upstairs, the **Portland Vase** presides over **Roman** ceramics and housewares. When discovered in 1582 the base had already been broken and replaced. In 1845, it was shattered by a drunken museum-goer; when it was put back together, 37 small chips were left over. Since then, the vase has been beautifully reconstructed twice, with more left-over chips being reincorporated each time—don't touch! *(Room 70.)*

NORTH GALLERIES. Revenge of the mummy: just when you thought you'd nailed Ancient Egypt, along come another 8 galleries. Rooms 62-63 contain painted wooden **sarcophagi** and bandaged **mummies** in various states of repair. *(Rooms 61-68, upper floor.)* More overflow from the West wing continues the Near Eastern theme; musical instruments and board games from the world's first city, **Ur,** show that life's priorities have changed little since. *(Rooms 51-59.)* The **African Galleries** are perhaps the best-presented in the museum, with the fabulous collection accompanied by soft chanting, video displays, and abundant documentation. *(Room 25, lower floor.)* The **Americas** collection has almost nothing from North America, but the **Mexican** gallery features some extraordinary Aztec artifacts. *(Rooms 26-27.)* Just off the Montague Pl. entrance is a fine collection of **Islamic art.** *(Room 34.)* Immediately above it, Room 33 (the largest in the museum) is dedicated to the art of **China,** the **South Asia,** and **Southeast Asia,** with some particularly fine Hindu sculpture. Upstairs, the highlight of the **Korean** display is a *sarangbang* house built on-site. *(Room 67.)* A teahouse, meanwhile, is the centerpiece of the **Japanese** galleries. *(Rooms 92-94.)*

SOUTH & EAST GALLERIES. The upper level of the museum's southeast corner is dedicated to ancient and medieval **Europe,** including most of the museum's British artifacts. A highlight of the collection is the treasure excavated from the **Sutton Hoo Burial Ship:** the magnificent inlaid helmet is the most famous example of Anglo-Saxon craftsmanship. With the ship is the extraordinary Mildenhall Treasure, a trove of brilliantly preserved Roman artifacts. *(Room 41.)* Next door are the enigmatic and beautiful **Lewis Chessmen,** an 800-year-old Scandinavian chess set mysteriously abandoned on Scotland's Outer Hebrides. *(Room 42.)* Also in this part of the museum are the frankly dull **Clock Gallery** *(Room 44)* and **Money Gallery** *(Room 68).*

NATIONAL GALLERY

⚑ LOCATION: *Main entrance on north side of* **Trafalgar Sq., Westminster:** *disabled access at Sainsbury Wing, on Pall Mall East* **WESTMINSTER QUICKFIND:** *Sights, p. 104; Museums & Galleries, p. 125; Food & Drink, p. 158; Pubs, p. 179.* **CONTACT:** *☎ 7747 2885; www.nationalgallery.org.uk.* **TUBE:** *Charing Cross or Leicester Square.* **OPEN:** *M-Tu and Th-Sa 10am-6pm, W 10am-9pm. Special exhibitions in the Sainsbury Wing occasionally open until 10pm.* **TOURS:** *Start at Sainsbury Wing info desk. 1hr. gallery tours daily 11:30am and 2:30pm, W also 6:30pm; free.* **AUDIOGUIDES:** *Free; £4 suggested donation.* **ADMISSION:** *Free; some temporary exhibitions £5-7, seniors £4-5, students and ages 12-18 £2-3.*

The National Gallery was founded by an Act of Parliament in 1824, with 38 pictures displayed in a townhouse; it became so popular that by 1838 a purpose-built gallery had to be constructed to house the collection. Since then, numerous additions have been made, the most recent (and controversial) being the massive Sainsbury Wing—Prince Charles described it as "a monstrous carbuncle on the face of a much-loved and elegant friend." The Sainsbury Wing holds almost all of the museum's large exhibitions—2004 will bring an **El Greco** show that promises to cover the full sweep of his career (Feb. 11-May 23). If you're pressed for time, head to the **Micro Gallery** in the Sainsbury Wing, where you can design and print out a personalized tour of the paintings you want to see.

SAINSBURY WING. The climate-controlled rooms of the gallery's newest extension house its oldest, most fragile paintings, dating from 1260 to 1510. The most famous of the many devotional **medieval** paintings on display is the *Wilton Diptych*, a 14th-century altarpiece made for (and featuring) Richard II. (Room 53) A stunning **early Renaissance** collection features Botticelli's *Venus and Mars*, an early plea to make love not war, and Piero della Francesca's *Baptism of Christ*. (Rooms 58 and 66) One of the museum's most famous works, the *Leonardo Cartoon* is a detailed preparatory drawing by Leonardo da Vinci for a never-executed painting. Other Leonardos on display include his second *Virgin on the Rocks*. (Room 51) Perhaps the finest of the Sainsbury Wing's offerings, however, is Van Eyck's masterpiece, the *Arnolfini Portrait*, which dominates Room 56.

WEST WING. With paintings from 1510 to 1600, the West Wing is dominated by the Italian **High Renaissance** and the first flowering of Flemish art, with a parallel move from exclusively religious themes in the first rooms to greater and greater attention to natural, secular themes. Room 4 has Holbein's *The Ambassadors* with its incredible optical illusion, while exquisite paintings by Moroni line the walls of room 6. In room 8, the artistic forces of Rome and Florence fight it out, with versions of the *Madonna and Child* by Bronzino and Correggio; room 9 and 10 focus on northern Italy, with the latter dominated by Titian. Room 12, featuring many early Flemish works, holds some stunning Gossaerts.

NORTH WING. Continuing this journey through time, the North Wing spans the **17th century,** with an exceptional display of Flemish and Spanish Renaissance works spread out over 10 rooms. The Vermeers in Room 16 are 2 of only 34 in the world, and Room 20 features some of the finest of Claude's work. Room 23 boasts no fewer than 18 Rembrandts, including his *Self Portrait at 34*. Room 29 is dominated by Rubens's *Samson and Delilah*, along with dozens of his other works. Velàzquez's super-sensuous *The Toilet of Venus* is at odds with the rest of his mostly religious output on show in room 30. Also housed here is a whole hall of Poissin mythologies.

EAST WING. The East Wing, home to paintings from **1700-1900,** is the most crowded in the gallery. The crowds focus primarily on, room 45, which features Van Gogh's *Sunflowers* and Cézanne's *Bathers*. Room 44 is also popular, containing a brilliant set of paintings by Seurat as well as work by Manet, Monet, and Renoir. A reminder that there was art on this side of the Channel too, room 34 flies the flag with portraits by Reynolds and Gainsborough, as well as six luminescent Turners, ranging from the stormy realism of *Dutch Boats in a Gale* to the proto-Impression-

in recent
news

MATERIAL GIRL

Usually, when Madonna and a wealthy American are linked in the news, everyone is happy. But this time, the Madonna in question is Raphael's *The Madonna of the Pinks*, which has been on loan to the National Gallery for the past ten years. The wealthy American? California's Getty Museum, which recently offered the Duke of Northumberland £35 million for it. The Duke jumped at the chance, and coolly informed the appalled director of the National Gallery that he was selling the Raphael.

Refusing to give up without a fight, the gallery is collecting donations, looking for sponsors, and doing everything possible to match the American offer.

The government has been appealed to for assistance, but Blair is wary of the political ramifications of contributing tax dollars to pay off an already-wealthy duke. Meanwhile, *The Madonna of the Pinks* remains in the National Gallery—a small, lovely painting, infused with delicate light and a distinctly Florentine grace. Its future home will not be decided for months yet, but Londoners who suspect that the news will not be good have been flocking to the gallery to pay their last respects.

ist blur of *Margate from the Sea*. Equally impressive is this room's collection of Constables, including *The Hay-Wain*.

TATE BRITAIN

⚑ LOCATION: *Millbank, near Vauxhall Bridge, in West-minster. Wheelchair access via Clore Wing.* **WEST-MINSTER QUICKFIND:** *Sights, p. 104; Museums & Galleries, p. 136; Food & Drink, p. 162; Pubs, p. 179.* **CONTACT:** ☎ *7887 8008; www.tate.org.uk.* **TUBE:** *Pimlico.* **AUDIOGUIDES:** *£3, concessions £2.50.* **TOURS:** *Art from 1500-1800 11am, 1800-1900 noon, Turner 2pm, 1900-2002 3pm; all free.* **Highlights Tour:** *M-F 11:30am, Sa 3pm.* **Turner:** *M-F 2:30pm.* **LUNCHTIME LECTURES:** *W or Th, Sa 1pm and Su 2:30pm. Regular events include:* **Gallery Talks,** *W-F lunchtime;* **Painting of the Month,** *M 1:15pm and Sa 2:30pm;* **Friday Lectures,** *F 1pm;* **Slide Lectures,** *Sa 1pm and Su 2:30pm.* **OPEN:** *Daily 10am-5:50pm, last admission 5pm.* **ADMISSION:** *Free; special exhibitions £3-9.*

Tate Britain now houses an excellent collection of British art—a tag which includes foreign artists working in Britain and Brits working abroad from 1500 to the present. The original Tate opened in 1897 to house Sir Henry Tate's collection of "modern" British art and was expanded to include the famed British painter's J.M.W. Turner bequest of 282 oils and 19,000 watercolors. The **Clure Gallery** continues to display Turner's extensive collection of hazy British landscapes while the bulk of the museum consists of the **Tate Centenary Development,** completed in late 2001, changing exhibits which loosely trace the chronology of art in Britain from 1500-2004 through themed subdivisions such as "British Artists & the Near East." These galleries feature significant holdings of the fervent work of William Blake, as well as the paintings by the Pre-Raphaelites John Everett Millais, William Hunt, and Dante Gabriel Rossetti. Additional artists on heavy display are John Constable, William Hogarth, Joshua Reynolds, Francis Bacon, and David Hockney. Other beloved works include Whistler's *Nocturne in Blue and Gold* and John Singer Sargent's *Carnation, Lily, Lily, Rose*. The bulk of modern British art is absent, having been transferred to the Tate Modern at Bankside in 1999 (see below), but that doesn't means that what remains here is static or stodgy. The annual **Turner Prize** for contemporary art is still held here, showcasing the vanguard of the art world. The shortlisted works go on show from late October to early January every year.

TATE MODERN

⚑ LOCATION: *Bankside, on the **South Bank**; main entrance and wheelchair access on Holland St.; secondary entrance on Queen's Walk.* **SOUTH BANK QUICKFIND:** *Sights, p. 95; Museums & Galleries, p. 123; Food & Drink, p. 157; Pubs, p. 177.* **CONTACT:** *☎ 7887 8000; www.tate.org.uk.* **TUBE:** *Southwark or Blackfriars.* **AUDIOGUIDES:** *4 tours including for children and the visually impaired. £1.* **TOURS:** *Meet on the gallery concourses; free.* **History/Memory/Society** *noon, level 5;* **Nude/ Body/Action** *11am, level 5;* **Landscape/Matter/Environment** *3pm, level 3;* **Still Life/Object/ Real Life** *2pm, level 3.* **TALKS:** *M-F 1pm. Meet at concourse on appropriate level; free.* **OPEN:** *Su-Th 10am-6pm, F-Sa 10am-10pm.* **ADMISSION:** *Free.*

Since opening in May 2000, Tate Modern has been credited with single-handedly reversing the long-term decline in museum-going numbers in Britain. The largest modern art museum in the world (until New York's MOMA re-opens in 2005), its most striking aspect is Giles Gilbert Scott's mammoth building, formerly the Bankside power station. The seventh floor has wraparound views of north and south London, and the old **Turbine Hall** is now an immense atrium that often overpowers the installations commissioned for it. A full one-third of the gallery space—all of level 4—is dedicated to temporary exhibitions. Rest areas around the galleries provide chairs, books, and recorded commentary by artists, intellectuals, and celebrities.

For all its popularity, the Tate has been criticized for its controversial curatorial method. By grouping works according to themes such as "Subversive Objects," the Tate has turned itself into a work of conceptual art—as many words are used to explain the logic behind each room's collection as the meaning behind the works themselves. Perhaps mindful of criticism, curators have stealthily begun arranging more works by period and artist; but officially, everything is still organized according to four themes: **Still Life/Object/Real Life** and **Landscape/Matter/Environment** on level 3, and **Nude/Action/Body** and **History/ Memory/Society** on level 5. This arrangement brings out some interesting contrasts: successes include the nascent geometry of Cézanne's *Still Life with Water Jug* juxtaposed with Howard Hodgkin's splotchy *Dinner at Smith Square* in the "Art of the Everyday" room of the Still Life/Object/Real Life, and Monet's indistinct *Waterlilies* paired with Patrick Heron's intense, piercing *Azalea Garden*, in Landscape/Matter/Environment. In other rooms, the purported theme is little more than a smokescreen for conventional arrangement: in Landscape/Matter/Environment, the "Inner Worlds" room might as well be called "Surrealism," with works by Dalí, Miró, Magritte, Ernst, and de Chirico. The greatest achievement of the thematic display is that it forces visitors into contact with a wide range of art. It's now impossible to see the Tate's more famous pieces, which include Picasso's *Weeping Woman*, without also confronting challenging and invigorating works by less well-known contemporary artists.

Special exhibits in 2004 include works by German artist **Sigmar Polke,** who creates distorted prints that reflect his interest in technologically marred images (until January 4), and the fourth in the **Unilever Series** of commissions for Turbine Hall: installations by **Olafur Eliasson** featuring natural materials like light, steam, and ice (until March 21).

VICTORIA & ALBERT MUSEUM

⚑ LOCATION: *Main entrance on Cromwell Rd., **Kensington**; wheelchair access on Exhibition Rd.* **KENSINGTON & EARL'S COURT QUICKFIND:** *Sights, p. 130; Museums & Galleries, p. 132; Food & Drink, p. 153; Pubs, p. 176.* **CONTACT:** *☎ 7942 2000; www.vam.ac.uk.* **TUBE:** *South Kensington.* **OPEN:** *Th-Tu 10am-5:45pm, W plus last F of month 10am-10pm.* **TOURS:** *Meet at rear of main entrance; free.* **Introductory tours:** *Daily 10:30, 11:30am, 1:30, 2:30pm; W also 4:30pm.* **Focus tours:** *Daily 12:30, 2:30pm. Subjects change every 6 weeks.* **TALKS & EVENTS:** *Meet at rear of main entrance.* **Gallery talks:** *Daily 1pm; 45-60min. Free.* **Late View Events:** *Talks, tours, and live music W from 6:30pm; last F of month also features live performances, guest DJs, late-night exhibition openings, bar, and food.* **ADMISSION:** *Free; additional charge for some special exhibitions.*

When the V&A was founded in 1852 as the Museum of Manufactures to encourage excellence in art and design, the original curators were deluged with objects from around the globe. Today, as the largest museum of the decorative (and not so decorative) arts in the world, the V&A rivals the British Museum for the sheer size and diversity of its holdings—as befits an institution dedicated to displaying "the fine and applied arts of all countries, all styles, all periods." Unlike that in the British Museum, the V&A's documentation is consistently excellent and thorough. Its five *million* square meters of galleries house the best collection of Italian Renaissance sculpture outside Italy, the largest array of Indian art outside India, and a gallery of fashion from the 16th century to the latest designer collections. Visitors should be aware that staff shortages can lead to the temporary closure of less-popular galleries without notice; it's best to call ahead on the day of your visit if you want to see a specific gallery. If you really want to see something in a cordoned-off gallery, try asking politely at the main entrance information desk: they may be convinced to send someone along to give you a private viewing.

BRITISH GALLERIES. The subject of a £31m refit, the vast British Galleries sprawl over 3 floors of reconstructed rooms documenting the progression of British taste and fashion from 1500 to 1900.

DRESS COLLECTION. Don't expect to find everyday clothing in the V&A's world-famous costume collection: it's nothing but the finest *haute couture* through and through. Men's suits and women's gowns are displayed on white mannequins, with panels describing the major designers of the 20th century, from John-Paul Gaultier to Issey Miyake.

EUROPE. The ground-floor European collections are staggering in their breadth. If you only see one thing in the museum, make it the **Raphael Gallery,** hung with eight massive cartoons (preliminary paintings) for tapestries commissioned by Leo X in 1515 to hang in the Sistine Chapel. The **Sculpture Gallery,** home to Canova's *Three Graces* (1814-17) and voluptuous *Sleeping Nymph* (1820-24), is not to be confused with the **Cast Courts,** two deceptive collections of the world's sculptural masterpieces, from Trajan's Column to Michelangelo's *David*—they're actually all plaster reproductions. The **Medieval Treasury** houses some extraordinary enamels and vestments, including the beautiful *Clare Chasuble* of 1272; rooms devoted to **Nothern Europe** display the fruits of the Late Middle Ages, including several Dürers.

ASIAN GALLERIES. If the choice of objects in the V&A's Asian collections seems to rely on national cliches (Indian temple carvings, Chinese porcelain), it says more about the way in which the V&A has formed opinion than followed it. The Turkish and Egyptian ceramics of the **Islamic Art** collection are overshadowed by the gigantic Ardabil carpet, woven in Iran in 1539 and containing an estimated 30 million knots. In addition to the requisite swords, armor, and paintings, the excellent **Japanese** gallery displays an array of contemporary ceramic sculpture and kimonos.

UPPER FLOORS. In contrast to the geographically organized ground floor, the upper levels are mostly arranged by material, with specialist galleries devoted to everything from musical instruments to stained glass. In the **textile** collection, where you can try on kimonos, long cabinets contain pull-out drawers with swatches of thousands of different fabrics. Turnstiles and solid steel doors protect the contents of the opulent **Jewelry** gallery. Two exceptions to the materially themed galleries are the **Leighton** gallery, with a fresco by the eponymous Victorian painter, and the sprawling **20th-century** collections. Here, arranged by period and style, are illustration and design classics from Salvador Dalí's 1936 sofa modeled on Mae West's lips to a pair of 1990s latex hotpants.

HENRY COLE WING. The 6-level Henry Cole wing is home to the V&A's collection of **British paintings,** including some 350 works by Constable and numerous Turners. Also here is a display of **Rodin** bronzes, donated by the artist in 1914, and the "world's greatest collection" of **miniature portraits,** including Holbein's *Anne of Cleves*. In the library-like **print room,** anyone can ask to see original works from the prodigious collection *(Print Room open Tu-F 10am-4:30pm, Sa 10am-1pm and 2-4:30pm).* The small **Frank Lloyd Wright** gallery contains a full-size recreation of the office commissioned by Edgar J. Kauffmann for his Pittsburgh department store in 1935.

MUSEUMS BY NEIGHBORHOOD

BLOOMSBURY

7 BLOOMSBURY QUICKFIND: Sights, *p. 74;* **Food & Drink,** *p. 148;* **Pubs,** *p. 173;* **Entertainment,** *p. 207;* **Shopping,** *p. 226;* **Accommodations,** *p. 254. For the* **British Museum,** *see Major Collections p. 119.*

■ BRITISH LIBRARY GALLERIES

SEE MAP, p. 362

7 Location: *96 Euston Rd.* **Contact:** ☎ *7412 7332; www.bl.uk.* **Open:** *M and W-F 9:30am-6pm, Tu 9:30am-8pm, Sa 9:30am-5pm, Su 11am-5pm.* **Audioguides:** *£3.50, concessions £2.50.* **Admission:** *Library free.*

Housed within the British Library (see p. 75) is an appropriately stunning display of books, manuscripts, and related artifacts from around the world and throughout the ages. Displays are arranged by theme: **Historical documents** include three original copies of the Magna Carta and pages from Leonardo da Vinci's notebook, as well as Saint Thomas More's last letter to Henry VIII. The **literature** section, as you'd expect, is very strong, from a first folio Shakespeare to the personally illustrated first copy of *Alice in Wonderland* that Lewis Carroll gave to his young muse. The **music collection** is more of a surprise, combining handwritten scores by the classical giants with an entire cabinet devoted to the Beatles. The **Bible display** contains the oldest works in the library, including the 2nd-century *Unknown Gospel* and the *Codex Sinaiticus,* one of the primary sources for the Greek text of the Gospels. The **Sacred Texts** and **Illuminated Manuscripts** are the highlights of the collection, including the luminous *Sherborne Missal* and the *Lindisfarne Gospel,* the best surviving Anglo-Saxon gospel and perhaps the loveliest work in the collection. In the **Printing** display, the *Million Charms of Empress Shotoku*—a scroll of Buddhist charms printed in 764—shares the same case as a magnificent *Gutenberg Bible* printed in 1454. To the rear of the exhibition, the **Turning the Page** computer gallery lets you get a closer look at some of the more famous works. Downstairs, the **Workshop of Sounds and Images** is aimed at a younger audience, with interactive displays charting the history of record-making, from parchment to TV.

OTHER PERMANENT COLLECTIONS

POLLOCK'S TOY MUSEUM. A maze of tiny rooms and passageways congested with antique playthings of high kitsch value; the emphasis here is on the Western world, but there are a number of interesting toys from Africa and Asia as well. Highlights include the oldest known teddy bear ("born" 1905), "Saucy Frauleins" who expose themselves at the tug of a string, and a room of elaborately furnished dollhouses that Barbie would kill for. None of the toys on display can be touched, which limits the museum's appeal for children; however, young'uns not totally dependent on computers will enjoy the old-fashioned toy shop by the entrance, with traditional playthings at, unfortunately, more modern prices. *(1 Scala St.; entrance on Whitfield St.* ☎ *7636 3452; www.tao2000.net/pollocks. Tube: Goodge St. Open M-Sa 10am-5pm; last admission 4:30pm. £3, concessions and under-18s £1.50. MC/V.)*

PERCIVAL DAVID FOUNDATION OF CHINESE ART. Heaven for lovers of Chinese porcelain; dull for most others. This Georgian townhouse boasts the finest collection of china outside of China. Temporary exhibitions, often using pieces from the collection to illustrate trends and themes in Chinese art, occupy the ground floor. The 1st floor houses superb early examples of imperial china, including 13 pieces of extremely rare Ru wares collected by Sir Percival himself. The 2nd floor features later examples of blue-and-white Ming and painted Qing work. *(53 Gordon Sq. ☎ 7387 3909; www.pdfmuseum.org.uk. Tube: Euston Square or Euston. Open M-F 10:30am-5pm. Free.)*

EXHIBITION SPACES

Brunei Gallery, 10 Thorhaugh St. *(☎ 7898 4915; www.soas.ac.uk/gallery).* Tube: Russell Square. On the campus of the School of Oriental and African Studies, this beautiful space is devoted to carefully and elaborately crafted exhibitions of African and Asian art and culture. As its patron is the Sultan of Brunei, you'd expect nothing less. Open M-F 10:30am-5pm when exhibitions are on; visit website or call for schedule. Free.

CHELSEA

SEE MAP, p. 363

🈁 *CHELSEA QUICKFIND: Sights, p. 76; Food & Drink, p. 150; Entertainment, p. 208; Shopping, p. 227. TRANSPORTATION: The only Tube station in Chelsea is Sloane Sq.; from here buses #11, 19, 22, 211, and 319 run down the King's Rd.*

NATIONAL ARMY MUSEUM. If you're not in a militaristic mindset when you get here, this museum will certainly get you into one—weapons point at visitors at every turn. Starting with the battle of Agincourt in 1415, the chronological displays use life-size recreations, videos, dioramas, and memorabilia to recreate combat though the ages. The wax figures occasionally border on the ridiculous, but do an admirable job of demonstrating the challenging nature of land warfare over the ages. Naturally, there's a large Waterloo display, complete with the skeleton of Napoleon's favorite horse, Marengo. *(Royal Hospital Rd. ☎ 7730 0717; www.national-army-museum.ac.uk. Open daily 10am-5:30pm. Free.)*

THE CITY OF LONDON

SEE MAP, p. 364

🈁 *THE CITY OF LONDON QUICKFIND: Sights, p. 78; Food & Drink, p. 150; Pubs, p. 174; Entertainment, p. 208.*

🏛 MUSEUM OF LONDON

🈁 *Location: London Wall; enter through the Barbican or from Aldersgate. Wheelchair users take elevator at Aldersgate entrance. Contact: ☎ 7600 3699; www.museumoflondon.org.uk. Tube: St. Paul's or Barbican. Open: M-Sa 10am-6pm, Su noon-6pm; last admission 5:30pm. Audioguides: £2. Events: Frequent demonstrations, talks, and guided walks; free-£10. Admission: Free.*

Perched in the corner of the Barbican complex (see **Sights**, p. 80), the Museum of London resembles a latter-day fortress from the outside. Enter from Aldersgate via a forbidding black tower in the center of a busy traffic roundabout as impassable as any moat. The engrossing collection traces the history of London from its Roman foundations to the present day, cleverly incorporating bits of architectural history, such as the adjacent ruins of the ancient city walls. The **London Before London** display is a little excessive (the Ice Age was a pretty dull time for the city), but the museum quickly heats up. The **Roman** galleries are particularly impressive, with a reconstructed dining room built over an original mosaic floor and the fascinating and well-documented Roman statuary from the Temple of Mithras (see **Sights,** p. 82). The Anglo-Saxon and Medieval collections are small but excellent, including a set of pewter pilgrim badges for towns from Compostella to Canterbury. Equally impressive are the 19th- and 20th-century displays, particularly the exhibit on poverty in the East End. The museum is worth a visit for the **Cheapside Hoard** alone, a 17th-century goldsmith's bounty uncovered in 1912, or for the **Lord Mayor's State Coach,** built in 1757 and dripping with gold carvings.

OTHER PERMANENT COLLECTIONS

▨ **BANK OF ENGLAND MUSEUM.** Housed within the Bank itself (see **Sights** p. 82), this surprisingly large museum traces its history from the Bank's foundation (1694) to the present day. Waxworks man a recreation of Sir John Soane's original Stock Office, while a display of banknotes includes a handwritten one from 1697 for the sum of £22—the ease of forgery and the annoyance of exchanging odd sums led to the introduction of standard printed notes soon after. An even more amusing set of waxworks stage a mock debate in the **Rotunda** over the relative merits of gold and paper currency. The whole experience culminates in a delightfully cheesy set of interactive screens in **The Bank Today** section, which provide a helpful primer on everything from supply and demand to the ins and outs of international finance. If you're a fan of bad animatronics, the Bank of England Museum is a lot cheaper than Mme Tussaud's, is more educational, and doesn't take itself nearly so seriously. *(Bartholomew Ln. ☎ 7601 5545; www.bankofengland.co.uk. Tube: Bank. Open M-F 10am-5pm. Free.)*

The British Museum

Tate Britain

▨ **GUILDHALL ART GALLERY.** This incredibly sumptuous new gallery is devoted to displaying the City's art collection—breeze over the aging portraits of forgotten Lord Mayors and head to the basement galleries, which hold a fine collection of Victorian and Pre-Raphaelite art with works by Constable, Tissot, Rossetti, and Millais. The first floor showcases John Singleton Copley's massive *The Defeat of the Floating Batteries*, while the undercroft houses the ruins of a Roman amphitheater on display in a bizarrely hi-tech gallery that seeks to recreate the gladiatorial experience in neon-green wireframes. Off the beaten track, but worth the trip. *(Guildhall Yard, off Gresham St. ☎ 7332 3700; www.guildhall-art-gallery.org.uk. Tube: St. Paul's, Moorgate, or Bank. Open M-Sa 10am-5pm, last admission 4:30pm; Su noon-4pm, last admission 3:45pm. Free all day F and Sa-Th after 3:30pm; otherwise £2.50, concessions £1, under 16 free.)*

THE CLOCKMAKERS' MUSEUM. A one-room museum measuring the 500-year history of London clockmakers through clocks, watches, chronometers, and sundials, including a watch

The National Gallery

belonging to Mary Queen of Scots and the one worn by Sir Edmund Hillary when he climbed Everest. *(Enter through Guildhall Library on Aldermanbury. ☎ 7606 3030. Tube: St. Paul's, Bank, or Moorgate. Open M-Sa 9:30am-4:45pm. Free.)*

EXHIBITION SPACES

Barbican Art Galleries (☎ 7638 8891; www.barbican.org.uk), between London Wall, Beech St., Aldersgate, and Moorgate. Tube: Barbican or Moorgate. The Barbican has two important gallery spaces, both of which will be closed until mid-2004 for major remodeling. The **Barbican Gallery** (Level 3) hosts innovative exhibitions of 20th-century and current art and design; recent shows have veered toward photography. Lesser-known international works are held in **The Curve**, a semicircular gallery that wraps around the back of the concert hall. Both are closed until mid-2004; call for hours.

CLERKENWELL

SEE MAP, p. 365

🏛 *CLERKENWELL QUICKFIND: Sights, p. 82; Food & Drink, p. 151; Pubs, p. 174; Nightlife, p. 185; Entertainment, p. 210; Accommodations, p. 259.*

MUSEUM OF ST. BARTHOLOMEW'S HOSPITAL. Bart's, as the hospital is known, was established in 1123, when Henry I's courtier Rahere founded both the hospital and nearby St. Bartholomew the Great (see p. 84). The tiny museum tells how William Harvey discovered circulation of the blood here in the 17th century. Two huge paintings by Hogarth (who was born in nearby Bartholomew Close) adorn the walls by the the Grand Staircase; for a close-up, you'll have to take the tour. Also on hospital grounds is the church of **St. Bartholomew the Less**, mostly an 1820s restoration but with a 15th-century tower. *(West Smithfield. ☎ 7601 8152. Tube: Barbican, Farringdon, or St. Paul's. Open Tu-F 10am-4pm. Free. Tours including Smithfield area F 2pm; £5, concessions £4.)*

HOLBORN

SEE MAP, p. 365

🏛 *HOLBORN QUICKFIND: Sights, p. 84; Food & Drink, p. 152; Pubs, p. 175; Nightlife, p. 187; Entertainment, p. 210; Shopping, p. 229.*

🏛 **SIR JOHN SOANE'S MUSEUM.** Eccentric architect John Soane let his imagination run free when designing this intriguing museum for his own collection of art and antiquities. Three separate homes in Lincoln's Field Rd. had to be joined together to accommodate the collection; the result is a bewildering, delightful maze. Soane manipulated perspectives and made the most of limited light sources with numerous round mirrors. Eclectic is the mildest adjective that could be applied to its holdings—items range from the mummified corpse of his wife's dog to an extraordinary sarcophagus of Seti I, for which Soane personally outbid the British Museum. The Picture Room houses Hogarth's *The Rake's Progress*. In addition to the permanent collection, the museum holds two to five exhibitions a year in its gallery space—which, in keeping with Soane's legacy, are nothing if not diverse. *(13 Lincoln's Inn Fields. ☎ 1405 2107. Tube: Holborn. Open Tu-Sa 10am-5pm, first Tu of month also 6-9pm. Tours Sa 2:30pm, tickets sold from 2pm; £3, students free. Free; £1 donation requested.)*

🏛 **HUNTERIAN MUSEUM.** Buried within the grandiose Royal College of Surgeons, this museum is not for the squeamish. John Hunter (1728-1793), considered the founder of modern surgery, had a keen interest in the anatomy of all living things. Only 3500 of his original 14,000 colorless pickled organs survived the Blitz, but that's enough to fill endless shelves. Among the viscera are some genuine marvels, generally of the freak-show variety—like the 7 ft. 7 in. skeleton of the 'Irish Giant' and the twisted bones of an anchylosed man. (35-43 Lincoln's Inn Fields; the street numbers aren't marked—enter via the columned main entrance to the RCS building. ☎ 7869 6560; www.rcseng.ac.uk/services/museums. Tube: Holborn. Closed for redevopment until late 2004; call for hours. Free.)

SOMERSET HOUSE

◪ Location: Strand, just east of Waterloo Bridge; **Tube:** Charing Cross or Temple.. **Open:** Daily 10am-6pm.

The elegant Somerset House (see **Sights**, p. 86) holds the Courtauld Institute Galleries, the Hermitage Rooms, and the Gilbert Collection (see below). Despite all having the same location and hours, each has its own separate admission price and contact information. Visitors receive £1 off tickets to both of the other collections after purchasing a ticket to one of the three.

▨ THE COURTAULD INSTITUTE GALLERIES. The Courtauld's small but outstanding collection ranges from 14th-century Italian religious works to 20th-century abstractions, with hallowed representatives from every period in between. Not limited solely to paintings, the three floors of the Courtald house sculpture, decorative arts, prints, and drawings. Works are arranged chronologically, emphasizing each artist's personal growth and the development of wider trends. The ground-floor **Renaissance** gallery features some of the finest triptychs in Europe. Diverse **15th- and 16th-century** works are on display on the first floor. Highlights include the Rubens room, Botticelli's *Christ on the Cross*, and Peter Brueghel's cold and eerie *Christ and the Woman Taken in Adultery*. The focus of the third floor is on **Impressionist and Post-Impressionist** art, and houses the undisputed gems of the collection: Manet's *A Bar at the Follies Bergères*, and van Gogh's *Self-Portrait with Bandaged Ear*, as well as works by Cézanne, Monet, Degas, Renoir, and Gauguin. The newly expanded top floor also contains over 100 new 20th-century works, including some exquisite sculptures by Rodin and an impressive collection of Kandinskys. (☎ 7420 9400; www.gilbert-collection.org.uk. 1hr. tours held Sa 2:30pm; £6.50, concessions £6, including admission. £5, concessions £4, disabled guests £4, under-18s free; free after 4:30pm.)

▨ THE GILBERT COLLECTION. The Gilbert Collection of Decorative Arts opened in 2000, the product of a spectacularly generous gift from Sir Arthur Gilbert to the British people. The emphasis here is on extraordinary detail, incomparable craftsmanship, and exquisite materials. The Gilbert Collection's 800 objects fall into three categories: mosaics, gold and silver, and snuffboxes. Sir Arthur's collection of the latter is considered by many to be among the finest in the world, with over 200 examples—including six made for Frederick the Great, each encrusted with diamonds, rubies, and emeralds. The collection of mosaics, the most comprehensive ever formed, is equally impressive, as are the over 7 ft. tall "Russian Gates." Be sure to spend time viewing the micromosaics carefully; to fully appreciate the brilliant craftsmanship of these pieces, you'll need to pick up a complimentary magnifying glass at the front desk. You can also access the King's Barge House, a reminder that the Thames once came up to the walls of Somerset House. (☎ 7420 9400; www.gilbert-collection.org.uk. 1hr. tours held Sa 2:30pm; £6.50, concessions £6, including admission. £5, concessions £4, disabled guests £4, under-18s free; free after 4:30pm.)

THE HERMITAGE ROOMS. A unique chance to get a taste of the renowned Hermitage art museum without going to St. Petersburg, Russia. The five rooms in the south wing of the Somerset House have been recreated as smaller replicas of the Winter Palace in St. Petersburg, down to the door fittings and floor patterns, all of which were done by Russian craftsmen. All this recreated elegance almost overshadows

The Tate modern

British Library

Antiquities Collection

the paintings on loan from the big brother in Russia, exchanged for new ones every six months to keep things fresh. In case you want to check your experience against the real thing, the main room has a live webcast from the museum in Russia. (☎ 7485 4630; www.hermitage-rooms.org.uk. £6, concessions £4, under 16 free.)

KENSINGTON & EARL'S COURT

🔢 KENSINGTON & EARL'S COURT QUICKFIND: Sights, p. 88; **Food & Drink,** p. 153; **Pubs,** p. 176; **Entertainment,** p. 210; **Shopping,** p. 229; **Accommodations,** p. 259. . For the **Victoria & Albert Museum,** see Major Collections, p. 123.

SEE MAP, pp. 366-367

South Kensington's Albertopolis (see p. 89) is home to three of London's biggest and best museums: the **Victoria & Albert Museum** (see p. 123), the **Natural History Museum,** and the **Science Museum.** While it's tempting to try and "do" them in a day, visiting more than two is a feat of superhuman stamina. While most people just take the signposted feeder tunnels from the Tube to the museums, it's just as quick (and far more pleasant in good weather) to use the overland route.

🏛 NATURAL HISTORY MUSEUM

🔢 Location: Cromwell Rd. **Contact:** ☎7942 5000; www.nhm.ac.uk. **Tube:** South Kensington. **Open:** M-Sa 10am-5:50pm; Su 11am-5:50pm; last admission 5:30pm. **Tours:** 45min. highlights tours hourly 11am-4pm; reserve places at the main info desk. Free. **Admission:** Free; special exhibits usually £5, concessions £3.

Architecturally the most impressive of the South Kensington trio, this cathedral-like Romanesque building has been a favorite with Londoners since 1880. The entrance hall is dedicated to the **Wonders of the Natural History Museum,** a series of historically important skeletons including a diplodocus and a moa. The **Life Galleries** offer insight into the minds of the curators—the relative importance of the displays perfectly mirrors the natural inclinations of school-aged children. The **Dinosaur** galleries will not disappoint the *Jurassic Park* generation: the animatronic T-Rex (complete with bad breath) is so popular that late 2003 sees an exhibit dedicated entirely to him.

The enormous **Human Biology** exhibition keeps adults and children intrigued with an endless succession of interactive and hi-tech displays, not to mention an extremely detailed reproduction gallery. Other galleries deal with their subjects more traditionally, with dozens of stuffed reptiles, birds, and mammals—the uncontested centerpiece of the mammalian display is the massive blue whale suspended from the ceiling. The **Origin of Species** display on the first floor offers a detailed explanation of evolution, from Darwin's finches to genetic engineering.

If anything, the **Earth Galleries** are even more engrossing, reached via a long escalator that pierces a giant model of the earth on its way to **The Power Within,** an exposition of the awesome volcanic and tectonic forces beneath the earth's surface. A walk-through model of a Japanese supermarket provides a literally earth-shaking recreation of the 1995 Kobe earthquake. On the same floor, **Restless Surface** explores the gentler action of wind and water in reshaping the world. The history of the Earth itself, from the big bang to the way life has shaped the environment, is the subject of **From the Beginning,** on the first floor, while the **Earth's Treasury** presents an enormous array of minerals, from sandstone to diamonds. Phase One of the cutting-edge **Darwin Center** on the ground floor opened in September 2002 and now houses 100 scientists and 22 million specimens, most of which are on display.

▨ SCIENCE MUSEUM

🔢 *Location:* Exhibition Rd. *Contact:* ☎ *0870 870 4868, IMAX* ☎ *0870 870 4771; www.science-museum.org.uk. Tube: South Kensington. Open: Daily 10am-6pm. Audiotours:* "Soundbytes" *audio stories covering* Power, Space, *and* Making the Modern World *£3.50.* **IMAX** *cinema: Shows usually every 75min., 10:45am-5pm daily; £7.10, concessions £5.95. Call to confirm showtimes and for bookings. Activities: Daily demonstrations and workshops in the basement galleries and theater. Admission: Free.*

Dedicated to the Victorian ideal of Progress (with a capital P), the Science Museum focuses on the transformative power of technology in all its guises. There's something for everyone in this mix of state-of-the-art interactive displays, priceless historical artifacts, and some truly mind-numbing galleries (standard weights and measures? light bulbs?). The gigantic **Making of the Modern World** entrance hall houses a collection of pioneering contraptions from "Puffing Billy" (1814), the oldest surviving steam locomotive, to the Apollo 10 command module, by way of Crick and Watson's original 1953 wire model of DNA, a beautiful chrome Lockheed Electra, and hundreds of other genuine artifacts. Nearby, **Space** makes do with mostly replica rockets, but video displays provide a thorough history of rocketry from Napoleonic artillery to modern missiles. The third-floor **Flight** gallery tells the story of air travel from Victorian attempts at steam-powered flight to jumbo jets, assisted by a supporting cast of dozens of airplanes and the hands-on **Flight Lab,** with a literally suck-it-and-see approach to aerodynamics. Children will love the basement: if the **Garden,** for kids aged 6 and under, and **Things,** for 7-11s, are of more entertainment than educational value, **Launch Pad** provides an enjoyable introduction to do-it-yourself science for adults and teens. Communicate across the room using giant sound dishes, try building an arch, or solve the "hangover problem." **The Science and Art of Medicine,** on the top floor, chronicles in impressive detail the history of medicine in its modern and cross-cultural incarnations. The newest part of the museum is the blue-lit **Wellcome Wing,** dominated by the overhead curve of the vast **IMAX** cinema. In the wing's main hall, consoles explain the wonders of cutting-edge technology while others provide a primer on global warming and its potential effects. September 2003 sees a *Lord of the Rings* exhibition featuring artwork and costumes from the movie trilogy (until spring 2004).

EXHIBITION SPACES

Serpentine Gallery, off West Carriage Dr., Kensington Gardens (☎ 7402 6075; www.serpentinegallery.org). Tube: South Kensington, Lancaster Gate, or High St. Kensington. This discreet, brick pavilion in the middle of the gardens is the unlikely venue for some of London's top contemporary art shows. Summer park nights in the pavilion include architecture talks, live readings, and open-air film screenings; most £5, concessions £4. Open daily 10am-6pm, F late-view until 10pm. Free.

MARYLEBONE & REGENT'S PARK

SEE MAP, p. 369

▶ MARYLEBONE & REGENT'S PARK QUICKFIND: *Sights,* p. 92; *Food & Drink,* p. 155; *Entertainment,* p. 211; *Accommodations,* p. 262.

▓ THE WALLACE COLLECTION

▶ Location: *Hertford House, Manchester Sq.* **Contact:** ☎ 7563 9500; www.wallace-collection.com. **Tube:** *Bond St. or Marble Arch.* **Open:** *M-Sa 10am-5pm, Su noon-5pm.* **Tours:** *W and Sa 11:30am and Su 3pm (1hr.); free.* **Talks:** *M-F 1pm and occasional Sa 11:30am; free.* **Admission:** *Free.*

Housed in palatial Hertford House, this stunning array of paintings, porcelain, and armor was bequeathed to the nation by the widow of Sir Richard Wallace in 1897. On the **ground floor,** the Front State Room retains its original appearance, with sumptuous furnishings and society portraits. China buffs will swoon at the collection of Sèvres porcelain in the Back State Room next door. Italian and Flemish works dominate the 16th-Century Galleries and Smoking Room, including some fascinating relief miniatures and a number of beautiful historiated initials. The pride of the ground floor, though, is the four **Armoury Galleries,** crammed with richly decorated weapons and burnished suits of armor. Don't miss the beautiful 15th-century German Gothic horse armor, a complete, recently refurbished suit of armor for horse and rider. The **first floor** is home to a world-renowned array of 18th-century French art, announced on the staircase by various works by Boucher, including the *Rising* and *Setting of the Sun,* all billowing clouds and trembling pink flesh. More Bouchers occupy the West Room and West Gallery, while the Small Drawing Room displays a series of Venice views by Canaletto and Guardi. The **Great Gallery** has a varied collection of 17th-century work, with works by van Dyck, Rembrandt, Rubens, and Velázquez as well as the collection's most celebrated piece, Frans Hals' *Laughing Cavalier.* In the modern basement, the **Conservation Gallery** has a small display on the manufacture of furniture and armor, including some pieces you can try on.

OTHER PERMANENT COLLECTIONS

SHERLOCK HOLMES MUSEUM. This museum claims to be the real 19th-century residence of Sherlock Holmes and Doctor Watson based on a few thin coincidences (and the belief that these fictional characters existed at all). It doesn't take a master sleuth to see that there is more fiction than fact here, but die-hard fans may find it worth the six quid. (*"221b Baker St."; actually at 239.* ☎ *7935 8866; www.sherlockholmes.co.uk. Tube: Baker St. Open daily 9:30am-6:30pm. £6, ages 7-16 £4.*)

THE SOUTH BANK

SEE MAP, pp. 370-371

▶ SOUTH BANK QUICKFIND: *Sights,* p. 95; *Food & Drink,* p. 157; *Pubs,* p. 177; *Entertainment,* p. 219; *Accommodations,* p. 263. For *Tate Modern,* see Major Collections, p. 123.

Anchored by the gigantic **Tate Modern** (see p. 123), the South Bank is home to some of London's top public contemporary art galleries, from established masters at the Hayward to promising newcomers at the Jerwood. In addition to the galleries listed below, there are also frequent exhibitions in the foyer and sculptural displays on the river terrace of the **Royal Festival Hall** (see p. 95). Design aficionados will drool at the **Design Museum** and the innovative works on show in the workshops and galleries of **OXO Tower Wharf** (see p. 97).

PERMANENT COLLECTIONS

DESIGN MUSEUM. Housed in a classic Art Deco riverfront building, this thoroughly contemporary museum is the brainchild of design maestro Terence Conran. Like those in the **Saatchi Gallery** (below), the ever-changing marvels in the Design Museum mostly cater to the young, hip, well-dressed crowd. Everyone will enjoy the **Interaction Space** on the bright and airy top floor, which includes a colorful variety of household items (some hands-on) and a bay of vintage video games (which you can play) that inspired contemporary gaming. Early 2004 will feature work by British architects and pop artists Peter and Alison Smithson (until February 29). The **Museum Café** on the first floor—not to be confused with the considerably pricier **Blue Print Café** one story up—serves an array of sweet treats as aesthetically pleasing as anything you'll find in the galleries upstairs. *(28 Shad Thames, Butlers Wharf. ☎ 7403 6933; www.designmuseum.org. Tube: Tower Hill or London Bridge. Open daily 10am-5:45pm, last entry 5:15pm. £6, students £4, under 15 and over-60s £4, family (2 adults and 2 children) £16.)*

THE CLINK PRISON MUSEUM. Satisfyingly onomatopoeic, the original jail on this site was so notorious that all English prisoners are said to be "in the clink." The Clink was the private prison of the Bishop of Winchester from the 13th century until rioters burned it down in 1780. Truly an equal-opportunity site, it was the first prison where women were confined for punishment. Now a Victorian warehouse occupies the site, but the mildly diverting museum in the basement attempts to chill visitors with tales of medieval punishments, complete with waxwork inmates and torture tools. Just past the museum on Clink St. stand the remains of the Bishop's **Winchester Palace.** *(1 Clink St. ☎ 7378 1558; www.clink.co.uk. Tours £1, on demand. Tube: London Bridge. Open daily 10am-6pm. £4, concessions £3, families £9.)*

EXHIBITION SPACES

Fashion and Textile Museum, 83 Bermondsey St. (☎ 7403 0222; www.ftmlondon.org). Brand-new space in an up-and-coming South Bank area that aims to collect and display the best of fashion and textiles from the 1950s to the present. Exhibits change about once every 3-4 months and cover all aspects of the fashion world, including photography. The gallery will also feature an upcoming permament collection; call or check website for exhibition dates and times. £6, concessions £4.

Hayward Gallery, South Bank Centre (☎ 7960 4242; www.hayward.org.uk). Tube: Waterloo, Embankment, or Temple. Behind the Royal Festival Hall, this stark modernist block, recognizable by its signature roof sculpture, is the South Bank Centre's appropriately high-powered artistic wing. Contemporary art predominates, with occasional forays into the early 20th century. Call ahead as the gallery closes between exhibitions. Open M, Th-Su 10am-6pm, W 10am-8pm. £7, concessions £5, under-12s free.

Saatchi Gallery, County Hall (☎ 7823 2363; www.saatchi-gallery.co.uk). Tube: Waterloo or Westminster. Charles Saatchi, famous for supporting young and provocative artists, relocated his gallery from North London to the South Bank in the spring of 2003. This enormous wood-panelled space in County Hall showcases some of the most innovative and most incendiary contemporary Britart. Past exhibitions have featured such YBAs (young British artists) as Damien Hirst, Marcus Harvey, and Chris Ofili. Primarily focused on Saatchi's own collection, the Saatchi Gallery is not for the faint-hearted. Open Su-Th 10am-6pm, F-Sa 10-10pm. £8.50, concessions £6.50.

Bankside Gallery, 48 Hopton St. (☎ 7928 7521; www.banksidegallery.com). Tube: Blackfriars. Entrance on Riverside Terr. Run jointly by the Royal Watercolour Society and the Royal Society of Painter Printmakers, this small gallery mostly displays members' works. The exception is the annual Open Exhibition (held in July), when anyone can submit watercolors for inclusion. Open Tu-F 10am-5pm, Sa-Su 11am-5pm. £3.50, concessions £2; some exhibitions free.

Jerwood Space, 171 Union St. (☎ 7654 0171; www.jerwoodspace.co.uk). Tube: Southwark or Borough. Also a center for performing arts, the Jerwood Space gives promising young artists a leg up, most famously by hosting the prestigious Jerwood Painting Prize exhibition (early May to mid-June). Six yearly exhibitions include works from the new Jerwood Artists Platform as well as the Sculpture Prize and Drawing Prize. Open Su 1-6pm, Tu-Sa 11am-6pm. Free.

THE WEST END

SEE MAP, p. 356

⊠ THE WEST END QUICKFIND: Sights, p. 98; **Food & Drink,** p. 158; **Pubs,** p. 178; **Nightlife** p. 188; **Entertainment,** p. 213; **Shopping,** p. 233; **Accommodations,** p. 263.

⊠ LONDON'S TRANSPORT MUSEUM

⊠ Location: Southeast corner of Covent Garden Piazza. **Contact:** ☎7565 7299; www.ltmuseum.co.uk. **Tube:** Covent Garden. **Open:** M-Th and Sa-Su 10am-6pm, F 11am-6pm; last admission 5:15pm. **Admission:** £6, concessions £4.50, under 16 free with adult.

The LTM is one of those rarest of museums—informative *and* fun. Adults will be engrossed in the history of London's public transportation system as children happily clamber over the buses, trams, and Tube trains; most of the interactive displays are conveniently located at kiddy-level. Tube simulators show firsthand how Underground trains have evolved from steam-powered relics to cutting-edge coasters, while the "Fast Forward" display explores the future of transport, from sci-fi hovercars to teleportation. The museum shop sells must-have "Angel" Tube-logo T-shirts (£13), as well as the world-famous London Underground posters (£5-10) whose design was originally rejected by London Transport. Eventually, designer Harry Beck was paid for his 1933 job—the handsome sum of £5.25.

THEATRE MUSEUM. The entrance hall, with a display of giant puppets, is the high point of a rather dry set of displays about the history of showbiz in London. Of note are the "Wind in the Willows" main gallery, which describes the process of producing a play, and an impressive selection of opera and ballet costumes, with original pieces from the *Ballets Russes* (Russian Ballet). Children will enjoy the make-up demos (daily 11:30am, Sa noon, 1, 2:30, 3:30, and 4:30pm) and costume workshops (12:30 and 2:30pm). (Russell St. ☎7943 4700; www.theatremuseum.org. Tube: Covent Garden. Open Tu-Sa 10am-6pm, last admission 5:30pm. Guided tours noon, 2, and 3:30pm. Free.)

EXHIBITION SPACES

⊠ Royal Academy of Art Burlington House, Piccadilly (☎7300 8000; www.royalacademy.org.uk). Tube: Piccadilly Circus or Green Park. Founded in 1768 as both an art school and meeting place for Britain's foremost artists, the Academy rapidly consolidated its position as the mouthpiece of the establishment. Rebellious young artists scorn it as the deathbed of innovation, only to swoon a few years later at the offer of becoming one of the 80 exalted Academicians who run the place. Exhibitions, whether in the ornate main galleries or the minimalist top-floor Sackler extension, are always of the highest standard. The **Summer Exhibition** (June-Aug.), held every year since 1769, is open-submission, providing an unparalleled range of contemporary art, much of which is available for purchase. Exhibitions for 2004 include: **Illuminating the Renaissance** (Nov. 29, 2003-Feb. 22, 2004); **Vuillard** (Jan. 31-Apr. 18, 2004); and **The Dog Ate My Homework**, a collection of Chris Orr's print work (starts May 23, 2004). F nights **free jazz** in Friends room after 6:30pm, and **candlelit suppers** in the cafe (2 courses £14, 3 courses £17). Open Sa-Th 10am-6pm, F 10am-10pm. Around £7 per exhibition; seniors £6, students £5.

⊠ Institute of Contemporary Arts (ICA), Nash House, the Mall (☎7930 3647; www.ica.org.uk). Tube: Charing Cross or Piccadilly Circus. A grand Neoclassical building just down the road from Buckingham Palace is the last place you'd expect to find Britain's national center for the subversion of the contemporary art world—but at least it's conveniently located for attacking the establishment. This arts complex contains galleries for temporary exhibitions, an avant-garde cinema, a theater, and a groovy late bar that hosts frequent club nights and gigs. Open M noon-11pm, Tu-Sa noon-1am, Su noon-10:30pm; galleries close 7:30pm. "Day membership," giving access to galleries and cafe/bar £1.50 M-F (concessions £1), £2.50 Sa-Su (concessions £1.50). Cinema £6.50, M-F before 5pm £5.50; concessions £5.50/£4.50.

MUSEUMS MUSEUMS BY NEIGHBORHOOD

The Photographers' Gallery, 5 and 8 Great Newport St. (☎ 7831 1772; www.photonet.org.uk). Tube: Leicester Sq. London's only public gallery devoted entirely to camerawork (including film and video). 2 exhibitions run concurrently at each location, addressing fine-art and social-documentary photography. The small bookshop (no. 8) has a good selection of photographic monologues. Also frequent talks and film screenings. Open M-Sa 11am-6pm, Su noon-6pm. Free.

COMMERCIAL GALLERIES & AUCTION HOUSES

Mayfair is the center of London's art market—and despite the genteel aura, it's not all Old Masters and Prince Charles's watercolors. **Cork St.,** running parallel to Old Bond St. between Clifford St. and Burlington Gdns., is lined with dozens of **commercial galleries** specializing in contemporary art. Nearby roads also have a number of avant-garde galleries. This is the place to pick up on new trends before the museums get in on the act; most exhibitions are of very high quality, and commercial galleries are always free to browsers.

Chinese Lantern

Annely Juda Fine Art, 23 Dering St. (☎ 7629 7578; www.annelyjudafineart.co.uk). Tube: Bond St. On the 3rd and 4th fl. (use elevator). Specializes in early Russian avant-garde and contemporary Japanese art, but also shows big Anglo-American artists like Anthony Caro and David Hockney. Open M-F 10am-6pm, Sa 10am-1pm. Free.

Christie's, 8 King St. (☎ 7839 9060; www.christies.com). Tube: Green Park. With a welcoming staff, Christie's is open to the public on the days before an auction to display what's up for grabs—galleries range from medieval manuscripts to European furniture. Open M-F 9am-4:30pm; during sales also Tu to 8pm and Su 2-5pm. Free.

British Museum Great Court

Gagosian Gallery, 8 Heddon St. (☎ 7292 8222). Tube: Piccadilly Circus. Holds solo shows of contemporary artists represented by their respected New York-based gallery. Open Tu-Sa 10am-6pm. Free.

Marlborough Fine Arts, 6 Albermarle St. (☎ 7629 5161; www.marlboroughfineart.com). Tube: Green Park. Spacious gallery presents variety of contemporary masters, from Lucian Freud to Frank Auerbach. Open M-F 10am-5:30pm, Sa 10am-12:30pm. Free.

Robert Sandelson, 5 Cork St. (☎ 7439 1001; www.robertsandelson.com). Tube: Bond St. or Green Park. 2 floors of big-time modern and contemporary artists. One 2002 show was devoted entirely to Andy Warhol. Open M-F 10am-6pm, Sa 11am-4pm. Free.

Sotheby's, 34-35 New Bond St. (☎ 7293 5000; www.sothebys.com). Tube: Bond St. Before each auction, the items to be sold are displayed for view-

Royal Academy of Art

Museum of London

National Gallery

ing in the many galleries. Anything and everything of value passes through these halls, from violins to Old Masters. Each sale is accompanied by a glossy catalog (£6-30); old catalogs usually half-price. Open for viewing M-F 9am-4:30pm, Sa and some Su noon-4pm. Free.

WESTMINSTER

SEE MAP, p. 372

🎗 **WESTMINSTER QUICK-FIND: Sights,** p. 104; **Food & Drink,** p. 162; **Pubs,** p. 179; **Entertainment,** p. 216; **Accommodations,** p. 264. For the **National Gallery,** see Major Collections, p. 121. For **Tate Britain,** see Major Collections, p. 122.

🎗 CABINET WAR ROOMS

🎗 **Location:** Clive Steps, King Charles St. **Contact:** ☎ 7766 0130; www.iwm.org.uk/cabinet. **Tube:** Westminster. **Open:** Apr.-Sept. daily 9:30am-6pm; Oct.-Mar. 10am-6pm; last admission 5:15pm. **Admission:** £7, concessions £5.50, disabled £2.70, under 16 free.

In 1938, as storm clouds gathered over Europe, work started on converting the coal cellars of the Ministry of Works into the bomb-proof nerve center of a nation at war. For six tense years, Churchill, his cabinet and generals, and dozens of support staff lived and worked in these dank, low-ceilinged quarters. The day after the war ended in 1945, they were abandoned, shut up, and left undisturbed for decades until their reopening in 1984 by Margaret Thatcher. A Churchillian-voiced audioguide talks you through the 19 rooms on show, supplemented with original recordings of Churchill's speeches and recreations that bring them to life. Highlights include "Churchill's personal loo"—a small room containing the top-secret transatlantic hotline—and the perfectly preserved Cabinet Room (accurate right down to the paperclips). The observant visitor will notice that all the clocks read two minutes before five, the moment Churchill called the Cabinet's first official meeting, one day after a German blitz on London. Plans are underway to open an elaborate **Churchill Museum** here in 2005.

NATIONAL PORTRAIT GALLERY

🎗 **Location:** St. Martin's Pl., at the start of Charing Cross Rd., Trafalgar Sq. **Contact:** ☎ 7312 2463; www.npg.org.uk. **Tube:** Leicester Sq. or Charing Cross. **Open:** M-W and Sa-Su 10am-6pm, Th-F 10am-9pm. **Wheelchairs:** Enter on Orange St. **Audioguides:** Free; £4 suggested donation. **Lectures:** Sa-Su 3pm,

The British Museum

Tu and Th 1:10pm; free, but popular events require tickets, available from the info desk. **Evening Events:** *Talks Th 7:30pm; free-£3. Live classical and jazz music every F 6:30pm; free.* **Admission:** *Free; exhibitions free-£6.*

This artistic *Who's Who* in Britain began in 1856 as "the fulfillment of a patriotic and moral ideal," and was recently bolstered by the addition of the sleek Ondaatje Wing. New facilities include a **Micro Gallery**, with computers allowing you to search for pictures and print out a personalized tour, and a 3rd-floor **restaurant** offering some of the best views in London—although the inflated prices (meals around £15) will limit most visitors to a coffee.

To see the paintings in historical order, take the escalator from the Ondaatje reception hall to the top-floor Tudor gallery, and work your way around and down to the contemporary works on the ground floor. The size of the collection, however, makes a complete tour of the gallery an exhausting prospect, not helped by endless galleries of bewhiskered Victorians. More popular highlights are few until you get to the 20th century and post-war galleries with Mike McCartney's snaps of his brother and friends, and Andy Warhol's portrait of the Queen.

OTHER PERMANENT COLLECTIONS

QUEEN'S GALLERY. "God Save the Queen" is the rallying cry at this recently-opened gallery dedicated to changing exhibitions of items from the Royal Collection. An extraordinary selection of Faberge's work will be on display until March 2004. Five exquisite rooms extol the glory of Her Majesty in numerous art forms—the finest pieces of the Royal Collection that the tourist can view, with the exception of the State Rooms. *(Buckingham Palace Rd. ☎ 7839 1377. Tube: St. James's Park. Open daily 10am-5:30pm, last admission 4:30pm. £6.50, concessions £5.)*

NORTH LONDON

▶ NORTH LONDON QUICKFIND: **Sights**, p. 107; **Food & Drink**, p. 163; **Pubs**, p. 180; **Nightlife**, p. 192; **Entertainment**, p. 216; **Shopping**, p. 240; **Accommodations**, p. 265.

THE IVEAGH BEQUEST. One of the finest small galleries in London, the impressive collection in Kenwood House was bequeathed to the nation by the Earl of Iveagh, who purchased the estate in 1922. Highlights include one of 35 Vermeers in the world, Rembrandt's most compelling self-portraits, and a beautiful Botticelli. The majority of these old masters are housed in the plush dining room. More consistent with the feel of the house are numerous Georgian society portraits by Reynolds, Gainsborough, and Romney. *(Kenwood House; for directions, see p. 109. ☎ 8348 1286. Audioguide £3.50, concessions £2.60, children £1.75; Open Apr.-Sept. Sa-Tu and Th 10am-6pm, W and F 10:30am-6pm; Oct. closes 5pm; Nov.-Mar. closes 4pm. Free.)*

ROYAL AIR FORCE MUSEUM. This enormous museum contains three huge hangars of planes, from the first plane made in Europe to 1980s Harriers. All can be viewed close-up. Details of each plane's combat missions add to the realism, though it still feels like an oversized model exhibition. Beyond the planes, galleries consist of the typical wax models and reconstructions, mixed with medallions and memorabilia. *Our Finest Hour*, a somewhat kitschy 15min. laser light show that starts on the hour, is probably only worth it if there is no wait. *(Grahame Park Way. ☎ 8205 2266; www.rafmuseum.com. Follow signs from the Tube: Colindale (Zone 4)—it's a 15min. walk. Open daily 10am-6pm; last admission 5:30pm. Free.)*

FREUD MUSEUM. The comfortable home in which Sigmund Freud spent the last year of his life after fleeing the Nazis evokes a little more than most celebrity houses. In his later years, Freud delved into cultural analysis, evidenced by the anthropological collection of masks and "old and dirty gods." He didn't drop his patients, however, and the infamous rug-covered couch in his study stands ready for the next session. Upstairs hangs Dalí's portrait of Freud alongside the room of Anna Freud, Sigmund's youngest daughter, who was an eminent psychoanalyst in her own right.

She practiced in the house until her death in 1982. *(20 Maresfield Gdns. ☎ 7435 2002; www.freud.org.uk. Tube: Swiss Cottage or Finchley Rd. Open W-Su noon-5pm; £5, concessions £2, under-12s free. Children over 12 can blame it on their parents.)*

ESTORICK COLLECTION. The Futurists' revolutionary manifesto included destroying old buildings, abolishing museums, celebrating the noise of machinery, reinventing food (recipes included sausage cooked in black coffee and perfume), and making the universe affordable for everyone. Ninety years after their heyday, their paintings, drawings, etchings, and sculptures are tastefully displayed in an 18th-century Georgian mansion with a secluded courtyard cafe. There are also works from the Metaphysical school. Temporary exhibitions change about every three months. *(39a Canonbury Sq. ☎ 7704 9522; www.estorickcollection.com. Tube: Highbury and Islington. Open W-Sa 11am-6pm, Su noon-5pm. £3.50, seniors £2.50, students and under 16 free.)*

THE JEWISH MUSEUM. Actually two complementary museums. The **Jewish Museum, Camden,** focuses on regalia and artifacts with the upstairs holding a display of table settings for each Jewish festival; pride of place goes to a magnificent 16th-century Venetian synagogue ark. *(129-131 Albert St. ☎ 7284 1997. Tube: Camden Town. Open M-Th 10am-4pm, Su 10am-5pm; closed Su in Aug. and Jewish holidays. £3.50, seniors £2.50, students and children £1.50, family £8.)* The **Jewish Museum, Finchley,** which is smaller but more compelling, focuses on 19th- and early 20th-century life in London's East End. The small Holocaust Education gallery is particularly moving, detailing the life of London-born Auschwitz survivor Leon Greenman, who visits the museum every Sunday to answer questions. *(80 East End Rd. ☎ 8349 1143. Tube: Finchley Central (Zone 4). Take the "Regent's Park Rd." exit from the Tube, turn left into Station Rd., then right into Manor View, which runs into East End Rd. by the museum; 10min. Open M-Th 10:30am-5pm, Su 10:30am-4:30pm; closed Su in Aug. and Jewish holidays. £2, concessions £1, children free.)*

EXHIBITION SPACES

Crafts Council, 44a Pentonville Rd. (☎ 7278 7700; www.craftscouncil.org.uk). Tube: Angel. Changing exhibitions on contemporary crafts showcase beautiful cutting-edge design by everyone from metalworkers to jewelers to glass artists. Previous exhibitions include *Boys Who Sew*, focusing on male textile artists. The council also displays the work of the Jerwood shortlist artists in the fall. The reference area upstairs includes a library and photo database. Gallery open Tu-Sa 11am-6pm, Su 2-6pm. Free.

SOUTH LONDON

◪ SOUTH LONDON QUICKFIND: Sights, *p. 111;* **Food & Drink,** *p. 166;* **Nightlife,** *p. 194;* **Entertainment,** *p. 219;* **Shopping,** *p. 241.*

▨ IMPERIAL WAR MUSEUM

◪ Location: *Lambeth Rd., Lambeth.* **Contact:** *☎ 7416 5320, recorded info ☎ 7416 5000; www.iwm.org.uk.* **Tube:** *Lambeth North or Elephant & Castle.* **Open:** *Daily 10am-6pm.* **Admission:** *Free.*

Massive 15-inch naval guns guard the entrance to the Imperial War Museum. Formerly the infamous lunatic asylum known as Bedlam, today it illustrates another type of human madness. The **Large Exhibits Hall** features an impressive array of military hardware, from "Little Boy" (dropped on Hiroshima) to Montgomery's tank to a V-2 rocket, all clearly labeled and carefully explained. In the basement, the **Trench Experience** and **Blitz Experience** recreate the conditions of WWI and life on the home front in WWII, respectively. On the first floor, the remarkably high-tech **Secret War** reveals little about intelligence operations—declassification hasn't proceeded much past WWII—but the grand finale, an astounding presentation on Operation NIMROD, makes it all worthwhile. The second-floor art collection, mostly the work of government war artists, is best skipped entirely. The best and most publicized display, the **Holocaust Exhibition,** provides an honest and poignant look at the Holocaust. *(Not recommended for children under 14.)* The **Women in Uniform** exhibit, on the role of women in 20th-century conflicts, will open in October 2003.

■ DULWICH PICTURE GALLERY

⚑ Location: *Gallery Rd., Dulwich.* **Contact:** *☎8693 5254; www.dulwichpicturegallery.org.uk.* **Rail:** *North Dulwich or West Dulwich, or* **Tube:** *Brixton and bus P4 to the door. From West Dulwich station, turn right onto Thurlow Park Rd., then left onto Gallery Rd. and follow the signs; from North Dulwich, cross East Dulwich Grove and follow Red Post Hill to Gallery Rd.* **Open:** *Tu-F 10am-5pm, Sa-Su 11am-5pm.* **Tours:** *Sa-Su 3pm; free.* **Admission:** *£4, seniors £3, students and under 16 free; F free.*

Dubbed "the most beautiful small art gallery in the world" by the *Sunday Telegraph*, England's first public gallery is the unlikely legacy of Polish misfortune. In 1790, the King of Poland decided to invest in a national art collection and commissioned two London dealers to buy up the best pictures available. Unfortunately for the dealers (not to mention the Poles), the partition of Poland in 1795 left them with a full-blown, unpaid-for collection in hand. Rather than selling the works they decided to put them on public display. The benefactors are buried in a domed mausoleum at the center of the gallery (designed by Sir John Soane), and the high-ceilinged halls house a stunning collection of mostly 17th- and 18th-century work from the Dutch, Spanish, Italian, French, and English schools of painting. Rubens and van Dyck feature prominently, while other Dutch masterpieces include Rembrandt's *A Girl at a Window.*

OTHER PERMANENT COLLECTIONS

HORNIMAN MUSEUM & GARDENS. This eccentric museum is the legacy of 19th-century tea merchant Frederick Horniman. The **African Worlds** gallery offers a small but rich selection of artifacts from past and present African cultures: Benin brass plaques are dwarfed by the world's largest *Ijele* (Nigerian masquerade costume). A marvel of taxidermy, the **Natural History** collection features stuffed animals and skeletons behind glass cases with an eye to the under-12 set. A colorful assortment of fish in waterfall tanks constitutes the tiny **Living Worlds** aquarium. The **Music Gallery,** which opened in 2002, displays instruments new and old alongside music boxes and other children's toys. The neighboring hillside **garden** holds a tiny domestic zoo and offers brilliant views of St. Paul's in the distance. *(100 London Rd. ☎8699 1872; www.horniman.ac.uk. Rail: Forest Hill plus a 15min. walk, or P4 bus (request stop) from Tube: Brixton. Open daily 10:30am-5:30pm. Free.)*

FLORENCE NIGHTINGALE MUSEUM. On the grounds of St. Thomas' Hospital, where Florence Nightingale's first school of nursing opened in 1860. The museum goes out of its way to show that nursing was just one of Florence's many pioneering talents. Precocious since childhood, she also reformed the army, designed hospitals, and lobbied for the foundation of a public health service in India. *(St. Thomas' Hospital, 2 Lambeth Palace Rd.; look for the ramp down to the museum near the corner of the hospital. ☎7620 0374; www.florence-nightingale.co.uk. Tube: Waterloo or Westminster. Open M-F 10am-5pm, Sa-Su 11:30am-4:30pm; last entry 1hr. before closing. £4.80, concessions £3.80, family (2 adults and 2 children) £12.)*

EAST LONDON

⚑ EAST LONDON QUICKFIND: Sights, *p. 112;* **Food & Drink,** *p. 167;* **Pubs,** *p. 181;* **Nightlife,** *p. 196;* **Entertainment,** *p. 219;* **Shopping,** *p. 242.*

GREENWICH

■ NATIONAL MARITIME MUSEUM

⚑ Location: *Trafalgar Rd., between the Royal Naval College and Greenwich Park.* **Contact:** *☎8858 4422; www.nmm.ac.uk.* **DLR:** *Cutty Sark.* **Open:** *June to early Sept. daily 10am-6pm; early Sept. to May 10am-5pm; last entry 30min. before closing.* **Admission:** *Free.*

The NMM's impressive displays cover almost every aspect of seafaring history. Child-friendliness is achieved with galleries designed to resemble a nautical theme park: the **Explorers** section recreates an Antarctic ice-cave and a ship's foredeck. Be careful—once children enter the **All Hands** interactive gallery, complete with steamship and canon-aiming simulators, it's hard to get them out. Not for the squeamish, but very enjoyable, the **Skin Deep** exhibit traces the history of tattooing from an encounter between Captain Cook's men and Polynesians up to the present day. Under the glass canopy, the **Future of the Sea** is a stark warning of how man's activities are affecting the maritime environment. The pride of the naval displays, naturally, is the **Nelson Room,** which tells the stirring tale of one 12-year-old midshipman's rise through the ranks—and displays the coat he died in, still stained with blood.

OTHER PERMANENT COLLECTIONS

▩ GEFFRYE MUSEUM. Billed as a "Museum of English Domestic Interiors," this very non-Shoho-esque establishment is surprisingly diverting. The setting—an elaborately restored terrace of 17th-century almhouses—showcases a set of connecting rooms, each painstakingly recreating a specific period in interior design. Yuppie lofts, Elizabethan parlors, and stark post-war sitting rooms are presented with a commendable attention to detail. The curators are not without a sense of humor: Avril Lavigne's voice can be heard from the radio in the "1990-2000" living room, and the table is strewn with glossy women's magazines. The space also houses excellent temporary exhibits and a Design Centre for local artists to display their craft. *(Kingsland Rd. ☎ 7739 9893; www.geffrye-museum.org.uk. Tube: Old St., then bus #243 or 10min. walk along Old St. and left into Kingsland Rd.; or Tube: Liverpool St. and bus #149 or 242. Open Tu-Sa 10am-5pm, Su noon-5pm. Free.)*

MUSEUM OF CHILDHOOD. In the original V&A building (transferred from Kensington to Bethnal Green in the 1860s), this museum is very popular with families. In order to make the museum more palatable to the thousands of children who visit it daily, the displays of historic toys are interspersed with play areas where children can try out a rocking horse, dress up in fabulous costumes, put on their own puppet show, play games, and generally exhaust their parents. Upstairs, the galleries tracking the history of childhood puzzle boys and girls alike with an invitation to try out a replica 15th-century birthing stool. *(Cambridge Heath Rd. ☎ 8980 2415; www.museumofchildhood.org.uk. Tube: Bethnal Green. Open M-Th, Sa-Su 10am-5:50pm. Free.)*

MAJOR EXHIBITION SPACES

▩ Whitechapel Art Gallery, Whitechapel High St. (☎ 7522 7888; www.whitechapel.org). Tube: Aldgate East. Long the sole artistic beacon in a culturally and materially impoverished area, now at the forefront of the buzzing art scene. Multiple televisions, DVDs, and slideshows emphasize visual appeal. Excellent and often controversial shows of contemporary art on two floors. Highlights for 2004 include "Faces in the Crowd," whch traces the story of figurative modern art and features work by Manet, Picasso, Kahlo, Hopper and Sherman. Open Tu-W and F-Su 11am-6pm, Th 11am-9pm.

Deluxe Gallery, 2-4 Hoxton Sq. Tube: Old St. Hoxton's only public exhibition space provides relief from the navel-gazing antics of many local galleries with a broad range of international contemporary art, often related to current new-media installations and various screenings. Open M-F 11am-6pm, Sa noon-5pm. Free.

COMMERCIAL GALLERIES

The small commercial galleries of Hoxton and Shoreditch, with outposts in Bethnal Green and Hackney, offer visitors their best chance to view the up-and-coming work of the "next big thing." Often controversial and generally free, dozens of these galleries dot the streets of Shoho and the surrounding districts. The best way to ferret out new shows and one-offs is to arm yourself with the determinedly artsy *Shoreditch Map*, available from most galleries and restaurants in the area, and start walking.

Victoria Miro, 16 Wharf Rd. (☎ 7336 8109; www.victoria-miro.com). Tube: Old St. Walk north up City Rd. toward Angel, then turn right after the McDonald's; ring the bell for entry. The curators of this cavernous former warehouse have maximized the impact of its stark interior by keeping exhibits spare and superb. Gallery list includes some of the finest contemporary artists in Britain, including Jake and Dinos Chapman, as well as Chris Ofili and Peter Doig. Open Sept.-July Tu-Sa 10am-6pm; Aug. Tu-W and F-Sa noon-6pm. Free

▨ **White Cube[2],** 48 Hoxton Sq. (☎ 7930 5373; www.whitecube.com). Tube: Old St. One of the small gems of Hoxton Sq., this recently-renovated space has showcased some of the biggest names in international contemporary art, with an emphasis on current British artists. This small but spectacular gallery has shown almost every major contemporary British artist. Open Tu-Sa 10am-6pm. Free.

Food & Drink

Forget stale stereotypes about British food: in terms of quality and choice, London's restaurants offer a gastronomic experience as diverse, stylish, and satisfying as you'll find anywhere on the planet—until you see the bill. For it's a sad truth that while the media scream about food being the new rock'n'roll, and chefs and restaurateurs have become household names, pound-for-pound restaurants in London charge what would be deemed exorbitant prices across the Atlantic or the Channel. Any restaurant charging under £9 for a main course is relatively cheap by London's standards. With drinks and service, the bill for this simple meal nudges £15. The price ranges that are represented by the five different **Price Diversity Icons** ❶, ❷, ❸, ❹, and ❺ are listed below.

ICON	❶	❷	❸	❹	❺
PRICE	under £5	£5-9	£9-12	£13-16	£17+

FOOD BY TYPE

TIPS FOR EATING CHEAPLY

It is possible to eat cheaply—and well—in London. The trick is knowing where and when to eat. If your hostel, B&B, or hotel includes a **"Full English Breakfast"** in its prices, you're half-way there—this cholesterol-laden feast of fried meat, eggs, and bread will probably mean a sandwich for lunch will suffice (see **On the Menu**, p. 149). If you want to spend a little more, lunchtime and early-evening special offers make it possible to dine in style affordably.

143

SANDWICHES. In many parts of central London sandwiches are the only affordable option. Chains such as Prêt-à-Manger and EAT (see p. 147) offer high-quality pre-packed sandwiches, while hundreds of snack bars offer made-to-order "sarnies" for under £2. Note that, if you ask for a ham sandwich, in most cases, you'll get a slice of ham between two pieces of buttered bread: no lettuce, no mayo, and certainly not "overstuffed" to American standards.

PUB GRUB. For a proper sit down meal without the high bill, pubs offer hope. Far more than mere drinking haunts, most pubs offer a range of hot and cold fare during the day and occasionally in the evenings; for around £6 you can lunch on traditional English specials like bangers and mash (sausage and mashed potato) or steak and kidney pie. "Pub grub" may be cheap but note that meals may be left under hot lamps for hours or microwaved from frozen. Find a pub where locals eat, and keep away from the tourist trail. For pub listings, see **Pubs**, p. 171.

EXOTIC TASTES. Many of the best budget meals are found in the amazing variety of **ethnic restaurants.** **Indian** food is recognized as being Britain's unofficial national cuisine—when Prince Charles was asked to describe the archetypal British meal, he shared popular taste and chose the classic Anglo-Indian hybrid chicken tikka masala. **Turkish** restaurants are also experts at cooking up low-budget feasts, while some of the cheapest and tastiest dinners in town are **Chinese.** Recently, **Japanese** cuisine has shed its upmarket image with a proliferation of noodle bars offering giant bowls of *ramen* for £5-6. For the best and cheapest ethnic food, head to the source: Whitechapel for Bengali baltis, Islington for Turkish *meze*, Marylebone for Lebanese *shwarma*, and Soho for Cantonese *dim sum*.

GROCERIES & SUPERMARKETS. Most hostels and student halls have kitchen facilities for residents, and cooking for yourself is almost always cheaper than eating out. The cheapest places to get the ingredients for your own meal in London are often the local markets; for listings of street markets see Shopping p. 223. For all your food under one roof, London's largest supermarket chains are **Tesco, Safeway,** and **Sainsbury's. Asda, Kwik-Save,** and **Somerfield** are "budget" supermarkets, while **Waitrose** and **Marks & Spencer** are more upmarket and a good source of fancier ingredients. For night owls, the branches of **Hart's** stay open 24 hours. And if you're willing to splurge, the food halls of **Harrods, Harvey Nichols, Selfridges,** and **Fortnum & Mason's** are attractions in their own right.

SNACKS. Favorite **chocolate bars** include Flake (a stick of flaky chocolate often stuck into an ice cream cone), Crunchie (honeycombed magic), and the classic Dairy Milk. **Sweets** come in many forms—the fizzy Refreshers, the chewy Wine Gums, or frosted Fruit Pastilles. **Crisps** (potato chips to Americans) come in a range of flavors, including prawn cocktail, cheese & onion, chicken, bacon, and salt & vinegar. All this sugar and salt can be washed down with Lilt, a pineapple and grapefruit flavored **fizzy drink** (soda), or a drinkbox-ful of Ribena, a super-sweet blackcurrant manna from heaven. This latter beverage belongs to a family of drinks known as **squashes**, fruit-based syrups watered down to drink. But the food that expatriate Britons miss most is **Marmite**, a yeast extract which is spread on bread or toast (see **On the Menu**, p. 154).

AFTERNOON TEA

Brown's, Albemarle St. (☎ 7493 6020). Tube: Green Park. Opened by Byron's butler in 1837, London's first luxury hotel still oozes old-fashioned charm. Take tea on comfy settees in the cozy, dark-panelled drawing room. Set tea £25. Dress code: no jeans or sneakers. M-F sittings at 2, 3:45, and 5:30pm (book 1 wk. ahead for Th-F); Sa-Su tea 3-4:45pm (no reservations). AmEx/MC/V.

🔳 **The Lanesborough,** Hyde Park Corner (☎ 7259 5599). Tube: Hyde Park Corner. This converted hospital astounds with both its opulent decor and its steep prices. Traditional afternoon tea served in the large, glass-ceilinged Conservatory, which was modelled on the Prince Regent's lurid oriental-fantasy Brighton Pavilion. You can also order a la carte (scones with jam and clotted cream £6.50), min. charge £9.50 per person. Set tea £24.50, champagne tea £32. Dress code is smart casual—no jeans or sneakers. Open 6:30am-midnight.

Fortnum & Mason, 181 Piccadilly (☎ 7734 8040; see p. 145). This locally popular patio restaurant overlooks the food hall of the Royals' official grocery store. Relatively affordable "special" tea (£12) served M-Sa 3-5:45pm. AmEx/MC/V.

St. Martin's Lane Hotel, 45 St. Martin's Ln. (☎ 7300 5588). Tube: Leicester Sq. Too cool for a sign (look for the yellow-lit revolving door), this white post-modern hotel ditches traditional for avant-garde. £14.50 gets you "Asian" (bento) or "Eurasian" tea. Bewilder your taste buds with the complex flavors. Dress code: casual. Tea served daily 3-5pm. AmEx/MC/V.

The Orangery, Kensington Palace (☎ 7938 1406). Tube: High St. Kensington. Built for Queen Anne's dinner parties, this airy Neoclassical building behind Kensington Palace is popular for light lunches (£8-9, set lunch £9) and afternoon teas (from £8) served to an admiring tourist-heavy clientele. Open daily noon-3pm for lunch, 3-6pm for tea. MC/V.

The Ritz, Piccadilly (☎ 7493 8181). Tube: Green Park. The most famous and popular place for afternoon tea, served near Palm Court's gilded fountains. Set tea £31. No jeans or sneakers; jacket and tie preferred for men. Arrive at noon for early tea. Reserve at least 6 weeks ahead for M-F, 3 months for Sa-Su. Sittings at 3:30 and 5pm daily. AmEx/MC/V.

The Savoy, Strand (☎ 7836 4343). Tube: Charing Cross. One of London's most famous hotels, popular for afternoon tea. Su a band plays hits from the 20s to the 40s as the floor is opened up to dancers. Set tea £24 M-F, £27 Sa-Su.; with champagne £31.50/ £34.50. Dress code: no jeans, shorts, or sneakers; jacket and tie preferred. Tea daily 3:30-5pm. Reserve 1-2 days ahead M-F, 2 weeks Sa-Su. AmEx/MC/V.

the BIG $plurge

Tea Total

Afternoon tea is perhaps the high point of English cuisine. A social ritual as much as a meal, at its best it involves a long afternoon of sandwiches, scones, pastries, tinkling china, and restrained conversation. And even a cup of tea.

The inherent qualities of "tiffin" notwithstanding, the main attraction of afternoon tea today is the chance to lounge in sumptuous surroundings that at any other time would be beyond all but a Sultan's budget. The Ritz is the most famous place to "take tea," but most of London's top hotels have got in on the act. It's a win-win situation: they get to charge over £20 for water, dried leaves, and cakes, and you get to relax in the kind of luxury you've only dreamed about. Note that you'll often need to book in advance, especially on weekends. Many hotels have a strict dress code; see listings for details.

Tea at any of these fancy establishments can be a daunting experience—for some teatime tips, see **From the Road,** p. 160.

AFTERNOON TEA

🅚 Brown's	Mayfair
Fortnum & Mason	Mayfair
🅚 The Lanesborough	Knightsbridge
The Orangery	Kensington
The Ritz	Mayfair
St. Martin's Lane Hotel	Soho
The Savoy	Strand

ASIAN

busaba eathai	West End ❷
Galangai Thai Canteen	North London ❷
Harbour City	West End ❷
Itsu	West End ❹
Jenny Lo's Teahouse	Knightsbridge ❷
Mandalay	Marylebone ❶
Mr. Kong	West End ❷
New Culture Revolution	North London ❶
Nusa Dua	West End ❷
Royal China	Bayswater, Marylebone ❷
Soba Noodle Bar	West End ❷
Yelo	East London ❶

BREAKFAST

🅚 Chelsea Bun Diner	Chelsea ❶
🅚 Chelsea Kitchen	Chelsea ❶

CAFES

Al's Café Bar	Clerkenwell ❷
Bar Italia	West End ❶
Bar Room Bar	North London ❷
🅚 Bluebird	Chelsea ❷
Blue Room Café	West End ❶
🅚 Books for Cooks	Notting Hill ❶
Café 7	South Bank ❷
Café 1001	East London ❶
🅚 Café Bar & Juice Bar	South London ❶
Café Emm	West End ❷
Candid Arts Trust Cafe	North London ❶
Crussh	Kensington ❶
Fluid	Notting Hill ❶
Gloriette	Knightsbridge ❷
The Island Café	South Bank ❶
Lazy Daisy Café	Notting Hill ❶
Lisboa Patisserie	Notting Hill ❶
Le Madeleine	West End ❷
Monmouth Coffee Co.	West End ❶
Raison d'Être	Kensington ❶
SW9	South London ❷

CARIBBEAN

🅚 Mango Room	West End ❷

EASTERN EUROPEAN

L'Autre	West End ❷
🅚 Bloom's	North London ❸
Patio	West London ❸
Trojka	North London ❷

FISH & CHIPS

George's Portobello Fish Bar	Notting Hill ❷

FRENCH

Bleeding Heart Bistro & Restaurant	Holborn ❺
La Brasserie	Kensington ❹
Le Cellier du Midi	North London ❺
Gloriette	Knightsbridge ❷
🅚 Gordon Ramsay	Chelsea ❺
La Lune	Chelsea ❷
La Madeleine	West End ❷
Maison Blanc	West London ❸
Le Mercury	North London ❷
Patisserie Valerie	West End ❶
Le Piaf	Notting Hill ❶
Poilâne	Knightsbridge ❶
Raison d'Être	Kensington ❶
🅚 Tartuf	North London ❷

GREEK

🅚 Aphrodite Taverna	Bayswater ❷

INDIAN

Aladin	East London ❷
🅚 Cafe Spice Namaste	The City ❷
Diwana Bhel Poori House	Bloomsbury ❶
Durbar Tandoori	Bayswater ❷
🅚 Masala Zone	West End ❷
🅚 Ophim	West End ❸
Tamarind	West End ❸
🅚 Zaika	Kensington ❹

ITALIAN

Cantina del Ponte	South Bank ❸
Carluccio's	West End ❷
Spighetta	Marylebone ❷
Tomato	West End ❷

LATE-NIGHT

Bar Italia	West End ❶
Brick Lane Beigel Bakery	North London ❶
Ranoush Juice	Marylebone ❶

MIDDLE EASTERN

Afghan Kitchen	North London ❶
Al Casbah	North London ❹
Alounak Kebab	Bayswater ❷
🅚 Café Zagora	West London ❷
🅚 Gallipoli	North London ❷
Manzara	Notting Hill ❶
🅚 Mô	West End ❸
Patogh	Marylebone ❶
Ranoush Juice	Marylebone ❶
Tas	South Bank ❷

MODERN BRITISH

Black & Blue	Kensington ❸
Buonasera, at the Jam	Chelsea ❸
🅚 Bleeding Heart Tavern	Holborn ❸
🅚 Bug	South London ❸
🅚 The Gate	West London ❸
Goddard's Pie & Mash	East London ❶
Grand Central	East London ❶
The Ivy	West End ❺

MODERN BRITISH (CONT.)	
People's Palace	South Bank ❷
St. John	Clerkenwell ❶/❹
Tiles	Westminster ❸

MONGOLIAN	
Tiger Lil's	Bayswater, North London ❷

PIZZA	
Bar Room Bar	North London ❷
☒ ECCo.	Bloomsbury, Westminster ❶
Gourmet Pizza Company	South Bank ❷
Pizzaria Oregano	North London ❷
Spighetta	Marylebone ❷

SEAFOOD	
Pescatori	Bloomsbury ❹

SNACKS & SANDWICHES	
Beigel Bake	East London ❶
☒ La Bottega del Gelato	Bayswater ❶
☒ Carmelli Bakery	North London ❶
☒ Le Creperie de Hampstead	North ❶
☒ Futures	The City ❶
The Grain Shop	Notting Hill ❶
Grand Central	East London ❶

SNACKS & SANDWICHES (CONT.)	
Marine Ices	North London ❶
Neal's Yard Bakery, Salad Bar, & Tearoom	West End, ❶
The Place Below	The City ❶
Poilâne	Kightsbridge ❶
Tom's Delicatessen	Notting Hill ❷
Wooley's	Holborn ❶

SPANISH/LATIN AMERICAN	
L'Autre	West End ❷
Café Dos Amigos	East London ❷
Cubana	South Bank ❷
Goya	Knightsbridge ❸
Navarro's Tapas Bar	Bloomsbury ❸

WINE BARS	
☒ Gordon's Wine Bar	West End ❷
Odette's Wine Bar	North London ❷
☒ Vats	Bloomsbury ❸

WORLD FOOD	
Giraffe	Marylebone, North London ❷

NOTABLE CHAINS

ASK (☎ 7486 6027). A recent pretender to Pizza Express's throne with a similar emphasis on hip, design-conscious restaurants. Not quite as dependable, but with much more menu variety. Pastas, salads, and thin-crust pizzas for £5-8. Open daily noon-11:30pm. MC/V. ❷

EAT (☎ 7222 7200). Despite the cheesy name (it stands for "Excellence And Taste"), this coffee bar/sandwich joint combo is a hit with Londoners. A small range of salads, soups, and sushi complements the sandwiches, all made fresh daily and preservative-free. Food £1.50-3.50; coffees from £1.10. Open M-F 7am-6pm, some Sa 10am-5pm. MC/V. ❶

Pizza Express (☎0189 561 8618). Once a mini-chain famed for crisp, Italian-style pizza and modern design, Pizza Express has massively expanded across Europe; their pizzas have simultaneously shrunk in size (now around 8 in. diameter) and in quality. Nonetheless, Pizza Express continues to offer reasonably priced food in reasonably attractive surroundings. Pizzas and salads £5-8. MC/V. ❷

Prêt-à-Manger (☎7827 8888). These bustling, chrome-adorned sandwich bars are mobbed for their sandwiches, baguettes, and salads (£2-3), all made daily on the premises without "obscure" additives and preservatives. Eat-in prices 17.5% higher. Most branches open approx. 7-7:30am, close 3-4pm in business districts, around 7pm in tourist areas. MC/V. ❶

Wagamama (www.wagamama.com). Pioneer of the noodle-bar revolution, Wagamama continues to pull in customers. It's not clear why, though—the transformation from one-hit wonder to international chain has brought with it a downward trend in food quality. That said, it's still good value (ramen from £6) and good fun. Wide vegetarian selection averages £6. Most branches open M-Sa noon-11pm, Su 12:30-10pm. MC/V. ❷

Yo!Sushi (www.yosushi.com). The original Yo!Sushi, at 52 Poland St. (Tube: Oxford Circus), pioneered conveyor-belt sushi in London, and the chain has spread like wildfire. Diners sit at an island bar, picking from a never-ending stream of small plates, color-coded by price (£1.50-3.50). There's no doubt that it's fun, but portions are paltry (a filling meal will come to around £15+ each), and there's no knowing how long that raw fish has been circling on the (unrefrigerated) conveyor belt. Open M-W noon-11pm, Th-Sa noon-midnight. AmEx/MC/V. ❹ **147**

RESTAURANTS BY NEIGHBORHOOD

BAYSWATER

SEE MAP, p. 361

🇼 BAYSWATER QUICKFIND: Pubs, p. 173; **Entertainment,** p. 207; **Shopping,** p. 226; **Accommodations,** p. 252.

Cheap and central, Bayswater was an immigrant magnet in the years after WWII, playing a pioneering role in developing Britain's tastebuds. The **Standard Tandoori,** on Westbourne Grove, was one of London's first Indian restaurants, while hummus, kebabs, and other Middle Eastern delights were also introduced to Londoners through Bayswater's large Arab population. **Westbourne Grove** and **Queensway** hold numerous cheap Chinese, Indian, and Persian restaurants, though many of the area's gems are on tiny side streets. For those with a less adventurous disposition, **Whiteleys** mall (see p. 226) has a good selection of upscale chain restaurants.

Aphrodite Taverna, 15 Hereford Rd. (☎7229 2206). Tube: Bayswater. Pantelis and Rosanna have been running this Greek restaurant for 20 years, and their expert touch is apparent everywhere, from the fabulous food to the warm, busy decor. Mains run from £7-15, chef specials £10-24. The cafe next door has some of the specialties at cheaper prices and a full sandwich menu. Restaurant open M-Sa noon-midnight. Cafe open daily 8:00am-5pm. AmEx/MC/V. ❷

La Bottega del Gelato, 127 Bayswater Rd. (☎7243 2443). Tube: Queensway. Now in his 70s, Quinto Barbieri still gets up at 4:30am every morning to make the best *gelati* this side of the Rubicon. Perfect to take on a stroll in the Kensington Gardens across the street. Scoops from £1.60. Open daily 10am-7pm; later in summer. Cash only. ❶

Alounak Kebab, 44 Westbourne Grove (☎7229 0416). Tube: Bayswater or Royal Oak. A discreet gem among the scads of Persian restaurants in the area, with low prices to boot. Much of the food is baked to order in the traditional clay oven by the door. All the dishes, including the succulent, slow-grilled kebabs (from £5.60), are served with mouthwateringly fluffy saffron rice or fresh *taftoon* bread. Open daily noon-11pm. MC/V. ❷

Durbar Tandoori, 84 Westbourne Grove. (☎7727 1947; www.durbartandoori.co.uk). Tube: Bayswater. Durbar's claim to fame is the extraordinary cooking of Shamin Syed, the former International Indian Chef of the Year. New location, same modest prices, with curries starting from £5 and a set menu for 2 going for £21.95. Open Sa-Th noon-3pm and 6pm-midnight. MC/V. ❷

Royal China, 13 Queensway (☎7221 2535). Tube: Bayswater or Queensway. Royal China's lacquered, swan-themed walls give it a glitzy flavor that isn't mirrored in the prices. Renowned for London's best dim sum (£2-3 per dish; 3-4 dishes each is enough), which is ordered from a menu rather than a trolley. On weekends, arrive early or expect to wait 30-45min. Meals start from £7-10. Dim sum served M-Sa noon-5pm, Su 11am-5pm. Open M-Th noon-11pm, F-Sa noon-11:30pm, Su 11am-10pm. AmEx/MC/V. ❷

Tiger Lil's, 75 Bishop's Bridge Rd. (☎7221 2622). Tube: Bayswater. Same formula as the branch in Islington, North London (see p. 164). ❷

BLOOMSBURY

SEE MAP, p. 362

🇼 BLOOMSBURY QUICKFIND: Sights, p. 74; **Museums & Galleries,** p. 125; **Pubs,** p. 173; **Entertainment,** p. 207; **Shopping,** p. 226; **Accommodations,** p. 254.

At the heart of London's student community, Bloomsbury is overflowing with top-notch budget food. Running parallel to Tottenham Court Rd., **Charlotte Street** (Tube: Goodge St.) has for decades been one of London's best-known foodie streets, with a range of fashionable restaurants at all price ranges. A string of extremely cheap Indian vegetarian eateries and sweet shops lines **Drummond**

148

Street, near Euston, while on the other side of Bloomsbury, bordering Holborn, **Sicilian Avenue** has some great sandwich and snack shops. A less obvious but equally rewarding area for cheap ethnic food is the stretch of **Euston Road** that runs directly north of the Warren St. Tube station.

ECCo (Express Coffee Company), 46 Goodge St. (☎ 7580 9250). Tube: Goodge St. Light-years ahead of its competition, ECCo puts Pizza Express to shame with delicious 11" pizzas, made to order, for an eye-popping £3.50. Sandwiches and baguettes, on in-store baked bread, start at £1.50 (rolls 50p). It's extremely popular with students, who are attracted by the good food, great prices, and bright, cheery atmosphere. Buy any hot drink before noon and get a free fresh-baked croissant. Sandwiches half-off after 4pm. Pizzas available from noon. Open M-Sa 7am-11pm, Su 9am-11pm. Cash only. ❶

Vats, 51 Lambs Conduit St. (☎ 7242 8963). Tube: Russell Square. Small front conceals a long romantic space. Friendly staff are happy to let you taste before you commit (at least for wines available by the glass). Food is pricey (starters £5-7, mains £10-16) but delicious and innovative. Vat's has too many wines to fit them all on their wine list, so if you have something particular in mind, don't be afraid to ask. The list leans towards Bordeaux, with "good ordinary claret" £3.50 per glass and £14.50 per bottle; Burgundy from £16. Open M-Sa noon-11:30pm; lunch served noon-2:30pm, dinner 6-9:30pm. AmEx/MC/V. ❸

Diwana Bhel Poori House, 121-123 Drummond St. (☎ 7387 5556). Tube: Euston or Euston Square. No frills or frippery here—just great, cheap south Indian vegetarian food and quiet, efficient service. Try the excellent lunch buffet (£5.95, served daily noon-2:30pm) or enjoy the ample portions of the regular menu. Outside buffet hours, *thali* set meals offer great value (£4-6). Open daily noon-11:30pm. AmEx/MC/V. ❶

Pescatori, 57 Charlotte St. (☎ 7580 3289). Tube: Goodge St. Don't let the tacky Tube ads fool you—Pescatori knows its fish. The seafood is consistently fresh and delicious, if pricey: pasta dishes run £8-16, mains £10-18; if you don't mind the lunchtime crowd, try the 2-course lunch special (£17.50). Open for lunch M-F noon-3pm, dinner M-Sa 6pm-11pm. MC/V. ❹

Navarro's Tapas Bar, 67 Charlotte St. (☎ 7637 7713). Tube: Goodge St. Bustling *tapas* restaurant, with traditional tiles and bright, handpainted furniture. The excellent food surpasses the slightly grouchy service—try the spicy and deliciously thick lentil stew. Each *tapas* is £4-6, and 2-3 *tapas* per person is plenty (£7.50 minimum). Open M-F noon-3pm and 6-10pm, Sa 6-10pm. AmEx/MC/V. ❸

Wagamama, 4A Streatham St. (☎ 7323 9223). Tube: Tottenham Ct. Rd. See p. 147. Original branch of the noodle empire, near the British Museum. ❷

Full English Breakfast

If you're after more food than you can imagine, there is little in life more fullfilling than a **full English breakfast** (a.k.a. the "fry-up") in the early morning. Variations abound, but an English breakfast typically consists of fried eggs and bacon in double servings, plus fried toast, baked beans and a selection of other foods, which can include pork sausages, liver, kidneys, black or white pudding (not actually pudding, but sausages of the blood and non-blood variety), grilled or fried tomato, and mushrooms—all washed down with coffee or tea (or beer if you're the hardy type).

It may be traditional English breakfast fare but very few British people actually eat a full English breakfast every morning—it's just too unhealthy to stomache daily. Quicker and healthier breakfast options have increasingly displaced the English breakfast, exiling it mostly to hotels, B&Bs, and neighborhood haunts like diners where it's readily consumed by tourists and working men looking for an early-morning cholesterol fix.

CHELSEA

SEE MAP, p. 363

CHELSEA QUICKFIND: Sights, *p. 76;* **Museums & Galleries,** *p. 126;* **Entertainment,** *p. 208;* **Shopping,** *p. 227.* **TRANSPORTATION:** *The only* **Tube** *station in Chelsea is Sloane Sq.; from here* **buses** *#11, 19, 22, 211, and 319 serve King's Rd.*

As with everything else in Chelsea, it's all happening on **King's Road.** The road is lined with a variety of eateries catering to a wide range of budgets and tastes, with a particularly high concentration between Sydney St. and the World's End kink. Most outdoor cafes are closer to Sloane Square.

Chelsea Bun, 9a Limerston St. (☎7352 3635). Airy and refreshingly casual diner that serves heaping portions. No need to set the alarm clock—early-bird specials available 7am-noon for £2-3. Sandwiches (£1.60-3.20) and breakfasts (from £3.70) are served until 6pm. Pasta, salads, burgers, and omelettes £6-8. Minimum £3.50 per person lunch, £5.50 dinner. Open M-Sa 7am-11:30pm, Su 9am-7pm. MC/V. ❶

Chelsea Kitchen, 98 King's Rd. (☎7589 1330). Dimly lit diner booths provide intimacy and a decadent feel at nondecadent prices. Mains, like the roast chicken and bountiful mozzarella salad, hover around £4. Wine is £1.50 per glass and £6.80 per bottle. Minimum charge £3 per person. Breakfast served until 11:30am. Open daily 7am-midnight. MC/V. ❶

Bluebird, 350 King's Rd. (☎7559 1222). An auto-shop turned gastronomic pit stop, this designer food emporium includes a flashy restaurant, a sprawling outdoor cafe, and a gourmet supermarket. The cafe offers creative salads, sandwiches, and steaks from £6.50-11. The restaurant touts more expensive fare, such as roast rabbit with prosciutto and spinach, starting at £16.25. Cafe open M-Sa 8am-11pm, Su 10am-6pm. Restaurant open M-F noon-3pm and 6-11pm, Sa 11am-3:30pm and 6-11pm, Su 11am-3:30pm and 6-10pm. Store open M-W 9am-8pm, Th-Sa 9am-9pm, Su 11am-5pm. AmEx/MC/V. Cafe ❷, restaurant ❹

Gordon Ramsay, 68 Royal Hospital Rd., (☎7352 4441). Tube: Sloane Square. Open M-F noon-2:20pm and 6:45-11pm. See The Big Splurge, right. ❺+

La Lune, 250 King's Rd., entrance on Sydney St. (☎7351 5351). This relaxed and chic cafe, restaurant, and juice bar spreads out around a beautiful sheltered courtyard. French-inspired sandwiches are the centerpiece (£6-10), alongside affordable smoothies (£3). Open daily 9:30am-5pm. MC/V. The **Phât Phúc** noodle bar shares the privileged seating, and the 3 dishes they decide to serve each day are just £4.95. Open daily noon-5pm. MC/V. ❷

Buonasera, at the Jam, 289a King's Rd. (☎7352 8827). The novelty of the bunk-style seating, patented by the owners, makes for a worthwhile experience in itself, as the waiters leap up the small ladders to your mid-air table. The fish and vegetables are bought at the market daily, which keeps the prices low and the ingredients fresh. Grilled fish and steak range from £7.90-11.50, while pasta dishes are even cheaper (£5-6). Reserve a week ahead for weekend nights and a day ahead for weekdays. Open Tu-F noon-3pm and 6pm-midnight, Sa-Su noon-midnight. MC/V. ❸

Pizza Express, 152 King's Rd. (☎7351 5031). See Notable Chains, p. 147. Perhaps the most impressive of Pizza Express's locations, The 3 atmospheric floors are located in the former home of dancer Princess Astafieva. A triumphal archway supported by caryatids and topped by a bronze chariot separates the large courtyard from the sidewalk. Open daily 11:30am-midnight. AmEx/MC/V. ❷

THE CITY OF LONDON

SEE MAP, p. 364

THE CITY OF LONDON QUICKFIND: Sights, *p. 78;* **Museums & Galleries,** *p. 126;* **Pubs,** *p. 174;* **Entertainment,** *p. 208.*

With almost none of the City's workforce sticking around for supper and with hardly any residents, it's not surprising that the vast majority of City eateries open only for weekday lunch—it's nearly impossible to find a decent dinner here. Even at lunchtime, the choice is limited: it comes down to either gulping down a sandwich, or feasting at a millionaire's banquet. If you're after the former, sandwich bars are on every corner (it helps to get off the main roads)—long queues will form outside the better establishments between noon and 1:30pm on weekdays. For something slightly different, the alleyways of **Leadenhall Market,** just south of Leadenhall, pack in numerous mid-range chain restaurants, cafes, and pubs (see p. 147).

🔲 **Café Spice Namaste,** 16 Prescot St. (☎ 7488 9242). Tube: Tower Hill or DLR: Tower Gateway. The standard bearer for a new breed of Indian restaurants. Bright, carnivalesque decoration brings an exotic feel to this old Victorian warehouse, as does the extensive menu of Goan and Parsee specialties. Meat dishes are on the pricey side (£11-13), but vegetarian meals are a bargain (£7-9). Outstanding service and attention to detail make this the pick of the City. Open M-F noon-3pm and 6:15-10:30pm, Sa 6:30-10pm. AmEx/MC/V. ❷

🔲 **Futures,** 8 Botolph Alley (☎ 7623 4529), between Botolph Ln. and Lovat Ln. Tube: Monument. Suits and their lackeys besiege this tiny takeaway, which dishes out a daily-changing variety of vegetarian soups (£2-3), salads (£3), smoothies (£1.40), and hot dishes (£4.10); for breakfast you'll find a wide variety of pastries for about 80p each, or porridges and cereals for about £1. Open M-F 7:30-10am and 11:30am-3pm. Cash only. ❶

The Place Below, Cheapside (☎ 7329 0789), in the basement of **St. Mary-le-Bow** (see p. 81). Tube: St. Paul's or Mansion House. Climb down the winding steps from the foyer of St. Mary-le-Bow, and you'll find yourself in a fantastic vegetarian restaurant, light-years away from the typical City sandwich joint. Fresh, elaborate sandwiches (£3-5), yummy porridge (£1.20), and a constantly changing menu of tasty mains (£4-6). Open M-F 7:30am-3:30pm. Cash only. ❶

CLERKENWELL

🔳 *CLERKENWELL QUICK-FIND: Sights,* p. 82; *Museums & Galleries,* p. 128; *Pubs,* p. 174; *Nightlife,* p. 185; *Entertainment,* p. 210; *Accommodations,* p. 259.

SEE MAP, p. 365

There's no shortage of fine dining in Clerkenwell—and even the best restaurants offer some affordable sustenance. For something light, try one of the many sandwich bars south of Farringdon station and on **Charterhouse Street.** There are also cheap snack bars, pubs, and Chinese takeaways on West Smithfield, just south of the market. For

the BIG $plurge

By Gordon!

Gordon Ramsay—eccentric artist, former footballer, and celebrity chef. Rumored to be abrasive inside, and sometimes outside the kitchen (food critics have been ejected from his restaurant), Gordon Ramsay is reputedly London's best chef. His food is light, innovative, and thoroughly anti-trendy. The food is French, but he avoids the butter and heavy creams that characterize much of French cooking, seeking brighter, livelier flavors with amazingly delicious results.

The £35 set lunch menu features such delights as pot-roasted pigeon on a bed of cabbage and truffle consommé. Dinner is pricier—a 7-course menu for £80 or 3 courses for £65—with numerous and tempting options including lobster ravioli poached in lobster bisque on a bed of crushed garden peas.

Decor is traditional, elegant, and relaxed. Service is unobtrusively impeccable. Wear a jacket or a suit, and tie. You can't reserve more than a month ahead, but getting a dinner reservation is still difficult (nearly impossible on Sa). Lunch is easier-book two weeks ahead and you should have no problems. (See **Gordon Ramsay** under **Chelsea.**)

a proper sit-down meal, your best bet is **Exmouth Market,** a pedestrian street north of Clerkenwell Rd. flanked on both sides by all manner of eateries, from pie'n'mash joints to some of London's priciest restaurants.

St. John, 26 St. John St. (☎7251 0848; www.stjohnrestaurant.com). Tube: Farringdon. St. John has stormed the London restaurant scene, winning countless prizes for its eccentric English cuisine—they call it "nose to tail eating," and certainly few body parts are wasted. Prices in the posh restaurant are high (mains £13-17.50), but you can enjoy similar bounty (in smaller quantities) in the airy bar outside the restaurant, which was formerly a smokehouse used by the butchers at Smithfield Market. Lamb and green sauce £4.50, roast bone-marrow salad £6.20, quail £4. A bakery at the back of the bar churns out delicious fresh loaves for £1.50. Restaurant open M-Sa 12pm-3pm, 6pm-11pm. Bar open M-Sa 11am-11pm. MC/V. ❹

Al's Café/Bar, 11-13 Exmouth Market (☎7837 4821). Tube: Angel or Farringdon. This maroon-hued cafe/bar (with a basement club) is a favorite hangout for journalists from the nearby *Guardian* newspaper, *Face* magazine, and *Arena* magazine. With comfortable seats and windows all around, Al's is a prime spot to lounge with a coffee (£1.60-2.00) and people-watch. Mains £6.50-9.50. All-day breakfast on weekends £1.50-6.50. Open M-F 8am-midnight, Sa 10am-2am, Su 8am-11pm. Last orders 1hr. before closing. MC/V (£10 minimum). ❷

HOLBORN

SEE MAP, p. 365

▶ *HOLBORN QUICKFIND:* **Sights,** *p. 84;* **Museums & Galleries,** *p. 128;* **Pubs,** *p. 175;* **Nightlife,** *p. 187;* **Entertainment,** *p. 210;* **Shopping,** *p. 229.*

In the 18th century, there was one tavern in Holborn for every five homes; they remain your best bet for nourishment in a district unusually devoid of restaurants and snack bars, cheap or otherwise. Some pubs have fallen to the dark side under pressure from Holborn's masses of "young professionals," but others (including some of London's oldest pubs) remain cozy enclaves of smoke-blackened wood, comfort food, and hand-pulled ales. If you're hungry and not up for pub grub, head for the maze of passageways between Holborn station and Lincoln's Inn Fields, home to a number of affordable eateries.

Bleeding Heart Tavern, corner of Greville St. and Bleeding Heart Yard (☎7404 0333). Tube: Farringdon. The name derives from the 1626 murder of Elizabeth Hatton by her jilted lover, the Spanish ambassador; the body was found in the yard, her heart "still pumping blood onto the cobblestones." This 2-level establishment is split between the friendly, slightly posh upstairs pub, with its polished wood floors and stone walls, and the luxurious restaurant below, whose thick tablecloths, fresh roses, and candles make a romantic backdrop to hearty and delicious English fare. Highlights include the roast suckling pig with delicately spiced shards of apple. Extraordinarily good service and fine ale round out your dining experience (mains £8-10). Open M-F noon-2:30pm and 6-10:30pm. Upstairs pub open M-F 11:30am-11pm. AmEx/MC/V. ❸

Bleeding Heart Bistro and Restaurant, Bleeding Heart Yard (bistro ☎7242 8238, restaurant ☎7242 2056). Tube: Farringdon. Around the corner from the Tavern (follow the signs). This duo ranks among London's finest French restaurants; the Restaurant boasts "one of the finest wine lists in the world." The Bistro features a prix-fixe menu of 3 courses for around £20; a la carte mains £8-16. Mains at the Restaurant run £11-19. Bistro and restaurant open M-F 11:30am-2:30pm and 6-10:30pm. AmEx/MC/V. Bistro ❹, Restaurant ❺

Woolley's, 33 Theobald's Rd. (☎7405 3028). Rear entrance on Lamb's Conduit Passage. Tube: Holborn. Narrow take-out joint in two parts: salads (£1.50-3.70) and jacket potatoes (£2.50-3.50) are dished out from the Theobald's Rd. side, whilst Lamb's Conduit supplies fresh sandwiches (£2-3). Woolley's cleanliness and impressive variety make it a standout. You can walk through to the Lamb's Conduit side and eat in the passage, which makes for great rush-hour people-watching, or take your order to the gardens of nearby Gray's Inn (p. 87). Open M-F 7:30am-3:30pm. Cash only. ●

KENSINGTON & EARL'S COURT

⚑ KENSINGTON & EARL'S COURT QUICKFIND: Sights, p. 88; **Museums & Galleries,** p. 130; **Pubs,** p. 176; **Entertainment,** p. 210; **Shopping,** p. 229; **Accommodations,** p. 259.

SEE MAP, pp. 366-367

Kensington proper is not known for food, budget or otherwise; the most attractive spot is **Kensington Court,** a short pedestrian street lined with budget and mid-range pavement cafes always popular on warm summer evenings. **Kensington High Street** is roughly split between overpriced yuppie hangouts and family-friendly pizzerias, both of which tend to be thoroughly mediocre. **South Kensington** is better; the area around the Tube station positively overflows with sandwich bars and cheap restaurants. On **Bute Street,** just opposite the Institut Francais's *lycée* (high school), you're as likely to hear French spoken as English in the sidewalk cafes, *pâtisseries*, and continental delis which provide some delicious cheap eats. In **Earl's Court,** both Earl's Court Rd. and Old Brompton Rd. have a good variety of affordable places to eat, though they tend to be scruffier than their northern and eastern neighbors.

⬛ Zaika, 1 Kensington High St. (☎7795 6533; www.zaika-restaurant.co.uk). Tube: High St. Kensington. Simply put, London's best Indian restaurant. About as far as can be imagined from the usual £4.95-lunch-buffet Indian dive: elegant decor, attentive service, and food that is original, beautiful, and sophisticated. Long, excellent wine list. Starters £3-10, mains £13-23, desserts £4-5 (2-course minimum for dinner). Lunch set menu £14.95 for 2 courses, £17.95 for 3. 5-course dinner menu £38, £57 with wine. Dinner reservations recommended. Dress up. Lunch daily noon-2:45pm; dinner M-Sa 6:30-10:45pm, Su 6:30-9:45pm. MC/V. ❹

The Orangery, Kensington Palace (☎7938 1406). Tube: High St. Kensington or Queensway. See **Afternoon Tea,** p. 144.

Raison d'Être, 18 Bute St. (☎7584 5008). Tube: South Kensington. One of many small cafes on Bute St. catering to the local French community, this comfortable, quiet cafe offers a bewildering range of filled *baguettes* and foccacia (£2.20-5) as well as *salades composées* (£3.50-4.70) and various other light dishes (like yogurt with fruit, £2.50), all made to order. After your meal, enjoy a divine *cafe au lait* under the canopy outside. Open M-F 8am-6pm, Sa 9:30am-4pm. Cash only. ❶

Black & Blue, 215-217 Kensington Church St. (☎7727 0004). Tube: High St. Kensington. Bears all the hallmarks of over-trendiness, yet manages to remain very laid-back, with comfortable booths and unpretentious food including all-day English breakfast (£8) and enormous burgers (£7-8). Appetizers and desserts £5, steaks £12-19. Open Su-Th noon-11pm, F-Sa noon-11:30pm. MC/V. ❸

La Brasserie, 272 Brompton Rd. (☎7581 3089). Tube: South Kensington. This bustling, cheerful French brasserie, famous for its oyster bar, serves large portions of very fresh pastas and meats. It's fairly pricey (appetizers £6-10, mains £12-17), but the prix-fixe dinner menus (£14/£17) offer great value and selection. Also serves breakfast and afternoon tea. Open daily 9am-11pm. MC/V. ❹

Crussh, 27 Kensington High St. (☎7376 9786). Tube: High St. Kensington. Fresh-squeezed smoothies and juices (£2.50-3.70) with optional vitamin boosters in pint-sized portions. Sip and soak up the cheery, colorful interior: comfy couches, bright chairs, and a giant fruit mural. Open M-F 8:30am-6pm, Th until 7pm, Sa 9am-6pm, Su 10am-6pm. ❶

ON THE MENU

So What's That Brown Stuff, Anyway?

It's named after a small French stock-pot (that remains on its label); it's enjoyed on toast, in sandwiches, and added to stews and casseroles. An excellent source of vitamin B-12 (which prevents anemia), riboflavin, niacin, and folic acid, it was shipped overseas during both World Wars as a dietary supplement to combat nutritional deficiency disorders. To most Britons, it's divine. To almost everyone else, it's nauseating.

"It" is **Marmite**, a strong-smelling, dark-brown, 100%-vegetarian paste made from spent brewer's yeast left over from the fermentation process. A German chemist realized that this yeast could be made into a food product, and attempts to manufacture the extract for commercial purposes culminated in the formation of the Marmite Food Company Limited in 1902, which set up a factory in Burton-on-Trent, then the center of the British brewing industry. The popularity of the spread grew steadily, and a new factory was established in 1907 at Camberwell Green, London. Almost a century later, CPC (now known as Best Foods, Inc.) took over both Marmite and Bovril Limited. Bovril, a meat extract, is second only to Marmite in the extract paste

KNIGHTSBRIDGE & BELGRAVIA

◪ KNIGHTSBRIDGE & BELGRAVIA QUICKFIND: Sights, p. 90; **Pubs,** p. 176; **Shopping,** p. 230; **Accommodations,** p. 154.

SEE MAP, p. 368

The jaw-dropping prices in Harrods's posh restaurants may deceive you into thinking that **Knightsbridge** is not promising territory for affordable eats. But cast your net a little wider, and you'll haul in the benefits. **Beauchamp** (BEE-cham) **Place**, off the Old Brompton Rd., is lined with cafes, noodle bars, and sandwich bars, and more bargains can be found in other side streets. **Belgravia** is a bit tougher—there's little chance of getting a sit-down meal for under £15. The mews behind **Grosvenor Place** cradle some popular pubs, and the gourmet delis and specialty food stores on **Elizabeth Street** will furnish a picnic basket fit for a prince.

KNIGHTSBRIDGE

▨ **The Lanesborough,** Hyde Park Corner (☎ 7259 5599). Tube: Hyde Park Corner. See **Afternoon Tea,** p. 144.

Gloriette, 128 Brompton Rd. (☎ 7584 1182). Tube: Knightsbridge. This venerable *pâtisserie* offers hot meals in a bright cafe atmosphere. Leaf teas £2 per pot, delicious cakes and pastries £3-3.60, sandwiches £5-7. More substantial fare includes a rich goulash soup with bread (£4.95) and 2- and 3-course set meals (£8.90 and £10.95). Open M-F 7am-8pm, Sa 7am-7pm, Su 9am-5pm. AmEx/MC/V. ❷

BELGRAVIA

▨ **Jenny Lo's Teahouse,** 14 Eccleston St. (☎ 7259 0399). Tube: Victoria. Long before noodle bars hit the big time, Jenny Lo's was offering stripped-down Chinese fare at communal tables. The modern interior bustles on weekdays, but the delicious *cha shao* (pork noodle soup; £5.50) and the broad selection of Asian noodles from Vietnamese to Beijing style (£5.50-7.50) make it well worth the wait. Teas, blended in-house, are served in attractive hand-turned stoneware (from 65p). Open M-F 11:30am-3pm and 6-10pm, Sa noon-3pm and 6-10pm. Cash only (£5 minimum). ❷

Goya, 2 Eccleston Pl. (☎ 7730 4299; www.goya-restaurant.co.uk). Tube: Victoria. London's most carefully prepared *tapas* menu (£3.50-6 per dish). Order 2-3 *tapas* per person, unless you order one of the larger *tapas*, like those with pork or octopus.

The other Spanish entrees (£10-15) offer excellent vegetarian and seafood options, all served by friendly staff in a spacious tiered dining room. Open daily 11:30am-11:30pm. AmEx/MC/V. ❸

Poilâne, 46 Elizabeth St. (☎7808 4910). Tube: Victoria or Sloane Square. Paris's most famous *boulangerie* brings freshly baked delights to Belgravia. The traditional round loaves can be as much as £6.50, but *pain au chocolat* is only 90p. Open M-F 7:30am-7:30pm, Sa 7:30am-6pm. MC/V. ❶

MARYLEBONE & REGENT'S PARK

🔟 *MARYLEBONE & REGENT'S PARK QUICKFIND: **Sights,** p. 92; **Museums & Galleries,** p. 132; **Entertainment,** p. 211; **Accommodations,** p. 262.* **MA**

SEE MAP, p. 369

Long regarded as something of a food wilderness, numerous fashionable restaurants and modern sandwich bars have cropped up around **Marylebone High Street** to challenge that reputation. Nevertheless, the Middle Eastern oasis of Edgware Rd. aside, this is not a place to go searching for great meals or great deals.

🍽 **Mandalay,** 444 Edgware Rd. (☎7258 3696). Tube: Edgware Rd. About 7min. walk north from Tube. Looks ordinary, tastes extraordinary. This down-to-earth Burmese restaurant is justly plastered with awards. Lunch specials are great value (curry and rice £3.70; 3 courses, including a banana fritter, £5.90). Be sure to ask for the full menu, which includes an explanation of Burmese cuisine. Most dishes are not spicy enough as they come, but ask the charming owner and he will gladly increase the heat. Mains £3-5. No smoking. Reservations recommended. Open M-Sa noon-2:30pm and 6-10:30pm. AmEx/MC/V. ❶

🍽 **Patogh,** 8 Crawford Pl. (☎7262 4015). Tube: Edgware Rd. Persian for "meeting place," Patogh is a culinary focal point for London's Iranian community. Space is limited, but the amazing food makes up for any discomfort from squeezing in. Order the understated "bread" and get a delicious 14 in. flatbread with sesame seeds and subtle spices for just £1.50; mains like *kebab-e-koobideh* (minced-lamb kebab) are £4-6 and worth every penny. Open daily 12:30pm-1:30am. Cash only. ❶

Giraffe, 6-8 Blandford St. (☎7935 2333; www.giraffe.net). Tube: Bond St. or Baker St. Second branch of the deservedly popular world-food micro-

market: sales of Marmite spread top £23.5m yearly.

Perhaps due to its popularity among the British, Marmite has spawned numerous knockoffs like Vegemite and Promite (which Britons consider vastly inferior to the original) mainly in Australia and New Zealand. Ever-imaginative, Brits also use the thick paste to flavor Walker's Crisps and Twiglets (preztel-like snacks). But be warned: unless you've been weaned on the stuff (as many British children are), it's highly unlikely that you'll form any lasting attachment to it.

The best way to eat Marmite:

Use toasted white bread. Butter the toast while it is still hot, so that it makes the bread slightly mushy on top; do not use margarine. Spread the Marmite thinly at first, coating the entire buttered area, leaving small random gaps if possible. Do not spend too much time applying the Marmite, or the toast will go soggy. Do not apply Marmite and butter to cold toast. And do not apply the Marmite too thickly, or the overwhelming taste will gag you.

MY best way to eat Marmite:

Don't.

—Tiffany Hsieh

chain, with the same winning combination of delicious global eats (mains £7-10), modern decor, and great music. Communal tables reduce privacy, but help make the atmosphere even more cheerful. Open daily noon-midnight. AmEx/MC/V. ❷

Ranoush Juice, 43 Edgware Rd. (☎7723 5929). Tube: Marble Arch. This tiny, affordable arm of the Maroush restaurant empire is commonly regarded as the best Lebanese joint on the Edgware Rd.—and that's up against some stiff competition. You don't need a sultan's ransom to enjoy lamb doner kebabs (£2.50-4). Open daily 9:30am-3am. Cash only. ❶

Spighetta, 43 Blanford St. (☎7486 7340). Tube: Baker St. This charming, easy-to-miss subterranean Italian restaurant off Baker St. cooks up deliciously crunchy pizza (£7-9.50) from a wood-fired oven. In additon to pasta (£7-8.50) and traditional Italian mainfare (£11-13), Spighetta also offers interesting chef's specials in a bright, laid-back setting. Open M-Th noon-2:30pm and 6:30-10:30pm, F-Sa noon-2:30pm and 6:30pm-11pm, Su 6:30-10:30pm. AmEx/MC/V. ❷

Royal China, 40 Baker St. (☎7487 4688). Tube: Baker St. Upscale branch of the micro-chain renowned for serving London's best *dim sum. Dim sum* is ordered from a menu rather than from a cart, gaining in freshness what it loses in charm. Keep your eyes open—this restaurant is crawling with MPs and minor celebs. If you're with a group and looking to splurge, the seafood 5-course prix-fixe is £36, while its standard and vegetarian versions ring in at £28. Most mains £8-18. Open M-Th noon-11pm, F-Sa noon-11:30pm, Su 11am-10pm. AmEx/MC/V. ❸

NOTTING HILL

SEE MAP, p. 361

🏲 **NOTTING HILL QUICKFIND: Sights,** p. 94; **Pubs,** p. 177; **Nightlife,** p. 187; **Entertainment,** p. 211; **Shopping,** p. 231.

Food in Notting Hill basically comes down to a choice between numerous overpriced, overhyped, and overtrendy media enclaves—such as Bridget Jones's favorite 192 and the Damien Hirst-designed Pharmacy (see Nightlife, p. 187)—and the cheap and often excellent eateries serving the market crowds around Portobello Rd. For the widest variety of food, hunt around at the southern end of the general market and under the Westway.

🔽 **George's Portobello Fish Bar,** 329 Portobello Rd. (☎8969 7895). Tube: Ladbroke Grove. George opened up here in 1961, and while the shop has had various incarnations (currently disguised as a 50s-style diner), the fish and chips is still as good as ever. Choose from the freshly fried fillets on display or ask the lineup of servers to rustle up a new piece (£4-5). Add a generous helping of chunky chips (£1) and wolf down the greasy goodness outside. Kebabs and burgers too. Open M-F 11am-midnight, Sa 11am-9pm, Su noon-9:30pm. Cash only. ❶

🔽 **Books for Cooks,** 4 Blenheim Crescent (☎7221 1992). Tube: Ladbroke Grove. At lunchtime, chef-owner Eric and his crew of culinary pros "test" recipes from new titles, filling the small store with warm, delicious smells (though the tables can make book-browsing a trifle tricky). There's no telling what will be on offer, but you can rely on the excellent cakes (£2). Food available M-Sa 10am-2:30pm or so. Bookstore open Tu-Sa 10am-6pm. Daily cookery workshops held in upstairs demo kitchen (£25; reservations essential). MC/V. ❶

Tom's Delicatessen, 226 Westbourne Grove (☎7221 8818). Tube: Ladbroke Grove or Notting Hill Gate. Short on space due to its popularity. The courteously efficient waitstaff rushes you in and out, while the table-sharing policy makes for some close encounters for those flying solo. One bite into the thick, fresh sandwiches (£6-9) reveals why this deli (complete with a small market downstairs) attracts a constant flow of customers. No smoking. Open M-F 11am-7pm, Sa 10:30am-6:30pm, Su noon-5pm. MC/V (£5 minimum). ❷

Lisboa Patisserie, 57 Golborne Rd. (☎8968 5242). Tube: Ladbroke Grove. Tiny Iberian bakery-cum-cafe, packed with nicotine-happy Portuguese and Moroccan men chatting football over their coffee (80p). Gets extremely stuffy on hot summer days, but the broad selection of cakes and pastries (from 45p) is hard to resist—don't miss the Portuguese custard pie. Open M-Sa 8am-8pm, Su 8am-7pm. Cash only. ❶

The Grain Shop, 269a Portobello Rd. (☎7229 5571). Tube: Ladbroke Grove. It's hard for passersby to ignore the aromatic invitation of this mini-bakery—or the line snaking out into Portobello Rd. The main attractions here are the generous homemade takeaway bakes and salads; mix as many dishes as you like for a small (£2.25), medium (£3.45), or gut-bustingly large (£4.60) box. Organic breads baked on-site (£1-2). Food available from noon onward. Open M-Sa 9am-6pm. MC/V. ❶

Le Piaf, 19/21 Notting Hill Gate (☎7727 8810). French panache with a laid-back touch in a breezy, open space. Feast your eyes on the colorful Impressionist art adorning the walls as you dine on light, understated French cuisine with Mediterranean influence (mains £8-11). Open daily 9am-11pm. AmEx/MC/V. ❸

Lazy Daisy Café, 59a Portobello Rd. (☎ 7221 8417). Tube: Notting Hill Gate. Tucked into an indoor alley: enter through the mint-green doors. This cheery cafe offers a healthy selection of salads and pastries. Breakfast is served all day, including a lazy fry-up (£5) and quiche (£4.25). Service runs on the leisurely side, but the wide range of periodicals and bin of toys keep customers of all ages happily occupied. Small menu for kids and child-sized portions of daily specials available. Open M-Sa 9am-5pm. ❶

Manzara, 24 Pembridge Rd. (☎7727 3062). Tube: Notting Hill Gate. Besides standard kebabs, this Turkish takeaway specializes in *pide,* rolled pizza-like pastries filled with various delicacies (£4.25 takeaway, £6 eat-in). Open daily 7am-11pm. Cash only. ❶

Fluid, 13 Elgin Crescent (☎7229 4871). Tube: Ladbroke Grove. Also at Vogue House, Hanover Sq. (☎7499 9052). Tube: Oxford Circus. Sleek, ultra-minimalist juice bar with no tables but a great fruity smell. Sizes run small. Single juices from £1.75, smoothies from £2.75. Open M-F 8:30am-6pm, Sa 9am-6pm, Su 10am-6pm. Cash only. ❶

THE SOUTH BANK

🄵 *THE SOUTH BANK QUICKFIND: Sights, p. 95; Museums & Galleries, p. 132; Pubs, p. 177; Entertainment, p. 212; Accommodations, p. 263.*

Until recently, no one would dream of going to the South Bank to eat—the choice was between overpriced restaurants in the big cultural complexes and the greasy spoons of Borough High St. But the rapid development of the area into a major cultural destination, not to mention increas-

SEE MAP, pp. 370-371

ing yuppification, have made this one of London's top spots for eating out—and the views are unbeatable. In addition to the places listed below, check out the **National Film Theatre** cafe under Waterloo Bridge (see p. 212) and the numerous pavement eateries of **Gabriel's Wharf,** between the National Theatre and the OXO Tower. Those who prefer to assemble their own meals can turn to the 🄼**Borough Market,** where stalls lay out fresh gourmet cheeses, breads, and cured meats. (Off Borough High St. Tube: London Bridge. Open F 11am-6pm, Sa 9am-4pm.)

🄼 **Cantina del Ponte,** 36c Shad Thames, Butlers Wharf (☎7403 5403). Tube: Tower Hill or London Bridge. Amazing riverside location by Tower Bridge. The Mediterranean mural inside takes you away from the Thames, but given the quality of the Italian food (especially the desserts), it's a trip worth taking. The set menu is a bargain at £11 for 2 courses, £13.50 for 3 (available M-F noon-3pm, 6-7:30pm); otherwise, pizzas are £7-8, mains £12-15. Open M-Sa noon-3pm and 6-10:45pm, Su noon-3pm and 6-9:45pm. MC/V/AmEx. ❸

🄼 **Tas,** 33 The Cut (☎7928 2111). Tube: Southwark. Also at 72 Borough High St. (☎7928 3300). Tube: London Bridge. Dynamic duo of stylish and affordable Turkish restaurants. Generous and tasty soups and baked dishes—many vegetarian—outshine the respectable kebabs. Mains £6-8; set menus include 2 courses for £7 and *mezes* (selection of starters) £7-10. Live music daily from 7:30pm. Evening reservations recommended. Open M-Sa noon-11:30pm, Su noon-10:30pm. AmEx/MC/V. ❷

■ **People's Palace,** Royal Festival Hall (☎ 7928 9999). Tube: Waterloo. Despite the Stalinist name, this is the swankiest of the Festival Hall's many eateries. Its chief virtue is the fantastic location on the 2nd fl. of the Hall, with vast windows overlooking the river; the Mediterranean food is also top-notch. While dinner is pricey (mains £13+), luncheon mains (served noon-3pm) like chicken with beetroot or roast salmon, are all £8. Bargains can be found on the pre-concert menu (5:30-7pm, starters from £6.25) or the children's menu (mains £6.50). Open daily noon-3pm and 5:30-11pm. MC/V. ❷/❹

Café 7, Tate Modern, Bankside (☎ 7401 5020). Tube: Southwark or Blackfriars. On the top (7th) fl. of Tate Modern (see **Museums & Galleries,** p. 123), windows on both sides provide stunning views of the city and south London, while specially commissioned murals cover the end walls. Slick and stylish, with artistically presented modern British cuisine: baked aubergine £8.25, braised ham hock £9. Sandwiches served in the afternoon start at £5.50. Open Su-Th 10am-5:30pm (last order), F-Sa 10am-9:30pm. AmEx/MC/V. ❷

Cubana, 48 Lower Marsh (☎ 7928 8778; www.cubana.co.uk.). Tube: Waterloo. Look for the giant salsa dancer dwarfing Uncle Sam. Generous *tapas* (£3.50-5) and mains (£7-10) take second place to the spiky cocktails (£5, 2-pint jug £15): sample some classic drinks like the "Sputnik," originally mixed with cheap Cuban rum, now with Bacardi and Martell cognac. At lunch, get 2 *tapas* for £5, a 2-course meal for £6, and 3 courses for £8. Reservations recommended. Happy hour daily 5-6:30pm. Salsa with live band F-Sa nights, £5 cover with free plate of *tapas.* Open M-Th noon-midnight, F noon-1am, Sa 6pm-1am. AmEx/MC/V. ❷

Gourmet Pizza Co., Gabriel's Wharf, 56 Upper Ground (☎ 7928 3188). Tube: Southwark or Waterloo. On the embankment, this adventurous pizzeria offers "tradition with imagination" in the form of pizzas with unexpected toppings, like thai chicken and eggplant (£6-9). Also serves standard Italian pastas and salads. Reserve for dinner or risk a long wait. Open M-Sa noon-11pm, Su noon-10:30pm. AmEx/MC/V. ❷

The Island Café, 1 Flat Iron Square (☎ 020 7407 2224). Tube: Southwark. At the junction of Union St. and Southwark Bridge Rd. One of the only places in the South Bank that serves lunch for under £4, the Island Café dishes up a full English breakfast for just £2.95 and classic lunchbox-style sandwiches as cheap as £1.70. Choose from a variety of fillings like tuna with sweet corn and egg salad, and complement your light meal with a candy bar, fruit, or crisps (35p each). Cash only. ❶

THE WEST END

SEE MAP, p. 356

OXFORD STREET & REGENT STREET

🔽 *OXFORD STREET & REGENT STREET QUICKFIND:* **Sights,** p. 98; **Museums & Galleries,** p. 134; **Pubs,** p. 178; **Nightlife,** p. 188; **Entertainment,** p. 213; **Shopping,** p. 233; **Accommodations,** p. 263.

Food on Oxford St. itself is as depressing and tourist-oriented as you'd expect, with fast-food chains competing with dodgy kebab and pizza vendors. Fortunately, side streets offer better food and wider selections. Londoners have long kept quiet about **St. Christopher's Place,** reached by an innocuous-looking alleyway opposite Bond St. Tube. This pedestrian Piazza just north of Oxford St. feels like a lost piece of the Mediterranean, ringed by the terrace seating of numerous budget and mid-range restaurants. Less picturesque but just as affordable, **Kingly Street,** between Regent St. and Carnaby St., is popular with local *boutiquiers.*

■ **Masala Zone,** 9 Marshall St. (☎ 7287 9966). Tube: Oxford Circus. Masala Zone's dramatically lit interior, varied seating arrangements, and open-kitchen design has a distinctly modern edge, but the food stems firmly from a South-Indian tradition, with an emphasis on *masala* or spices. The menu has typical favorites (£5-6) as well as *tapas*-style "street food," which comes in small bowls (£2.75-4.40), or large Thali platter, which allows you to sample a variety of dishes (£8-11). No smoking. Open M-F noon-2:45pm and 5:30-11pm, Sa 12:30-3pm and 5-11pm, Su 12:30-3:30pm and 6-10:30pm. MC/V. ❷

Mô, 23 Heddon St. (☎ 7434 3999). Tube: Piccadilly Circus or Oxford Circus. A "salad bar, tea room, and bazaar," Mô is functionally and aesthetically a slice of Marrakesh. The interior is hung with traditional lanterns and festooned with Moroccan crafts, all for sale. The carved chairs, floor cushions, and low tables used by diners add to the unique experience. Mix and match from their *tapas*-style dishes (£6-£7.50), and wash it down with some mint tea (£2). No reservations, but very popular—arrive early or late. Open M-Th 11am-11pm, F-Sa noon-11:30pm. AmEx/MC/V. ❸

Carluccio's, St. Christopher's Pl. (☎ 7935 5927; www.carluccios.com). Tube: Bond St. Refined, no-frills Italian cooking in a bright and bustling environment. The short menu is simple but diverse. Choose from shared tables on the ground floor, the more formal basement seating, or a *piazza*-style patio. Antipasti £4-7, main dishes £5-10.50. Also sandwiches and *calzone* for takeaway (£3-4) and a gourmet deli with Italian hams, gourmet pastas, and olive oils. Open M-F 8am-11pm, Sa 10am-11pm, Su 11am-10pm. AmEx/MC/V. ❷

Soba Noodle Bar, 38 Poland St. (☎ 7734 6400; www.soba.co.uk). Tube: Oxford Circus. Also at 11/13 Soho St. (☎ 7827 7300; Tube: Tottenham Court Rd.). This narrow noodle bar with a long yellow communal table, bench seating, and walls covered with corrugated plastic is minimalist with a Japanese flair. Great for a quick meal. Big bowls of noodles £6-6.50, rice plates £5.30-6.50. Drop by during Happy Hour when all mains go for £4, M-W 5:30pm-7pm, Sa noon-5pm, Su all day. Open M-F noon-3:30pm and 5:30pm-11pm, Sa noon-10pm, Su noon-9pm. MC/V. ❷

MAYFAIR & ST. JAMES'S

🚶 **MAYFAIR & ST. JAMES'S QUICKFIND: Sights,** *p. 100;* **Museums & Galleries,** *p. 134;* **Pubs,** *p. 178;* **Entertainment,** *p. 213;* **Shopping,** *p. 235;* **Accommodations,** *p. 263.*

One of the most pleasant places to eat and drink is in and around the pedestrian alleys of **Shepherd Market.** Within easy reach of the restaurants around Oxford St. and Regent St. and Soho, Mayfair provides a pleasant alternative to the noise and bustle of the city.

L'Autre, 5b Shepherd St., in Shepherd's Market (☎ 7499 4680). Tube: Hyde Park Corner or Green Park. Given its French name, English decor, and mixed menu, this small Polish-Mexican bistro has a surprisingly defined character. The cozy interior and hearty Polish fare (£9-12.50) are perfect for a cold winter's day; in summer, sit on the pavement and munch the Mexican food (£8-12) which was requested by the Mexican embassy around the corner. Specializes in fresh game in season. Open M-F noon-2pm and 5:30-10:30pm, Sa-Su 5:30-10:30pm. AmEx/MC/V. ❷

La Madeleine, 5 Vigo St. (☎ 7734 8353). Tube: Piccadilly Circus. Sit back, sip a perfectly brewed leaf tea (£1.30), and rejoice in a little bit of *temps perdu* in this casual, classy cafe. Lunchtime menu includes a daily changing *plat du jour* (£7), omelettes (£7-8), and a 2-course set meal with wine (£10.50). Open M-Sa 8am-8pm, Su 11am-7pm. AmEx/MC/V. ❷

Tamarind, 20 Queen St. (☎ 7629 3561). Tube: Green Park. 1 of only 2 Indian restaurants in the UK to receive a Michelin star, and the award-winning North Indian cuisine won't break the bank. Vegetarian dishes start at £6, while meat kebabs run from £13-22. For the best deal come for the 3-course set lunch for £16.50. Open M-Sa noon-2:45pm and 6-11:15pm, Su 6-10:30pm. AmEx/MC/V. ❸

AFTERNOON TEA

▨ **Brown's,** Albemarle St. (☎ 7493 6020). Tube: Green Park. See **Afternoon Tea,** p. 144.

Fortnum & Mason, 181 Piccadilly (☎ 7734 8040). See **Afternoon Tea,** p. 144.

The Ritz, Piccadilly (☎ 7493 8181). Tube: Green Park. See **Afternoon Tea,** p. 144.

SOHO

🚶 **SOHO QUICKFIND: Sights,** *p. 101;* **Museums & Galleries,** *p. 134;* **Pubs,** *p. 178;* **Nightlife,** *p. 189;* **Entertainment,** *p. 213;* **Shopping,** *p. 237;* **Accommodations,** *p. 263.* **TRANSPORTATION:** *All listings are near Tube: Piccadilly Circus, Leicester Sq., Tottenham Court Rd., and Oxford Circus.*

Tea at Brown's

Afternoon tea at Brown's is essential to any visit to London, however short. Here are some hints to make it less daunting:

1. Whenever possible, let your waiter pour your tea for you.

2. If you pour yourself a cup, do not forget to use the strainer provided. It is not optional. This fearless writer found herself with a cup full of silt, and hopes that you will learn from her error.

3. There is no way to drop sugar cubes in your tea without making a loud "plopping" noise, unless you were born an Englishman. I now limit myself to milk.

4. If you manage to finish any one of your three tiers of food, your waiter will bring you another one momentarily—they will feed you until you tell them to stop.

5. Make sure to stop by the bathroom, if only to sit in the armchairs and gawk at the full-length gilded mirrors.

6. People-watching is expected, but be subtle. Remember—if you appear aloof, you may be mistaken for a minor celebrity.

7. Dress appropriately—no jeans, no trainers. Do not, however, show up in full evening dress.

8. Finally, you did not "have" tea at Brown's. You "took" tea at Brown's. Good for you.

—Nicole Cliffe

One of the best places in London to eat and drink, Soho has restaurants, cafes, and bars to suit every taste and budget. Bustling **China-town's** main attractions are the dozens of Cantonese and other Asian restaurants. While **Gerrard Street** is considered Chinatown's heart, its eateries cater just as much to non-Chinese tourists; those on **Lisle Street,** one block south towards Leicester Sq., are often cheaper, less crowded, and more "authentic." Various late-night and 24-hr. options on **Wardour Street** and the southern side of **Shaftesbury Avenue,** just north of Gerrard St., feed hungry post-clubbers, and the outdoor cafes near Soho Sq. are perfect for lounging the afternoons away.

busaba Eathai, 106-110 Wardour St. (☎7255 8686). Brought to you by the founder of Wagamama; unlike its sibling, this wildly popular eatery has kept quality up and prices down. *Busaba* is a Thai flower, and *eathai...* well, you get the picture. Locals and students queue for marvelous Thai food (£5-10) at shared square tables in a wood-paneled room delicately perfumed with incense. Open M-Th noon-11pm, F-Sa noon-11:30pm, Su noon-10pm. AmEx/MC/V. ❷

Ophim, 139 Wardour St. (☎7434 9899; www.ophim.com). You don't even have to place an order at this gorgeous new Indian establishment: they bring you a platter of starters and then small bowls of unique, tasty mains; just ask for unlimited portions of whatever you like best. All-you-can-eat lunch £7.50, dinner £13.50. Vegetarian platters also available. Downstairs bar and lounge is delightfully atmospheric, with hookahs (5 different flavors) and huge squishy pillows in the exotic red-tinted booths. Delicious fruity cocktails are expensive (£5-6) but well worth it. Open daily noon-3pm, 5pm-midnight. AmEx/MC/V. ❸

Café Emm, 17 Frith St. (☎7437 0723; www.cafeemm.com). Cheap, generous portions in an unpretentious bistro setting with lots of vegetarian dishes. Main courses (£6-8) range from enormous salads (which come with extras) to rump steak. Open M-Th noon-2:30pm and 5:30-10:30pm, F noon-2:30pm and 5-11:30pm, Sa 1-4pm and 5-11:30pm, Su 1-4pm and 5-10:30pm. MC/V. ❷

Itsu, 103 Wardour St. (☎7479 4794). A genuinely ground-breaking eating experience in a stylish retro-modern interior. A steel monorail shuttles color-coded fusion delights and more traditional raw-fish plates (£2.50-3.50) right to your table. The perfection of *kaiten-sushi* (conveyor-belt sushi)—if only the monorail were chilled. Expect to spend about £15 each. Take-out available in boxes both inside and outside. Open M-Th noon-11pm, F-Sa noon-midnight, Su 1-10:30pm. AmEx/MC/V. ❹

Nusa Dua, 11 Dean St. (☎ 7437 3559). Named after a luxury Balinese resort, this is a prime destination for affordable Javanese and Singaporean cooking. If you can, opt for the bright, airy ground floor, which is less crowded than the downstairs rooms. Fish tanks and Indonesian carvings complement the flavorful cuisine. Plentiful chicken and vegetarian dishes £5-7, duck and seafood £6-8. Open daily noon-midnight. Minimum charge £15. AmEx/MC/V. ❷

Patisserie Valerie, 44 Old Compton St. (☎ 7437 3466; www.patisserie-valerie.co.uk). Branches at 27 Kensington Church St., 215 Brompton Rd., Sloane Sq., 8 Russell St. and 105 Marylebone High St. Opened in 1926, this continental patisserie has become a London institution. The excellent pastries are better than the snooty service. The recently opened upstairs restaurant offers more luxury, but without the sweet aromas of the bakery on the ground floor. Patrons swear the croissants (90p) are better than any French rival. Cakes and pastries £1.20-3.50, mains £2.50-7. Open M-F 7:30am-8pm, Sa 8am-8pm, Su 9am-6pm. AmEx/MC/V. ❶

Bar Italia, 22 Frith St. (☎ 7437 4520). A fixture of the late-night Soho scene. Despite its name, you won't find anything stronger than an espresso here (£1.80), but it's still *the* place for a post-club *panini* (£4-6) or pizza (£6-9). As long as the restaurant is open, the loud TV is never turned off—appropriate, since John Logie Baird gave the first-ever demonstration of television upstairs in 1922. Diplomatic Bar Italia accepts the euro. Open 7am-5am daily. AmEx/MC/V (£10 minimum). ❶

Tomato, 54 Frith St. (☎ 7437 0666; www.tomatogroup.com). Quintessential Italian fare with decent-sized pizzas and pasta dishes (mains £6-13). Lunch and pre-theater menu 2 courses for £9.50. Dimly lit modern interior brightened up by a wall colored—you guessed it—tomato-red. Open daily noon-11pm. MC/V. ❷

Blue Room Café, 3-5 Bateman St. (☎ 7437 4827, www.blueroomcafe.com). Cosmopolitan regulars relax on the leather couches of this tiny laid-back hangout, absorbing the mellow music, sipping on smoothies (£2.50-3.25), and munching on sandwiches (£3-5) and salads (£3-5). Take-away prices 17% lower. Open M-F 8am-10:30pm, Sa 10am-10:30pm, Su noon-10pm. Cash only. ❶

Yo!Sushi, 52 Poland St. See p. 147 and also **Nightlife,** p. 189. ❹

CHINATOWN

🚇 *Tube:* Leicester Sq.

🦐 **Mr. Kong,** 21 Lisle St. (☎ 7437 7341). If you're up for some duck's web with fish lips (£12) or spicy pig's knuckles with jelly fish (£8.80), this is the place to go. Less-adventurous eats (from £6), like fried Mongolian lamb, sound less impressive but are equally delicious. £7 min. for dinner. Open daily noon-3am. AmEx/MC/V. ❷

Harbour City, 46 Gerrard St. (☎ 7439 7859). Its name sounds Western, but this is Gerrard St.'s best and biggest Cantonese restaurant. Extremely popular for menu-ordered *dim sum* (£2-3), served daily noon-5pm. The giant noodle dishes (£4-6) could feed 2 hungry giants; other dishes £5.50-12. Open M-Th noon-11:30pm, F-Sa noon-midnight, Su 11am-10:30pm. AmEx/MC/V. ❷

COVENT GARDEN

🚇 *CONVENT GARDEN QUICKFIND:* **Sights,** p. 103; **Museums & Galleries,** p. 134; **Pubs,** p. 178; **Nightlife,** p. 190; **Entertainment,** p. 213; **Shopping,** p. 238; **Accommodations,** p. 263. **TRANSPORTATION:** Tube: Covent Garden unless stated otherwise.

Despite, or perhaps because of, its trendiness, Covent Garden is not known for its cuisine. The Piazza has mostly unremarkable tourist-oriented cafes and overpriced restaurants catering to the theater- and opera-goers, while sandwich bars and theme pubs prevail on the side streets. An exception is **Neal's Yard,** a small open courtyard that has evolved into a wholesome haven of vegetarian, vegan, and organic delights.

St. Martin's Lane Hotel, 45 St. Martin's Ln. (☎ 7300 5588). Tube: Leicester Sq. See **Afternoon Tea,** p. 144.

Neal's Yard Bakery, Salad Bar & Tearoom, 1, 2, 8-10 Neal's Yard (☎ 7836 3233). A small, open-air counter sells fresh organic breads (loaves from £1.60) as well as vegan favorites like bean burgers (£3 eat-in, £2.50 takeaway). The salad bar has more substan-

the BIG
$plurge

The Ivy

Noel Coward, Lawrence Olivier, and Madonna didn't become regulars at the West End's most celebrity-ridden restaurant because of glitter or glamour. They came because the team here manages to do modest British traditions to standards that no one else seems able to match. While The Ivy's reputation has recently dropped a bit because it has become so popular (weekend nights sometimes require a month's advance booking), the place can't seem to lose the title of Best Restaurant in London. Perhaps it's because the staff is still friendly, and the kitchen keeps making British food into gourmet cuisine. Stick with reasonably-priced favorites like shepherd's pie (£12.50) or fresh picks from the seafood menu—the popular salmon fishcake is only £11.75. The manageable wine menu is split up by nationality, and the laid-back waitstaff can always help you find a suitable vintage. The 3-course set lunch on Sa and Su provides numerous choices for each course (£18.50). (See **The Ivy**, under **Covent Garden**.)

tial vegan and vegetarian meal options, including quiches and bruschetta. Wash it all down with a glass of fresh Brazilian juice (£3.50). Seating upstairs in the dim tea room or right outside in Neal's Yard, where you can duke it out with the pigeons. Eat-in minimum £1.50 M-F noon-3pm and Sa noon-4:30pm. Bakery open M-Sa 9:30am-5pm, salad bar and tea room M-Sa 10:30am-4:30pm. ❶

The Ivy, 1-5 West St. (☎ 7838 4751). Tube: Leicester Sq. Open daily noon-3pm and 5:30pm-midnight. AmEx/MC/V. See **the Big Splurge,** p. 162. ❺

Monmouth Coffee Company, 27 Monmouth St. (☎ 7645 3562). A refreshing change from the impersonal Starbucks on every street corner. Monmouth has huge sacks of beans, tiny wooden booths, and 17 different coffees to choose from. Coffee £1.50, double espresso £1. Get a bag of beans to go, or savor an aromatic cup in the "sample room" at the back. Branch at 2 Park St. Open M-Sa 9am-6:30pm. MC/V (£5 minimum). ❶

THE STRAND

The Strand shares Covent Garden's culinary shortcomings, being dominated by American chains, tourist traps, and expensive establishments like the old-fashioned *Simpsons in the Strand*. Fortunately, **Craven Passage** and **Villiers St.,** between the Strand and Victoria Embankment, have a number of pleasant bars and pubs serving fairly priced standards.

Gordon's Wine Bar, 47 Villiers St. (☎ 7930 1408). Tube: Embankment or Charing Cross. A wine bar has been on the site since 1364, and the history is written on the walls—they are plastered with a century of newspaper articles about long-past coronations and marriages. Gordon's outdoor seating is limited, and the real attraction is the honeycomb of low, candle-lit vaults dripping with dark, smoky atmosphere. Choose a main dish, then pile on as much as you like from the self-serve salad bar for £7-9. Sherry and port are decanted from wood barrels (around £3 per glass), while the wide selection of wine comes in glasses (£3.60) or bottles (£12.95). Open M-Sa 11am-11pm, Su noon-10pm. MC/V (£10 minimum). ❷

The Savoy, Strand (☎ 7836 4343). Tube: Charing Cross. See **Afternoon Tea,** p. 144.

WESTMINSTER

🏛 *WESTMINSTER QUICK-FIND: Sights,* p. 104; *Museums & Galleries,* p. 136; *Pubs,* p. 179; *Entertainment,* p. 216; *Accommodations,* p. 264.*

SEE MAP, p. 372

With one of London's highest concentrations of office workers, from tens of thousands of poorly paid clerks and civil servants to ministers, Lords, and business leaders, Westminster has no shortage of restaurants at every price range—at least for a weekday lunch. In the evenings, sandwich bars shut up and restaurants raise their prices, while many places shut entirely over weekends. **Strutton Ground,** a short pedestrian road between Victoria and Great Peter St., is particularly rich in budget pickings, from sandwich and salad bars to Chinese buffets. South of Victoria, **Tachbrook Street** also has a number of cheap eats, as well as a tiny but superior food market. (Market open M-Sa 9am-5pm.) **Trafalgar Square's** eateries are hidden away inside its various historic buildings—**Crivelli's** restaurant, in the National Gallery (see p. 121), combines affordable Italian favorites with a view of the Square. For cheaper fare, you may prefer the cafe in the crypt of St. Martin-in-the-Fields.

▧ **ECCo (Express Coffee Company),** 40 Strutton Ground (☎7233 0557). Tube: Victoria or St. James's Park. The same great deals as the Bloomsbury original (see p. 149), including made-to-order 11" pizzas for just £3 and flavored french bread options (£1-2), all served by a remarkably friendly staff. Buy any hot drink before noon and get a free croissant. Open M-F 7am-7pm, Sa-Su 7am-4pm. Cash only. ❶

▧ **Goya,** 34 Lupus St. (☎7976 5309). Tube: Pimlico. Corner *tapas* bar, with earnest Spanish waiters serving snacks and drinks to a chattering crowd of diverse locals. Mirrors and large windows give the interior a deceptively spacious feel. Generous, meticulously prepared *tapas* mostly £4-5; 3 per person is more than enough. Goya's special sangria £2.50; alcohol is only served with food. Open daily noon-11:30pm. AmEx/MC/V. ❸

▧ **Tiles,** 36 Buckingham Palace Rd. (☎7834 7761). Tube: Victoria. Within spitting distance of Buckingham Palace. Upstairs, small round tables grace the blue-and-white tiled floor, and large mirrors add to the airy atmosphere. Downstairs, exposed brick, thick linen tablecloths, candles, and secluded couches raise the level of intimacy. Modern British cooking with a twist of French makes for an eclectic menu with mains averaging £9.50. Wine from £2.50 per glass. Open M-F 11am-11pm, kitchen noon-2:30pm and 5:30-10:30pm. AmEx/MC/V. ❸

NORTH LONDON

▞ **NORTH LONDON QUICKFIND: Sights,** p. 107; **Museums & Galleries,** p. 137; **Pubs,** p. 180; **Nightlife,** p. 192; **Entertainment,** p. 216; **Shopping,** p. 240; **Accommodations,** p. 265.

ISLINGTON

▞ *Tube: Angel unless otherwise noted.*

Upper Street has over 100 restaurants, and there are close to 200 nearby. Naturally, all the big chains are out in force, but they face tough competition from cheaper down-market eateries at Islington Green on **Essex Road,** which still preserves some of the old Islington feel. For a real taste of the old days, head to **Chapel Market,** just off Liverpool St. opposite Angel Tube, where a traditional English meal can be had for under £2 in tiny roadside cafes. For the truly adventurous, **M. Manze,** at 70 Chapel Market, will give you a ladleful of hot eels smothered in green gravy, with a dollop of mash, for £2.70. One taste of this authentic London fare will suffice to explain how Indian food gained such rapid acceptance in England.

▧ **Tartuf,** 88 Upper St. (☎7288 0954). Have a simply divine cutlery-free experience with Alsatian *tartes flambées* (£5-6), a cross between a crepe and a pizza, only much tastier. Pick your own toppings from scrumptious salty and sweet selections. Before 6:30pm get 1 savory and 1 sweet *tarte* for £6.90; all-you-can-eat is always £11.90 per person. Open M-Th 6-11pm, F 6pm-midnight, Sa noon-midnight, Su noon-11pm. MC/V. ❷

▧ **Gallipoli,** 102 Upper St., and **Gallipoli Again,** 120 Upper St. (☎7359 0630). Patterned wall tiles and hanging lamps provide the authentic background to spectacular Turkish delights like "Iskender Kebap" (grilled lamb with yogurt and marinated pita bread in a top-secret sauce, £5.95). They've opened two branches on the same block—essentially the same restaurant, though Again has an outdoor patio in the back. Reserve F-Sa. Open M-Th 10:30am-11pm, F-Sa 10:30am-midnight, Su 10:30am-11pm. MC/V. ❷

Le Mercury, 140a Upper St. (☎7354 4088). This sunny little corner restaurant offers delicious and delightfully presented French food at extremely affordable prices—a great deal in London. Dinner mains £5.95. Reservations recommended for evenings. Open daily noon-12:30am. MC/V. ❷

Pizzeria Oregano, 18-19 St. Alban's Place (☎7288 1123). Hidden away from Upper St. and its trendy chains, Oregano foregoes the stream of tourists for a devoted crowd of regulars that comes for the carefully prepared pasta and pizza that spills off the plate (£7-8) and the excellent, friendly service. Open Tu-F 5:30-11pm, Sa 12:30-11pm, Su 1-11pm. MC/V. ❷

Afghan Kitchen, 35 Islington Green (☎7359 8019). The tiny kitchen and small menu mean that the owners can pay more attention to both. "Traditional Afghan home cooking" equals small, manageable portions of extra-spicy meat and vegetarian dishes; most are £5-6. Enjoy the food while sitting on stools and wooden planks. Open Tu-Sa noon-3:30pm and 5:30-11pm. Cash only. ❶

Giraffe, 29-31 Essex Rd. (☎7359 5999). The same successful formula as the Hampstead original (see p. 166). Open M-F 8am-11pm, Sa-Su 9am-11pm. AmEx/MC/V. ❷

Tiger Lil's, 270 Upper St. (☎7226 1118). Tube: Highbury and Islington. This Mongolian buffet chain allows you to gather your own (raw) ingredients before they stir-fry them with your choice of sauce. It's a clever way for a restaurant to avoid coming up with recipes, though they do offer some mains (£5-8). If you make the wrong choices you can go back as many times as you want during dinner (£12.50); lunch (£5) is only one serving, so there's less room for error. Open M-F noon-3pm and 6-11pm, Sa-Su noon-11pm. MC/V. ❷

Candid Arts Trust Cafe, 3 Torrens St. (☎7837 2437). It's the door beneath the horse sculpture; go up 2 floors to reach the cafe. Quirky antique furniture and serene, sexually provocative paintings form the perfect background for serious discussions and romantic overtures. Huge sandwiches from £2.80; other dishes, like quiches and lasagna, £6-7. Open M-Sa noon-10pm, Su noon-5pm. Cash only. ❶

CAMDEN TOWN

🔲 *Tube:* Camden Town unless otherwise noted.

Camden Lock and **Camden Canal** markets combine a fair selection of stands with some canalside seating, but the widest range of world food is in **Stables Market.** Outside the market, Camden has no shortage of restaurants, though it's important to get off Camden High St. to find the best ones; **Parkway,** running from the Tube toward Regent's Park, is home to several noodle bars and old stalwarts. Away from the hubbub, **Regent's Park Rd.** towards posh Primrose Hill has a burgeoning concentration of mid-priced restaurants catering to more refined tastes.

Mango Room, 10-12 Kentish Town Rd. (☎7482 5065). A neighborhood favorite in an area where few restaurants last more than a year. The small Caribbean menu heavily favors fish, complemented with plenty of mango, avocado, and coconut sauces (mains £9-12). A wide array of potent tropical drinks, but only at night. Reserve for weekends. Open M 6pm-midnight, Tu-Sa noon-3pm and 6pm-midnight, Su noon-11pm. MC/V. ❶

Galangai Thai Canteen, 29-31 Parkway (☎7485 993). Simple and sleek with a spicy edge, this Thai restaurant certainly does not look anything like a canteen, though the prices are reasonably canteen-like. Pad thai starts at £5.20, while mains like samui chicken and deep-fried tilapia fish run from £5-7. Open M-F noon-3pm and 6pm-11pm, Sa 1:30pm-11:30pm, Su 1pm-10pm. MC/V. ❷

Marine Ices, 8 Haverstock Hill (☎7482 9003). Tube: Chalk Farm. The Mansi family have been in charge since 1930, and now supply their superb *gelati* to 1500 restaurants in and around London. Get it at the source for £1.50 for a single scoop; more elaborate ice cream concoctions start at £2.50. The family-friendly restaurant also offers Italian standards (pastas, pizzas, and meats £6-9). *Gelateria* open M-Sa 10:30am-11pm, Su 11am-10pm. Restaurant open M-F noon-3pm and 6-11pm, Sa noon-11pm, Su noon-10pm. MC/V. ❷

New Culture Revolution, 43 Parkway (☎7267 2700). Prophetically named—when this small restaurant first opened in 1994, serving steaming bowls of noodles in a modern, functional setting, it upgraded Londoners' perceptions of East Asian food. What's lost in authenticity is made up for with a clean, quiet environment and relatively healthy offerings. Cantonese noodles and dumplings, including lots of fish and vegetables, make up the bulk of the menu, all under £6. Open M-Th noon-3:30pm and 5:30-11pm, F noon-11pm, Sa-Su 1-11pm. AmEx/MC/V. ❶

Odette's Wine Bar, 130 Regent's Park Rd. (☎ 7586 5486). Tube: Chalk Farm. Odette's Restaurant, upstairs, is one of London's best restaurants, with a modern British menu from £7-19, and a plush but airy eating area. The wine bar in the basement offers a cozy, romantic setting and an exceptional range of wines, including many half bottles. House wine starts at £12 per bottle. Open M-F 12:30-3:30pm and 5:30-10:30pm, Sa 5:30-10:30pm, Su 12:30-3:30pm. MC/V. ❷

Trojka, 101 Regent's Park Rd. (☎ 7483 3765). Ostensibly a Russian tea room, the 3-horse trap of its name could refer to the Russian, Ukrainian, and Polish influences tugging on the menu. If your budget doesn't stretch to the ossetra caviar *blinis* (£46), the salmon caviar makes an affordable substitute (£8); *Pelmeni* (pierogi; £6.50) are perfect for a light supper. Open daily 9am-10:30pm. MC/V. ❷

Old Compton St., Soho

HAMPSTEAD & HIGHGATE

🚩 *Tube:* Hampstead *unless otherwise noted.*

Hampstead High Street has no shortage of eating opportunities for the area's wealthy residents, and most of the establishments know they have to maintain their quality to retain customers, making the area perfect for a culinary splurge. For a small cluster of cheap restaurants, head to South End Rd. near the Hampstead Heath train station. **Highgate** is short on eating opportunities.

📷 **Le Crêperie de Hampstead,** 77 Hampstead High St. (metal stand on the side of the King William IV; www.hampsteadcreperie.com). Don't let the perpetual slow-moving line deter you; these phenomenal crepes are worth any wait. The savory crepes are great for a quick meal, the sweet crepes are straight from heaven, and all are served in a customized tear-away cone that minimizes mess. Among many other varieties, mushroom in tarragon cheese goes for £3.20, while the "Banana Butterscotch Cream Dream" is £2.60. 40p gets you gooey Belgian chocolate (plain, milk, or white) instead of syrup. Open M-Th 11:45am-11pm, F-Su 11:45am-11:30pm. Cash only. ❶

Old Spitalfields Market

Giraffe, 46 Rosslyn Hill (☎ 7435 0343). With a menu as deliberately international as the world music they play, Giraffe orients itself toward young citizens of the world. There are dishes from most continents, ranging from Jamaican red vegetable curry (£6.95) to salmon fish fingers (£8.95). M-F 5-7pm get 2 courses for £6.95 (7-11pm, £8.95) and 2-for-1 drinks. Family-friendly—for better or worse. Open M-F 8am-11:30pm, Sa 9am-11:30pm, Su 9am-11pm. AmEx/MC/V. ❷

Wagamama Noodle

Al Casbah, 42 Hampstead High St. (☎7431 6356). The Moroccan chef cooks up an array of *tajine* meat casseroles (£15-16) and couscous dishes (£14.50-17.50) large enough for two. Patrons lounge on the low-slung couches with ornate pillows, although eating at the not-so-low tables is a bit awkward. Sa they bring in a belly dancer—semi-ironically, of course, and all in keeping with their young, hip attitude. Open daily 10am-11pm. MC/V. ❹

Bar Room Bar, 48 Rossyln Hill (☎7431 8802). A consciously hip but laid-back bar and art gallery. Ponder the bizarre teacup chandelier, or head out to the heated rear garden. Su live jazz from 8pm. Pizzas £5-7.25; 2-for-1 pizza special Tu. Open M-Sa 11am-11pm, Su noon-10:30pm. MC/V. ❷

Le Cellier du Midi, 28 Church Row (☎7435 9998). A secret lair where French tradition is kept safe. The rich wooden bistro interior complements the rich sauces, meats, and wines. You pay for all of this, but you won't go away hungry. Choose from the 3-course meal (£21.75) or the 2-course meal (£18.75)—both of which allow you to mix and match any items on the menu. Single entree £15.75. Open daily 6:30-11pm. AmEx/MC/V. ❺

GOLDERS GREEN

🚇 **Tube:** *Golders Green (Zone 3). From the Tube exit, walk up to the big intersection and bear right.*

🍴 **Carmelli Bakery,** 128 Golders Green Rd. (☎8455 2074). Carmelli's golden, egg-glazed challah (£1.25-1.85) is considered the best in London; the bagels and sinfully good pastries (£1.50) aren't far behind. Packed F afternoons, as every Jewish mother in London scrambles to get bread for the Sabbath. Hours are flexible, but generally open daily 6am-1am; Th and Sa 24 hours. ❶

🍴 **Bloom's,** 130 Golders Green Rd. (☎8455 1338). Gloomy waiters in white dinner jackets and black bow ties have been an essential part of the Bloom's experience since 1920. The mains are primarily varieties of roasted meat (£8.50-14.90)—simple, but delicious. Jewish favorites like gefilte fish (£3.50) and latkas (£1.90) served as side orders. Open Su-Th noon-10:30pm, F 11am-2 or 3pm. ❸

SOUTH LONDON

🚇 **SOUTH LONDON QUICKFIND: Sights,** *p. 111;* **Museums & Galleries,** *p. 138;* **Nightlife,** *p. 194;* **Entertainment,** *p. 219;* **Shopping,** *p. 241.*

Brixton's mix of rich and poor means that there's very little between dodgy Caribbean dives and trendy, expensive new openings. Come during market hours (see p. 242) for traditional delights like curry goat.

🍴 **Bug,** (☎7738 3366) in the crypt of St. Matthew's Church, Brixton Hill. Tube: Brixton. Formerly Bah Humbug. Eerie lighting and decor give this small dining room and lounge a uniquely gothic atmosphere. Prices for the mostly vegetarian and fish mains are high (£9-11), but Sunday's special "Bug Roast" gets you 2 courses for £13.50. Evening reservations essential. Open Tu-Th 5-11pm, F-Sa 5-11:30pm, Su 1-9pm. MC/V. ❸

🍴 **Café Bar and Juice Bar,** 407 Coldharbour Ln. (☎7738 4141). Tube: Brixton. Plop into a deep leather chair or perch atop a (surprisingly ergonomic) upended bucket in the makeshift bar. On fine days, take a seat outside this quirky little cafe to enjoy fresh smoothies (£4) alongside soups (£4.50), organic quiches (£4.50), and open sandwiches (£4.50). Generous portions are made to order and show strong Caribbean influence. Open daily 10am-midnight. MC/V. ❶

SW9, 11 Dorrell Pl. (☎7738 3116). Tube: Brixton. A stylish hangout for rich new Brixtonians, who congregate at the tables outside to consume heaping plates of food, cocktails, and pints of ale. Sundays DJ Mez spins 70s, 80s, and 90s pop music. Breakfasts £6-7 (M-F until 2pm, Sa-Su until 3pm), meals £6.50-8 (11am to 10pm). Open Su-W 10am-11:30pm, Th 10am-midnight, F-Sa 10am-1am. MC/V. ❷

EAST LONDON

☞ EAST LONDON QUICKFIND: Sights, p. 112; **Museums & Galleries,** p. 139; **Pubs,** p. 181; **Night-life,** p. 196; **Entertainment,** p. 219; **Shopping,** p. 242.

WHITECHAPEL & THE EAST END

☞ TRANSPORTATION: Tube: Shoreditch (open rush hour and Su morning), or a 10min. walk from Tube: Aldgate East or Liverpool St.

Mention Whitechapel and food to a Londoner, and they'll immediately reply "Brick Lane" and "curry." While that's a fairly accurate summing up of the situation—for dirt-cheap Bangladeshi food **Brick Lane** can't be beat—it ignores the burgeoning popularity of **Spitalfields Market** (see Sights, p. 112). Here, the Edwardian market hall has a number of international food stalls offering day-time market browsers everything from pad thai to crepes; there's even a dedicated seating area. Most food stalls open only for lunch and close Saturdays.

Aladin, 132 Brick Ln. (☎7247 8210). One of Brick Ln.'s more popular balti joints—even the Prince of Wales has been here. You may not get the royal treatment, but you will get a reasonably priced and well-prepared meal. Mains from £3-7. BYOB. Open Su-Th noon-11:30pm, F-Sa noon-midnight. Cash only. ❷

Beigel Bake, 159 Brick Ln. (☎7729 0616). One of the last remaining Jewish businesses in what was once the heartland of Jewish London, this bagel sanctuary invites customers off the street with its infectious doughy aroma. The neighborhood has changed, but the prices haven't—bagels at 12p each. Also platzels, filled bagels, challah, brownies, and pastries, all under £1. Open daily 24hr. Cash only. ❶

Café 1001, Dray Walk, off Brick Ln. (☎7247 9679). Hipster hangout in the Truman Brewery complex, where 20-somethings gather on sofas to unwind to bumping garage beats. Parma ham and mozzarella sandwiches £3.20, smoked chicken salad £2.20. Smoothies £2.50. Food served until 8pm. Open M-F 8am-11pm, Sa-Su 10am-midnight. Cash only. ❶

HOXTON & SHOREDITCH

Shoho's tone is shifting from can't-afford-to-eat artists to can't-be-bothered-to-cook media types, but the best meal remains the bar food in trendy drinking haunts.

Yelo, 8-9 Hoxton Sq. (☎7729 4629). Tube: Old St. This popular Thai restaurant pulls off style, good service, and generous portions at an affordable price. Noodles, curries, rice dishes, and salads for £4-5. Small bowl of rice £1.50 extra. Eat out overlooking the square in summer, or make new friends at the communal wooden benches. Open M-Th noon-3pm and 6-11pm, F noon-3pm and 6-11pm, Sa 2-11pm, Su 2-10:30pm. ❶

Grand Central, 93 Great Eastern St. (☎7613 4228). Tube: Old St. This determinedly hip gas-trobar is wildly popular with hungry pre- and post-clubbers, who tuck into smoked ham and cheese sandwiches (£5.85), and wild salmon hash (£7.80). Replete with music, brunch, and Bloody Marys, Su *Plasma Sessions* are designed to combat your hangover. Open M-F 8am-midnight, Sa 5pm-midnight, Su 11am-5pm. MC/V. ❶

GREENWICH

There's no shortage of places to eat in Greenwich, but many have a distinctly touristy feel—this is one of the few places in London where visitors outnumber locals. Ignore the dodgy snack and fish and chips bars along Greenwich Church St. and duck into the market.

Goddard's Pie & Mash, 45 Greenwich Church St. (☎8293 9313). DLR: Cutty Sark. Saved from closure by a local campaign, Goddard's has been serving the good folk of Greenwich since 1890. All the original London working-class favorites are dished up on the wooden benches: pies 95p (takeaway), eat-in lunch special pie with mash £2.00, fruit pie and ice cream £1.20. The adventurous can try various eels, jellied and otherwise (£2-4), the newest addition to the menu. Open M-F 10am-6:30pm, Sa-Su 10am-8pm. Cash only. ❶

Café Dos Amigos, 33 Greenwich Church St. (☎8853 4880). DLR: Cutty Sark. Delicious hot and cold *tapas* (£3-5) and mouthwatering desserts—try *capriccio* chocolate (£3). Open daily noon-midnight. MC/V. ❷

WEST LONGON

🚩 *WEST LONDON QUICKFIND: Sights, p. 115; Entertainment, p. 220; Shopping, p. 243; Accommodations, p. 266.*

Shepherd's Bush offers the most variety on Goldhawk Rd. (Tube: Goldhawk Rd.), with a wealth of cheap ethnic eateries. **Hammersmith** is famous for the riverside pubs along the Upper and Lower Malls, west of the bridge. During the annual boat race between Oxford and Cambridge universities (late Mar./early Apr.), thousands gather here to drink and watch the rowers speed by at the race's halfway point.

🍴 **Café Zagora,** 38 Devonshire Rd. (☎8742 7922). Tube: Turnham Green. From the Tube, walk south to Chiswick High Rd.; turn right, then left onto Devonshire Rd. From the attentive, discreet service to the warm North African interior (complete with mosaic tabletops and embroidered pillows), Café Zagora positively oozes elegance. You'll feel like you're paying a lot more than you are, which is not much—the Lebanese-Moroccan cuisine is priced very reasonably, with mains £7-13. Share several small dishes at £2.50-4 each. Deserts are £3.50 and worth every penny—the mint tea is heavenly and comes with pillowy baklava that melts in your mouth. Open daily 5-11pm. MC/V. ❷

🍴 **The Gate,** 51 Queen Caroline St. (☎8748 6932). Tube: Hammersmith. Go through the garden gate and up the external stairs on the right. One of London's top vegetarian restaurants, the Gate has an interesting, tasty menu, served up by friendly and knowledgeable staff. Plenty of vegan options as well. Mains £8-10, starters £4-5. Deservedly popular at all times; reserve a table for dinner. Open M-F noon-3pm and 6-11pm, Sa 6-11pm. AmEx/MC/V. ❸

Maison Blanc, 26-28 Turnham Green Terr. (☎8995 7220). Tube: Turnham Green. An unexpectedly delightful little patisserie/boulangerie, featuring spectacular freshly made pastries and breads, with an emphasis on quality ingredients. Maison Blanc is authentically French—from the menu to the staff's impenetrable accents. Try the croquettes (£3-5). Open daily 8am-6pm. MC/V. ❸

At Docklands

In Chinatown

Old Spitalfields Market

Patio, 5 Goldhawk Rd. (☎8743 5194). Tube: Goldhawk Rd. A popular destination for hungry City workers, who travel from far afield for Patio's friendly service and massive portions of solid Polish mainstays. For the best value, attempt to finish the 3-course special (£11.90). "Light meals," e.g. filled pancakes, run £4.50-7; meat and fish mains £8-10. Open M-F noon-3pm and 6pm-midnight, Sa-Su 6pm-midnight. AmEx/MC/V. ❸

Pubs

It's impossible to visit London and not see a pub—almost everywhere in the city is within a few blocks of one. Pubbing in London can be an incredible experience, allowing you to explore the different ways this 800-year-old institution has adapted to the present, while simultaneously downing some of the world's finest beer. Pubbing can be a bit daunting for the novice, but the following pages should make it all a bit clearer.

PUBBING TIPS

WHAT TO AVOID

Avoid drinking in **chain pubs.** Most pubs are owned by big breweries, but the owners usually leave the publican to his own devices. Not so in chain pubs, whose proliferation in London is both worrying and inexplicable. Why anyone would want to drink in these giant, characterless monstrosities is beyond us—especially since you can usually find a real pub with better food within a few blocks. The most common chain pubs are **All Bar One, Pitcher & Piano, Slug & Lettuce, O'Neil's,** and **It's A Scream;** avoid them all. Outposts of the **Firkin** chain all have "Firkin" in the title to warn you off.

DRINK

BEERS. Every pub keeps a range of different beers on tap and has dozens more in bottles. There are three basic types of beer: lagers, stouts, and bitters. **Lagers** are light, gassy beers with little substance—most American beers are lagers. **Stouts** are dark and heavy; Guinness is the best-known stout, and one of the darkest. **Bitters** lie in the middle—they are rich and full-bodied with very little gas. Bitters are served at slightly below room temperature, and are normally hand-pulled from casks in the cellar. The bitter is the classic pub beer and what almost every Englishman drinks when he's at a pub. Most pubs have a half-dozen different bitters on tap; two of our favorites are ▧**Old Speckled Hen** and ▧**Adnams**.

OTHER DRINKS. All pubs have a fully stocked bar in addition to their beer taps. **Cider** is an alcoholic drink, about as strong as beer. A **Martini** in Britain is not a cocktail—it's just a glass of vermouth. **Lemonade** in Britain is a carbonated drink similar to ginger ale. Lemonade and beer can be mixed to form a **shandy,** which is very refreshing and perfect for a summer afternoon—but only an afternoon, thanks to...

THE UNWRITTEN RULES. It is considered effeminate for a **man** to drink anything except beer; ordering a cocktail will elicit strange looks and maybe some heckling. Shandies are especially girly. These rules relax during the afternoon, especially during the summer, when it's too hot to down a pint of bitter; in the evening, order that Bacardi Breezer at your own peril. **Women** are expected to shun beer in favor of wine, mixed drinks and bottled cocktails, though this is not a hard-and-fast rule. While most pubs are perfectly friendly, **solo females** may feel unwelcome at some very traditional pubs. Almost all the pubs we list in *Let's Go* are very friendly toward solo women.

HOW TO GET YOUR DRINK. Pubs have no waitstaff. You must order at the bar—try to catch the barman's eye, and wait your turn. If you're in a group, have one person order and pay for the entire group. You must pay in cash when you order. Order at the bar, pay the bartender (never tip), and carry your drink anywhere in the pub. Most pubs reward exploration with deliciously cozy nooks and galleries. Note that almost no pubs serve alcohol after 11pm; a bell will ring to announce last orders.

FOOD

WHAT TO EXPECT. Standard pub grub consists of sandwiches and maybe soup in the afternoon, and British classics in the evening: sausages, meat pies, jacket potatoes, etc. Snack foods like chips, nuts, and crisps are usually available all day. The menu usually is written on a chalkboard above the bar, though there may also be printed menus. If there's a glossy color menu, beware: you're probably in a chain pub, and the food is probably lousy. Gastropubs like ▧**The Eagle** (p. 174) offer trendy, modern takes on traditional British cuisine, usually with excellent results. The food at non-gastropubs is usually cheaper, but you never know whether it'll be microwaved-from-frozen—again, avoiding chain pubs will help. Most of the pubs we list serve excellent food.

HOW TO GET YOUR FOOD. Pubs have no waitstaff. Choose your meal from the chalkboard menu, then order and pay at the bar. Bring your drink back to your table; the bartender will bring you your food when it's ready. Never tip.

PUBS BY NEIGHBORHOOD

BAYSWATER

🗐 **BAYSWATER QUICKFIND:**
Food & Drink, p. 148; **Enter-**
tainment, p. 207; **Shopping,**
p. 226; **Accommodations,** p.
252.

SEE MAP, p. 361

Mitre, 24 Craven Ter. (☎7262
5240). Tube: Bayswater. This
comfortable, sprawling Victo-
rian pub is perfect for a lazy afternoon. Board games are
available from the bartender. Food (£6-9) is served M-Sa
noon-3pm and 6pm-9:30pm, Su noon-9:30pm. Quiz Nite
M 8:30pm. Jazz & blues Th-F 7-11pm. Open daily 11am-
11pm. MC/V.

BLOOMSBURY

🗐 **BLOOMSBURY QUICKFIND:**
Sights, p. 74; **Museums &**
Galleries, p. 125; **Food &**
Drink, p. 148; **Entertainment,**
p. 207; **Shopping,** p. 226;
Accommodations, p. 254.

SEE MAP, p. 362

🗒 **The Queen's Larder,** 1
Queen's Square. (☎7837 5627). Tube: Russell Square.
A pub has stood on the premises since 1710; the
present incarnation dates to the late 1700s, when
Queen Charlotte rented out the cellar to store food for
her ailing husband, King George III; the friendly proprietor
is more than happy to tell the story. In good weather, the
crowd spills out the door and onto the sunny patio. Traditional English fare, including a popular roast with Yorkshire pudding, is available in the tiny upstairs restaurant
(mains £6-7). Open M-F 11am-11pm, Sa noon-11pm,
Su noon-10:30pm. AmEx/MC/V.

The Museum Tavern, 49 Great Russell St. (☎7242
8987). Tube: Tottenham Court Rd., Russell Sq., or
Holborn. Don't let the name fool you—this pleasant,
wood-paneled pub is not a ploy to extort business
from thirsty tourists on their way out of the British
Museum (directly across the street.) Founded the
same year as the Museum itself (1759) the Tavern
has a friendly and down-to-earth atmosphere, with
decent pub grub (mains £5-7), an excellent array of
bitters, and a stunning 1869 interior. Open M-Sa
11am-11pm, Su noon-10:30pm. AmEx/MC/V.

The Jeremy Bentham, 31 University St. (☎7387
3033). Tube: Goodge St. With 2 floors packed with
students from nearby University College London, the

Dogs & Ducks &
Lambs & Bulls &...

With titles like "The Dog &
Duck," pub names appear to
be mysteriously unrelated to
the offerings inside. That's
not usually the case. Pub
names with the word "bell" in
them often referred to nearby
church or monastery ringers;
Christian religious icons such
as lambs and doves soon
found their way onto pub
signs, then into the names
themselves. Even the unlikely
name "The Bull" has a religious derivative, "bull" being
a corruption of the Latin word
for monastery.

Pubs also tried to align
themselves with nobility;
some, like the "King William
IV" pub, are named after individual royal figures. It was
often too impractical, however, to constantly shift
names with the political
tides, so many pubs adopted
general terms associated
with the monarchy, such as
"The Crown" and "The King's
Head." To align themselves
with noble families, pubs
often took the names of the
creatures that appeared on a
family coat-of-arms; the lion
was a popular example of
this phenomenon.

friendly staff, superior food. and wide selection of ales make this an extremely popular little pub. In fine weather, the crowd spills onto the patio and pavement at front. Sandwiches and burgers from £4. Open M-F 11am-11pm, Sa noon-11pm, Su noon-10:30pm.

The Lamb, 94 Lamb's Conduit St. (☎7405 0713). Tube: Russell Square. Popular with doctors from the many nearby hospitals and barristers from nearby Holborn, this quiet and deliciously cozy pub is also a celebrity hangout—regulars include Peter O'Toole. The swiveling "snob screens" around the bar originally hid "respectable" men meeting with ladies of ill repute, though ladies of any sort are a rare sight here: this old-fashioned establishment still feels like an old boy's club, and solo females will probably feel unwelcome. The usual staples served M-Sa noon-2:30pm and daily 6-9pm. Open M-Sa 11am-11pm, Su noon-10:30pm. MC/V.

THE CITY OF LONDON

SEE MAP, p. 364

🛈 **THE CITY OF LONDON QUICKFIND: Sights,** p. 78; **Museums & Galleries,** p. 126; **Food & Drink,** p. 150; **Entertainment,** p. 208.

Simpson's, Ball Crt., off 38½ Cornhill (☎7626 9985). Tube: Bank. "Established 1757" says the sign on the alley leading to this pub; it remains so traditional that an employee stands in the door to greet you. Different rooms divide the classes: quaffers populate the basement wine bar (sandwiches £2-4), drinkers the standing-only ground-floor bar, and diners the ground-floor and upstairs restaurants, with long wood tables and benches (traditional main dishes £6-7); all are comfortable, packed, and welcoming. Open M-F 11:30am-3:30pm.

The Black Friar, 174 Queen Victoria St. (☎7236 5650). Tube: Blackfriars. The Black Friar's claim of being "London's most unique pub" rests upon its Art Deco imitation of the 12th-century Dominican friary that once occupied this spot. Very popular with the post-work crowd, and it's easy to see why—this is one of the City's coziest pubs. Food served 11:30-9pm, mains £6-7. Open daily 11:30am-11pm.

The Samuel Pepys, Stew Ln., off High Timber St. (☎7634 9841). Tube: Mansion House. Worth a look for the view alone. This recently renovated gastro-pub juts out over the Thames, offering a sweeping vista south to the Tate Modern and west along the river to Westminster. The modernist decor disguises a remarkably relaxed atmosphere. Respectable array of ales, a solid wine list, and excellent sandwiches on ciabatta (£5-6). Food served noon-9pm. Open M-F noon-11pm. AmEx/MC/V.

The Hung Drawn and Quartered, 27 Great Tower St. (☎7626 6123). Tube: Tower Hill. Named for—surprise, surprise—a Sam Pepys quotation, this spacious and pleasant establishment is that rarest of beasts: a City pub open on the weekend. Its key location, just a block from the Tower, means that Beefeaters have been known to stop in wearing full regalia. Serves jacket potatoes (£3-5), and solid English standards (£4-6). Food served M-F noon-7pm, Sa-Su noon-4pm. Open M-F 11am-11pm, Sa-Su noon-5pm. AmEx/MC/V.

CLERKENWELL

SEE MAP, p. 365

🛈 **CLERKENWELL QUICKFIND: Sights,** p. 82; **Museums & Galleries,** p. 128; **Food & Drink,** p. 151; **Nightlife,** p. 185; **Entertainment,** p. 210; **Accommodations,** p. 259.

▨ **The Eagle,** 159 Farringdon Rd. (☎7837 1353). Tube: Farringdon. As the original gastropub, the always-packed Eagle kicked off the whole stripped-wood, mismatched-furniture craze, transforming pubs from blue-collar boozers into hipster hangouts. The Eagle offers tasty Mediterranean dishes (£10) and a down-to-earth atmosphere that appeals to both lunching businessmen and lingering locals. Open M-F 12:30-3pm and 6:30-10pm, Sa 12:30-2:30pm and 6:30-10:30pm, Su 12:30-3:30pm. MC/V.

▨ **The Jerusalem Tavern,** 55 Britton St. (☎7727 7985; www.stpetersbrewery.co.uk). Tube: Farringdon. Located in a former coffeehouse, this Dickensian pub offers three seating areas and many little niches, including a small balcony-like platform across from the bar. The broad beer selection rewards the adventuresome with specialty ales (£2.40) like grapefruit, cinnamon and apple, and the delicious Suffolk Gold. Popular amongst the locals, the small space fills up quickly at night, and the crowd spills onto the sidewalk during the summer. Open M-F 11am-11pm. MC/V.

The Three Kings, 7 Clerkenwell Close. (☎ 7253 0483). Tube: Farringdon. The bright tri-colored exterior captures the merry, laid-back atmosphere of this cozy local favorite. The pub is eccentrically decorated—check out the metal rhino head over the mantle and the authentic 1940s jukebox upstairs. Loud and crowded around the bar area, the pub affords more privacy in the two upper-level rooms. Open M-Th noon-11pm, F-Sa 7pm-11pm. Cash only.

Fox & Anchor, 115 Charterhouse St. (☎ 7253 5075). Tube: Farringdon. One of the only places in London where you can get a beer with your breakfast (£7.50), this pub is great for an early morning fix. It does a roaring trade in the mornings thanks to loyal locals and power-breakfasting businessmen—reservations are recommended, especially Th-F. Open M-Th 7am-5pm, F 7am-11pm; may close earlier.

HOLBORN

☞ HOLBORN QUICKFIND:
Sights, p. 84; **Museums & Galleries,** p. 128; **Food & Drink,** p. 152; **Nightlife,** p. 187; **Entertainment,** p. 210; **Shopping,** p. 229.

SEE MAP, p. 365

Ye Olde Mitre Tavern, 1 Ely Ct. (☎ 7405 4751). Between Ely Pl. and Hatton Garden. Tube: Chancery Ln. To find the alley where this pub hides, look for the street lamp on Hatton Garden bearing a sign of a mitre. This classic pub fully merits its "ye olde"—it was built in 1546 by the Bishop of Ely. The corner still holds the cherry tree planted to divide the Bishop's land from that he rented to Christopher Hatton, namesake of Hatton Garden. With dark oak beams and spun glass, the two pint-sized rooms are perfect for nestling up to a bitter—for a time, you can forget the bustle of Holborn Circus entirely. No hot meals, but bar snacks and superior sandwiches (£1.75) served until 9:30pm. Open M-F 11am-11pm.

Ye Olde Cheshire Cheese, Wine Office Ct. (☎ 7353 6170; www.yeoldecheshirecheese.com). By 145 Fleet St., not to be confused with The Cheshire Cheese on the other side of Fleet St. Tube: Blackfriars or St. Paul's. A dark labyrinth of oak-paneled, low-ceilinged rooms on 3 floors, dating from 1667. One-time haunt of Johnson, Dickens, Mark Twain, and Theodore Roosevelt. Drink in the small front bar; munch on sandwiches (£4-5) in the Cheshire bar at the back; tuck into meaty traditional dishes in the Chop Room

Enjoy a Cold Pint

Friend at Hand Pub

Girly Drinks

(mains £7-10); sup on daily hot specials (£4.95) on the long wooden benches of the down-stairs Cellar Bar; or savor fancier cuisine on the 2nd fl. Johnson Room (£7-13). Front bar open M-F 11am-11pm, Sa 11am-3pm and 5:30-11pm, Su noon-3:30pm. Cellar Bar open daily 11am-3pm, as well as M-Th and Sa 5:30-11pm. Chop Room open daily noon-9:30pm. Johnson Room open M-F noon-2pm and 5:30-9:30pm. AmEx/MC/V.

Cittie of Yorke, 22-23 High Holborn St. (☎7242 7670). Next to the Gray's Inn gatehouse on High Holborn. Tube: Chancery Ln. Cittie of Yorke, with its towering raftered ceilings and chandelier from 1695, has served such patrons as Charles Dickens and Samuel Johnson. Three separate bars offer a choice between a bustling front room overlooking High Holborn, and the larger but more secluded back bar, overlooking Gray's Inn. Here, private tables resemble dark wood carriages set into the wall. Downstairs, the Cellar Bar's excellent lunch special (£4.95) features solid English fare with good vegetarian options. Open M-F 11am-11pm. AmEx/MC/V (£10 minimum).

The Old Bank of England, 194 Fleet St. (☎7430 2255). Tube: Temple. Next to the Royal Courts of Justice and directly across from the entrance to The Temple. Opened on the pre-mises of the 19th-century Bank of England, this enormous pub takes full advantage of its predecessor's towering ceilings, massive oil paintings, and impressive chandeliers. Sweeney Todd, "The Demon Barber of Fleet St.," killed his victims in the tunnels beneath the modern pub; his mistress turned them into meat pies next door. The Old Bank of England is "extremely proud" of its own meat pies (£6.75). Mains £5-10, sandwiches £3-4. Reserva-tions recommended for lunch. Open M-F 11am-11pm, kitchen closes at 9pm. AmEx/MC/V.

The Punch Tavern, 99 Fleet St. (☎7353 6658). Tube: Blackfriars. This laid-back, skylit pub occupies the old site of the Punch and Judy show—decor includes a funky set of puppets, and other interesting dramatical touches. Popular enough for lunch that some reserve tables. Dishes such as salmon fishcakes or scampi £5.50, sandwiches £3.50, jacket pota-toes £3.50. Open M-F 11am-11pm. AmEx/MC/V.

KENSINGTON & EARL'S COURT

SEE MAP, pp. 366-367

🚩 *KENSINGTON & EARL'S COURT QUICKFIND: Sights, p. 88; Museums & Galleries, p. 130; Food & Drink, p. 153; Entertainment, p. 210; Shopping, p. 229; Accommodations, p. 259.*

The Scarsdale, 23a Edwardes Sq. (☎7937 1811). Tube: High St. Kens-ington. The pub is hidden down the alleyways off Earl's Court Rd.—turn onto Earl's Walk and follow it to the end, then turn right. Built by a French speculator to house Napoleon's officers following the inevitable conquest of Britain, it's now a picture-perfect pub, welcoming local crowds to a sea of flowers outside and hanging lanterns inside. Always fantastically popular (dinner reservations are essential, even during the week) and for good reason, considering the elaborate food and great decor. Mains (£10-16) served noon-3pm and 6-10pm, bar food (salads and sandwiches, £6-9) served until 9pm. Open daily noon-11pm. MC/V.

The Troubadour, 265 Old Brompton Rd. (☎7370 1434; www.troubadoureclectic.com). Tube: Earl's Court. Brightly colored teapots sitting in the window provide a warm welcome to this combination coffee shop, pub, and deli, all under the same ownership. You can sit all day in this quirkily decorated, intimate establishment, from espresso shots in the morning to vodka shots at night. Open daily 9am-midnight.

KNIGHTSBRIDGE & BELGRAVIA

SEE MAP, p. 368

🚩 *KNIGHTBRIDGE & BELGRAVIA QUICKFIND: Sights, p. 90; Food & Drink, p. 154; Shopping, p. 230; Accommodations, p. 262.*

Grouse & Claret, Little Chester St. (☎7235 3438). Tube: Hyde Park Corner or Victoria. Traditional (though newish) pub on a quiet Belgravia mews, with lots of frosted-glass booths and polished wood. Food depends whether a roast is cooked that day; they always have freshly carved, hot gammon (roast pork steak) sandwiches (£3.15) and dinners (£6). Open M-Sa 11am-11pm. MC/V.

The Talbot, Little Chester St. (☎ 7235 1639). Cheerful, bright, and airy, the Talbot beckons both the errant traveler blundering into the Grosvenor mews and the smartly clad professional Londoner taking a lunch break. Meals are simple, hot, and cheap: sandwiches with three fillings are £3.25 and hot meals just £5.50. On a hot afternoon, share an icy pitcher of Pimm's and lemonade for £10. Open M-F 9am-11pm. MC/V.

NOTTING HILL

⚐ NOTTING HILL QUICKFIND:
Sights, p. 94; **Food & Drink,** p. 156; **Nightlife,** p. 187; **Entertainment,** p. 211; **Shopping,** p. 231.

SEE MAP, p. 361

Prince Albert Pub, 11 Pembridge Rd. (☎ 7727 5244). Tube: Notting Hill Gate. Euro-trendy meets blue-collar at the comfortably crowded Prince Albert's, where stained-glass windows preside over the cordial culture-cross. Take your pint to the breezy backyard patio. Open daily noon-11pm.

Portobello Gold, 95-97 Portobello Rd. (☎ 7460 4900). Tube: Notting Hill Gate. Classic pub with a convenient twist: along with a healthy selection of draughts and ales (£2.30-3), Portobello Gold has Internet terminals (£1 for half an hour) so punters can surf and drink at the same time. The picturesque restaurant area boasts a glass ceiling. Open daily 10am-10:30pm. MC/V.

THE SOUTH BANK

⚐ SOUTH BANK QUICKFIND:
Sights, p. 95; **Museums & Galleries,** p. 132; **Food & Drink,** p. 157; **Entertainment,** p. 212; **Accommodations,** p. 263.

SEE MAP, pp. 370-371

🕮 The Royal Oak, 44 Tabard St. (☎ 7357 7173). Tube: Borough. Voted the Best Pub of 2003 by the Campaign for Real Ale, the Royal Oak is one of the most pleasant establishments in London. Family-run, with an intensely loyal group of local patrons, it manages to be nostalgically traditional, yet extremely welcoming to outsiders. Superior pub grub (mains £4-6) served from noon-2:15pm and 6pm-9:15pm. Open M-F 11:30am-11pm. MC/V.

🕮 The George Inn, 77 Borough High St. (☎ 7407 2056). Tube: London Bridge. With a mention in Dickens's "Little Dorritt" and the honor of being the

GREAT BRITISH BEER FESTIVAL

The beer-lover's dream come true, the annual Great British Beer Festival brings over 450 ales under roof. If it's beer, and it's good, you'll find it here. The festival is organized by the Campaign for Real Ale (CAMRA) every year in early August. Obscure micro-breweries, big names, and international brands are all represented. Some breweries, including Courage, Fuller, and 🕮 Adnams, even have their own bars. The budding connoisseur can learn from the experts with tutored beer tastings (tickets go quickly, book in advance). The prestigious annual Champion Beer of Britain awards are also handed out for milds, bitters, best bitters, strong bitters, specialty beers, and real ales. The Champion award is considered the consumer's top choice award, and those at the festival get first taste of the winners.

Beer is the main focus of the festival, but food, entertainment, and even nonalcoholic drinks get some space. Food stalls sell international fare, plus traditional pub foods like cornish pasties, sausages, and pork scratching. Entertainment includes live music, pub games, and street theatre, including the popular balloon twiddlers. For tickets or more information, go to www.camra.org.uk or call ☎ 2786 7201.

only remaining galleried inn in London, the George Inn takes great pride in its historical tradition. A deceptively tiny interior leads out into a popular patio, full of migrants from the City across the river. The ale is excellent, the atmosphere is relaxed, and the proprietor is pleased to hold forth on his pub's storied past. Open M-Sa 11am-11pm, Su noon-10:30pm. AmEx/MC/V.

THE WEST END

SEE MAP, p. 356

⚑ WEST END QUICKFIND: Sights, p. 98; **Museums & Galleries,** p. 134; **Food & Drink,** p. 158; **Nightlife,** p. 188; **Entertainment,** p. 213; **Shopping,** p. 233; **Accommodations,** p. 263.

⚑ Lamb and Flag, 33 Rose St. (☎7497 9504). Once commonly called the "Bucket of Blood" in honor of the bare-knuckle fights held upstairs, a tradition documented by numerous framed sketches. The dark-wood interior, the quality ale, and the harried but friendly staff combine to make it one of the best places to enjoy a nice pint in Covent Garden—and everyone knows it. Regularly packed, but everyone's too happy to even notice. Food daily noon-3pm. Live jazz upstairs Su from 7:30pm. Open M-Th 11am-11pm, F-Sa 11am-10:45pm, Su noon-10:30pm.

⚑ Dog and Duck, 18 Bateman St. (☎7494 0697). Tube: Tottenham Court Rd. This historic establishment occupies the site of the Duke of Monmouth's Soho house. The smallest and oldest pub still standing in Soho, its name recalls the area's hunting past. The theme continues in the original Victorian tiled interior—look out for the dog-and-duck tiles lower down opposite the bar and the matching mosaic underfoot at the Frith St. entrance. Now you can order classic pub-grub (steak and ale pie £7.50) at the bar. Open M-Sa noon-11pm, Su noon-10:30pm.

Freedom Brewing Co., underneath Thomas Neal's at 41 Earlham St. (☎7240 0606). This pub is one of London's few microbreweries and a winner of numerous awards. Most of the post-work professional crowd stakes out space on the stylish, translucent red chairs. Pints from £3, sampler gives you a sip of 3 beers for £1.70. Food is standard, if pricey, pub fare: sandwiches £7, main dishes £7-11. Happy Hour M-F 6-8pm, £2 pints. £5 lunches M-F, includes pint of Pilsner or glass of wine. Open M-Sa noon-11pm, Su noon-10:30pm. AmEx/MC/V.

Maple Leaf, 41 Maiden Ln. (☎7240 2843). Need a break from the local blokes? In this pub, start a rousing chorus of "O Canada" as you down Alberta beefburgers (£6.45), *quebecois poutine* (fries with cheese and gravy, £4). Molson on tap (£2.95), and 20p chicken wings M 6-9pm. Hope that your arteries will hold out long enough for you to appreciate all the Canadian pride. Hockey nights W-Th from 7pm. Open M-Sa 11am-11pm, Su noon-10:30pm. AmEx/MC/V.

The Cross Keys, 31 Endell St. (☎7836 5185). It's all about ambience in this small, dark pub half-hidden by wildly flowering plants: gold lamps cast an eerie glow over framed photographs and brass pots dangling from the ceiling. Far from being intimidating, however, the decor only enhances the cozy feel. If you're missing the sunlight, take a pint of ale to one of the benches outside. Food served noon-2:30pm daily. Open M-Sa 11am-11pm, Su noon-10:30pm.

The Toucan, 19 Carlisle St. (☎7437 4123). Tube: Tottenham Court Rd. Small, snug, tight-knit pub right outside of Soho Sq., bursting with Irish pride and with blowzy, affable men swigging Guinness. Arrive before the early-evening crowds, stake out a place at the bar, and stay for the camaraderie—and the whiskey. Open M-F 11am-11pm, Sa noon-11pm.

Comptons of Soho, 53 Old Compton St. (☎7479 7461). Tube: Leicester Sq. or Piccadilly Circus. The rainbow flag flies with pride outside Soho's oldest gay pub, which fills early with a male crowd of all ages. Horseshoe-shaped bar encourages meaningful glances, while the upstairs lounge (opens 6:30pm) offers a more mellow scene with pool table. Open M-Sa noon-11pm, Su noon-10:30pm. MC/V.

The Shepherds Tavern, 50 Hertford St. (☎7499 3017). Tube: Hyde Park Corner or Green Park. In 1735, Edward Shepherd of Shepherd Market fame also lent his name to this local watering hole, which today attracts a diverse clientele of tired shoppers and locals. Thoroughly unglamorous (except for the random chandeliers hanging from the bright red ceiling), it feels like a worn-in couch—nothing snazzy, just a comfortable, relaxed atmosphere. Kitchen (open until 30min.

before closing) serves traditional favorites like shepherd's pie (£7.50). Open M-Sa 11am-11pm, Su noon-3pm and 7-10:30pm. AmEx/MC/V.

Admiral Duncan, 54 Old Compton St. (☎ 7437 5300). Tube: Leicester Sq. or Piccadilly Circus. Proclaimed as the gay "Cheers!", everyone knows your name at this popular hangout, which attracts a diverse mix of men and women. At night, this narrow standing-room pub fills with a laid-back male crowd. Open noon-11pm daily.

The Duke of York, 7 Dering St. (☎ 7629 0319). Tube: Bond St. Generic name aside, this pub packs in plenty of fun while you pack down the pints (£2.60-3). The three floors are connected by a tight, dramatic spiral staircase—the ground floor holds the bar, the first floor feels like a restaurant, and the basement "comfort zone" is perfect for some lazy lounging or a game of pool or darts. Open M-Sa 11am-11pm; Su noon-10:30pm. MC/V.

WESTMINSTER

The Grapes Ale House

⏻ WESTMINSTER QUICK-FIND: Sights, p. 104; **Museums & Galleries,** p. 136; **Food & Drink,** p. 162; **Entertainment,** p. 216; **Accommodations,** p. 264.

SEE MAP, p. 372

⚑ The Cask and Glass, 39-41 Palace St. Tube: St. James's Park. The proprietor claims that this is the "second smallest pub in London," and it's certainly among the coziest. This pleasant, quiet establishment is a second home to a loyal troop of patrons, that claims to treat outsiders "with grace." Not to be missed. Decent sandwiches £3.50, ploughman's lunch £4.25. Open M-F 11am-11pm, Sa noon-8pm.

Red Lion, 48 Parliament St. (☎ 7930 5826). Tube: Westminster. *The* politicians' pub. TVs carrying the Parliament cable channel allow MPs to listen to the debates over a warm pint, while a "division bell" alerts them to drink up when a vote is about to be taken. Even the decor—predominantly political cartoons—reminds you that Parliament is just across the street. Despite the distinguished clientele, the food (sandwiches £3, hot dishes £6) is decidedly ordinary. Food served daily noon-3pm. Open M-Sa 11am-11pm, Su noon-7pm. MC/V.

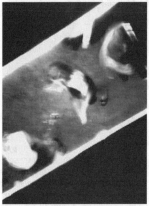

Mingling

The Old Shades, 37 Whitehall. (☎ 7321 2801). Tube: Charing Cross. If the clubby atmosphere of the Red Lion becomes too much for you, you may want to try this bustling, pleasant pub in the heart of Whitehall. Lunchtime crowds aside, The Old Shades offers up a great assortment of bitters, and an extremely spacious interior—the perfect break from the throngs in Trafalgar Sq. The food is a cut above the usual pub standard, serving solid British fare (£5-7). Open M-Sa 11am-11pm, Su noon-3pm and 7-10:30pm. MC/V.

A Little vino

179

Sherlock Holmes, 10-11 Northumberland St. (☎7930 2644). Tube: Charing Cross. In the former Northumberland Hotel, as mentioned in the *Hound of the Baskervilles*. Numerous Holmesian "artifacts" are displayed in the pub, and diners in the excellent upstairs restaurant (mains £9-13) can view a replica of Holmes's study. Cheaper pub food is served downstairs. Sherlock Holmes Ale £2.30, sandwiches £3-5, hot meals £6. Food served daily noon-10pm. Open M-Sa 11am-11pm, Su noon-10:30pm. Restaurant open M-Th noon-3pm, and 5:30-10pm; F-Su noon-10pm. MC/V.

NORTH LONDON

🔌 *NORTH LONDON QUICKFIND: Sights, p. 107; Museums & Galleries, p. 137; Food & Drink, p. 163; Nightlife, p. 192; Entertainment, p. 216; Shopping, p. 240; Accommodations, p. 265.*

🏶 **The Wenlock Arms,** 26 Wenlock Rd. Tube: Old St. or Angel. One of the best-kept secrets in London, this fantastic traditional pub is the real deal, with an unbeatable array of real ales, and the best hot salt beef sandwich in the city (£3). The atmosphere is warm and relaxed, and the crowd of noisy and congenial locals are all mates. One of the very best pubs in London. Food served "until we run out of bread." Open Tu-F 11am-7pm, Sa 10am-4pm. MC/V.

🏶 **Compton Arms,** 4 Compton Ave. (☎7359 6883; www.comptonarms.net). Tube: Highbury and Islington. This charming, cozy pub is removed enough from Upper St. to escape the hectic crowds. Low ceilings and multicolored bar stools enhance the friendly, amiable atmosphere. The tiny "beer garden" in back is actually a picturesque outdoor patio where locals enjoy their sausages and mash. Su comedy video night. Food served daily noon-2pm and 6-8pm. Open M-Sa noon-11pm, Su noon-10:30pm.

Camden Head, 2 Camden Walk (☎7359 0851). Tube: Angel. Chintzy rose wallpaper and plenty of etched glass give this large, comfortable pub a traditional Victorian atmosphere far removed from most Islington yuppie hangouts. The only thing that makes it better are the wonderfully cheap prices. Jug of Pimms with vodka and Red Bull £10; food served noon-9:30pm daily, and you can get 2 meals for £6. Also offers comedy nights every night upstairs starting around 9pm. Open M-Sa 11am-11pm, Su noon-10:30pm.

The World's End, 174 Camden High St. (☎7482 1932). Tube: Camden Town. Smack in the middle of all the Camden Town action, this sprawling pub is permanently buzzing. With two bar areas (one with traditional pub decor and the other in an open indoor arcade), a fine dining area, and upper-level balcony seating, World's End lives up to its claim of being "probably the largest pub in the world." Located below the pub, The Underworld venue hosts live bands. Open M-Th 11am-11pm, F-Sa 11am-midnight, Su noon-10:30pm.

The Flask, 77 Highgate West Hill (☎8348 7346). Bus #214 from Kentish Town or #210 from Archway. Built in 1663, the low-ceilinged, intricate interior of this pub is perfect for winter evenings, while summer drinkers regularly spill over from the beer garden onto the green in front. The changing menu mixes Olde English (sausage and mash £8) with modern British (sandwiches around £5). Open M-Sa 11am-11pm, Su noon-10:30pm. MC/V.

Duke of Cambridge, 30 St. Peter's St. (☎7359 3066). Dedicated to the art of environmentally responsible dining, even much of the alcohol in this gastropub is organic. Specializing in fresh fish dishes, the kitchen changes the menu twice a day to keep you on your toes. Mains £7-13. Dinner M-Sa 6:30-10:30pm, Su 6:30-10pm; lunch M-F 12:30-3pm, Sa-Su 12:30-3:30pm. Open M-Sa noon-11pm, Su noon-10:30pm. AmEx/MC/V.

King William IV (KW4), 77 Hampstead High St. (☎7435 5647). The rainbow flag fluttering outside the well-kept, 18th-century facade says it all—a rocking gay bar in the body of a Victorian pub. The most popular event here is the traditional British Sunday lunch (£6.50). During the summer KW4 hosts barbecues in the sizable beer garden Sa-Su. Otherwise, pub food served daily noon-4pm. Open M-Sa noon-11pm, Su noon-10:30pm.

Freemason's Arms, 32 Downshire Hill (☎7433 6811). Tube: Hampstead. All that you'd expect from a pub, but much larger, with a fuller menu and a sizable beer garden right next to the heath. The inside was designed by Erno Goldfinger in what was obviously one of his boring, traditional moments. Open M-Sa noon-11pm, Su noon-10:30pm. AmEx/MC/V.

EAST LONDON

🛈 EAST LONDON QUICKFIND: Sights, *p. 112;* **Museums & Galleries,** *p. 139;* **Food & Drink,** *p. 167;* **Nightlife,** *p. 196;* **Entertainment,** *p. 219;* **Shopping,** *p. 242.*

▧ Prospect of Whitby, 57 Wapping Wall (☎ 7481 1095). Tube: Wapping. This fantastic 1570 pub would be worth a visit just for the spectacular river view, but it has the added advantage of a weathered stone floor and a highly-polished old pewter bar. Mains £5-7, sandwiches £3-4. Food M-Sa noon-9pm, Su noon-3pm and 6-9pm. Open M-F 11:30am-11pm, Su noon-10:30pm. AmEx/MC/V.

Cat and Canary, 1-24 Fisherman's Walk (☎ 7512 9187). DLR: Canary Wharf. A fairly standard yet pleasant Fuller's pub, the Cat and Canary benefits from a superb river view and a large, classy interior. Standard pub grub (£5-7). Open M-Sa 11am-11pm, Su noon-10:30pm. Food served M-F 11am-11pm, Sa 11am-4pm. AmEx/MC/V.

Nightlife

NIGHTLIFE BY TYPE

BARS (DRINKING)

In London these days, drinking is the new dancing, and bars are the new nightclubs. An explosion of club-bars has invaded the previously forgotten zone between pubs and clubs, offering seriously stylish surroundings and top-flight DJs together with plentiful lounging space and a wide selection of bottled lagers (the current "in" drink). Often incorporating both restaurants and dance floors, the new bars are designed as one-stop nightspots, combining all you need for an evening's entertainment under one roof. Usually, club-bars are open from noon or early evening, allowing you to skip the cover charge (if there is one) by arriving early and staying put as the scene shifts around you. On the other hand, they tend to close earlier than clubs, usually between midnight and 2am, so you'll need to move on to a "real" nightclub for late night early morning action.

NIGHTCLUBS (DANCING)

Every major DJ in the world either lives in London or makes frequent visits to the city. While the US may have introduced house music to the world, the UK has taken the lead in developing and experimenting with new types of dance music, and club culture in London is all pervasive—18- to 30-year-old Londoners live to party. Such is the variety and fast-changing nature of London nightlife that even weekly publications have trouble keeping up—even *Time Out*, the Londoner's clubbing bible, only lists about half the club happenings in London on any given night.

DRESS. London clubs often fall into one of two categories: those for dancing, and those for posing. In the former, dress codes are generally relaxed; it's not uncommon to find clubbers dressed in nothing fancier than jeans, a stylish T-shirt, and trainers (sneakers), although women are usually expected to make more of an effort and pulling on a pair of "proper" shoes never hurts your chances. At posers' clubs, however, dress is crucial, and what's expected depends very much on the scene. If you're not sure what to wear, call up the club beforehand (although answers like "New York super-funk glam" aren't always that helpful); otherwise, black and slinky is generally safe. The exception to the categorization are theme nights, especially retro clubs—you're unlikely to get in unless you look like an extra from *Saturday Night Fever*. If a bouncer says it's "members and regulars only," he thinks you're not up to scratch; however, persistence can pay off, especially when accompanied by a sob story—like how it's your best friend's birthday and she's already inside.

PLANNING. Planning is important for the discriminating clubber. Look before you leap, and especially before you drink. Avoid the bright glitzy clubs of Leicester Sq. (e.g. Equinox and Hippodrome), in which no Londoner would be seen dead—they're crowded with out-of-town English youth looking to get lucky. Instead, comb through listings in *Time Out* which also prints the weekly "TOP" club pass (look in the clubbing section). The latter gives you discounts on entry to many of the week's shenanigans. For popular clubs, it's worth learning the names of the DJs (not to mention the type of music) just to prove to the bouncer that you're part of the scene. Working out **how to get home** afterwards is crucial; remember that the Tube and regular buses stop shortly after midnight, and after 1am black cabs are like gold dust. If there's no convenient night bus home, ask the club in advance if they can order a minicab (unlicensed taxicab) for you on the night; otherwise, order your own (see p. 334 for phone numbers). Although it's technically illegal for minicabs to ply for hire, whispered calls of "taxi, taxi" or honking horns signal their presence outside clubs and in nightlife-heavy neighborhoods—however, you've no guarantee that the driver is reputable or even insured. If you have no other option, agree on a price before you get in, and never ride alone.

SELECTED CLUB NIGHTS

London clubbing revolves around promoters and the nights they organize rather than the bricks-and-mortar clubs themselves. This gives London clubbing both its incredible range and its infuriating ephemeral nature, as promoters arrange one-off events, move regular nights between clubs, or just get married and find a "proper" job. While some locations have a music policy that favors one genre of clubbing over another—the Ministry of Sound is solidly house-based, for example—in most clubs what's on one night has nothing to do with what's on the next. Below is a selection of particular club nights that we think are something special; however, it's inevitable that some will move to different clubs or different nights, shift from weekly to monthly, or simply fold altogether. Always call ahead to check the details still hold, and don't forget that these listings barely scrape the surface of what's offered.

GAY NIGHTS

G-A-Y, see Soho, p. 190.

Love Muscle, every other Sa at the Fridge (see p. 195). As big and brash as they come, led by Yvette and her stage troupe of "horny and hunky, spunky studs." "Hot and steamy fun"–their words. Open 10pm-6am, followed by after-party at Fridge Bar, cover £6 (see p. 194). Cover £13.

Popstarz, F at Scala (see p. 193). A long-running gay/mixed extravaganza. Covers the whole musical spectrum: the Rubbish Room is devoted to the most embarrassing hits of the 80s, the Love Lounge hosts 70s funk and disco, indie lives in Common Room, while house stays home in the Big Beat Bar. Open 10pm-5am. Cover £8; free with flyer before 11pm.

DANCE

Shake, Sa at the Electric Ballroom (see p. 194). Over 1000 people pack the 3 floors, grooving to a range of 70s, 80s, and 90s disco music. Open 10:30pm-3am. Cover £10.

FUNK AND JAZZ

Deep Funk, F at Madame Jojo's (see p. 189). Resident Keb Darge's legendary funk jam night: funkier than an evening with James Brown, plumbing the depths of 60s and 70s music. Most of the laid-back student crowd is content to sit back and watch the amazing feats of the dedicated movers and shakers on the floor. Things get churning around 11:30pm. Open 10pm-3am. Cover £8; £6 before 11pm.

THIS! (That's How It iS), M at Bar Rumba (see p. 189). It's been a while since the Bar Rumba's Saturday heyday, but on a Monday you won't do better than THIS! Jazzy sounds swing uptempo through the evening, from Miles Davis to dancy, eclectic jazz-funk—you could listen all night, and most people do, though there's no shortage of freestylers bopping and swerving on the floor. Open 9pm-3:30am. Cover £5.

HOUSE AND GARAGE

Escape From Samsara, F at the Fridge (☎8889 5221). Is everyone raving mad, or are they just in a trance? Massive night out, with a midnight stage show and stilt walkers moving among the fluorescent hangings. Around the dance floor, stalls sell essentials like glo-sticks (£2.50 each) and king-size Rizlas (£1), plus anything else that fluoresces under UV. Dress code fairly relaxed, but the brighter, tighter, and spanglier the better. If you want more, escape to the Fridge Bar afterparty (see p. 194). Open 10pm-6am. Cover £14; £9 before 11pm.

INDIE & ALTERNATIVE

Full Tilt, F at the Electric Ballroom (see p. 194). London's oldest and best-known alternative night; goths flock to this festival of leather, ripped lace, and pierced flesh. Industrial techno and punk goth. Open 10:30pm-3am. Cover £7.

Feet First, Tu at Camden Palace (see p. 194). Popular Indie/alternative/rock midweeker, with a mix of leather-clad goths and T-shirted students thrashing wildly to heavy guitar sounds. Be warned—queue starts early and much of the crowd looks barely 15. 30min. live band at 12:30am—Pulp, Blur, and Feeder all played here before hitting the big time. Jumbo ice pops £1. Cover £5, students £3.

RETRO

School Disco, see sidebar, p. 188.

NIGHTLIFE BY NEIGHBORHOOD

CLERKENWELL

▌ *CLERKENWELL QUICKFIND: Sights, p. 82; Museums & Galleries, p. 128; Food & Drink, p. 151; Pubs, p. 174; Entertainment, p. 210; Accommodations, p. 259.*

SEE MAP, p. 365

If London's fashionable epicenter has shifted east to Hoxton, so much the better for Clerkenwell—less posing, more partying! Most nightspots are found around Charterhouse St. and St. John's St., with a lower concentration on Clerkenwell Rd. Be aware that this isn't the most pleasant area to walk at night; while it doesn't have a particularly dangerous reputation, the streets tend to be narrow, winding, and dark, so you may feel uncomfortable walking by yourself.

the hidden deal

Cheap Soles

Like many things in London, clubbing is an expensive pastime. Cover charges run £10-15, and you'll probably spend as much again on drinks—even a beer will set you back £3-5. Add in a taxi home, and an evening's out can easily set you back £50.

There are ways of limiting the damage. First, **arrive early**—cover charges rise after 10 or 11pm. Since most clubs don't get busy until midnight, though, it's easy to lose the savings in extra drinks until the dance floor fills up.

Bring a **club flyer** along. Usually available in dance-music shops, presenting a flyer can often save you pounds on the door. Alternatively, if you're a student try showing an **ISIC card**—most clubs only give discounts to NUS (National Union of Students) card holders, but it's worth a try.

Avoid weekends and instead opt for **midweek clubbing,** when cover charges are lower—though there are fewer options, London has enough students, slackers, and devoted party people to pack a few clubs even Su-W.

Alternatively, skip nightclubs altogether and head to a **club-bar.** Increasingly popular, these have smaller dance floors (and more couches), but still attract top DJs for covers that vary from free to £5.

DRINKING

Cafe Kick, 43 Exmouth Market (☎7837 8077; www.cafekick.co.uk). Tube: Farringdon or Angel. Dedicated to the twin goals of drinking and football (soccer), this is a cantina most men would call heaven. There's a jovial, Latin American feel to this cafe-bar, dominated by multiple foosball tables (50p per game) which play host to monthly table football contests. Happy Hour 4-7pm daily (beer of the day £1.50). Otherwise, beers and cocktails £2.50-5.50. Open M-Sa 11:30am-11pm, Su noon-11pm.

Match EC1, 45-47 Clerkenwell Rd. (☎7250 4002; www.matchbar.com). Tube: Farringdon. With an original drinks list full of exclusive concoctions created by Match bartenders and Dale DeGroff ("The King of Cocktails"), Match has made its reputation with quality cocktails (£6-6.50). The family-style "big bowl" dishes (£7-20) are ideal for group meals, while the sunken bar and plush setting make it an ideal spot for lounging. Open M-Sa 11am-midnight. AmEx/MC/V.

DANCING

✪ **Fabric,** 77a Charterhouse St. (☎7336 8898; www.fabriclondon.com). Tube: Farringdon. One of London's premier clubbing venues, Fabric is as large and loud as it gets, featuring a vibrating main dance floor that is actually one giant speaker. Chill-out beds, multiple bars, and three dance floors crammed with up to 1900 dance-crazed Londoners. F *Fabric Live* (hip-hop, breakbeat; 9:30pm-5am; cover £12), Sa *Fabric* (house, techno; 10pm-7am; £15), Su *DTPM* polysexual night (house; 10pm-5am; £15).

Fluid, 40-42 Charterhouse St. (☎7253 3444). Tube: Farringdon. Sushi bar by day, intimate nightclub by night, Fluid is the perfect antidote to megaclub madness. The basement dance floor, adorned with a Tokyo cityscape at one end and a glowing bar at the other, is too small for serious dancing. Instead, chill upstairs on the fabu leather couches under the soft projections. Th *Orient Exxpress* beats and breaks; F *Fluid Session* friendly funk; Sa *Eye Candy* funky house. Generally free before 10pm (Sa 11pm), then cover £3. Restaurant open M-W noon-midnight, Th-F noon-3pm and 5-10pm; club Th-Sa 8pm-2am.

Turnmills, 63 Clerkenwell Rd. (☎7250 3409; www.turnmills.co.uk). Tube: Farringdon. Clubbing Tomb-Raider style: enter through a Spanish restaurant into a subterranean maze of themed zones, from post-industrial jungle to French bistro. The glammed-up, affluent crowd is more intent on eyeing up than getting down. Tu Salsa (classes from 6:30pm on); F *The Gallery* hard and funky house with art show (10:30pm-7:30am; £10); Sa monthlies and one-offs (10pm-5am; £15-20).

HOLBORN

⛶ *HOLBORN QUICKFIND: Sights, p. 84; Museums & Galleries, p. 128; Food & Drink, p. 152; Pubs, p. 175; Entertainment, p. 210; Shopping, p. 229.*

SEE MAP, p. 365

DRINKING

Na Zdrowie, 11 Little Turnstile (☎7831 9679). Hidden in the alleyways behind the Holborn Tube station—when you see Pu's Brasserie, look to the left. Tube: Holborn. The minimalist decor—including a wall of fragmented mirrors and a row of chrome Polish eagles—marks Na Zdrowie out as an oddity among the generally dour Holborn restaurants, as do the over 65 vodkas on offer for around £2 a shot. The latter makes the establishment fantastically popular in the evening, but at quieter times patrons dive into the sandwiches (£2.50-3) and hearty Polish fare (£5-6). The name (nah-ZDROVE-yeh) is a Polish toast. Open M-F 12:30-11pm, Sa 6-11pm. MC/V.

NOTTING HILL

⛶ *NOTTING HILL QUICKFIND: Sights, p. 94; Food & Drink, p. 156; Pubs, p. 187; Entertainment, p. 211; Shopping, p. 231.*

SEE MAP, p. 361

DRINKING

▨ **The Market,** 240A Portobello Rd. (☎7229 6472). Tube: Ladbroke Grove. Consistently the loudest spot on Portobello—which is no mean feat—The Market has a rowdy, unpretentious atmosphere in tune with the local Caribbean vibe. A perfect location to take in market sights while downing a cool Cuban punch (£3). Jazz Su 5-8pm. Open M-Sa 11am-11pm, Su noon-12:30am.

192, 192 Kensington Park Rd. (☎7229 0482). Tube: Ladbroke Grove. The 192 of *Bridget Jones* fame is filled to the brim with the young and fashionable, who lounge on plush red couches. Stylishly trendy with low lighting and more class than it knows what to do with. Range of reasonable wines (£3-6 per glass), smaller selection of pricey food (£14). Bar open M-Sa 12:30-11pm, Su 12:30-10:30pm. Restaurant open M-Sa 12:30-11:30pm, Su 12:30-11pm. MC/V.

Pharmacy, 150 Notting Hill Gate (☎7221 2442). Tube: Notting Hill Gate. The talk of the town when it first opened, Damien Hirst's pharmacy-themed bar has lost its controversial edge, and now thrives comfortably in yuppieland. Clinical environment of bright lights and medicine cabinets makes for a strangely ideal place to strut and pose. The takeaway cafe next door is named, of course, Outpatients. Caters to deep pockets: mains £7.50-24, cocktails £6-7.50. Bar open Su-Th noon-3pm and 5pm-1am, F noon-3pm and 5:30pm-2am, Sa noon until Su opening. Restaurant open M-F noon-2:35pm and 7pm-close, Sa 7pm-close. AmEx/MC/V.

DANCING

▨ **Notting Hill Arts Club,** 21 Notting Hill Gate (☎7460 4459). Tube: Notting Hill Gate. With turntables on folding tables, 1 dance floor, and no decoration beyond projections and art left over from daytime exhibitions, this no-frills basement still manages to rock the house. A friendly, casual venue for rock stars and Rastafarians to sip cocktails (£2.50-3.15) and groove to a range of eclectic music. Acts vary daily. Open M-W 6pm-1am, Th-F 6pm-2am, Sa

Night School

Recently, Londoners have grown used to seeing groups of youngsters, still dressed in school uniform, queuing up for 18+ nightclubs and cavorting with each other in ways their mothers certainly wouldn't approve of. Rather than calling the police, though, more and more people are joining in: we're not talking about an epidemic of teenage delinquency, but rather the newest (and craziest) craze in London clubbing—**School Disco.**

Since starting in a small restaurant in 1999, the original School Disco has moved and expanded as it has grown in popularity, now running two nights a week spawning a host of imitators. Londoners, it seems, can't wait to pull on those itchy polyester skirts, trousers, ties, and jackets most were only too glad to dump a few years before, and dance to cheesy 80s chart hits and get down to serious business in the snogging room. So if you never found out why high school was meant to be "the best days of your life," now's your chance to make up (and make out).

School Disco (☎0871 872 1234; www.school-disco.com) is held F at **Heaven** (see p. 192; 9pm-3am, £15) and Sa at **Po Na Na Hammersmith,** 242 Shepherd's Bush Rd. (Tube: Hammersmith. 10pm-3am, £12.50). Strict "school uniform" dress code: check the website for details and a list of school outfitters.

4pm-2am, Su 4pm-12:30am. M cover £4, free before 9pm; Tu-Th £5, free before 8pm; F £6, free before 8pm; Sa-Su £5, free before 6pm.

THE WEST END

OXFORD ST. & REGENT ST.

🏠 *OXFORD ST. & REGENT ST.* QUICKFIND: *Sights,* p. 98; *Museums & Galleries,* p. 134; *Food & Drink,* p. 158; *Pubs,* p. 178; *Entertainment,* p. 213; *Shopping,* p. 233; *Accommodations,* p. 263.

SEE MAP, p. 356

DRINKING

The Social, 5 Little Portland St. (☎7636 4992; www.thesocial.com). Tube: Oxford Circus. This small DJ-driven bar packs a happening crowd into its maze of narrow spaces. Upstairs fosters a low-key fluorescent-lit diner atmosphere with eccentric pub food whereas downtairs has a harder edge. Cocktails £5.10, shooters £3. DJs nightly from 7pm. Open M-Sa noon-11pm. No cover.

Propaganda, 201 Wardour St. (☎7434 3820). Tube: Oxford Circus or Tottenham Court Rd. Ultra-plush moody club-bar with two uber-hip glowing bars. With waitress service, you won't even need to get up; when you see the bill (shots £6), you won't be able to. If you dare, join the fashionable set on the pop-art dance floor; on weekends the dancing extends into the club downstairs (open W, F-Su). The adjoining restaurant (snacks £3.50-5, mains £6.50-8) stays open all night. Open M-Sa noon-3am, Su noon-midnight. Cover £5-15 on club nights.

DANCING

🕺 **Strawberry Moons,** 15 Heddon St. (☎7437 7300; www.strawberrymoons.co.uk). Tube: Piccadilly Circus or Oxford Circus. Eccentric, hip bar-club with theatrical lighting effects, an animatronic talking moose head, a "time machine," and a staff that performs impromptu dance routines. The fun starts early, with an enthusiastic crowd dancing and singing loudly to a non-stop hit parade from every decade and genre. All the fun of prom, with none of the unnecessary drama. Tu hip hop, garage, R&B (cover £5, ladies free before midnight); Th *Reach for the Stars* mixed hits, karaoke (free before 10pm, £5 after); F *Body Heat* (free before 9pm, £5 9-10pm, £7 after 10pm); Sa *Fever!* chart classics (free before 8pm, 8pm-9pm £5, 9pm-10pm £7, after 10pm £9). Open M and W 5pm-11pm, Tu and Th-Sa 5pm-3am.

SOHO

🆘 SOHO QUICKFIND: Sights, p. 101; Museums & Galleries, p. 134; Food & Drink, p. 159; Pubs, p. 178; Entertainment, p. 213; Shopping, p. 237; Accommodations, p. 263.

DRINKING

Point 101, 101 New Oxford St. (☎7379 3112). Tube: Tottenham Court Rd. Underneath the signature Centrepoint office tower, 101 has a cosmopolitan and impersonal 1970s look and feel, with low steam-moulded plywood chairs and tables, and long vinyl booths in the balcony bar (accessed via a separate door). The 70s theme ends there—nightly DJ's, starting around 9pm, tends towards chill-out jazz, latin, and soul. Turnouts are big, but the sprawling space dilutes the crowd factor. Open M-Th 8am-2am, F-Sa 8am-2:30am, Su 8am-11:30pm. AmEx/MC/V.

Yo!Below, 52 Poland St., below Yo!Sushi (☎7439 3660). Tube: Piccadilly Circus. Another concept-driven Yo! venture (see p. 147). Professionals unwind at futuristic blue booths and tables sunk into the floor, complete with self-service beer taps (£1.30 for a small glass). Staff belt out karaoke, give tarot readings, and egg on *Jenga* participants. Since the public got jealous, Tu night *Karayo!ke* has been added to the weekly quirky repertoire. Impressive selection of sake sticks (£5-5.50). Open daily 5pm-1am, food to 11pm. AmEx/MC/V.

DANCING

Bar Rumba, 36 Shaftesbury Ave. (☎7287 2715; www.barrumba.co.uk). Tube: Piccadilly Circus. Long *the* place to be in London, Rumba now lures a fresh, young crowd that makes good use of the industrial-strength interior. The sound system goes for high fidelity over volume. Arrive early or risk spending most of the night waiting in line. M *This!* (see p. 185) starts off the week with a bang. Tu latin with salsa-rap and techno-merengue (9pm-3am; cover £4, students £3); W 70s-00s classics (£5, £3 students, £4 with flyer); Th perpetual sexy drum&bass (8:30pm-3am; £6, £3 before 10pm); F global house (9pm-4am; £10, £6 before 11pm, free before 10pm); Sa US garage night (9pm-5am; £12, £7 before 11pm); Su street soul and R&B (8pm-1:30am; £5, women free before 10pm).

Madame Jojo's, 8-10 Brewer St. (☎7734 3040; www.madamejojos.com). Tube: Piccadilly Circus. The home of deep funk. Intimate bordello-style red-hued club, with a sunken dance floor inviting grand entrances down the staircase. Th deep beats with DJs Trouble and Funkie P; cover £7, £5 before 11. F *Deep Funk* says it all (see p. 185), Sa *Groove Sanctuary* deep soulful house, nu-jazz, samba soul, and latin (10pm-3am; £8, £6 before 11). Also Sa, Soho's premiere drag cabaret, "Kitsch Cabaret" (doors open 7pm).

Sound, 10 Wardour St. (☎7287 1010). Tube: Leicester Sq. or Piccadilly Circus. In keeping with its commercial Leicester Sq. location, this maze of a club is both glitzy and glittery, with a large, loud main room and balcony bar on the 1st and 2nd floors, and the Sound Bar on the ground floor. The basement restaurant and the posh Blue Room have separate entrances through the Swiss Centre on Leicester Sq. After a recent about-face, this club has hyped up and now periodically attracts some of the biggest names in Europe. Th *Starlight Live* is the people's night with a full stage show and talent contest (10pm-3am; cover £8, £5 before 11pm).

Rouge, 144 Charing Cross Rd., down the alleyway (☎7240 1900; www.rougeclublondon.com). Tube: Tottenham Court Rd. After merging with the live-music Studio Club, Rouge is now a revamped warehouse-style venue with four floors, five bars, and aspirations to chic-ness. Cocktails £4.40 singles, £6.60 doubles. W old skool live music; Th 3 rooms of R&B, disco, electropop, live cabaraet and jam session (£10); F funky house, R&B, club classics, eclectic beats (£15, guests £10); Sa R&B, old skool hip-hop, funky house, Brazilian beats (£15, guests £10). Open 8pm-4am nightly.

GAY & LESBIAN

BarCode, 3-4 Archer St. (☎7734 3342). Tube: Piccadilly Circus. On a dark alley in the seedier side of Soho is this bustling, cruisy men's—men's only—bar. The only thing better groomed than the tightly-dressed, no-nonsense clientele is the impeccable inte-

the local story

ERIC MILLER, DJ

Mr. Miller has been DJing in the UK for over 20 years. He founded "nu funky people," a group that encourages experimental musicians.

LG: What are your favorite venues in London?

A: Among others, I enjoy the Tongue&Groove, because it's a very intimate venue, and it feels like you're dancing with the crowd in there, which is very unusual. It reminds you that you're there having fun and it's great—though not when people spill drinks on you, of course.

LG: Why do you think the clubbing scene is so big in London?

A: In London, everything is extremely fast-paced and cosmopolitan, and I think it's reflected in the music. You go to a techno night, and you could have a Brazilian techno DJ who puts latin sounds in his music. The eclecticism here really makes a difference.

LG: What do you think of pop music?

A: I tend to go for good songwriting and mucisianship. I've got nothing against pop music; I just don't like the churned-out, conveyor-belt, boy/girl band crap. My favorite genre is jazz, as well as drum&bass, anything funky. That's one of the beauties of dance music today: people

rior. F-Sa the action shifts to the downstairs dance floor, open starting at 10pm. Comedy club Tu evenings. Open daily 4pm-1am.

Ku Bar, 75 Charing Cross Rd. (☎ 7437 4303; www.ku-bar.co.uk). Tube: Leicester Sq. Don't be fooled by the naked-lady mosaic; this fashionable hangout is definitely gay. Staff that looks vacuum-packed into impossibly tight T-shirts and jeans pours drinks (cocktail pitchers £7 before 9pm) for well-dressed men. Get your tickets to *G-A-Y.* (see below) and Heaven here and skip the queue. Bottled beer from £2.90. Open M-Sa 1-11pm, Su 1-10:30pm.

Vespa Lounge, St. Giles Circus (☎ 7836 8956). Tube: Tottenham Court Rd. Above the Conservatory restaurant, at the foot of Centrepoint tower. Newly refurbished, relaxed lesbian lounge bar with blue walls, comfy seats, and a pleasant outdoor terrace. Gay men welcome as guests. Spirits and mixers £2.75 all day, every day. DJ G.I. Jo M and Th nights from 8pm. Open daily noon-midnight, upstairs 6pm-midnight.

G-A-Y (☎ 7434 9592; www.g-a-y.co.uk). M and Th at the Mean Fiddler (formerly LAII), 165 Charing Cross Rd., F-Sa at the Astoria. Tube: Tottenham Court Rd. London's biggest gay/lesbian night, 4 nights a week. Frequently besieged by teenage girls on weekends—the Spice Girls and Boyzone both played here. M *Pink Pounder* 90s classics with 70s-80s faves in the bar (10:30pm-4am; cover £1 with flyer or ad, available at most gay bars, students free); Th *Music Factory* house, dance, and a little pop (11pm-4am; £1 with flyer or ad, students free); F *Camp Attack* attitude-free 70s and 80s cheese and a second room devoted to 90s music (11pm-4am; £2 with flyer, £3 after midnight); Sa *G-A-Y* big night out, rocking the capacity crowd with commercial-dance DJs and live pop performances (10:30pm-5am; £10, £8 with flyer).

COVENT GARDEN

🛈 *COVENT GARDEN QUICKFIND: Sights,* p. 103; *Museums & Galleries,* p. 134; *Food & Drink,* p. 161; *Pubs,* p. 178; *Entertainment,* p. 220; *Shopping,* p. 238; *Accommodations,* p. 263.

As with restaurants, Covent Garden's popularity with tourists means easy money for bars and clubs, which translates into high prices and low quality. The many Commonwealth expat hangouts in the streets near the Piazza may provide a good night out—if you're Canadian, Australian, or South African. Otherwise, while the Piazza makes a great place for a drink on a warm evening, it won't be long before you're heading down to Soho.

DRINKING

Freud, 198 Shaftesbury Ave. (☎7240 9933). Not to be confused with the metalworks store on the ground floor, this offbeat basement hipster hangout is accessed via a dodgy set of stairs. The sandblasted walls occasionally echo to live jazz (M starting at 4pm). Invigorate your psyche with cheap cocktails (from £3.40) that beat an hour on the couch. All bottled beers less than £3. Light meals noon-4:30pm (£3.50-6). Open M-Sa 11am-11pm, Su noon-10:30pm. MC/V.

The Spot, 29 Maiden Ln. (☎7379 5900). Frequent live acts, from singers to stand-up, at this 3-floor club-bar; dance in the velvet-trimmed basement, drink in the sparkling bar, lounge in the wood-paneled Oval Room. Weekday after-work business crowd gives way to young, dance-happy revelers on weekend nights. DJs spin dance music (soul, R&B, some garage) W-Su. Open daily noon-1am. Cover £5 F-Su after 9pm. Happy Hour daily noon-7pm (beers from £2.20). AmEx/MC/V.

Detroit, 35 Earlham St. (☎7240 2662; www.detroit-bar.com). A set of imposing double doors swings open to reveal a snug subterranean den that's perfect for drinking your way to oblivion. Low ceilings, powerful speakers, and futuristic lighting add to the cavernous appeal. Top-notch cocktails £4-7. DJs start spinning deep house and funky house around 8pm on weekend nights. Open M-Sa 5pm-midnight, restaurant open 5:30pm-10:30pm (2 courses £11). AmEx/MC/V (£10 minimum).

DANCING

Africa Centre, 38 King St. (☎7836 1973). Tube: Covent Garden. Community centre by day, party hotspot by night. With a bar reminiscent of a school canteen and a warehouse-like dance floor, the Center gets plenty of bang for its buck, attracting a racially diverse crowd for carefree weekend nights. F *Limpopo Club* follows a live African band (10pm-3am. Cover £8, £7 in advance); Sa various one-offs, including live music and poetry.

AKA, 18 West Central St. (☎7836 0110; www.aka-london.com), next to The End (see below). Tube: Tottenham Court Rd. or Holborn. From Holborn, walk west along High Holborn and turn right onto Museum St.; look for the lavender building. This uber-chic, innovative DJ-bar straddles 2 floors (perfect for people-watching from above) and attracts a laid-back, trendy clientele. Cocktails £5-10. Dress: casual. M hip hop and R&B (no cover). Tu Games Night with board games (no cover). W R&B, funk, and videos thrown in the mix (£3 after 11pm). Th tech-house (£5 after 11pm). F DJs from the four corners of London (£7 after 11pm). Sa joins with The End for *As One* (£10 after 9pm for AKA only,

are a lot more open-minded about these different genres.

LG: What do you think of the Ministry of Sound?

A: I would like to do it just for the sound system. They were one of the pioneers of bringing the dance floor to the masses. They were quite businesslike about their approach, so what they did was introduce the whole club culture to the masses, which I think is a good thing. In a way, it's like a popular culture that's an alternative to pop music.

LG: Do you get a lot of chicks as a DJ?

A: Well, yes. You're approached by *lots* of girls—you're on stage, you're like a mini-god for a while, and it's very exciting. But they don't do that when I'm not working.

LG: Why London?

A: There's also this sense here that anything goes; that you're free to do what you want to do. There's no set way of living here. I've lived in Hoxton, Islington, Notting Hill—and then I fell in love with South London when I first came. There's a real sense of community here, even if everyone's from different parts of the world; that's why I came to London in the first place.

£15 for both clubs). First Su of every month joins up with The End for *Clandestino:* house from 10pm until late. Check website for details. Open Su-F 6pm-3am; Sa 7pm-7am; club nights start at 10pm.

The End, 16A West Central St. (☎ 7419 9199; www.the-end.co.uk), next to AKA. Tube: Tottenham Court Rd. or Holborn. With speaker walls capable of earth-shaking bass, a huge dance floor, and a second lounge bar, The End is a cutting-edge clubber's paradise, thankfully hidden from most tourists. M *Trash* glam rock to disco (10pm-3am; cover £4). W Fabio (transplanted from the defunct Velvet Room) lays big beats over samba sounds to create toe-tapping, funky drum & bass (10pm-3am, £5 after 11pm). Th mixed/gay clubbing (10pm-4am; cover £7, £5 before midnight); Happy Hour 10-11:30pm. Sa *As One* joins up with AKA (see above) to provide 3 floors and 4 bars of futuristic dance (7pm-7am).

GAY

The Box, 32-34 Monmouth St. (☎ 7240 5828). Definitely not boxed-in. Recently renovated, this spacious gay/mixed bar-brasserie has a stylish media/fashion clientele and an equally stylish staff. Food specials change daily (mains £8-9). Also sells club tickets. Food served until 5pm. Open M-Sa 11am-11pm, Su noon-10:30pm. MC/V.

THE STRAND

⚑ THE STRAND QUICKFIND: Sights, p. 103; *Museums & Galleries,* p. 134; *Food & Drink,* p. 161; *Pubs,* p. 178; *Entertainment,* p. 213; *Shopping,* p. 238; *Accommodations,* p. 263.

DANCING

Heaven, The Arches, Craven Terrace (☎ 7930 2020; www.heaven-london.com). Tube: Charing Cross or Embankment. Though it runs regular mixed nights, "the most famous gay nightclub in the world" dispels any doubts about its orientation with the ubiquitous *boyz* magazine. Intricate interior rewards explorers—try every unguarded door to discover the fantastically lit main floor, two additional bars/dance floors, a coffeebar with Internet access, and an elusive chill-out room. M mixed *Popcorn* with chart-toppers, 70s-80s disco hits, commercial house, and £1.50 drinks (cover £4); W gay *Fruit Machine* house, garage, soul, and swing (£6, £2 before 11:30pm); F *School Disco* (£15); Sa gay/lesbian *Heaven* dance, trance, house, and disco (£12). Open M, W, F 10:30pm-3am, Sa 10pm-5:30am.

T.S. Queen Mary, Victoria embankment. (☎ 7240 9404). Tube: Embankment or Temple. This 1930s Turbine Steamer, now moored permanently on the north bank of the Thames, provides a relaxingly breezy drinking experience. While the occasionally swaying deck and loud creaking noises can be disconcerting, after a few pints, you'll barely notice. On weekends T.S. becomes a floating disco. Open M-Th noon-11pm, F-Sa noon-2am, Su noon-10:30pm (6pm in the winter). Cover £7 F-Sa after 9pm.

NORTH LONDON

⚑ NORTH LONDON QUICKFIND: Sights, p. 107; *Museums & Galleries,* p. 137; *Food & Drink,* p. 163; *Pubs,* p. 180; *Entertainment,* p. 216; *Shopping,* p. 240; *Accommodations,* p. 265.

Nightlife in **Islington** mostly means bar-hopping around Upper St. With Clerkenwell's superclubs just a short jaunt away, there's little booty-shaking—although the seedy area on the Islington side of King's Cross has developed a few superclubs of its own. Famous as a proving ground for new bands, and with swarms of young people in the area every weekend, it comes as a surprise that **Camden Town's** late-night scene is limited to a handful couple of clubs and club-bars. The local council is loathe to hand out late licenses; the burgeoning bar scene is abruptly cut short at 11pm, which helps explain why it's more popular with local professionals than with Camden's pierced youth.

DRINKING

Filthy MacNasty's Whiskey Café, 68 Amwell St. (☎ 7837 6067). Tube: Angel. Shane MacGowan, U2, and the Libertines have all played in this laid-back Irish pub. The last two still drop by periodically; Shane just lives here. It's actually 2 spaces with separate entrances, linked by the passage marked "toilets." Live music on most Th and occasional literary readings fuel the pub's erudite bad-boy atmosphere. 14 different whiskies all go for around £2. Bar food mostly £5-6. Open M-Sa noon-11pm, Su noon-10:30pm.

Bar Vinyl, 6 Inverness St. (☎ 7681 7898). Tube: Camden Town. The first bar in London with its own decks. DJs play mostly dance music in a narrow space dominated by the concrete counter. The cheery red and orange decor makes for a great place to have a few drinks before hitting the Camden clubs. During the day, a relaxed spot for a coffee or lunch, with an open kitchen at the rear (ciabatta sandwiches from £3.25). Absinthe £5. DJs W-F night and Sa-Su from 3pm. Food served until 9pm. Open M-Sa noon-11pm, Su noon-10:30pm.

Blakes, 31 Jamestown Rd. (☎ 7482 2959). Tube: Camden Town. Stripped-down modern pub/bar with a more classy and subdued atmosphere than the Camden standard. Mirrors and loud abstract paintings look down at couples and serious-looking 20- to 30-somethings. Cocktails £4.50-£5.50. Bar food (around £5) served until 10:30pm. Open M-Sa 11am-11pm, Su noon-10:30pm.

The Purple Turtle, 61-65 Crowndale Rd. (☎ 7383 4976). Tube: Mornington Crescent. The name says it all. A young, eclectic crowd frequents this eccentric, purple drinking haven. Even if the strangely psychedelic music isn't exactly your thing, there's always the foosball table, not to mention close to 50 shooters to choose from. Open M-Th and Su noon-midnight; F-Sa noon-1am.

The Garden, 179 Upper St. (☎ 7226 6276). Tube: Angel. Until 11pm the sizable outdoor patio swarms with the international yuppies who fill Islington. From Th-Sa this crowd moves inside for the DJs who spin from the lacquered library cove starting around 9pm. On Th student nights, many drinks go for £1.50. The eclectic pub menu (most items £6) offers more than your standard pies and mash. Open M-W noon-11pm, Th-Sa noon-1am, Su noon-midnight.

DANCING: KING'S CROSS

Scala, 275 Pentonville Rd. (☎ 7833 2022, tickets 0870 060 0100; www.scala-london.co.uk). Tube: King's Cross. Brilliant nights in a seedy area guaranteed to scare out-of-towners—what more could a Londoner ask for? The huge main floor embraces its movie-theater past: DJs spin from the projectionist's box, tiered balconies make great people-watching, and giant screens pulse with mood-enhancing visuals as enormous speakers detonate the bass. Room 2 is larger than most clubs' room 1s, while the tiny floor and bar by the entrance provide sweaty relief. F *Popstarz* is a classic night of gay/mixed eclectica (see p. 185); on Sa *Cookies and Cream* brings a blend of hip-hop and R&B (no caps, sneakers, or sportswear; £14, £10 before 11); every Su before bank holidays *Latin 8* provides 6 hr. of hip-swinging salsa (8pm-2am; £8). Occasional live events during the week. Dress up.

Bagley's Studios, King's Cross Freight Depot, off York Way (☎ 7278 2777; www.bagleys.net). Tube: King's Cross. Walk up York Way (to the right of King's Cross station), turn left on Goods Way, then right about 100m later through the iron gates, and follow the road left and down (10min.). Prostitutes and drug dealers frequent this area after dark; **travel in groups or take a taxi** (Bagley's can arrange taxis home). Soon to be renamed Canvas, Bagley's is a former movie studio and London's biggest club venue, accommodating over 2000 people on up to five cavernous, minimalist dance floors. Dress is funky and mostly casual. F music is usually old skool drum & bass, happy hardcore, garage; Sa *Smile* hard house and euphoric trance, with bubbles, pyrotechnics, and glitter bombs (10:30pm-7am; £13).

DANCING: CAMDEN TOWN

Electric Ballroom, 184 Camden High St. (☎ 7485 9006; www.electric-ballroom.co.uk). Tube: Camden Town. No one can remember the last time the Ballroom was fashionable, but no one here cares—they're just out for a good time. You won't find the latest sound systems or particularly stylish decor, but free Sega Dreamcast machines, not to mention foosball and pinball, more than make up for the lack of style. There are 2 floors of dancing and 1 floor for relaxing with an expensive drink. F *Full Tilt* (see p. 194) attracts a regular crowd of Goths while Sa *Shake* (see p. 194) provides a generic 70s and 80s night.

Camden Palace, 1a Camden High St. (☎7387 0428). Tube: Mornington Crescent. In a converted Victorian theater with ornate plasterwork and multiple balconies that overlook the huge dance floor. The entire building shakes when they turn up the bass. Completely off the fashion-scene radar, but good for a fun night out. A favorite with students, foreign and British alike. F *Peach* house/trance (10pm-6am; £12, £9 before 11pm); Sa nights vary but usually stick to techno favorites like old school, hard house, and drum & bass (10pm-6am; cover £10-20); Tu *Feet First* Indie night (see p. 185).

Jazz Café, see Entertainment, p. 217.

WKD, 18 Kentish Town Rd. (☎7267 1869; www.wkd.co.uk). Tube: Camden Town. The trinity of "Wisdom Knowledge Destiny" meets that of "cafe-music-club." Two self-consciously cool floors host funky flavored live music and DJs at night. *Tapas* (£3-6) served during the day. To maintain the edge, they never settle down into predictable nights, but generally bands Su-Tu, beats Th-F. Open M-Th 3pm-2am (restaurant until 8pm), F-Sa 1pm-3am (restaurant until 9pm), Su 1pm-midnight. Cover M-Th £5, F-Su £9.

GAY

The Black Cap, 171 Camden High St. (☎7428 2721; www.theblackcap.com). Tube: Camden Town. North London's most popular gay bar and cabaret draws an eclectic male and female crowd. Upstairs pub and rooftop patio could pass for any London local; live shows downstairs every Tu-Sa night 12:30am, Su 10:30pm. Cover £3, £2 before 11pm; F-Sa £4, £3 before 11pm; M nights drinks £1.50 plus £1.50 cover. Food served daily noon-6pm. Open M-Th noon-2am, F-Sa noon-3am, Su noon-midnight.

Bar Fusion, 45 Essex Rd., Islington (☎7688 2882). Tube: Angel. Laid-back gay and lesbian bar with comfy black sofas and mellow purple walls gets raucous on the weekends—jump on the sinuous bar and dance, or chill by the pool table at the back. Open M-Th 3:30pm-midnight, F-Sa 2pm-1am, Su 1pm-midnight. MC/V.

SOUTH LONDON

🔁 *SOUTH LONDON QUICKFIND: Sights,* p. 111; *Museums & Galleries,* p. 138; *Food & Drink,* p. 166; *Entertainment,* p. 219; *Shopping,* p. 241.

Nightlife features most prominently in Brixton's renaissance, with an ever-increasing number of bars and clubs luring London's largest concentration of under-40s. Lounging takes priority over dancing, though the proliferation of DJ-bars signals a shift back to good old-fashioned booty-shaking. While many nightspots are little different from their Hoxton or Clerkenwell brethren, there are still plenty of places that have escaped yuppification. Outside Brixton, south London's undisputed megaclub is the ▨**Ministry of Sound,** now one of the biggest players in the world club scene.

DRINKING

Fridge Bar, Town Hall Parade, Brixton Hill (☎7326 5100; www.fridge.co.uk). Tube: Brixton. Next to the Fridge nightclub (see below). Stylish Brixtonians from both sides of the fence mingle in this narrow bar, occasionally nipping downstairs to the dance floor, where strobe lights weirdly illuminate the geometric pastel walls. DJs spin from 9:30pm every night: M roots and reggae, Tu hip-hop, W classic reggae, Th dirty R&B, raw garage, ghetto rap (22+), F-Sa soul and R&B (F 22+, Sa 23+), and Su 70s-80s faves (24+). Sa-Su mornings, after-parties continue the previous night's fun from The Fridge club (see p. 195). M-Th no cover; F-Su £5-8 after 9pm; after-parties £6. Open M-Th 6pm-2am, F 6pm-4am, Sa 5:30am-noon and 6pm-4am, Su 5:30am-noon and 6pm-2am.

Satay Bar, 447-455 Coldharbour Ln. (☎7326 5001; www.sataybar.com). Tube: Brixton. Sharing space with an Indonesian restaurant (mains £5-6), one of Brixton's more relaxed bars. All strata of local society mix beneath Balinese masks and modern art. During Happy Hour (daily 5-7pm), cocktails are £3.50, with £10 jugs. No cover. Restaurant open M-Th noon-3pm and 6-11pm, F noon-3pm and 6pm-1:30am, Sa 1pm-1:30am, Su 1-11pm; bar open M-Th noon-11pm, F noon-2am, Sa 1pm-2am, Su 1-11pm. MC/V.

Living, 443 Coldharbour Ln. (☎7326 4040). Tube: Brixton. This popular newcomer to the Brixton party scene is regularly packed even on weekday nights. The upstairs dance floor has club pretensions, but it's ultimately a DJ-driven drinking den for 20-something new Brixtonians homesick for the sofa-bars of North London. F-Sa cover £5 after 10pm; no cover Su-Th. Open M-Th 5pm-2am, F 5pm-4am, Sa noon-4am, Su noon-2am. Music starts pumping around 9pm nightly. Live comedy W 7pm.

DANCING

◼ **Ministry of Sound,** 103 Gaunt St. (☎7378 6528; www.ministryofsound.co.uk). Tube: Elephant and Castle. Take the exit for South Bank University. Mecca for serious clubbers worldwide—arrive before it opens or queue all night. Emphasis on dancing rather than decor, with a massive main room, smaller second dance floor, and overhead balcony bar. Dress code generally casual, but famously unsmiling door staff make it sensible to err on the side of smartness (*no* jeans or sneakers, especially on Saturdays). Friday *Smoove* garage and R&B (10:30pm-5am; £12); Sa *Rulin* US and vocal house (11pm-8am; £15).

◼ **Tongue&Groove.** 50 Atlantic Rd. (☎7274 8600; www.tongueandgroove.org). Tube: Brixton. Unselfconsciously trendy club-bar so popular and narrow that people dance on the speakers. Soak up the brothel chic—huge black leather sofas lining one wall, red lighting, and chandeliers—and anticipate ecstatic early-morning partying. Do *not* underestimate the cocktails (£4.50 doubles)! W rare groove, soul, and funk; Th sexy US house; F house-based mix of African, Cuban, and Brazilian vibes; Sa soulful house, jazz breaks, some disco; Su rare grooves and deep house. Cover £4 F, Sa after 10:30; £3 Su after 10:30. Open 9pm-5am nightly.

◼ **Bug Bar,** Crypt, St. Matthew's Church (☎7738 3184; www.bugbrixton.co.uk). Tube: Brixton. The antithesis of most self-labeled "cool" nightspots, the intimate space in this whitewashed former church crypt holds an extremely laid-back, friendly crowd. The single dance floor is nowhere near big enough to contain all the chilled-out movers and shakers. W live acts, from poetry slams to break-beats (cover £4-5, free before 8pm); Th funk, jazz, and R&B (free before 8pm, £2 before 10pm, £5 after 10pm); F rare beats and breaks and old skool house (£6, £4 before 11pm, free before 9pm); Sa one-offs (£6, £4 before 11pm, free before 9pm); Su garage, R&B, funk, hip-hop, and "boogie classics" (£3, free before 10pm). Open W-Th 7pm-1am, F-Sa 8pm-3am, Su 7pm-2am.

Brixton Academy, see Entertainment, p. 219. Massive venue that flattens out the auditorium for occasional F-Sa club nights, sometimes open until 6am. Call for dates and details.

The Dogstar, 389 Coldharbour Ln. (☎7733 7515; www.thedogstar.com). Tube: Brixton. One of the first nightspots to cash in on Brixton's new-found popularity as a bohemian hang-out for aspiring media-types. Every night around 9pm the bar transforms into a full-out club with projectors and a good-sized dance floor. M *Bueno Disco* indie music; Tu DJ Billy (R&B and hip-hop); W Salsa night; Th Breaks and electro from A1 People, Fuel, Hunk-Papa; F-Sa varied electro-, breaks-, and house-oriented nights; Su 60s-80s pop. Cover £3 daily after 11pm. Open Su-Th noon-2am, F-Sa noon-4am.

The Fridge, Town Hall Parade, Brixton Hill, SW2 (☎7326 5100; www.fridge.co.uk). Tube: Brixton. The giant split-level dance floor and the stepped wraparound balcony bar give it away as a former cinema. Hard benches in the "restaurant" dissuade loungers, though there's plenty of seating upstairs. F usually hard dance, techno trance; Sa usually trance and hard house. Dress code fairly relaxed, but the whiter, tighter, and spanglier the better. cover £5-15, sometimes more at the door. After-party gets going Sa-Su mornings from 5:30am at the Fridge Bar, £6 (see above).

Mass, St. Matthew's Church, Brixton Hill (☎7733 7515; www.massclub.co.uk), upstairs from the Bug Bar. Tube: Brixton . Renovated in early 2003 and now billed as the "New Mass," these two funkily decorated rooms fill quickly with a happy crowd intent on gyrating the night away. Constantly changing line-up heavy on the house, trance, and drum and bass; last F of the month is *Torture Garden*, Europe's foremost fantasy fetish night, with a very strict dress code. Hours and cover depend on the event and promoter; usually open F-Sa 10pm-6am, cover £10-17, sometimes less before 10:30pm.

EAST LONDON

🔟 *EAST LONDON QUICKFIND: Sights, p. 112; Museums & Galleries, p. 139; Food & Drink, p. 167; Pubs, p. 181; Entertainment, p. 219; Shopping, p. 242.*

As the self-proclaimed capital of the London scene—and there aren't too many dissenters—**Shoreditch** and **Hoxton**, or "Shoho" as their trendier elements prefer to call it, is now London's main nighttime destination outside Soho. However, the scene here is quite different from that of the West End—in Shoho, dancing takes definite second place to lounging, and in some bars and clubs the navel-gazing crowds aren't as friendly as you might like. Of course, fashion was always about exclusivity, so you can hardly complain if locals scowl at you for crashing the party—instead, get a spiky blue haircut, dress to the nines in art-student chic, and pout right back.

DRINKING

Cargo, Kingsland Viaduct, 83 Rivington St. (☎ 7739 3440; www.cargo-london.com). Tube: Old St. With great acoustics, an intimate candlelit lounge, a hopping outside patio, and 2 enormous arched rooms, this immensely popular pre- and post-club hangout is chock-full of Beautiful People. Generally swamped by two separate waves of patrons, the place is always kicking by 9:30pm. A mix of DJs and live music, usually with a Latin focus, manages to drag even the most determined lounger onto the dance floor. On-site restaurant serves world food day and night (£3-5). Open M-Th noon-1am, F noon-3am, Sa 6pm-3am, Su noon-midnight. Live music M-Sa from 8pm, Su from 6pm. Cover £4-10.

🍸 Cantaloupe, 35-42 Charlotte Rd. (☎ 7613 4411; www.cantaloupe.co.uk). Tube: Old St. Archetypal we're-so-hip Shoho hangout, with dim lighting and funky chairs made from wood off-cuts. The young, hip crowd of regulars lines Charlotte Rd. on warm summer nights. *Tapas* £3-4, great cocktails £5.50. Open M-F 11am-midnight, Sa noon-midnight, Su noon-11:30pm. AmEx/MC/V.

🍸 Vibe Bar, 91-95 Brick Ln. (☎ 7247 3479; www.vibe-bar.co.uk). Tube: Aldgate East or Liverpool St. One of the Truman Brewery's 2 nightspots, this young, fun clubby bar has an interior straight out of a style mag. DJs spin M-Sa from 7:30pm and Su from 6:30pm; in summer, fun extends outside with a 2nd DJ working the shady courtyard. The diversity of the crowd is reflected in the music, which includes hip-hop, soul, acoustic, funk, and jazz. Plop on a comfy sofa, or check your email for free when you buy a drink. Open Su-Th noon-11:30pm, F-Sa noon-1am. Free on weeknights, £3 F-Sa after 8pm.

Hoxton Square Bar & Kitchen, 2-4 Hoxton Sq. (☎ 7613 0709). Tube: Old St. This long, dark space, with raw gray concrete walls adorned with funky photographs, is London's first gastrobar. Incredibly popular with young artists and alternative types who sink into retro swivel chairs and low-slung leather couches. The pleasant outdoor patio is packed with spiky-haired drinkers every evening. Mediterranean food served in the open-plan kitchen (mains £7-9, sandwiches £5-6, served all day). Open M-Sa noon-midnight, Su noon-10:30pm. MC/V.

DANCING

93 Feet East, 150 Brick Ln. (☎ 7247 3293; www.93feeteast.com). Tube: Aldgate East or Liverpool St. Part of the Truman Brewery complex, 93 benefits from East London's danger-cool image while being far enough from Shoho to be off the wannabe radar. Each of the 3 rooms has a different feel: the stark, barn-like main floor is primarily a dance space, packed even on weeknights; the sofa-strewn upstairs room combines dancing and lounging; while the hard-to-find 3rd room (go back to the club entrance and follow the "bar" sign) is a candle-lit chill-out space, with curved wooden benches topped with bean-bag cushions perfect for intimate encounters. Music style changes virtually every night; call or check website for details.

333, 333 Old St. (☎ 7739 1800; www.333mother.com). Tube: Old St. Although no longer the cornerstone of Shoho nightlife, this massive 3-floor venue can still pack them in with a vengeance. The oddly shaped main room, complete with airline seating, literally bounces to the beat of the dance floor; the plain basement feels like a sweaty student venue, and the heaving upstairs is visibly a former pub, despite the wraparound Manhattan mural. Most notorious monthly is 1st Sa *Revolver* which brings eclectic funky dance on the main floor and basement, while in true Warhol fashion anyone can get 15min. of fame upstairs—BYO music (cover £10, £5 before 11pm; 10pm-5am.).

Herbal, 12-14 Kingsland Rd. (☎ 7613 4462; www.herbaluk.com). Tube: Old St. Herbal is less studiedly hip than most of its Shoho neighbors, and often more fun as a result. The action is divided onto two floors—the smaller, loft-like upstairs room is popular with loungers. Wide range of one-offs and rotating monthlies, never over £7; check website or call. Fixtures include 1st F of the month *Red Alert* "all sorts of sleaze and funky shit" (cover £6) and the pounding drum & bass *Grace* (4th Su; £7) as well as *Warm Leatherette* punk, disco, and electronica (4th Sa; £6). Open daily 7:30pm-2am.

Entertainment

When a man is tired of London, he is tired of life; for there is in London all that life can afford.
—Samuel Johnson, 1777

On any given day or night in London, you can choose from the widest range of entertainment a city can offer. The West End is perhaps the world's theater capital, supplemented by an adventurous "fringe" and a justly famous National Theatre, while new bands spring eternal from the fountain of London's many music venues. Dance, film, comedy, sports, and countless more happenings will leave you amazed by the continual variety on offer.

ENTERTAINMENT BY TYPE

CINEMA		CINEMA (CONT.)	
Barbican Cinema	The City	Renoir	Bloomsbury
BFI London IMAX	The South Bank	⬛ Riverside Studios	West London
Curzon Soho	The West End	⬛ Tricycle Cinema	North London
⬛ Electric Cinema	Notting Hill		
Everyman Cinema	North London	**COMEDY**	
Gate Cinema	Notting Hill	Canal Cafe Theatre	North London
ICA	The West End	Chuckle Club	Holborn
⬛ National Film Theatre	The South Bank	⬛ Comedy Cafe	East London
Prince Charles	The West End	⬛ Comedy Store	The West End

COMEDY (CONT.)

Donwstairs at the King's Head	North

DANCE

See also Opera & Ballet

Peacock Theatre	Holborn
The Place	Bloomsbury
Sadler's Wells	Clerkenwell

MUSIC: CLASSICAL

Barbican Hall	The City
City of London Festival	The City
Music on a Summer Evening	North
🎵 The Proms	Kensington
Purcell Room	The South Bank
Queen Elizabeth Hall	The South Bank
Royal Albert Hall	Kensington
Royal Festival Hall	The South Bank
St. John's Smith Square	Westminster
St. Martin-in-the-Fields	Westminster
Wigmore Hall	Marylebone

MUSIC: FOLK & WORLD

Cargo	East
Hammersmith Irish Centre	West
Spitz	East
The Swan	South

MUSIC: JAZZ

100 Club	The West End
🎵 606 Club	Chelsea
Jazz Café	North
Pizza Express Jazz Club	The West End
Ronnie Scott's	The West End

MUSIC: ROCK & POP

Borderline	The West End
Brixton Academy	South
Cargo	East
Dublin Castle	North
Forum	North
The Garage	North
London Arena	East
London Apollo	West
London Astoria (LA1)	The West End
Sheperd's Bush Empire	West
🎵 The Water Rats	Bloomsbury

OPERA AND BALLET

English National Opera	The West End
Holland Park Opera	Kensington
Royal Opera House	The West End

PUPPETRY

Puppet Theatre Barge	Northwest

THEATER: "WEST END"

Adelphi	The West End
Aldwych Theatre	The West End
Apollo Victoria	Westminster
Barbican Theatre	The City
Criterion Theatre	The West End
Duke of York's Theatre	The West End
Fortune Theatre	The West End
Her Majesty's Theatre	The West End
London Apollo	West
London Palladium	The West End
Lyceum	The West End
National Theatre	The South Bank
Old Vic	The South Bank
Open-Air Theatre	Regent's Park
Palace Theatre	The West End
Phoenix Theatre	The West End
Prince Edward Theatre	The West End
Prince of Wales	The West End
🎵 Royal Court Theatre	Chelsea
St. Martin's Theatre	The West End
🎵 Shakespeare's Globe	The South Bank
Strand	The West End
Theatre Royal Drury Lane	The West End
Wyndhams Theatre	The West End

THEATER: "OFF-WEST END"

Almeida	North
Battersea Arts Centre	South
Donmar Warehouse	The West End
Hackney Empire	East
Hampstead Theatre	North
Lyric Hammersmith	West
RADA	Bloomsbury
🎵 Riverside Studios	West
Soho Theatre	The West End
Tricycle Theatre	Northwest
Young Vic	The South Bank

THEATER: FRINGE

Bush Theatre	West
Etcetera Theatre	North
The Gate	Notting Hill
The King's Head	North
New End Theatre	North
The Old Red Lion	North

OTHER

BBC Television Centre	West
Cycle Rickshaws	The West End
Earl's Court Exhibition Centre	Earl's Court
Firstbowl (Bowling & Ice Skating)	Bayswater
London's Skate Centre	Bayswater

THEATER

The stage for a national dramatic tradition over 500 years old, London theaters maintain unrivaled breadth of choice. Knowing what's on is easy enough: pick up the week's *Time Out*, look through the newspapers' weekend sections, or check out www.officiallondontheatre.co.uk. Knowing what to pick, however, is tougher. For many people, a visit to London isn't complete with going to see a big musical, for others it requires a trip to the National Theatre or Royal Shakespeare Company; in both cases, you're unlikely to be disappointed. Of the enormous variety in between, much is inevitably dross. At a **West End** theater (a term referring to all the major stages, whether or not they're actually in the West End), you can expect a professional, if mainstream production, top-quality performers, and (usually) comfortable seats. **Off-West End** theaters usually present more challenging work, while remaining every bit as professional as their West End brethren; indeed some, such as the Almeida and the Donmar Warehouse, can attract big-name Hollywood stars the West End can only dream of. The **Fringe** is refers to the scores of smaller, less commercial theaters, often just a room in a pub basement with a few benches and a team of dedicated amateurs. With so many fringe productions, few even get reviewed by newspapers and magazines; it's hit-or-miss whether you stumble across the next Tom Stoppard, but even if it turns out to be a flop, you're rarely more than £5 the worse for it.

LONG-RUNNING SHOWS

London's West End is dominated by musicals and plays that run for years, if not decades; below we have listed both shows that have proved their staying power, plus recent arrivals that look set to settle down for the long haul. Despite what the ever-increasing number of ticket peddlers would have you believe, you'll almost always get the best deal by going to the theater directly—phone bookings (and virtually all transactions through an agent) will attract a supplementary fee of £1-3 per ticket. The one exception is the **tkts** booth in Leicester Square (see p. 215), which is run by the theaters themselves and releases half-price tickets on the day of the show. **Ticket touts** who hawk tickets outside theaters charge sky-high prices for tickets of dubious authenticity or of obstructed views; moreover, selling (and by extension buying) tickets from an unauthorized source is a crime.

Blood Brothers, Phoenix Theatre, Charing Cross Rd. (☎ 7369 1733). Tube: Tottenham Court Rd. Willy Russell's musical about identical twins growing up apart. Songs are as memorable as the carefully tangled plot. Shows M-Sa 7:45pm plus Th 3pm, Sa 4pm. £14.50-37.50, student and senior standby £15 1hr. before curtain.

Take Your Seats

Americans can easily be confused by the terminology used in English theaters and concerts. First, seating terminology: **Stalls** are what Americans call orchestra seats, and are nearest the stage. The **dress circle** is the first tier of balcony above the stalls, often with better views of the stage; both stalls and dress circle are usually the most expensive seats. Above the dress circle comes the **upper circle,** while the cheapest seats at the top of the theater are **slips** or in the **balcony.** Patrons usually refer to them as **the gods,** a reference to their closeness to heaven.

The **interval** is the time for gin or the loo; within seconds the entire theater empties into the appropriately named **crush bar.** Instead of joining the undignified scramble, you can order interval drinks before the show and find them waiting for you—usually on an unguarded side table marked with your name. Fortunately, London theatergoers do not seem to be of the drink-snatching variety.

Bombay Dreams, Apollo Victoria, 17 Wilton Rd. (☎0870 400 0650). Tube: Victoria. Bollywood comes to the West End, in the guise of an old-fashioned love story with stunning music. Shows Tu-Sa 7:45pm, also W, Sa-Su 3pm. £14-45, student and senior standby 1hr. before curtain.

Chicago, The Adelphi, Strand (☎7344 0055). Tube: Charing Cross. Backstage backstabbing and leggy blondes are the twin attractions of this mega-hit musical about the seedy show-biz world. Puts a premium on glitz and glamour. M-Th and Sa 8pm, F 5 and 8:30pm, plus Sa 3pm. £15-40.

Chitty Chitty Bang Bang, London Palladium, Argyll St. (☎0870 890 1108). Tube: Oxford Circus. A flying car and some mad scientists make for a crowd-pleasing spectacle. Great fun for children. Shows M-Sa 7:30pm, also W, Sa 2:30pm. £11-40.

The Complete Works of William Shakespeare (Abridged) and **The Complete History of America (Abridged),** Criterion Theatre, Piccadilly Circus (☎7413 1437). Tube: Piccadilly Circus. Monumental topics in only two hours in a light-hearted, energetic and irreverent manner. *Shakespeare* W and F-Sa 8pm, plus Th 3pm, Sa 5pm, Su 4pm; *America* Tu 8pm. £10-33.

Fame—The Musical, The Cambridge Theatre, Earlham St. (☎7449 5080). Tube: Covent Garden. Based on the Oscar-winning musical about New York dance students, with lots of high-octane dancing. Shows M-Th 7:30pm, F 5:30 and 8:30pm, Sa 3 and 7:30pm. £13-35, F matinee half-price.

The Full Monty, Prince of Wales, 31 Coventry St. (☎7839 5972). Tube: Piccadilly Circus. The original British film about unemployed miners has been transplanted to Buffalo, NY for this musical look at the lengths to which men will go to keep a job. Shows M-Sa 7:30, plus F, Sa 3pm. £15-40.

The Lion King, Lyceum Theatre, Wellington St. (☎0870 243 9000). Tube: Covent Garden. Disney has adapted their movie into a surprisingly innovative and aesthetically pleasing show, while still retaining the Disney pop appeal. Shows Tu-Sa 7:30pm plus W and Sa 2pm, Su 3pm. £17.50-40. Standing-room tickets released at noon the day of the show.

Mamma Mia!, Prince Edward Theatre, Old Compton St. (☎7447 5400). Tube: Leicester Sq. A revue of ABBA's music strung together with a simple plotline. Perpetually sold out, so much that it spawned a tawdry imitator down the street. Shows M-Th and Sa 7:30pm, F 5 and 8:30pm, Sa 3pm. £18.50-45.

Les Misérables, Palace Theatre, Shaftesbury Ave., entrance on Charing Cross Rd. (☎7434 0909). Tube: Leicester Sq. A rather polarized look at good and evil in 19th-century France, but with music like this, who needs subtlety? Shows M-Sa 7:30pm, plus Th and Sa 2:30pm. £10-43.

The Mousetrap, St. Martin's Theatre, West St. (☎7836 1443). Tube: Leicester Sq. By Agatha Christie. After half a century on the stage, is there anyone left in London who doesn't know whodunnit in the world's longest-running play? Shows M-Sa 8pm plus Tu 2:45pm and Sa 5pm. £12-29.

Phantom of the Opera, Her Majesty's Theatre, Haymarket (☎7494 5400). Tube: Piccadilly Circus. This tale of misdirected love at the Paris Opera never loses its thrill, musical ingenuity, and romantic appeal. Shows M-Sa 7:30pm plus W and Sa 2:30pm. Box office M-Sa 10am-8pm. £10-43.

Stones in His Pockets, New Ambassador's Theatre, West St. (☎7369 1761). Tube: Leicester Sq. or Covent Garden. Humorously and deftly recounts the collision between a small Irish town and a Hollywood film crew with false expectations of rural Ireland. Shows M-Sa 7:30pm, plus Th and Sa 3:30pm. £15-32.50.

The Woman in Black, Fortune Theatre, Russell St. (☎7369 1737). Tube: Covent Garden. Proving that good writing is scarier than any amount of cinematic gore, an aging detective recalls the ghost of a dead woman. Shows M-Sa 8pm plus Tu 3pm and Sa 4pm. £10-30; student and senior standby £10 1hr. before curtain.

We Will Rock You, Dominion Theatre, Tottenham Court Rd. (☎7413 3546). Tube: Tottenham Court Rd. Adapted from Ben Elton's book and incorporating the songs of Queen, this futuristic tale pits a rock rebel against a globalized, conformist world. Shows M-Sa 7:30pm, plus Sa and last W of the month 2:30pm. £7.50-50.

FILM

London's film scene offers everything. The heart of the celluloid monster is **Leicester Square** (p. 213), and the surrounding streets, which are literally lined with cinemas. It's best to avoid cinemas on the square itself, given that prices are generally £2-3

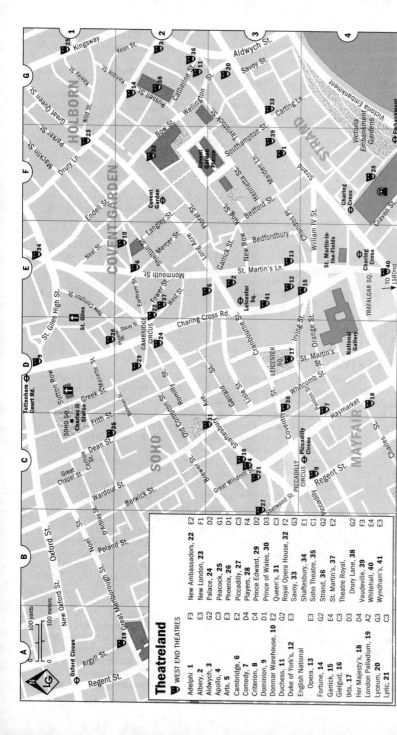

higher than anywhere else. The dominant cinema chain is **Odeon** (☎ 0870 5050 007; www.odeon.co.uk); Odeon does much more than just mainstream fare and each branch has its own character. Tickets to West End cinemas cost £5-10; weekday screenings before 5pm are usually cheaper and many cinemas offer regular student discounts. The annual **London Film Festival** (www.lff.org.uk), held in November, takes place at the National Film Theatre (see p. 212). While Hollywood shows are released much later in London than in the US, film buffs will be pleased at the large number of repertory cinemas screening classics and obscure arthouse works. The two most prolific theaters for independent flicks are the **ICA** (p. 134) and **NFT** (p. 212), which both tend to have different movies every single night. *Time Out* publishes reviews and schedules for all cinemas, as do many other newspapers.

COMEDY

Capital of a nation famed for its sense of humor, London takes its comedy seriously. On any given night of the week, you'll find at least 10 comedy clubs in operation; **stand-up** is the mainstay, but **improvisation** is also hot. Most clubs and nights only run once a week or once a month, with a different line-up every time—check listings in *Time Out* or a newspaper to keep up to speed. However, as comedy goes more mainstream, there's an increasing number of purpose-built, full-time comedy venues, of which the **Comedy Store** (p. 214) is the most famous.

Summertime comedy seekers should note that London empties of comedians in **August,** when most head to Edinburgh to take part in the annual festival (trying to win an award); but **July** is full of feverish comic activity as performers test out new material prior to heading north.

MUSIC

CLASSICAL

Home to four world-class orchestras, three major concert halls, two opera houses, two ballet companies, and more chamber ensembles than Simon Rattle could shake his baton at, London is renowned for serious music—and there's no need to break the bank. The London Symphony Orchestra remains the marquee orchestra but has competition from the Philharmonia, London Philharmonic, and the Royal Philharmonic, all of which play at the **Barbican Centre** (see p. 209) and **South Bank Centre** (see p. 212). Smaller chamber groups like the Academy of St. Martins in the Fields and the Gabrieli Consort provide different classical pleasures. The serious opera buffs who populate "the Gods" (so called because the seats are so far from the stage, you may as well be in heaven) in the **Royal Opera House** (p. 214) and the **Coliseum** (p. 214) wouldn't dream of descending to rub shoulders with the wealthy posers below. Every evening for most of July and August queues snake around the Royal Albert Hall for the **Proms** (p. 210), the world's largest festival of classical music; others brave the elements to enjoy some outdoor **Music on a Summer Evening** (p. 217) on Hampstead Heath. Beyond the major concert halls, smaller venues offer music of all periods and standards—almost every church in central London has a regular concert program, often for free. To hear some of the world's top choirs, head to Westminster Abbey (p. 65) or St. Paul's Cathedral (p. 68) for Evensong—as a double bonus, you'll also get into the cathedral for free.

JAZZ, FOLK & WORLD

London's jazz scene is small but serious; this ain't Chicago, but hallowed clubs like **Ronnie Scott's** (p. 214) pull in big-name performers from across the world, while the **606 Club** (p. 208) focuses on hot local players in a priceless setting. For the most part, the scene is low-key and home-grown, with performances taking place in various bars and pubs around town, often in the suburbs. The **Pizza Express** chain of restaurants (p. 147) often features jazz in its larger and swankier branches, in addition to operating a full-time jazz club (p. 215).

Folk (which in London usually means ⬛Irish) and **world** music keep an even lower profile, though big-name acts make occasional appearances at major concert venues—the **South Bank Centre** (p. 212) runs a strong and varied program in its three halls. In general, folk and world outings are restricted to pubs and community centers. The **Swan Stockwell** (p. 219) and the **Hammersmith Irish Centre** (p. 220) are two of the best-known venues for Celtic music, while the **Africa Centre** (see Nightlife, p. 191) has a weekly music spot.

ROCK & POP

Birthplace of the Rolling Stones, the Sex Pistols, Madness, and the Chemical Brothers, home to Madonna and Paul McCartney, London is a town steeped in rock'n'roll history. Every major band and singer in the world has played at least one of its major venues; dates for the biggest acts are usually booked months in advance and often sell out within days of tickets being released, so you need to start planning well before arriving in London to have a chance of bagging a place.

Stadium-filling acts are only the tip of the giant iceberg of London's music scene. For the best of the bands that can't sell out whole arenas yet check out the **London Astoria** (see p. 215) or the **Forum** (see p. 217). Other well-known traveling acts frequently stop at the **Borderline** (p. 215). Every night in dozens of pubs and smaller venues, hopeful bands play to a devoted crowd of followers and friends, hoping the record-company scout is somewhere in the audience. The ⬛**Water Rats** (p. 207) and the **Dublin Castle** (p. 217) are both pubs with good records of welcoming talented new acts.

SPECTATOR SPORTS

Many evils arise which God forbid.
—Edward II, banning football in London in 1314

Britain may not produce the best sportsmen in the world—it's been over 60 years since a local won Wimbledon, 35 since the English team lifted the football World Cup, and almost 20 since they last won the Ashes in cricket—but they count among the world's most enthusiastic spectators. While this has occasionally been less than positive (football hooliganism comes to mind), for the most part watching sports is an essential part of English social cohesion.

FOOTBALL

Whether or not football (the term "soccer" is an abbreviation of Association Football) was invented here—the Italians also lay claim to it—there's no doubt that the sport in its current form is an English creation. During the 2003/2004 season (August 16 to May 15 for the Premier League, August 9 to May 9 for League Division 1), over half a million people attend professional matches dressed with fierce loyalty in team colors. The vast majority of fixtures take place on Saturdays, with some on Sundays and the odd mid-week matches. Though violence at stadiums have dogged the game for years, the atmosphere has become tamer now that stadiums sell seats rather than standing spaces and with the increasing (though still tiny) number of women attending matches. Most of these fans attend the matches of one of five London teams in England's **F.A. Premier League**.

The big three London teams are **Arsenal,** Highbury Stadium, Avenell Rd. (☎ 7413 3366; Tube: Arsenal, Zone 2), **Chelsea,** Stamford Bridge, Fulham Rd. (☎ 7386 7799; Tube: Fulham Broadway, Zone 2), and **Tottenham Hotspur,** White Hart Ln. (☎ 8365 5000; Tube: Seven Sisters, Zone 3 or Rail: White Hart Ln.). Generally tickets are £10-40, but they are never easy to get on short notice. The odds of your getting a ticket may be better for one of London's other Premiership teams, though travel times to the stadia are usually greater: **Charlton**, The Valley (☎ 8333 4010; Rail: Charlton or DLR: North Greenwich, Zone 3 plus bus: #422, 472 or 486), and **Fulham**, Loftus Rd.

Dust to Dust...

"In affectionate remembrance of English Cricket, which died at the Oval on 29th August, 1882, deeply lamented by a large circle of sorrowing friends and acquaintances, R.I.P. N.B. The body will be cremated and the ashes taken to Australia." —Sporting Times, 1882

In most sports, every player's dream is to win a heavy silver urn or receive a gold medal. English cricketers, however, fantasize about getting their hands on 120-year-old charred wood—the Ashes.

It all started in 1882, when the first international Test series resulted in defeat for an over-confident English team against a bunch of upstart Australians. This shocked the English establishment so greatly that the *Sporting Times* published the now immortal obituary notice as seen above.

The following year, the English captain swore to bring back these metaphorical ashes. His wish took a literal turn when some Australians burned a stump used in one of the games and presented it to him following the English victory.

Today, the ashes permanently reside in a terracotta urn in the Lord's Museum despite the fact that England hasn't won since 1986. England has a chance to put an end to its losing streak Nov. 2003 to Jan. 2004 in the biennial Ashes Test Series, but they go to Australia as the overwhelming underdog. R.I.P. Indeed.

(☎ 7442 1234; Tube: White City). Generally teams not in the Premiership have greater ticket availability. For the best of the next rung of teams try **West Ham**, Upton Park (☎ 8548 2700; Tube: Upton Park, Zone 3), or **Crystal Palace** and **Wimbledon,** who both play at Selhurst Park, Whitehorse Ln. (☎ 8771 8841; Rail: Selhurst).

RUGBY

Rugby was allegedly created when an inspired (or confused) Rugby School student picked up a regular football and ran it into the goal. Never as popular in London as it is in the north, locals still turn out loyally to support the four big London teams who play their season from August to May on weekend afternoons: **London Wasps** (☎ 8993 8298); **NEC Harlequins** (☎ 8410 6000); **Saracens** (☎ 0192 347 5222); and **London Broncos** (☎ 090683 3303). Jan.-Mar. bring the **Six Nations Championship** (featuring England, Scotland, Wales, Ireland, France, and Italy). Tickets for the matches at **Twickenham** (☎ 8892 2000; Rail: Twickenham) are nearly impossible to get.

CRICKET

For non-Commonwealth visitors who have no understanding of the game, cricket can seem baffling—matches amble on for days and often end in draws. But who cares? The sun is (hopefully) shining, the beer is warm, and there's little enough action that you can read the newspaper and still not miss a thing. In a bid to attract younger viewers, one-day matches have been introduced, with risk-taking players dressed in gaudy colors, but purists complain that it's just not cricket. During the summer there are matches nearly every day at the famous **Lord's Cricket Grounds** (see Sights, p. 110) and the **Oval,** in south London (☎ 7582 7764; Tube: Oval, Zone 2). Many matches (bar the **International Test Matches**) are free or affordable.

TENNIS

Every year, for the last week of June and the first week of July, tennis buffs all over the world focus their attention on **Wimbledon.** If you're only interested in seeing the marquee matches you have to reserve months ahead or arrive by 7am (gates open 10:30am) to secure one of the coveted, but expensive 500 Centre and no. 1 court tickets sold every morning (£19-60) except the last four days. On the first Saturday of the championships, 500 extra Centre Court tickets are put up for sale at the "bargain" price of £30. For the best bargain, purchase a "grounds" ticket (£9-11) to the outer courts, where notable players may appear in earlier rounds or doubles matches. You can then enter the queue atop "Henman Hill" where returned Centre Court and no. 1 court tickets are resold for a cool £5 at 5pm for early evening action. (All England Lawn Tennis Club. ☎8971 2473. Tube: Southfields, Zone 3 or Rail: Wimbledon.)

ENTERTAINMENT BY NEIGHBORHOOD

BAYSWATER

⊓ BAYSWATER QUICKFIND: Food & Drink, p. 148; **Pubs,** p. 173; **Shopping,** p. 226; **Accommodations,** p. 252.

SEE MAP, p. 361

Hyde Park and Kensington Gardens next door provide for perfect lazy summer days; when it rains, try the UCI cinema in Whiteleys (see p. 226).

Firstbowl, 17 Queensway (☎7229 0172). Tube: Queensway or Bayswater. There's something for everyone in this all-in-one entertainment center: central London's only ice rink, 12 lanes of 10-pin bowling, a video-game arcade, pool tables, and a bar. Bowling open daily 10am-11:30pm, £4.50 per game, children £3.50 before 6pm; £1 shoe hire. Ice rink sessions daily 10am-2pm, 2-5pm, and 5-7pm, M-Th 8-11pm, Su 8-10pm. £5.50 per session, £6.50 F-Sa nights; £1 skate hire. Live DJ skating sessions Th-Su.

London's Skate Centre, 35 Queensway (☎7727 4669). For those tired of walking or eager for some wheels, this boards-and-blades store rents in-line skates by the day (£7 for 2 hours, £10 per day, £15 overnight; only day rentals on weekends). Deposit required: passport, photo ID with credit card, or £100 cash. Open Tu-F 12pm-6pm, Sa-Su 11am-6:30pm. MC/V (£12 minimum).

BLOOMSBURY

⊓ BLOOMSBURY QUICKFIND: Sights, p. 74; **Museums & Galleries,** p. 125; **Food & Drink,** p. 148; **Pubs,** p. 173; **Shopping,** p. 226; **Accommodations,** p. 254.

SEE MAP, p. 362

⊠ The Water Rats, 328 Grays Inn Rd. (☎7837 7269). Tube: King's Cross St. Pancras. A hip, laid-back pub-cafe by day, a stomping venue for top new talent by night—this is where young indie-rock bands come in search of a record deal. Oasis was signed here after performing their first London gig. Open for coffee M-F 8am-midnight. Excellent, generous gastro-pub lunches (£5-6) M-F noon-3pm, and music M-Sa 8-"late." Cover £5, £4 with the band's flyer.

Renoir, Brunswick Sq. (☎7837 8402). Tube: Russell Sq. This independent movie house has a strong emphasis on European, especially French, cinema's latest releases. There are only two screens, but the regular turnover makes this a standout. Doors and bar/cafe from 30min. before each screening. £7.50; 1st performance of the day M-F £5, concessions £3.

RADA (Royal Academy of the Dramatic Arts), 62-64 Gower St., entrance on Malet St. (☎7908 4800; www.rada.org). A cheaper alternative to West End theaters, Britain's most famous drama school has 3 on-site theaters, with productions throughout the academic year—catch the next Ken Branagh or Ralph Fiennes before they hit the big time. Box office open M-F 10am-6pm, 7:30pm on performance nights. Call ahead for event details. Tickets £8.50, concs £7.50. Also regular Foyer events, with plays, music, and readings M-Th at 7 or 7:30pm (free-£4).

The Place, 17 Duke's Rd. (☎7387 0031; www.theplace.org.uk). Tube: Euston or King's Cross St. Pancras. Britain's top venue for contemporary dance, attracting companies from both the UK and abroad. Seasons run Jan.-July and Sept.-Nov. Box office/phone bookings

the local story

West End Star

Liz Robertson, Madame Giry in The Phantom of the Opera, winner of the "Most Popular Musical Audience Award" in the 2002 Olivier Awards.

Q: How long have you been on the cast?

A: About 5 months—150 shows.

Q: Do you remember night #1?

A: Yes, it was frightening, but thankfully uneventful. What the audience doesn't know is that we enter the show fairly cold with only enough time for one real dress rehearsal.

Q: What is your view like?

A: A sea of faces staring at you—quite a thrill—but it's hard to see the audience much because it's so dark. Bruce Willis was here one night, others in the cast spotted him and were pointing him out, but I couldn't find him. Maybe it's my eyesight.

Q: You've acted in plays before. How does that compare to musicals?

A: Musicals are a huge high—the music is so uplifting! With a play, unless it's a comedy, it's hard to tell if the audience is hooked. Musicals are so rewarding because audiences cheer each number.

open M-F 10:30am-6pm, Sa 12:30-6pm; until 8pm on performance nights. Performances £5-15, depending on how far in advance you book; students and concessions £7 in advance. Standbys (£7) available from 6pm on performance nights. MC/V.

CHELSEA

SEE MAP, p. 363

CHELSEA QUICKFIND: *Sights,* p. 76; *Museums & Galleries,* p. 126; *Food & Drink,* p. 150; *Shopping,* p. 227. **TRANSPORTATION:** *The only Tube station in Chelsea is Sloane Sq.; from here buses #11, 19, 22, 211, and 319 run down the King's Rd.*

Royal Court Theatre, Sloane Sq. (☎7565 5000; www.royalcourttheatre.com). Called "the most important theater in Europe" by *The New York Times,* this venerable stage is dedicated to challenging new writing and innovative interpretations of classics. As part of their project they sponsor young writers' contests and workshops; they've helped launch the careers of many influential playwrights. Main auditorium £7.50-26; £9 concessions buy the best seats in the house; standing room 10p 1hr. before curtain. Upstairs £12.50-15, concessions £9. M all seats £7.50, though you can only book M upstairs tickets on the day of the performance.

606 Club, 90 Lots Rd. (☎7352 5953; www.606club.co.uk). Hard to find; look for the brick arch with a light bulb opposite the power station and ring the doorbell by the metal grille door to be let downstairs. The intrepid will be rewarded with brilliant British and European jazz in a smoky, candle-lit basement venue. Alcohol is served only with the pricey meals (£11-16), and only diners can reserve tables. For everyone else, grab a seat and a coffee. A music charge (£6-8) is only added to your bill if you've spent a substantial amount on food. Making money comes second to enjoying the music. Closing times are for the kitchen—the music continues until the musicians don't want to play anymore. M-W doors open 7:30pm, 1st band 8-10:30pm, 2nd 10:45pm-1:00am; Th doors open 8pm, music 9:30pm-1:30am; F-Sa doors open 8pm, music 10pm-2am; Su (vocalists) doors open 8pm, music 8:30pm-11:30pm.

THE CITY OF LONDON

SEE MAP, p. 364

THE CITY OF LONDON QUICKFIND: Sights, p. 78; **Museums & Galleries,** p. 126; **Food & Drink,** p. 150; **Pubs,** p. 174.

With 39 churches, the City is not short of venues for lunchtime concerts or choral evensong; see separate church listings under **Sights,** p. 78, for details. Less well-known as venues are the 24 **livery halls**—occasional concerts provide the only opportunity for most people to see inside these bastions of tradition. Contact the **City Music Society** (☎ 7628 6228) or the **City of London Information Centre** (☎ 7332 1456) for information. In June and July, the **City of London Festival** (see below) provides another occasion to get into places like the Mansion House and Middle Temple Hall. The City's primary entertainment venue, though, is the massive **Barbican** arts complex.

Barbican Centre, Barbican; main entrance on Silk St. (box office ☎ 7638 8891; cinema ☎ 7382 7000; www.barbican.org.uk). Tube: Barbican or Moorgate. See also Sights, p. 80, and Museums & Galleries, p. 128. Equally famous for the quality of its offerings and the impossibility of its layout, the Barbican is a one-stop cultural powerhouse. Currently under massive redevelopment, the details for the venues below remain largely up in the air for 2004. Be sure to call ahead before making any plans, or consult the website for updates.

> **Barbican Theatre:** A futuristic auditorium that hosts touring companies and short-run shows, as well as frequent one-off and short-run **contemporary dance** performances. Prices vary considerably by seat, day, and production; £6-30, cheapest M-F evening and Sa matinee. Student and senior standbys from 9am day of performance in person or by phone.

> **The Pit:** A small, intimate theater used primarily for new and experimental productions. £10-15 depending on production.

> **Barbican Hall:** Recently refurbished, the Barbican Hall is one of Europe's leading concert halls, with excellent acoustics and a nightly performance program. The resident **London Symphony Orchestra,** currently celebrating their Centenary, plays here frequently; the hall also hosts concerts by international orchestras, jazz artists, and world musicians. £6-35.

> **Barbican Cinema:** 2 smallish screens, offer a mix of latest blockbusters with occasional art-house, international, and classic movies. £7, seniors and students £5.50, under 15 £4.

City of London Festival (box office ☎ 7638 8891; www.colf.org). From June 21 to July 8 2004, the City will explode with activities, many in otherwise forbidden spaces: concerts and operas play in livery halls, banks open up their art collections, and walks take you into the City's hidden corners. Pick up the festival guide at the Barbican (see above) or tourist information centers. Booking for events starts in late April; buy tickets through the Barbican box office.

Q: You've also performed on Broadway. Is there a difference between audiences in America and The West End?

A: The American audience is there to love and appreciate you. But, if you do happen to get a standing ovation in the West End, you know you've accomplished a great feat—it's definitely a little more testing in London.

Q: Have you had any embarrassing moments on stage?

A: I've fallen quite a few times. My worst moment was during a curtain call. I stepped backwards but my heel caught on my frock. I went down in a heap; it was spectacular.

Q: You must dislike cell phones.

A: Yes, and they always seem to go off at the most inopportune times. We've also had the most disgusting nose-blowing and belching incidents. They must think that they can't be heard. But oh, they can!

Liz Robertson has starred in many West End shows including The Mitford Girls, Song and Dance, *and* Stepping Out*. She played Eliza in* My Fair Lady *at the Adelphi Theatre in 1979, and received rave reviews.*

The Phantom of the Opera, *which opened October 1986, is playing at Her Majesty's Theatre, Haymarket.*

CLERKENWELL

SEE MAP, p. 365

🔢 **CLERKENWELL QUICKFIND; Sights,** *p. 94; **Museums & Galleries,** p. 128; **Food & Drink,** p. 151; **Pubs,** p. 174; **Nightlife,** p. 185; **Accommodations,** p. 259.*

Sadler's Wells, Rosebery Ave. (☎ 7863 8000; www.sadler-swells.com). Tube: Angel. Recently rebuilt as a hulking brick-and-glass megalith, historic Sadler's Wells remains London's premier dance theater, with everything from classical ballet to contemporary tap, plus occasional operas. 10/10 for transportation: Sadlers Wells Express (SWX) bus to Waterloo via Farringdon and Victoria leaves 8min. after the end of each evening show (£1.50, £1 with period Travelcard); those arriving by regular bus can have their fare refunded (and get cash for the journey home) at the box office. Box office open M-Sa 9am-8:30pm. £10-45; student, senior, and under-16 standbys £10-18.50 1hr. before curtain (cash only). AmEx/MC/V.

HOLBORN

SEE MAP, p. 365

🔢 **HOLBORN QUICKFIND: Sights,** *p. 84; **Museums & Galleries,** p. 128; **Food & Drink,** p. 152; **Pubs,** p. 175; **Nightlife,** p. 187; **Shopping,** p. 229.*

Chuckle Club, at the Three Tuns Bar, Houghton St. (☎ 7476 1672; www.chuckleclub.com). Tube: Holborn. From Holborn walk south on Kingsway and turn left onto Aldwych, then turn left onto Houghton St.; it's in LSE's Clare Market Bldg. on the right. Located in a dingy basement bar, this is not one of those "comedy-is-hip" clubs. A changing lineup of at least 3 headline acts and many tryouts guarantees more belly laughs than chuckles. Expect quality heckling from student-heavy audience. Show Sa 8:30pm; doors 7:45pm, line up 15min. earlier. £12, students £10.

Peacock Theatre, Portugal St. (☎ 7863 8222; www.sadlers-well.com). Tube: Holborn. The (almost) West End outpost of Sadler's Wells (see Clerkenwell, p. 210), London's leading dance venue. Program leans toward contemporary dance, ballet, and popular dance-troupe shows. Some wheelchair accessible seats (£7.50) can be booked 24hr. in advance. Box office open M-Sa 10am-6:30pm, noon-8:30pm on performance days. £10-35; cheaper rates M-Th and Sa matinee. Standbys for students, seniors, and under 16 from 1hr. before performance. Small discount on online bookings.

KENSINGTON & EARL'S COURT

SEE MAP, pp. 366-367

🔢 **KENSINGTON & EARL'S COURT QUICKFIND: Sights,** *p. 88; **Museums & Galleries,** p. 130; **Food & Drink,** p. 153; **Pubs,** p. 176; **Shopping,** p. 229; **Accommodations,** p. 259.*

MUSIC: CLASSICAL & OPERA

☑ **The Proms** (accessibility info ☎ 7589 3853; www.bbc.co.uk/proms), at the Royal Albert Hall (see below). The summer season of classical music has been held every year since 1895, with concerts every night from mid-July to mid-Sept. "Promenade" refers to the tradition of selling dirt-cheap standing tickets, and it's the presence of up to 1000 dedicated prommers that gives the concerts their unique, informal atmosphere—that and the lack of AC. Seats for popular concerts can sell out months in advance, while lines for standing places often start mid-afternoon. The **arena,** immediately in front of the orchestra, tends to be most popular; the **gallery** has more space, but you need binoculars to see the musicians. The famous **Last Night** is an unabashedly jingoistic celebration complete with Union Jack-painted faces, flag-waving, and mass sing-a-longs of "Rule Britannia." Regarded with horror by "serious" music lovers, it's so popular that you have to have attended at least six other concerts before they'll let you take part in a lottery for tickets. Tickets go on sale in mid-May (£5-30; occasional discounts for under 16); standing places sold from 90min. before the concert (£4). Season ticket £160 arena, £135 gallery; half-season £90/£75. All concerts are transmitted live on BBC Radio 3 (91.3FM), and the Last Night is broadcast on a big screen in Hyde Park.

Holland Park Theatre, Holland Park (☎7602 7856, box office ☎0845 230 9769; www.rbkc.gov.uk/hollandpark). Tube: High St. Kensington or Holland Park. Open-air performance space in the grounds of a Jacobean mansion, with a generally conservative program tailored to its generally conservative patrons. No need to fear the rain—everything is held under a huge white canopy. Performances for 12 weeks from mid-June to early Aug. Tu-Sa 7:30pm, occasional matinees Sa 2:30pm. Box office located in the Old Stable Block just to the west of the opera; open from mid-Apr. M-Sa 10am-6pm or 30min. after curtain. Tickets £30, £36, £40; concessions (F evening and Sa matinee only) £31 and £25. There is a special allocation of tickets for wheelchair users. AmEx/MC/V.

GENERAL VENUES

Earl's Court Exhibition Centre, Warwick Rd. (☎7385 1200; www.eco.co.uk). Tube: Earl's Court (follow signs for Exhibition Centre exit). London's main venue for trade fairs and mega-expos, from the London Car Show to the Great British Beer Festival (see *All Play No Work*, p. 177). Also popular with pop acts: Radiohead and the Stereophonics played here in 2003, and Dec.-Jan. 2004 features Justin Timberlake.

Royal Albert Hall, Kensington Gore (see p. 89 for details). 5300-seat Victorian mega-venue holding anything from trade fairs to pop concerts. From mid-July to mid-Sept., the hall rocks to the sound of the **Proms** (see above).

MARYLEBONE & REGENT'S PARK

▶1 MARYLEBONE & REGENT'S PARK QUICKFIND: Sights, *p. 92; **Museums & Galleries,** p. 132; **Food & Drink,** p. 155; **Accommodations,** p. 262.*

Open-Air Theatre, Inner Circle, Regents Park (☎7486 2431; www.openairtheatre.org). Tube: Baker St. Bring blankets and waterproofs to this open-air stage—performances only get cancelled in the most extreme weather conditions. Program runs early June to early Sept. and always includes two Shakespeare plays, a musical, and a

SEE MAP, p. 369

children's performance. Barbecue before evening shows. Performances: M-Sa 8pm; matinees most Th and every Sa 2:30pm. £9-26; discounts for groups and for under 16; student and senior standby £9 from 1hr. before curtain.

Wigmore Hall, 36 Wigmore St. (☎7935 2141; fax 7935 3344; www.wigmore-hall.org.uk). Tube: Oxford Circus. London's premier chamber-music venue, in a beautiful setting with excellent acoustics; occasional jazz recitals. Seats neither raked nor staggered; shorter patrons will spend time contemplating the ornate mural above the stage. Box office phone bookings (£1 extra) open mid-Mar. to Oct. M-Sa 10am-7pm, Su 10:30am-6:30pm; Nov. to mid-Mar. M-Sa 10am-7pm, Su 10:30am-4pm. Concerts most nights 7:30pm, no concerts late July-Aug. £8-22, student and senior standby £8-10 1hr. before start (cash only). Daytime concerts Su 11:30am (£10, including refreshments) and M 1pm (£8, seniors £6).

NOTTING HILL

▶1 NOTTING HILL QUICKFIND: Sights, *p. 94; **Food & Drink,** p. 156; **Pubs,** p. 177; **Nightlife,** p. 187; **Shopping,** p. 231*

Electric Cinema, 191 Portobello Rd. (☎7908 9696, tickets 7229 8688; www.the-electric.co.uk). Tube: Ladbroke Grove. London's oldest purpose-built cinema (built 1910), recently reopened after a 15-year hiatus. It combines the baroque splendor of a stage theater with the buzzing effects of a big screen. Red

SEE MAP, p. 361

leather armchairs and ottomans make for an extra-luxurious cinematic experience. Independent and international films, including classics and recent raves. Double bills Su 2pm (£7.50). Kids Club films Sa 1pm (£4.50). M £7.50, Tu-Su £12.50; 2-seat sofa M £20, Tu-Su £30; front three rows M £5, Tu-Su £10.

The Gate, 11 Pembridge Rd. (☎7229 0706). Tube: Notting Hill Gate. In a tiny room above the Prince Albert pub, the Gate bills itself as the "home of international drama"—they often premiere new foreign works (in English translation) even before they've been given in their home countries. Performances M-Sa 7:30pm. Happy Mondays: first 30 customers "pay what you can" at the door. Box office open for phone bookings M-Sa 10am-6:30pm, in person from 7pm. £12, concessions £6.

Gate Cinema, 87 Notting Hill Gate (☎7727 4043; www.picturehouses.co.uk). Tube: Notting Hill Gate. Opened in 1911, Gate's unbecoming exterior is a result of post-war reconstruction. Fortunately, the Victorian interior remains intact. Viewers can admire the exquisite ceiling details while waiting for the film to start. This box-like theater hosted the world premiere of "Notting Hill." Art-house and discerning Hollywood flicks. £7, 1st show M-F £4, concessions £3.50 M-F before 6pm and F-Sa after 11pm. MC/V (50p surcharge).

THE SOUTH BANK

▶ SOUTH BANK QUICKFIND: Sights, p. 95; **Museums & Galleries,** p. 132; **Food & Drink,** p. 157; **Pubs,** p. 177; **Accommodations,** p. 263.

SEE MAP, pp. 370-371

When it comes to highbrow entertainment, the South Bank is hard to beat; it offers the most concentrated array of theater, music, and serious film in Britain, if not the world. If you're in the mood for something more light-hearted, try out the massive BFI IMAX cinema, or relax to the free jazz that often fills the South Bank Centre foyers. Organized by the community developers responsible for much of the South Bank's vitality, the **Coin Street Festival** (☎7401 3610) runs during the summer months. A sporadic succession of independent events, the festival celebrates ethnic diversity, modern design, and world music in and around Gabriel's Wharf and OXO Tower Wharf (see p. 97), finishing off in mid-September with the **Mayor's Thames Festival** along the South Bank embankment.

CINEMA

National Film Theatre (NFT; ☎7928 3232; www.bfi.org.uk/nft). Tube: Waterloo, Embankment, or Temple. Underneath Waterloo Bridge. One of the world's leading cinemas, with a mind-boggling array of films from Hollywood blockbusters to European art-house retrospectives. 6 different shows hit 3 screens every evening (9 shows on the weekends), starting around 6pm. The sprawling cafe and bar on the ground floor belie the zero-tolerance food and drink policy in the theaters. Annual membership (£22, concessions £14) gives £1 off movies, priority booking, and a free ticket when you join. All films £7.50, concessions £5.70.

BFI London IMAX Cinema, 1 Charlie Chaplin Walk (☎7902 1234; www.bfi.org.uk/imax). Tube: Waterloo. At the south end of Waterloo bridge, accessed via underground walkways from the South Bank. Get the ultimate 3-D experience in this stunning glass drum, which houses the UK's biggest screen: at 20m high and 26m wide, it's taller than 5 double-decker buses stacked on top of each other. Shows start every 1-1¼hr.; last show 9pm daily. £7.50, concessions £6.20, under 16 £4.95; extra film £4.20.

MUSIC: CLASSICAL, WORLD & JAZZ

The South Bank Centre (☎7960 4201; www.rfh.org.uk). Tube: Waterloo or Embankment. This megaplex of concert halls features all kinds of music. Tickets for all events can be purchased from the Royal Festival Hall box office (open daily 11am-8pm, until 9pm on performance days); Queen Elizabeth Hall and Purcell Room box offices open 45min. before performance. Some discounts for concessions and under-18s; some standbys from 2hr. before performance (check for availability ☎7921 0973).

Royal Festival Hall: 2700-seat concert hall with the best acoustics in London. Some of the cheapest seats are the choir benches, which put you right behind the orchestra. The 2 resident orchestras, the **Philharmonia** and the **London Philharmonic,** predominate, but big-name jazz, latin, and world-music groups also visit. The hall converts to a theater when dance and ballet troupes drop by. Classical concerts £6-35; others £10-30.

Queen Elizabeth Hall: Mid-sized venue used for smaller musical ensembles; more varied program than the Festival Hall. World-class jazz soloists and Indian DJs share the space with choirs and classics; also occasional literary evenings. £10-25.

Purcell Room: Intimate hall for chamber music, soloists, and small groups, with the usual varied South Bank repertoire. £15.

THEATER

⚑ Shakespeare's Globe Theatre, 21 New Globe Walk (☎7401 9919; www.shakespeares-globe.org). Tube: Southwark or London Bridge. Innovative, top-notch performances at this faithful reproduction of the original 16th-century playhouse where Shakespeare himself performed. Choose among three covered tiers of hard, backless wooden benches (cushions £1 extra) or stand through a performance as a "groundling." The latter costs less, allows a historical communion with the Elizabethan peasantry, and puts you much closer to the stage. Should it rain, however, the show *must* go on, and umbrellas are prohibited. For tours of the Globe, see p. 95. Wheelchair accessible and child-friendly. Performances mid-May to late Sept. Tu-Sa 7:30pm; Su 6:30pm; June-Sept. also Tu-Sa 2pm, Su 1pm. Box office open M-Sa 10am-6pm, 8pm on performance days. Seats £12-27, concessions £10-24, yard (i.e. standing) £5. Raingear £2.50.

National Theatre (info ☎7452 3400, box office ☎7452 3000; www.nationaltheatre.org.uk). Tube: Waterloo or Embankment. Founded by Laurence Olivier, the National Theatre opened in 1976 and has been at the forefront of British theater ever since. Popular musicals and hit plays, which often transfer to the West End, are mostly staged on the **Olivier,** which seats 1160 in a fan-shaped open-stage layout; the 890-seat **Lyttleton** is a proscenium theater, while the **Cottesloe** offers flexible staging for new works. Box office open M-Sa 10am-8pm. Complicated pricing scheme: Olivier/Lyttelton £10-34, Cottesloe £10-27, standby (2hr. before curtain) £15 all theaters, standing places (only available if all seats sold) £6. Numerous concessions include: matinees seniors £16, under-18s £10; M-Th evenings under-25s £15; disabled £8-16; student standbys £8 from 45min. before curtain.

Old Vic, Waterloo Rd. (☎7369 1722, www.oldvictheatre.com). Tube: Waterloo. Still in its original 1818 hall (the oldest theater in London), the Old Vic is one of London's most historic and most beautiful theaters. These days, it hosts touring companies like the Royal Shakespeare Company, which set their own prices and show schedules. Check website for listings.

Young Vic, 66 The Cut (☎7928 6363; www.youngvic.org). Tube: Waterloo. Close to the Old Vic but completely independent, the Young Vic is a pointed contrast to its older cousin: both interior and exterior are rather plain. The "in-the-round" theater itself—with only 8 rows of seats surrounding the flat stage—is conducive to experimental theater. One of London's top off-West End companies, with a focus on younger writers and younger viewers. Box office open M-Sa 10am-7pm. Unreserved seating; only 2 tickets per customer on day of performance. £19, concessions £9.50, school groups £7.50 (get 11th ticket free).

THE WEST END

⚐ WEST END QUICKFIND: Sights, p. 98; **Museums & Galleries,** p. 134; **Food & Drink,** p. 158; **Pubs,** p. 178; **Nightlife,** p. 188; **Shopping,** p. 233; **Accommodations,** p. 263.

So prominent is the West End in London's entertainment industry that the term "West End Theatre" now refers to any major mainstream London theater, whether or not it's actually in the West End. **Shaftesbury Avenue** in Soho, **Drury Lane** and the **Aldwych** in Covent Garden, and the **Strand** have been

SEE MAP, p. 356

synonymous with the London stage for centuries. **Leicester Square** is home to the essential **tkts** (see p. 215), which peddles coveted discount tickets to budget the-

213

atergoers, and London's largest first-run cinemas. If you worry that the entertainment in the West End is too mainstream, Off-West End and fringe theaters lie just yards from *Mamma Mia!* and *Les Misérables*, and art-house and repertory indie films play just a stone's throw from Leicester Sq. and Piccadilly Circus.

CINEMA

Cinemas abound in the West End, most of them concentrated in gaudy Leicester Sq. Unless you've booked early for a premiere, it's best to avoid the megaplex cinemas on the square itself—they all charge a few pounds more than those on the surrounding streets.

Curzon Soho, 93-107 Shaftesbury Ave. (☎ 7734 2255). Tube: Leicester Sq. After *Time Out* readers voted it London's best cinema in 2001, it keeps getting bigger and better with an added bar and restaurant. It retains the same good taste in good films. Ground floor theaters underwent more renovations in 2003. Independent and international films, plus Su classic and repertory double bills. Frequent talks and Q&A sessions from big-name indie directors. Tu-Su £8.50; M all day and Tu-F before 5pm £5.50; Su matinees and double bills £6; M-Th concessions £5.50; under 14 £4.50.

Prince Charles Cinema, 7 Leicester Pl. (☎ 7957 4009 or 7420 0000; www.princecharlescinema.com). Tube: Leicester Sq. Just off blockbuster-ridden Leicester Sq., the Prince Charles couldn't offer more of a contrast. They host the offbeat sing-a-long screenings of *The Sound of Music* (F 7:30pm; £13.50) and *Annie* (F 7:30pm, Su 2pm; £13.50, children £10) with a costumed host and dress competitions (www.singalonga.com). Other times during the week feature second-run Hollywood films and recent independents for unbelievably low prices. Tickets £2.50-3.50.

ICA Cinema, Institute of Contemporary Arts. See p. 134.

COMEDY

Comedy Store, 1a Oxendon St. (Tickets: TicketMaster booking number ☎ 0870 060 2340; www.thecomedystore.co.uk). Tube: Piccadilly Circus. The UK's top comedy club sowed the seeds that gave rise to *Ab Fab, Whose Line is it Anyway?*, and *Blackadder*, while Robin Williams did frequent improv acts here in the 80s. Tu *Cutting Edge* (contemporary satire), W and Su ▨ *Comedy Store Players* improv, Th-Sa standup. Grab food at the bar before shows and during interval (burger £5.60), and bring it back to your seat. Loosen up before the show with Happy Hour 6:30-7:30pm. Shows Tu-Su 8pm plus midnight F-Sa. Book ahead. Over-18s only. Tu and W £12, concessions £8; Th, F early show, and Sa £15, no concessions; F late show and Su £13, concessions £8.

MUSIC: CLASSICAL, OPERA & BALLET

English National Opera, the Coliseum, St. Martin's Ln. (☎ 7632 8300; www.eno.org). Tube: Charing Cross or Leicester Sq. In London's largest theater, re-opening in January 2004 for its centennial celebration. Known for both innovative productions of the classics and contemporary, avant-garde work. All performances in English. Box office open M-Sa 10am-8pm. £5-55; under-18s half-price with adult. Cheap standbys bookable on performance days, by phone from 9am, 1 per person.

Royal Opera House, Bow St. (☎ 7304 4000; www.royaloperahouse.org). Tube: Covent Garden. Known as "Covent Garden" to the aficionado, the Royal Opera House is also home to the **Royal Ballet.** Productions tend to be conservative but lavish, just like the patrons. Prices for the best seats (orchestra stalls) regularly top £100, but standing room and restricted-view seating in the upper balconies can be under £5. Tickets unsold 4 hr. before curtain available at half-price to everyone; student, senior, and under-18s standby £12.50 ballet, £15 opera. 67 seats available from 10am on day of performance, limit one per person. Box office open M-Sa 10am-6pm.

MUSIC: JAZZ

Ronnie Scott's, 47 Frith St. (☎ 7439 0747; www.ronniescotts.co.uk). Tube: Tottenham Court Rd. or Leicester Sq. The reputation justifies the prices. This intimate venue is London's oldest and most famous jazz club, having hosted everyone from Dizzy Gillespie to

Jimi Hendrix. 2 bands alternate 4 sets every night M-Sa, the support starting at 9:30pm, the headline act around 11pm; Su brings lesser-known bands from 7:30pm. Table reservations essential for big-name acts, though there's limited unreserved standing room at the bar—if it's sold out, try coming back at the end of the main act's first set, around midnight. Ask for a non-smoking table to be (probably) right by the stage. Food £5-25, cocktails £7-8. Box office open M-Sa 11am-6pm. Club open M-Sa 8:30pm-3am, Su 7:30-11pm. £15 M-Th, £25 F-Sa, £8-12 Su; students £10 M-W. AmEx/MC/V.

100 Club, 100 Oxford St. (☎7636 0933). Tube: Tottenham Court Rd. Stage, audience, and bar are all bathed in sallow orange light in this jazz venue that makes frequent excursions into indie rock. Punk burst onto the scene at a legendary gig here in 1976, when the Sex Pistols, the Clash, and Siouxsie and the Banshees all shared the stage in one evening. Regular nights include Sa night swing, M night *Stompin'*. Open for free jazz on F noon-3pm. Open Su-Th 7:30pm-midnight, F-Sa 7:30pm-2am. Cover £7-12, concessions £5-10.

Pizza Express Jazz Club, 10 Dean St. (☎7439 8722; www.pizzaexpress.co.uk). Tube: Tottenham Court Rd. Underneath a branch of the popular chain (see p. 147), sophisticated diners tuck into their pizzas while feasting their ears on music. Surprisingly one of the best places to hear innovative contemporary jazz, with the classy trappings of an old-time jazz club. Table reservations recommended, especially F-Sa. Doors normally open 7:45pm, with music 9-11:30pm; some F-Sa have 2 shows, with doors opening at 6 and 10pm. Cover (£12-20) added to the food bill. AmEx/M/V.

MUSIC: ROCK & POP

London Astoria (LA1), 157 Charing Cross Rd. (☎7344 0044; www.londonastoria.com). Tube: Tottenham Court Rd. Former pickle factory, strip club and music hall before turning to full-time rock venue in the late 1980s. Now basking in an air of somewhat faded glory, the 2000-capacity venue hosts hip, not-quite-big acts Su-W (£12-25) and the popular G-A-Y clubnight (see p. 200) Th-Sa.

Borderline, Orange Yard, off Manette St. (☎7734 5547; www.borderline.co.uk), box office 1 block away under Salsa restaurant, 96 Charing Cross Rd. Tube: Tottenham Court Rd. Warm, funky, smoky basement space used for well-known groups with a strong folk-rock flavor. Music M-Sa usually from 7pm-3am. Box office open M-F 11am-5pm. £5-16 in advance.

THEATER

tkts, on the south side of Leicester Sq.—look for the long lines. (www.tkts.co.uk). Tube: Leicester Sq. Run jointly by London theaters, tkts (formerly the Half-Price Ticket Booth) is the only place where you can be sure your half-price tickets are genuine. The catch is that theaters only release the most expensive tickets to the booth, which means that it's a good deal for the best seats in the house, but rarely provides a ticket for under £15 (most musicals around £23, plays £20-22). In addition, you can only buy tickets on the day of the performance, in person and in cash, and there's little choice in seating. There's no way of knowing in advance what shows will have tickets available that day, but they almost always have a wide range. Noticeboards display what's going on; up to £2.50 booking fee per ticket. No limit on the number of tickets you can buy. Open M-Sa 10am-7pm, Su noon-3pm.

Donmar Warehouse, 41 Earlham St. (☎7369 1732; www.donmarwarehouse.com). Tube: Covent Garden. Serious contemporary theater. With productions starring the likes of Nicole Kidman and Colin Firth, it's not surprising that this nondescript warehouse rarely has difficulty filling its 251 seats. £13 -29; concessions and under-18s standby £12 30min. before curtain; £5 standing-room tickets available once performance is sold out.

Soho Theatre, 21 Dean St. (☎7478 0100; www.sohotheatre.com). Tube: Tottenham Court Rd. With a focus on new writers and plenty of low-priced tickets, this populist, modern fringe theater intends to introduce people of all ages to theater. The associated writers' center will read any script you send them and provide comments. Plays £5 matinees and M nights; Tu-Th £14, concessions £10; F-Sa £15, £12.50. Online prices Tu-Th £12. Late night stand-up comedy £6-15.

Long-running shows, see p. 201.

ENTERTAINMENT ENTERTAINMENT BY NEIGHBORHOOD

Map: See **Theatreland** Map.

The Adelphi, Strand. *Chicago.*

Aldwych Theatre, Aldwych St. *Fame: The Musical.*

Criterion Theatre, Piccadilly Circus. *The Complete Works of William Shakespeare (Abridged)* and *The Complete History of America (Abridged).*

Dominion Theatre, Tottenham Court Rd. *We Will Rock You.*

Duke of York's Theatre, St. Martin's Ln. *Stones in His Pockets.*

Fortune Theatre, Russell St. *The Woman in Black.*

Her Majesty's Theatre, Haymarket. *Phantom of the Opera* (see The Local Story).

London Palladium, Argyll St. *Chitty Chitty Bang Bang.*

Lyceum Theatre, Wellington St. Disney's *The Lion King.*

Palace Theatre, Shaftesbury Ave. *Les Misérables.*

Phoenix Theatre, Charing Cross Rd. *Blood Brothers.*

Prince Edward Theatre, Old Compton St. *Mamma Mia!*

Prince of Wales, Coventry St. *The Full Monty.*

St. Martin's Theatre, West St. *The Mousetrap.*

Theatre Royal, Drury Lane, Catharine St. *My Fair Lady.*

Wyndham's Theatre, Charing Cross Rd. *Art.*

OTHER

■ **Cycle Rickshaws** (☎ 7437 5696; www.londonpedicabs.com) bring a touch of Bangkok to an area now largely denuded of strip joints and sex shops. If you'd rather not explore Soho on foot, flag down a pedicab driver to cart you around. Marvel as your driver nimbly evades cars screeching past. Rickshaws congregate at various points around the West End, but the most popular pick-up spot is the corner of Frith St. and Old Compton St. (Tube: Piccadilly Circus or Leicester Sq.), Su-Th 6pm-1am, F-Sa 6pm-4am. Short spins around Soho £2.50-3 per person; longer trips £5 per person per mi. Agree to a price before you go. Cash only.

WESTMINSTER

SEE MAP, p. 372

⚑ **WESTMINSTER QUICKFIND: Sights,** p. 104; *Museums & Galleries,* p. 136; *Food & Drink,* p. 162; *Pubs,* p. 179; *Accommodations,* p. 264.

Long-running shows, (see p. 201):

Apollo Victoria, Wilton Rd. *Bombay Dreams.* **Map:** See **Theatreland**

St. John's, Smith Square, Smith Sq. (☎ 7222 1061). Tube: Westminster or St. James's Park. A former church (see p. 107), now a full-time concert venue with a program weighted toward chamber and early music; little-known, but highly regarded by critics. Concerts Sept. to mid-July daily, mid-July to Aug. 1-2 per week. Performances generally start 7:30pm. £5-15; concessions sometimes available. Box office open M-F, 10am-5pm.

St. Martin-in-the-Fields, Trafalgar Sq. (see p. 105; box office ☎ 7839 8362). Frequent concerts and recitals are given in this ornate 18th-century church, home to the acclaimed Academy of St. Martin-in-the-Fields, which occasionally plays here. Free lunchtime concerts most M-Tu and F 1:05pm. Tourist-oriented candlelit evening concerts Th-Sa 7:30pm; reserved seating £10-17, unreserved places £6-8.

NORTH LONDON

216 ⚑ *NORTH LONDON QUICKFIND: Sights,* p. 107; *Museums & Galleries,* p. 137; *Food & Drink,* p. 163; *Pubs,* p. 180; *Nightlife,* p. 192; *Shopping,* p. 240; *Accommodations,* p. 265.

CINEMA

▧ Tricycle Cinema, see Tricycle (below) for details; entrance on Buckley Rd. Gorgeous large-screen luxury cinema specializing in independent and foreign films, with the occasional Hollywood blockbuster. Recline on the plush pink seats and enjoy the show. Singles night 1st Th of the month including pre-movie champagne and post-movie bar (£12, concessions £9). Family films Sa 1pm (£4, concessions £3). Supercheap matinees Th 2:30pm, £3, concessions £2.50. Regular features £7, £4.50 M and Tu-F before 5pm; concessions £1 less M-F before 8pm and Sa-Su before 5pm.

Everyman Cinema, 5 Holly Bush Vale (☎08700 664 777; www.everymancinema.com). Tube: Hampstead. One of London's oldest movie theaters, this 1930s picture house was recently revamped. Lean back on the leather sofas on the "luxury" balcony, or snuggle into one of the velvet stall seats. Mostly new independent films. Cafe/bar open M-F 5:30pm-11pm, Sa-Su 2pm-11pm. Standard/stalls £8, concessions £7; luxury seats £13.

COMEDY

Canal Cafe Theatre, above the Bridge House pub, Delamere Terr. (☎7289 6054). Tube: Warwick Ave. One of the few comedy venues to specialize in sketch, as opposed to stand-up, comedy. Grab dinner below and enjoy your drinks around the small tables while you laugh. Box office opens 30min. before performance. Weekly changing shows W-Sa 7:30pm (£5, concessions £4). *Newsrevue,* Th-Sa 9:30pm and Su 9pm, is London's longest-running comedy sketch show, presenting an irreverent weekly take on current events since 1970 (£9, concessions £7). Both shows together cost £12. £1 membership included in ticket price.

Downstairs at the King's Head, 2 Crouch End Hill (☎8340 1028). Bus #W7 from Finsbury Park or #41 from Archway (Zone 3). One of London's oldest and most reliable comedy clubs, in a cozy space under a pub. Shows start 8:30pm, doors 8pm, Su 7:45pm. Try-outs every Th give up to 16 new acts their 15min. of fame (£4, concessions £3); Sa-Su "comedy cabarets" mix up to 5 acts, from stand-up to songs to ventriloquism (£7, concessions £5).

MUSIC: CLASSICAL, FOLK & JAZZ

Jazz Café, 5 Parkway (☎7344 0044; www.jazzcafe.co.uk). Tube: Camden Town. With a crowded front bar and balcony restaurant overlooking the large dance floor and stage, this popular, pricey nightspot boasts a top line-up of jazz, hip-hop, funk, and Latin performers (£10-30). Jazzy club nights follow the show F-Sa (£8-9), going until 2am. Jam session Su noon-4pm (£1). Open M-Th 7pm-1am, F-Sa 7pm-2am, Su 7pm-midnight. MC/V.

Music on a Summer Evening, in Kenwood, Highgate (see p. 108; ☎7413 1443; www.picnicconcerts.com). Popular classics and lakeside fireworks held July-Aug. Aficionados will shrink from the amplified sound system. If a view of the orchestra isn't important, stay outside the enclosure and listen for free—music is audible for miles around. Deckchairs £20-24, concessions £18-22; promenade (no seat—bring a groundsheet or risk a wet bum) £16, concessions £14.

MUSIC: ROCK & POP

Dublin Castle, 94 Parkway. There's music in the back of this pub every night, but Tu nights (*Club Fandango* or *Bug Bear)* get particularly intense as record execs and talent scouts descend looking for the next big thing. W-Sa after the bands finish the pub turns into a dance club until 1am. 3 bands nightly 8:45-11pm; doors open 8:30pm. Cover £5, students £4.

Forum, 9-17 Highgate Rd. (☎7284 1001, box office ☎7344 0044; www.meanfiddler.com). Tube: Kentish Town. Turn right out of Tube station, go over the crest of the hill and bear left—you'll see the marquee. Lavish Art Deco theater turned top venue, with great sound and good views, that attracts some of the biggest bands: Van Morrison, Bjork, Oasis, Jamiroquai, and many others have played this 2000-capacity space.

The Garage, 20-22 Highbury Corner. Enter on Holloway Rd. (box office ☎7344 0044; www.meanfiddler.com). Tube: Highbury and Islington. Hard core and indie rock groups play 5 nights a week, with a smattering of American punk and emo bands. Lesser acts play the **217** upstairs room. Music 8-11pm, F-Sa followed by an indie clubnight until 3am (included in gig

Shakespeare's Globe Theatre

Royal Opera House

Electric Cinema

ticket; clubnight alone F £6, Sa £5). F night *Statik*, eclectic contemporary music; Sa night *International Hi-Fi*, more of the same. Gigs £5-15.

THEATER

The Almeida, Almeida St. (☎7359 4404; www.almeida.co.uk). Tube: Angel or Highbury and Islington. The top fringe theater in London, if not the world; Hollywood stars, including Kevin Spacey and Nicole Kidman, queue up to prove their acting cred here. The sparkling bar and foyer areas testify to expensive renovations that culminated in spring 2003 with a new executive director. Shows M-Sa at 7:30pm, Sa matinees 3pm. Tickets £6-27.50, concessions £10 M, F and Sa matinees.

Etcetera Theatre, upstairs at the Oxford Arms, 265 Camden High St. (☎7482 4857). Tube: Camden Town. 5 rows of seats leading straight onto a good-sized stage, with 2 plays per night. Mostly experimental stuff from new writers and unsolicited scripts, though local mega-dramatist Alan Bennett *(The Madness of King George III)* has premiered a couple of pieces here. Box office opens 30min. before the show. Shows M-Sa 7:30 and 9:30pm, Su 6:30 and 8:30pm. £8-10, concessions £5-8; includes 1yr. membership giving £1.50 off future tickets. Cash only.

Hampstead Theatre, 98 Avenue Rd. (☎7722 9301; www. hampsteadtheater.com). Tube: Swiss Cottage. Take the Eton Ave. Tube exit. Recently re-opened in a brand-new, ultra-modern space, this theater features works selected from hundreds of unsolicited scripts by budding unknowns from around the UK. Acting alumni include John Malkovich. Shows M-Sa 7:45pm and Sa 3pm. M £12, Tu-F and Sa 3pm £16, Sa 8pm £19. Limited student tickets (£5) available in advance for some F-Sa 3pm shows; day-of-tickets for £8.

The King's Head, 115 Upper St. (☎7226 1916). Tube: Angel or Highbury and Islington. Above a hip pub, the theater focuses on new writing. Successful productions often transfer to the West End. Alums include Hugh Grant, Gary Oldman, and *Ab Fab's* Joanna Lumley. 3-course meal (£14) is available to ticket holders 1hr. before the show. Shows Tu-Sa 8pm and Sa 3:30pm; £9-13, concessions M-Th and matinees £5-10. Lunchtime shows £5-10. Slightly cheaper, short-run show plays Su (matinee)-M.

New End Theatre, 27 New End (☎7794 0022; www.newendtheatre.co.uk). Tube: Hampstead. Thought-provoking new work skillfully produced by local and touring companies Tu-Sa night (Sa-Su matinee). Box office open M-F 10am-7pm, Sa 1-7pm, Su noon-3pm. £12-16, concessions available in advance £10-14.

The Old Red Lion, 418 St. John St. (☎ 7837 7816). Tube: Angel. New writing and adaptations in a tiny theater above the pub, with occasional film screenings and readings from new scripts. Performances Tu-Su 7:45 or 8pm (£12, Su and Tu-Th concessions £10), poetry or comedy M (£5/£4). Call or drop by in advance.

Puppet Theatre Barge, colorful barge moored in Little Venice next to Blomfield Rd. (☎ 7249 6876; www.puppetbarge.com). Tube: Warwick Ave. Puppet and shadow-puppet shows beneath the bright red-and-yellow awnings of this Little Venice institution have thrilled children for years, while occasional adult-oriented shows recall the long and ribald history of puppetry as a serious performance art. Children's shows most weekends and daily during holidays at 3pm; call for program. £7, children and concessions £6.50.

Tricycle, 269 Kilburn High Rd. (☎ 7328 1000; www.tricycle.co.uk). Tube: Kilburn or Rail: Brondesbury Park. A marvelous 3-in-1, with cinema (see above), art gallery, and a theater known for new minority playwrights. January 2004 will feature the return of the West End smash-hit musical *Kat and the Kings*. Box office open M-Sa 10am-9pm, Su 2-9pm. Performances M-F 8pm, Sa 4 and 8pm, Su 5pm (*Kat and the Kings* only). £9-16; concessions Th-F £2 less, M and Sa 4pm pay-what-you-can (first 30 seats); W students £5; Su 5pm £14.

SOUTH LONDON

🔃 *SOUTH LONDON QUICKFIND:* **Sights,** *p. 111;* **Museums & Galleries,** *p. 138;* **Food & Drink,** *p. 166;* **Nightlife,** *p. 194;* **Shopping,** *p. 241.*

Battersea Arts Centre (BAC), Old Town Hall, 176 Lavender Hill (☎ 7223 2223, www.bac.org.uk). Rail: Clapham Junction. From Clapham Junction, take the shopping center exit, turn left and walk straight up Lavender Hill for 10min. BAC is right after the junction with Latchmere Rd. One of London's top off-West End venues, best known for experimental theater. Also hosts comedy, opera, and "mainstream works" (radical corruptions of Shakespeare and other canonical texts). Plenty of family-friendly selections. On occasional 'Scratch Nights,' guinea pigs can see works in progress for free (advance booking essential). Tickets usually around £13, concessions £7.

Brixton Academy, 211 Stockwell Rd. (bookings on Ticketweb, ☎ 7771 2000; www.brixton-academy.co.uk). Tube: Brixton. Beautiful 4300-seat 1929 Art Deco ex-cinema; sloping floor ensures even those at the back have a chance to see the band. Covers all the bases from the Pogues to Marilyn Manson. Occasional club nights. Box office open only on performance evenings. £15-20, sometimes up to £33. Cash only at the door.

The Swan, 215 Clapham Rd. (☎ 7978 9778; www.theswanstockwell.com). Tube: Stockwell. Opposite the Tube. Large, dark pub with shabby but comfortable furnishings and a devoted crowd of regulars. Th "Thank God It's Thursday" essential rock, pop, and indie dance anthems; F live bands, Sa-Su rock and indie bands. Music starts 10pm. Open Th 6pm-2am, F 6pm-3am, Sa 7pm-3am, Su 7pm-2am. Th free; F £3, free before 8pm; Sa £6, £3 before 9pm; Su £3, free before 10pm, no admittance after 1am.

EAST LONDON

🔃 *EAST LONDON QUICKFIND:* **Sights,** *p. 112;* **Museums & Galleries,** *p. 139;* **Food & Drink,** *p. 167;* **Pubs,** *p. 181;* **Nightlife,** *p. 196;* **Shopping,** *p. 242.*

🎭 **Comedy Cafe,** 66 Rivington St. (☎ 7739 5706; www.comedycafe.co.uk). One of London's best venues for stand-up; come see both established stars and hot young talent. Skip the food (burgers £7) and save up your cash for beers (£2.70). You may run up a substantial bar bill, but at least you'll be laughing all the way to the ATM. Reserve F-Sa. W free try-out night, Th cover £5, F £10, Sa £14. Group packages W-Sa £15-25. F-Sa nights include disco music and dancing. Doors open 7pm, show 9pm, dancing to 1am. MC/V.

Cargo, Kingsland Viaduct, 83 Rivington St. See **Nightlife,** p. 196. Club-bar triples as a venue; diverse live acts intermixed with club DJs most nights, starting 8pm. £3-10.

Hackney Empire, 291 Mare St. (☎ 8985 2424; www.hackneyempire.co.uk). Rail: Hackney Central or Tube: Bethnal Green, then bus #D6, 106, or 253. An unlikely location for such an ornate theater, but it's pulled in the stars for years. Charlie Chaplin performed here early in

219

his career, and it features comedy, musicals, opera, and drama. The Empire is currently closed and under construction; a multi-million-pound overhaul will include technological upgrades. It will reopen in September 2003 with a shift in focus away from comedy and toward theater. Call or check website for shows and prices.

Greenwich and Docklands International Festival (☎8305 1818, bookings 8858 7755; www.festival.org). Two weeks in early July (July 2-15 in 2004) bring international musicians, dancers, and theatrical troupes to outdoor stages and alternative venues all over East London, culminating in a spectacular fireworks display. Individual events free-£20.

London Arena, Limeharbour (☎7538 1212 or 0870 512 1212 24hr.; www.londonarena.co.uk). DLR: Crossharbour and London Arena. Giant shed-like space that since a multi-million pound refurbishment in 1998 has established itself as London's leading megavenue for commercial pop. At other times, the arena serves as the base of the London Knights hockey team. Box office open M-F 9am-8pm, Sa 10am-6pm. £10-25.

Spitz, 109 Commercial St. (☎7392 9032; www.spitz.co.uk). Tube: Liverpool St. Above a restaurant in Spitalfields market, this venue hosts an eclectic range of live music, from klezmer, jazz, and world music to indie pop and rap. All profits go to help Bosnian and Kosovar children through the Dandelion Trust. Music most nights at 8pm. Check the website for details. Cover £5-15.

WEST LONDON

🔼 *WEST LONDON QUICKFIND: **Sights**, p. 115; **Food & Drink**, p. 168; **Shopping**, p. 243; **Accommodations**, p. 266.*

🖼 **Riverside Studios,** Crisp Rd. (☎8237 1111; www.riversidestudios.co.uk). Tube: Hammersmith. From the Tube, take Queen Caroline St. under the motorway and follow it right past the Apollo (15min.) to the Thames. One of the best, if least-known, entertainment venues in London. The 2 **theaters** offer international work, as well as home-grown fringe productions and comedy. The superb, plush 🖼 **cinema** plays international art-house, with an excellent program featuring many classics (some with live piano) and frequent double bills. Box office open daily noon-9pm. Plays £12-18, concessions £5-12; films £5.50/£4.50.

BBC Television Centre, Wood Ln. (see **Sights,** p. 115; ☎8576 1227; www.bbc.co.uk). Tube: White City. The BBC records over 600 shows with live studio audiences every year. Book 5 weeks ahead, though less-popular shows often have tickets available nearer showtime. With the exception of children's shows, participants must be 18+. Apply by phone or write to: Audience Services, P.O. Box 3000, BBC Television Centre, London W12 7RJ. Send your name, address, daytime phone, number of tickets requested, and the age range of those attending; you will be added to a waiting list. If approved, your tickets will arrive 2 weeks before the date of the show. You can also apply online—www.bbc.co.uk/tickets. Free.

Bush Theatre, Shepherd's Bush Green (☎7610 4224; www.bushtheatre.co.uk). Tube: Shepherd's Bush. Above a branch of O'Neill's. This theatre's off-beat and controversial programs derive from their policy of actively encouraging unsolicited submissions from new writers. Telephone booking M-Sa 10am-7pm. Box office open M-Sa 5-8pm, 1:30-8pm on performance days. £3.50-10.

Hammersmith Irish Centre, Black's Rd. (info ☎8563 8232, tickets ☎8741 3211; www.lbhf.gov.uk/irishcentre). Tube: Hammersmith. Run by the local council, this claims to be London's foremost Irish cultural center. It is also home to a small Irish lending library, an art gallery, and frequently screens Irish films. The large hall hosts Irish bands, trad guitar sessions, and *ceilidhs,* as well as comedians and literary readings. Library open Th-F 11am-4pm. Most performances F-Sa 8:15pm. Free-£10.

Lyric Hammersmith, King St. (☎08700 500 511; www.lyric.co.uk). Tube: Hammersmith. Behind a concrete facade, this ornate 1895 theater is known for classy, controversial productions. Above the main theater, the small **Lyric Studio** stages experimental drama. Box office open M-Sa 10am-8pm, until 6pm on performance nights. Theater £10-20, students and concessions £7-9. Studio usually £7, concessions £5. M all £7.

Shepherd's Bush Empire, Shepherd's Bush Green (☎0905 020 3999; bookings on Ticketweb, ☎7771 2000; www.shepherds-bush-empire.co.uk). Tube: Shepherd's Bush. Turn-of-the-century theater once famous for hosting BBC gameshows, now a surprisingly intimate music venue (capacity 2000). Everyone has played here—from Radiohead to Melanie C. Box office open M-Sa noon-5pm. £13.50-28, most £15-18.

Carling Apollo Hammersmith, Queen Caroline St. (book via 24hr. Ticketmaster ☎0870 606 3400; www.cclive.co.uk). Tube: Hammersmith. In the shadow of the Hammersmith Flyover, this venue hosts musical and theatrical diversions, from the Nutcracker to Pokémon Live. Box office only open on performance days, from 4pm-start of show. £18.50 and up, depending on show.

Shopping

From its earliest days, London has been a trading city, its wealth and power built upon commerce. Today even more so than at the Empire's height, London's economy is truly international—and thanks to the outward-looking and eclectic nature of Londoners' diverse tastes, the range of goods on offer is unmatched anywhere in the world. From Harrods's proud boast to supply "all things to all people," to African crafts on sale in Brixton market, you could shop for a lifetime.

The major mainstream shopping areas in Central London are Covent Garden, Oxford St., Carnaby St., Bond St. **(The West End)**; King's Rd. **(Chelsea)**; Old Brompton Rd. and Sloane St. **(Knightsbridge & Belgravia)**; Kensington High St. **(Kensington & Earl's Court)**; and Tottenham Court Rd. **(Bloomsbury).** For the market-oriented shopper Central London offers Portobello Market **(Notting Hill)** while Greater London has Camden Market **(North London)**, Brick Ln. and Petticoat Ln. Markets **(East London).**

The shopping areas vary greatly in character. At the beginning of each Neighborhood entry is an overall outline of what to expect. Find what you want and fulfill those spending impulses, or just window-shop and browse to your heart's content.

SHOPPING BY TYPE

ALCOHOL		BOOKS, CONT.	
The Beer Shop	East London	Fosters Bookshop	West End
Gerry's	West End	Foyles	West End
		Gay's the Word	Bloomsbury
BOOKS		Hatchard's	West End
Blackwell's	West End	Mega City Comics	North London
Books for Cooks	Notting Hill		

BOOKS (CONT.)

Southeran's of Sackville St.	North London
Stanfords	West End
The Travel Bookshop	Notting Hill
Unsworths	Bloomsbury
Waterstone's	West End, Bloomsbury
Zwemmer	West End

CHEESES

☒ Neal's Yard Dairy	West End

CLOTHES: NEW

Ad Hoc	Chelsea
☒ Apple Tree	West End
Backstage	Chelsea
☒ The British Hatter	Kensington
Browns Labels for Less	West End
☒ Cyberdog	West End, North London
Daisy & Tom	Chelsea
Diesel Stylelab	West End
Diesel	West End
Hoxton Boutique	East London
Jauko	Kensington
Joy	South London
The Laden Showroom	East London
Mango	West End
Miss Sixty	West End
Nothing	Notting Hill
Oscar Milo	West End
Paul Smith Sale Shop	West End
Proibito Sale Shop	West End
Savage London	West End
Teaze	Notting Hill
Ted Baker	West End
Therapy	West End
Unique Leatherwear	East London
Urban Outfitters	Kensington
Willma	Notting Hill
World's End	Chelsea
Zara	West End

CLOTHES: VINTAGE

Annie's	North London
Cinch	West End
☒ Delta of Venus	Bloomsbury
Dolly Diamond	Notting Hill
One of a Kind	Notting Hill
Pandora	Knightsbridge
☒ Steinberg & Tolkien	Chelsea

DEPARTMENT STORES

Barkers	Kensington
Fortnum & Mason	West End
☒ Hamley's	West End
Harrods	Knightsbridge
Harvey Nichols	Knightsbridge
John Lewis	West End
Liberty	West End
Marks & Spencer	West End
Selfridges	West End

GIFTS & MISCELLANY

Butler and Wilson	West End
☒ James Smith & Sons	Bloomsbury
L. Cornelissen & Son	Bloomsbury
Neal's Yard Remedies	West End
☒ Paperchase	Bloomsbury
Penhaligon's	West End
Purves & Purves	Bloomsbury
The Tea and Coffee Plant	Notting Hill
Twining's	Holborn

MARKETS

Brick Lane	East London
Brixton Market	South London
Camden Markets	North London
Camden Passage	North London
Chapel Market	North London
Greenwich Markets	East London
Jubilee Market Hall	West End
Petticoat Lane	East London
Portobello Market	Notting Hill
Spitalfields	East London

MUSIC

Black Market	West End
Blacker Dread Muzik Store	South London
HMV	West End
Honest Jon's	Notting Hill
Intoxica!	Notting Hill
☒ Music Zone	West End
Out on the Floor	North London
Reckless Records	West End
Rough Trade	Notting Hill
Tower Records	West End
Turnkey	West End
Vinyl Addiction	North London
Virgin Megastore	West End

SHOES

Dr. Marten's	West End
Office	West End
Sukie's	Chelsea
Swear	West End
Tabio	Chelsea

SPORTING GOODS

Lillywhite's	West End
Niketown	West End

NOTABLE CHAINS

As in almost any major city, London retailing is dominated by chains. Fortunately, local shoppers are picky enough that buying from a chain doesn't mean abandoning the flair and quirky stylishness for which Londoners are famed. Stores must have an eagle eye for trends and change lines often enough to keep punters coming back. Most chain stores have a flagship on or near Oxford St., often with a second branch in Covent Garden. The different branches of chains will have slightly different hours, but almost all the stores listed below are open daily 10am-7pm, starting later (noon) on Su and staying open an hour later one night of the week (usually Th).

Lush (☎01202 668 545; www.lush.co.uk). 7 London locations including 123 King's Rd. (Tube: Sloane Sq.); Covent Garden Piazza (Tube: Covent Garden); 40 Carnaby St. (Tube: Oxford Circus); 96 Kensington High St. (Tube: High St. Kensington); Quadrant Arcade, 80-82 Regent St. (Tube: Piccadilly Circus); and the concourses of Victoria Station (Tube: Victoria) and Heathrow. All-natural cosmetics look good enough to eat: soap is hand-cut from blocks masquerading as cakes and cheeses (£2-5), and facial masks are scooped from guacamole-like tubs. Giant, fizzing bath-beads too. Vegan cosmetics are marked with a green dot.

Karen Millen (☎01622 664 032; www.karenmillen.co.uk). 8 central London locations including: 262-264 Regents St. (Tube: Oxford Circus); 22-23 James St. (Tube: Covent Garden); 33 Kings Rd. (Tube: Sloane Sq.); 57 South Molton St. (Tube: Bond St.); and Barker's Arcade (Tube: High St. Kensington). Best known for richly embroidered brocade suits and evening gowns, but recently edging towards a more casual line.

FCUK, flagship 396 Oxford St. (☎7529 7766; www.frenchconnection.com). Tube: Bond St. 14 branches in London. Home of the advertising coup of the 90s offers an extensive collection of their vaguely offensive, mildly subversive moniker. AmEx/MC/V.

Jigsaw, flagship 126-127 New Bond St. (☎7491 4484; www.jigsaw-online.com). Tube: Bond St. 17 branches in London. The essence of Britishness, distilled into quality mid-priced womenswear. Restrained, classic cuts that prize elegance over fad-based fashions, though they've recently begun to move towards more edgy designs. AmEx/MC/V.

Muji (www.muji.co.uk). 8 London locations including 187 Oxford St. (☎7437 7503; Tube: Oxford Circus), 41 Carnaby St. (☎7287 7323; Tube: Oxford Circus); 135 Long Acre (☎7379 0820; Tube: Covent Garden); 157 Kensington High St. (☎7376 2484; Tube: High St. Kensington); 118 King's Rd. (☎7823 8688; Tube: Sloane Sq.); and 6-17 Tottenham Ct. Rd. (☎7436 1770; Tube: Tottenham Court Rd.). Minimalist lifestyle stores, with a sleek Zen take on everything from chilled oolong tea to futons. AmEx/MC/V.

Oasis, flagship 292 Regent St. (☎7323 5978; www.oasis-stores.com). Tube: Oxford Circus. 19 London branches. Colorful, sexy clothes for work and play, plus shoes and accessories. A favorite with students and 20-somethings. AmEx/MC/V.

Shellys, 266-270 Regent St. (☎7287 0939; www.shellys.co.uk). Tube: Oxford Circus. Smaller stores at: 159 Oxford St. and 44-45 Carnaby St. (both Tube: Oxford Circus); 40 Kensington High St. (Tube: High St. Kensington); 14-18 Neal St. (Tube: Covent Garden); 163 King St. (Tube: Hammersmith); and 124b King's Rd. (Tube: Sloane Sq.). The Topshop of shoes, with a good selection of reasonably priced, funky footwear. Women's selection better than men's. AmEx/MC/V.

Topshop/Topman/Miss Selfridge, flagship 214 Oxford St. (☎7927 2158). Tube: Oxford Circus. Dozens of locations in central London. Cheap fashions for young people—over-25s will feel middle-aged. The flagship store brings them all under 1 roof, though Topshop dominates with a huge range of strappy shoes and skimpy clubwear spread over 3 floors. Miss Selfridge, on the ground floor, has an even younger feel; Top Man is all shiny Ts, cargo pants, and polyester suits. 10% student discount. AmEx/MC/V.

UNIQLO, 84-86 Regent St. (☎7014 0100; www.uniqlo.co.uk). Tube: Piccadilly Circus. Also at 163-169 Brompton Rd. (Tube: Knightsbridge). "The clothes store from Japan" offers simple, casual clothing for men, women, and children. Similar to GAP clothing but more affordable. AmEx/MC/V.

SHOPPING BY NEIGHBORHOOD

BAYSWATER

🗺 **BAYSWATER QUICKFIND: Food & Drink,** *p. 148;* **Pubs,** *p. 173;* **Entertainment,** *p. 207;* **Accommodations,** *p. 252.*

As with eating, shopping in Bayswater is largely confined to two streets. Most of the stores on **Queensway** and **Westbourne Grove,** however, peddle a generic range of tourist paraphernalia, electronics, and high-street chain clothing.

SEE MAP, p. 361

Whiteleys Shopping Centre, Queensway (☎7229 8844; www.whiteleys.com). Tube: Bayswater. Upscale shopping mall with over 70 restaurants and stores including Oasis, Karen Millen, Jigsaw, and Muji, along with a Marks & Spencer **grocery store** and a **UCI** multiplex cinema. Open M-Sa 10am-8pm, Su noon-6pm.

BLOOMSBURY

🗺 **BLOOMSBURY QUICKFIND: Sights,** *p. 74;* **Museums & Galleries,** *p. 125;* **Food & Drink,** *p. 148;* **Pubs,** *p. 173;* **Entertainment,** *p. 207;* **Accommodations,** *p. 254.*

As home to the British Library and most of London's academic institutions, Bloomsbury's main commodity is **books;** the streets around the British Museum are crammed with specialist and cut-price bookshops, while the Waterstone's on Gower St. (see below) is one of London's largest. If you're after **electronics** equipment, head to **Tottenham Court Road** Don't be afraid to haggle with the salespeople, especially if you're paying cash or have seen the item cheaper elsewhere. If you're contemplating a serious purchase, do a quick price-checking jaunt up and down the road—you may find a much better deal.

SEE MAP, p. 362

BOOKS

Gay's the Word, 66 Marchmont St. (☎7278 7654; www.gaystheword.co.uk). Tube: Russell Sq. The UK's largest specialist gay and lesbian bookstore, GTW boasts an amazingly well-informed and friendly staff, and a large enough inventory to devote entire sections to such arcanities as queer detective fiction. Includes erotic postcards, serious movies, and free magazines. Noticeboard with accommodations listings. Open M-Sa 10am-6:30pm, Su 2-6pm. AmEx/MC/V.

Waterstone's, 82 Gower St. (☎7636 1577). Tube: Goodge St. Cafe, infinite magazines, and frequent signings are additional attractions of this 5-floor behemoth. Make sure to check the large used and remaindered section on the second floor, and the excellent travel section on the ground floor. Open M and W-F 9:30am-8pm, Tu 10am-8pm, Sa 9:30am-7pm, Su noon-6pm. AmEx/MC/V.

Unsworths, 12 Bloomsbury St. (☎7436 9836; www.unsworths.com). Tube: Tottenham Court Rd. Up to 90% off publishers' prices on a wide range of literature and academic books, with an emphasis on the humanities. An excellent used selection upstairs, rare and antiquarian books in the basement. Open M-Sa 10am-8pm, Su 11am-7pm. AmEx/MC/V.

CLOTHES

Delta of Venus, 151 Drummond St. (☎7387 3037; www.deltaofvenus.co.uk). Tube: Euston or Euston Square. A small but unbeatable array of vintage clothes for both sexes spanning the 60s to the early 80s. Dresses £18-40, shirts £10-18, men's jackets from £20—it's not cheap, but it's worth every penny. Just as exciting as the clothes is the small but mouth-watering selection of vinyl, with everything from the Doors to the Sex Pistols to Velvet Underground at great prices (most LPs £8-15). Be sure to chat with the friendly and knowledgeable proprietor. Open M-Sa 11am-7pm. MC/V.

GIFTS & MISCELLANY

James Smith & Sons, 53 New Oxford St. (☎ 7836 4731; www.james-smith.co.uk). Tube: Tottenham Court Rd. Groucho Marx once quipped that he hated London when it wasn't raining. The Smith family, in the umbrella business since 1830, must agree. Signature handmade gentlemen's brollies (from £35) come in any color, so long as it's black. Also a variety of colorful ladies' and cheaper mass-produced models, as well as a display of hand-carved walking sticks. Open M-F 9:30am-5:25pm, Sa 10am-5:25pm, Su 10am-5:25pm. AmEx/MC/V.

Paperchase, 213 Tottenham Court Rd. (☎ 7467 6200; www.paperchase.co.uk). Tube: Goodge St. A massive 1-stop for artsy types. Unbeatable selection of cards, giftwrap, and stylish desktop accessories on the ground floor; pens, some interior design accessories, and frames on the 1st; art and graphics supplies on the 2nd, including paper by the sheet, from Tibetan bark paper to frosted Mylar. Accessories of all sorts (candles, brushed-steel pencil cases, decorated boxes, handmade notebooks, etc.) scattered throughout the store. Open M, W, F 9:30am-7pm, Tu 10am-7pm, Th 9:30am-8pm, Sa 10am-7pm, Su noon-6pm. AmEx/MC/V.

Purves & Purves, 220-224 Tottenham Court Rd. (☎ 7580 8223; www.purves.co.uk). A temple to modern living, Purves is *the* shop for design aficionados. There are some affordable items (funky magazine racks, £13; too-cool-to-ever-use playing cards, £6), but the biggest thrill is sitting in the sexy furniture without having to shell out thousands. Open M-W and F 10am-6pm, Th 10am-7:30pm, Sa 9:30am-6pm, Su 11:30am-5:30pm. MC/V.

L. Cornelissen & Son, 105 Great Russell St. (☎ 7636 1045). Tube: Tottenham Court Rd. With its original 1855 interior, Cornelissen's looks more like an apothecary's than an art store. Jars of raw pigment, crystals, and lumps of evil-smelling "dragon's blood" reach to the ceilings, while mahogany drawers hide a fantastic array of brushes, nibs, paints, and crayons. An artist's dream. Open M-F 9:30am-5:30pm, Sa 9:30am-5pm. MC/V.

CHELSEA

⚑ CHELSEA QUICKFIND: Sights, *p. 76;* **Museums & Galleries,** *p. 126;* **Food & Drink,** *p. 150;* **Entertainment,** *p. 208.* **TRANSPORTATION:** *The only Tube station in Chelsea is Sloane Sq.; from here buses #11, 19, 22, 211, and 319 run down the King's Rd.*

SEE MAP, p. 363

the hidden deal

Sale Crazy

Twice a year, in January and July, London goes sale crazy. Prices are slashed in almost every shop and crowds take full advantage of extended opening hours. Real pros scout out what's on offer in the days leading up to the sale—staff can normally tell you what will be reduced and by how much—and then turn up early on the first day of the sale to ensure success (there are often queues outside Harrods). Some department stores will even (unofficially) sell items at their sale prices a day or two before the sale officially starts—it can't hurt to ask.

On the other hand, if you're willing to cope with a reduced choice, it pays to wait—in the last days of the sales prices are slashed even further, often up to 80%. One word of warning, though: if a bargain looks too good to be true, it probably is. Many more expensive shops order lower-quality merchandise especially for the sales that they wouldn't dream of offering their regular customers.

the BIG $plurge

Precious Clothing

Steinberg & Tolkien offers London's largest collection of vintage American and European clothing. The ground floor is like a museum, full of exquisitely decorated bags, antique costume jewelry, and stunningly beautiful gowns carefully arranged for display-but the basement level is where the bulk of the collection lies. Organized by decade in a colorful array, the glamor of the past is right at your fingertips-there's even a rack of Victorian dresses. It's all available for touching, trying, and buying. The designer clothing section boasts high-end names like Christian Lacroix, Giorgio Armani, and Sonia Rykiel.

Even at the second-time-around, price tags for designer brands can still be hefty-but prices vary greatly: on the Victorian rack, a £700 2-piece gown hangs next to a £130 dress. Much of the collection hovers in the very splurgable £100-300 range. Many pieces go as low as £50-60, especially in the two half-off sale rooms in the back. With a little time and money, you can bring a bit of old-time Chelsea glamor home.

193 King's Rd. (☎ 7376 3660). Open M-Sa 11am-7pm, Su noon-6pm. MC/V.

No serious shopper can come to London and ignore Chelsea, even if it's lost much of its edge. **Sloane Square** is extremely Sloaney (the English equivalent of American Preppy), and one would hardly guess that **King's Road** gave us both the miniskirt and the Sex Pistols—alternative styles have given way to trendy, if traditional, cuts. The eastern end of the street, where it comes out of Sloane Sq., has a few mid-priced chains and the massive **Peter Jones** department store (a branch of John Lewis, p. 234); the rest of King's Rd. is full of one-off boutiques, which bring it a vitality and diversity lost in many other London shopping meccas.

CLOTHES

Steinberg & Tolkien, 193 King's Rd. (☎ 7376 3660). Open M-Sa 11am-7pm, Su noon-6pm. MC/V. See **Precious Clothing**, left.

Ad Hoc, 153 King's Rd. (☎ 7376 8829; www.adhoclondon.com). With glitter and confetti spilling out into the sidewalk, Ad Hoc is the closest thing to alternative left on King's Rd. Baggy cargoes, ultra-short minis, and a rainbow collection of wigs dominate the cluttered space. Check out the plastic retro jewelry (£5-10) and the basket of irreverent pins (50p) by the register. Clothing mostly £20-50. Open M-Tu and Th-Su 10am-6:30pm, W 10am-7pm. MC/V.

Backstage, 207 King's Rd. (☎ 7351 2373). Trendy without the cliché, this cheerfully pink boutique carries Peter Golding's line of fun, street-savvy women's clothing at street-sensible prices (from £20). Open M-Sa 10:30am-6pm, Su noon-5pm. MC/V.

World's End, 430 King's Rd. (☎ 7352 6551). This small store's past legendary incarnations include SEX and Let it Rock, but other than the huge clock spinning wildly backwards, not much remains of the punk store that launched the careers of the Sex Pistols. Owned by the notorious Vivienne Westwood, the shop is now an unassuming showplace for Westwood's line of clothing (most items £100-300). Open M-Sa 10am-6pm. AmEx/MC/V.

Daisy & Tom, 181 King's Rd. (7352 5000; www.daisyandtom.com). This multi-level kiddie paradise stocks toys, books, nursery goods, clothing, and even a hairdressing salon. The in-store carousel and marionette shows (every 30min. in the clothing department) are bound to please. Open M-W and F 9:30am-6pm, Th and Sa 10am-7pm, Su 11am-5pm. MC/V.

SHOES

Sukie's, 285 and 289 King's Rd. (☎ 7352 3431, 7376 7129). Too much style for just one store, Sukie's two locations carry a brilliant selection of funky-to-formal footwear, in both classic and contemporary styles with unusual colors, materials, and textures. Many were designed specifically for the store. For groovers and shakers of both sexes. Shoes starting from £30. Open M-Sa 10am-6:30pm, Su 1-6pm. MC/V.

Tabio, 94 King's Rd. (☎ 7591 1960; www.tabio.co.uk). Two levels of perfectly arranged socks (starting at £6.50) in every imaginable color. The yin-yang rock garden at the foot of the stairs hints at the store's Japanese roots. Open M-Sa 10am-7pm, Su noon-6pm. MC/V.

HOLBORN

▶ HOLBORN QUICKFIND: Sights, *p. 84; **Museums & Galleries,** p. 128; **Food & Drink,** p. 152; **Pubs,** p. 175; **Nightlife,** p. 187; **Entertainment,** p. 210.*

With Covent Garden so close—and barristers not renowned for their dress sense— Holborn is not a top shopping destination. **High Holborn** is a busy road with a few common high-street chains, while **Fleet Street** has a number of indistinguishable clothing shops serving lawyers who just spilled port down their shirtfronts.

SEE MAP, p. 365

GIFTS & MISCELLANY

Twining's, 216 Strand (☎ 7353 3511). Tube: Temple. Proportionately London's narrowest shop, Twining's is the oldest family-run business in Britain to stay on the same premises (since 1706), and takes its legacy seriously. In addition to a small tea museum in the back, Twining's has its own epic lay, including the stirring: "Note, by the way, it was not *Twining's* tea / The Boston rebels tossed into the sea." The real draw is, of course, the tea: rows of Earl Grey (£1.70 per 125g), Prince of Wales (£1.90 per 100g), and other noble blends recall the Queen's offical patronage. Open M-F 9:30am-4:45pm. AmEx/MC/V.

KENSINGTON & EARL'S COURT

▶ KENSINGTON & EARL'S COURT QUICKFIND: Sights, *p. 88; **Museums & Galleries,** p. 130; **Food & Drink,** p. 153; **Pubs,** p. 176; **Entertainment,** p. 210; **Accommodations,** p. 259.*

Some people prefer **Kensington High St.** to Oxford St. It offers a similar, albeit more limited, range of mid-priced UK and international chains as its West End rival in a smaller and less crowded area. Karen Millen, Monsoon, Next, Diesel, Zara... if you've heard of it, it's probably here. On the other hand, it lacks the

SEE MAP, pp. 366-367

trendy one-off boutiques, and **Barkers,** the only department store, is positively tiny compared to the West End behemoths—if you're looking for anything other than mainstream clothes, go elsewhere. **Kensington Church Street** provides a mildly alternative, if pricey, experience—it's mostly clothing stores in the south, crafts and specialty shops in the middle, and antiques and oriental art as it winds north towards Notting Hill Gate.

CLOTHES

The British Hatter, 36 Kensington Church St. (☎ 7361 0000). Tube: High St. Kensington. Attending a smart wedding or the Royal Ascot? Pamela Bromley's superb hats will make sure that your headgear complements you perfectly—you'll emerge from this exquisite store looking altogether British. You'll find hats of all shapes and sizes and colors here, festooned with feathers, ribbons, and bows; also stocks accessory essentials: pins and combs to anchor your hat that discreetly in place. They also stock a small selection of men's hats. Hats from £98-£190. Open M-Sa 10:30am-6pm, Th 11am-6:30pm. AmEx/MC/V.

Jauko, 34c Kensington Church St. (☎ 7376 1408). Tube: High St. Kensington. Like its name says, the clothes in this tiny boutique are a clever melding of Japanese, UK, and Korean styles from Hello Kitty and Astro Boy-logo tees to bright flower-print dresses. All

the BIG $plurge

°LIFE CENTRE

Tired of walking? To escape the insanity of Portobello Marke, try **The Life Centre**, a bonafide relaxation haven. The Life Centre offers a wide range of soothing therapies perfect for the weary, back-pack-laden, jetlagged traveler.

The complex philosophy behind many of the therapies may not make much sense, but the word "massage" transcends all belief systems. An hour of deep tissue massage, aromatherapy, therapeutic massage, or reflexology will set you back at least £55. For a truly deep and relaxing experience, try the chavutti thirumal massage, originated from India, in which the therapist uses his feet to massage the body (£75 for 1½ hours). An Indian head massage (£25-30 for 30 minutes) covers the scalp, face, and shoulder areas. Walk-ins are welcome as long as there are therapists available. Massage therapies are all cash-only.

The center also offers 6 yoga classes daily (£9 an hour) daily at varying skill levels which are also available on a drop-in basis. Each class has 27 spaces.

☎ 7221 4602; www.thelife-centre.org. 15 Edge St. Open M-F 6:30am-10pm, Sa-Su 9am-8pm.

delightfully feminine, with soft, flowing lines. Prices run from £30-300. Also carries some adorable handbags. Open M-Sa 10am-6pm. MC/V.

Urban Outfitters, 36-38 Kensington High St. (☎ 7761 1001). Tube: High St. Kensington. 5-level deconstructed megastore, with raw concrete columns still bearing the scars of previous incarnations. Clothes, accessories, and random housewares for the young, hip, and plastic-obsessed at the usual sky-high prices (some exclusive designer tees go for over £100). Records can be found in the sub-basement. Open M-Sa 10am-7pm, Th until 8pm, Su noon-6pm. MC/V.

KNIGHTSBRIDGE & BELGRAVIA

⚑ KNIGHTSBRIDGE & BELGRAVIA QUICKFIND: Sights, p. 90; **Food & Drink,** p. 154; **Pubs,** p. 176; **Accommodations,** p. 262.

SEE MAP, p. 368

Brompton Road dominates Knightsbridge's shopping arteries, with representatives of most upmarket chains between Harvey Nichols and Harrods. Explore the side streets for spectacular deals on designer clothing, or blow a cool thousand on ultra-exclusive **Sloane Street,** which rivals Bond St. for designer boutiques. Armani, Chanel, Dior, Gucci, Hermès, Kenzo, Versace, and Yves St. Laurent all have storefronts here.

CLOTHES

Pandora, 16-22 Cheval Pl. (☎ 7589 5289). Tube: Knightsbridge. Chanel suits, Gucci handbags, and Gaultier sunglasses for as little as a quarter of their original price. A dress agency, Pandora resells clothes and accessories on behalf of unnamed wealthy women and celebrities whose appetites for hâute couture exceed their closet space. Designer garments are all "seasonally correct," under 2 years old, and often barely worn. Open M-Sa 9am-6pm. MC/V.

DEPARTMENT STORES

Harrods, 87-135 Old Brompton Rd. (☎ 7730 1234; www.harrods.com). Tube: Knightsbridge. Big things start small: in 1849, Mr. Harrod opened a small grocery store, and by 1901 had done well enough to construct the terra-cotta behemoth that now bears his name. In the Victorian era, this was the place for the wealthy to shop; over a century later, decadence still permeates this massive store. Given the sky-high prices, it's no wonder that only tourists and oil sheiks actually shop here. Prices near normal during sales in Jan. and July. If nothing else, ride the Egyptian escalator in the middle, which leads down to the eerie "Diana and Dodi" memorial, with Diana's engagement ring and a wine glass she drank out of her last night alive. Open M-Sa 10am-7pm. AmEx/MC/V.

Harvey Nichols, 109-125 Knightsbridge (☎ 7235 5000; www.harveynichols.com). Tube: Knightsbridge. Imagine Bond St., Rue St-Honoré, and Fifth Ave. all rolled up into one store. 6 of its 7 floors are devoted to the sleekest, sharpest fashion, from the biggest names to the hippest unknowns. Needless to say, the prices discourage much more than starry-eyed browsing. 5th-floor food hall has a swanky restaurant, a Yo!Sushi (see p. 147), and the chic 5th Floor Café; there's a juice bar on the main floor and a Wagamama in the basement (see p. 147). Open M-Tu and Sa 10am-7pm, W-F 10am-8pm, Su noon-6pm. AmEx/MC/V.

NOTTING HILL

🖪 *NOTTING HILL QUICKFIND: Sights, p. 94; Food & Drink, p. 156; Pubs, p. 177; Nightlife, p. 187; Entertainment, p. 211.*

SEE MAP, p. 361

The best reason to visit Notting Hill is the world-renowned **Portobello Market,** which brings color to an otherwise gentrified area. Portobello Rd. is home to a number of distinct markets, occupying different parts of the street and operating on different days. It all comes together in a mile-long row of stalls on Saturdays. The **antiques market** is what most people associate with Portobello Rd.; it stretches north from Chepstow Villas to Elgin Crescent. Most of what's on display outside is cheap bric-a-brac. *(Tube: Notting Hill Gate. Sa 7am-5pm.)* Farther north, from Elgin Crescent to Lancaster Rd., is the **general market,** with food, flowers, and household essentials. Gourmet stalls selling continental breads and organic produce show up on Saturdays. *(Tube: Westbourne Park or Ladbroke Grove (both Zone 2). M-W 8am-6pm, Th 9am-1pm, F-Sa 7am-7pm.)* North of Lancaster Rd., with arms stretching along the Westway, is the **clothes market,** with a wide selection of second-hand clothes, ethnic gear, and kitsch fashions, oddly interspersed with dodgy used electronics. *(Tube: Ladbroke Grove. F-Sa 8am-3pm.)* Finally, north of the Westway, the **Golborne Rd. market** has a dowdier, local air, while Golborne Rd. itself shows Moroccan influence with stalls selling gourmet olives, steaming couscous, and Berber handicrafts. *(Tube: Ladbroke Grove. M-Sa 9am-5pm; busiest Sa.)*

BOOKS

The Travel Bookshop, 13-15 Blenheim Crescent (☎ 7229 5260; www.thetravelbookshop.co.uk). More than just a Grantophile destination, the specialist bookshop featured in *Notting Hill* is packed with all the books you need to plan your next trip. They also carry a small selection of fiction. Open M-Sa 10am-6pm. MC/V.

Books for Cooks, 4 Blenheim Crescent. See p. 156.

CLOTHES & ACCESSORIES

Dolly Diamond, 51 Pembridge Rd. (☎ 7792 2479). Tube: Notting Hill Gate. Jackie Onassis or Audrey Hepburn? Choose your look from Dolly's great selection of classic 50s-70s clothing and elegant 20s-40s evening gowns. Dresses £50-120, ball gowns from £75. Smaller selection of men's formalwear upstairs. Open M-F 10:30am-6:30pm, Sa 9:30am-6:30pm, Su noon-6pm. MC/V, cash preferred.

One of a Kind, 259 Portobello Rd. (☎ 7792 5853). Tube: Ladbroke Grove. Vintage clothing, shoes, and accessories line every available inch of wall space, with more hanging from the ceiling. Shoes start at £25, clothes around £35, and rise rapidly into the stratosphere—some pieces on display are literally priceless. Also at 404 King's Rd. Open daily 11am-6pm. MC/V.

the hidden deal

Market Economy

Unlike Paris, Milan, and New York, London's fashion scene has always been a bottom-up affair, starting out in the street before percolating through to the catwalks. For your best bet of seeing where fashion is going, you need to hit the **markets**—trends are born in **Camden Market** (p. 240) and **Portobello Market** (p. 230), the two biggest destinations for fashionistas on a budget.

It's not just clothes you'll find here, either: antiques, books, music, shoes, and almost anything you'll ever need (and many you won't) are up for sale in the streets, and bargaining is part of the fun. However, some traders will try to take advantage of foreigners; to make sure you know the difference between a bargain and a rip-off, check up high-street prices before hitting the markets—and make sure you like what you buy, since the chance of getting a refund from a market trader is virtually nil.

Willma, 339 Portobello Rd. (☎8960 7296; www.willma.co.uk). Fluorescent cases present an exclusive range of intricate accessories and clothes. All are sourced from up-and-coming designers around the world, mostly one-offs. Prices run high, with some affordable pieces mixed in: tops from £20, novelty knickers from £10. Open Tu-Sa 11am-6pm. MC/V.

Nothing, 230 Portobello Rd. (☎7221 2910; www.nothingshop.co.uk). In line with designer Carla Portman's "nothing complicated, nothing cluttered" aesthetic, this small boutique carries women's wear (from £30) in light colors and soft fabrics. Cuts are stylish but functional. Open M-F 11am-7pm, Sa 10:30am-6:30pm, Su noon-5pm. MC/V.

Teaze, 47 Pembridge Rd. (☎7727 8358). Tube: Notting Hill Gate. Wide range of anti-slogan T-shirts with sexual overtones; novelty lingerie, with themes from Che Guevara to Playboy; and last but not least, tubs of liquid latex (£13) for the true skin-tight look. Bondage tape (£5) also available. Open M-Sa 10:30am-6:30pm, Su 1-5pm. AmEx/MC/V.

GIFTS & MISCELLANY

The Tea and Coffee Plant, 182 Portobello Rd. (☎7221 8137). Tube: Ladbroke Grove. An overpowering smell of freshly ground coffee permeates this tiny shop, which offers a wide selection of coffees and teas (£1-3). All are fairly traded and organic—the staff in this politically charged shop wouldn't have it any other way. Chew a bean before committing to a kilo (£8-11), or sip on a fresh espresso (75p). Mail order available. Open M-Sa 9am-6pm.

MUSIC

Honest Jon's, 276-278 Portobello Rd., W10 (☎8969 9822). Tube: Ladbroke Grove. Still loud and funky after all these years. Subterranean 276 holds an impressive jazz, latin, and world-music collection, while 278 carries a wide selection of reggae, hip-hop, house, and garage on vinyl and CD, as well as some soul and funk. Open M-Sa 10am-6pm, Su 11am-5pm. AmEx/MC/V.

Intoxica!, 231 Portobello Rd. (☎7229 8010; www.intoxica.co.uk). Tube: Ladbroke Grove. All vinyl. Enviable stock of surf-rock, rockabilly, soundtracks, and funk. Downstairs, jazz, blues, and 60s soul reign. Many pricey 60s originals (£20-60), and contemporary indie. Open M-F 10:30am-6:30pm, Sa 10am-6:30pm, Su noon-4pm. AmEx/MC/V.

Rough Trade, 130 Talbot Rd. (☎7229 8541). Tube: Ladbroke Grove. Branch at 16 Neal's Yard (☎7240 0105; Tube: Covent Garden), under Slam City Skates. Choosing from the wide selection of music is made easier by the small reviews tacked to most CDs and records (£5-13). Try out the in-store turntables. Open M-Sa 10am-6:30pm, Su 1-5pm. AmEx/MC/V.

THE WEST END

OXFORD STREET & REGENT STREET

⚑ OXFORD STREET & REGENT'S STREET QUICKFIND: Sights, p. 98; **Museums & Galleries,** p. 134; **Food & Drink,** p. 158; **Pubs,** p. 178; **Nightlife,** p. 188; **Entertainment,** p. 213; **Accommodations,** p. 263.

SEE MAP, p. 356

A bona-fide shopping nirvana, **Oxford St.** has an amazing atmosphere and buzz—"crowded" would be a ridiculous understatement. Tourists and Londoners alike flock to the flagships of all the mainstream British chains—from Marks & Spencer to FCUK—on what is essentially a massive British High Street. The street's popularity is undoubtedly a part of the priceless Oxford St. experience; if you prefer a less frenetic atmosphere, try High St. Kensington. Many Londoners head to Oxford St. for the massive **department stores** that line its northern edge (between Oxford Circus and Marble Arch) and the fashionable boutiques of **South Molton St.,** stretching south into Mayfair from Bond St. Tube. East of Oxford Circus, especially near Tottenham Court Rd., things are much more downmarket, with budget chains and dodgy "sale shops" alongside the Virgin and HMV **music megastores.**

Regent St. is altogether a more refined affair, despite the presence of a Disney Store. There are plenty of shops aimed at rich tourists, but it's balanced with venerable names such as Aquascutum and Liberty, not to mention the toyshop of the gods, Hamley's. **Oxford Circus,** where Regent St. and Oxford St. cross, is home to mega-flagships of international brands such as Nike and Benetton. Behind Regent St., **Carnaby St.** has a decent selection of youth fashions from famous-but-still-credible brands such as Diesel, though you'll find more interesting and obscure designer pickings in nearby **Foubert's Pl.** and **Newburgh St.**

CLOTHES

Cinch, 5 Newburgh St. (☎7287 4941). Tube: Oxford Circus. Specializes in classic Levi's cuts from the 40s to the 70s, with a mixture of both vintage and modern gear. Pick up an unworn pair of 1960s 505s for £850, but there are also affordable pairs from £50. The showcase of strategically hung clothing also includes limited edition Kubrick t-shirts (£50). Open M-Sa 11am-6:30pm. MC/V.

Mango, 106-112 Regent St. (☎7240 6099). Tube: Piccadilly Circus. Also at 225-235 Oxford St. (Tube: Oxford Circus) and 8-12 Neal St. (Tube: Covent Garden). A UK foothold for a Spanish fashion empire, Mango's keenly priced female line is cut with classy, sensible designs appropriate for all occasions. Most casual tops and bottoms go for under £40. Open M-W and F-Sa 10am-8pm, Th 10am-9pm, Su noon-6pm. AmEx/MC/V.

Ted Baker, 5-7 Foubert's Pl. (☎7437 5619). Tube: Oxford Circus. Also at 1-4 Langley Ct., Covent Garden (☎7497 8862; Tube: Covent Garden). Mid-priced modern classics for both sexes, from one of Britain's best-known and most influential names. Shirts £45-70, jeans £70-90. Open M-W and F-Sa 10:30am-7pm, Th 10:30am-7:30pm, Su 11am-5pm. MC/V.

Therapy, 318 Oxford St. (☎7529 4700), lower ground floor of the House of Fraser. All the high street women's fashion brands in one place, with flashing lights and in-store DJ. Clothes from Diesel and DKNY to budget high-street names like Morgan and Warehouse. Open M-Tu 10am-7pm, W-F 10am-8pm, Sa 9:30am-8pm, Su noon-6pm. AmEx/MC/V.

Zara, 118 Regent St. (☎7534 9500). Tube: Piccadilly Circus. Also at 242-248 Oxford St. (☎7318 2700; Tube: Oxford Circus); 333 Oxford St. (☎7518 1550; Tube: Oxford Circus); 52-56 Long Acre (☎ 7438 9900; Tube: Leicester Sq.); and 48-52 Kensington High St. (☎7368 4680; Tube: High St. Kensington). Yet another Stylish Spanish brand that has taken Europe by storm with its sleek, inexpensive clothing. Prices similar to its neighbor Mango, but with brighter and younger designs. Menswear is especially popular. Open M-W and F-Sa 10am-7pm, Th 10am-8pm, Su noon-6pm. AmEx/MC/V.

CLOTHES: SALE SHOPS

Browns Labels for Less, 50 South Molton St. (☎7514 0052). Tube: Bond St. Remainders from the Browns mini-empire that's taking over South Molton St. The range is small, especially for menswear, but high fashion is reduced to low prices: D&G jeans dropped to £50, and trouser suits for £99. Open M-W and F-Sa 10am-6:30pm, Th 10am-7pm. AmEx/MC/V.

Proibito Sale Shop, 42 South Molton St. (☎7941 3244) Tube: Bond St. Casual-, club-, and jeanswear from top designer names for up to 70% off—get a pair of Moschino jeans for only £39. Also stocks D&G, Valentino, and Versace for both men and women. Open daily 10am-6:30pm. AmEx/MC/V.

DEPARTMENT STORES

Hamley's, 188-189 Regent St. (☎7734 3161). Tube: Oxford Circus. 7 floors filled with every conceivable toy and game, plus dozens of strategically placed product demonstrations to tempt the young (and not-so-young) with flying airplanes and rubber bugs that stick to the walls. The Bear Factory lets you personalize a stuffed toy by choosing the animal and voice; it's then stuffed and sewn on the site (from £15). 4th fl. has enough model cars, planes, and trains for even the most die-hard enthusiast; the basement has Lego stations and video game consoles. Open M-F 10am-8pm, Sa 9:30am-8pm, Su noon-6pm. AmEx/MC/V.

Selfridges, 400 Oxford St. (☎0870 837 7377; www.selfridges.com). Tube: Bond St. The total department store—tourists may flock to Harrods, but Londoners head to Selfridges every time. Fashion departments are not cheap, but run the gamut from traditional tweeds to space-age clubwear. They have departments specializing in every product imaginable, from antiques to scented candles, and it's all carefully modern and stylish. With 18 cafes and restaurants, a hair salon, a bureau de change, and even a hotel, shopaholics need never leave. Massive January and July sales. Open M-F 10am-8pm, Sa 9:30am-8pm, Su noon-6pm. AmEx/MC/V.

Liberty, 210-220 Regent St. (☎7734 1234; www.liberty.co.uk), main entrance on Gt. Marlborough St. Tube: Oxford Circus. Liberty's timbered, Tudor chalet (built in 1922) sets the tone for this unique department store. The focus on top-quality design and handicrafts makes it more like a giant boutique than a full-blown department store. Liberty is famous for custom fabric prints—now 10,000 Liberty prints in the archive—sewn into everything from shirts to pillows, but they also have a wide array of other high-end contemporary designer lines. Open M-W 10am-6:30pm, Th 10am-8pm, F-Sa 10am-7pm, Su noon-6pm. AmEx/MC/V.

Marks & Spencer, (www.marks-and-spencer.co.uk). Hundreds of stores: flagship at 458 Oxford St. (☎7935 7954; Tube: Bond St. or Marble Arch.) Universally known as M&S or Marks & Sparks, this icon has fallen on hard times, as label-conscious consumers eschew its solid but unexciting clothing line. The gourmet supermarket is still going strong: millions rely on its perfectly packaged microwave meals, pre-washed salads, and fresh sandwiches. Open M-F 9am-9pm, Sa 8:30am-7:30pm, Su noon-6pm. AmEx/MC/V.

John Lewis, 300 Oxford St. (☎7629 7711). Tube: Oxford Circus. The employees collectively own John Lewis, with predictable results. They have a somewhat questionable fashion sense but are famed for service and guarantees, with a "Never Knowingly Undersold" policy that will refund you the difference if you find the same item cheaper elsewhere. Great for houseware and electronics, and the best haberdashery department in London. Open M-W, F-Su 9:30am-7pm, Th 9:30am-8pm. MC/V.

GIFTS & MISCELLANY

Butler and Wilson (B&W), 20 South Molton St. (☎7409 2955; www.butlerandwilson.com). Tube: Bond St. A magpie's paradise and a masterpiece of Oriental kitsch. Brilliant range of costume jewelry (most pieces £35-90), including ornate chokers, tiaras, pendants, and body chains. Also Indian-style beaded handbags, colorful print tops, and "vintage Chinese jackets" (£178). Open M-W and F-Sa 10am-6pm, Th 10am-7pm, Su noon-6pm. AmEx/MC/V.

MUSIC

HMV, 150 Oxford St. (☎ 7631 3423). Tube: Oxford Circus. 3 massive floors with a huge range of new vinyl on the ground floor, especially dance music. Level 1 games department has free consoles from every game maker. Open M, W, F-Sa 9am-8pm, Tu 9:30am-8pm, Th 9am-9pm, Su noon-6pm. AmEx/MC/V.

Virgin Megastore, 14-16 Oxford St. (☎ 7631 1234). Tube: Tottenham Court Rd. With 4 floors, fully deserves its name (the 2nd half, at least). Covers the entire musical spectrum, including books, magazines, and posters, plus lots of DVDs, videos, and computer games on the 1st fl. Internet cafe on ground fl. (£1 per hr. before noon, £1 for 30 min. after). Open M-Sa 9am-9pm, Su noon-6pm. AmEx/MC/V.

SPORTING GOODS

Niketown, 236 Oxford St. (☎ 7612 0800). Tube: Oxford Circus. Less a store than a mega marketing exercise and a temple to Nike culture, with a mind-boggling array of swoosh-emblazoned sportswear. Open M-W 10am-7pm, Th-Sa 10am-8pm, Su noon-6pm. AmEx/MC/V.

MAYFAIR & ST. JAMES'S

⚐ MAYFAIR & ST. JAMES'S QUICKFIND: Sights, p. 100; **Museums & Galleries,** p. 134; **Food & Drink,** p. 159; **Pubs,** p. 178; **Entertainment,** p. 213; **Accommodations,** p. 263.

Nowhere is Mayfair's aristocratic pedigree more evident than in the scores of high-priced boutiques, many bearing Royal Warrants to indicate their status as official palace suppliers. **Bond Street** is the location of choice for the biggest designer names. Its southern end (called Old Bond St.) is equally renowned for its jewelers and silversmiths. Less mainstream designers— like Vivienne Westwood, Alexander MacQueen, and Yohji Yamamoto—set up shop on **Conduit Street,** where Old Bond St. meets New Bond St. **Savile Row,** which runs south off Conduit St., and **Jermyn Street,** one block south of Piccadilly, are the home of old-fashioned elegance, with tailormade suits whose understated style belies their four-figure price-tags. Near Piccadilly, a number of Regency and Victorian **arcades** are lined with boutiques whose wares have changed little in the last hundred years.

BOOKS

Hatchard's, 187 Piccadilly (☎ 7439 9921; www.hatchards.co.uk). Tube: Green Park. Although London's oldest bookshop (est. 1797) has been bought by

from the road

BOOKWORMING

I had supposed that much of my spare time in London would be spent rummaging through used books, finding bargain gems and rare editions of cherished favourites. Then I walked into a Waterstone's. I emerged six weeks later, slightly more learned and substantially poorer. I had been looking for a bathroom, but I had found a substance abuse problem.

New books in London are appallingly expensive, but as a result, publishing houses in Britain churn out extraordinarily beautiful volumes. Even the trashiest pulpy novels look classy. I found myself actually judging (and buying) books by their covers.

I remember the moment that I finally admitted I had a problem—standing in front of the cash register, holding two separate editions of *Vanity Fair.* Not only do I already own a copy of this novel, purchased back home for 75 cents, but in order to lug even one 900-page tome on the plane, I was going to have to buy new luggage.

So I did. Strangely enough, the suitcase vendor hunkered down on the street outside the Waterstone's in Piccadilly Circus didn't seem that surprised to see me coming. Apparently, it's the best location in town.

—Nicole Cliffe

235

the hidden deal

The Other Music Store

Oxford St. is home to the grand trio of music megastores, but it also quietly houses the only London branch of a home-grown UK independent music chain. Founded by Russ Grainger, **Music Zone** is dedicated to bringing music to the people at an affordable price. Grainger first gained experience selling albums from a Longsight market stall in Manchester, and jumped at the chance to start a store, using the same "if you sell it cheaply, they will come" philosophy. His business formula has turned Music Zone into the UK's fastest growing music chain, with 40 locations already—but only one in London area. Music Zone lives up to its mascot "Underdog" by consistently undercutting the larger chains.

At a "measly" two levels, the Oxford St. Music Zone is like the sale section of HMV, only with a better selection and lower prices. All albums sell at £12 or less, with many going for £10. The store is dominated by the £5 section which is actually made up of recognizable artists and albums rather than the random junk offered elsewhere. There are no contingency sales that lure you into buying unwanted albums. £5 for an album—period.

See **Music Zone** *under Covent Garden.*

Waterstone's, it remains the most respected literary bookshop in London. Renowned for its selection of signed bestsellers, many by authors who frequent the store. The knowledgeable staff can guide you to specific books; the fiction and royalty sections are particularly strong—as you'd expect from Prince Charles's official bookseller. Open M and W-Sa 9:30am-6:30pm, Tu 10am-6:30pm, Su noon-6pm. AmEx/MC/V.

Sotheran's of Sackville Street, 2-5 Sackville St. (☎7439 6151; www.sotherans.co.uk). Tube: Piccadilly Circus. Founded in 1761 in York, Sotheran's moved to London in 1815, when Dickens began to frequent these silent stacks. The book selection of collectible and rare books hasn't changed much since that time. While the hushed atmosphere and locked shelves give an impression of exclusivity, there are affordable newer books (£5-30). Antique prints available downstairs. Open M-F 9:30am-6pm, Sa 10am-4pm. AmEx/MC/V.

Waterstone's, 203-206 Piccadilly (☎7851 2400; www.waterstones.co.uk). Tube: Piccadilly Circus. The 8 floors house Europe's largest bookshop, with specialty sections in just about everything. In addition to the prerequisite cafe, there's a swanky basement restaurant. The top floor is dedicated to events, including book signings by big-name authors (£2-4). Open M-Sa 10am-10pm, Su noon-6pm. AmEx/MC/V.

CLOTHES

Oscar Milo, 19 Avery Row (☎7495 5846). Tube: Bond St. Fantastic menswear boutique with clothes that may not be cheap (separates and shoes £50-110), but are a bargain for what you get: beautifully cut trousers and shirts and seriously smooth footwear. Open M-W and F-Sa 10:30am-6:30pm, Th 10am-7pm, Su noon-6pm. AmEx/MC/V.

Paul Smith Sale Shop, 23 Avery Row (☎7493 1287). Tube: Bond St. Small range of last-season and clearance items, plus some made-for-sale-shop stuff, from the acknowledged master of modern British menswear. At least 30% off original prices: grab a shirt or a pair of jeans for £45. Open M-W and F-Sa 10am-6pm, Th 10am-7pm. AmEx/MC/V.

DEPARTMENT STORES

Fortnum & Mason, 181 Piccadilly (☎7734 8040; www.fortnumandmason.com). Tube: Green Park or Piccadilly Circus. Founded in 1707, Fortnum's is famed for its sumptuous food hall, with liveried clerks, chandeliers, and fountains. This is the official grocer to the royal family, but don't come here to do the weekly shopping—prices aside, the focus is very much on gifts and luxury items, especially chocolates, preserves, and teas. Open M-Sa 10am-6:30pm, Su noon-6pm (food hall and patio restaurant only). AmEx/MC/V.

MUSIC

Music Zone, 104/106 Oxford St. (☎ 7631 5393; www.musiczone.co.uk). Tube: Tottenham Court Rd. Open M-W, F-Sa 10am-7:30pm, Th 10am-9pm, Su noon-6pm. See Hidden Deal, left.

Tower Records, 1 Piccadilly Circus (☎ 7439 2500; www.tower.co.uk). Tube: Piccadilly Circus. London's first music megastore has lower prices and better discount sections than most. Tower also has a particularly good alternative selection, as well as every other type of media imaginable. Open M-Sa 9am-11pm, Su noon-6pm. AmEx/MC/V.

SPORTING GOODS

Lillywhite's, 24-36 Lower Regent St. (☎ 0870 0333 9600). Tube: Piccadilly Circus. A 7-floor sporting goods mecca, selling everything from polo mallets to Polo™ shirts. With slow lifts and no escalators, only the sportiest will ever make it to the top floor. Open M-F 10am-9pm, Sa 9:30am-9pm, Su noon-6pm. AmEx/MC/V.

SOHO

🚩 SOHO QUICKFIND: Sights, p. 101; **Museums & Galleries,** p. 134; **Food & Drink,** p. 159; **Pubs,** p. 178; **Nightlife,** p. 189; **Entertainment,** p. 213; **Accommodations,** p. 263.

Despite Soho's eternal trendiness, its shopping options are decidedly mediocre—between all the bars and cafes, there's precious little space left for boutiques. The main exceptions to this rule in central Soho are the record stores of **D'Arblay** and **Berwick Street,** not surprising given the area's integral position in the British media industry. **Denmark Street,** on the eastern fringe of Soho, has been dubbed London's "Tin Pan Alley" due to its many musical instrument and equipment shops. **Charing Cross Road,** meanwhile, remains London's bookshop central.

ALCOHOL

🚩 Gerry's, 74 Old Compton St. (☎ 7734 2053). Tube: Piccadilly Circus or Leicester Sq. Gerry's stocks a staggering selection of beer and hard liquor, in all sizes from miniatures to magnums. With 50 different tequilas, 150 vodkas, a revolving bottle display, and an incendiary Bulgarian absinthe that's 89.9% alcohol by volume (half-liter £38), you can get drunk just looking. Open M-F 9am-6:30pm, Sa 9am-5:30pm. Cash or check only.

BOOKS

Blackwell's, 100 Charing Cross Rd. (☎ 7292 5100; www.blackwell.co.uk). Tube: Tottenham Court Rd. or Leicester Sq. Get blissfully lost in the London flagship of Oxford's top academic bookshop, with everything on one enormous floor. Go for the postmodern theory, stay for the huge selection of fiction. Open M-Sa 9:30am-8pm, Su noon-6pm. AmEx/MC/V.

Foyles, 113-119 Charing Cross Rd. (☎ 7437 5660; www.foyles.co.uk). Tube: Tottenham Court. Rd. or Leicester Sq. With over 30 miles of shelving, this self-proclaimed "world's greatest bookshop" is at least the largest in Europe. The 5 floors can make finding the book you want quite a challenge, but you can be sure it's there somewhere. There's also a strong sheet music department and a small art gallery (newly renovated in 2003). Relax with a new book in Ray's Jazz and a cafe, on the first floor. Open M-Sa 9:30am-8pm, Su noon-6pm. AmEx/MC/V.

Zwemmer, 72 and 80 Charing Cross Rd. (☎ 7240 4158; www.zwemmer.com). Tube: Leicester Sq. Two stores specializing in books on all types of art. 80 Charing Cross Rd. focuses on media (mainly film and photography) with a generous fashion spread downstairs; 72 Charing Cross Rd. covers graphic design and typography. Both open M-Sa 10am-6:30pm, Th 10am-7pm, Su noon-5pm. AmEx/MC/V.

MUSIC

Black Market, 25 D'Arblay St. (☎ 7437 0478; www.blackmarket.co.uk). Tube: Oxford Circus. Metal-clad walls and massive speakers characterize this all-vinyl dance emporium. House and garage upstairs, phenomenal drum & bass section below with more underground garage. Give the turntables on the counters a spin. Also sells club tickets and own-label merchandise, T-shirts and hats £15-40. Open M-W and Sa 11am-7pm, Th-F 11am-8pm.

Reckless Records, 26 and 30 Berwick St. (☎7437 3362 and 7437 4271; www.reckless.co.uk). Tube: Tottenham Court Rd. or Oxford Circus. It may not be under the same roof, but Reckless covers it all. #30 is the DJs' favorite exchange shop, with bucketfuls of used vinyl and CDs running the gamut from disco to soul. #26 is big in the hip-hop/rap department, including rarities. **Branches** at 92 Camden High St. and 79 Upper St. Open daily 10am-7pm. AmEx/MC/V.

Sister Ray, 94 Berwick St. (☎7287 8385; www.sisterray.com). Tube: Oxford Circus, Piccadilly Circus, or Tottenham Court Rd. Rare, usually crowded outlet for indie and alternative music on both vinyl and CD; lots of goth, metal, and punk. Also decent dance selection, with ambient, trance, techno, and beats. Open M-Sa 9:30am-8pm, Su 11am-5pm. MC/V.

Uptown Records, 3 D'Arblay St. (☎7434 3639; www.uptownrecords.co.uk). Tube: Oxford Circus. Ever wondered what top DJs do in the daytime? Descend a rickety spiral staircase in this small all-vinyl store and you'll find lots of them huddled in the basement, advising shoppers on the latest house, garage, and hip-hop happenings. Bags and DJ equipment £50-100. Open M-Sa 10:30am-7pm. MC/V.

MUSIC: EQUIPMENT

Turnkey, 114-116 Charing Cross Rd. (☎7419 9999; www.turnkey.co.uk). Tube: Tottenham Court Rd. A creative dance DJ's paradise, with a basement crammed with synthesizers, turntables, PA machines, and a mix station. Upstairs, play to your heart's content on dozens of dedicated analyzers, processors, and PCs. You'll also find a massive range of guitars and keyboards on the first floor. Open M-Sa 10am-6pm. AmEx/MC/V.

COVENT GARDEN

🚩 *COVENT GARDEN QUICKFIND: Sights, p. 103; Museums & Galleries, p. 134; Food & Drink, p. 161; Pubs, p. 178; Nightlife, p. 190; Entertainment, p. 213; Accommodations, p. 263. TRANSPORTATION: All listings are nearest Tube: Covent Garden unless otherwise noted.*

Once the hottest proving ground for new designers, Covent Garden is gradually being overtaken by large clothing chains: almost every store with an eye on the youth market has a second shop in the area, in addition to its main branch around Oxford and Regent Sts. Mid-priced chains fill the **Piazza**, though there are still enough quirky specialty shops left to make it worth a wander. Still a top destination for funky footwear and mid-priced clubwear, **Neal Street** led the regeneration of Covent Garden back in the 90s but is now uncannily indistinguishable from Carnaby St. (see p. 233). The fashion focus has shifted to nearby streets such as **Short's Gardens** to the east for chic menswear and **Earlham** and **Monmouth Street** to the west for a similarly stylish selection of women's clothing.

BOOKS

Stanfords, 12-14 Long Acre (☎7836 1321; www.stanfords.co.uk). The self-proclaimed best map store in the world, Stanfords covers every corner, nook, and cranny of the universe. With a staggering range of hiking maps, city maps, road maps, flight maps, star maps, wall maps, and globes, you'll never be lost again. Also a massive selection of travel books (including the full series of ▨ *Let's Go*). Open M-F 9am-7:30pm, Sa 10am-7pm, Su noon-6pm. Branch at 1 Regent St. MC/V.

CHEESES

▨ **Neal's Yard Dairy,** 17 Short's Gdns. (☎7240 5700). You'll smell it from a mile off—and that's a good thing. Enormous array of mostly British and Irish cheeses, all produced in small farms by traditional methods; massive wheels of stilton and cheddar line the shelves and countertops. Also sells preserves, organic milk, and yogurts. Drop in just to escape the summer heat—the chilly shop is essentially a walk-in refrigerator to keep the cheese fresh. Open M-Sa 9am-7pm. MC/V.

CLOTHES

Apple Tree, 51 and 62 Neal St. (☎7836 6088; www.appletree.uk.com). Locations across the street from each other. Cute, wildly colorful clothing that verges on the punk, with an emphasis on cartoon-character designs from Hello Kitty to Pucca. So gaudy and garish that it's 150% hip. Pick up a pair of Powerpuff Girls pajamas (£20), underwear (£6), a matching wallet and purse (£17), and save the world before bedtime. Open M-Sa 10am-7:30pm, Su 11am-6:30pm. MC/V.

Cyberdog, 9 Earlham St. (☎7836 7855; www.cyberdog.net). Tube: Leicester Sq. Main store in Camden Town (see p. 239). A must for the aspiring cyberpunk, or just for next Friday's rave. Power Rangers meet Marilyn Manson in these delightfully wacky, predominantly black-and-fluorescent clothes, which can only be defined as futuristic clubgear. Open M-Sa 11am-7pm, Su noon-6:30pm. AmEx/MC/V.

Diesel StyleLab, 12 Floral St. (☎7836 4970; www.dieselstylelab.com). This new label tries its darndest to recapture the original anarchic spirit that first propelled Diesel to fame—and mostly succeeds. Fantastically funky patterns and offbeat cuts for men's and women's fashions at regular Diesel prices—in a word, expensive (£40-100+). Has surpassed the original without going too trendy. Open M-Sa 11am-7pm, Su noon-6pm. AmEx/MC/V.

Diesel, 43 Earlham St. (☎ 4797 5543; www.diesel.com). Though it's now rather overpriced and mainstream, Diesel still remains popular among the young and hip. This three-level store (men's ground floor, women's first floor) carries a bunch of wild T-shirts, shoes, and other goodies with the brand name, now synonymous with must-have expensive jeans. Don't expect to find any article of clothing under £25. Open M-W and F-Sa 10am-7pm, Th 10am-8pm, Su noon-6pm. AmEx/MC/V.

Miss Sixty, 39 Neal St. (☎7836 3789; www.misssixty.com). The newest Italian streetwise clothing. Eye-catching and skin-hugging women's fashions in a sassy, sexy style. Long and skinny jeans around £60, shirts around £30. Similar genre and prices at their new menswear store, **Energie**, 47-49 Neal St. Open M-W and F-Sa 10am-6:30pm, Th 10am-7:30pm, Su noon-6pm. AmEx/MC/V.

Savage London, Unit 14, Covent Garden Market Pl. (☎7240 4582; www.savagelondon.com). Small corner store that focuses on funny, funky printed t-shirts (all £20). Logos range from neighborhood pride ("Brixton") to the irreverent ("Jesus loves hip-hop"). Also carries a small selection of purses and urbanwear, baggy sweatshirts, and jackets. Open M-Sa 10am-7pm, Su 11am-5pm. Branch at 14a Newburgh St. AmEx/MC/V.

COSMETICS & TOILETRIES

Neal's Yard Remedies, 15 Neal's Yard (☎7627 1949; www.nealsyardremedies.com). A fragrant alternative medicine mecca, therapy rooms included. Jars behind the counter hold every conceivable herb, from basil and mint to bladder wrack and pilewort, while cobalt-blue bottles of essential oils, soaps, and lotions fill the shelves of this glorified Body Shop. Gift boxes from £10. Herb and healthcare literature also available. Open M-Sa 10am-7pm, Su 11am-6pm. AmEx/MC/V.

Penhaligon's, 41 Wellington St. (☎7836 2150; www.penhaligons.co.uk). Branches on Bond St. and Piccadilly Circus. Founded by a former palace barber, this aristocratic shop still provides the royals with aftershave. Churchill never left home without a dab of the English classic *Blenheim Bouquet*—get a jar of shaving cream for £24. Also sells female fragrances, scented candles, and exquisite, incredibly expensive toilette accessories. Open M-W and F-Sa 10am-6pm, Th 10am-7pm, Su noon-6pm. AmEx/MC/V.

MARKETS

Jubilee Market Hall, south side of Covent Garden Piazza. Large covered market, purportedly antique on M and arts and crafts Tu, Th, F, and Su; in reality a rather commonplace mix of clothes, souvenirs, and other goods from aspiring designers. Open daily 10am-7pm.

SHOES

Office, 57 Neal St. (☎7379 1896). The largest outlet of London's foremost fashion footwear retailer. Office's broad range of high heels, low heels, and no heels is colorful, stylish, *and* wearable (well, most of it, at least). Most women's shoes run £20-145, men's £60-130. The **239**

Dockland Shoes

Harrods

Camden Market

sale shop at 61 St. Martin's Ln. (☎ 7497 0390; Tube: Leicester Sq.) has good deals but a more limited, conventional selection. Neal St. store open M-W and F-Sa 10am-7:30pm, Th 10am-8pm, Su noon-6pm. Sale shop open M-Sa 10am-7pm, Su noon-6pm. MC/V.

Swear, 61 Neal St. (☎ 7240 7673; www.swear-net.net). Once the headquarters of platforms, this footwear boutique has gone flat and somewhat monotonous, but still draws a trendy clientele. Open M-F 11am-7pm, Sa 10:30am-7pm, Su 2-6pm. AmEx/MC/V.

NORTH LONDON

🔁 **NORTH LONDON QUICKFIND: Sights,** p. 107; **Museums & Galleries,** p. 137; **Food & Drink,** p. 163; **Pubs,** p. 180; **Nightlife,** p. 192; **Entertainment,** p. 216; **Accommodations,** p. 265.

North London has some of the best cheap, non-chain shopping. **Camden Town**—renowned for its markets that radiate out from Camden High St.—is like a market itself, with stores spilling out onto the street. Most of the stores are alternative, concentrating on cheap clothes and accessories for a young crowd. Even if it's not your style, you're bound to find something you want. Serious music shoppers will also revel here, particularly those interested in records. **Islington** also has a few markets that are smaller but offer more choice goods. These markets spread out from the lower part of Upper St., around the Angel Tube station. Moving north on Upper St. brings you to scads of boutiques catering to yuppies.

CAMDEN TOWN

Camden Markets. Make a sharp right out of the Tube station to reach Camden High St. where most of the markets start. Tube: Camden Town.

Cyberdog, arch 14, Stables Market (☎ 7482 2842). Tube: Camden Town. Ever wonder what the world would be like if it happened in the mind of a clubber? These people made that world. Endless caverns with flashing lights, pumping music, and glowing clubbing clothes in museum-like displays. The reason to go is not so much to buy but to wander and wonder. They also have an enormous dance floor in the silver-plated entrance lobby, where guest DJs spin on Sa. Open M-F 10:30am-6pm, Sa-Su 10am-7:30pm. AmEx/MC/V.

Stables Market, farthest from the station and the best of the bunch. A free map of the market is available at the main entrance. Towards the back, at the horse hospital, you'll find some of the few remaining independent artists. The railway arches hold outrageous club- and fetish-wear, plus a good selection of vintage clothes. Open F-Sa, with a few shops open daily.

Camden Canal Market, down the tunnel opposite Camden Lock. Little more than cheap club gear and tourist trinkets. Open F-Su.

Camden Lock Market, extends from the railway bridge to the canal. The original market and still the place to catch a bite along Regent's Canal. The non-tourist stores focus on carpets, furniture, and household goods. Open daily 10am-6pm.

The Camden Market, the nearest to Camden Town Tube stop, and correspondingly the most crowded and least innovative. Oriented toward teenagers, with jeans, sweaters, and designer fakes at average prices. Open daily 9:30am-5:30pm, though not everything opens during the week.

Inverness Street Market, off Camden High St. opposite the Tube. A daily fruit'n'veg market unconnected to the madness surrounding it, though some clothing and trinket stalls have spilled over. Open M-Sa 8am-5pm.

Mega City Comics, 18 Inverness St. (☎7485 9320; www.megacitycomics.co.uk). Tube: Camden Town. Comics in mint condition, from collector's items to the latest foreign imports, starting at 50p. Mostly American stuff, but still covers a decent range from Tintin to erotic Manga; also animated videos and DVDs and t-shirts with comic book characters. Open M-W and Sa-Su 10am-6pm, Th-F 10am-7pm. MC/V (£10 minimum).

Out on the Floor, 10 Inverness St. (☎7267 5989). Tube: Camden Town. Used records and CDs, specializing in 60-70s rock, soul, reggae, and funk on vinyl, as well as vintage posters from the same eras. Open daily 10am-6pm. MC/V.

Vinyl Addiction, 6 Inverness St. (☎7482 1230). Tube: Camden Town. Underneath Bar Vinyl (see p. 193); a shop for professional DJs and those who wish to be. Many records have a staff description of the beats on the jacket, and there are numerous tables with mixers to take a test spin. Open daily 11am-7:30pm.

ISLINGTON

Camden Passage Market, Islington High St. Tube: Angel. Turn right from the Tube; it's the alleyway that starts behind "The Mall" antiques gallery on Upper St. Not to be confused with Camden Market (see above). *The* place for antiques; smaller items may dip into the realm of the affordable, especially old prints and drawings. Stalls are only open W and Sa 8:30am-6pm; most stores are open daily, and shops vastly outnumber the stalls.

Annie's, 12 Camden Passage (☎7359 0796). *Vogue* and *Elle* regularly use these vintage frocks in their photo shoots. 1920s dresses are pricey (£350-600), but the less flashy 1930s pieces are more affordable (£60-150). Bags start at £30. Open M-Tu and Th-F 11am-6pm, W and Sa 8:30am-6pm. AmEx/MC/V.

Chapel Market, Chapel Market. Tube: Angel. A living reminder of Islington's pre-yuppie past, this down-to-earth street market is all about practical needs. Stalls hawk fruit'n'veg, household goods, and clothes. No-frills budget eateries line the road behind the market stalls. Open M-Sa 9am to mid-afternoon.

SOUTH LONDON

◪ *SOUTH LONDON QUICKFIND: Sights, p. 111; Museums & Galleries, p. 138; Food & Drink, p. 166; Nightlife, p. 194; Entertainment, p. 219.*

If you're looking for the fruits of West Indian cultures or cheap club-wear, **Brixton** is the place to be. Shops along Brixton Rd. and Coldharbour Ln. blast hip-hop and reggae and peddle skanky tops, tight pants, and gaudy accessories perfect for a night out on the town.

CLOTHES

Joy, 432 Coldharbour Ln. (☎7787 9616) Tube: Brixton. Funky, seductive, bold, and decadent—or so their cards proclaim. In reality, this happy-go-lucky chain caters specifically to young clubbers, offering them a brightly colored outfits and retro-futuristic accessories. Playboy-bunny playing cards (£3) and cartoon-logo handbags (£12) are among the eclectic goods, which include lots of vinyl and rubber. Open M-Sa 10am-7:30pm, Su 1-7pm. MC/V. **241**

MARKETS

Brixton Market, along Electric Ave., Pope's Rd., and Brixton Station Rd., and inside markets in Granville Arcade and Market Row. Tube: Brixton. To experience Brixton fully in the daytime, stroll through the crowded streets of the market, where stalls hawk everything from cheap household items to bootlegged Blaxploitation films. Negotiate with the vendors for some unbelievable deals on meat and fruit. Open daily 8am-6pm.

MUSIC

Blacker Dread Muzik Store/CD Link, 404/406 Coldharbour Ln. (☎7274 5095; www.blacker-dreadmuzikstores.co.uk). Tube: Brixton. Plastered wall-to-wall with record and CD covers, these two tiny shops literally vibrate with Carribbean beats and boast a remarkable selection of R&B, hip-hop, UK garage, gospel, and soul. Specializes in pre-relases: singles around £3, albums around £15. Mail-order service also available. Open M-W 9:30am-9pm, Th-Sa 9:30am-10pm, Su noon-6pm.

EAST LONDON

🔳 *EAST LONDON QUICKFIND: Sights, p. 112; Museums & Galleries, p. 139; Food & Drink, p. 167; Pubs, p. 181; Nightlife, p. 196; Entertainment, p. 219.*

In East London, the **street-market** tradition is alive and well, helped along by large immigrant communities; the South Asian-dominated Brick Ln. and Petticoat Ln. are justly famous. In **Hoxton, Shoreditch,** and especially the stretch of **Brick Ln.** just north of the Truman Brewery, independent young designers have opened up boutiques frequented by local artists and arty pretenders. Corporate **Docklands** has gone in the opposite direction, with the huge Cabot Place and Canada Place shopping malls offering the full range of British and international clothing chains and mainstream designer stores.

ALCOHOL

🔳 **The Beer Shop,** 14 Pitfield St. (☎7739 3701). Tube: Old St. Over 600 beers from around the world line the walls of this store, whose hoppy smell comes from the all-organic brewery next-door ("Eco Warrior" ale £2.25 per 0.5L). The friendly staff is happy to make recommendations and guide you through the overwhelming selection. Home-brewing equipment, bottles and glasses, and organic wines and ciders. Open T-F 11am-7pm, Sa 10am-4pm. MC/V.

CLOTHES & ACCESSORIES

Hoxton Boutique, 2 Hoxton St. (☎7684 2083; www.hoxtonboutique.co.uk). Tube: Old St. If the thought of hitting the Shoho club scene in your current gear terrifies you, let this pricey but ultra-hip boutique funkify you. Most items £50-100. Open M-F 10am-6pm, Sa 11am-5pm, Su noon-5pm. MC/V.

The Laden Showroom, 103 Brick Ln. (☎7247 2431; www.laden.co.uk). Tube: Aldgate East or Liverpool St. "Where fashion is a lifestyle," this unassuming store is a fitting favorite of celebs like Posh Spice. Up-to-the-minute casual and clubwear by up-and-coming London designers. Staff is dedicated and highly trend-conscious. Both new and recently used items, most under £50, all dripping with irony. Open M-Sa noon-6pm, Su 10:30am-6pm. AmEx/MC/V.

Unique Leatherwear, 151 Brick Ln. (☎7729 9859). Tube: Aldgate East or Shoreditch. The Petticoat Ln. market may be lined with cheap leather jacket vendors, but this is the real deal. You can choose from the existing coats, or have one tailor-made for you. Short leather jackets start at just £35—no, that's not a misprint. Open M-F 11am-6pm, some Sa, Su 10am-2pm. MC/V.

MARKETS

Spitalfields Market. Tube: Shoreditch or Liverpool St. Formerly one of London's main wholesale vegetable markets, now a new-agey crafts market with a range of food stalls, plus an organic food market twice a week. On Su, the foodstuffs share room with burgeoning independent clothing designer stalls. Crafts market M-F 11am-3:30pm, Su 10am-5pm. Organic market F and Su 10am-5pm.

Brick Lane Market. Tube: Shoreditch or Aldgate East. At the heart of Whitechapel's sizeable Bangladeshi community, Brick Ln. hosts a large weekly market with a South Asian motif (food, rugs, spices, bolts of fabric, strains of sitar) in addition to its perennial supply of curry houses, colorful textile shops, and grocers. Open Su 8am-2pm.

Greenwich Markets. Numerous weekend markets converge on Greenwich, which on Su is blanketed with stalls and shoppers seeking the ultimate bargain.

> **Antiques Market,** Greenwich High Rd. Rail: Greenwich. Mostly 20th-century stuff; busiest in the summer. Open Sa-Su 9am-5pm.

> **Greenwich Market,** in the block surrounded by King William Walk, Greenwich Church St., College Approach, and Romney Rd. DLR: Cutty Sark. Antiques and collectibles Th, arts & crafts F-Su. Open Th-Su 10am-6pm.

> **Village Market,** Stockwell St. DLR: Cutty Sark. Food court, clothes, bric-a-brac. Indoor stalls F-Sa 10am-5pm, Su 10am-6pm; outdoor market Sa 7am-6pm, Su 7am-5pm.

Petticoat Lane Market. Tube: Liverpool St., Aldgate, or Aldgate East. Streets of stalls, mostly cheap clothing and household appliances, with lots of leather jackets around Aldgate East. Hectic shopping scene begins at about 9:30am. Open Su 9am-2pm; starts shutting down around noon.

WEST LONDON

🚩 *WEST LONDON QUICKFIND: Sights,* p. 115; *Food & Drink,* p. 168; *Entertainment,* p. 220; *Accommodations,* p. 266.

BOOKS

Fosters Bookshop, 183 Chiswick High Rd. (☎8995 2768). Tube: Turnham Green. One of the most delightful used book shops in London, this small family-run business is a treasure trove for serious (and not so serious) readers of all ages. From vintage children's literature to antique angler's manuals. Open Th-Sa 10:30am-5pm. MC/V.

Accommodations

Sorry folks, but this isn't going to be pretty. Just as real estate prices make Londoners clutch their heads and scream, London's hotels and hostels are incredibly expensive. The price ranges that are represented by the five different **Price Diversity Icons** ❶, ❷, ❸, ❹, and ❺ are listed below.

ICON	❶	❷	❸	❹	❺
PRICE	under £20	£21-34	£35-49	£50-74	£75+

ACCOMMODATIONS TIPS

PLAN AHEAD. No matter where you plan to stay, it is essential to plan ahead, especially in summer. In a pinch, tourist offices can help you find a room (see **Service Directory**, p. 329), while private hostels will usually grant you a patch of floorspace if all else fails. When reserving in advance, it's worth the price of a phone call or fax to confirm a booking. Almost all accommodations require a deposit to secure the reservation; the proprietor should specify the amount (usually one night's stay) and advise on the best way to make payment (usually by credit card). Be sure to check the cancellation policy before handing over the deposit; most require 24hr. notice, but some are entirely non-refundable.

DISCOUNTS. Most B&Bs offer discounted rates for **long-term** stays (over a week), though not all advertise the fact—be sure to ask, and insist, if necessary—while most private hostels offer super-cheap weekly rates for guests staying over a month. Another

good source of discounts is traveling in the **low season,** October through March, excepting Christmas. September, April, and May are slow enough that you may be able to wrangle a few pounds' discount too with a little gentle persuasion. If you're brave enough to arrive in London without prearranged accommodation and lucky enough to find a hotel with a vacancy in the afternoon or early evening, you're in a strong bargaining position—if you don't take the room, it will likely go empty.

PAYMENT. It's perfectly normal (though not defensible) for accommodations in London to demand full payment on arrival—that way, you can't just up and leave if you don't like the room or find somewhere nicer. For this reason, always insist on being shown the room before handing over any money; that way, you'll only lose your one-night deposit should the room turn out to be unacceptable.

The vast majority of accommodations accept payment by either cash, credit card, or sterling travelers checks—note that almost nowhere will accept travelers checks made out in foreign currency, and those that do use horrendous exchange rates to make the conversion. A number of lower-end accommodations don't take credit cards, so be sure to find out before checking in; those that do often levy a 3-5% surcharge for those paying by plastic. Conversely, you may be able to negotiate a small reduction for cash payments (but don't count on it).

TYPES OF ACCOMMODATION

HOSTELS

Hostels offer travelers a bed in a shared dormitory and are a great way of meeting fellow travelers; if you're traveling alone, a hostel is almost certainly your cheapest option. Shared dorms can hold anything from 3 to 20 beds, typically on a sliding

price scale with smaller rooms being more expensive. Hostels in London are either run by the **Youth Hostel Association** (YHA), an affiliate of Hostelling International (HI), or are independent **private hostels;** the difference is explained below.

YHA/HI HOSTELS

YHA hostels (www.yha.org.uk) are invariably more expensive than private ones, but are generally better kept, with well-maintained baths, more facilities, and knowledgeable staff; reductions for under-18s make them popular with families. On the other hand, they tend to be more institutional-feeling, and draw a less bohemian crowd. While bedding is included in the price at all London hostels, towels are not; some hostels offers towels for sale, otherwise you must supply your own. All hostel rooms are equipped with large lockers that require your own padlock (available for purchase at hostels; £3). Most YHA hostels operate cheap cafeterias for dinner, and can supply a picnic lunch; all have laundry facilities and well-equipped kitchens.

MEMBERSHIP. To take full advantage of YHA hostels, you need to be a member of the YHA or another HI-affiliated hostelling association, such as the American Youth Hostels (AYH). Non-members can stay in YHA hostels, but must purchase a "Welcome Stamp" (£2 per night stayed until payment equals £13), after which you become a full member for one year; you can also purchase membership straight away. In addition to being able to stay at YHA hostels, HI members are eligible for a range of discounts on sights and activities in London. *(Adults, 1-parent families, and groups £12.50; under-18 £6.25; family £25.)*

RESERVATIONS. YHA hostels in London are invariably oversubscribed; in the summer, beds fill up months in advance, and sometimes hostels have not been able to accommodate every written request for reservations, let alone walk-ins. However, hostels occasionally hold a few beds free until a few days before, and

Welcome to

Abbey House

Hospitality, Quality & Genuine Value in the Heart of London.

If you are planning a trip to England and looking for a B&B in London Abbey House is the place to stay. Situated in a quiet garden square adjacent to Kensington Palace, this elegant Victorian house retains many of its original features including the marble entrance hall and wrought iron staircase. Once the home of a Bishop and a member of Parliament it now provides well maintained quality accommodation for the budget traveller who will be well looked after by its owners the Nayachs.

Write or call for a free colour brochure.

Recommended by more travel guides than any other B&B.

ABBEY HOUSE HOTEL
11 Vicarage Gate, Kensington, London W8 4AG
Reservations: 020-7727 2594
Fax: 020-7727 1873

www.AbbeyHouseKensington.com

in a large hostel there's a good chance that someone will fail to show up or check-out early—it's always worth asking. If you want to risk it without reservations, turn up as early as possible and expect to queue.

PRIVATE HOSTELS

Private hostels vary widely in price and quality, but as a rule are cheaper and have a more "fun" feel than their YHA equivalents—with a few exceptions, they also have fewer facilities and a less family-friendly atmosphere (many have a minimum age of 16 or 18). On the other hand, a lack of formal rules and the general laissez-faire attitude means that those who value privacy, quiet, and tidiness should think again about staying at a private hostel—though a few are as well-run as any YHA equivalent. As with YHA hostels, prices generally include sheets but not towels, and most have kitchens in various states of repair.

RESIDENCE HALLS

Over summer vacation, many of London's universities and college turn their student residences into vast budget hotels, offering B&B-style accommodation at hostel prices. Most residence halls have student-priced bars, TV lounges, and games rooms with pool, ping-pong, and foosball tables. The downside is that rooms tend to be fairly ascetic—standard student digs—and shared baths feel rather institutional; additionally, the bulk of accommodation is single rooms, with the occasional twin and triple, so they're not ideal for couples or large groups. All halls have shared "pantries" (small kitchens), but they're mostly designed for students to hear tins of baked beans in; kitchenware, crockery, and cutlery are rarely supplied.

Given their low prices, great locations, and good facilities, it's not surprising that residence halls fill extremely rapidly; it's often necessary to book months in advance. Moreover, many halls don't take walk-ins, so some form of advance booking is required, even if just the night before. Many of London's colleges run a **central accommodations office:**

University College London Residential Services, 24-36 Bidborough St., (☎7554 7780; fax 7554 7781). Tube: King's Cross St. Pancras. Runs 8 halls, mostly around Bloomsbury. Rooms available Apr. and mid-June to mid-Sept. Office open M-F 9am-5pm.

King's Campus Vacation Bureau, 127 Stamford St. (☎7928 3777; www.kcl.ac.uk). Tube: Waterloo. Accommodations at the halls of King's College London, mostly located on the South Bank. Office open M-F 9am-5pm.

B&BS & HOTELS

Bed and Breakfasts—or B&Bs—are smallish hotels, usually in a converted townhouses, run by a family or a proprietor. The term "B&B" encompasses accommodations of wildly varying quality and personality, often with little relation to price. Some are nothing more than budget hotels that serve breakfast, with small, dreary, and bare rooms. Others (often on the same street as their nightmarish doubles) are unexpected oases of comfort, beautifully decorated and with excellent facilities. A **basic room** means that you share the use of a shower and toilet in the hall. A room **with bath** contains a private shower or bath and a toilet, and tends to cost £10-20 more. Be aware, however, that in-room showers are often awkward prefab units jammed into a corner. **Family room** in B&B lingo generally means a quad or quint with at least one double bed and some single beds. Most B&Bs serve **English breakfasts**—eggs, bacon, toast, fried bread, baked beans, tomato (baked or stewed), and tea or coffee (see p. 149). **Continental breakfast** means some form of bread, cereal, and a hot drink.

Apart from B&Bs, a few **hotels** descend into the realms of the affordable—or at least, overlap in price with London's ridiculously expensive B&Bs. In general, these fall into two categories. The first is once-grand hotels that never modernized. On the one hand, you've got lifts, bars, restaurants, and sometimes even bellhops; on the other, it can be like a trip back in time to the 1970s, with aging decor, dodgy plumbing, and a radio pre-set to stations that haven't broadcast for 20 years. The second category are the increasingly numerous and ultra-modern **chain hotels**, which offer large well-equipped rooms. The downside to these, aside from a lack of character, is that they're only economic for travelers in groups of two or more, since they usually charge a flat rate per room; additionally, breakfast is rarely included in the prices. Advance booking is strongly recommended.

ACCOMMODATIONS BY PRICE

UNDER £20 (PRICE ICON ❶)	
⬛ Ashlee House	Bloomsbury
⬛ The Generator	Bloomsbury
Hyde Park Hostel	Bayswater
International Student House	Marylebone
Leinster Inn	Bayswater
Palace Hotel	Bayswater
Pickwick Hall International Backpackers	
	Bloomsbury
Quest Hotel	Bayswater
St. Christopher's Inn	North London
YHA Earl's Court	Earl's Court
YHA Holland House	Kensington
YHA Oxford St.	The West End

£20-34 (PRICE ICON ❷)	
Carr-Saunders Hall	Bloomsbury
City University Finsbury Residence	
	Bloomsbury
Commonwealth Hall	Bloomsbury
⬛ High Holborn Residence	The West End
Indian YMCA	Bloomsbury
LSE Bankside House	The South Bank
⬛ Melbourne House	Westminster
Passfield Hall	Bloomsbury
Rosebery Hall	Clerkenwell
Windsor Guest House	West London
⬛ YHA Hampstead Heath	North London
YHA St. Pancras International	Bloomsbury

£35-49 (PRICE ICON ❸)	
Abbey House Hotel	Kensington
Admiral Hotel	Bayswater
⬛ Alexander Hotel	Westminster
Balmoral House Hotel	Bayswater
Cardiff Hotel	Bayswater
Crescent Hotel	Bloomsbury

Dalmacia Hotel	West London
Edward Lear Hotel	Marylebone
Garden Court Hotel	Bayswater
Georgian House Hotel	Westminster
Hotel Orlando	West London
Hyde Park Court Hotel	Bayswater
Jurys Inn	North London
⬛ Kandara Guesthouse	North London
⬛ The Langland Hotel	Bloomsbury
Luna Simone Hotel	Westminster
Morgan House	Belgravia
Mowbray Court Hotel	Earl's Court
⬛ Oxford Hotel	Earl's Court
Philbeach Hotel	Earl's Court
⬛ Star Hotel	West London
Vicarage Private Hotel	Kensington
⬛ Westminster House Hotel	Belgravia

£50-74 (PRICE ICON ❹)	
Accommodation Outlet	The West End
George Hotel	Bloomsbury
Hadleigh Hotel	Marylebone
Hamstead Village Guest House	North London
James and Cartref House	Belgravia
⬛ Jenkins Hotel	Bloomsbury
Kensington Gardens Hotel	Bayswater
Mentone Hotel	Bloomsbury
Royal National Hotel	Bloomsbury
Seven Dials Hotel	The West End
⬛ Swiss House Hotel	Kensington
Thanet Hotel	Bloomsbury
Travel Inn County Hall	South Bank
Vancouver Studios	Bayswater

£75+ (PRICE ICON ❺)	
Amsterdam Hotel	Earl's Court
⬛ Five Sumner Place Hotel	Kensington

ACCOMMODATIONS BY NEIGHBORHOOD
BAYSWATER

SEE MAP, p. 361

🔃 *BAYSWATER QUICKFIND: Food & Drink, p. 148; Pubs, p. 173; Entertainment, p. 207; Shopping, p. 226.*

Bayswater is your best bet for a cheap, convenient bed. Almost every side street is lined with converted Victorian houses offering rooms. The greatest variety of rooms, and all the cheaper hostels, are on roads around **Queensway,** such as **Inverness Terrace, Kensington Square Gardens,** and **Leinster Square.** On the other side of Bayswater, the area around **Paddington** is convenient for travelers arriving on the Heathrow Express: **Sussex Gardens** is lined with affordable hotels.

A word of warning: almost all the establishments are in converted 5- or 6-story townhouses with **very steep staircases.** Those who may have physical difficulty making the climb should ask for a room on a lower floor.

HOSTELS

Hyde Park Hostel, 2-6 Inverness Terr. (☎7229 5101; www.astorhostels.com). Tube: Queensway or Bayswater. Despite flimsy mattresses and cramped quarters (though the big dorms are relatively spacious), this colorful, backpacker-friendly hostel is tons of fun. The recently renovated, jungle-themed basement bar and dance space hosts DJs and theme parties (open W-Sa 8pm-3am). Continental breakfast and linen included. Kitchen, laundry, TV lounge, secure luggage room. Ages 16-35 only. Reserve 2 weeks ahead for summer; 24hr. cancellation policy. Internet access. Online booking with 10% non-refundable deposit. 10- to 12-bed dorms £11-13.50; 8-beds £14.50-15.50; 6-beds £15.50-16.50; 4-beds £16.50-17.50; twins £42-45. 10% ISIC discount. MC/V. ❶

Quest Hostel, 45 Queensborough Terr. (☎7229 7782; www.astorhostels.com). Tube: Bayswater or Queensway. Another in the Astor chain, but with more comfortable, snazzy bunkbeds and more space than the Hyde Park Hostel (see above). Dorms are mostly mixed-sex, and many have baths; those that don't could be 2 floors from a shower. Laundry, kitchen available. Continental breakfast, linen, and lockers included. 4- to 8-bed dorms £14-16; twins £40. MC/V. ❶

Leinster Inn, 7-12 Leinster Sq. (☎7229 9641; www.astorhostels.com). Tube: Bayswater. A basic hostel with nothing exciting but everything you need. Small bar that stays open M-F until 4am, Sa-Su until 5am. TV/pool room. Internet access. Linen and Continental breakfast included. Safe-deposit boxes, kitchen, luggage room, laundry. £10 key deposit. 4- to 8-bed dorms £14, with shower £18; single £25/29; twins £35/40; triples £57/£60. MC/V. ❶

Palace Hotel, 48-49 Princes Sq. (☎ 7229 1729). Tube: Bayswater. Catering to a quieter crowd, Palace offers decent-sized rooms equipped with wardrobe, sink, fridge, and table. No private baths. Linen included. Laundry, internet access, large kitchen, TV room, garden. Book at least one week ahead in summer. 8-bed dorms £8; 4-to 6-bed dorms £10; doubles £14; single (only one) £20. Cash only. ❶

HOTELS AND BED & BREAKFASTS

Admiral Hotel, 143 Sussex Gdns. (☎7723 7309; www.admiral-hotel.com). Tube: Paddington. Beautifully kept family-run B&B, with bath, TV, and kettle, decorated in summer colors. Some baths are covered in linoleum—ask for one with tiled baths. Non-smoking. English breakfast included. Call 10-14 days ahead in summer; 4-day cancellation policy. Singles £45; doubles £65; triples £90; quads £100; quints £120. MC/V. ❸

Balmoral House Hotel, 156-157 Sussex Gdns. (☎7723 4925; www.balmoralhousehotel.co.uk). Tube: Paddington. Classy, well-kept rooms with spacious interior. All rooms have private baths, satellite TV, kettle, and hair dryer. English breakfast included. Singles £40; doubles £65; triples £80; family suites for 4 £100, for 5 £120. MC/V (5% surcharge). ❸

Cardiff Hotel, 5-9 Norfolk Sq. (☎ 7723 9068; www.cardiff-hotel.com). Tube: Paddington. All rooms have TV, kettle, and phone. Professionally run with enthusiastic staff and elegant, reasonably sized rooms. Singles can run on the small side. English breakfast included. 48hr. cancellation policy. Singles with shower £49, with bath £55-69; doubles with bath £79; triples with bath £90; quads with bath £110. MC/V. ❸

Garden Court Hotel, 30-31 Kensington Gdns. Sq. (☎ 7229 2553; www.gardencourthotel.co.uk). Tube: Bayswater. Rooms vary widely in size (the quad is an especially tight fit), but all are tastefully decorated and equipped with sink, TV, hair dryer, and phone. Guests have access to the patio garden. English breakfast included. Strict 14-day cancellation policy. Singles £39, with bath £58; doubles £58/£88; triples £72/£99; family quad (2 double beds) £82/£120. MC/V. ❸

Vancouver Studios, 30 Prince's Sq. (☎ 7243 1270; www.vienna-group.co.uk/vancouver). Tube: Bayswater. Boasting the "convenience of a hotel, with the privacy of an apartment," Vancouver Studios offers fully-serviced studios. The light, airy rooms are large, with kitchenette, TV, hair dryer, phone, and daily maid service; all have private bath and access to laundry facilities and the garden. Studio for 1 £75; for 2 £97 (small), £112 (large); for 3 £137. Single studio F-Su £60. AmEx/MC/V. ❹

Kensington Gardens Hotel, 9 Kensington Gdns. Sq. (☎ 7221 7790; www.kensingtongardenshotel.co.uk). Tube: Bayswater. Handsomely decorated, well-equipped rooms with kettle, TV, phone, mini bar, fan and hair dryer on demand, and even a bowl of snacks. Rooms are similarly sized, so singles feel more spacious. All rooms have private bath; the 4 shower-only singles share 3 hall toilets. Continental breakfast included; English breakfast £5.50. 48hr. cancellation policy. Singles £55-58; doubles £75-79; triples £95. £5 discount after 7 days. AmEx/MC/V. ❹

Hyde Park Court Hotel, 48 Norfolk Sq. (☎ 7723 3050; www.hydeparkcourthotel.com). Tube: Paddington. Though decor is a bit bland, rooms are reasonably sized with baths, TV, and phone. The ingenious, duplex-style family rooms are especially spacious and fun. Continental breakfast included, but the lack of a self-contained dining room means eating on an elevated platform across from the reception desk. Singles £36-50; doubles £52-70; triples £60-80; family rooms £71-95. AmEx/MC/V. ❸

THE CARDIFF HOTEL

IDEAL CENTRAL LOCATION

Run by the Davies family for 40 years, the Cardiff Hotel overlooks a quiet tree-lined square. Enjoy our friendly service and become one of our regular visitors. 60 + rooms.

Singles: £45 - £55   Doubles: £65 - £79

DELICIOUS ENGLISH BREAKFAST INCLUDED

150 metres to Heathrow Express & Paddington Station

5, 7, 9 Norfolk Square London W2 1RU
Tel: (020) 7723 9068 / 7723 3513   Fax: (020) 7402 2342
e-mail: stay@cardiff-hotel.com
www.cardiff-hotel.com
Int'l Tel: + 44 20 7723 9068 Int'l Fax: + 44 20 7402 2342

BLOOMSBURY

SEE MAP, p. 362

BLOOMSBURY QUICKFIND: Sights, p. 74; **Museums & Galleries,** p. 125; **Food & Drink,** p. 148; **Pubs,** p. 173; **Entertainment,** p. 207; **Shopping,** p. 226.

Bloomsbury's quiet squares and Georgian terraces are now home to an endless assortment of accommodations of every size, shape, and variety—from dodgy places near King's Cross charging by the hour to London's self-appointed "coolest" hotel (the pricey myhotel, on Bedford Sq.). If you opt for a hostel or B&B in the King's Cross area, be warned that the local nightlife consists mainly of drug-dealing and prostitution. The southern part of Bloomsbury, by contrast, is close to the more socially acceptable nightlife of the West End.

HOSTELS

The Generator, Compton Pl., off 37 Tavistock Pl. (☎7388 7655; www.the-generator.co.uk). Tube: Russell Sq. or King's Cross St. Pancras. The ultimate party hostel. Under-14s not allowed, under-18s restricted to the quieter private rooms upstairs. Mixed-sex dorms, a hopping bar, cheap pints, dinner specials, and large well-equipped common rooms have earned this former police barracks a well-deserved reputation for excellence amongst young hostellers. All rooms have mirrors and washbasins; private doubles have tables and chairs. Continental breakfast included. Fax and photocopy machines, luggage storage, lockers (free—bring your own lock), towels and linens (free and changed on request), laundry. Internet access. Reserve 1 week ahead for weekends. Single-sex dorms available. 8-bed dorms £15 per person; 6-bed £16; 4-bed £17, and cheaper weekly rates apply. Mar.-Oct. singles £42; doubles £53; triples £67.50; quads £90; quints £112.50. Smaller rooms are cheaper in the off-season. Discounts for long stays, online booking, or VIP Backpacker card-holders. Credit card required with reservation. MC/V. ❶

Ashlee House, 261-265 Gray's Inn Rd. (☎ 7833 9400; www.ashleehouse.co.uk). Tube: King's Cross St. Pancras. Clean, brightly painted rooms crammed with blue steel bunks. It's "backpackers only," and the enthusiastic staff work hard to ensure a quiet, friendly atmosphere. This is definitely not a party hostel, but the crowd is friendly, young, and diverse. King's Cross location may not be the most pleasant, but it's massively convenient. Lift, TV room, continental breakfast included. Luggage room, safe (free), linen included, towels £1, laundry, kitchen. No lockers, but all rooms lock. 2-week max. stay. Internet access. May-Sept. 16-bed dorms £15; 8- to10-bed £17; 4- to 6-bed £19. Singles £36; doubles £48. Oct.-Apr. dorms £13/£15/£17, singles £34, doubles £44. MC/V. ❶

Indian YMCA, 41 Fitzroy Sq. (☎ 7387 0411; www.indianymca.org). Tube: Warren St. or Great Portland St. Standard student-dorm affairs, with desk and phone, and shared baths have an institutional (and somewhat musty) feel, but with prices this low, including both continental breakfast and an Indian dinner, who needs charm? Laundry, lounge, and games room. Deluxe rooms are subtantially larger and feature TV, fridge, and kettle. Reserve 1 month in advance. £1 temporary membership fee payable on arrival. 1-night deposit required with reservations. £10 fee for cancellations. Dorms £20 per person. Singles £34; doubles £49, with bath £55; deluxe doubles with bath £72. AmEx/MC/V. ❷

Pickwick Hall International Backpackers, 7 Bedford Pl. (☎ 7323 4958). Tube: Russell Sq. or Holborn. Aside from a single six-bed room, most accommodation is in 3- to 4-bed single-sex "dorms." Rooms are clean, and recently redecorated by the friendly new owner. Rules include no smoking, no food in the dorms, and no guests. Continental breakfast

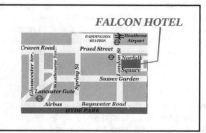

and linen included. Laundry room, kitchen, TV lounge. Reception approx. 8am-10pm. Call 2-3 days ahead, 6 weeks ahead for July-Aug. Singles £25; doubles £50 with bathroom; triples £66 with bathroom. Discounts available for longer stays. AmEx/MC/V. ❶

YHA St. Pancras International, 79-81 Euston Rd. (☎ 7388 9998; stpancras@yha.org.uk). Tube: King's Cross St. Pancras. Away from the seediest part of King's Cross, opposite the British Library. Triple glazing and comfortable wooden bunks provide a sound night's sleep. Most of the dorms have private bath and A/C; all have lockers (bring your own lock). Lounge with video games, dinner 6-9pm (£5.40). Guests must be members of Hostelling International, or pay a small surcharge. English breakfast and linen included. Laundry. Kitchen. Internet access. 10-day max. stay. Reserve 2 weeks ahead for summer, 1 month ahead for doubles. Dorms £24 per person, under-18s £20. Doubles £52, with bath £57.50; quads with bath for families with a child under 18, £84.50. AmEx/MC/V. ❷

RESIDENCE HALLS

Commonwealth Hall, 1-11 Cartwright Gdns. (☎ 7685 3500; cwh@lon.ac.uk). Tube: Russell Sq. Post-war block housing 425 basic, recently refurbished student singles with telephones; a good value, especially with the included English breakfast. Pantry on each floor, elevators, bar, cafeteria, tennis and squash courts. Open Easter (Mar. 22-Apr. 26) and mid-June to mid-Sept. Reserve at least 3 months ahead for July-Aug.; no walk-ins. Singles £23, half-board £27; UK students half-board £20. MC/V. ❷

Carr-Saunders Hall, 18-24 Fitzroy St. (☎ 7580 6338; www.lse.ac.uk/vacations). Tube: Warren St. Large hall shows its age in places, but rooms are larger than in most student halls and have sink and phone. TV lounge, games room, and elevator to all floors, including panoramic roof terrace, used for breakfast. English breakfast included. Reserve 6-8 weeks ahead for July-Aug. Internet access. Open Easter (Mar. 22-Apr. 26) and mid-June to mid-Sept. 30% deposit required. Discount for stays over 5 weeks. Singles £27 summer, £24 Easter; doubles £45/£40, with bath £50/£45. MC/V. ❷

Passfield Hall, 1-7 Endsleigh Pl. (☎ 7387 3584; www.lse.ac.uk/vacations). Tube: Euston or Euston Square. Three converted Georgian blocks arranged around a garden courtyard. Singles fairly small, but with sink and phone; doubles and triples are much bigger. Unisex baths and kitchen on each floor. TV lounge, games room, laundry. English breakfast included. Open Easter (Mar. 22-Apr. 26) and summer (July 6-Sept. 28). Book at least 1 month ahead. Singles £27; doubles £48; triples £62. MC/V. ❷

Graffiti

Virginia Woolf's

Heathrow

HOTELS AND BED & BREAKFASTS

Jenkins Hotel, 45 Cartwright Gdns., entry on Barton Pl. (☎7387 2067; www.jenkinshotel.demon.co.uk). Tube: Euston or King's Cross St. Pancras. Airy, pleasant rooms with large windows and antique-style furniture have a bright, summery feel whatever the weather. Guests can use the tennis courts in Cartwright Gardens. All rooms have TV, kettle, phone, fridge, hair dryer, and safe. English breakfast included. Completely non-smoking. Reserve 1-2 months ahead. Singles £52, with bath £72; doubles with bath £85; triples with bath £105. MC/V. ❹

The Langland Hotel, 29-31 Gower St. (☎7636 5801; www.langlandhotel.com). Tube: Goodge St. Family atmosphere, competitive rates, wood-framed beds, solid furniture, and plenty of spacious, sparkling baths (cleaned twice daily) help this B&B stand out from its neighbors. Guests have access to the garden and to a comfortable lounge with satellite TV. All rooms have TV, kettle, and fan, and have been recently refurbished. English breakfast included. Singles £40, with bath £55; doubles £50/£75; triples £70/£90; quads £90/£110; quint (no bath) £100. Discounts available for longer stays, for students, and in winter. AmEx/MC/V. ❸

Crescent Hotel, 49-50 Cartwright Gdns. (☎7387 1515; www.crescenthoteloflondon.com). Tube: Russell Sq. A family-run hotel, with artistically decorated rooms (some with their original fireplaces) and antiques in the hallways. All rooms have TV, kettle, washbasin, and phone. Bathrobes lent out with £30 deposit; racquets and balls are available for the tennis courts in front of the hotel. English breakfast included. 1-night deposit required. Reserve 3 weeks ahead for weekends. 7-day cancellation policy. Singles £46, with only shower £51, with bath £73; doubles with bath £89; triples with bath £99; quads with bath £108. Discounts for stays over 3 nights. MC/V. ❸

Thanet Hotel, 8 Bedford Pl., Russell Sq. (☎7636 2869; www.thanethotel.co.uk). Tube: Russell Sq. or Holborn. Bright, clean rooms in the small, family-run B&B have TV, hair dryer, kettle, and phone. Experienced and friendly staff are available 24hr. and more than willing to help. Rooms at the back of the hotel are away from the noise of the street and have a beautiful view of the leafy garden. All rooms have private shower and WC. Continental and full English breakfast included. Reserve 1 month in advance. Singles £69; doubles £94; triples £102; quads £112. AmEx/MC/V. ❹

George Hotel, 58-60 Cartwright Gdns. (☎7387 8777; www.georgehotel.com). Tube: Russell Sq. Meticulous rooms with satellite TV, kettle, phone, and sink, plus hair dryers and iron on request. The forward-facing 1st-floor rooms are the best, with high ceilings and tall

. Continental breakfast included. Reserve a week ahead; 24hr. cancellation policy. Sir, 5, with bath £52; doubles £56/£67; triples £69/£80; quads £84/£95; quints £100/1 tuples £115/£125. Discounts for stays of 7 nights or more. AmEx/MC/V. ❸

ilbeach Hotel, 30-31 Philbeach Gdns. (☎7373 1244; www.philbeachho freeserve.co.uk). The rooms in London's largest gay and lesbian B&B vary greatly: "bud- singles" are very basic (phone and sink), while 1 double with private bath features a t-iron bedframe, desk, and full bay window. Standard rooms have TV, phone, kettle, and . Continental breakfast included, served in the Thai restaurant downstairs. Reserve 1-2 eks ahead; 48hr. cancellation policy. Budget singles £35. Singles £55, with bath £65; bles £70/£90; triples £85/£117.50. Stay 7 nights, get 1 free. AmEx/MC/V.❸

NIGHTSBRIDGE & BELGRAVIA

🖪 KNIGHTSBRIDGE & BELGRAVIA QUICKFIND: Sights, p. 90; **Food & Drink,** p. 154; **Pubs,** p. 176; **Shopping,** p. 230.

Belgravia's B&Bs are concentrated on **Ebury St.,** a fairly busy road of Georgian terraces as close to Victoria and Sloane Sq. as it is to Belgravia proper. That's not a disadvantage—on the contrary, with Westminster's sights and Chelsea's shops within walking distance, you'd be hard pressed to do better.

SEE MAP, p. 368

◪ Westminster House Hotel, 96 Ebury St. (☎7730 7850; w.westminsterhousehotel.co.uk). Tube: Victoria. Extreme cleanliness, prime location, ◪ a charming family staff make this a standout. The 10 spotless rooms have TV, trays ◪ tea, coffee and hot chocolate, and almost all have private bath. English breakfast uded. 48hr. cancellation policy. Singles £55, with bath £60; doubles £75/£85; tri- s with bath £95; quad with bath £105. AmEx/MC/V. ❸

es and Cartref House, 108 and 129 Ebury St. (☎7730 7338, 7730 6176; www.jamesandcar co.uk). Tube: Victoria. Really two separate B&Bs on opposite sides of Ebury St. under the same ily's ownership. Both have sparkling rooms and well-kept hallways. The James has a bright kfast room overlooking the garden; the Cartref feels older but has more rooms with private bath an ornate dining room with fireplace. All rooms come with TV, kettle, hair dryer, and fan. English kfast included. Reserve with 1-night deposit; 10% non-refundable, the rest refundable with 2 notice. Singles £52, with bath £62; doubles £70/£85; triples £95/£110; family room (1 dou- and 2 bunks for under-12s) with bath £135. AmEx/MC/V. ❹

rgan House, 120 Ebury St. (☎7730 2384; www.morganhouse.co.uk). Tube: Victoria. sts are housed in 11 somewhat small rooms with TV, kettle, and phone for incoming s (pay phone downstairs); a few have fireplaces. English breakfast included. Reserve months ahead. 48hr. cancellation policy. Singles £46; doubles £66/£86; triples 0; quad with bath £122. MC/V. ❸

ARYLEBONE & REGENT'S PARK

🖪 MARYLEBONE & REGENT'S PARK: Sights, p. 92; **Museums & Galleries,** p. 132; **Food & Drink,** p. 155; **Entertainment,** p. 211.

Marylebone's West End-fringe location means that it has plenty of accommodations; however, they're usually beyond the price range of those not on corporate expense accounts. There are a number of B&Bs, but don't expect facilities or rooms to be up to, say, Bloomsbury standards. Here, you're paying to be in walking distance of Oxford St. Though little

SEE MAP, p. 369

pens after dark, you're never more than a short night-bus ride away from Soho.

STELS

rnational Student House, 229 Great Portland St. (☎7631 8300; www.ish.org.uk). Tube: t Portland St. A thriving international metropolis in a great location near Regent's Park and utes from Oxford Circus. Most rooms are of similar size, varying primarily in the number of

---

windows; basement and rear rooms are darker. The lounge (with Internet terminal) and dining room are both delightful. Full English breakfast included. Reserve 3 weeks ahead for summer; 48hr. cancellation policy. Singles £50, with shower only £65, with shower and WC £75; doubles £69.50/£77/£90; triples £83/£91.50/£105; basic quads £95. 10% discount for stays over 5 days. MC/V. ❹

Mentone Hotel, 54-56 Cartwright Gdns. (☎7387 3927; www.mentonehotel.com). Tube: Russell Sq. Bright rooms are furnished in a variety of styles, from Louis XIV to modern, all spotlessly clean with TV, phone, and kettle. All rooms have private bath. English breakfast and free broadband Internet access included. Reserve 1-2 weeks ahead. 48hr. cancella- tion policy. Apr.-Sept. singles £60; doubles £85; triples £95; quads (2 double beds) £105. Oct.-Mar. £55/£75/£85/£95. Discounts on stays over 1 week. AmEx/MC/V. ❹

Royal National Hotel, Bedford Way (☎7637 2488; reservations ☎7278 7871; www.imperialho- tels.co.uk). Tube: Russell Sq. London's largest hotel, with 1335 rooms, the Royal National occupies almost an entire block, with 2 lobbies and corridors that vanish into the horizon. Recently redeco- rated, the hotel offers meticulously clean, attractive rooms. All rooms have satellite TV and bath. Continental breakfast included. Singles £66; doubles £85; triples £102.50. MC/V. ❹

CLERKENWELL

🖪 CLERKENWELL QUICKFIND: Sights, p. 94; **Museums & Galleries,** p. 128; **Food & Drink,** p. 151; **Pubs,** p. 174; **Nightlife,** p. 185; **Entertain- ment,** p. 210.

City University Finsbury Residences, 15 Bastwick St. (☎7040 8811; www.city.ac.uk/ems). Tube: Barbican. Don't judge a build- ing by its facade—this might be a grim 1970s tower block, but the inside is freshly renovated, and it's within walking distance of City sights, Islington restaurants, and Clerkenwell nightlife. Standard singles in the main building. English breakfast included. Evening meals available (£4.70). Rooms available late June to mid-September. £21, students £19. MC/V. ❷

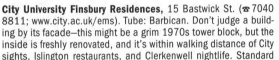

SEE MAP, p. 365

Rosebery Hall, 90 Rosebery Ave. (☎7278 3251; www.lse.ac.uk). Tube: Angel. Exit left from the Tube, cross the road, and take the 2nd right onto Rosebery Ave. Buzz for entry. Modern student residence in 2 buildings arranged around a sunken garden. Plain but sleek with phone, sink, and narrow beds. "Economy twins" are singles with an extra bed. Rooms in the newer block are more spacious, with handicap-accessible baths. TV lounge, laundry, and bar. English breakfast included. Open Easter and mid-June through Sept. Reserve 6 weeks ahead for July with 1 night or 25% deposit; £10 cancellation fee. Singles £26-31; doubles £46, economy £35, with bath £58; triples £55. MC/V. ❷

KENSINGTON & EARL'S COURT

🖪 KENSINGTON & EARL'S COURT QUICKFIND: Sights, p. 88; **Museums & Galleries,** p. 130; **Food & Drink,** p. 153; **Pubs,** p. 176; **Entertain- ment,** p. 210; **Shopping,** p. 229.

For such a posh neighborhood, Kensington is not entirely devoid of affordable accommodations. Then again, it's a big place and a "Kensington" address doesn't necessarily put you within walking distance of the main sights and shops. Decid- edly less exclusive **Earl's Court** remains popular with back- packers and budget travelers, with good transportation compensating for the slightly out-of-the-way location.

SEE MAP, pp. 366-367

KENSINGTON

◪ Five Sumner Place Hotel, 5 Sumner Pl. (☎7584 7586; www.sumnerplace.com). Tube: South Kensington. Sumner Place boasts all the amenities of a luxury hotel without losing the charm of the converted Victorians in the area. All accessible by lift, the spacious rooms have

King George

Tower Hill

Kensingtown Garden

elegant ceiling moldings and large windows; all have private bath, TV, fridge, phone, and hair dryer. Add to these an unbeatable location, and it's no surprise one award for the best small hotel in London landed here. English breakfast served in the beautiful conservatory dining room. 14-day cancellation policy; book 1 month ahead in summer. Singles £85; doubles £130. AmEx/MC/V. ❺

Swiss House Hotel, 171 Old Brompton Rd. (☎7373 2769; www.swiss-hh.demon.co.uk). Tube: Gloucester Rd. or South Kensington. On a quiet, shady part of Old Brompton Rd. All of the large, wood-floored rooms have TV, phone, fan, and bath. Book 1 month ahead for summer. Continental breakfast included; English breakfast £6.50. Singles £71, with shower only £51; doubles £89-104; triples £120; quads £134. 5% discount for stays over 7 nights and cash payments. AmEx/MC/V. ❹

Vicarage Private Hotel, 10 Vicarage Gate, (☎7229 4030; www.londonvicaragehotel.com). Tube: High St. Kensington. Beautifully kept Victorian house with ornate hallways, TV lounge, and charming bedrooms: all have solid wood furnishings and luxuriant drapes, with kettle and hair dryer (rooms with private bath also have TV). English breakfast included. Reserve several months ahead with 1 night's deposit; US$ personal checks accepted for deposit with at least 2 months notice. Singles £46, £75 with private facilities; doubles £78/£102; triples £95/£130; quads £102/140. Cash only. ❸

Abbey House Hotel, 11 Vicarage Gate, (☎7727 2594; www.abbeyhousekensington.com). Tube: High St. Kensington. Spacious, pastel-themed rooms with TV, desk, and sink. 5 baths between 16 rooms. 24hr. free tea, coffee, and ice room. English breakfast included. Hospitable staff will gladly provide you with bus routes and sightseeing directions. Singles £45; doubles £74; triples £90; quads £100. Winter discounts available. No credit cards; personal checks in US$ or Euros accepted for deposit with at least 1 month notice. ❸

YHA Holland House, Holland Walk, (☎7937 0748; fax 7376 0667; hollandhouse@yha.org.uk). Tube: High St. Kensington or Holland Park. On the edge of Holland Park, accommodation is split between a picturesque 17th-century mansion and an ugly 1970s unit; dorms in both are similar and standard, with 12-20 interlocking metal bunks. Caters mostly to groups. Facilities include Internet, TV room, luggage storage, lockers, laundry, and kitchen. Breakfast included. Until Feb. 2004, get 5 nights for the price of 4. Book 2-3 weeks ahead in summer. £21, under-18s £18.75. AmEx/MC/V. ❶

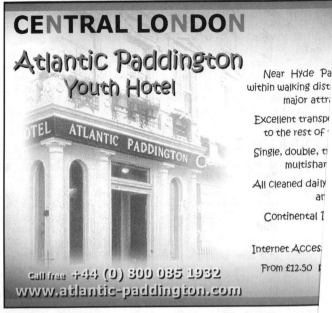
EARL'S COURT

🚇 Tube: all Earl's Court.

Oxford Hotel, 24 Penywern Rd. (☎7370 1161; www.the-oxford-hote bright rooms with enormous windows that let in tons of light. Sparkling-cl nishing is minimal but high-quality, with comfortable beds, TV, kettle, s clothes rail. Continental breakfast in the beautiful breakfast area include weeks ahead for June. Singles with shower only £36, with bath £50; dou triples £69/£79; quads £87/£93; quints £105/£115. Discount on sta AmEx/MC/V. ❸

Amsterdam Hotel, 7 Trebovir Rd. (☎7370 2814; www.amsterdam-hotel.c dations are split into rooms and suites, and further between "standard" Suites are gorgeous, with kitchenette and sitting area; rooms are less lovely. Executive rooms are slightly bigger. All rooms have private batl phone, and are served by an elevator. Continental breakfast included. £74, executive £82; doubles £84/£98; triple £108/£112. Suites: studi executive £101; doubles £102/£115; triples £129/£140; 2-bedroom discount on stays 7 nights or more. AmEx/MC/V. ❺

YHA Earl's Court, 38 Bolton Gdns. (☎7373 7083; fax earlscourt@yha.org.uk). Rambling Victorian townhouse that's considerab than most YHAs. The bright, tidy, single-sex dorms (4-8 people) have wo ers (bring your own lock), and sink. Features a garden, kitchen, 2 spacio luggage storage. Linen and laundry included. Internet access available. only for private rooms; otherwise £3.50. 2-week max stay. 24hr. canc cancellation charge. Dorms £19; under-18s £18.75. Private rooms (on book at least 48 hours in advance): doubles £52; quads £76. AmEx/M

Mowbray Court Hotel, 28-32 Penywern Rd. (☎7373 8285; www.m-c-hotel B&B making a bid for hotel status with elevator, TV lounge, and bar. Rooms enormous, but facilities include TV, trouser press, hair dryer, safe, and phor

beds—singles seem huge, bunk-bedded quads less so—and have desk, sink, phone, and fridge. Spartan 8- to 10-bed dorms have sink and lockers. Facilities include 3 bars (open F-Sa to 3am), nightclub/venue, cheap cafeteria, fitness center (£3 per day), cinema (Su only), and laundry. Internet access £2 per hr. 3 wk. max stay. Continental breakfast included except for dorms (£2); English breakfast £3. £10 key deposit. Reserve 3 months ahead during the summer; singles and doubles are mostly booked throughout the school year. All dorms £12. Singles £31, with bath £33; doubles £50/£52; triples £60; quads £72. MC/V. ❶

BED & BREAKFASTS

Edward Lear Hotel, 28-30 Seymour St. (☎ 7402 5401; www.edlear.com). Tube: Marble Arch. This was once the home of Ed Lear, though no owls nor pussycats here. Clean, cheerful rooms in a pretty location. Each room has phone, kettle, and TV and comes with English breakfast and free e-mail lounge. Singles £47.50, with shower only £60; doubles £66.50/£74, with full bath £83; triples £79/£89/£99; family quad with shower only £99, with full bath £105. 10% discount on stays of 3-4 nights, 15% 5 nights. MC/V. ❸

Hadleigh Hotel, 24 Upper Berkeley St. (☎ 7262 4084). Tube: Marble Arch. Rooms are pleasant, spacious, and equipped to executive standard. In addition to baths, TVs, telephones, and kettles, all have an extra in-room sink, minibar, safe, and even an iron with fold-out board. Continental breakfast included. Reserve at least 1 month ahead during the summer. Singles £65; doubles £75-85; triples £95; 2-bedroom apartment £138. AmEx/MC/V. ❹

THE SOUTH BANK

▶ **THE SOUTH BANK QUICKFIND: Sights,** p. 95; **Museums & Galleries,** p. 132; **Food & Drink,** p. 157; **Pubs,** p. 177; **Entertainment,** p. 212.

Though the South Bank has some of the best views in the city, its cheaper hotels don't—still, where else in London could you roll out of bed and be breakfasting by the Thames in five minutes? What it lacks in nightlife it makes up for in art, and with the City, West End, and Westminster all just a bridge away, you'd be hard pressed to find a more convenient base for sightseeing.

SEE MAP, pp. 370-371

Travel Inn County Hall, Belvedere Rd. (☎ 0870 238 3300; www.travelinn.co.uk). Tube: Westminster or Waterloo. Though it's in County Hall (see p. 95), expect no grand views (the river front is hogged by a Marriott) but you're seconds from the South Bank and Westminster. All rooms are clean and modern with bath and color TV. Facilities include elevator, restaurant, and bar. Prices by the room make it a great deal for families. Reserve at least 1 month ahead; cancel by 4pm on day of arrival. Continental breakfast £5, English £6, Singles/doubles and family rooms (2 adults and 2 children) M-Th £83, F-Su £80. AmEx/MC/V. Family ❶, individual ❹.

LSE Bankside House, 24 Sumner St. (☎ 7107 5750; www.lse.ac.uk/vacations). Tube: Southwark or London Bridge. One of London School of Economics' well-kept student halls, facing the back of the Tate Modern. Over 800 rooms, all with phone. Facilities include elevator, laundry, TV lounge, games room, restaurant, and bar. Open July 6-Sept. 20, 2004. English breakfast included. Singles £28, with bath £44; doubles with bath £50; triples with bath £63; quads with bath £84. MC/V. ❷

THE WEST END

▶ **THE WEST END QUICKFIND: Sights,** p. 98; **Museums & Galleries,** p. 134; **Food & Drink,** p. 158; **Pubs,** p. 178; **Nightlife,** p. 188; **Entertainment,** p. 213; **Shopping,** p. 233.

Accommodations in the West End are scarce at any budget—unless you book months in advance, you won't find a bed here. If you want to be close to the Soho action, don't forget that many Bloomsbury accommodations are but a walk away.

SEE MAP, p. 356

High Holborn Residence, 178 High Holborn (☎7379 5589; www.lse.ac.uk/vacations). Tube: Holborn or Tottenham Court Rd. One of the nicest university dorms that converts into a hostel during the summer, with a great location for Covent Garden exploits. Accommodations are organized into clusters of 4-5 rooms, each with phone, sharing well-equipped kitchen and bath; rooms with private bath are much larger, though all are decent-sized. Some rooms wheelchair-enabled. Bar, elevator, laundry, TV room, and games room. Continental breakfast included. Open July 5-Sept. 29 in 2004. Singles £30; twins £48, with bath £58; triples with bath £68. MC/V. ❷

Accommodation Outlet, 32 Old Compton St. (☎7734 7216; www.outlet4holidays.com). Tube: Piccadilly Circus or Leicester Sq. Organizes shared accommodations around Old Compton St. for gays, lesbians, and gay-friendly travelers. Double bedroom (gay/lesbian only) from £50, £65 with private bath. Studio apartments from £75 per night, 1-bedroom from £100, 2-bedroom from £120, 3-bedroom from £150. Office open M-F 10am-7pm, Sa noon-5pm. Up to 30% discount for long stays. Related organization (www.outlet4homes.com) also helps find long-term apartments. MC/V. ❹

Seven Dials Hotel, 7 Monmouth St. (☎7240 0823; fax 7681 0792). Tube: Covent Garden or Holborn. The fantastic location of this tiny B&B compensates for pleasant but dowdy decor and smaller-than-average rooms. Front rooms are brighter, with triple glazing to keep out the noise, and have better views. All have TV, phone, kettle, and sink; most have ceiling fan. English breakfast included. Reserve well ahead; 72hr. cancellation policy. Singles £65, with shower £75, with bath £85; doubles £75/£85/£95; twin with bath £100; triple with bath £115. AmEx/MC/V. ❹

YHA Oxford Street, 14-18 Noel St. (☎0870 770 5984; www.yha.org.uk). Tube: Oxford Circus. Small, clean rooms with limited facilities but an unbeatable location for Soho nightlife. Triple-decker bunk beds may feel cramped once the novelty wears off. TV lounge, Internet terminal, and well-equipped kitchen. Linen included. Towels £3.50. Prepacked continental breakfast £3.40. Reserve at least 1 month ahead. 3- to 4-bed dorms £24, under-18s £19.75; 2-bed dorms £26. ❶

WESTMINSTER

SEE MAP, p. 372

⚑ WESTMINSTER QUICKFIND: Sights, p. 104; **Museums & Galleries,** p. 136; **Food & Drink,** p. 162; **Pubs,** p. 179; **Entertainment,** p. 216.

Pimlico, south of Victoria station, is a grid-like district of towering late Georgian and early Victorian terraces that are home to dozens of B&Bs—among them some of London's best. Very few have elevators, so if stairs are a problem, be sure to request a ground-floor room. While Pimlico itself has little to offer the visitor, Westminster Abbey, Parliament, and Buckingham Palace are close by, and Victoria's fantastic transportation links put all of London within easy reach.

▨ Alexander Hotel, 13 Belgrave Rd., SW1V 1RB (☎7834 9738; www.alexanderhotel.co.uk). Tube: Victoria. Recently renovated rooms, eclectically and lavishly furnished with quality fittings, solid oak dressers, comfy beds, and satellite TV. A halberd-wielding suit of armor keeps order in the sunny and pleasant breakfast room. Prices vary according to demand. Singles £45; doubles £65; triples from £75; quads and quints £120. MC/V. ❸

▨ Melbourne House, 79 Belgrave Rd. (☎7828 3516; www.melbournehousehotel.co.uk). Tube: Pimlico. A clean, well-kept, and recently refurbished establishment with a superbly friendly staff. Non-smoking rooms all with TV, phone, coffee-maker, and kettle; the pride and joy is the luxurious basement double, with triangular bathtub large enough for 2. Continental breakfast included. Reserve 2 weeks ahead; 48hr. cancellation policy. Singles £30, with bath £55; doubles with bath £75; triples with bath £95; quad with bath £110. MC/V (payment on arrival; cash preferred). ❷

Luna Simone Hotel, 47/49 Belgrave Rd. (☎7834 5897; www.lunasimonehotel.com). Tube: Victoria or Pimlico. Stuccoed Victorian facade conceals pleasant yellow rooms with TV, phone, kettle, safety deposit box, and hair dryer. Internet access. Meticulously clean bathrooms. On the downside, some singles are cramped. English breakfast included. Reserve 2 weeks ahead; 48hr. cancellation policy. Singles £40, with bath £55; doubles £75, triples £100. 10% discount for stays over 7 nights in low season. AmEx/MC/V. ❸

Georgian House Hotel, 35 St. George's Dr. (☎7834 1438; www.georgianhousehotel.co.uk). Tube: Victoria. Large, well equipped rooms, with TV, phone, hair dryer, kettle, and matching furniture. Top-floor "student" rooms, available to all, are smaller with fewer fittings. Lounge-room portraits commemorate the family in charge since 1851. English breakfast included. Internet access. Reserve 1 month ahead for Sa-Su and student rooms. Singles £38.50, student £28.50, with bath £49.50; doubles £52.50/44.50/68.50; triples £72.50/66.50/86.50; quads student £76.50, with bath £96.50. MC/V. ❸

NORTH LONDON

🏴 **NORTH LONDON QUICKFIND: Sights,** *p. 107; **Museums & Galleries,** p. 137; **Food & Drink,** p. 163; **Pubs,** p. 180; **Nightlife,** p. 192; **Entertainment,** p. 216; **Shopping,** p. 240.*

🏠 **YHA Hampstead Heath,** 4 Wellgarth Rd. (☎8458 9054; fax 8209 0546; hampstead@yha.org.uk). Deceptively named hostel is actually near Tube: Golders Green (Zone 3). This gorgeous manorial hostel is surrounded by lovely shaded gardens. Rooms are fresh and relatively spacious. Great for those traveling in large groups or with children. Common rooms (both smoking and nonsmoking), lockers, laundry, currency exchange, kitchen, and snack bar. Linen and breakfast included. 24hr. reception. Internet access. 4- to 8-bed dorms £20.40; doubles £47; triples £67; quads £84; quints £103.50; 6-beds £124; 7-beds £144. Families with 1 child under 18 get significant discounts on the larger rooms. AmEx/MC/V. ❷

Kandara Guesthouse, 68 Ockendon Rd. (☎ 7226 5721; www.kandara.co.uk). From Tube: Angel take bus #38, 56, 73, 341, or 476 to Essex and Ockendon—be alert, it's a small stop. Far from the Tube (around 20min. walk)—but with so many buses to the West End, it's a blessing in disguise. Classically decorated family-run B&B, with sparkling clean rooms and a friendly, bustling atmosphere. 5 baths between 11 rooms keeps waiting to a minimum. Breakfast included. Hairdryer and iron on request. Reserve ahead; call for family quad. Singles £41-47; doubles/twins £51-62; triples £64-72 MC/V. ❸

Hampstead Village Guest House, 2 Kemplay Rd. (☎ 7435 8679; www.hampsteadguesthouse.com). Tube: Hampstead. 8 good-sized rooms in a charming, well-maintained Victorian house with a touch of old-fashioned elegance. All rooms have TV, fridge, phone, iron, and kettle. The studio apartment, in a converted garage, sleeps 5 and has a small kitchen. English breakfast £7. Reservations essential. Singles £48-54, with bath £66; doubles £72/84; studio £90 for 1 person, £120 for 2, £138 for 3, £150 for 4, £162 for 5. ❹

St. Christopher's Inn, 48-50 Camden High St. (☎ 7388 1012; www.st-christophers.co.uk). Tube: Mornington Crescent. The reception in Belushi's Bar downstairs serves as a fitting entrance to this party-friendly, backpacker hostel. They get you started right with 10% off all food and drinks at the bar, and it's well located for late nights out at the nearby Camden Town clubs. Even with the commotion, the rooms are surprisingly fresh and cheerful, and all have private bath. Luggage room, safe deposit boxes, lockers. Linen and continental breakfast included. Laundry and common rooms. 24hr. reception. Internet access. 10-bed dorms £15, book online £7.50; 8-bed £16; 6-bed £17. ❶

Jurys Inn, 60 Pentonville Rd. (☎ 7282 5500; www.jurys.com). Tube: Angel. Steps from the Tube, this business hotel offers 3-star luxury for B&B prices—at least if you're in a group of 3. Naturally, private bath, TV, kettle, A/C, and hair dryer are standard. Nonsmoking except for 5th fl. English breakfast £8.50. Room-only rates for up to 3 adults, or 2 adults and 2 children, £94 per night; when you book online all rooms are £59. AmEx/MC/V. ❸

WEST LONDON

🔢 *WEST LONDON QUICKFIND: Sights, p. 115; Food & Drink, p. 168; Entertainment, p. 220; Shopping, p. 243.*

Reasonably central and relatively cheap, with good transport links, Shepherd's Bush is popular with budget travelers (especially Australians), but they have to compete with builders and other workers who also favor the B&Bs on **Shepherd's Bush Rd.**

Star Hotel, 97-99 Shepherd's Bush Rd. (☎ 7603 2755; www.star-hotel.net). Tube: Hammersmith. Rooms are relatively spacious; all have TV, kettle, hair dryer, and large bath, as well as solid wood furniture and new carpeting. This is how a family-run B&B should feel—kindly and comfortable. English breakfast included, served in a sky-lit dining area. Book 2 months ahead July-Aug. and Easter. 48hr. cancellation policy. Singles £42; doubles £62; triples £75; quads £95. Stays over 2 nights receive a substantial discount. MC/V (3% surcharge). ❸

Hotel Orlando, 83 Shepherd's Bush Rd. (☎/fax 7603 4890; www.hotelorlando.co.uk). Tube: Goldhawk Rd. Clean, pleasant rooms are decently-sized, with sparkling modern baths. Friendly and considerate staff. All rooms have TV, phone, and bath. Most have a mini-fridge. English breakfast included. 5-day cancellation policy. Singles £40; doubles £52; triples £70; family (1 double and 2 single beds) £88. AmEx/MC/V. ❸

Dalmacia Hotel, 71 Shepherd's Bush Rd. (☎ 7603 2887; www.dalmacia.co.uk). Tube: Goldhawk Rd. The aspiring-rock-star accommodation of choice (Nirvana stayed here before they became famous), the Dalmacia provides each room with kettle, TV, phone, and hair dryer. English breakfast included. Internet access. Singles £49; doubles £69; triples £81. 30% discount with cash or if staying 2 or more nights. MC/V. ❸

Windsor Guest House, 43 Shepherd's Bush Rd. (☎/fax 7603 2116; neven@windsorghs.freeserve.co.uk). Tube: Goldhawk Rd. Small, unpretentious family-run B&B catering to a mixture of tourists and workmen. Rooms are small, but are well kept and have TV; baths are reasonably clean and modern. English breakfast included, served in an airy and attractive conservatory looking onto a small, nicely tended garden. Reserve 2 months ahead in summer. Singles £30; doubles £50; triples £67.50. Cash only. ❷

windows; basement and rear rooms are darker. The lounge (with Internet terminal) and dining room are both delightful. Full English breakfast included. Reserve 3 weeks ahead for summer; 48hr. cancellation policy. Singles £50, with shower only £65, with shower and WC £75; doubles £69.50/£77/£90; triples £83/£91.50/£105; basic quads £95. 10% discount for stays over 5 days. MC/V. ❹

Mentone Hotel, 54-56 Cartwright Gdns. (☎7387 3927; www.mentonehotel.com). Tube: Russell Sq. Bright rooms are furnished in a variety of styles, from Louis XIV to modern, all spotlessly clean with TV, phone, and kettle. All rooms have private bath. English breakfast and free broadband Internet access included. Reserve 1-2 weeks ahead. 48hr. cancellation policy. Apr.-Sept. singles £60; doubles £85; triples £95; quads (2 double beds) £105. Oct.-Mar. £55/£75/£85/£95. Discounts on stays over 1 week. AmEx/MC/V. ❹

Royal National Hotel, Bedford Way (☎7637 2488; reservations ☎7278 7871; www.imperialhotels.co.uk). Tube: Russell Sq. London's largest hotel, with 1335 rooms, the Royal National occupies almost an entire block, with 2 lobbies and corridors that vanish into the horizon. Recently redecorated, the hotel offers meticulously clean, attractive rooms. All rooms have satellite TV and bath. Continental breakfast included. Singles £66; doubles £85; triples £102.50. MC/V. ❹

CLERKENWELL

🔳 *CLERKENWELL QUICKFIND: Sights, p. 94; Museums & Galleries, p. 128; Food & Drink, p. 151; Pubs, p. 174; Nightlife, p. 185; Entertainment, p. 210.*

City University Finsbury Residences, 15 Bastwick St. (☎7040 8811; www.city.ac.uk/ems). Tube: Barbican. Don't judge a building by its facade—this might be a grim 1970s tower block, but the inside is freshly renovated, and it's within walking distance of City sights, Islington restaurants, and Clerkenwell nightlife. Standard

SEE MAP, p. 365

singles in the main building. English breakfast included. Evening meals available (£4.70). Rooms available late June to mid-September. £21, students £19. MC/V. ❷

Rosebery Hall, 90 Rosebery Ave. (☎7278 3251; www.lse.ac.uk). Tube: Angel. Exit left from the Tube, cross the road, and take the 2nd right onto Rosebery Ave. Buzz for entry. Modern student residence in 2 buildings arranged around a sunken garden. Plain but sleek with phone, sink, and narrow beds. "Economy twins" are singles with an extra bed. Rooms in the newer block are more spacious, with handicap-accessible baths. TV lounge, laundry, and bar. English breakfast included. Open Easter and mid-June through Sept. Reserve 6 weeks ahead for July with 1 night or 25% deposit; £10 cancellation fee. Singles £26-31; doubles £46, economy £35, with bath £58; triples £55. MC/V. ❷

KENSINGTON & EARL'S COURT

🔳 *KENSINGTON & EARL'S COURT QUICKFIND: Sights, p. 88; Museums & Galleries, p. 130; Food & Drink, p. 153; Pubs, p. 176; Entertainment, p. 210; Shopping, p. 229.*

For such a posh neighborhood, Kensington is not entirely devoid of affordable accommodations. Then again, it's a big place and a "Kensington" address doesn't necessarily put you within walking distance of the main sights and shops. Decidedly less exclusive **Earl's Court** remains popular with back-

SEE MAP, pp. 366-367

packers and budget travelers, with good transportation compensating for the slightly out-of-the-way location.

KENSINGTON

🔳 **Five Sumner Place Hotel,** 5 Sumner Pl. (☎7584 7586; www.sumnerplace.com). Tube: South Kensington. Sumner Place boasts all the amenities of a luxury hotel without losing the charm of the converted Victorians in the area. All accessible by lift, the spacious rooms have

King George

Tower Hill

Kensingtown Garden

elegant ceiling moldings and large windows; all have private bath, TV, fridge, phone, and hair dryer. Add to these an unbeatable location, and it's no surprise one award for the best small hotel in London landed here. English breakfast served in the beautiful conservatory dining room. 14-day cancellation policy; book 1 month ahead in summer. Singles £85; doubles £130. AmEx/MC/V. ❺

▨ **Swiss House Hotel,** 171 Old Brompton Rd. (☎7373 2769; www.swiss-hh.demon.co.uk). Tube: Gloucester Rd. or South Kensington. On a quiet, shady part of Old Brompton Rd. All of the large, wood-floored rooms have TV, phone, fan, and bath. Book 1 month ahead for summer. Continental breakfast included; English breakfast £6.50. Singles £71, with shower only £51; doubles £89-104; triples £120; quads £134. 5% discount for stays over 7 nights and cash payments. AmEx/MC/V. ❹

Vicarage Private Hotel, 10 Vicarage Gate, (☎7229 4030; www.londonvicaragehotel.com). Tube: High St. Kensington. Beautifully kept Victorian house with ornate hallways, TV lounge, and charming bedrooms: all have solid wood furnishings and luxuriant drapes, with kettle and hair dryer (rooms with private bath also have TV). English breakfast included. Reserve several months ahead with 1 night's deposit; US$ personal checks accepted for deposit with at least 2 months notice. Singles £46, £75 with private facilities; doubles £78/£102; triples £95/£130; quads £102/140. Cash only. ❸

Abbey House Hotel, 11 Vicarage Gate, (☎7727 2594; www.abbeyhousekensington.com). Tube: High St. Kensington. Spacious, pastel-themed rooms with TV, desk, and sink. 5 baths between 16 rooms. 24hr. free tea, coffee, and ice room. English breakfast included. Hospitable staff will gladly provide you with bus routes and sightseeing directions. Singles £45; doubles £74; triples £90; quads £100. Winter discounts available. No credit cards; personal checks in US$ or Euros accepted for deposit with at least 1 month notice. ❸

YHA Holland House, Holland Walk, (☎7937 0748; fax 7376 0667; hollandhouse@yha.org.uk). Tube: High St. Kensington or Holland Park. On the edge of Holland Park, accommodation is split between a picturesque 17th-century mansion and an ugly 1970s unit; dorms in both are similar and standard, with 12-20 interlocking metal bunks. Caters mostly to groups. Facilities include Internet, TV room, luggage storage, lockers, laundry, and kitchen. Breakfast included. Until Feb. 2004, get 5 nights for the price of 4. Book 2-3 weeks ahead in summer. £21, under-18s £18.75. AmEx/MC/V. ❶

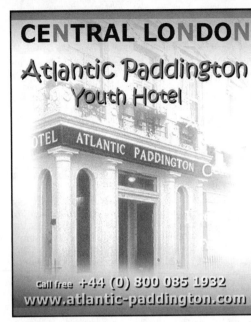

CENTRAL LONDON

Atlantic Paddington Youth Hotel

Near Hyde Park and within walking distance of major attractions.

Excellent transport links to the rest of the city.

Single, double, triple and multishare rooms.

All cleaned daily with TV and phone.

Continental Breakfast included.

Internet Access and Bar.

From £12.50 per person

Call free **+44 (0) 800 085 1932**
www.atlantic-paddington.com

EARL'S COURT

⚑ *Tube: all Earl's Court.*

🏨 **Oxford Hotel,** 24 Penywern Rd. (☎7370 1161; www.the-oxford-hotel.com). Large, bright rooms with enormous windows that let in tons of light. Sparkling-clean baths. Furnishing is minimal but high-quality, with comfortable beds, TV, kettle, safe, chair, and clothes rail. Continental breakfast in the beautiful breakfast area included. Reserve 2-3 weeks ahead for June. Singles with shower only £36, with bath £50; doubles £57/£67; triples £69/£79; quads £87/£93; quints £105/£115. Discount on stays over 1 week. AmEx/MC/V. ❸

Amsterdam Hotel, 7 Trebovir Rd. (☎7370 2814; www.amsterdam-hotel.com). Accommodations are split into rooms and suites, and further between "standard" and "executive." Suites are gorgeous, with kitchenette and sitting area; rooms are less luxurious but still lovely. Executive rooms are slightly bigger. All rooms have private bath, TV, kettle, and phone, and are served by an elevator. Continental breakfast included. Singles standard £74, executive £82; doubles £84/£98; triple £108/£112. Suites: studios standard £98, executive £101; doubles £102/£115; triples £129/£140; 2-bedroom £150/£160. 10% discount on stays 7 nights or more. AmEx/MC/V. ❺

YHA Earl's Court, 38 Bolton Gdns. (☎7373 7083; fax 7835 2034; earlscourt@yha.org.uk). Rambling Victorian townhouse that's considerably better-equipped than most YHAs. The bright, tidy, single-sex dorms (4-8 people) have wooden bunks, lockers (bring your own lock), and sink. Features a garden, kitchen, 2 spacious TV lounges, and luggage storage. Linen and laundry included. Internet access available. Breakfast included only for private rooms; otherwise £3.50. 2-week max stay. 24hr. cancellation policy; £5 cancellation charge. Dorms £19; under-18s £18.75. Private rooms (only bookable online; book at least 48 hours in advance): doubles £52; quads £76. AmEx/MC/V. ❶

Mowbray Court Hotel, 28-32 Penywern Rd. (☎7373 8285; www.m-c-hotel.mcmail.com). Large B&B making a bid for hotel status with elevator, TV lounge, and bar. Rooms vary from smallish to enormous, but facilities include TV, trouser press, hair dryer, safe, and phone. Baths are ugly but

261

big. Continental breakfast included. Reserve a week ahead; 24hr. cancellation policy. Singles £45, with bath £52; doubles £56/£67; triples £69/£80; quads £84/£95; quints £100/110; sextuples £115/£125. Discounts for stays of 7 nights or more. AmEx/MC/V. ❸

Philbeach Hotel, 30-31 Philbeach Gdns. (☎7373 1244; www.philbeachho-tel.freeserve.co.uk). The rooms in London's largest gay and lesbian B&B vary greatly: "bud-get singles" are very basic (phone and sink), while 1 double with private bath features a cast-iron bedframe, desk, and full bay window. Standard rooms have TV, phone, kettle, and sink. Continental breakfast included, served in the Thai restaurant downstairs. Reserve 1-2 weeks ahead; 48hr. cancellation policy. Budget singles £35. Singles £55, with bath £65; doubles £70/£90; triples £85/£117.50. Stay 7 nights, get 1 free. AmEx/MC/V.❸

KNIGHTSBRIDGE & BELGRAVIA

SEE MAP, p. 368

🔟 **KNIGHTSBRIDGE & BELGRAVIA QUICKFIND: Sights,** p. 90; **Food & Drink,** p. 154; **Pubs,** p. 176; **Shopping,** p. 230.

Belgravia's B&Bs are concentrated on **Ebury St.,** a fairly busy road of Georgian terraces as close to Victoria and Sloane Sq. as it is to Belgravia proper. That's not a disadvantage—on the contrary, with Westminster's sights and Chelsea's shops within walking distance, you'd be hard pressed to do better.

🔲 **Westminster House Hotel,** 96 Ebury St. (☎7730 7850; www.westminsterhousehotel.co.uk). Tube: Victoria. Extreme cleanliness, prime location, and a charming family staff make this a standout. The 10 spotless rooms have TV, trays with tea, coffee and hot chocolate, and almost all have private bath. English breakfast included. 48hr. cancellation policy. Singles £55, with bath £60; doubles £75/£85; tri-ples with bath £95; quad with bath £105. AmEx/MC/V. ❸

James and Cartref House, 108 and 129 Ebury St. (☎7730 7338, 7730 6176; www.jamesandcar-tref.co.uk). Tube: Victoria. Really two separate B&Bs on opposite sides of Ebury St. under the same family's ownership. Both have sparkling rooms and well-kept hallways. The James has a bright breakfast room overlooking the garden; the Cartref feels older but has more rooms with private bath and an ornate dining room with fireplace. All rooms come with TV, kettle, hair dryer, and fan. English breakfast included. Reserve with 1-night deposit; 10% non-refundable, the rest refundable with 2 wk. notice. Singles £52, with bath £62; doubles £70/£85; triples £95/£110; family room (1 dou-ble and 2 bunks for under-12s) with bath £135. AmEx/MC/V. ❹

Morgan House, 120 Ebury St. (☎7730 2384; www.morganhouse.co.uk). Tube: Victoria. Guests are housed in 11 somewhat small rooms with TV, kettle, and phone for incoming calls (pay phone downstairs); a few have fireplaces. English breakfast included. Reserve 2-3 months ahead. 48hr. cancellation policy. Singles £46; doubles £66/£86; triples £110; quad with bath £122. MC/V. ❸

MARYLEBONE & REGENT'S PARK

SEE MAP, p. 369

🔟 **MARYLEBONE & REGENT'S PARK: Sights,** p. 92; **Museums & Galleries,** p. 132; **Food & Drink,** p. 155; **Entertainment,** p. 211.

Marylebone's West End-fringe location means that it has plenty of accommodations; however, they're usually beyond the price range of those not on corporate expense accounts. There are a number of B&Bs, but don't expect facilities or rooms to be up to, say, Bloomsbury standards. Here, you're paying to be in walking distance of Oxford St. Though little happens after dark, you're never more than a short night-bus ride away from Soho.

HOSTELS

International Student House, 229 Great Portland St. (☎7631 8300; www.ish.org.uk). Tube: Great Portland St. A thriving international metropolis in a great location near Regent's Park and minutes from Oxford Circus. Most rooms are of similar size, varying primarily in the number of beds—singles seem huge, bunk-bedded quads less so—and have desk, sink, phone, and fridge. Spartan 8- to 10-bed dorms have sink and lockers. Facilities include 3 bars (open F-Sa to 3am), nightclub/venue, cheap cafeteria, fitness center (£3 per day), cinema (Su only), and laundry. Internet access £2 per hr. 3 wk. max stay. Continental breakfast included except for dorms (£2); English breakfast £3. £10 key deposit. Reserve 3 months ahead during the summer; singles and doubles are mostly booked throughout the school year. All dorms £12. Singles £31, with bath £33; doubles £50/£52; triples £60; quads £72. MC/V. ❶

BED & BREAKFASTS

Edward Lear Hotel, 28-30 Seymour St. (☎ 7402 5401; www.edlear.com). Tube: Marble Arch. This was once the home of Ed Lear, though no owls nor pussycats here. Clean, cheerful rooms in a pretty location. Each room has phone, kettle, and TV and comes with English breakfast and free e-mail lounge. Singles £47.50, with shower only £60; doubles £66.50/£74, with full bath £83; triples £79/£89/£99; family quad with shower only £99, with full bath £105. 10% discount on stays of 3-4 nights, 15% 5 nights. MC/V. ❸

Hadleigh Hotel, 24 Upper Berkeley St. (☎ 7262 4084). Tube: Marble Arch. Rooms are pleasant, spacious, and equipped to executive standard. In addition to baths, TVs, telephones, and kettles, all have an extra in-room sink, minibar, safe, and even an iron with fold-out board. Continental breakfast included. Reserve at least 1 month ahead during the summer. Singles £65; doubles £75-85; triples £95; 2-bedroom apartment £138. AmEx/MC/V. ❹

THE SOUTH BANK

🔊 **THE SOUTH BANK QUICKFIND: Sights,** p. 95; **Museums & Galleries,** p. 132; **Food & Drink,** p. 157; **Pubs,** p. 177; **Entertainment,** p. 212.

Though the South Bank has some of the best views in the city, its cheaper hotels don't—still, where else in London could you roll out of bed and be breakfasting by the Thames in five minutes? What it lacks in nightlife it makes up for in art, and with the City, West End, and Westminster all just a bridge away, you'd be hard pressed to find a more convenient base for sightseeing.

SEE MAP, pp. 370-371

🛏 **Travel Inn County Hall,** Belvedere Rd. (☎ 0870 238 3300; www.travelinn.co.uk). Tube: Westminster or Waterloo. Though it's in County Hall (see p. 95), expect no grand views (the river front is hogged by a Marriott) but you're seconds from the South Bank and Westminster. All rooms are clean and modern with bath and color TV. Facilities include elevator, restaurant, and bar. Prices by the room make it a great deal for families. Reserve at least 1 month ahead; cancel by 4pm on day of arrival. Continental breakfast £5, English £6, Singles/doubles and family rooms (2 adults and 2 children) M-Th £83, F-Su £80. AmEx/MC/V. Family ❶, individual ❹.

LSE Bankside House, 24 Sumner St. (☎ 7107 5750; www.lse.ac.uk/vacations). Tube: Southwark or London Bridge. One of London School of Economics' well-kept student halls, facing the back of the Tate Modern. Over 800 rooms, all with phone. Facilities include elevator, laundry, TV lounge, games room, restaurant, and bar. Open July 6-Sept. 20, 2004. English breakfast included. Singles £28, with bath £44; doubles with bath £50; triples with bath £63; quads with bath £84. MC/V. ❷

THE WEST END

🔊 **THE WEST END QUICKFIND: Sights,** p. 98; **Museums & Galleries,** p. 134; **Food & Drink,** p. 158; **Pubs,** p. 178; **Nightlife,** p. 188; **Entertainment,** p. 213; **Shopping,** p. 233.

Accommodations in the West End are scarce at any budget—unless you book months in advance, you won't find a bed here. If you want to be close to the Soho action, don't forget that many Bloomsbury accommodations are but a walk away.

SEE MAP, p. 356

High Holborn Residence, 178 High Holborn (☎7379 5589; www.lse.ac.uk/vacations). Tube: Holborn or Tottenham Court Rd. One of the nicest university dorms that converts into a hostel during the summer, with a great location for Covent Garden exploits. Accommodations are organized into clusters of 4-5 rooms, each with phone, sharing well-equipped kitchen and bath; rooms with private bath are much larger, though all are decent-sized. Some rooms wheelchair-enabled. Bar, elevator, laundry, TV room, and games room. Continental breakfast included. Open July 5-Sept. 29 in 2004. Singles £30; twins £48, with bath £58; triples with bath £68. MC/V. ❷

Accommodation Outlet, 32 Old Compton St. (☎7734 7216; www.outlet4holidays.com). Tube: Piccadilly Circus or Leicester Sq. Organizes shared accommodations around Old Compton St. for gays, lesbians, and gay-friendly travelers. Double bedroom (gay/lesbian only) from £50, £65 with private bath. Studio apartments from £75 per night, 1-bedroom from £100, 2-bedroom from £120, 3-bedroom from £150. Office open M-F 10am-7pm, Sa noon-5pm. Up to 30% discount for long stays. Related organization (www.outlet4homes.com) also helps find long-term apartments. MC/V. ❹

Seven Dials Hotel, 7 Monmouth St. (☎7240 0823; fax 7681 0792). Tube: Covent Garden or Holborn. The fantastic location of this tiny B&B compensates for pleasant but dowdy decor and smaller-than-average rooms. Front rooms are brighter, with triple glazing to keep out the noise, and have better views. All have TV, phone, kettle, and sink; most have ceiling fan. English breakfast included. Reserve well ahead; 72hr. cancellation policy. Singles £65, with shower £75, with bath £85; doubles £75/£85/£95; twin with bath £100; triple with bath £115. AmEx/MC/V. ❹

YHA Oxford Street, 14-18 Noel St. (☎0870 770 5984; www.yha.org.uk). Tube: Oxford Circus. Small, clean rooms with limited facilities but an unbeatable location for Soho nightlife. Triple-decker bunk beds may feel cramped once the novelty wears off. TV lounge, Internet terminal, and well-equipped kitchen. Linen included. Towels £3.50. Prepacked continental breakfast £3.40. Reserve at least 1 month ahead. 3- to 4-bed dorms £24, under-18s £19.75; 2-bed dorms £26. ❶

WESTMINSTER

SEE MAP, p. 372

🞄 WESTMINSTER QUICKFIND: Sights, p. 104; **Museums & Galleries,** p. 136; **Food & Drink,** p. 162; **Pubs,** p. 179; **Entertainment,** p. 216.

Pimlico, south of Victoria station, is a grid-like district of towering late Georgian and early Victorian terraces that are home to dozens of B&Bs—among them some of London's best. Very few have elevators, so if stairs are a problem, be sure to request a ground-floor room. While Pimlico itself has little to offer the visitor, Westminster Abbey, Parliament, and Buckingham Palace are close by, and Victoria's fantastic transportation links put all of London within easy reach.

🞖 Alexander Hotel, 13 Belgrave Rd., SW1V 1RB (☎7834 9738; www.alexanderhotel.co.uk). Tube: Victoria. Recently renovated rooms, eclectically and lavishly furnished with quality fittings, solid oak dressers, comfy beds, and satellite TV. A halberd-wielding suit of armor keeps order in the sunny and pleasant breakfast room. Prices vary according to demand. Singles £45; doubles £65; triples from £75; quads and quints £120. MC/V. ❸

🞖 Melbourne House, 79 Belgrave Rd. (☎7828 3516; www.melbournehousehotel.co.uk). Tube: Pimlico. A clean, well-kept, and recently refurbished establishment with a superbly friendly staff. Non-smoking rooms all with TV, phone, coffee-maker, and kettle; the pride and joy is the luxurious basement double, with triangular bathtub large enough for 2. Continental breakfast included. Reserve 2 weeks ahead; 48hr. cancellation policy. Singles £30, with bath £55; doubles with bath £75; triples with bath £95; quad with bath £110. MC/V (payment on arrival; cash preferred). ❷

Luna Simone Hotel, 47/49 Belgrave Rd. (☎7834 5897; www.lunasimonehotel.com). Tube: Victoria or Pimlico. Stuccoed Victorian facade conceals pleasant yellow rooms with TV, phone, kettle, safety deposit box, and hair dryer. Internet access. Meticulously clean bathrooms. On the downside, some singles are cramped. English breakfast included. Reserve 2 weeks ahead; 48hr. cancellation policy. Singles £40, with bath £55; doubles £75, triples £100. 10% discount for stays over 7 nights in low season. AmEx/MC/V. ❸

Georgian House Hotel, 35 St. George's Dr. (☎7834 1438; www.georgianhousehotel.co.uk). Tube: Victoria. Large, well equipped rooms, with TV, phone, hair dryer, kettle, and matching furniture. Top-floor "student" rooms, available to all, are smaller with fewer fittings. Lounge-room portraits commemorate the family in charge since 1851. English breakfast included. Internet access. Reserve 1 month ahead for Sa-Su and student rooms. Singles £38.50, student £28.50, with bath £49.50; doubles £52.50/44.50/68.50; triples £72.50/66.50/86.50; quads student £76.50, with bath £96.50. MC/V. ❸

NORTH LONDON

🗹 **NORTH LONDON QUICKFIND: Sights,** p. 107; **Museums & Galleries,** p. 137; **Food & Drink,** p. 163; **Pubs,** p. 180; **Nightlife,** p. 192; **Entertainment,** p. 216; **Shopping,** p. 240.

🏠 **YHA Hampstead Heath,** 4 Wellgarth Rd. (☎8458 9054; fax 8209 0546; hampstead@yha.org.uk). Deceptively named hostel is actually near Tube: Golders Green (Zone 3). This gorgeous manorial hostel is surrounded by lovely shaded gardens. Rooms are fresh and relatively spacious. Great for those traveling in large groups or with children. Common rooms (both smoking and nonsmoking), lockers, laundry, currency exchange, kitchen, and snack bar. Linen and breakfast included. 24hr. reception. Internet access. 4- to 8-bed dorms £20.40; doubles £47; triples £67; quads £84; quints £103.50; 6-beds £124; 7-beds £144. Families with 1 child under 18 get significant discounts on the larger rooms. AmEx/MC/V. ❷

Kandara Guesthouse, 68 Ockendon Rd. (☎ 7226 5721; www.kandara.co.uk). From Tube: Angel take bus #38, 56, 73, 341, or 476 to Essex and Ockendon—be alert, it's a small stop. Far from the Tube (around 20min. walk)—but with so many buses to the West End, it's a blessing in disguise. Classically decorated family-run B&B, with sparkling clean rooms and a friendly, bustling atmosphere. 5 baths between 11 rooms keeps waiting to a minimum. Breakfast included. Hairdryer and iron on request. Reserve ahead; call for family quad. Singles £41-47; doubles/twins £51-62; triples £64-72 MC/V. ❸

Hampstead Village Guest House, 2 Kemplay Rd. (☎ 7435 8679; www.hampsteadguesthouse.com). Tube: Hampstead. 8 good-sized rooms in a charming, well-maintained Victorian house with a touch of old-fashioned elegance. All rooms have TV, fridge, phone, iron, and kettle. The studio apartment, in a converted garage, sleeps 5 and has a small kitchen. English breakfast £7. Reservations essential. Singles £48-54, with bath £66; doubles £72/84; studio £90 for 1 person, £120 for 2, £138 for 3, £150 for 4, £162 for 5. ❹

St. Christopher's Inn, 48-50 Camden High St. (☎ 7388 1012; www.st-christophers.co.uk). Tube: Mornington Crescent. The reception in Belushi's Bar downstairs serves as a fitting entrance to this party-friendly, backpacker hostel. They get you started right with 10% off all food and drinks at the bar, and it's well located for late nights out at the nearby Camden Town clubs. Even with the commotion, the rooms are surprisingly fresh and cheerful, and all have private bath. Luggage room, safe deposit boxes, lockers. Linen and continental breakfast included. Laundry and common rooms. 24hr. reception. Internet access. 10-bed dorms £15, book online £7.50; 8-bed £16; 6-bed £17. ❶

Jurys Inn, 60 Pentonville Rd. (☎ 7282 5500; www.jurys.com). Tube: Angel. Steps from the Tube, this business hotel offers 3-star luxury for B&B prices—at least if you're in a group of 3. Naturally, private bath, TV, kettle, A/C, and hair dryer are standard. Nonsmoking except for 5th fl. English breakfast £8.50. Room-only rates for up to 3 adults, or 2 adults and 2 children, £94 per night; when you book online all rooms are £59. AmEx/MC/V. ❸

WEST LONDON

🔲 *WEST LONDON QUICKFIND: Sights, p. 115; Food & Drink, p. 168; Entertainment, p. 220; Shopping, p. 243.*

Reasonably central and relatively cheap, with good transport links, Shepherd's Bush is popular with budget travelers (especially Australians), but they have to compete with builders and other workers who also favor the B&Bs on **Shepherd's Bush Rd.**

Star Hotel, 97-99 Shepherd's Bush Rd. (☎ 7603 2755; www.star-hotel.net). Tube: Hammersmith. Rooms are relatively spacious; all have TV, kettle, hair dryer, and large bath, as well as solid wood furniture and new carpeting. This is how a family-run B&B should feel—kindly and comfortable. English breakfast included, served in a sky-lit dining area. Book 2 months ahead July-Aug. and Easter. 48hr. cancellation policy. Singles £42; doubles £62; triples £75; quads £95. Stays over 2 nights receive a substantial discount. MC/V (3% surcharge). ❸

Hotel Orlando, 83 Shepherd's Bush Rd. (☎/fax 7603 4890; www.hotelorlando.co.uk). Tube: Goldhawk Rd. Clean, pleasant rooms are decently-sized, with sparkling modern baths. Friendly and considerate staff. All rooms have TV, phone, and bath. Most have a mini-fridge. English breakfast included. 5-day cancellation policy. Singles £40; doubles £52; triples £70; family (1 double and 2 single beds) £88. AmEx/MC/V. ❸

Dalmacia Hotel, 71 Shepherd's Bush Rd. (☎ 7603 2887; www.dalmacia.co.uk). Tube: Goldhawk Rd. The aspiring-rock-star accommodation of choice (Nirvana stayed here before they became famous), the Dalmacia provides each room with kettle, TV, phone, and hair dryer. English breakfast included. Internet access. Singles £49; doubles £69; triples £81. 30% discount with cash or if staying 2 or more nights. MC/V. ❸

Windsor Guest House, 43 Shepherd's Bush Rd. (☎/fax 7603 2116; neven@windsorghs.freeserve.co.uk). Tube: Goldhawk Rd. Small, unpretentious family-run B&B catering to a mixture of tourists and workmen. Rooms are small, but are well kept and have TV; baths are reasonably clean and modern. English breakfast included, served in an airy and attractive conservatory looking onto a small, nicely tended garden. Reserve 2 months ahead in summer. Singles £30; doubles £50; triples £67.50. Cash only. ❷

FINDING SOMEWHERE TO LIVE

There's a good reason that every year a long-ignored, distant suburb is "outed" as the Next Big Thing in London living—inexorably rising property prices are pushing the urban hip further and further from the center of town. It's the same old story: struggling artists move to a long-depressed borough, then a few years later it's "discovered" by the style magazines and the next thing you know it's all bankers, Starbucks, and BMWs. The people who made it hip, meanwhile, have long since been forced to move to a more distant zone. This year's hapless neighborhood is Hoxton; next on the list looks to be Bethnal Green. Luckily, London is large enough that there are still enough terminally uncool neighborhoods where you might actually be able to afford to live; if you're lucky, you might pick just at the start of the upswing.

COST

Take a deep breath. If you want to live alone, you'll most probably end up in a **bedsit**, a single room, typically in a converted townhouse, typically miniscule, and typically with a shared kitchen and bath. For this privilege, you won't get away paying less than £60 per week in the most distant, depressed suburb; count on at least £100 for anywhere within striking distance of the center. You won't save money by being sociable, either: **flatshares** (shared apartments) cost £60-80 per week in the suburbs, £100-150 in a more fashionable area. **Short-term** housing is pricier and harder to find; it's almost impossible to rent for under a month. When deciding how much you can afford, don't forget to figure in **transport costs;** if you work in the center, living in the suburbs could add £30-50 to your monthly Travelcard cost; if you work outside Zone 1, you'll save if you don't have to go through Zone 1 to get there.

COUNCIL TAX. Local taxes are another factor that shouldn't be ignored when choosing a place to live. In England, council tax is levied on each "dwelling", with the amount owed being set by the local council and dependent on the market price of the dwelling. A dwelling is defined as any self-contained living unit—so a house converted into independent flats counts as numerous dwellings, but a house converted into bedsits that share kitchen and bathroom facilities counts as only one dwelling. Who is liable to pay the tax is a complicated matter; in rented flats it's generally the tenant, though if the landlord lives on the premises, he or she is normally liable. In any case, who is responsible for paying the tax should be clearly worked out before moving into any flat. If everyone in the dwelling is a full-time student, or earns less than a certain amount, it may be exempt from council tax; however this is not an automatic exemption and must be applied for. If your dwelling is liable for council tax, expect to pay around £600 per year for a small flat.

TENANTS' RIGHTS

🛈 *For free advice on housing rights, or if you have a dispute with your landlord, go to your local* **Citizens' Advice Bureau (CAB)**, *or check www.nacab.org.uk.*

All tenants have certain rights: for example, the landlord is responsible for keeping the accommodation in habitable condition and paying for necessary repairs; it's also illegal for landlords to threaten or harass tenants, or to cut off utilities for late rent payment. Asserting your rights is another matter. Few tenants can afford a court dispute with a landlord, and some may even face eviction. It's best to get advice from your local CAB before demanding action. Note that terms set out in the **tenancy agreement** (lease) cannot override rights laid out by law. Oral agreements have the force of law, but are hard to enforce; it's best to get a signed document.

RESOURCES

🛈 *For a listing of accommodations agencies in London, see the Service Directory, p. 329.*

Do-it-yourselfers willing to put in some time and footwork should rush to the newsagent the morning that London's **small-ads papers** are published, and immediately begin calling. **Loot** is published daily, as is the **Evening Standard** (which, despite its name, can be bought in the morning). Both have the best listings for short rentals (1-2 month). Other sources of vacancies are **Time Out** (published Tu) and **NME** (Th). Bulletin boards in **newsagents** frequently list available rooms, as do the classified sections of major and local newspapers. Beware of ads placed by **letting agencies;** they may try to sell you something more expensive when you call. Though they save a lot of legwork, agencies generally charge one to two weeks' rent as a fee, and it's in their interest to find high-priced accommodations. There are few laws regulating letting agencies, and tales of unscrupulous practices are common—make sure to only deal with agencies that are members of the **National Approved Letting Scheme (NALS),** which must adhere to a strict set of standards. Always thoroughly read the contract before signing anything—you might find yourself responsible for repairs that are normally the landlord's responsibility. Note that agencies may legally charge you only once you rent a room through them—don't pay just to register, or to get a list of rooms available. Many London boroughs run **information offices,** which often have listings of reliable local agencies.

Daytripping

For all the capital's many and varied charms, even the most die-hard London-lover needs to get out of the city occasionally. With Britain's comprehensive transportation network capable of spiriting you anywhere in the country in under a day, there's no excuse for staying cooped up in London when the historic and bucolic charms of England await. But first, a word of explanation about the organization of this chapter. **Short Daytrips Near London** covers sights and towns that are close (and small) enough to be easily covered in a day; you can leave after breakfast and return in time for dinner without breaking a sweat. If you're pressed for time, **Overnight Trips** could be done as long full-day trips, but their distance and/or size make it worth staying over. Most of the sights listed as being **"Near"** overnight trip destinations also make excellent short daytrips direct from London.

SHORT DAYTRIPS FROM LONDON

HAMPTON COURT

🏃 *Travel time from central London: 32min. from Waterloo by train; 4hr. by boat.* **Contact:** ☎ 0870 752 7777; www.hrp.org.uk. **Open:** *late Mar. to late Oct. M 10:15am-6pm, Tu-Su 9:30am-6pm; late Oct. to late Mar. closes 4:30pm; last admission 45min. before closing. Gardens open until dusk or 9pm.* **Admission:** *Palace and gardens £11.30, concessions £8.50, children £7.40, family (2 adults and 3 kids) £34; Maze or South Gardens only £3.50, children £2.50; gardens (excl. South Gardens) free. Free admission for worshippers at Chapel Royal services, held Su 11am and 3:30pm.*

HAMPTON COURT PALACE. Although a monarch hasn't lived here for 250 years, Hampton Court still exudes regal charm. The sprawling palace and carefully manicured gardens appeal to everyone from nature lovers to history buffs to art fans to horticulturalists. Cardinal Thomas Wolsey built the first structure here in 1514, showing young Henry VIII how to act the part of a splendid and powerful ruler—a lesson Henry learned quite well, confiscating the palace in 1528 and embarking on a massive building program. His rooms remain the most grandiose and magnificent parts of the palace. In 1689, William III and Mary II employed Christopher Wren to bring Hampton Court up to date, utilizing a more subdued Baroque style. The development of English architecture can be traced throughout these multiple rebuildings.

The palace itself is arrayed around three central courtyards. Visitors enter through the **Base Court,** which survives from Wolsey's original Tudor-style building; Henry VIII's own apartments are off this courtyard. Many of Henry's private rooms were demolished in the later renovations, but the glorious Great Hall survives, where many of his courtiers ate, slept, and waited eagerly to talk to Henry. Below the royal apartments are the **Tudor Kitchens,** which appear as they might have before a Midsummer's Day feast, and the enormous wine cellar.

The **Clock Court** is so named because of the colorful astronomical clock built for Henry in 1540. Half of the Tudor yard has been overtaken by Wren's colonnades, which lead to the apartments of King William III and the Wolsey Rooms. The latter have been renovated to look as they did in Wolsey's time; they also hold the impressive Renaissance picture gallery, which includes a self-portrait by Raphael.

The last courtyard, the **Fountain Court,** is the only Baroque courtyard completed by William and Mary, who had intended to tear the whole palace down and rebuild it in this style. Just off this courtyard are the **Queen's Apartments** and the **Georgian Rooms,** which were used by George II and Queen Caroline the last time they stayed at the Palace in 1737. Guides in full historical costume lead several free tours that start in the Fountain Courtyard.

HAMPTON COURT GARDENS. On a fine day, the palace has to compete with the equally lavish gardens. Palace tickets are required for entry to the **South Gardens,** the first of which is the ornate Privy Garden, built for the private enjoyment of William III. Nearby, the giant Great Vine is the world's oldest vine, planted sometime between 1768 and 1774; it still produces about 500 pounds of grapes every year. Secreted away in the neighboring Lower Orangery is Andrea Mantegna's series *The Triumphs of Caesar* (1484-1505). Among the most important works of the Italian Renaissance, the nine paintings are displayed in semi-darkness to protect the fragile colors. The rest of the gardens are open to all. The Home Park stretches beyond the yews and fountains of the **East Front Gardens.** North of the palace, the **Wilderness,** a pseudo-natural area earmarked for picnickers, holds the ever-popular Maze, planted in 1690. Another popular area here is the **Tiltyard Tearoom,** where jousting matches used to take place—it's really a sandwich cafeteria with beautiful seating by the gardens. The palace also hosts the annual Hampton Court Palace Flower Show every August.

GETTING THERE. The fastest way is to take the **train** to Hampton Court from Waterloo; the palace is a 5min. walk. *(32min., every 30min. Day return £4.90; reductions with Travelcard.)* More relaxing, scenic, and slower, **boats** from Westminster run April thorugh October. It's a 4hr. trip; to leave time to see the Palace take it one-way and return by train, or board at Kew (p. 116) or Richmond (p. 273) instead. *(Westminster Passenger Association, Westminster Pier. ☎7930 2062; www.wpsa.co.uk. Tube: Westminster. Departures mid-Apr. to Sept. daily 10:30, 11:15am, noon, and 2pm returning 3, 4, and 5pm. Tides may affect schedules; call to confirm. £12, return £18; ages 5-15 £6/£9; 33% discount with Travelcard.)*

HATFIELD HOUSE

🚩 *Travel time from central London:* 20min. from King's Cross by train; 1hr. from Victoria Coach Station by bus. Take a train that calls at Hatfield Station; the House is right across the street from the rail station exit. *Contact:* ☎0170 728 7010; www.hatfield-house.co.uk. *Open:* House open

Easter to Sept. 30 daily noon-4pm. Grounds open Easter to Sept. 30 daily 11am-5:30pm. **Tours:** *House is presented by guided tour only; check for the sign in front of the entrance for times.* **Admission:** *House, park, and gardens £7.50, children £4. Park and gardens £4.50/£3.50. Park only £2/£1. Prices rise for "Connoisseurs Friday," when tours are longer and more gardens are open. £10.50, grounds only £6.50.*

Built for the Bishop of Ely in 1497, Hatfield was acquired by Henry VIII as a residence for the royal children. Elizabeth I is most associated with Hatfield; it was here that she turned from prisoner to Queen upon the death of her sister, Mary I. Keep an eye out for Liz's fanciful, 22-yard-long family tree, tracing her lineage to Adam and Eve via Noah, Julius Caesar, and King Arthur. All that remains of Elizabeth's palace is the Great Hall; the rest was razed to make way for the magnificent mansion that dominates the estate today, which, in a final homage to Elizabeth, was designed in the shape of an 'E' by chief minister to James I and first Earl of Salisbury Sir Robert Cecil. Tours cover the rooms not currently inhabited by the Cecil family. Most of the 45 acres of gardens are open to the public; be prepared to battle the bugs.

GETTING THERE. Trains arrive from **King's Cross**—just take any train that calls at Hatfield Station; the house is right across the street from the station exit. *(20min., approx. every 30min.)* **National Express buses** arrive from **Victoria Coach Station.** *(☎ 0870 580 8080. 1hr., every hr. £8.)*

RICHMOND

⚑ *Travel time from central London: 50min. by Tube; 2hr. by boat.*

Richmond is where London ends and the countryside begins, a leafy suburb along the Thames that, while accessible by Tube, is a town in its own right. Edward III built the first royal palace here in 1358, but a major fire in 1497 literally took the Sheen off the area—that's what it was called until 1501, when Henry VII named the rebuilt palace (later destroyed by Cromwell) after his earldom in Yorkshire. For a great view of the upper Thames valley, climb the incline of **Richmond Hill.** So many artists set up their easels on the 17th-century terrace that Parliament has declared it a protected site.

⬛ **RICHMOND PARK.** Perhaps the most breathtakingly beautiful area in all of greater London. The largest city park in Europe, Richmond's lush and beautiful 2500 acres were first enclosed by Charles I, who in 1637 generously built a wall around other people's property. Heading right along the main footpath from Richmond Gate will bring you to **Henry VIII's Mound,** actually a bronze-age barrow. Look through a small hole cut into the foliage at the top of the mound for a glimpse of St. Paul's in the distance. Bertrand Russell grew up in **Pembroke Lodge,** an 18th-century conversion job by the versatile Sir John Soane that's now a popular cafe. Deeper into the park, the **Isabella Plantation** bursts with color in the spring. Make sure to explore some of the smaller footpaths—not only do you have a better chance of seeing the free-roaming **deer,** you're less likely to be run over by cyclists and joggers. *(Main gate at the top of Richmond Hill. Bus # 371 from Richmond (70p). Park office ☎ 020 8948 3209. Open Mar.-Sept. daily 7am-dusk; Oct.-Feb. daily 7:30am-dusk.* **Health warning:** *Tick-borne Lyme disease is a risk in the park; wear long trousers.)*

HAM HOUSE. Some way downriver of Richmond, Ham House sits among resplendent gardens. William Murray received the house as a reward for being Charles I's "whipping boy"—he took the punishment whenever the future king misbehaved. Today, the house has been returned to the height of its glory, filled with 17th-century portraits, furniture, and tapestries, though the gardens are the main attraction. The **Cherry Garden** is actually a diamond lattice of lavender, santolina, and hedges with not a cherry tree in sight. **The Wilderness** is even less aptly named, an orderly array of trimmed hedges surrounding nooks of roses and wildflowers—plans are in the works to restore the original 17th-century statuary. A new attraction is the recently spruced-up **Kitchen Garden,** with rows of fresh fruit and vegetables. *(At the bottom of*

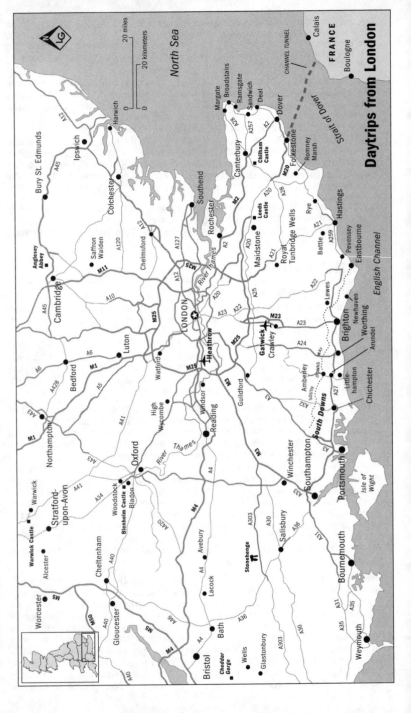

Daytrips from London

Sandy Ln., Ham. Bus #65 or 371 from Richmond station, or a beautiful 30min. walk along the Thames. A ferry crosses the river from Marble Hill, Twickenham, Sa-Su 10am-6:30pm or dusk; Feb.-Oct. also M-F 10am-6pm; 60p, children 30p. ☎8940 1950. House open Apr.-Oct. M-W and F-Su 1-5pm, gardens year-round M-W and F-Su 11am-6pm or dusk. House and gardens £7, children £3.50, family £17.50; gardens only £3/£1.50/£7.50.)

OTHER SIGHTS. Quite the hidden treasure, the ⬛**Museum of Richmond** has a small but fascinating array of exhibits on the history of Richmond, from the days of Queen Elizabeth to its Blitz legacy. (Whittaker Ave. ☎8332 1141; www.museumofrichmond.com. Open Tu-Sa 11am-5pm; May-Sept. also Su 1-4pm. Free.) Across the river from Ham House, **Marble Hill** was built in 1724 by Henrietta Howard, using an allowance from her former lover, George II. (Marble Hill Park, Richmond Rd. Bus #33, H22, R68, R70, or 490 from Richmond; alternatively, a ferry crosses from Ham House, Richmond (see above), or 15min. walk from the town center—walk west on Bridge St., then left onto Richmond Rd. ☎020 8892 5115. House open Apr.-Sept. daily 10am-6pm; Oct. daily 10am-5pm. Grounds open daily 7am-dusk. £3.50, concessions £3, kids £2.) Only James Gibbs's richly decorated Octagon Room survives of 18th-century **Orleans House.** Louis Philippe, Duc d'Orleans, rode out the French Revolution here before becoming king in 1830. (Riverside, Twickenham. Transportation as for Marble Hill. ☎8892 0221. House open Tu-Sa 1-5:30pm, Su 2-5:30pm. Grounds open daily 9am-dusk. Free.)

PRACTICALITIES

GETTING THERE. Richmond is at the end of the District line; the quickest route there is by **Tube** or **Silverlink train** (Zone 4). For a more leisurely, scenic journey, **boats** make the 2hr. cruise upriver from Westminster. Travelcard holders receive a 33% discount on most riverboat fares—be sure to ask. (Westminster Passenger Association, Westminster Pier. ☎020 7930 2062; www.wpsa.co.uk. Tube: Westminster. Departures mid-Apr. to Sept. daily 10:15, 10:30, 11:15am, noon, and 2:00pm; returning 4, 5, and 6pm. Tides may affect schedules; **call to confirm.** £10.50, return £16.50; concessions £7/£11; ages 4-15 £5.25/£8.25.)

ORIENTATION & PRACTICAL INFORMATION. From **Richmond** station, turn left onto The Quadrant, which becomes George St. and then Hill St. Turning right from Hill St. onto Bridge Rd. takes you across Richmond Bridge into **Twickenham,** while bearing left onto Hill Rise leads to Richmond Hill and Richmond Park. Running from Hill St. to the river, Whittaker Ave. is home to the **Tourist Information Centre,** where you can pick up your best friend—a **free map** of the town and the surrounding sites. (Old Town Hall, Whittaker Ave. ☎020 8940 9125; www.richmond.gov.uk. Open May-Sept. M-Sa 10am-5pm, Su 10:30am-1:30pm; Oct.-Apr. M-Sa 10am-5pm.)

WINDSOR & ETON

🎫 **Travel time from central London:** 50min. from Victoria and Paddington by train.

The town of Windsor and its attached village of Eton are completely overshadowed by two bastions of the British class system, Windsor Castle and Eton College. Windsor itself is filled with specialty shops, tea houses, and pubs, which for all their charm pale beside the fortress high above the Thames.

WINDSOR CASTLE. Built by William the Conqueror in the 1070 and 80s as a fortress rather than a residence, Windsor is the largest inhabited castle in the world. The castle's main attractions are found in the **Upper Ward.** Stand in the left queue as you enter to detour past **Queen Mary's Doll House,** an exact replica of a grand home down to tiny books in its library handwritten by their original authors. The **state apartments** are filled with works by Holbein, Rubens, Rembrandt, Van Dyck, and Queen Victoria herself. A stroll to the **Lower Ward** brings you to the 15th-century **St. George's Chapel,** with delicate vaulting and exquisite stained glass. The site of Edward and Sophie's wedding, 10 sovereigns lie here, including George V, Edward IV, Charles I, and Henrys VI and VIII. (24hr. info ☎01753 831 118. As a "working cas-

Fountain Court, Hampton Court

Pond Gardens

East Front Gardens

tle," large areas may be closed at short notice. Open daily Apr.-Oct. 10am-5:30pm, last entry 4pm; Nov.-Mar. 10am-4pm, last entry 3pm. Audioguide £3.50. £11.50, seniors £9.50, children £6, family £29.)

ETON COLLEGE. Founded by Henry VI in 1440 as a school for paupers, Eton is now England's preeminent public (i.e. private) school. Pupils still wear tailcoats to every class and raise one finger in greeting to any teacher they pass. For all its air of privilege, Eton has shaped some notable dissidents, including Aldous Huxley and George Orwell. (Across Windsor Bridge, and along Eton High St. ☎01753 671 177. Tours daily 2:15 and 3:15pm; £4, under 16 £3.10. Open daily July-Aug. and late Mar. to mid-Apr. 10:30am-4:30pm; mid.-Apr. to June and Sept. to late Mar. 2-4:30pm. Schedule can vary due to academic calendar. £3, children £2.25.)

PRACTICALITIES

GETTING THERE. Windsor has two train stations, both in walking distance of the castle. Trains to **Windsor** and **Eton Central** arrive from both **Victoria** and **Paddington** stations via **Slough,** while those to **Windsor** and **Eton Riverside** come direct from **Waterloo.** (☎08457 484 950. All services 50min., 2 per hr., day return £6.90.)

ORIENTATION & PRACTICAL INFORMATION. Windsor village slopes downhill in an elegant crescent from the foot of its castle. **High Street,** which becomes **Thames Street** at the statue of Queen Victoria and continues downhill to the Thames, spans the top of the hill; the main shopping area, **Peascod Street,** meets High St. at the statue. The **Tourist Information Centre,** near Queen Victoria, has numerous free brochures and sells local maps, guides, and tickets to Legoland. (24 High St. ☎01753 743 900; www.windsor.gov.uk. Open May-June daily 10am-5pm; July-Aug. M-F 9:30am-6pm, Sa 10am-5:30pm, Su 10am-5pm; Sept. M-Sa 10am-5pm, Su 10am-4pm; Oct.-Apr. Su-F 10am-4pm, Sa 10am-5pm.)

OVERNIGHT TRIPS

BATH

◪ Travel time from central London: 1½hr. from Paddington by train; 2¼hr. from Waterloo by train; 3hr. from Victoria Coach Station by bus.

A visit to the elegant spa town of Bath remains de rigueur, even if it is now more of a museum—or perhaps a museum's gift shop—than a resort. Romans built an elaborate complex of baths to house the curative waters at the town they called

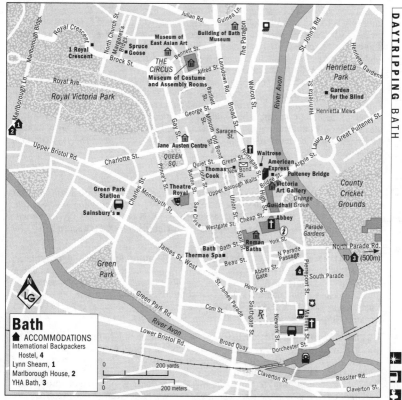

Bath

ACCOMMODATIONS
International Backpackers
Hostel, **4**
Lynn Shearn, **1**
Marlborough House, **2**
YHA Bath, **3**

Aquae Sulis, and the excavated remains of that complex draw in visitors today. Queen Anne's visit to the hot springs here in 1701 reestablished the city's prominence, making it a meeting place for 18th-century artists, politicians, and intellectuals.

ROMAN BATHS. Bath flourished for nearly 400 years as a Roman spa city, but it was not until 1880 that sewer diggers inadvertently uncovered the first glimpse of advanced Roman engineering. Underneath the baths, the **▨museum** features exhibits on Roman building design, including central heating and internal plumbing. Penny-pinching travelers can view one of the baths in the complex for free by entering through the **Pump Room.** *(Stall St. ☎01225 477 759. Open July-Aug. daily 9am-10pm; Apr.-June and Sept. 9am-6pm; Oct.-Mar. 9:30am-5:30pm; last admission 1hr. before close. £8.50, children £4.80, family £22.)*

BATH ABBEY. An anomaly among the city's Roman and 18th-century Georgian sights, the 15th-century abbey still towers over its neighbors. The abbey saw the crowning of Edgar, "first king of all England," in AD 973. *(Next to the Baths. ☎01225 422 462. Open Apr.-Oct. M-Sa 10am-6pm, Su 1-2:30pm and 4:30-5:30pm; Nov.-Mar. M-Sa 9am-4pm, Su between services. Free; suggested donation £2.50.)* Below the abbey, the **Heritage Vaults** detail the abbey's history and its importance to Bath. *(Open M-Sa 10am-4pm; last admission 3:30pm. £2.50, concessions £1.50.)*

OTHER SIGHTS. The Museum of Costume hosts a dazzling, albeit motionless, parade of 400 years of catwalk fashions, with everything from silver tissue garments to the revealing Versace dresses worn by J.Lo and Geri Haliwell. *(Bennett St. ☎01225 477* **277**

789. Open daily 10am-5pm. £5.50, concessions £4.50, children £3.75, family £15.) The museum is in the basement of the **Assembly Rooms,** which staged fashionable events in the 18th century. (☎01225 477 789. Open daily 10am-5pm. Free.) The **Jane Austen Centre** invites dilettantes to experience the city as it was in 1806. Tours of the sights in her novels run daily 1:30pm from Abbey Churchyard. (40 Gay St. ☎01225 443 000. Open M-Sa 10am-5:30pm, Su 10:30am-5:30pm. £4.45, concessions £3.65, children £2.45, family £12. Tours £3.50/£2.50/£2/£8.) Walk up Gay St. to **The Circus,** which has attracted illustrious residents for two centuries. Blue plaques mark the houses of Gainsborough, Pitt the Elder, and Dr. Livingstone. Proceed from there up Brock St. to **Royal Crescent,** a half-moon of Georgian townhouses. The interior of **1 Royal Crescent** has been painstakingly restored to a replica of a 1770 townhouse. (☎01225 428 126. Open mid-Feb. to Oct. Tu-Su 10:30am-5pm; Nov. Tu-Su 10:30am-4pm. £4, concessions £3.50, family £10.)

PRACTICALITIES

GETTING THERE. Trains from **Paddington** are the fastest way to get to Bath, but those from **Waterloo** are much cheaper. (Railway Pl., at the south end of Manvers St. Paddington: 1½hr., 2 per hr., £32. Waterloo: 2¼-3hr., 3 per day, £21.) Even slower and cheaper are **National Express buses** from **Victoria Coach Station.** (☎0870 580 8080. 3hr., every hr., £14.)

ORIENTATION & PRACTICAL INFORMATION. Beautiful **Pulteney Bridge** and **North Parade Bridge** span the River Avon, which bends around the city. The **Roman Baths,** the **Pump Room,** and **Bath Abbey** cluster in the city center, while the **Royal Crescent** and **The Circus** lie to the northwest. The **Tourist Information Centre** offers the usual services. (Abbey Chambers. ☎0870 444 6442; www.visitbath.co.uk. Open May-Sept. M-Sa 9:30am-6pm, Su 10am-4pm; Oct.-Apr. M-Sa 9:30am-5pm, Su 10am-4pm.)

ACCOMMODATIONS. B&Bs cluster on **Pulteney Road** and **Pulteney Gardens.** From the stations, walk up Manvers St., which becomes Pierrepont St., right onto North Parade Rd., and past the cricket ground to Pulteney Rd. For a more relaxed (and more expensive) setting, continue past Pulteney Gdns. (or take the footpath from behind the train station) to **Widcombe Hill. ■Prior House ❸** has friendly proprietors and inviting rooms, complete with board games and hairdryers. (3 Marlborough Ln. Take bus #14 from the station to Hinton Garage or walk 15min. ☎01225 313 587; www.greatplaces.co.uk/priorhouse. Doubles from £45, with bath £50.) **Marlborough House ❺** is a classic B&B with themed rooms, from Georgian to Victorian to Oriental-fantasy "bamboo." All rooms come with fresh flowers and sherry. (1 Marlborough Ln. ☎01225 318 175; www.marlborough-house.net. Breakfast included. Doubles £75-85; extra person £10.) **YHA Bath Youth Hostel ❶** is in a secluded Italianate mansion overlooking the city. In summer, reserve a week ahead. (Bathwick Hill. From North Parade Rd., turn left onto Pulteney Rd., right onto Bathwick Hill, and then 40min. up a steep footpath, or take bus #18 or #418 (6 per hr., return £1.20) from the bus station or the Orange Grove roundabout. ☎01225 465 674. Dorms £11.50, under 18 £8.25.) **International Backpackers Hostel ❶** has a more convenient location, up the street from the stations and three blocks from the baths. (13 Pierrepont St. ☎01225 446 787; www.hostels.co.uk. Dorms £12, doubles £30.)

BRIGHTON

🚩 *Travel time from central London:* 1¼hr. by train from Victoria; 2hr. by bus from Victoria Coach.

The undisputed home of the dirty weekend, Brighton sparkles with a risqué, tawdry luster. Back in 1784, the future George IV sidled into town for some hanky-panky. Having staged a fake wedding with a certain "Mrs. Jones" (Maria Fitzherbert), he headed off to the farmhouse known today as the Royal Pavilion, and the royal rumpus began. Kemp Town (jokingly called Camp Town), among other areas of Brighton, has a thriving gay population, while the immense student crowd, augmented by flocks of foreign youth purportedly learning English, feeds Brighton's decadent clubbing scene. Lovingly known as "London-by-the-Sea," Brighton's open demeanor and youthful spirit make it a memorable visit for adventurous travelers.

SIGHTS. In 1750, Dr. Richard Russell wrote a treatise on the merits of drinking seawater and bathing in brine. Thus began the transformation of sleepy Brighthelmstone into a fashionable town with a hedonistic bent, led by the most decadent layabout of them all, the Prince Regent (soon to be George IV). **The Royal Pavilion** is the epitome of Brighton gaudiness; the prince enlisted John Nash to turn an ordinary farmhouse into the Oriental/ Indian/Gothic/Georgian palace visible today. (☎ 01273 290 900. Open June-Sept. daily 10am-6pm; Oct.-May 10am-5pm. Guided tours 11:30am and 2:30pm, £1.25. Audio tour £1. £5.20, students & seniors £3.75, children £3.20.) The Pavilion's gaudiness reaches the beachfront, where the **Palace Pier** has slot machines and video games galore, with a roller coaster thrown in for good measure. Farther along, the now decrepit **West Pier** lies abandoned out in the sea. Even though Brighton was the original seaside resort, don't expect too much from the **beach**—the weather can be nippy even in summer, but yet on sunny days visitors have to fight for a patch of rock. Inland, fishermen's cottages once thrived in **the Lanes**, a jumble of 17th-century streets south of North St. constituting the heart of Old Brighton. Those looking for fresher shopping opportunities should head towards **North Laines,** off Trafalgar St., where alternative merchandise and colorful cafes still dominate.

Ashmolean Museum

NIGHTLIFE. Even Londoners come to club in Brighton. For the latest happenings, check *The Punter*, a local monthly, and *What's On*, a poster-sized flysheet. Gay and lesbian venues are found in the *Gay Times* (£2.50) and *Capital Gay* (free). Most clubs are open M-Sa 10pm-2am. **The Beach** adds big beats to the music on the shore. (171-181 King's Rd. Arches ☎ 02173 722 272.) **Event II** is among the most technically armed, crammed with the London crowds looking for wild thrills. (West St. ☎ 01273 732627.) Gay clubbers flock to zany **Zanzibar.** (129 St. James's St. ☎ 01273 622 100.)

Catte Street

PRACTICALITIES

GETTING THERE. Two trains per hour leave from London's Victoria Station. (☎ 08457 484 950; 1¼hr., £11.90.) The Brighton Train Station is uphill at the northern end of Queen's Rd. **National Express buses** stop at Pool Valley, at the southern angle of Old Steine; buy tickets from **One Stop Travel.** (16 Old Steine. ☎ 01273 700 406; National Express ☎ 08705 808080. 2hr., 15 per day, £14.50 return.)

St. Mary's Church

ORIENTATION & PRACTICAL INFORMATION. Queen's Road connects the train station to the English Channel, becoming **West Street** at the intersection with **Western Street.** Funky stores and restaurants cluster around **Trafalgar Street.** The narrow streets of **the Lanes,** left off Prince Albert St., provide an anarchic setting for Brighton's nightlife. **Old Steine,** a road and a square, runs in front of the Royal Pavilion, while **King's Road** runs along the waterfront. The **Tourist Information Centre** runs **walking tours** June-Aug. *(10 Bartholomew Sq. ☎0906 711 2255; www.visit-brighton.com. Walking tours £3. Open Mar.-Oct. M-F 9am-5pm, Sa 10am-5pm, Su 10am-4pm; Nov.-Feb. M-F 9am-5pm, Sa 10am-5pm.)*

ACCOMMODATIONS. Frequent conventions make rooms scarce—book early or consult the TIC upon arrival. Many mid-range B&Bs line **Madeira Place;** shabbier B&Bs and hotels collect west of **West Pier** and in Kemp Town east of **Palace Pier.** ◪**Baggies Backpackers ❶** has live jazz, spontaneous parties, murals, and spacious dorms, plus some doubles. *(33 Oriental Pl. ☎01273 733 740. Key deposit £5. Dorms £12, doubles £30.)* At ◪**Hotel Pelirocco ❹**, rock-star longings are fulfilled with over-the-top, hip-to-be-camp style. 19 individually themed swanky rooms. *(10 Regency Sq. ☎01273 327 055. Singles £50-55; doubles £85-125.)* Lively and social **Brighton Backpackers Hostel ❶** has a great location with many rooms overlooking the ocean. *(75-76 Middle St. ☎01273 777 717. Dorms £11-£12; doubles £25-£30.)* **Cavalaire Guest House ❷** has comfortable rooms ideal for a lazy weekend in town. *(34 Upper Rock Gdns. ☎01273 696 899. Singles £29; doubles from £70.)*

CAMBRIDGE

🚊 *Travel time from central London: 50min. from King's Cross by train; 1½hr. from Liverpool St. by train; 2hr. from Victoria Coach Station by bus.*

Cambridge was a typical market town until the 13th century, when an academic schism sent Oxford's refugees to the banks of the Cam. In contrast to metropolitan Oxford, Cambridge is determined to retain its pastoral academic robes; as a town it's smaller, quieter, and more beautiful. Visitors can enter most colleges from 9am to 5:30pm, though virtually all close during the exam period from May to mid-June.

KING'S PARADE TO ST. JOHN'S ST. Founded twice—by Queen Margaret of Anjou in 1448 and again by Elizabeth Woodville in 1465—**Queens' College** has the only unaltered Tudor court in Cambridge. *(Silver St. ☎01223 335 511. College open Mar.-Oct. daily 10am-4:30pm. Closed during exams. £1.30.)* The most famous colleges are found along the east side of the Cam between Magdalene Bridge and Silver St. Founded, along with Eton, by Henry VI, **King's College** features most heavily on postcards thanks to its soaring chapel, perhaps the finest piece of Perpendicular architecture in the world. *(King's Parade. ☎01223 331 100. Chapel and grounds open M-Sa 9:30am-4:30pm, Su 10am-5pm. Evensong 5:30pm most nights. Contact TIC for tours. £3.50, concessions £2.50, under 12 free.)* Behind King's chapel, **Senate House** is where graduation ceremonies are held. *(Closed to visitors.)* Just opposite, you can climb the tower of **Great St. Mary's,** the university's official church, for a view of the greens and the colleges. Pray that the 12 bells don't ring while you're ascending. *(Tower open M-Sa 9:30am-5pm, Su 12:30-5pm. £1.85, children 60p, family £4.20.)* Founded by Henry VIII, **Trinity College** is the largest and wealthiest college. Isaac Newton heads a list of alumni including Byron, Tennyson, Nabokov, Russell, Wittgenstein, and Nehru. The pride of the college is Christopher Wren's Library, whose treasures include A.A. Milne's handwritten manuscript of *Winnie the Pooh* and Newton's own *Principia*. *(Trinity St. ☎01223 338 400. Chapel and courtyards open daily 10am-5pm. Library open M-F noon-2pm. Easter-Oct. £2, concessions £1; otherwise free.)* Next to Trinity, arch-rival **St. John's College** is established in 1511 by Henry VIII's mother. The Bridge of Sighs connects the older part of the college to the neo-Gothic extravagance of New Court. The oldest complete building in Cambridge, School of Pythagoras's 12th-century pile of wood and stone hides in the college gardens. *(St. John's St. ☎01223 338 600. Open daily 10am-5:30pm. £2, concessions £1.20, family £4.)*

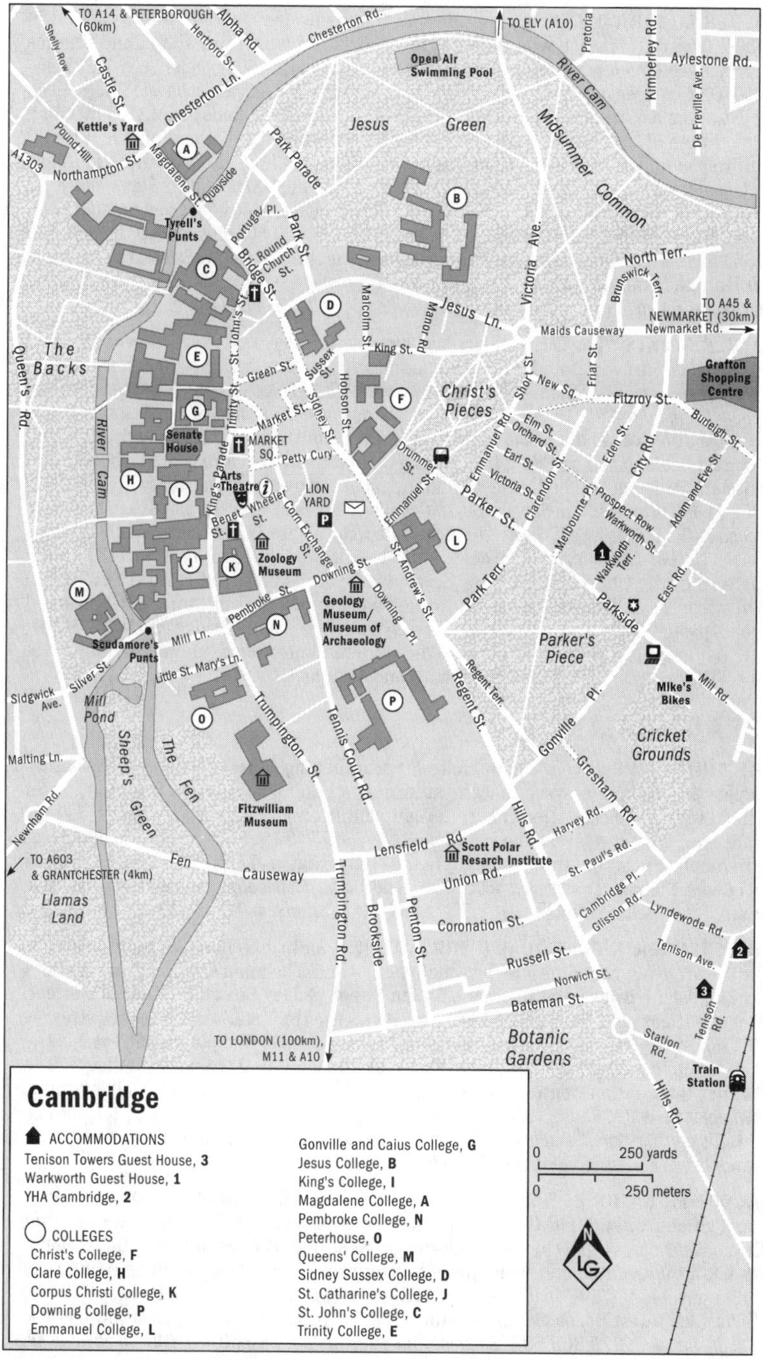

TO A14 & PETERBOROUGH (60km)
TO ELY (A10)
TO A45 & NEWMARKET (30km)
TO A603 & GRANTCHESTER (4km)
TO LONDON (100km), M11 & A10
Shelly Row
Castle St.
Hertford St.
Alpha Rd.
Chesterton Rd.
Chesterton Ln.
Open Air Swimming Pool
Pretoria
Kimberley Rd.
Aylestone Rd.
De Freville Ave.
River Cam
Jesus Green
Midsummer Common
Kettle's Yard
Pound Hill
A1303
Northampton St.
Magdalene St.
Quayside
Park Parade
Tyrell's Punts
Portugal Pl.
Round Church St.
Bridge St.
Park St.
North Terr.
Brunswick Terr.
Victoria Ave.
Malcolm St.
Manor Rd.
Jesus Ln.
Maids Causeway
Newmarket Rd.
St. John's St.
King St.
Friar St.
Short St.
Grafton Shopping Centre
The Backs
Queen's Rd.
Green St.
Sussex St.
Hobson St.
Christ's Pieces
New Sq.
Fitzroy St.
Trinity St.
Market St.
Sidney St.
Emmanuel Rd.
Elm St.
Orchard St.
Burleigh St.
River Cam
Senate House
MARKET SQ.
Petty Cury
Drummer St.
Earl St.
Eden St.
City Rd.
King's Parade
Arts Theatre
LION YARD
Emmanuel St.
Victoria St.
Clarendon St.
Prospect Row
Adam and Eve St.
Benet St.
Wheeler St.
Corn Exchange St.
Parker St.
Melbourne Pl.
Warkworth St.
Warkworth Terr.
Zoology Museum
Downing St.
St. Andrew's St.
Park Terr.
East Rd.
Pembroke St.
Geology Museum/ Museum of Archaeology
Downing Pl.
Parkside
Scudamore's Punts
Mill Ln.
Parker's Piece
Little St. Mary's Ln.
Regent Terr.
Mike's Bikes
Mill Rd.
Sidgwick Ave.
Silver St.
Mill Pond
Regent St.
Trumpington St.
Tennis Court Rd.
Gonville Pl.
Cricket Grounds
Malting Ln.
Sheep's Green
The Fen
Fitzwilliam Museum
Gresham Rd.
Newnham Rd.
Hills Rd.
Harvey Rd.
Lensfield Rd.
Scott Polar Resarch Institute
Fen Causeway
St. Paul's Rd.
Union Rd.
Llamas Land
Trumpington Rd.
Brookside
Penton St.
Cambridge Pl.
Glisson Rd.
Lyndewode Rd.
Coronation St.
Tenison Ave.
Russell St.
Norwich St.
Bateman St.
Tenison Rd.
Botanic Gardens
Station Rd.
Train Station
Hills Rd.
Cambridge
ACCOMMODATIONS
Tenison Towers Guest House, 3
Warkworth Guest House, 1
YHA Cambridge, 2
COLLEGES
Christ's College, F
Clare College, H
Corpus Christi College, K
Downing College, P
Emmanuel College, L
Gonville and Caius College, G
Jesus College, B
King's College, I
Magdalene College, A
Pembroke College, N
Peterhouse, O
Queens' College, M
Sidney Sussex College, D
St. Catharine's College, J
St. John's College, C
Trinity College, E
0 250 yards
0 250 meters
N
LG

OTHER MAJOR COLLEGES. Founded as "God's-house" in 1448 and renamed in 1505, **Christ's** has since won fame for its association with John Milton and Charles Darwin—his rooms were on G staircase in First Court. *(St. Andrews St. ☎01223 334 900. Gardens open in summer M-F 9:30am-noon; term-time M-F 9:30am-noon and 2-4pm. Free.)* Occupying a 15th-century Benedictine hostel, **Magdalene College** (MAUD-lin), one time home of C.S. Lewis, is renowned for its traditionalism—the dining hall is still entirely candlelit. The **Pepys Library** in the second court houses the diarist's journals. *(Magdalene St. ☎01223 332 100. Library open Easter-Aug. 11:30am-12:30pm and 2:30-3:30pm; Sept.-Easter M-Sa 2:30-3:30pm. Free.)* **Peterhouse** is the oldest and smallest college, founded in 1294. *(Trumpington St. ☎01223 338 200.)* **Corpus Christi**, founded in 1352 by townspeople, contains the snazziest collection of Anglo-Saxon manuscripts in England, including the *Anglo-Saxon Chronicle.* Alums include Sir Francis Drake and Christopher Marlowe. *(Trumpington St. ☎01223 338 000.)*

OTHER SIGHTS. The ▓**Fitzwilliam Museum** has a fine array of Impressionists and some Blake drawings and woodcuts, along with ancient statuary, medieval armor, and far-eastern porcelain. *(Trumpington St. ☎01223 332 900. Tours Sa 2:45pm; £3. Open Tu-Sa 10am-5pm, Su 2:15-5pm. Free, suggested donation £3.)* The former house of Tate curator Jim Ede, **Kettle's Yard** hardly resembles a museum at all; the early 20th-century art is displayed as Ede left it, among a homely atmosphere of beds, books, and trinkets. Adjacent to the house, a modern gallery shows contemporary art. *(☎01223 352 124. House open Apr.-Sept. Tu-Su 1:30-4:30pm; Oct.-Mar. Tu-Su 2-4pm. Gallery open year-round Tu-Su 11:30am-5pm. Free.)* The **Round Church,** where Bridge St. meets St. John's St., is one of five surviving circular churches in England, first built in 1130 on the pattern of the Church of the Holy Sepulchre in Jerusalem. *(☎01223 311 602. Free.)* On warm days, Cambridge takes to the river on **punts,** traditional flat-bottomed boats propelled by a pole. You can rent at **Tyrell's,** Magdalene Bridge *(☎01480 394 941; £12 per hr. plus a £60 deposit)* or take the student-punted **tours** (about £10). Inquire at the TIC for a complete list of companies and options.

PRACTICALITIES

GETTING THERE. Every 30min. **trains** leave from **King's Cross** (50min.) and from **Liverpool St.** (1¼hr.); beware that the station is a good 30min. walk from the center (head to the end of Station Rd., turn right, and keep going), and city buses (£1) are rare after 6pm and on Sundays. *(Station Rd. ☎08457 484 950. Day return £15.60.)* **Buses** are much slower, but drop you right in the center; **National Express** arrives from **Victoria Coach Station.** *(Drummer St. ☎08705 808 080. 2hr., 17 per day, from £9.)* **Taxi** services in Cambridge include Cabco *(☎01223 312 444)* and Camtax *(☎01223 313 131)*, both 24hr.

ORIENTATION & PRACTICAL INFORMATION. Cambridge has two main avenues, both suffering from multiple personality disorder. The main shopping street starts at **Magdalene Bridge** and becomes **Bridge Street, Sidney Street, St. Andrew's Street, Regent Street,** and finally **Hills Road** as it nears the train station. The other street—**St. John's Street,** then **Trinity Street, King's Parade,** and **Trumpington Street**—is the academic thoroughfare, parallel to the river but separated from it by colleges. The **Tourist Information Centre,** a block south of Market Sq., runs 2hr. **walking tours.** *(Wheeler St. ☎09065 862 526; www.tourismcambridge.com. Walking tour £7.50, children £4.25; call for times. Open Apr.-Oct. M-F 10am-5:30pm, Sa 10am-5pm, Su 11am-4pm; Nov.-Mar. M-F 10am-5:30pm, Sa 10am-5pm.)*

ACCOMMODATIONS. Hostel and B&B reservations are essential in summer. Pick up a guide from the TIC (50p) or check the comprehensive list in the window after it closes. Located two blocks from the train station, ▓**Tenison Towers Guest House** ❷ is an impeccable and welcoming house; breakfast includes homemade bread and marmelade. *(148 Tenison Rd. ☎01223 566 511. Singles £20-25; doubles £40-50.)* ▓**Warwick Guest House** ❸ offers sunny, ensuite rooms near the bus station. *(Warkworth Terr. ☎01223 363 682. Singles from £40, twins from £60)* At **YHA Cambridge** ❶,

the staff fosters a relaxed atmosphere, although more showers wouldn't hurt. *(97 Tenison Rd. ☎ 01223 354 601. Reserve ahead. 3- to 4-bed dorms £16, under-18s £12.)*

CANTERBURY

the staff fosters a relaxed atmosphere, although more showers wouldn't hurt. *(97 Tenison Rd. ☎ 01223 354 601. Reserve ahead. 3- to 4-bed dorms £16, under-18s £12.)*

CANTERBURY

⏱ Travel time from central London: *1½hr. from Victoria, Waterloo, and Charing Cross by train; 2hr. from Victoria Coach Station by bus.*

Flung somewhere between the cathedral and the open road, the soul of Canterbury is as flighty as the city's itinerant visitors. Saint Thomas à Becket met his demise in Canterbury Cathedral after an irate Henry II asked, "Will no one rid me of this troublesome priest?" and a few of his henchmen took the hint. In the near millennium since, the site has become the focus of many pilgrimages dedicated to the "the hooly blisful martir."

Pembroke College

█ CANTERBURY CATHEDRAL. The focal point of English Christianity since St. Augustine consecrated it in the 6th century, Canterbury Cathedral became the nation's primary pilgrimage destination following the 1170 murder of Archbishop (now Saint) Thomas à Becket. The murder site is closed off by a rail—a kind of permanent police line—around the Altar of the Sword's Point. In the adjacent **Trinity Chapel,** a solitary candle marks where Becket's body lay until 1538, when Henry VIII burned his remains and destroyed the shrine to show how he dealt with bishops who crossed the king. In a structure plagued by fire and rebuilt time and again, the 12th-century **crypt** remains intact. The **Corona Tower,** 105 steps above the easternmost apse, is recently renovated. *(☎ 01227 762 862. Cathedral open M-Sa 9am-5pm, Su 12:30-2:30pm. Evensong M-F 5:30pm, Sa-Su 3:15pm. Tours £3.50, concessions £2.50.)*

St. John's College

OTHER SIGHTS. Inevitably, someone would come up with an attraction called **The Canterbury Tales.** Let the gap-toothed Wife of Bath and her waxen companions entertain you with abbreviated versions of the tales. *(St. Margaret's St. ☎ 01227 479 227. Open daily 10am-5pm. £6.75, concessions £5.50, family £19.)* Soaring arches, crumbling walls, and silent altars are all that remain of **St. Augustine's Abbey,** founded in AD 598. Don't miss St. Augustine's humble tomb under a pile of rocks. *(Outside the city wall near the cathedral. ☎ 01227 767 345. Open Apr.-Oct. daily 10am-6pm; Nov.-Mar. 10am-4pm. £3, concessions £2.30, children £1.50.)* Just around the corner from St. Augustine's on North Holmes St.

All Soul's College

the staff fosters a relaxed atmosphere, although more showers wouldn't hurt. *(97 Tenison Rd. ☎ 01223 354 601. Reserve ahead. 3- to 4-bed dorms £16, under-18s £12.)*

stands the **Church of St. Martin.** King Ethelbert married the Christian Princess Bertha here in AD 562, paving the way for England's conversion to Christianity. Joseph Conrad lies in an underground heart of darkness. *(North Holmes St.* ☎*01227 459 482. Open daily 9am-5pm. Free.)* The **Museum of Canterbury** spans Canterbury's history from its earliest days to beloved children's-book character Rupert Bear. *(Stour St.* ☎*01227 452 747. Open June-Sept. M-Sa 10am-5pm, Su 1:30-5pm; Nov.-May M-Sa 10:30am-5pm. £3, concessions £2.)* England's first Franciscan friary, **Greyfriars** was built over the River Stour in 1267 by Franciscan monks who arrived in the country in 1224, two years before Saint Francis of Assisi died. A museum and chapel are found inside the building. *(Stour St. Open summer M-F 2-4pm. Free.)* Near the city walls to the southwest lie the remnants of **Canterbury Castle,** built for the Conqueror himself.

PRACTICALITIES

GETTING THERE. Canterbury has two **train** stations. **Connex South** runs to **Canterbury East** from **Victoria.** *(Station Rd. East, off Castle St. Station open M-Sa 6:10am-8:20pm, Su 6:10am-9:20pm. National Rail Enquiries* ☎*08457 484950. 1½hr.; 2 per hr.; £16.50, day return £16.20.)* Connex also serves **Canterbury West** from **Charing Cross** and **Waterloo.** *(Station Rd. West, off St. Dunstan's St. Station open M-F 6:15am-8pm, Sa 6:30am-8pm, Su 7:15am-9:30pm. 1½hr., every hr. 1½hr.; 2 per hr.; £16.50, day return £16.20.)* **National Express buses** arrive at St. George's Ln. from **Victoria Coach Station.** *(*☎*08705 808080. 2hr., every hr., £10.50.)*

ORIENTATION & PRACTICAL INFORMATION. Canterbury is roughly circular, as defined by the eroding city wall. An unbroken street crosses the city from northwest to southeast, changing names from **St. Peter's St.** to **High St.** to **The Parade** to **St. George's St.** The **tourist information centre** gives out a free mini-guide. *(The Buttermarket, 12/13 Sun St.* ☎*01227 378 100. Bed booking £2.50 and 10% deposit. Open M-Sa 9:30am-5:30pm, Su 10am-4pm.)*

ACCOMMODATIONS. Reserve ahead, or arrive mid-morning to grab recently vacated rooms. B&Bs are concentrated around the lanes stemming from High St., with quite a few scattered near West Station. Oh-so-wittily named, ◪**Kipps, A Place to Sleep ❶** is a 5-10min. walk from the city center, with a variety of accommodations and a terrific kitchen. *(40 Nunnery Fields.* ☎*01227 786 121. Key deposit £10. Dorms £11-13; singles £17.50; doubles £30.)* **YHA Canterbury ❶** is ¾ mi. from East Station and ½ mi. southeast of the bus station; book at least two weeks ahead in summer. *(54 New Dover Rd.* ☎*01227 462 911; canterbury@yha.org.uk. Reception 7:30-10am and 3-11pm. Dorms £15.50, under-18s £8.)* The **Castle Court Guest House ❷** is a few minutes from Eastgate in the old town. *(8 Castle St.* ☎*/fax 01227 463 441. Singles £25, doubles £40-50. 5% discount for Let's Go users.)*

NEAR CANTERBURY: LEEDS CASTLE

�🔟 ☎*01622 765 400 or 0870 600 8880. Castle open Mar.-Oct. daily 11am-7:30pm; Nov.-Feb. 10:15am-5:30pm. Grounds open Mar.-Oct. daily 10am-7pm; Nov.-Feb. 10am-5pm. Last admission 2hr. before close. Castle and grounds £12, concessions £10.50, children £8.50, family £35. Grounds only £9.50/£8/£6.20/£27.*

Billed as "the Loveliest Castle in the World," Leeds Castle was built immediately after the Norman Conquest. Henry VIII made it a lavish dwelling whose woodlands and gardens still host unusual waterfowl, including black swans. Outside, lose yourself in a **maze** of 2400 yew trees; the sculpted grounds, vivid gardens, and forests, meanwhile, are almost a maze in themselves.

GETTING THERE. Leeds Castle is 23 mi. southwest of Canterbury on the A20 London-Folkestone road near Maidstone. Take the train to **Bearsted** from **Canterbury West** or **London Victoria;** a shuttlebus runs to the castle (£3.40).

OXFORD

🚌 *Travel time from central London:* 1hr. from Paddington by train; 1¾hr. from Victoria Coach Station, Marble Arch, and near Baker St. by bus.

Oxford had been a center of learning for a century before Henry II founded the university in 1167. Though tourists now outnumber scholars, Oxford has irrepressible grandeur and pockets of tranquility, most famously the perfectly maintained quadrangles ("quads") of the university's 39 colleges. Most colleges are free to enter, though some charge admission in high season; opening hours for visitors are restricted, however, especially April to early June as students prepare for exams.

■ **ASHMOLEAN MUSEUM.** Opened in 1683, the Ashmolean was Britain's first public gallery, and now plays host to familiar favorites including Leonardo, Monet, Manet, Van Gogh, Michelangelo, Rodin, and Matisse. Renovated galleries also house ancient Islamic, Greek, and Far Eastern art. *(Beaumont St. From Carfax, head up Cornmarket St., which becomes Magdalene St.; Beaumont St. is on the left. ☎01865 278 000. Open Tu-Sa 10am-5pm, Su 2-5pm; Th until 7:30pm in summer. Free.)*

MAJOR COLLEGES. Christ Church, grand enough for Charles I to make it his capital during the Civil War, is centered around Tom Quad, named for the bell which has rung at 9:05pm (the original student curfew) every evening since 1682. The college's art gallery includes works by Tintoretto and Vermeer, with Leonardo and Michelangelo occasionally coming out of hiding. *(Just down St. Aldates St. from Carfax; for gallery only, enter at Canterbury Gate off Oriel St. College ☎01865 286 573, gallery 01865 276 172. College open M-Sa 9am-noon and 2:30-5:15pm, Su 9:45am-noon and 2:30-4:45pm; in winter closes 4:30pm. No entry after 4pm. Gallery open Apr.-Sept. M-Sa 10:30am-1pm and 2-5:30pm, Su 2-5:30pm; Oct.-Mar. closes 4:30pm. College £4, concessions £3; gallery £2/£1.)* **Merton College** has Oxford's oldest quad, the 14th-century Mob Quad, and an equally ancient library holding the first printed Welsh Bible. *(Merton St. ☎01865 276 310. Open M-F 2-4pm, Sa-Su 10am-4pm. Closed around Easter and Christmas. Free.)* **University College** dates from 1249 and vies with Merton for the title of oldest college; misbehaving alums include Shelley, expelled for his pamphlet *The Necessity of Atheism,* and a non-inhaling Bill Clinton. *(High St. ☎01865 276 676.)* Around since 1341, **Queen's College** was later rebuilt by Wren and Hawksmoor in orange, white, and gold. A trumpet call summons students to dinner. *(High St. ☎01865 279 121. Open only to tours.)* **Magdalen College** (MAUD-lin), with flower-laced quads and a private deer park, is considered Oxford's handsomest, and thus a natural choice for budding aesthete Oscar Wilde. *(On High St. near the River Cherwell. ☎01865 276 000. Open daily 1-6pm. £2, concessions £1.)* Founded in 1555, **Trinity College** has a splendid Baroque chapel, with a limewood altarpiece, cedar lattices, and cherubim everywhere. *(Broad St. ☎01865 279 900. Open M-F 10am-noon and 2-4:30pm. £1.50.)* Founded in 1379, **New College** is actually one of Oxford's oldest colleges. The bell tower has equally grotesque gargoyles of the Seven Deadly Sins on one side and the Seven Virtues on the other. "Spoonerisms" are named for former warden William Spooner, who once rebuked a student that he had "tasted the whole worm." *(New College Ln. ☎01865 279 555. Open daily Easter to mid-Oct. 11am-5pm; Nov.-Easter 2-4pm, use the Holywell St. Gate. £1.50 in the summer, free otherwise.)*

OTHER SIGHTS. The **Bodleian** was endowed in 1602 and is Oxford's principal library. No one has ever been allowed to take out even one of its five million volumes. Only scholars may enter the reading rooms; student ID may suffice, but an academic letter of introduction is recommended. *(Catte St. Take High St. and turn left on Catte. ☎01865 277 224. Tours start at the Divinity School, across the street; in summer M-F 4 per day, Sa-Su 2 per day; in winter 2 per day. £3.50. Library open M-F 9am-6pm, Sa 9am-1pm; 2-day reader ticket £3.)* A teenage Christopher Wren designed the Roman-style **Sheldonian Theatre,** now the site of graduation ceremonies; its cupola affords an inspiring view. The stone heads on the fence behind the theater are a 20th-century study of beards. *(Broad St. ☎01865 277 299. Open approx. M-Sa 10am-12:30pm and 2-4:30pm. £1.50, under*

285

Royal Blenheim

Sheldonian Theatre

Shopping in Oxford

15 £1.) A hike up the medieval **Carfax Tower's** 99 spiral stairs gives a fantastic view of the city. *(Corner of Queen and Cornmarket St. ☎01865 792 653. Open Apr.-Oct. M-Sa 10am-5pm, Su 11am-5pm. £1.40, under 16 70p.)* Haul yourself past the rural banks of the rivers Thames (called Isis in Oxford) and Cherwell on a traditional **punt.** Magdalen Bridge Boat Co. rents from March to November. *(Magdalen Bridge. ☎01865 202 643. M-F £9 per hr., Sa-Su £10 per hr.; deposit £20 plus ID. Open Mar.-Nov. daily 10am-9pm.)*

PRACTICALITIES

GETTING THERE. The railway station, a 10min. walk from the historic center, is served by **Thames Trains** from **Paddington.** *(Botley Rd., down Park End. Trains ☎08457 484 950. 1hr., 2-4 per hr., day return £14.30.)* **Oxford CityLink** runs 3 buses per hr. from London. *(☎01865 785 400. 1¾hr., £10 next day return.)* Oxford Tube operates 6 buses per hr. to **Victoria Coach Station.** *(Bus station, Gloucester Green. Oxford Tube ☎01865 772 250. 2 hr., next-day return £8.50).*

ORIENTATION & PRACTICAL INFORMATION. While Oxford is a fair-sized town, the historic center is easily walkable. The easiest way to orient yourself is to locate the colossal **Carfax Tower,** from which most colleges lie to the east. The **Tourist Information Centre,** beside the bus station, sells a £1 street map and guide with a valuable index. *(15-16 Broad St., Gloucester Green. ☎01865 726 871; www.visitoxford.org. Open M-Sa 9:30am-5pm, Su 10am-3:30pm.)*

ACCOMMODATIONS. Book at least a week ahead June-September. The superbly located **YHA Oxford ❶** is an immediate right from the station onto Botley Rd. *(2a Botley Rd. ☎01865 727 275. Breakfast included. 4- to 6-bed dorms £19, under 18 £14.)* **Heather House ❷** has sparkling rooms and exceptionally helpful staff. *(192 Iffley Rd. Walk 20min. or take the "Rose Hill" bus from the bus or train station or Carfax Tower (70p). ☎/fax 01865 249 757. Singles £33, doubles £66; discounts on longer stays.)* The recently refurbished **Falcon Private Hotel ❸** offers TV, phone, and shower in rooms. *(88-90 Abingdon Rd. ☎01865 511 122. Singles £36; doubles £58-72, triples from £80.)*

NEAR OXFORD: BLENHEIM PALACE

⌨ ☎01993 811 091. Open daily mid-Mar. to Oct. 10:30am-5:30pm, last entry 4:45pm; grounds open daily 9am-9pm. Free tours every 10min. £10.50, concessions £7.50, children £5, family £27.

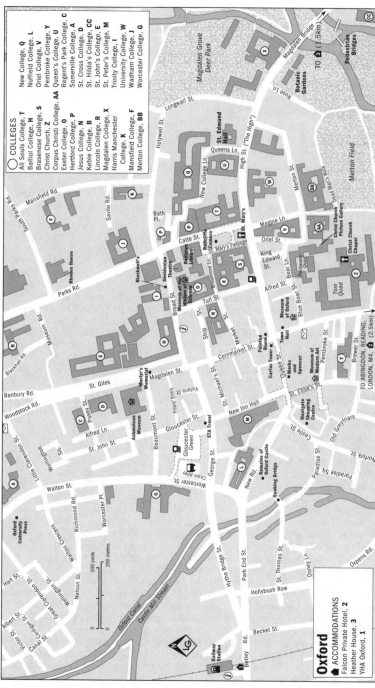

COLLEGES

All Souls College, **T**	New College, **Q**
Balliol College, **H**	Nuffield College, **L**
Brasenose College, **S**	Oriel College, **V**
Christ Church, **Z**	Pembroke College, **Y**
Corpus Christi College, **AA**	Queen's College, **U**
Exeter College, **O**	Regent's Park College, **C**
Hertford College, **P**	Somerville College, **A**
Jesus College, **N**	St. Cross College, **D**
Keble College, **B**	St. Hilda's College, **CC**
Lincoln College, **R**	St. John's College, **E**
Magdalen College, **X**	St. Peter's College, **M**
Harris Manchester	Trinity College, **I**
College, **K**	University College, **W**
Mansfield College, **F**	Wadham College, **J**
Merton College, **BB**	Worcester College, **G**

Oxford

▲ ACCOMMODATIONS

Falcon Private Hotel, **2**
Heather House, **3**
YHA Oxford, **1**

287

The largest private home in England, Blenheim (BLEN-em) was built in appreciation of the Duke of Marlborough's victory over Louis XIV at the Battle of Blenheim in 1704. Another family scion, **Winston Churchill** grew up here; his baby curls are on display, while he rests in the nearby village churchyard of Bladon. **Capability Brown** designed the 2100 acres of gardens.

GETTING THERE. The palace is in **Woodstock,** 8 mi. north of Oxford; take the **Stagecoach** from Gloucester Green bus station. (☎01865 772 250. 30-40min., every 30min. 8:15am-5pm, return £3.50.)

SALISBURY & STONEHENGE

🚩 *Travel time from central London:* 1½hr. from Waterloo by train; 2¾hr. from Victoria Coach Station by bus.

Salisbury's fame comes from two remarkable historic monuments: its cathedral, with the highest spire in Europe, and the mysterious monoliths of nearby Stonehenge.

SALISBURY CATHEDRAL. Salisbury Cathedral rises from its grassy close to a neck- and record-breaking height of 404 ft. Built in just 38 years, starting in 1320, the cathedral has a singular and weighty design. The bases of the marble pillars bend inward under the strain of 6400 tons of limestone. Nearly 700 years have left the cathedral in need of structural and surface repair, and scaffolding shrouds parts of the outer walls where the stone is disintegrating. The chapel houses the oldest functioning mechanical clock, a strange collection of wheels and ropes that has ticked 500 million times over the last 600 years. Much to King John's chagrin, the best-preserved of four surviving copies of the *Magna Carta* rests in the Chapter House. (33 The Close. ☎01722 555 120. Cathedral open June-Aug. M-Sa 7:15am-8:15pm, Su 7:15am-6:15pm; Sept.-May daily 7:15am-6:15pm. Chapter House open June-Aug. M-Sa 9:30am-5:30pm, Su noon-5:30pm; Sept.-May daily 9:30am-5:30pm. 1½hr. tours of the roof and tower May-Sept. M-Sa 11am, 2, 3pm, and Su 4:30pm; June-Aug. M-Sa also 6:30pm. Suggested donation £3, concessions £2.)

STONEHENGE. A ring of submerged colossi amid swaying grass and indifferent sheep, Stonehenge stands unperturbed by whipping winds. The present stones—22 ft. high—comprise the fifth temple constructed on the site. The first probably consisted of an arch and circular earthwork furrowed in 3050 BC, and was in use for about 500 years. Its relics are the **Aubrey Holes** (white patches in the earth) and the **Heel Stone** (the rough block standing outside the circle). The current monument is still more impressive considering that its stones, weighing up to 45 tons, were hauled all the way from Wales and erected by a tedious process of rope-and-log leverage—legend holds that the stones were magically transported here by Merlin. In 300 BC, Celts arrived from the Continent and claimed Stonehenge as their shrine; today, Druids are permitted to enter Stonehenge on midsummer to perform ceremonial exercises. (☎01980 624 715. Open June-Aug. daily 9am-7pm; mid-Mar. to May and Sept. to mid-Oct. 9:30am-6pm; mid-Oct. to mid-Mar. 9:30am-4pm. £4.40, concessions £3.30, children £2.20, family £11.) Getting to Stonehenge from Salisbury doesn't require much effort—as long as you don't have a 45-ton rock in tow. **Wilts and Dorset bus** #3 runs from Salisbury station (☎01722 336 855. 40min., return £5.25). An **Explorer** ticket ($5.25) allows you to travel all day on any bus, including those stopping by **Avebury,** Stonehenge's less-crowded cousin. The most scenic **walking** or **cycling** route from Salisbury is the **Woodford Valley Route.** Go north on Castle Rd., bear left just before Victoria Park onto Stratford Rd., and follow the road over the bridge through Lower, Middle, and Upper Woodford. After about 9 mi., turn left onto the A303 for the last mile. If Stonehenge isn't enough rock for you, look over your right for Sting's Jacobean mansion.

PRACTICALITIES

GETTING THERE. Trains leave every 30min. from **Waterloo.** *(South Western Rd., across the Avon.* ☎ *08457 484 950. 1½hr., £22-30.)* **National Express buses** make the trip from **Victoria Coach Station.** *(8 Endless St. Bus station* ☎ *01722 336 855; National Express* ☎ *08705 808 080. 2¾hr., 4 per day. Return £13.10.)*

ORIENTATION & PRACTICAL INFORMATION. That all roads in Salisbury seem to lead to its cathedral gates is no accident—the streetplan was charted by Bishop Poore in the 13th century. The **Tourist Information Centre** is in the Guildhall, Market Sq., and runs 1½hr. **city tours.** *(Fish Row.* ☎ *01722 334 956; www.visitsalisbury.com. Tours Apr.-Oct. 11am and 8pm, June-Aug. also 6pm; £2.50, children £1. Open June-Sept. M-Sa 9:30am-6pm, Su 10:30am-4:30pm; Oct.-Apr. M-Sa 9:30am-5pm; May M-Sa 9:30am-5pm, Su 10:30am-4:30pm.)*

ACCOMMODATIONS. Salisbury's proximity to Stonehenge breeds B&Bs, most of them comfortable and reasonably priced, though they fill quickly in summer. **YHA Salisbury ❶** is tucked into a cedar grove; reserve ahead in the summer. *(Milford Hill House, Milford Hill.* ☎ *01722 327 572. Lockout 10am-1pm. Dorms £14.50, under-18s £11.25.)* **Matt and Tiggy's ❶** is a welcoming 450-year-old house with warped floors and ceiling beams and an overflow house nearby. Mellow, hostel-style, 2- to 4-person rooms. *(51 Salt Ln., just up from the bus station.* ☎ *01722 327 443. Breakfast £2.50. Sheets £1. Dorms £11-12.)* **Farthings B&B ❷** is a peaceful haven with a lovely garden. *(9 Swaynes Close, a 10min. walk from city center.* ☎ *01722 330 749. Singles £25-27; doubles £46-55.)*

STRATFORD-UPON-AVON

🖪 *Travel time from central London: 2¼hr. from Paddington by train; 3hr. by bus.*

Shakespeare lived here. Admittedly, he got out as soon as he could, but even so millions make the pilgrimage here every year, showing their dedication by purchasing "Will Power" T-shirts, dining on faux-Tudor fast food, and dutifully traipsing through all the many sights vaguely connected to the Bard and his family. Yet for all that Stratford has milked its one cow, it still deserves a visit for the grace of the weeping Avon and the excellence of the Royal Shakespeare Company's productions.

SHAKESPEAREAN SIGHTS. Two combination tickets are available for Will-seekers. The **Three In-Town Houses** ticket covers the "official" Shakespeare sights in town—the Birthplace, Hall's Croft, and Nash's House and New Place. *(£9, concessions £8, children £4.50, family £29.)* For fanatics, the **All Five Houses Ticket** throws in the more distant Anne Hathaway's Cottage and Mary Arden's House. *(£13, concessions £12, children £6.50, family £21.)* The least crowded way to pay homage is to visit the Bard's tiny grave in **Holy Trinity Church,** though groups still pack the arched door at peak hours. *(Trinity St. £1, students & children 50p.)* **Shakespeare's Birthplace** is now half period recreation and half life-and-about exhibition. *(Henley St.* ☎ *01789 204 016. Open Nov.-Mar. M-Sa 10am-4pm, Su 10:30am-4pm; Apr.-May and Sept.-Oct. M-Sa 10am-5pm, Su 10:30am-5pm; June-Aug. M-Sa 9am-5pm, Su 9:30am-5pm. £6.50, concessions £5.50, children £2.50, family £15.)* **Hall's Croft** follows the work of Dr. John Hall, who aside from being Shakespeare's son-in-law was one of the first doctors to keep detailed records of his patients. *(Old Town.* ☎ *01789 292 107. Open Nov.-Mar. daily 11am-4pm; Apr.-May and Sept.-Oct. daily 11am-5pm; June-Aug. M-Sa 9:30am-5pm, Su 10am-5pm. £3.50, concessions £2.70, children £1.70, family £8.50.)* The first husband of Shakespeare's granddaughter Elizabeth, Thomas Nash has only a tenuous connection to the bard, but a ticket to **Nash's House** also gets you a peek at what little remains of **New Place,** Stratford's hippest home when Shakespeare bought it in 1597. *(Chapel St. Open as Hall's Croft (above). £3.50, concessions £3, children £1.70.)* Will's wife's birthplace, **Anne Hathaway's Cottage** is one mile north of Stratford along ill-marked footpaths. This is the thatched cottage on all the posters; if you've seen the birthplace, there's little need to go inside. *(*☎ *01789 292 100. £5, concessions £4, children £2, family £12.)*

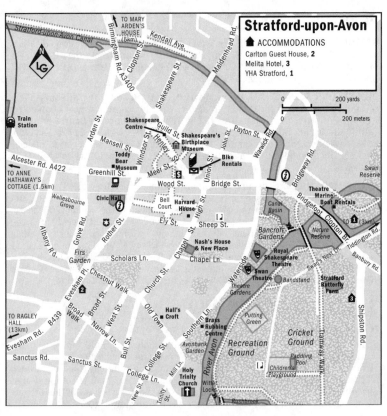

Stratford-upon-Avon

🏠 ACCOMMODATIONS

Carlton Guest House, **2**
Melita Hotel, **3**
YHA Stratford, **1**

THE PLAY'S THE THING. One of the world's finest repertory companies, the acclaimed **Royal Shakespeare Company (RSC)** is what makes Stratford more than an exploitative tourist trap. They even perform plays by other dramaturges, but only the Bard's work graces the stage at the towering **Royal Shakespeare Theatre,** Waterside. Renaissance and restoration plays are given at the neighboring **Swan Theatre,** built to resemble a 16th-century playhouse. If you don't manage to get tickets in advance, join the queue for the main box office about 20min. before opening for same-day sales. A happy few get returns and standing-room tickets for evening shows; queue 1-2hr. before curtain. The RSC also conducts **backstage tours** that cram camera-happy groups into the wooden "O"s of the RST and the Swan. *(Tours: ☎01789 403 405. Daily 5:30pm, 11am on matinee performance days and also M-Sa 1:30pm and Su noon, 1, 2, 3pm. £4, concessions £3. Box office: ☎01789 403 403, www.rsc.org.uk. Open M-Sa 9am-8pm. RST tickets £5-40, Swan £5-36. Standing places £5. Same-day tickets ½ price for those under 25, some at £8-12 for concessions)*

PRACTICALITIES

GETTING THERE. Thames Trains serve Stratford's rail station from **Paddington.** *(Station Rd., off Alcester Rd. ☎08457 484 950. 2¼hr., 7 per day, return £22.50.)* **National Express buses** stop at Riverside Car Park, off Bridgeway Rd. near the Leisure Centre; buy tickets at the tourist centre. *(☎08705 808 080. 3hr., 3 per day, £12.)*

ORIENTATION & PRACTICAL INFORMATION. To get to the **Tourist Information Centre** from the train station, turn left onto Alcester Rd., which becomes Greenhill St., Wood St., Bridge St., and finally Bridgefoot. *(☎01789 293 127. Maps, guidebooks, tickets, and accommodations list. Books rooms for £3 and 10% deposit. Open Apr.-Oct. M-Sa 9am-5pm, Su 10:30am-4:30pm; Nov.-Mar. M-Sa 9am-5pm.)* There is another **branch** in the Civic Hall. *(14 Rother St. ☎299 866. Same hours as above.)*

ACCOMMODATIONS. Be sure to make reservations well ahead in summer. **B&Bs** in the £15-26 range line Grove Rd., Evesham Pl., and Evesham Rd.; if that fails, try Shipston Rd. and Banbury Rd. across the river. **YHA Stratford ❶** is 2 mi. from town, but makes up with attractive grounds, a 200-year-old building, and friendly staff. *(Hemmingford House, Wellesbourne Rd., Alveston. Follow the B4086 road for 35min., or take the hourly #X18 bus from Bridge St. (return £1.80). ☎01789 297 093. Midnight lockout. Breakfast included. Dorms £16, under 18 £11.50.)* For more privacy, **Carlton Guest House ❷** offers spacious rooms and spectacular service at a great price. *(22 Evesham Pl. ☎01789 293 548. Singles £20-26, doubles £40-52.)* **Melita Hotel ❸** is an upscale B&B with a gorgeous garden. *(37 Shipston Rd. ☎01789 292 432. Singles £39; doubles £72.)*

NEAR STRATFORD: WARWICK CASTLE

🄽 ☎01926 495 421, 24hr. recording 01926 406 600. Open Sept. daily 10am-6pm; Oct.-Mar. 10am-5pm. May to mid-Sept. £12.50, seniors £9, students £9.40, children £7.40, family £33; mid-Sept. to April £1-2 less.

Many historians, architects, and fire-breathing dragons regard Warwick Castle as England's finest medieval fortress. Climb the 530 steps to the top of the towers and see the countryside unfold like a fairy-tale kingdom full of hobbits and elves. The dungeons are filled with wax figures of soldiers, and "knights" and "craftsmen" talk about their trades. Also host to medieval games, storytelling by the "Red Knight," and seasonal events such as summer jousting tournaments and Christmas festivals.

GETTING THERE. Trains come from **Stratford** and **London Marylebone.** *(Stratford: 20-40min., 1 every 2hr., £2.70. Marylebone: 2½hr., 2 per hr., £20.50.)* **National Express buses** make the journey from **Stratford** and **Victoria Coach Station.** *(Stratford: 3 per day, 20min., day return £2. London: 3hr., 3 per day, £11.)* For cabs, try **B&R Taxi** *(☎01926 495 000).*

Planning Your Trip

In a city as perennially popular with tourists as London, it's essential to plan your trip in advance—a week or two in the low season, up to two months ahead for the summer, Easter, and Christmas periods. Traveling in the low season can also save you money, and will give you more room to enjoy the city—though with 8 million "locals," tourists are rarely in a majority outside visitor attractions. This section is designed to help you prepare for your trip--after you arrive in London, you can ignore this section and turn instead to **Once in London** (p. 23).

WHEN TO GO

WEATHER

Summers tend to be mild, though London has its occasional hot day. It's just as rainy during the summer as it is the rest of the year. Winters aren't terribly cold; prepare for blustery wind and rain, not snow. London, by the way, isn't very foggy—the famed London fog (actually smog) was banished by clean-air legislation in the 1960s, which turned the city into a smoke-free zone.

Most temperatures in the UK are quoted using the Celsius scale, though many older people still prefer Fahrenheit. To convert from °C to °F multiply by 9/5 and add 32. To convert from °F to °C subtract 32 and multiply by 5/9.

AVGERAGE TEMPERATURE. (HIGH/LOW), PRECIPITATION

JANUARY			APRIL			JULY			OCTOBER		
°C	°F	mm	°C	°F	mm	°C	°F	mm	°C	°F	mm
6/2	43/36	54	13/6	55/43	37	22/14	72/57	59	14/8	57/46	57

2004 HOLIDAYS & FESTIVALS

Winter

Dec. 25	Christmas
Dec. 26	Boxing Day
Dec. 31	New Year's Eve
Jan. 1	New Year's Day
Jan. 22	Chinese New Year

Spring

Mar. 17	St. Patrick's Day
Mar. 28	Oxford & Cambridge Boat Race
Apr. 9	Good Friday
Apr. 12	Easter Monday
Apr. 18	London Marathon
May 1-31	Museums and Galleries Month
May 22	FA Cup Final
May 3	May Day Bank Holiday
May 21-24	Chelsea Flower Show

Summer

Mid June - Mid Aug.	Royal Academy Summer Exhibition
June 4-5	Epsom Derby Day
Mid-Late June	Spitalfields Festival
June 7	Trooping the Color
June 15-19	Royal Ascot
June 21-July 4	Wimbledon Lawn Tennis Championships
June 30-July 4	Henley Royal Regatta
July 16-Sept. 18	BBC "Proms"
Early Aug.	Great British Beer Festival
Aug. 29-30	Notting Hill Carnival
Aug. 30	Summer Bank Holiday

Autumn

Late Sept.	London Open House
Mid. Nov.	London Jazz Festival
Early-Mid Nov.	State Opening of Parliament
Early-Mid. Nov.	London Film Festival
Nov. 5	Bonfire Night
Nov. 13	Lord Mayor's Show
Nov. 9	Remembrance Sunday

EMBASSIES & CONSULATES

BRITISH CONSULAR SERVICES ABROAD

🔰 *For up-to-date information on entry requirements and British consular services, check the Foreign Office (www.fco.gov.uk). For **foreign consular services in London**, see **Once In London**, p. 34.*

For addresses of British embassies in countries not listed here, consult the **Foreign and Commonwealth Office** (☎020 7270 1500; www.fco.gov.uk) or your local telephone directory. Some large cities have a local British consulate that can handle most of the same functions as an embassy.

Australia: British High Commission, Commonwealth Ave., Yarralumla, Canberra, ACT 2600 (☎02 6270 6666; www.uk.emb.gov.au). Consulate-General, Level 10, SAP House, Canberra, ACT 2601 (☎19 0294 1555). Consulates-General in Brisbane, Melbourne, Perth, and Sydney; Consulate in Adelaide.

Canada: British High Commission, 80 Elgin St., Ottawa, ON K1P 5K7 (☎613-237-1530; www.britain-in-canada.org). British Consulate-General, College Park, 777 Bay St., Suite 2800, Toronto, ON M5G 2G2 (☎416-593-1290). Consulates-General also in Montreal and Vancouver; Consulates in Calgary, St. John's, Quebec City, Dartmouth, Winnipeg.

France: British Embassy, 35 Rue du Faubourg-St-Honoré, 75383 Paris CEDEX 08 (☎01 44 51 31 00; www.amb-grandebretagne.fr). Consulate-General, 18 bis rue d'Anjou, 75008 Paris (☎01 44 51 31 00). Consulates-General also in Bordeaux, Lille, Lyon, and Marseille.

Ireland: British Embassy, 29 Merrion Rd., Ballsbridge, Dublin 4 (☎01 205 3700; www.britishembassy.ie).

New Zealand: British High Commission, 44 Hill St., Thorndon, Wellington 1 (☎04 924 2888; www.britain.org.nz); mailing address P.O. Box 1812, Wellington. Consulate-General, 17th fl., NZI House, 151 Queen St., Auckland 1 (☎09 303 2973); mailing address Private Bag 92014, Auckland 1.

South Africa: British High Commission, 91 Parliament St., Cape Town 8001 (☎021 405 2400); also at 255 Hill St., Pretoria 0002 (☎012 483 1200; www.britain.org.za). Consulate-General in Durban; Consulate in Port Elizabeth.

US: British Embassy, 3100 Massachusetts Ave. NW, Washington, D.C. 20008 (☎202-588-6500; www.britainusa.com). Consulate-General, 845 3rd Ave., New York, NY 10022 (☎212-745-0200). Other Consulates-General in Atlanta, Boston, Chicago, Houston, Los Angeles, and San Francisco. Consulates in Dallas, Denver, Miami, and Seattle.

DOCUMENTS & FORMALITIES

PASSPORTS & VISAS

ENTRY REQUIREMENTS. Citizens of European Union countries need only a valid national identity card to enter the UK; citizens of all other countries must be in possession of a valid passport and, if necessary, visa (see below). Note that while the Common Travel Area has abolished regular checks on travel between the UK and Ireland, travelers may still be required to produce the necessary documentation on arrival. Britain does not allow entrance if the holder's passport expires in under six months; returning home with an expired passport is illegal, and may result in a fine.

VISAS. EU citizens do not need a visa to enter the UK. Citizens of Australia, Canada, New Zealand, South Africa, and the US do not require visas for visits of under six months; for a complete list of countries with visa-free travel to the UK, check http://ukvisas.gov.uk. Tourist visas cost £35, and can be obtained from the British consulates listed on p. 295. A visa or relevant permit is required by all non-EU citizens intending to **work** or **study** in the UK, or who intend to stay longer than 6 months for whatever reason. EU citizens staying over 3 months must apply for a residence permit after their arrival in the UK. For details of long-term visas and work, study, and residence permits, see **Alternatives to Tourism**, p. 322.

PHOTOCOPIES. Be sure to photocopy the page of your passport with your photo, passport number, and other identifying information, as well as visas, travel insurance policies, plane tickets, and traveler's check numbers. Carry one set of copies in a safe place, apart from the originals, and leave another set with someone back at home. Consulates also recommend that you carry an expired passport or an official copy of your birth certificate in a part of your baggage separate from other documents.

LOST PASSPORTS. If you lose your passport, immediately notify local police and your nearest national embassy or consulate. To expedite its replacement, you will need to know all information previously recorded and show ID and proof of citizenship. In some cases, a replacement may take weeks to process, and may be valid only for a limited time. Any visas in your old passport will be irretrievably lost. In an emergency, ask for temporary traveling papers that will permit you to re-enter your home country. Your passport is a public document belonging to your nation's government. You may have to surrender it to a foreign government official, but if you don't get it back in a reasonable amount of time, inform your nearest consulate.

IDENTIFICATION

When you travel, always carry at least two forms of identification on your person, including at least one photo ID; a passport combined with a driver's license or birth certificate is usually adequate. Never carry all of your IDs together; split them up in case of theft or loss, and keep photocopies of them in your luggage and at home.

STUDENT, YOUTH, & TEACHER IDENTIFICATION. The **International Student Identity Card (ISIC),** the most widely accepted form of student ID, provides discounts on some sights, accommodations, food, and transport; access to 24hr. emergency helpline (in North America call ☎877-370-ISIC; elsewhere call US collect ☎+1 715-345-0505); and insurance benefits for US cardholders (see **Insurance,** p. 300). Applicants must be degree-seeking students of a secondary or post-secondary school and must be of at least 12 years of age. Because of the proliferation of fake ISICs, some services (particularly airlines) require additional proof of student identity.

The **International Teacher Identity Card (ITIC)** offers teachers the same insurance coverage as well as similar but limited discounts. For travelers who are 25 years old or under but are not students, the **International Youth Travel Card (IYTC)** also offers many of the same benefits as the ISIC. Similarly, the **International Student Exchange ID Card (ISE)** provides discounts, medical benefits, and the ability to purchase student airfares.

Each of these identity cards costs US$22 or the equivalent. ISIC and ITIC cards are valid for roughly one and a half academic years; IYTC cards are valid for one year from the date of issue. Many student travel agencies (see p. 302) issue the cards; for a list of issuing agencies, or for more information, contact the **International Student Travel Confederation (ISTC),** Herengracht 479, 1017 BS Amsterdam, The Netherlands (☎+31 20 421 28 00; www.istc.org).

CUSTOMS

Upon entering the UK, you must declare certain items from abroad and pay a duty on the value of those articles that exceeds the allowance established by the EU customs service. Note that goods and gifts purchased at duty-free shops abroad are not exempt from duty or sales tax at your point of return and thus must be declared as well; "duty-free" merely means that you need not pay a tax in the country of purchase. Duty-free allowances were abolished for travel between EU member states on July 1, 1999 but still exist for those arriving from outside the EU. Upon returning home, you must similarly declare all articles acquired abroad and pay a duty on the value of articles in excess of your home country's allowance. In order to expedite your return, make a list of any valuables brought from home; registering this list with customs before your departure and having an official stamp will avoid import duty charges and ensure an easy passage on your return. Also be sure to keep receipts for all goods acquired abroad.

MONEY

CURRENCY & EXCHANGE

The currency chart below is based on August 2003 exchange rates between United Kingdom pounds and Australian dollars (AUS$), Canadian dollars (CDN$), Irish pounds (IR£), New Zealand dollars (NZ$), South African Rand (ZAR), US dollars (US$), and European Union euros (EUR€). Check the currency converter on financial websites such as www.bloomberg.com and www.xe.com, or a large newspaper for the latest exchange rates.

THE POUND (£)		
AUS$1 = £0.40	£1 = AUS$2.49
CDN$1 = £0.45	£1 = CDN$2.23
NZ$1 = £0.35	£1 = NZ$2.86
ZAR1 = £0.08	£1 = ZAR13.12
US$1 = £0.62	£1 = US$1.61
EUR€1 = £0.71	£1 = EUR€1.41

It's usually cheaper to convert money in London than at home. While currency exchange is always available in your arrival airport, it's wise to bring enough foreign currency to last for the first 24 to 72 hours of a trip. You'll get the best exchange rates by paying with a credit card or debit card, or by using an ATM card to withdraw money from your home account while in London.

When changing money abroad, try to go only to banks or bureaux de change with no more than a 5% spread between their buy and sell prices. Since you lose money with every transaction, **convert large sums, but no more than you'll need.**

If you use traveler's checks, carry some in small denominations (the equivalent of US$50 or less) for times when you are forced to exchange money at disadvantageous rates, but bring a range of denominations since there may be a fee charged per check cashed. Store your money in a variety of forms; you will be best off carrying some cash, some traveler's checks, and a debit and/or credit card.

TRAVELER'S CHECKS

🔏 *For traveler's check* **refund hotline** *numbers, see the Service Directory, p. 331.*

Traveler's checks are one of the safest means of carrying funds, though they're far less convenient than a debit or credit card. American Express, Travelex/Thomas Cook, and Visa are the most widely recognized brands in London. Many banks and agencies sell them for a small commission. Check issuers provide refunds if the checks are lost or stolen, and many provide additional services, such as toll-free refund hotlines, emergency message services, and stolen credit card assistance.

American Express: Checks available with commission at select banks and all AmEx offices. US residents can also purchase checks by phone (☎888-269-6669) or online (www.aexp.com). AAA offers commission-free checks to its members. Checks available in British pounds. *Cheques for Two* can be signed by either of 2 people traveling together. For purchase locations or more information contact AmEx's service centers: In the US and Canada ☎800-221-7282; in the UK ☎0800 521 313; in Australia ☎800 25 19 02; in New Zealand 0800 441 068; elsewhere US collect ☎+1 801-964-6665.

Visa: At banks worldwide, generally with commission. For the location of the nearest office, call Visa's service centers: In the US ☎800-227-6811; in the UK ☎0800 89 50 78; elsewhere UK collect ☎+44 020 7937 8091. Checks available in US, British, Canadian, and Japanese currencies, and the Euro.

Travelex/Thomas Cook: In the US and Canada call ☎800-287-7362; in the UK call ☎0800 62 21 01; elsewhere call UK collect ☎+44 1733 31 89 50.

CREDIT, DEBIT & ATM CARDS

CREDIT CARDS. Where accepted, credit cards often offer superior exchange rates—up to 5% better than the retail rate used by banks and other currency exchange establishments. Credit cards may also offer services such as insurance or emergency help, and are sometimes required to reserve hotel rooms or rental cars. **MasterCard** and **Visa** are most welcomed; **American Express** cards are rarely accepted, **Diners Club** and **Discover** almost never. Credit cards are also useful for **cash advances,** which allow you to withdraw local currency from associated banks and ATMs abroad. If you intend to use your credit card extensively in London, alert your card issuer before leaving; otherwise, automated systems could block your card for "suspicious activity." If you will also be making cash advances through cash machines in London, you will need to ask your card issuer for a 4-digit PIN.

ATM CARDS. Cash machines are common in London, and you should have no problems withdrawing money from your home bank account. Your access to other ATM functions (e.g., checking account balances or moving money between accounts), however, may be limited. The wholesale exchange rate offered is the same as credit cards; there is often a limit on the amount of money you can withdraw per day (around US$500), and the issuing bank usually charges US$1-5 per withdrawal. Before you leave, memorize your PIN in numeric form: British cash machines do not have letters on their keys. British ATMs only accept four-digit pins; if your PIN is longer than four digits, ask your bank whether you need a new number.

DEBIT CARDS. Debit cards are as convenient as credit cards but withdraw money directly from your bank account. A debit card can be used wherever its associated credit card company (usually Mastercard or Visa) is accepted, yet the money is withdrawn directly from the holder's checking account. Debit cards often also function as ATM cards and can be used to withdraw cash from associated banks and ATMs throughout Britain and Ireland. The two major international money networks are **Cirrus** (to locate ATMs US ☎ 800-424-7787 or www.mastercard.com) and **Visa/PLUS** (to locate ATMs US ☎ 800-843-7587 or www.visa.com). ATMs of major British banks (including Barclays, HSBC, Lloyds TSB, National Westminster, and Royal Bank of Scotland) usually accept both networks.

COSTS

It's a good idea to work out a daily budget and stick to it. Based on the estimates below, you could get away with spending £35 (US$50) a day, sharing a cheap B&B room, buying food in supermarkets, only hitting the free sights, and staying home at night, but £50 (US$80) is a more reasonable minimum if you want to fully experience London.

Accommodations: count on spending at least £15 per person night in a dorm or a shared hotel room. For **longer stays** (over a week), you should be able to negotiate a discount.

Food: by shopping in supermarkets and eating frugally, you could get away with spending £8 per day; at restaurants you're unlikely to spend less than £15, even if you're careful.

Admissions charges: London's major museums (including the Tate Modern, the British Museum, and the National Gallery) are all free. Sights range from free to over £10, so ask yourself if you really need to see that wax model of Elvis.

Entertainment & Nightlife can really add up: club covers are rarely under £10, and a pint of beer is about £3. Theater and concert tickets range from £5 for student standbys at off-West End locations to £20+ for cheaper tickets to a well-known show.

Transport: At a bare minimum, 2 bus rides a day will cost £2; for any serious sightseeing you should invest in a Travelcard (see p. 27), at least £4 a day or £15.90 a week.

TIPS FOR SAVING MONEY. Some simpler ways include searching out opportunities for free entertainment, splitting accommodation and food costs with other trustworthy fellow travelers, and buying food in supermarkets rather than eating out. Do your laundry in the sink (unless you're explicitly prohibited from doing so). With that said, don't go overboard with your budget obsession. Though staying within your budget is important, don't do so at the expense of your health or a great travel experience.

HEALTH

🛈 For advice on obtaining **urgent treatment** in the UK, see **Once in London,** p. 40. For listings of **clinics** and **emergency rooms** see **Service Directory,** p. 331 and **late-night chemists** (pharmacies), p. 330.

Common sense is the simplest prescription for good health while you travel. Drink lots of fluids to prevent dehydration and constipation, and wear sturdy, broken-in shoes and clean socks.

BEFORE YOU GO

In your **passport,** write the names of any people you wish to be contacted in case of a medical emergency, and list any allergies or medical conditions. Matching a prescription to a foreign equivalent is not always easy, safe, or possible, so carry up-to-date, legible prescriptions or a statement from your doctor stating the medication's trade name, manufacturer, chemical name, and dosage. While traveling, be sure to keep all medication with you in your carry-on luggage. For tips on packing a basic **first-aid kit** and other health essentials, see p. 301.

PRE-EXISTING CONDITIONS. Those with medical conditions may want to obtain a **Medic Alert** ID tag (first year US$35, annually thereafter US$20), which identifies the condition and gives a 24hr. collect-call number. Contact the Medic Alert Foundation, 2323 Colorado Ave, Turlock, CA 95382, USA (☎1-888-633-4298; www.medicalert.org). **Diabetics** can contact **Diabetes UK** (☎020 7424 1030) or the **American Diabetes Association,** 1701 North Beauregard St., Alexandria, VA 22311 (☎1-800-232-3472; www.diabetes.org), to receive copies of the article "Travel and Diabetes" and a diabetic ID card. Those down under can contact **Diabetes Australia,** Churchill House, 1st fl., 218 Northbourne Ave., Braddon, ACT 2612 (☎02 6230 1155).

IMMUNIZATIONS & PRECAUTIONS

Travelers over two years old should make sure that the following vaccines are up to date: MMR (for measles, mumps, and rubella); DTaP or Td (for diptheria, tetanus, and pertussis); OPV (for polio); HbCV (for haemophilus influenza B); and HBV (for B).

USEFUL ORGANIZATIONS & PUBLICATIONS

The US **Centers for Disease Control and Prevention** (CDC; US☎877-394-8747; toll-free fax 888-232-3299; www.cdc.gov/travel) maintains an international travelers' hotline and an informative website. The CDC's comprehensive booklet *Health Information for International Travel,* an annual rundown of disease, immunization, and general health advice, is free online or US$30 via the Public Health Foundation (☎877-252-1200). Consult the appropriate government agency of your home country for consular information sheets on health, entry requirements, and other issues for various countries. For quick information on health and other travel warnings, call the **Overseas Citizens Services** (☎202-647-5225), or contact a passport agency, embassy, or consulate abroad. US citizens can send a self-addressed, stamped envelope to the Overseas Citizens Services, Bureau of Consular Affairs, #4811, US Department of State, Washington, D.C. 20520. For information on medical evacuation services and travel insurance firms, see the US government's website at http://travel.state.gov/medical.html or the **British Foreign and Commonwealth Office** (www.fco.gov.uk).

For detailed information on travel health, including a country-by-country overview of diseases, try the **International Travel Health Guide,** by Stuart Rose, MD (US$24.95; www.travmed.com). For general health info, contact the **American Red Cross** (☎800-564-1234; www.redcross.org).

INFECTIOUS DISEASES

Rabies: Transmitted through the saliva of infected animals; fatal if untreated. By the time symptoms (thirst and muscle spasms) appear, the disease is in its terminal stage. If you are bitten, wash the wound thoroughly, seek immediate medical care, and try to have the animal located. A rabies vaccine, which consists of 3 shots given over a 21-day period, is available but is only semi-effective.

Hepatitis B: A viral infection of the liver transmitted via bodily fluids or needle-sharing. Symptoms, which may not surface until years after infection, include jaundice, loss of appetite, fever, and joint pain. A 3-shot vaccination sequence is recommended for health-care workers, sexually-active travelers, and anyone planning to seek medical treatment abroad; it must begin 6 mo. before traveling.

Hepatitis C: Like Hepatitis B, but the mode of transmission differs. IV drug users, those with occupational exposure to blood, hemodialysis patients, and recipients of blood transfusions are at the highest risk, but the disease can also be spread through sexual contact or sharing items like razors and toothbrushes that may have traces of blood on them.

AIDS, HIV & OTHER STDS

For detailed information on **Acquired Immune Deficiency Syndrome (AIDS)** in London, call the **US Centers for Disease Control's** 24hr. hotline at ☎800-342-2437, or contact the **Joint United Nations Programme on HIV/AIDS (UNAIDS)**, 20, ave. Appia, CH-1211 Geneva 27, Switzerland (☎+41 22 791 3666; fax 22 791 4187).

Sexually transmitted diseases (STDs) such as gonorrhea, chlamydia, genital warts, syphilis, and herpes are easier to catch than HIV and can be just as deadly. **Hepatitis** B and C can also be transmitted sexually (see above). Though condoms may protect you from some STDs, oral or even tactile contact can lead to transmission. If you think you may have contracted an STD, see a doctor immediately.

INSURANCE

Travel insurance generally covers four basic areas: medical/health problems, property loss, trip cancellation/interruption, and emergency evacuation. Although your regular insurance policies may well extend to travel-related accidents, you may consider purchasing travel insurance if the cost of potential trip cancellation/interruption is greater than you can absorb. Prices for travel insurance purchased separately generally run about US$50 per week for full coverage, while trip cancellation/interruption may be purchased separately at a rate of about US$5.50 per US$100 of coverage.

Medical insurance (especially a university policy) often covers costs incurred abroad; check with your provider. **US Medicare** does not cover foreign travel. **Canadians** are protected by their home province's health insurance plan for up to 90 days after leaving the country; check with the provincial Ministry of Health or Health Plan Headquarters for details. **Australians** traveling in the UK are entitled to many of the services that they would receive at home as part of the Reciprocal Health Care Agreement. **Homeowners' insurance** (or your family's coverage) often covers theft during travel and loss of travel documents (passport, plane ticket, railpass, etc.) up to US$500.

ISIC and **ITIC** (see p. 296) provide basic insurance benefits, including US$100 per day of in-hospital sickness for up to 60 days, US$3000 of accident-related medical reimbursement, and US$25,000 for emergency medical transport. Cardholders have access to a toll-free 24hr. helpline (run by the insurance provider **TravelGuard**) for medical, legal, and financial emergencies overseas (US and Canada ☎877-370-4742, elsewhere call US collect ☎+1 715-345-0505). **American**

Express (US ☎ 800-528-4800) grants most cardholders automatic car rental insurance (collision and theft, but not liability) and ground travel accident coverage of US$100,000 on flight purchases made with the card.

INSURANCE PROVIDERS. Council and **STA** (see p. 302) offer a range of plans that can supplement your basic coverage. Other private insurance providers in the US and Canada include: **Access America** (☎ 800-284-8300); **Berkely Group/ Carefree Travel Insurance** (☎ 800-323-3149; www.berkely.com); **Globalcare Travel Insurance** (☎ 800-821-2488; www.globalcare-cocco.com); and **Travel Assistance International** (☎ 800-821-2828; www.europ-assistance.com). Providers in the **UK** include **Columbus Direct** (☎ 020 7375 0011). In **Australia**, try **AFTA** (☎ 02 9264 3299).

PACKING

Pack lightly: lay out only what you absolutely need, then take half the clothes and twice the money.

LUGGAGE. Be sure that you can carry your luggage up and down stairs, as steep staircases are unavoidable at most Tube stops and in many B&Bs and hostels.

CLOTHING. A **rain jacket** in essential year-round. Londoners generally dress conservatively and darkly—a pair of black trousers will help you blend in. Be sure to pack some semi-dressy trousers and shoes, especially if you plan to go clubbing: many clubs ban jeans and sneakers. **Flip-flops** are must-haves for grubby hostel showers.

CONVERTERS & ADAPTERS. In the UK, electricity is 240 volts AC, enough to fry any 110V North American appliance. **Americans** and **Canadians** should buy an **adapter** (which changes the shape of the plug) and a **converter** (which changes the voltage; US$20). Don't make the mistake of using only an adapter; the only exception is laptops, which often contain internal power converters. **New Zealanders** and **South Africans** (who both use 220V at home) as well as **Australians** (who use 240/250V) won't need a converter, but will need a set of adapters to use anything electrical. For more on all things adaptable, check out http:// kropla.com/electric.htm.

FIRST-AID KIT. For a basic first-aid kit, pack: bandages, pain reliever, antibiotic cream, a thermometer, a Swiss Army knife, tweezers, moleskin, decongestant, motion-sickness remedy, diarrhea or upset-stomach medication (Pepto Bismol or Imodium), an antihistamine, sunscreen, and burn ointment.

FILM. Film is expensive in London (upwards of £3 for a roll of 24 color exposures) and developing can be exorbitant (up to £6 for 24 prints), so consider bringing along enough film for your entire trip and developing it at home. Despite disclaimers, airport X-rays *can* fog film, so buy a lead-lined pouch at a camera store or ask security to hand-inspect it. Always pack film in your carry-on luggage, since higher-intensity X-rays are used on checked luggage.

IMPORTANT DOCUMENTS. Don't forget your passport, traveler's checks, ATM and/ or credit cards, adequate ID, and photocopies of all of the above in case these documents are lost or stolen (see p. 296).

TOILETRIES. Toothbrushes, towels, cold-water soap, talcum powder (to keep feet dry), deodorant, razors, and tampons are easily available, but are often much more expensive in London than at home, so bring extras along. **Contact lense solution** is extremely expensive in London. Also bring your glasses and a copy of your prescription in case you need emergency replacements. If you use heat-disinfection, either switch temporarily to a chemical disinfection system (check first to make sure it's safe with your brand of lenses), or buy a converter to 220V.

GETTING TO LONDON

BY PLANE

When it comes to airfares, a little effort can save you a bundle. If your plans are flexible enough to deal with the restrictions, courier fares are the cheapest. Tickets bought from consolidators and standby seating are also good deals, but last-minute specials and charter flights often beat these fares. The key is to hunt around, to be flexible, and to ask persistently about discounts. Only those traveling on expense accounts should ever pay full price for a ticket.

AIRFARES

Airfares to London peak between June and mid-September, and again from early December to New Year. Fares are almost always much higher for trips that do not include a Saturday night. "Open return" tickets are normally pricier than fixing a return date when buying the ticket. Round-trip flights are the cheapest; "open-jaw" (arriving in and departing from different cities) tickets tend to be pricier. On commercial airlines, patching one-way flights together is the most expensive way to travel; however many "budget" airlines charge independently for each segment. Depending on route and season, **fares** for roundtrip flights to London range: US$250-600 from the eastern USA and Canada, US$300-800 from the west; AUS$1300-1800 from Australia; NZ$2000-3500 from New Zealand; and ZAR4000-6000 from South Africa.

BUDGET & STUDENT TRAVEL AGENCIES

Travelers holding **ISIC, ITIC,** or **IYTC** cards (see p. 296) qualify for discount fares from student travel agencies. Most flights from budget agencies are on major airlines, but in peak season some may sell seats on less reliable chartered aircraft. A major advantage of student tickets over similarly-priced bucket-shop deals is that dates of travel can normally be changed for a small fee (US$20-40). Most of the following agencies have London offices; these are listed in the **Service Directory,** p. 334.

usit world (www.usitworld.com). Over 50 **usit campus** branches in the UK, including 52 Grosvenor Gardens, **London** SW1W 0AG (☎0870 240 10 10); **Manchester** (☎0161 273 1880); and **Edinburgh** (☎0131 668 3303). Nearly 20 **usit NOW** offices in Ireland, including 19-21 Aston Quay, O'Connell Bridge, **Dublin** 2 (☎01 602 1600; www.usitnow.ie), and **Belfast** (☎02 890 327 111; www.usitnow.com). Offices also in **Athens, Auckland, Brussels, Frankfurt, Johannesburg, Lisbon, Luxembourg, Madrid, Paris, Sofia,** and **Warsaw.**

Council Travel (www.counciltravel.com). Countless US offices, including branches in **Atlanta, Boston, Chicago, L.A., New York, San Francisco, Seattle,** and **Washington, D.C.** Check the website or call 800-2-COUNCIL (226-8624) for the office nearest you. Also an office at 28A Poland St. (Oxford Circus), **London,** W1V 3DB (☎0207 437 77 67).

CTS Travel, 44 Goodge St., **London** W1T 2AD, UK (☎0207 636 0031; fax 0207 637 5328; www.ctstravel.co.uk).

STA Travel, 7890 S. Hardy Dr., Ste. 110, Tempe AZ 85284, US (24hr. reservations and info ☎800-781-4040; www.sta-travel.com). A student and youth travel organization with over 150 offices worldwide (check their website for a listing of all their offices), including US offices in **Boston, Chicago, L.A., New York, San Francisco, Seattle,** and **Washington, D.C.** Ticket booking, travel insurance, railpasses, and more. In the UK, walk-in office 11 Goodge St., **London** W1T 2PF or call 0207-436-7779. In New Zealand, Shop 2B, 182 Queen St., **Auckland** (☎09 309 0458). In Australia, 366 Lygon St., **Carlton** Vic 3053 (☎03 9349 4344).

Travel CUTS (Canadian Universities Travel Services Limited), 187 College St., **Toronto,** ON M5T 1P7 (☎416-979-2406; www.travelcuts.com). Offices across Canada and the United States in Seattle, San Francisco, Los Angeles, New York and elsewhere. Also in the UK, 295-A Regent St., **London** W1R 7YA (☎0207-255-1944).

Wasteels, Skoubogade 6, 1158 Copenhagen K. (☎3314 4633; fax 7630-0865; www.wasteels.com). A huge chain with 180 locations across Europe. Sells Wasteels BIJ tickets discounted 30-45% off regular fare, 2nd-class international point-to-point train tickets with unlimited stopovers for those under 26 (sold only in Europe).

DIRECT AIRLINE BOOKING

COMMERCIAL AIRLINES

The commercial airlines' lowest regular offer is the **APEX** (Advance Purchase Excursion) fare, which provides confirmed reservations and allows "open-jaw" tickets. Generally, reservations must be made seven to 21 days ahead of departure, with seven- to 14-day minimum-stay and up to 90-day maximum-stay restrictions. These fares carry hefty cancellation and change penalties (fees rise in summer). Book peak-season APEX fares early; by May you will have a hard time getting your desired departure date. Use **Microsoft Expedia** (http://msn.expedia.com) or **Travelocity** (www.travelocity.com) to get an idea of the lowest published fares, then use the resources outlined here to try and beat those fares. Low-season fares should be appreciably cheaper than the high-season (mid-June to September) ones listed here.

Finnair: US ☎800-950-5000; www.us.finnair.com. Cheap round-trips from New York, and Toronto to Helsinki (June, July and Aug. only); connections throughout Europe.

Icelandair: US ☎800-223-5500; www.icelandair.com. Stopovers in Iceland for no extra cost on most transatlantic flights. New York to London May-Sept. US$500-730; Oct.-May US$390-$450. For last-minute offers, subscribe to their email Lucky Fares.

Martinair: US ☎800-627-8462; www.martinairusa.com. Florida (Miami and Orlando) to Amsterdam, then connect throughout Europe. Mid-June to mid-Aug. US$880; mid-Aug. to mid-June US$750.

EUROPEAN DISCOUNT AIRLINES

Travelers from Ireland and the continent can take advantage of the numerous no-frills budget airlines criss-crossing Europe. By only taking direct bookings, flying between lesser-known airports and cutting back on free drinks, food, and sometimes baggage allowances, this new breed of carrier offer regular services at prices that are often lower than trains and ferries, let alone commercial airlines.

buzz: UK ☎0870 240 7070; www.buzzaway.com.

easyJet: UK ☎0870 6 000 000; www.easyjet.com.

go: UK ☎0870 60 76 543, elsewhere call UK +44 1279 66 63 88; www.go-fly.com.

Ryanair: Ireland ☎01 870 1569 569, UK 0870 156 95 69; www.ryanair.ie.

CHEAP ALTERNATIVES

AIR COURIER FLIGHTS

Those who travel light should consider courier flights. Couriers help transport cargo on international flights by using their checked luggage space for freight. Generally, couriers must travel with carry-ons only and deal with complex flight restrictions. Most flights are round-trip only, with short fixed-length stays (usually one week) and a limit of a one ticket per issue. Most of these flights also operate only out of major gateway cities, mostly in North America. Round-trip courier fares from the US to London run about US$300-700. Most flights leave from New York, Los Angeles, San Francisco, or Miami in the US; and from Montreal, Toronto, or Vancouver in Canada. Generally, you must be over 21 (in some cases 18). In summer, the most popular destinations usually require an advance reservation of about two weeks (you can usually book up to two months ahead). Super-discounted fares are common for "last-minute" flights (three to 14 days ahead).

Round-trip courier fares from the US to Western Europe run about US$200-500. Most flights leave from New York, Los Angeles, San Francisco, or Miami in the US; and from Montreal, Toronto, or Vancouver in Canada. The organizations below provide members with lists of opportunities and courier brokers for an annual fee. Prices quoted below are round-trip.

Air Courier Association, 350 Indiana St. #300, Golden, CO 80401 (☎800-282-1202; www.aircourier.org). Ten departure cities throughout the US and Canada to London, Madrid, Paris, Rome, and throughout western Europe (high-season US$150-360). One-year membership US$49.

International Association of Air Travel Couriers (IAATC), PO Box 980, Keystone Heights, FL 32656 (☎352-475-1584; fax 475-5326; www.courier.org). From 9 North American cities to Western European cities, including London, Madrid, Paris, and Rome. One-year membership US$45.

Global Courier Travel, PO Box 3051, Nederland, CO 80466 (www.globalcouriertravel.com). Searchable online database. Six departure points in the US and Canada to Amsterdam, Athens, Brussels, Copenhagen, Frankfurt, London, Madrid, Milan, Paris, and Rome. Lifetime membership US$40, 2 people US$55.

STANDBY FLIGHTS

Traveling standby requires considerable flexibility in arrival and departure dates and cities. Companies dealing in standby flights sell vouchers rather than tickets, along with the promise to get to your destination (or near your destination) within a certain window of time (typically 1-5 days). You call in before your specific window of time to hear your flight options and the probability that you will be able to board each flight. You can then decide which flights you want to try to make, show up at the appropriate airport at the appropriate time, present your voucher, and board if space is available. Vouchers can usually be bought for both one-way and round-trip travel. You may receive a monetary refund only if every available flight within your date range is full; if you opt not to take an available (but perhaps less convenient) flight, you can only get credit toward future travel. Carefully read agreements with any company offering standby flights as tricky fine print can leave you in a lurch. To check on a company's service record in the US, call the Better Business Bureau (☎212-533-6200). It is difficult to receive refunds, and clients' vouchers will not be honored when an airline fails to receive payment in time.

TICKET CONSOLIDATORS

Ticket consolidators, or **"bucket shops,"** buy unsold tickets in bulk from commercial airlines and sell them at discounted rates. The best place to look is in the Sunday travel section of any major newspaper (such as the *New York Times*), where many bucket shops place tiny ads. Call quickly, as availability is typically extremely limited. Not all bucket shops are reliable, so insist on a receipt that gives full details of restrictions, refunds, and tickets, and pay by credit card (in spite of the 2-5% fee) so you can stop payment if you never receive your tickets. For more info, see www.travel-library.com/air-travel/consolidators.html.

TRAVELING FROM THE US & CANADA

Travel Avenue (☎800-333-3335; www.travelavenue.com) searches for best available published fares and then uses several consolidators to attempt to beat that fare. **NOW Voyager,** 74 Varick St., Ste. 307, New York, NY 10013 (☎212-431-1616; fax 219-1793; www.nowvoyagertravel.com) arranges discounted flights, mostly from New York, to Barcelona, London, Madrid, Milan, Paris, and Rome. Other consolidators worth trying are **Interworld** (☎305-443-4929; fax 443-0351); **Pennsylvania Travel** (☎800-331-0947); **Rebel** (☎800-227-3235; travel@rebeltours.com; www.rebeltours.com); **Cheap Tickets** (☎800-377-1000; www.cheaptickets.com). Yet more consolidators on the web include the **Internet Travel Network** (www.itn.com); **Flights.com** (www.flights.com);

TravelHUB (www.travelhub.com); and **The Travel Site** (www.thetravelsite.com). Keep in mind that these are just suggestions to get you started in your research; *Let's Go* does not endorse any of these agencies. As always, be cautious, and research companies before you hand over your credit card number.

CHARTER FLIGHTS

Charters are flights a tour operator contracts with an airline to fly extra loads of passengers during peak season. Charter flights fly less frequently than major airlines, make refunds particularly difficult, and are almost always fully booked. Schedules and itineraries may also change or be cancelled at the last moment (as late as 48 hours before the trip, and without a full refund), and check-in, boarding, and baggage claim are often much slower. However, they can also be cheaper.

Discount clubs and **fare brokers** offer members savings on last-minute charter and tour deals. Study contracts closely; you don't want to end up with an unwanted overnight layover. **Travelers Advantage**, Trumbull, CT, USA (☎203-365-2000; www.travelersadvantage.com; US$60 annual fee includes discounts and cheap flight directories) specializes in European travel and tour packages.

BY CHANNEL TUNNEL

Traversing 27 mi. under the sea, the Chunnel is undoubtedly the fastest, most convenient, and least scenic route from the continent to Britain.

BY TRAIN. Eurostar, Eurostar House, Waterloo Station, London SE1 8SE (UK ☎0990 186 186; US ☎800-387-6782; elsewhere call UK +44 20 7928 5163; www.eurostar.com) runs frequent trains between London and the continent. 10-28 trains per day run to **Paris** (3hr.; US$75-159, 2nd class), **Brussels** (3hr.; 50min.; US$75-159, 2nd class), and **Eurodisney.** Routes include stops at **Ashford** in England, and **Calais** and **Lille** in France. Book at major rail stations in the UK, at the office above, by phone, or on the web.

BY CAR. Eurotunnel, P.O. Box 2000, Folkestone, Kent CT18 8XY (www.eurotunnel.co.uk) shuttles cars and passengers between Kent and Nord-Pas-de-Calais. Return fares for vehicle and all passengers range from £219-317 with car, £259-636 with campervan. Same-day return costs £110-150, five-day return £139-195. Book online or via phone. Travelers with cars can also look into sea crossings by ferry (see below).

BY BOAT

The following fares listed are **one-way** for adult foot passengers unless otherwise noted. Though standard return fares are in most cases simply twice the one-way fare, **fixed-period returns** (usually within five days) are almost invariably cheaper. Ferries run year-round unless otherwise noted. **Bikes** are usually free, although you may have to pay up to £10 extra in high-season. For a **camper/trailer** supplement, you will have to add anywhere from £20-140 to the "with car" fare. A directory of ferries in this region can be found at www.seaview.co.uk/ferries.html.

DFDS Seaways: UK ☎08705 33 30 00; www.dfdsseaways.co.uk. **Harwich** to **Hamburg** (20hr.) and **Esbjerg, Denmark** (19hr.). **Newcastle** to **Amsterdam** (14hr.); **Kristiansand, Norway** (19hr.); and **Gothenburg, Sweden** (22hr.).

Fjord Line: Norway ☎55 54 88 00, UK ☎0191 296 1313; www.fjordline.no. **Newcastle, England** to **Stavanger** (19hr.) and **Bergen** (26hr.), Norway (UK£50-110, students £25-110).

Hoverspeed: UK ☎0870 240 8070, France ☎008 00 1211 1211; www.hoverspeed.co.uk. **Dover** to **Calais** (35-55min., every hr., UK£24) and **Ostend, Belgium** (2hr., 5-7 per day, UK£28). **Newhaven** to **Dieppe, France** (2¼-4¼hr., 1-3 per day, UK£28).

P&O Stena Line: UK ☎087 0600 0611, from Europe +44 13 04 86 40 03; customer.services@posl.com; www.posl.com. **Dover** to **Calais** (1¼hr., every 30min.-1hr., 30 per day; UK£24). **305**

SeaFrance: UK ☎0870 571 1711, France ☎08 03 04 40 45; www.seafrance.co.uk. **Dover** to **Calais** (1½hr., 15 per day, UK£15).

Stena Line: UK ☎+44 1233 64 68 26; www.stenaline.co.uk. **Harwich** to **Hook of Holland** (5hr., UK£26). **Fishguard** to **Rosslare** (1-3½hr.; UK£18-21, students £14-17). **Holyhead** to **Dublin** (4hr.; UK£23-27, students £19-23) and **Dún Laoghaire** (1-3½hr.; £23-27, students £19-23). **Stranraer** to **Belfast** (1¾-3¼hr.; UK£14-36, students £10)

SPECIFIC CONCERNS

The **National Emergency** number is **999**. To talk confidentially about emotional problems, the **Samaritans** number in the UK is ☎0845 790 9090. Open 24hr., it can also refer you to the appropriate sources. The **Rape Crisis Federation Wales and England** (☎0115 900 3560; www.rapecrisis.co.uk) provides referrals to local rape crisis and sexual abuse counseling services throughout the UK.

WOMEN TRAVELERS

🚹 *Resources for women in London are listed in the* **Service Directory,** *p. 335.*

Even in a city as cosmopolitan and liberal as London, women exploring on their own face some additional safety concerns. Most hostels offer women-only rooms or will make one up on request; you should also be sure in any hostel or hotel that your door locks properly from the inside. If a hostel has communal showers, check them out before booking. By choosing centrally located accommodations, you'll help avoid solitary late-night treks and Tube rides. Look as if you know where you're going and approach older women or couples for directions if you're lost or uncomfortable; always carry extra money for a phone call, bus, or taxi just in case, and memorize or write down the number of a local taxi firm before going out.

Generally, the less you look like a tourist, the better off you'll be. Wearing a conspicuous wedding band or mentioning a husband waiting back at the hotel may help prevent unwanted overtures.

The best answer to verbal harassment is no answer at all; feigning deafness, sitting motionless, and staring straight ahead at nothing in particular will do a world of good that reactions usually don't achieve. The extremely persistent can sometimes be dissuaded by a firm, loud, and very public "Go away!" Don't hesitate to seek out a police officer or a passerby if you are being harassed. Memorize the emergency number (☎**999**), and consider carrying a whistle or airhorn on your keychain; mace and pepper sprays are illegal throughout the UK.

A self-defense course will not only prepare you for a potential attack, but will also raise your level of awareness of your surroundings as well as your confidence. **Impact, Prepare, and Model Mugging** can refer you to local self-defense courses in the US (☎800-345-5425). Visit the website at www.impactsafety.org for a list of nearby chapters. Workshops (2-3hr.) start at US$50; full courses (20hr.) run US$350-500.

TRAVELING ALONE

There are many benefits to traveling alone, including independence and greater interaction with locals. On the other hand, any solo traveler is a more vulnerable target of harassment and street theft. As a lone traveler, try not to stand out as a tourist, look confident, and be especially careful in deserted or very crowded areas. If questioned, never admit that you are traveling alone. Maintain regular contact with someone at home who knows your itinerary. For more tips, pick up *Traveling Solo* by Eleanor Berman (Globe Pequot Press, US$17) or subscribe to **Connecting: Solo Travel Network,** 689 Park Rd., Unit 6, Gibsons, BC V0N 1V7, Canada (☎604-886-9099; www.cstn.org; membership US$35). **Travel**

Companion Exchange, P.O. Box 833, Amityville, NY 11701, USA (☎631-454-0880, or in the US ☎800-392-1256; www.whytravelalone.com; US$48), will link solo travelers with companions with similar travel habits and interests.

OLDER TRAVELERS

Travelers aged 60 or over are eligible for a wide range of discounts on transportation, museums, movies, theaters, concerts, restaurants, and accommodations; look for rates marked **concessions, concs,** or **OAP** (Old Age Pensioner). If you don't see a discount listed, it doesn't hurt to ask. Older travelers should be aware that London is not friendly to the mobility-impaired: many B&Bs and almost all Tube stops have many unavoidable stairs. See **Travelers with Disabilities** (p. 308) for more details.

The books *No Problem! Worldwise Tips for Mature Adventurers,* by Janice Kenyon (Orca Book Publishers; US$16) and *Unbelievably Good Deals and Great Adventures That You Absolutely Can't Get Unless You're Over 50,* by Joan Rattner Heilman (NTC/Contemporary Publishing; US$13) are both excellent resources. For more information, contact one of the following organizations:

Elderhostel, 11 Ave. de Lafayette, Boston, MA 02111, USA (☎877-426-8056; www.elderhostel.org). Organizes 1- to 4-week "educational adventures" in London on varied subjects for those 55+.

The Mature Traveler, P.O. Box 15791, Sacramento, CA 95852, USA (☎800-460-6676; www.thematuretraveler.com). Deals, discounts, and travel packages for the 50+ traveler. Subscription $30.

BISEXUAL, GAY & LESBIAN TRAVELERS

⁊ *For gay and lesbian* **resources** *in London, see the* **Service Directory,** *p. 332.*

Soho, particularly around Old Compton St., is London's gay nexus, though gay bars and pubs can be found throughout the city; *Let's Go* has included numerous rainbow-toting cafes, bars, and nightclubs in neighborhood listings. Newspaper resources include *The Pink Paper* (free) available from newsagents; *Gay Times* (£3) which covers political issues; and *Diva* (£2.25), a monthly lesbian lifestyle magazine with an excellent mix of features and good listings. *Boyz* (www.boyz.co.uk) is the main gay listings and lifestyle magazine for London (free from gay bars and clubs), while www.gingerbeer.co.uk offers the lesbian lowdown.

RESOURCES

British Tourist Authority (US ☎800-462-2748) devotes a portion of its American site (www.travelbritain.org) to gay and lesbian travel information and publishes the guide *Britain: Inside & Out.* Visit www.gaybritain.org.

Gay's the Word, 66 Marchmont St., London WC1N 1AB, UK (☎020 7278 7654; www.gaystheword.co.uk). The largest gay and lesbian bookshop in the UK, with both fiction and nonfiction titles. Mail-order service available.

Giovanni's Room, 1145 Pine St., Philadelphia, PA 19107, USA (☎215-923-2960; www.queerbooks.com). An international gay and lesbian bookstore; mail-order service.

FURTHER READING

Spartacus International Gay Guide 2003-2004. Bruno Gmunder Verlag (US$33).

Damron's Accommodations and *The Women's Traveller.* Damron Travel Guides (US$16-23).

Ferrari Guides' Gay Travel A to Z, Ferrari Guides' Men's Travel in Your Pocket, and *Ferrari Guides' Inn Places.* Ferrari Publications (US$19-20). Purchase online at www.amazon.com. **307**

TRAVELERS WITH DISABILITIES

⚑ Resources *for disabled travelers in London are listed in the* **Service Directory**, *p. 331. For information on accessibility on* **public transportation**, *see* **Once in London**, *p. 29.*

London makes few concessions to disabled travelers. Transport for London Access & Mobility (☎ 020 7941 4600) can provide information on public transportation within the city. For those who wish to rent cars, some major **car rental** agencies (Hertz, Avis, and National), as well as local agencies, such as Wheelchair Travel in Surrey (☎ 01483 233 640), can provide and deliver hand-controlled cars. The National Rail website (www.nationalrail.co.uk) provides general information for travelers with disabilities as well as assistance phone numbers for individual rail companies. The Tube is almost entirely out-of-bounds to those who cannot handle stairs, buses and taxis are rarely wheelchair enabled, and few hostels, B&Bs, and inexpensive hotels have lifts. Though refurbishment has rendered some theaters and concert halls accessible, the majority remains without wheelchair bays or elevators. Those with disabilities should inform airlines and hotels of their disabilities when making reservations; some time may be needed to prepare special accommodations. Call ahead to restaurants, museums, and other facilities to find out if they are handicapped-accessible.

Guide dogs fall under the UK's strict PETS regulations. Pets coming from EU countries, Australia, and New Zealand can avoid quarantine by being microchipped, vaccinated, bloodtested, and certified against tapeworm and ticks before entering the UK. All other animals will be quarantined for six months. Call the PETS helpline at ☎ 0870 0241 1710 or consult www.defra.gov.uk/animalh/quarantine for details.

The London Tourist Board's *London For All* leaflet, available at London Visitor's Centres (see p. 334), includes information on accessibility in London. *Access in London,* by Gordon Couch (Quiller Press; $12) is an in-depth guide to accommodations, transport, and accessibility in London.

USEFUL ORGANIZATIONS

Mobility International USA (MIUSA), P.O. Box 10767, Eugene, OR 97440, USA (☎ 541-343-1284, voice and TDD; www.miusa.org). Provides a variety of books and other publications containing information for travelers with disabilities.

Society for the Advancement of Travel for the Handicapped (SATH), 347 Fifth Ave., #610, New York, NY 10016, USA (☎ 212-447-7284; www.sath.org). An advocacy group that publishes free online travel information and the travel magazine *OPEN WORLD* (US$18, free for members). Annual membership US$45, students and seniors US$30.

TOUR AGENCIES

Directions Unlimited, 123 Green Ln., Bedford Hills, NY 10507, USA (☎ 800-533-5343). Books individual and group vacations for the physically disabled; not an info service.

The Guided Tour, Inc., 7900 Old York Rd., #114B, Elkins Park, PA 19027, USA (☎ 800-783-5841; www.guidedtour.com). Organizes travel programs for persons with developmental and physical challenges in London.

MINORITY TRAVELERS

Minority travelers in London should have no problems at all—London's as multiracial and tolerant as cities come. The **Commission for Racial Equality (CRE),** Elliot House, 10-12 Allington St., London SW1E 5EH (UK☎ 020 7828 7022; www.cre.gov.uk), offers a wide variety of publications on diversity and race relations and can provide advice to minority travelers who encounter harassment or discrimination.

TRAVELERS WITH CHILDREN

🔼 For information on child and family discounts on **transportation** in London, see p. 27.

Family vacations require that you slow your pace and plan ahead. If you decide to stay in a B&B or small hotel, call ahead and make sure it's child-friendly. If you rent a car, make sure the rental company provides a car seat for younger children. **Be sure that your child carries some sort of ID** in case of an emergency or in case he or she gets lost.

Many museums, shows, and tourist attractions offer discounts for children, often at the same "concession" rate as students and seniors, as well as "family" tickets (normally for two adults and two children, not necessarily related). Most large museums in London also offer special activity packs and tours for children. B&Bs and hotels typically offer discounts for children sharing an adult's room, while restaurants will often be willing to prepare special child-sized portions. Infants under two generally fly for 10% of the adult fare on international flights when sitting on an adult's lap, while those aged 2-11 get a seat for 75% of the adult fare.

The London Tourist Board publishes the pamphlet *Where to Take Children*, available at London Visitor's Centres and filled with child-friendly sights, restaurants, and services. For more general info, consult one of the following books:

Adventuring with Children: An Inspirational Guide to World Travel and the Outdoors, Nan Jeffrey. Avalon House Publishing (US$15).

Backpacking with Babies and Small Children, Goldie Silverman. Wilderness Press (US$10).

Gutsy Mamas: Travel Tips and Wisdom for Mothers on the Road, Marybeth Bond. Travelers' Tales, Inc. (US$8).

Have Kid, Will Travel: 101 Survival Strategies for Vacationing With Babies and Young Children, Claire and Lucille Tristram. Andrews McMeel Publishing (US$9).

How to take Great Trips with Your Kids, Sanford and Jane Portnoy. Harvard Common Press (US $10).

Trouble Free Travel with Children, Vicki Lansky. Book Peddlers (US$9).

DIETARY CONCERNS

In a country battered by foot-and-mouth disease and besieged by mad cows, it's not surprising that one in five Britons aged under 25 is vegetarian. Almost all restaurants offer a range of vegetarian dishes. *Let's Go* notes restaurants with good vegetarian selections. For more information about vegetarian travel, contact **The Vegetarian Society of the UK** (☎ 0161 925 2000; www.vegsoc.org). South Indian **bhel poori** and **Thai-Chinese Buddhist** buffets are increasingly popular with budgetarians of all dietary persuasions for their cheap, filling, and wholesome fare, including plenty for vegans.

Bhel poori and Buddhist restaurants are also a boon to **kosher** travelers, since they offer religiously exacting standards and a complete absence of meat products. Jews with a taste for meat, or who prefer to eat in rabbinically certified establishments, will spend most of their mealtimes in the enclaves of North London, particularly **Golders Green** (see p. 110). For more information, check out the *Jewish Travel Guide,* edited by Michael Zaidner (Vallentine Mitchell; US$17). Travelers who keep **halal** will have little trouble eating well in London, as long as they have a good appetite for North Indian, Turkish, and middle-eastern food. **Marylebone** and **Bayswater** have the highest concentration of Lebanese restaurants and Islington the most Turkish. Indian restaurants are fairly ubiquitous (though not all are *halal*), and the **East End** is known for its large Bangladeshi community.

ADDITIONAL INFORMATION

TOURIST OFFICES

◪ *Tourist information tailored to visitors from specific countries can be found at www.visit-britain.com. For **tourist information offices in London**, see the **Service Directory**, p. 334.*

London is represented abroad by the **British Tourist Authority** (BTA), and in the UK by the **London Tourist Board.** BTA offices abroad supply advance tickets to major attractions and travel passes as well as information on how to get to Britain, where to stay, and what to do. They also sell the **Great British Heritage Pass,** which gives entrance to almost 600 sights around Britain. (7 days £35, 15 days £46, 1 month £60.) BTA offices are found in:

Australia, Level 16, Gateway, 1 Macquarie Pl., Sydney NSW 2000 (☎02 9377 4400; fax 9377 4499). Open M-F 9:30am-4:30pm; phones M and W-F 9am-5pm, Tu 9:30am-5:30pm.

Canada, 5915 Airport Rd., Suite 120, Mississauga, Ontario L4V 1T1 (☎888-VISIT UK or 905-405-1840; fax 905-405-1835). Open M-F 9am-5pm; phones M-F 10am-6pm.

Ireland, 18-19 College Green, Dublin 2 (☎01 670 8000; fax 670 8244). Open M and W-Th 9am-5:30pm, Tu 10am-5:30pm, F 9am-5pm, Sa 10am-2pm.

New Zealand, Level 17, 151 Queen St., Auckland 1 (☎09 303 1446; fax 09 377 6965). Open M-F 9am-5pm.

South Africa, Lancaster Gate, Hyde Park Ln., Hyde Park 2196, Johannesburg; mailing address P.O. Box 41896, Craighall 2024 (☎011 325 0343; fax 011 325 0344).

United States, 7th fl., 551 Fifth Ave., **New York,** NY 10176-0799 (☎800-462-2748). Open M-F 9am-6pm. Also 625 N. Michigan Ave., Suite 1001, **Chicago,** IL 60611 (☎800-462-2748). Open M-F 9am-5pm. Also 10880 Wilshire Blvd, Suite 570, **Los Angeles,** CA 90024 (☎310-470-2782).

USEFUL PUBLICATIONS

▨ **London A-Z:** Geographers Map Co. (£5). The world's best map, for the world's best city.
Time Out Weekly: Entertainment, nightlife, and exhibitions listings. On sale every W; £2.20.

WORLD WIDE WEB

How to See the World: www.artoftravel.com. Tips on how to travel cheap.

Backpacker's Ultimate Guide: www.bugeurope.com. Tips on packing, transport, and where to go. Also country-specific travel info.

INFORMATION ON LONDON

London Tourist Board: www.londontouristboard.com. Information for visitors, including addresses of London Visitor Centers.

LondonTown: www.londontown.com. Tourist information, special offers, maps, listings, and resources for travelers with special needs.

Visit Britain: www.visitbritain.com. The British Tourist Association website. Lots of useful information about visiting Britain and London.

Transport For London: www.tfl.gov.uk. Comprehensive information on public transportation in London, including ticket prices and current service reports.

London Theatre Guide: www.londontheatre.co.uk. Reviews, listings, tickets, chatrooms, and theater seating plans.

AND OUR PERSONAL FAVORITE...

 Our website, www.letsgo.com, now includes introductory chapters from all our guides and a wealth of information on a monthly featured destination. As always, our website also has info about our books, a travel forum buzzing with stories and tips, and additional links that will help you make the most of a trip to London.

Alternatives to Tourism

When we started out in 1961, about 1.7 million people in the world were traveling internationally each year; in 2002, nearly 700 million trips were made, projected to be up to a billion by 2010. The dramatic rise in tourism has created an interdependence between the economy, environment, and culture of many destinations and the tourists they host. Eight percent of London's GDP is produced by tourist dollars, along with eight percent of employment. One-fourth of the people using the Tube in central London are tourists, a whopping 20% of these tourists coming from the US.

Since the economic downturn of 2001, London has seen some strain on its citizen's pockets and patience. This past year London markets have followed the dips in share value experienced on Wall Street. During the past two years, London has seen strikes by British Airways workers, London Underground and Rail Drivers, and even British firefighters. London also suffers from an increase in Graduate unemployment (up to 6.3% in 2003), affecting the finance, IT, engineering and technology industries the most strongly. Yet at the same time, the city endeavors to push through reforms to improve the standard of living. Blair's Labour government along with local councils are currently in the process of improving the state of London's schools, particularly in the poorer boroughs of Islington, Hackney, Southwark, and Lambeth. The debate, however, continues as to whether improvement could best be achieved through local fundraising and monitoring or nationalization. Other reforms aim to improve the local commute around town. Central London's infamously congested roads may be headed for a change as London experiments with "congestion charges" of £5 for driving at certain hours.

In the spirit of sustainable tourism, *Let's Go* aims to offer travelers a chance to give back to the cities and communities they visit. We've watched the growth of the 'ignorant tourist' stereotype with dismay, knowing that the majority of travelers care passionately about the state of the communities and environments they explore—but also knowing that even conscientious tourists can inadvertently damage natural wonders and cultural enclaves. We believe the philosophy of **sustainable travel** is among the most important travel tips we could impart to our readers, to help guide fellow backpackers and on-the-road philanthropists. In this chapter we describe the social, political, and economic issues facing London along with listings of volunteer organizations dedicated to these concerns.

As the political center of the country, London is the place for movers and shakers to make an impact on representatives in Westminster. For those interested in **political activism** we provide the contact information for nine of the largest or most influential parties in Parliament; from the well-known Labour and Conservative parties, to the nationalist parties of Ireland, Scotland and Wales, to the non-affiliated Trade Justice movement. Contact the party offices to inquire how they can become involved in London campaigns. For those interested in **environmental issues,** we list those organizations at the forefront of current concerns, including the GM food debate, the protection of endangered species, conservation legislation ratified through the European Union, urban pollution, and waste management. Finally, we list organizations dedicated to **community assistance,** acknowledging the poor of London. Because London poverty is concentrated most in those areas with high populations of West African refugees, South Asians, and southern Europeans, it is a concern closely intertwined with continuing high rates of immigration. However, altruists can choose organizations which focus on a variety of different community segments, including recent immigrants, homeless youth and persons under the wing of religious institutions. Later in this section, we recommend how to find organizations that best suit your interests, whether you're looking to pitch in for a day or a year.

Studying at a college or language programs is another way to integrate yourself into the London scene. Many travelers also structure their trips by the **work** that they can do along the way—either odd jobs as they go, or full-time stints in cities where they plan to stay for some time. **Internships, teaching,** and **au pair** opportunities await the persistent or with the help of temp agencies, a job in the service or clerical sector is yours for the taking, provided you have the right visa documentation.

For those who seek more active involvement, Earthwatch International, Operation Crossroads Africa, Cross Cultural Solutions, and Habitat for Humanity offer fulfilling volunteer opportunities all over the world. For more on volunteering, studying, and working in London and beyond, consult Let's Go's alternatives to tourism website, **www.beyondtourism.com**.

Before handing your money over to any volunteer or study abroad program, make sure you know exactly what you're getting into. It's a good idea to get the names of **previous participants** and ask them about their experience, as some programs sound much better on paper than in reality. The **questions** below are a good place to start:

-Will you be the only person in the program? If not, what are the other participants like? How old are they? How much will you be expected to interact with them?

-Is room and board included? If so, what is the arrangement? Will you be expected to share a room? A bathroom? What are the meals like? Do they fit any dietary restrictions?

-Is transportation included? Are there any additional expenses?

-How much free time will you have? Will you be able to travel around the island?

-What kind of safety network is set up? Will you still be covered by your home insurance? Does the program have an emergency plan?

A NEW PHILOSOPHY OF TRAVEL

We at *Let's Go* have watched the growth of the 'ignorant tourist' stereotype with dismay, knowing that the majority of travelers care passionately about the state of the communities and environments they explore—but also knowing that even conscientious tourists can inadvertently damage natural wonders, rich cultures, and impoverished communities. We believe the philosophy of **sustainable travel** is among the most important travel tips we could impart to our readers, to help guide fellow backpackers and on-the-road philanthropists. By staying aware of the needs and troubles of local communities, today's travelers can be a powerful force in preserving and restoring this fragile world.

Working against the negative consequences of irresponsible tourism is much simpler than it might seem; it is often self-awareness, rather than self-sacrifice, that makes the biggest difference. Simply by trying to spend responsibly and conserve local resources, all travelers can positively impact the places they visit. Let's Go has partnered with **BEST (Business Enterprises for Sustainable Travel,** an affiliate of the Conference Board; see www.sustainabletravel.org), which recognizes businesses that operate based on the principles of sustainable travel. Below, they provide advice on how ordinary visitors can practice this philosophy in their daily travels, no matter where they are.

TIPS FOR CIVIC TRAVEL: HOW TO MAKE A DIFFERENCE

Travel by train when feasible. Rail travel requires only half the energy per passenger mile that planes do. On average, each of the 40,000 daily domestic air flights releases more than 1700 pounds of greenhouse gas emissions.

Use public mass transportation whenever possible; outside of cities, take advantage of group taxis or vans. Bicycles are an attractive way of seeing a community firsthand. And enjoy walking—purchase good maps of your destination and ask about on-foot touring opportunities.

When renting a car, ask whether fuel-efficient vehicles are available. Honda and Toyota produce cars that use hybrid engines powered by electricity and gasoline, thus reducing emissions of carbon dioxide. Ford Motor Company plans to introduce a hybrid fuel model by the end of 2004.

Reduce, reuse, recycle—use electronic tickets, recycle papers and bottles wherever possible, and avoid using containers made of styrofoam. Refillable water bottles and rechargable batteries both efficiently conserve expendable resources.

Be thoughtful in your purchases. Take care not to buy souvenir objects made from trees in old-growth or endangered forests, such as teak, or items made from endangered species, like ivory or tortoise jewelry. Ask whether products are made from renewable resources.

Buy from local enterprises, such as casual street vendors. In developing countries and low-income neighborhoods, many people depend on the "informal economy" to make a living.

Be on-the-road-philanthropists. If you are inspired by the natural environment of a destination or enriched by its culture, join in preserving their integrity by making a charitable contribution to a local organization.

Spread the word. Upon your return home, tell friends and colleagues about places to visit that will benefit greatly from their tourist dollars, and reward sustainable enterprises by recommending their services. Travelers can not only introduce friends to particular vendors but also to local causes and charities that they might choose to support when they travel.

Officer of the Law

Apostrophe Protectorate

Double Decker

VOLUNTEERING

Volunteering can be one of the most fulfilling experiences you have in life, especially if you combine it with the thrill of traveling in a new place. London offers a rich array of options, from environmental activism, to political campaigning, to poverty relief. Volunteer jobs are fairly easy to secure. However, if you receive room and board in exchange for your labor, you are "employed" and must get a **work visa.** To avoid the nasty high application fees charged by agency organizations try contacting the individual organizations directly.

Most people who volunteer in London do so on a short-term basis, at organizations that make use of drop-in or once-a-week volunteers. There are two main types of organizations—religious and non-sectarian—although there are rarely restrictions on participation for either. More intensive volunteer services may charge you a fee to participate. These costs can be surprisingly hefty (although they frequently cover airfare and most, if not all, living expenses). Most people choose to go through a parent organization that takes care of logistical details and frequently provides a group environment and support system. A good place to begin your search for openings in London is on **www.volunteerabroad.com,** which allows you to search specifically within the city. Another useful engine for broadening your search is **www.idealist.org.**

ENVIRONMENTALISM

Wary of oversized tomatoes? Protests are mounting in London over GM (genetically modified) foods. Advocates for GM praise their potential for lowering costs, improving the quality and size of produce, and aiding farmers by reducing the need for pesticides. Environmental groups, on the other hand, raise concerns over the long-term consequences of GM foods, calling for more extensive research. The organizations listed below participate in a variety of environmental issues both including and beyond the GM debate.

British Trust for Conservation Volunteers (BTCV), 36 St. Mary's St., Wallingford, Oxfordshire OX10 0EU (☎01491 821 600; www.btcv.org). The largest volunteer organization in Britain, BTCV also sponsors community and school programs, training for employment, as well as regular sessions of conservation activities through Green Gym.

Friends of the Earth, 26-28 Underwood St., London, N1 7JQ (☎ 7490 1555; www.foe.co.uk). Circulates news events, networks with local groups.

Greenpeace UK, Canonbury Villas, London, N1 2PN (☎ 7865 8100; www.greenpeace.uk). Active in a wide range of regional campaigns; contact the London central office for calendar and volunteer openings.

Sustain, 94 White Lion St., London, N1 9PF (☎ 7837 1228; www.sustainweb.org). Launched in 1999 as a merger of the National Food Alliance and the Sustainable Agriculture Food and Environment (SAFE) Alliance, Sustain relies on volunteers to maintain a network of over 100 organizations committed to safe and sane food production.

FARMING OPTIONS

The classic country vs. city conflict is especially poignant in London, where farms struggle for subsidies, trade protection, and representation within the GM food debate. If you're inspired to get first-hand exposure to the green beyond, consider the following organizations:

Future Farmers of America (FFA) Global, P.O. Box 68960, 6060 FFA Drive, Indianapolis, IN 46268 (☎ 317-802-4220; www.ffa.org/international). Sponsors international exchange and work experience programs, including Agricultural Ambassadors to the UK.

Global Outreach, P.O. Box 25883, Alexandria, VA 22313, USA (☎ 703-299-9551; www.globaloutreach.net). Arranges short and long-term international exchange programs. Program fees US$800-2500.

World Wide Opportunities on Organic Farms (WWOOF), UK Main Office, P.O. Box 2675, Lewes, East Sussex BN7 1RB (www.wwoof.org.uk). Arranges volunteer work with independent host farms across Britain and Ireland. £15.00 membership fee.

POLTICAL ACTIVISM

For those with a tendency towards politics, London is the ideal place to participate in a party campaign. Your best bet is to contact the party directly to inquire what kind of tasks are needed. Often volunteers are recruited for clerical support, fundraising, and publicity. Usually no fee is required to participate, though you may be solicited to contribute to "the cause." *Let's Go* does not endorse the views of any of these parties, though we do have a soft spot for the Monster Raving Loony Party.

The Conservative Party, 32 Smith Sq., London SW1P 3HH (☎ 7984 8162; www.conservative-party.org.uk). The oldest political party in the world, the Tories hold sway over the moderate right, having locked horns with Labour over social and fiscal spending for a decade.

The Labour Party, 16 Old Queen St., London, SW1H 9HP (☎ 7490 4904; www.londonlabor.org.uk). Currently Her Majesty's government, Labour is led by Prime Minister Tony Blair. Originally founded by the Labour Movement, the now center-left Labour party continues to advocate for increased social services, such as health care and education, though recently it has been criticized by most Leftist groups for its moderation.

Liberal Democrats, 4 Cowley St., London, SW1P 3NB (☎ 7227 1335; www.libdems.org.uk). Britain's third-largest political party, the center-left Liberal Democrats advocate changing the voting system for a "fairer distribution of power" and has aggressively lobbied for improved public transportation in London. Check out www.getlondonmoving.org.

Communist Party of Britain, 94 Camden Rd., London NW1 9EA (☎ 7428 9300; www.communist-party.org.uk). Advocating unabashed socialism for the past 83 years, the Communist party remains vehemently opposed to the so-called right-wing tactics of the Labour Party.

The Green Party of England and Wales, 1a Waterlow Rd., London N19 5NJ (☎ 7272 4474; www.greenparty.org.uk). Aiming for a "just and sustainable society", this ecologically-minded, leftist party advises volunteers to mail an application to the Green Party Volunteer Manager.

UK Independence Party, Bridgeman House, 54 Broadwick St., London W1F 7AH (☎/fax 7434 4559; mail@ukip.org). If the EU doesn't do it for you, join the party that seeks UK's withdrawal from the European Union.

Scottish National Party Headquarters, 107 McDonald Rd., Edinburgh EH7 4NW, Scotland (☎131 525 8900; www.snp.org.uk). Like most nationalist parties, the SNPH endorses decentralized government, and increasing the power of local assemblies.

Plaid Cymru, (Westminster Office) 4/5 Norman Shaw Bank, Victoria Embankment, London, SW1A 2JF (☎029 2064 6000, post@plaidcymru.org). Plaid Cymru promotes the revival of the Welsh language, along with a platform of "decentralist socialism." Head office is located (surprise!) in Wales at Ty Gwynfor, 18 Park Grove, Cardiff, CF10 3BN, Wales.

Trade Justice Movement (secretariat ☎7404 0530; www.tradejusticemovement.org.uk). An umbrella organization for numerous British, Scottish, and Welsh charity organizations dedicated to fighting world poverty and promoting fair trade. Political campaigns often address the UK's position in the WTO. In June 2003, Radiohead demonstrated their support by encouraging UK MPs to join the TJM lobby marathon. TJM website provides links to member organizations, including Save the Children, Action Aid, and the World Development Movement. Volunteer positions, when available, are usually at the Fairtrade Foundation offices in central London. Email your CV to mail@tjm.org.uk.

Apostrophe Protection Society, 23 Vauxhall Rd., Boston, Lincs. PE21 0JB (johnrichards20@beeb.net). Begun in 2001 by current Chairman John Richards, this society aims to preserve the correct use of this "much abused" punctuation mark.

Monster Raving Loony Party, The Dog & Partridge, 105 Reading Road, Yateley, Hampshire, GU46 7LR, (☎012 5287 8382; www.omrlp.com). Questions why there is only one female Smurf and pressures the Olympics to include The Egg and Spoon Race and The Annual Witch-ducking Championships.

POVERTY

Large economic discrepancies exist within London. Last year, Mayor Ken Livingstone reported that after housing costs are taken into account, 41 percent of London children live in poverty, the vast majority coming from minority groups, such as the Pakistani, Bangladeshi and persons of African descent. The following organizations focus on relief for all age groups.

Alone in London, 188 Kings Cross Rd., London WC1X 9DE (☎7278 4224 or 7841 3725 for volunteering; www.als.org.uk). Committed to the young homeless in London and specializing in family support, ALS volunteer posts are for 3 to 6 months and require an application.

Church on Poverty, Central Buildings, Oldham St., Manchester M1 1JT (☎016 1236 9321; www.church-poverty.org.uk). A national Christian social justice charity based in Manchester, CAP operates throughout the UK with churches and directly with those in poverty. Also maintains a Parliamentary Office in Westminster.

Community Service Volunteers (CSV), Head Office, 237 Pentonville Rd., London N1 9NJ (☎7278 6601; www.csv.org.uk). Offers both full and part-time volunteer positions, including teaching citizenship courses, broadcasting, and support for troubled youth and the homeless. Several local offices in London, check website for local listings. CSV cannot guarantee placement in a specific location but can offer help obtaining visas (only after placement). Provides £27.00 allowance plus free room and board. No fee.

Concordia International Volunteer Projects, Heversham House, 20-22 Boundary Rd., Hove, BN3 4ET, England (☎012 7342 2218; www.concordia-iye.org.uk). A small, not-for-profit charity, Concordia sponsors volunteer projects chiefly for residents of the UK, worldwide and locally. Volunteers pay a subscription fee of £6-10, a project fee of £75-80.

Oxfam, UK Poverty Programme, Central office, 274 Banbury Rd., Oxford OX2 7DZ (☎18 6531 3184; www.oxfam.co.uk). The UK's largest secular organization supporting the poor; contact Oxfam for your nearest regional office. Download an application online. No fee.

The Salvation Army UK Headquarters, 101 Newington Causeway, London SE1 6BN (☎0845 634 0101 or 7367 4500; www.salvationarmy.org.uk). A Christian organization dedicated to providing emergency and social services, including youth programs and family tracing. Open M-F 8:15am-4:30pm.

Volunteers for Peace, 1034 Tiffany Rd., Belmont, VT 05730, USA (☎802-259-2759; www.vfp.org). Arranges 2-3 week placements in work camps. Membership required for registration. Programs average US$200-500.

STUDYING

Study abroad programs in London range from basic language and culture courses to college-level classes, often for credit. In order to choose a program that best fits your needs, research all you can before making your decision—determine costs and duration, as well as what kind of students participate in the program and what sort of accommodations are provided. A good resource for finding programs that cater to your particular interests is **www.studyabroad.com,** which has links to various semester abroad programs based on a variety of criteria, including desired location and focus of study. Other useful links include **www.studyabroaddirectory.com** and **www.internationalstudent.com.** .

STUDENT VISAS

Non-EU nationals intending to study in the UK generally must be enrolled by a qualifying British educational institution before applying for student status. **Non-visa nationals** (foreigners who do not require visas to enter the UK as visitors) are permitted to enter the country as tourists and then apply for student status once they have been admitted to a course of study. If they have already been accepted on a course, they may apply for student status when entering the UK. To do this, you will need to show at the port of entry a letter of admittance from the school, university, or college and proof of adequate financial support to cover tuition and maintenance. **Visa nationals** are required to obtain a student visa from their local British Consulate before entering the country; to do so, they must provide proof of admittance to a course of study and financial support.

WORKING ON A STUDENT VISA. Non-EU students may work up to 20hr. per week during term-time, and full-time in vacation. However, longer hours may be authorized if deemed a necessary part of the course of study (e.g., as part of medical school training). EU citizens enjoy the same working rights as British citizens.

UNIVERSITIES

With dozens of institutions, from the sprawling colleges of the University of London and the vast collections of the British Library, you can study almost any subject at any level in London. It's not surprising that every year tens of thousands of international students choose to make London their academic home-away-from-home. Even if you didn't come to London to study, taking evening courses—whether in medieval architecture, Italian cookery, or jazz dance—can be a great way to broaden your horizons and meet similarly minded people. For a comprehensive list of part-time and evening classes, the annual **Floodlight** directory lists over 40,000 courses in Greater London. (www.floodlight.co.uk. Available from news agents. £3.75.). Some American schools still require students to pay them for credits obtained elsewhere.

The following is a list of organizations that can help place students in university programs abroad, or have their own branch in London

AMERICAN PROGRAMS

American Institute for Foreign Study, College Division, River Plaza, 9 West Broad St., Stamford, CT 06902, USA (☎800-727-2437, ext. 5163; www.aifsabroad.com). Organizes programs for high school and college study in universities in Britain and Ireland.

Arcadia University for Education Abroad, 450 S. Easton Rd., Glenside, PA 19038, USA (☎866-927-2234; www.arcadia.edu/cea). Operates programs both within London and throughout Britain and Ireland. Costs range from $2200 (summer) to $29,000 (full-year).

Association of Commonwealth Universities (ACU), John Foster House, 36 Gordon Sq., London WC1H OPF (☎+44 020 7380 6700; www.acu.ac.uk). Publishes information about Commonwealth universities which include the United Kingdom and Canada.

Center for Cultural Interchange, 17 North Second Avenue, St. Charles, IL 60174, (☎888-227-6231; www.cci-exchange.com). High school abroad program, independent homestay, internship program.

Central College Abroad, Office of International Education, 812 University, Pella, IA, 50219, USA (☎800-831-3629 or 641-628-5284; www.central.edu/abroad). Offers internships, as well as summer, semester, and year-long programs in London and throughout Britain. US$25 application fee.

Council on International Educational Exchange (CIEE), 633 3rd Ave., 20th floor, New York, NY 10017-6706 (☎800-407-8839; www.ciee.org/study) sponsors work, volunteer, academic, and internship programs in London and throughout Britain and Ireland.

International Association for the Exchange of Students for Technical Experience (IAESTE), 10400 Little Patuxent Pkwy. Suite 250, Columbia, MD 21044-3519, USA (☎410-997-2200; www.aipt.org). 8- to 12-week programs in London and throughout Britain and Ireland for college students who have 2 yrs. of technical study. US$25 application fee.

Institute for the International Education of Students (IES), 33 N. LaSalle St., 15th fl., Chicago, IL 60602, USA (☎800-995-2300; www.IESabroad.org). Offers year-long, semester, and summer programs in London for college students. Internships offered. US$50 application fee. Scholarships available.

School for International Training, College Semester Abroad, Admissions, Kipling Rd., P.O. Box 676, Brattleboro, VT 05302, USA (☎800-336-1616 or 802-257-7751; www.sit.edu). Semester- and year-long programs in Western Europe, including Ireland, run US$10,600-13,700. Also runs the **Experiment in International Living** (☎800-345-2929; www.usexperiment.org), 3- to 5-week summer programs that offer high-school students cross-cultural homestays, community service, ecological adventure, and language training in London and throughout Britain and Ireland. Cost: US$1900-5000.

PROGRAMS IN LONDON

Between themselves, the University of London and the London Institute encompass the vast majority of London's universities and colleges, though there are also numerous independent specialist institutions. Many offer **special programs** for international students on exchange visits, semesters abroad, and **summer schools.**

Enrolling for a **degree course** can present problems to those raised in a different system. UK universities will want to see evidence that you have attained the same educational standard as British 18-year-olds, either by passing the British A-level exams or a recognized equivalent, such as the International Baccalaureate; EU credentials are generally admissible. Americans may have problems, since SAT scores and high-school diplomas are not normally accepted; frequently, students must have completed a year of college in the US before being considered equivalent to European school graduates. The **British Council** (see p. 321) can often arrange for people to take British exams in their home countries.

Fees for degree programs for non-EU students depend on the subject and school, from around £8500 per year for humanities to £18,000 for medicine; EU residents pay the same as UK students, currently £1050 per year for all subjects. All foreign students need to show they have access to at least £8250 per year for **living expenses.**

EducationUK, (www.educationuk.org), a slick website run by the British Council (see below) to explain the British education system and persuade international students to buy British.

The London Institute, 65 Davies St., London W1K 5DA (☎ 7514 6000; www.linst.ac.uk) runs 5 of London's best-known art and design schools, including Central St. Martins College, Chelsea College of Art, and the London College of Fashion.

Universities and Colleges Admissions Services (UCAS), P.O. Box 28, Cheltenham, Gloucestershire, GL52 3ZA (☎ 01242 227 788; www.ucas.ac.uk). The centralized admissions service for all undergraduate degree courses in the UK. Also provides impartial information to international students on the application process.

University College London, Gower St., London WC1E 6BT (☎ 7679 7765; www.ucl.ac.uk) is the biggest of UofL's schools (and one of the UK's top universities), with a complete academic curriculum. Special programs are offered for international **affiliate students** on semester or 1yr. leaves from their home universities; affiliates must normally have completed 2yr. of university at time of admission to UCL.

The University of London (www.lon.ac.uk) is an umbrella organization uniting the vast majority of London's academic institutions, with 17 constituent universities and colleges.

THE BRITISH COUNCIL

The British Council is the arm of the government charged with promoting education opportunities in Britain, among other responsibilities. Its offices are an invaluable source of information for those intending to study in Britain at a secondary school or university level, or for those enrolling in language classes in Britain. They also offer the opportunity to take British exams for university admission. For branches in countries not listed here, call the London office or check www.britishcouncil.org.

London: 10 Spring Gdns., London SW1A 2BN (☎ 7389 4383, inquiries 0161 957 7755; general.enquiries@britcoun.org).

Australia: P.O. Box 88, Edgecliff NSW 2027 (☎ 016 301 204; www.bc.org.au).

Canada: 80 Elgin St., Ottawa, Ontario K1P 5K7 (☎ 613-237-1530; www.ca.britishcouncil.org).

Ireland: Newmount House, 22/24 Lower Mount St., Dublin 2 (☎ 01 676 4088 or 01 676 6943; www.britishcouncil.org/ireland).

New Zealand: 44 Hill St., P.O. Box 1812, Wellington 6001 and 151 Queen St., Private Bag 92014, Auckland 1001 (both ☎ 04 472 6049; www.britishcouncil.org.nz).

South Africa: 76 Juta St., Braamfontein, Johannesburg 2001; send mail to P.O. Box 30637, Braamfontein, 2017 (☎ 011 403 3316; www.britishcouncil.org/southafrica).

United States: British Embassy, 3100 Massachusetts Ave. N.W., Washington, D.C. 20008 (☎ 800-488-2235 or 202-588-6500; www.britishcouncil-usa.org).

LANGUAGE SCHOOLS

Unlike American universities, language schools are frequently independently run organizations or divisions of foreign universities that rarely offer college credit. Language schools are a good alternative to university study if you desire a deeper focus on a new language or a slightly less-rigorous courseload. **Eurocentres** at 101 N. Union St. Suite 300, Alexandria, VA 22314, USA (☎ 703-684-1494; www.eurocentres.com) or in Europe, Head Office, Seestr. 247, CH-8038 Zurich, Switzerland (☎ +41 1 485 50 40; fax 481 61 24), offers language programs for beginning to advanced students with homestays in London, Brighton, Cambridge, London, and Oxford.

SUMMER & SHORT VOCATIONAL PROGRAMS

Many of London's elite **art, music,** and **drama** academies supplement their income by offering part-time and summer courses to motivated amateurs. Typically there are no admissions requirements (though some courses fill up

ALTERNATIVES TO TOURISM LANGUAGE SCHOOLS

quickly); the flipside is that you will rarely receive any recognition other than a certificate of attendance for the work you put in. Always check whether you'll be taught by the same master artists who teach the colleges' regular offerings—often the famous name hides the fact that a course is being taught by a part-time teacher they wouldn't dream of subjecting degree-seeking students to. Numerous private **vocational schools** also run short courses that are wildly popular with an international crowd.

Central St. Martins College of Art and Design, Southampton Row, London WC1B 4AP (☎7514 7015; www.csm.linst.ac.uk), offers dozens of evening courses throughout the year as well as a comprehensive summer program covering all aspects of fine art, graphic design, fashion, and film (£150-300 per week).

Courtauld Institute, Somerset House, Strand, London WC2R ORN (☎7848 2413; www.courtauld.ac.uk), offers 12 week-long summer courses in art history. Courses include gallery visits, focusing on the Courtauld's own impressive collections. Also offers a 1yr. Master's program in Art History and Art Restoration (see also **Museums,** p. 129).

London School of Journalism, 22 Upbrook Mews, London W2 3HG (☎7706 3790; www.lsj.org), offers 3-month full-time and 6-month part-time post-graduate diploma courses (from £2750) and a 4-week summer school (£1295). All courses are recognized by the National Union of Journalists, entitling students to NUJ membership.

Royal Academy of the Dramatic Arts (RADA), 62-64 Gower St., London WC1E 6ED (☎7636 7076; www.rada.org). The alma mater of Ralph Fiennes, Kenneth Branagh, and Anthony Hopkins offers 4- and 8-week summer courses in acting, set design, and scriptwriting (around £2250 per 4 weeks). Applicants must be at least 18; no experience required.

Slade School of Fine Art, part of University College London, Gower St., London WC1 E6BT (☎7679 7772; www.ucl.ac.uk/slade). Offers a range of general and specialized art courses over the summer, lasting 1-10 weeks. The 2-month Alternative Foundation offers a complete introduction to drawing, painting, sculpting, and printing (£2500).

Vidal Sassoon Academy, 56-59 Davies Mews, London W1Y 1AS (☎7318 5202). As many students come here for the scene as for the teaching. 8-month diploma course for beginners £10,750; shorter advanced courses up to £1000.

COURSES IN ARCHAEOLOGY

Every quest for the Holy Grail should begin with a trustworthy guide. In your case that guide should be *Current Archaeology* (www.archaeology.co.uk), a reliable publication on current and upcoming excursions and innovations in the UK.

Birkbeck College, Faculty of Continuing Education, 26 Russell Sq., London, WC1B 5DQ (☎7631 6627; www.bbk.ac.uk/fce). Offers courses in field archaeology and Egyptology, day and weekend schools and surveying courses. Be sure to check out their annual urban training excavation during June/July (£155 per week).

Bromley & West Kent Archaeological Group, 5 Harvest Bank Rd., West Wickham, Kent, BR4 9DL (☎/fax 020 8462 4737) Opportunities for volunteers to participate in weekend excavations and as guides at the Crofton Roman Villa in Orpington. Open to the public Apr.-Oct.

Bloomsbury Summer School or **Bloomsbury Academy,** University College London, Gower St., London WC1E 6BT (☎7679 3622; www.egyptology-uk.com/bloomsbury). Offers intensive summer courses on Eygptology.

WORKING

With unemployment in the UK at its lowest level for decades, ranging from 3-6%, there's never been a better time to find work in London. **Casual work,** such as bartending, baby-sitting, and waiting tables is the easiest to find, though it remains poorly paid. Unscrupulous employers will often take on foreigners without work permits for lower wages. Be warned that as an illegal employee your right of redress against any malpractice by your employer will be severely limited. If you work legally, you will enjoy the protection of UK labor laws. You'll pay 23% tax and 10% National Insurance on all but the lowest-paid jobs.

YOUR RIGHTS. The **minimum wage** varies with age and length of employment. 18- to 21-year-olds and those receiving accredited training within six months of starting a new job may not be paid less than £3.60 per hr.; otherwise the rate is £4.20. **Full-time workers** may not be forced to work over 48hr. per week, 13hr. per day, or six days per week. They are also entitled to 4 weeks paid vacation per year. **Part-time workers** are now entitled to many of the benefits an employer accords full-time employees, including paid vacation on a pro-rated basis. For more information, including details of **maternity leave** and **anti-discrimination laws,** the **Tailored Interactive Guide on Employment Rights** (TIGER; www.tiger.gov.uk) offers comprehensive information on employment law in the UK.

COMMONWEALTH CITIZENS. Commonwealth citizens aged 17-27 are eligible for a **working holidaymaker visa,** allowing them to stay and work in the UK for up to two years provided that employment is "incidental to a holiday." Essentially, this means that no more than half your stay can be spent in full-time work. (See FCO form INF 5 for details.) Those aged 17 or over and who have at least one **UK-born grandparent** (including Ireland if born before March 31, 1922) are eligible for a **UK Ancestry Visa,** which gives the right to reside and work in the UK for an initial period of four years. (See FCO form INF 7 for details.) Canadian citizens should also refer to the **Student Work Abroad Programme** (SWAP; www.swap.ca), which has 40 offices in Canada administered by the Canadian Universities Travel Service. This program is similar to the BUNAC program available to US citizens (see below).

US STUDENTS. In general, US citizens are required to have a work permit (see below) to work in the UK. However, American citizens who are full-time students and are older than 18 can apply for a special permit from the **British Universities North America Club (BUNAC),** which allows them to work for **up to six months.** Contact BUNAC at: P.O. Box 430, Southbury, CT 06488 (US ☎ 203-264-0901; UK ☎ 020 7251 3472; www.bunac.org.uk). BUNAC also offers limited assistance in finding housing and employment in the UK and organizes regular social events. You will need to enter

Punk Girl

Look Right

Black Cab

the UK within one semester of graduation, and have at least US$1000 on entry. BUNAC also has a very helpful bulletin board in their London office, 16 Bowling Green Ln. (☎7251 3472), with housing and job postings.

STUDENTS AT UK INSTITUTIONS. Full-time students at UK educational institutions have a limited right to part-time and vacation work. See p. 319 for details.

WORK PERMITS & WORK VISAS. If you do not fall into one of the above categories, you will need a **work permit** in order to work in the UK. If you require a visa to travel to the UK, you will also need a **work visa.** You must already have a job set up in the UK before obtaining a work permit, which can only be applied for through your employer. For further information, consult **Work Permits (UK),** Department of Education and Employment, W5 Moorfoot, Sheffield, S1 4PQ (☎0114 259 4074; www.workpermits.gov.uk).

> **VISA INFORMATION**
> The **Foreign and Commonwealth Office's (FCO)** Joint Entry Clearance Unit (JECU; www.ukvisas.gov.uk) has info on visa and work permit requirements and downloadable application forms. Information for visitors already in the UK is also available from the **Home Office Immigration and Nationality Directorate** (www.ind.homeoffice.gov.uk). The **Immigration Advisory Service,** County House, 190 Great Dover St., London SE1 4YB (☎7357 6917; www.iasuk.org) is an independent charity that provides free advice and assistance to people applying for UK visas.

LONG-TERM WORK

If you're planning on spending a substantial amount of time (more than three months) working in London, search for a job well in advance. Currently teachers and specialists in the medical field, such as nurses, doctors and paramedics are in particularly high demand. For those outside the UK, a good place to begin your search online is on **www.tntmagazine.com/uk/jobs.**

INTERNSHIPS

Finding an internship in London is not difficult—finding a paid one is. If you are interested in interning,,, use college career offices and the Internet to investigate options. London's status as a financial hub means that there are hundreds of overpaid summer positions in banks and consultancies, but competition is fierce: applications must normally be completed by February for work starting in June. There is a smaller number of (normally unpaid) internship positions in media and publishing companies, though duties will typically be limited to menial tasks. Be wary of advertisements or companies abroad that claim the ability to get you a job for a fee—their listings are often available online or in newspapers, or even out-of-date. Some reputable companies include:

Council Exchanges, 52 Poland St., London W1F 7AB, UK (☎7478 2000, in the US 888-268-6245; www.councilexchanges.org), charges a US$300-475 fee for arranging short-term working authorizations (generally valid for 3-6 months) and provides extensive information on different job opportunities in London.

Hansard Scholar Programme, St. Philips, Building North, Sheffield St., London WC2 2EX (☎7955 7459; www.hansard-society.org.uk). Combines classes at the London School of Economics with internships in British government.

IAESTE—US, 10400 Little Patuxent Pkwy., Ste. 250L, Columbia, MD 21044, USA (☎410-997-3068; www.aipt.org/iaeste.html). Arranges internships, especially in technical fields.

interExchange, 161 Sixth Ave., New York, NY 10013, USA (☎212-924-0446; www.interexchange.org). US students only. Pay US$950 to get paid $5-6 per hr. in a London hotel; room and board not included. $1250 for an unpaid internship. Fees include BUNAC Blue Card work permit (see **US Students,** p. 323).

International Exchange Programs (IEP), 196 Albert Rd., South Melbourne, Victoria 3205, Australia (☎03 9690 5890), and P.O. Box 1786, Shortland St., Auckland, New Zealand (☎09 366 6255; www.iepnz.co.nz). Helps Aussies and Kiwis on working holidaymaker visas (see p. 324) find work, lodging, and friends. AU$300/NZ$340 fee.

Tate, 7 Hanover Sq., London W1S 1HQ (☎7408 0424; www.tate.co.uk), arranges secretarial placements for foreigners in London.

University of North London, Office of International Programs, 228 Miller Bldg., Box 2000, SUNY Cortland, Cortland, NY 13045, USA (☎697-753-2209; www.cortland.edu/html/ipgms.html). Offers fall and spring internship openings in London. Students pay SUNY tuition costs plus program fees (US$4500-5500).

TEACHING

Teaching jobs abroad are rarely well-paid, although some elite private American schools can pay somewhat competitive salaries. Volunteering as a teacher in lieu of getting paid is also a popular option; teachers often get some sort of a daily stipend to help with living expenses. In almost all cases, you must have at least a bachelor's degree to be a full-fledged teacher, although college undergraduates can often get summer positions teaching or tutoring. The British school system is comprised of state (public, government-funded), "public" (independent, privately funded), and international (often for children of expatriates in the UK) schools, as well as universities. Applications to teach at state schools must be made through the local government; independent and international schools must be applied to individually. University positions are typically only available through fellowship or exchange programs. Placement agencies are often a good way to find teaching jobs in Britain, although vacancies are also listed in major newspapers. The alternative is to make contacts directly with schools or just to try your luck once you get there. If you are going to try the latter, the best time of the year is several weeks before the start of the school year. The following organizations may be of help in your search:

Independent Schools Information Service, 56 Buckingham Gate, London SW1E 6AG (☎7630 8793; www.iscis.uk.net). A list of British independent schools and further information on teaching opportunities.

International Schools Services (ISS), 15 Roszel Rd., Box 5910, Princeton, NJ 08543-5910, USA (☎609-452-0990; www.iss.edu). Candidates should have experience teaching or with international affairs. 2yr. commitment expected.

European Council of International Schools, 21B Lavant St., Petersfield, Hampshire GU32 3EL (☎0730 268 244; www.ecis.org). Contact details for British international schools, as well as placement opportunities.

AU PAIR WORK

Au pairs are typically women, aged 18-27, who work as live-in nannies, caring for children and doing light housework in exchange for room, board, and a small spending allowance or stipend (around £40-70 per week). Typically they work 25-40hr. per week with one or two nights off. Citizens of certain countries may not be eligible for au-pair work in the UK, but may find placement instead as a **mother's helper.** Mother's helpers work 40-50 hours per week caring for children under the supervision of a parent. They are also responsible for light housework and a few nights of babysitting. People with childcare qualifications can find much more lucrative work as **live-in nannies,** making up to £250 per week in addition to food and lodging. Most former au pairs speak favorably of their experience, and of how it allowed them to get to know the country without the high expenses of traveling. Drawbacks include long hours of constantly being on-duty and the somewhat mediocre pay. Much of the au pair experience really does depend on the family you're placed with. The agencies below are a good starting point for looking for employment as an au pair.

Accord Cultural Exchange, 750 La Playa, San Francisco, CA 94121, USA (☎415-386-6203; www.cognitext.com/accord). Hefty US$750 to arrange au pair and guest-teacher positions, US$1200 unpaid internships. US$40 application fee.

Au Pair Homestay, World Learning, Inc., 1015 15th St. NW, Suite 750, Washington, DC 20005, USA (☎800-287-2477). Covers Britain and Ireland.

Au Pair in Europe, P.O. Box 68056, Blakely Postal Outlet, Hamilton, Ontario, Canada L8M 3M7 (☎905-545-6305; www.princeent.com). Covers Britain and Ireland.

Childcare International, Ltd., Trafalgar House, Grenville Pl., London NW7 3SA (☎8906 3116; www.childint.co.uk). Arranges childcare placements for Commonwealth and European applicants. Au pairs work 25-30 hrs. per week, receive full board, lodging, and £40 per week spending allowance. Those with prior childcare experience can work as mothers' helpers (40-50 hrs. per week) in return for board, lodging, and £100 per week. Qualified nannies can make £230 per week. No application fee.

InterExchange, 161 Sixth Ave., New York, NY 10013, USA (☎212-924-0446; www.interexchange.org).

SHORT-TERM WORK

A good place for foreigners to get their start is by checking newspapers such as *The Guardian, The Times,* and *The Evening Standard.* Other good (and free!) employment-specific publications include **TNT Magazine UK,** which appears every Monday, and the **Metro,** can be found in blue bins at Tube stations. The jobs published may vary by day: Secretarial on Mondays, Financing on Tuesdays, etc. Most often, these short-term jobs are found by word of mouth, or simply by talking to the owner of a hostel or restaurant. Many places, due to the high turnover in the tourism industry, are eager for help, even if temporary.

HOTEL/CATERING. There's no shortage of jobs in London waiting tables, tending bars, or filling less glamorous behind-the-scenes roles in kitchen and cleaning positions. What these all have in common is that they are poorly paid (typically minimum wage—as little as $3.60 per hr.—or even less for illegal employees) with antisocial hours. And don't expect to boost that much with tips: bartenders are not tipped in the UK, and many restaurants have "service included" in their prices—money which may or may not find its way into your pay. Another popular option is to work several hours a day at a **hostel** in exchange for free or discounted room and/or board. You can also begin your search with the **Blue Speed Employment Agency,** which specializes in the hotel and leisure industries. (☎/fax 084 564 433 04; www.bluespeed.co.uk).

SECRETARIAL WORK. If you can type like a demon, then **temping** can be a good way to pay the bills. Temps are temporary secretaries on short-term placements (from as little as one day to a few weeks); you'll need to register with a temping agency who'll match available positions to your skills.

ACCOUNTING, INVESTMENT BANKING, & INFORMATION TECHNOLOGY. These employment agencies are usually seeking professionals or semi-professionals. However, some agencies offer openings for temporary and contract staff.

Badenock & Clark, (☎7583 6073; accounting@badenockandclark.com).

Cameron Kennedy, 125 High Holborn, London, WC1V 6ZX (☎7430 001; fax 7404 4333).

Joslin Rowe, Bell Court House, 11 Blomfield St., London, EC2M 7AY (☎7786 6927; temporaries@joslinrowe.com).

Should Britain Stay in the EU?

Ever since Jean Monnet and Robert Schuman dreamed up the European Coal and Steel Community—the forerunner of today's European Union—back in 1950, the UK has suffered from a prolonged case of attraction/repulsion syndrome towards European integration. Britain only joined the then-European Community in 1973 (which became the EU in 1993), having had its application vetoed twice in the 1960s by de Gaulle's France, thus having been kept out of (or, some say, having missed out on) the formative years of European integration. While having been unable to offer a *yea* or *nay* on fundamental, early efforts at creating the common market may explain Britain's continuing ambivalence (and intermittent obstructiveness) toward the EU, its oft-vaunted 1000 years of independence may go further in illuminating its ongoing love-affair with its sovereignty.

After World War II, Britain's political and economic attachments were felt to lie elsewhere—with its then-empire and within the emerging Commonwealth, as well as in its "special relationship" with the US. Indeed, the fact that Britain arrogantly ignored the developments on the European continent perhaps justified the EC's spiteful rejection of Britain's early attempts at courtship. When Britain finally joined, the Thatcher government almost immediately started to cause trouble, calling into question Britain's significant contribution to the EC's budget and specifically the cherished Common Agricultural Policy (a gargantuan agglomeration of subsidies to Europe's farmers, most of which did not apply to a country like the UK whose agricultural economy is based largely on, well...sheep). Thatcher famously asked for Britain's money back before demanding a massive financial overhaul of Europe, largely provoking the black days when politicians and academics on both sides of the Atlantic questioned whether European integration would ever be attained.

By 1988, Britain had experienced the largest reorientation of its trade toward the EU of all member states—a remarkable demonstration of just how much Britain needed the EU, if it did not really love the idea of it. Britain (with Denmark) nevertheless continues to be Europe's most awkward partner, cherry-picking policies of which it approves and fiercely negotiating opt-outs of those of which it doesn't—most famously, the common travel area and the Euro. Given its reluctance to play like a true European, some even speculate that Britain might be better suited to membership of NAFTA. An all-or-nothing choice between the rapacious capitalism of the North Americans and the mellower mix of mandated job stability, long vacations, and comprehensive social services enjoyed by most European continentals is, however, not a straight-forward one for Britain to make.

Should Britain stay in the EU? Although membership is technically politically reversible, it may not be so economically. Extracting itself from the EU's treaties and legislation adopted to date, as well as from the customs-free European web of trade, would be a Herculean task for Britain. While Britain's pensioners and punters on the street (25% of whom, in a recent poll, didn't even know that Britain was a member of the EU) might proudly rejoice at such a reclamation of self-determination, the City of London's financiers and businessfolk would likely revolt at the idea. The UK's current Labour government has, further, been the most Europhilic in recent times, and is contemplating a referendum on joining the Euro in the year to come. While the advantages of a single currency become evident to Britons as soon as they head out for their next holiday to Spain, France, or Greece, their deep attachment to the Pound Sterling as the last plank of Britishness in a sea of eroding sovereignty still runs high. Continuing to opt out of the Euro, as well as other unwearable policy areas, will keep Britain semi-detached and out of Europe's inner core for some time to come, as well as continue to position the nation as the Euro-Atlantic area's idiosyncratic middle ground. Thus, the question of Britain's membership in the EU may be less one of "should I stay or should I go?", but rather how long its partners in the ever-closer Union will continue to tolerate Britain's consternating fickleness.

Jeremy Faro wrote for Let's Go: Britain & Ireland 1995. *He worked in London as a Senior Consultant for Interbrand, and is now a Master's student in European Studies at the University of Cambridge.*

Service Directory

ACCOMMODATION AGENCIES

Jenny Jones, 40 South Molton St., W1K 5RW (☎7493 4801; fax 7495 2912; www.jenny-jonesagency.co.uk). Tube: Bond St. One agency that you can trust. No fee (landlord charged). Some 3 mo. rentals, most 6 mo. minimum. Open M 2-5pm, Tu-Th 9:30am-1:30pm and 2:30-5pm, F 9:30am-1pm.

Accommodation Outlet. Short- and long-term apartments for gays and lesbians. See p. 264.

University of London Accommodations Office, Senate House, Room B, Malet St. (☎7862 8880; fax 7862 8084; www.lon.ac.uk/accom). Tube: Russell Square. Keeps a list of summer room and apartment vacancies, only available by going into the office. Information on residence halls on website. Services available only during vacations to students with valid ID. Other services only available to University of London students. Open M-F 9:30am-5:30pm.

AIRPORTS

See **Once in London,** p. 23.

BANKS

See **Once In London,** p. 37.

BICYCLE & SCOOTER RENTAL

Bikepark, 63 New King's Rd. (☎7731 7012). Tube: Fulham Broadway. £12 1st day, £6 2nd, £4 per day thereafter. Credit-card deposit. Open M-F 8:30am-7pm, Sa 9am-6pm, Su 11am-5pm.

London Bicycle Tour Company, 1a Gabriel's Wharf, off 56 Upper Ground (☎7928 6838; www.londonbicycle.com). Tube: Blackfriars or Waterloo. Bikes and blades £2.50 per hr. £12 for first 24hr., £6 per day thereafter. Credit-card deposit. Open Apr.-Oct. daily 10am-6pm; call ahead Nov.-Mar. AmEx/MC/V.

Scootabout, 1-3 Leeke St. (☎7833 4607). Tube: King's Cross. Moped and scooter rentals. Riders must have already had some experience. 21+ only; rates depend on age and include insurance coverage. 50-125cc bikes £20 per day; 2-day minimum. Credit-card deposit. Helmets occasionally available (£2); inquire when booking. MC/V.

BUDGET TRAVEL AGENCIES

Make sure any travel agencies you use are members of the Air Travel Organizer's License so that your ticket will still be good if the agency goes bankrupt.

CTS Travel, 44 Goodge St. (☎ 7636 0031, 7636 0032; www.ctstravel.co.uk). Tube: Goodge St. Open M-F 9:30am-6pm.

Flightbookers, 177 Tottenham Court Rd. (☎ 7757 2504; www.ebookers.com). Tube: Warren St. Budget travel agency for non-students. Open M-F 9am-7pm, Sa 9am-6pm, Su 10am-5pm.

STA Travel (☎ 0870 1600 599; www.statravel.co.uk). 14 London branches; largest at 85 Shaftesbury Ave. (☎ 7432 7474). Tube: Piccadilly Circus. Open M-W and F 11am-7pm, Th 11am-8pm, Sa 11am-5pm. Other branches at 11 Goodge St.; 86 Old Brompton Rd.; 117 Euston Rd.; London School of Economics, East Building.

Travel CUTS, 295A Regent St. (☎ 7255 1944). Tube: Oxford Circus. Open M-W and F 9am-6pm, Th 9am-7pm, Sa 11am-4pm. Other branch at International Student House (☎ 7436 0459; p. 262).

BUSES

See **Transportation,** p. 334.

CALLING CARDS

See **Telephone Services,** p. 334.

CAR RENTAL

Foreigners over 17 may drive in the UK for up to one year if in possession of a valid driving licence (some exceptions apply).

Budget (☎ 08701 56 56 56; www.budget.co.uk). Locations include Heathrow Airport (☎ 845 606 6669; fax 208 750 2525), Gatwick Airport (☎ 845 606 6669; fax 1293 562 613), and numerous London branches. Minimum age 25.

easyRentACar.com (www.easyrentacar.com). Internet-only rentals. 3 central London locations. Minimum age 21. From £7 per day, plus £5 preparation fee.

Europcar (☎ 0870 607 5000; fax 01132 429 495; www.europcar.com). 5 London locations, including 30 Woburn Pl. Tube: Euston. Minimum age 23.

Wheelchair Travel. See **Disability Resources,** p. 331.

CHEMISTS

Most chemists keep standard store hours (approx. M-Sa 9:30am-5:30pm); one "duty" chemist in each neighborhood will also open on Sunday, though hours may be limited. Late-night and 24hr. chemists are extremely rare; two are given below.

Bliss, 5-6 Marble Arch (☎ 7723 6116). Tube: Marble Arch. Open daily 9am-midnight.

Zafash Pharmacy, 233 Old Brompton Rd. (☎ 7373 2798). Tube: Earl's Court. Open 24hr.

CINEMA

West End Cinemas: see also **Entertainment,** p. 213.

The Empire, Leicester Sq. (☎ 0870 010 2030).

Odeon Leicester Sq., Leicester Sq. (☎ 7930 6111).

CLINICS

See also **Hospitals,** p. 332.

Jefferiss Centre for Sexual Health, St. Mary's Hospital, Praed St. (☎ 7725 6619). Tube: Paddington. Free and confidential sexual health services and supplies, including free condoms and dental dams, STD and HIV tests, and counseling. Open for walk-ins M 8:45am-4:30pm, Tu and Th 8:45am-6pm, W 11:45am-6pm, F 8am-1pm.

West London Center for Sexual Health, Charing Cross Hospital, Fulham Palace Rd. (☎ 8846 1576). Tube: Baron's Court or Hammersmith. NHS-run sexual and women's health clinic. By appointment only.

COMMUNITY & CULTURAL CENTERS

See **Gay & Lesbian Services,** p. 332; **Minority Resources,** p. 333; **Religious Resources,** p. 334.

CONSULATES

See **Embassies & Consulates,** p. 331.

CRISIS LINES

See **Helplines,** p. 332.

CURRENCY EXCHANGE

See also **Once In London,** p. 329.

American Express (www.americanexpress.com). For **traveler's check refunds,** call toll-free 24hr. ☎ 0800 52 13 13. 30 London locations including:

    102-104 Victoria St. (☎ 7802 4701). Tube: Victoria. Open M-F 9am-5:30pm, Sa 9am-4pm.

84 Kensington High St. (☎ 7795 6703). Tube: High St. Kensington. Open M-Sa 9am-5:30pm.

Paddington Station (☎ 7706 7127). Tube: Paddington. Open M-F 7:30am-7:30pm, Sa 8am-6pm, Su 9am-6pm.

30-31 Haymarket (☎ 7484 9610). Tube: Piccadilly Circus. Open M-F 9am-7pm, Sa 9am-6pm, Su 10am-5pm.

Terminal 3 & 4 Heathrow (☎ 8897 0134). Tube: Heathrow Terminal 4 (Zone 6). Open daily 5:15am-10pm.

Thomas Cook (☎ 01733 41 65 65; www.thomascook.com). Numerous currency-exchange bureaux in London; call to locate one. Cashes Thomas Cook Mastercard traveler's checks commission free. For **traveler's check refunds,** call ☎ 0800 622 101.

DENTAL CARE

Dental Emergency Care Service (☎ 7955 2186). Refers callers to the nearest open dental surgery. Open M-F 8:45am-3:30pm.

Dental Accident & Emergency, Guy's Hospital, 23 fl., Guy's Tower, St. Thomas St. (☎ 7955 4317). Tube: London Bridge. Free walk-in treatment for dental emergencies. Adults treated up until patient quota (usually M-F 9-11am), children M-F 9am-noon and 2-4pm. Sa-Su and holidays use paying services at **Emergency Dental Clinic** (ground floor). Open Sa-Su and holidays 9am-6pm.

Eastman Dental Hospital, 256 Gray's Inn Rd. (☎ 7915 1000; fax 7915 1012). Tube: Russell Square, Chancery Ln., or King's Cross. Leading specialist hospital. By appointment only.

DISABILITY RESOURCES

Artsline, 54 Charlton St., NW1 1HS (☎ 7388 2227; www.artsline.org.uk). Disability access information service for London arts and entertainment. Open M-F 9:30am-5:30pm.

Direct Mobility Hire, 8 Cheapside, North Circular Rd. (☎ 8807 9830; www.directmobility.co.uk). Short-term rentals of wheelchairs, mobility scooters, walking aids, chairs, beds, and bathing aids. Minimum rental 1 wk. Delivery/pick-up anywhere in London within 24hr.

London Disability Arts Forum, Diorama Arts Center, 34 Osnaburgh St. NW1 3ND (☎ 7916 5484; www.ldaf.net). Organizes the annual Disability Film Festival; also publishes the **DAIL** (Disability Arts in London) listings magazine (available in braille and on audiocassette).

RADAR (Royal Association for Disability and Rehabilitation), 12 City Forum, 250 City Rd., London EC1V 8AF (☎ 7250 3222; www.radar.org.uk). Network of 500 charities offering advocacy, information, and support for the handicapped. Also administers the nationwide disabled-toilet key scheme, which gives access to disabled toilets around the UK. Call for details.

Wheelchair Travel, 1 Johnston Green, Guildford, Surrey GU2 6XS (☎ 01483 233 640; www.wheelchair-travel.co.uk). Rents hand-controlled and accessible cars (from £46 per day), lift-enabled minivans (from £90 per day). Delivery to anywhere in UK (extra charge). Meet & greet service £138 for 2hr.

EMBASSIES & CONSULATES

Australia: Australia House, Strand (☎ 7379 4334; www.australia.org.uk). Tube: Temple. Open M-F 9am-5pm; consular services available 9:30am-3:30pm. In an **emergency,** dial ☎ 0500 890 165 toll-free to contact the Foreign Affairs Dept.'s Consulate Officer in Canberra.

Canada: MacDonald House, 1 Grosvenor Sq. (☎ 7258 6600; www.dfait-maeci.gc.ca/london). Tube: Bond St. Open M-F 8:30am-5pm.

Ireland: 17 Grosvenor Pl. (☎ 7235 2171). Tube: Hyde Park Corner. **Consular** services at Montpelier House, 106 Brompton Rd. (☎ 7225 7700). Tube: Knightsbridge. Open M-F 9:30am-4:30pm.

New Zealand: New Zealand House, 80 Haymarket (☎ 7930 8422; www.nzembassy.com). Tube: Piccadilly Circus. Consular section open M-F 10am-4pm.

South Africa: South Africa House, Trafalgar Sq. (☎ 7451 7299; www.southafricahouse.com). Tube: Charing Cross. **Consular** services nearby at 15 Whitehall (☎ 7925 8901). Open M-F 8:45am-12:45pm.

United States: 24 Grosvenor Sq. (☎ 7499 9000; www.usembassy.org.uk). Tube: Bond St. or Marble Arch. Open M-F 8:30am-5:30pm. Phones answered 8am-10pm.

EMERGENCY SERVICES

In an emergency, dial ☎ 999 from any fixed phone or ☎ 112 from a mobile to reach ambulance, police, and fire services. See also **Helplines,** p. 332; **Hospitals,** p. 332; and **Police,** p. 333.

FINANCIAL SERVICES

See **Currency Exchange,** p. 330, and **Once In London,** p. 37.

GAY & LESBIAN RESOURCES

GAY to Z (www.gaytoz.co.uk). Online and printed directory of gay-friendly resources and businesses throughout Britain. Print version available at gay bookstores, or send £3 (overseas US$10) to: GAY to Z Directories Limited, 41 Cooks Rd., London, SE17 3NG.

Gay's the Word. The largest gay and lesbian bookshop in the UK. See p. 226.

gingerbeer.co.uk. Lesbian web portal for London, with listings of clubs, bars, restaurants, and community resources.

London Lesbian & Gay Switchboard (☎7837 7324; www.queery.org.uk). 24hr. helpline and information resource.

Accommodation Outlet. Finds accommodations for gays and lesbians. See p. 264.

HEALTH & FITNESS

London has hundreds of fitness clubs, from council-run gyms to lavish private clubs. Use Yellow Pages (under "Leisure Centres") or call **Sportsline** (☎7222 8000) to find one near you.

Barbican YMCA, 2 Fann St. (☎7628 0697). Tube: Barbican. Weights, Nautilus machines, treadmills, and bikes. Non-members £5 per session. Membership £55 per yr.; £27 for 3 mo., plus £3.50 per use; £35 unlimited use per mo. Open M-F 7am-9:30pm, Sa-Su 10am-6pm.

Chelsea Sports Centre, Chelsea Manor St. (☎7352 6985). Tube: Sloane Square or South Kensington. Pool, solarium, gym, tennis, ping-pong, volleyball, basketball, football, and badminton. Numerous classes. Open M-F 7am-10pm, Sa 8am-6:30pm, Su and holidays 8am-10pm. Call for prices.

Kensington Leisure Centre, Walmer Rd. (☎7727 9747). Tube: Ladbroke Grove. In Notting Hill, despite the name. Pool, sauna, weights, badminton, and squash, plus aerobics, self-defense, and scuba-diving classes. Hours as for Chelsea Sports Centre.

Queen Mother Sports Centre, 223 Vauxhall Bridge Rd. (☎7630 5522). Tube: Victoria. 1hr. induction course (non-members £28) required for use of weights. Pool open M-Tu 6:30am-8pm, W-F 6:30am-7:30pm, Sa-Su 8am-5:30pm. Membership £40 per mo.; non-members £2.45 per use. Open M-F 6:30am-10pm, Sa 8am-8pm.

HELPLINES

Rape Crisis Centre: ☎7837 1600.

Samaritans: ☎08457 90 90 90. Emotional support for depression and suicide. 24hr.

Victim Support: ☎0845 303 0900. Emotional help and legal advice for crime victims. Open M-F 9am-9pm, Sa-Su 9am-7pm.

HOSPITALS

For urgent care, go to one of the 24hr. **Accident & Emergency** departments listed below. For non-urgent care, or to see a specialist, you will need a referral from your primary care doctor. See also **Clinics,** p. 330, and **Emergency Services,** p. 331.

Charing Cross, Fulham Palace Rd., entrance on St. Dunstan's Rd. (☎8846 1234). Tube: Baron's Court or Hammersmith.

Chelsea and Westminster, 369 Fulham Rd. (☎8746 8000). Tube: Fulham Broadway, or South Kensington then bus #14 or 211.

Royal Free, Pond St. (☎7794 0500). Tube: Belsize Park or Rail: Hampstead Heath.

St. Mary's, Praed St. (☎7725 6666). Tube: Paddington.

St. Thomas's, Lambeth Palace Rd. (☎7928 9292). Tube: Waterloo.

University College Hospital, Grafton Way (☎7387 9300). Tube: Warren St.

Whittington, Highgate Hill (☎7272 3070). Tube: Archway.

HOTLINES

See **Helplines,** above.

INTERNET ACCESS

Independent cyber cafes are on almost every business street in London. If you're paying more than £2 per hour you're paying too much. The big chains are listed below.

easyEverything (☎7241 9000; www.easyeverything.com). 5 locations, each with hundreds of terminals: 9-16 Tottenham Court Rd. (Tube: Tottenham Court Rd.); 456/459 Strand (Tube: Charing Cross); 358 Oxford St. (Tube: Bond St.); 9-13 Wilson Rd. (Tube: Victoria); 160-166 Kensington High St. (Tube: High St. Kensington); Unit G1, King's Walk, King's Rd. (Tube: Sloane Square). Prices vary with demand, from £1 per 15min. during busy times; minimum charge £2. Open 24hr.

Virgin Megastore, Oxford St. See p. 235.

BT Multi.phones, installed in Tube and rail stations throughout London. Internet-enabled payphones with touch-screen control.

Internet Exchange, (☎0800 9175 425) has 22 locations in the London area, including central locations at 37 Covent Garden Market (Tube: Covent Garden); 47-49 Queensway (Tube: Bayswater); 125-127 Baker St. (Tube: Baker St.). Generally £1 per hr. and £1 membership (or £2 per hr. for non-members).

LEGAL RESOURCES

Embassies may provide legal advice and services to citizens under arrest.

Citizen's Advice Bureaux (www.nacab.org.uk). Independent nationwide network of offices giving free advice on legal and consumer issues. London bureaux include 140 Ladbroke Grove (☎8960 3322; Tube: Ladbroke Grove); 32 Ludgate Hill (☎7236 1156; Tube: Blackfriars); 135 Upper St. (☎7359 06139; Tube: Angel (Zone 1) or Highbury & Islington). Opening hours very limited and appointments often necessary; call ahead.

Community Legal Service (www.justask.org.uk). Government-run online advice service and directory of legal advisors.

Police Complaints Authority, 10 Great George St., SW1P 3AE (☎7273 6450; www.pca.gov.uk). For reporting police misconduct. Be sure to note the offending officer's number (worn on the shoulder).

Release: ☎7729 9904. Advice and info on the law and drugs. Open daily 10am-5:30pm.

Victim Support. See **Helplines,** p. 330.

LOST PROPERTY

See also **Police,** p. 333.

Public Carriage Office, 15 Penton St. (☎7833 0996). Tube: Angel. For articles left in licensed taxicabs (black cabs). Open M-F 9am-4pm.

Transport for London Lost Property Office, 200 Baker St., NW1 5RT (fax 7918 1028). Items left on public transport are first held 48hr. at the bus garage or the Tube station where they were found, then forwarded to the above address. To reclaim an item, write or fax with a Lost Property Enquiry form, available from Tube stations, or go in person. Open M-F 9:30am-2pm. Fee on reclamation.

MAIL SERVICES

See **Postal Services,** p. 334.

MEDICAL SERVICES

See **Clinics,** p. 330; **Dental Care,** p. 331; and **Hospitals,** p. 332.

MINICABS

See also **Taxis,** p. 334.

Teksi (☎7267 0267, 8455 9999; www.teksi.com). 24hr. pick-up anywhere in London. Cash rates: £3 for first mi., £1.30 additional mi. (£5 for first 2½ mi., £1.30 additional mi. in West End and City). Airport rates: Heathrow £23, Gatwick £42, Stansted/Luton £35, plus parking and waiting at £10 per hr. AmEx/V/MC; £5 surcharge.

Lady Cabs (☎7254 3501). Not limited to women passengers, provides a female driver on request. Pick-up North London only. Open M-F 8am-10pm, Sa 9am-10pm, Su 10am-10pm.

Liberty Cars, 330 Old St. (☎7734 1313). Shoreditch-based cab service catering to gays and lesbians. Pick-up anywhere in London. 24hr. West End to Airport: Heathrow £30, Gatwick £40, Stansted/Luton £45; £10 more for pick-up at airport.

MINORITY RESOURCES

See also **Gay & Lesbian Services,** p. 332, and **Religious Resources,** p. 334.

Africa Centre, 38 King St. (☎7836 1973; www.africacentre.org.uk). Tube: Covent Garden. Pan-African cultural center, with a full program of events. Also runs regular nightclub evenings (see p. 191).

Black Cultural Archives, 378 Coldharbour Ln. (☎7738 4591). Tube: Brixton.

BLINK (www.blink.co.uk). Web resource for the UK's Black and Asian communities, from art and culture to human rights.

MOVIE THEATERS

See **Cinema,** p. 330

PHARMACIES

See **Chemists,** p. 330.

POLICE

In an **emergency,** dial ☎999 from any land phone, or ☎112 from a mobile phone. London is covered by two police forces: the **City of London Police** (☎7601 2222; www.cityof-london.police.uk) for the City, and the **Metropolitan Police** (☎7230 1212; www.met.police.uk) for the rest.

For **general inquiries,** write to: New Scotland Yard, Broadway, London SW1H OBG. In the event of police misconduct, contact the **Police Complaints Authority** (see **Legal Resources,** p. 332). There is at least one police station in each of the 32 boroughs open 24hr. (call 24hr. ☎7230 1212 to find the nearest station).

POSTAL SERVICES

For information on **Royal Mail** services, see **Once In London,** p. 34.

FedEx (☎0800 123 800). Cheapest express service is International Priority. 500g envelope £25-35 depending on destination.

RELIGIOUS RESOURCES

Anglican/Episcopal: The vast majority of churches in London; there's almost always one within walking distance. **London Diocese,** London Diocesan House, 36 Causton St. (☎7932 1100; www.london.anglican.org), for London north of the Thames. **Southwark Diocese,** 4 Chapel Ct., Borough High St. (☎7939 9400; www.dswark.org), for South London.

Buddhist: Buddhapadipa Temple, Calonne Rd., Wimbledon Parkside (☎8946 1357). Tube: Wimbledon Park (Zone 3).

Hindu: Shree Swaminarayan Mandir, 105-119 Brentfield Rd. (☎8965 2651). Tube: Neasden (Zone 3). Also **cultural center.**

Jewish: Orthodox: Central Synagogue, Great Portland St. (☎7580 1355; www.brijnet.org/centralsyn). Tube: Great Portland St. or Oxford Circus. Can also advise on kosher restaurants and hotels. **Reform:** West London Synagogue, 33 Seymour Pl. (☎7723 4404; www.wls.org.uk). Tube: Marble Arch.

Muslim: London Central Mosque, 146 Park Rd. (☎7724 3363; www.islamicculturalcentre.co.uk). Tube: Baker St. Also houses the **Islamic Cultural Centre.**

Roman Catholic: Vaughn House, 46 Francis St. (☎7798 9009; www.rcdow.org.uk).

SPORTS CLUBS

See **Health & Fitness,** p. 332.

TAXIS

The listings below refer to licensed taxicabs ("black cabs"). All operate throughout London and charge the same rates (see **Once in London,** p. 31). For **Minicabs,** see p. 333. **Computer Cabs:** ☎7286 0286.

Dial-a-Cab: ☎7253 5000.
Radio Taxis: ☎7272 0272.

TELEPHONE SERVICES

For info on making calls in Britain and useful numbers, see **Once In London,** p. 36.

Let's Go has recently partnered with **ekit.com** to provide a calling card that offers a number of services, including email and voice messaging. Before purchasing any calling card, always be sure to compare rates with other cards, and to make sure it serves your needs (a local phonecard is generally better for local calls, for instance). For more information, visit www.letsgo.ekit.com.

Calling card access numbers: If calling from a British Telecom phone, use ☎0800; if using Cable & Wireless, use ☎0500.

AT&T: see calling card for details.
Canada Direct: ☎0800/0500 890 016.
MCI Worldcom: ☎0800/0500 890 222.
Telecom NZ Direct: ☎0800/0500 890 064.
Sprint: ☎0800/0500 890 877.
Telkom South Africa: ☎0800 890 027.
Telstra Australia: ☎0800 890 061.

TICKETS

Ticketmaster (☎7344 4444; www.ticketmaster.co.uk) is the UK's largest telephone ticketing agency. Tickets to almost every event, show, mainstream movie theater, and major nightclub in the country—just beware of the booking fee. Book directly from the venue if you can.

tkts, Leicester Sq. Half-price theater tickets to almost every play on the day. See p. 215.

TOURIST INFORMATION

Britain Visitor Centre (www.visitbritain.com), 1 Regent St. Tube: Oxford Circus. Run by the British Tourist Association. Open M 9:30am-6:30pm, Tu-F 9am-6:30pm, Sa-Su 10am-4pm.

TOURS

See **Sights,** p. 61.

TRANSPORT INFORMATION

For information on transportation, see **Once In London,** p. 27. For listings, see also **Bicycle Rental,** p. 329; **Car Rental,** p. 330; **Minicabs,** p. 333; and **Taxis,** p. 334.

Transport for London (info ☎ 7222 1234; www.londontransport.co.uk) operates information centers in 8 central London Tube stations and also at Heathrow Airport and Greenwich. For specific locations see **Travel Info,** p. 27.

WOMEN'S RESOURCES

See also **Clinics,** p. 330, and **Helplines,** p. 332.

West London Center for Sexual Health, health clinic. See **Clinics,** p. 330.

Lady Cabs. Taxi service for women. See **Minicabs,** p. 333.

INDEX

C

F

G

Gabriel's Wharf 97, 157
Gagosian Gallery 135
Gainsborough, Thomas 50
Galangai Thai Canteen 164
Galleries
    see Museums & Galleries
Gallipoli 163
Gallipoli Again 163
The Garage 217
garage club nights 185
Garden Court Hotel 253
The Garden 193
The Gate 168
Gate Cinema 212
The Gate theatre 212
Gatwick 25
G-A-Y 190
gay
    nightlife 184
Gay, John 49
Gay's the Word 226
Geffrye Museum 140
The Generator 254
George Hotel 258
George I 49
George III 50, 63, 75
The George Inn 177
George IV 51, 64, 75, 105, 278
George V 275
George's Portobello Fish Bar 156
Georgian House Hotel 265
Gerry's 237
getting around London 27
    bike 33
    car 32
    public transportation 27
    taxicab 31
    walking 32
Getting to London 302–??
    by boat 305
    by Channel tunnel 305
    by plane 302
Gibbon, Edward 50
Gibbons, Grinling 100, 114
    grave 103
Gibbs, James 87, 105
Gilbert Collection 129
Giraffe restaurant 155, 164, 165
Globe Theatre 48, 95, 213

Gloriette 154
glossary 32, 33, 34
Goddard's Pie & Mash 167
Gog and Magog 88
Golden Hinde 97
Golders Green 110
    Crematorium 110
Goldfinger, Erno 94, 109
Gordon Ramsay 150, 151
Gordon's Wine Bar 162
Gourmet Pizza Co. 158
Goya 154, 163
The Grain Shop 157
Grand Central 167
Grand Old Duke of York 101
Grand Union Canal 108
Grant, Hugh 5
Gray's Inn 87
Great British Beer Festival 177
Great British Heritage Pass 310
Great Exhibition 88, 89
Great Fire 48, 68
Great Plague 48
Great Stink 52
Green Line 27
Green Park 106
Greenwich 14, 113
    Food & Drink 167
    Park 115
Greenwich and Docklands
    International Festival 220
Greenwich Markets 243
Grey, Lady Jane 72
grocery stores
    see supermarkets
Grosvenor Square 101
Grouse & Claret pub 176
Guildhall 80
    Art Gallery 127
Guildhall School of Music 80
Guildhall Yard 79
Gutenberg Bible 125
gyms 332
Gypsy Moth 114

H

Hackney Empire 219
Hadleigh Hotel 263
halal food 309
halls of residence
    see residence halls
Hamley's 234
Hammersmith 14, 115
    Food & Drink 168
Hammersmith Irish Centre 220
Hampstead 12, 108
    Food & Drink 165
    Heath 109
Hampstead Theatre 218
Hampstead Village Guest House
    266
Hampton Court 271
Handel, George Frederick 49, 105
    grave 67
Harbour City 161
Hardy, Thomas 111
Harold of Wessex 46
Harrods 230
Harvard, John
    grave 96
Harvey Nichols 231
Harvey, William 128
Hatchard's 235
Hatfield House 272
Hatton Garden 86
Hawksmoor, Nicholas 82
Hay's Galleria 97
Hayward Gallery 133
health 40, 299–301
    immunizations 299
    pre-existing conditions 299
    sexually transmitted diseases
        300
Heathrow 23
Heaven 192
Helplines
    legal 330
helplines 332
Henry II 283
Henry III 71
Henry V 47
Henry VI 47, 275, 276
Henry VII 273
Henry VIII 47, 66, 106, 272, 273,
    280, 284

I

J

K

L

M

N

O

P

S

V

W

Y

Z

Map Appendix

MAP LEGEND

✛ Hospital	✈ Airport
🚓 Police	🚌 Bus Station
✉ Post Office	🚂 Train Station
ⓘ Tourist Office	⊖ TUBE STATION
💲 Bank	⚓ Ferry Landing
Embassy/Consulate	✝ Church
▪ Site or Service	✡ Synagogue
Library	☪ Mosque
Entertainment	⚔ Castle

🏛 Museum	▲ Mountain
🏠 Hotel/Hostel	Park
🍎 Food	
🛍 Shopping	Beach
★ Nightlife	
🍺 Pub	Water
💻 Internet Café	
℞ Pharmacy	The Let's Go compass always points NORTH.
·········· Pedestrian Zone	

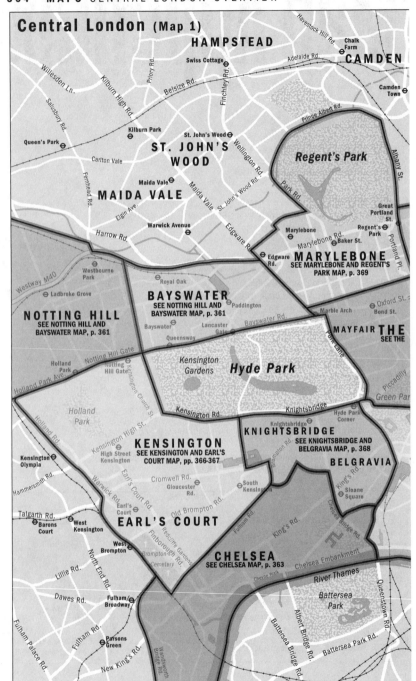

Central London (Map 1)

HAMPSTEAD

Havestock Hill Rd.

Chalk Farm

CAMDEN

Swiss Cottage

Adelaide Rd.

Willesden Ln.

Priory Rd.

Belsize Rd.

Finchley Rd.

Camden Town

Kilburn High Rd.

Salusbury Rd.

Prince Albert Rd.

Albany St.

Kilburn Park

St. John's Wood

Queen's Park

ST. JOHN'S WOOD

Regent's Park

Carlton Vale

Wellington Rd.

Great Portland St.

Fernhead Rd.

Maida Vale

Park Rd.

Regent's Park

MAIDA VALE

Maida Vale

St. John's Wood Rd.

Marylebone

Marylebone Rd.

Baker St.

Portland Pl.

Elgin Ave.

Warwick Avenue

Edgware Rd.

Edgware Rd.

MARYLEBONE
SEE MARYLEBONE AND REGENT'S PARK MAP, p. 369

Harrow Rd.

Westway M40

Westbourne Park

Royal Oak

BAYSWATER
SEE NOTTING HILL AND BAYSWATER MAP, p. 361

Paddington

Marble Arch

Oxford St.
Bond St.

Ladbroke Grove

NOTTING HILL
SEE NOTTING HILL AND BAYSWATER MAP, p. 361

Bayswater

Lancaster Gate

Bayswater Rd.

MAYFAIR THE
SEE THE

Queensway

Holland Park

Notting Hill Gate

Notting Hill Gate

Kensington Gardens

Hyde Park

Park Lane

Piccadilly

Green Par

Holland Park Ave.

Kensington Church St.

Kensington Rd.

Knightsbridge

Hyde Park Corner

Holland Rd.

Holland Park

Kensington High St.

Kensington Rd.

Knightsbridge

KNIGHTSBRIDGE
SEE KNIGHTSBRIDGE AND BELGRAVIA MAP, p. 368

Kensington Olympia

High Street Kensington

KENSINGTON
SEE KENSINGTON AND EARL'S COURT MAP, pp. 366–367

Brompton Rd.

BELGRAVIA

Hammersmith Rd.

Warwick Rd.

Earl's Court Rd.

Cromwell Rd.

Gloucester Rd.

South Kensington

King's Rd.

Sloane Square

Talgarth Rd.

Barons Court

West Kensington

Earl's Court

Old Brompton Rd.

Fulham Rd.

EARL'S COURT

West Brompton

Redcliffe Gardens

Finborough Rd.

Brompton Cemetery

King's Rd.

Chelsea Bridge Rd.

Lillie Rd.

North End Rd.

CHELSEA
SEE CHELSEA MAP, p. 363

Chelsea Embankment

Cheyne Walk

River Thames

Queenstown Rd.

Dawes Rd.

Fulham Broadway

Wandsworth Bridge Rd.

Battersea Park

Albert Bridge Rd.

Battersea Bridge Rd.

Battersea Park Rd.

Fulham Palace Rd.

Fulham Rd.

Parsons Green

New King's Rd.

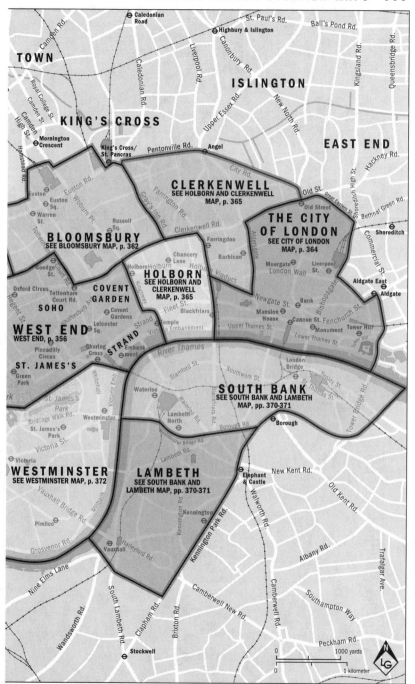

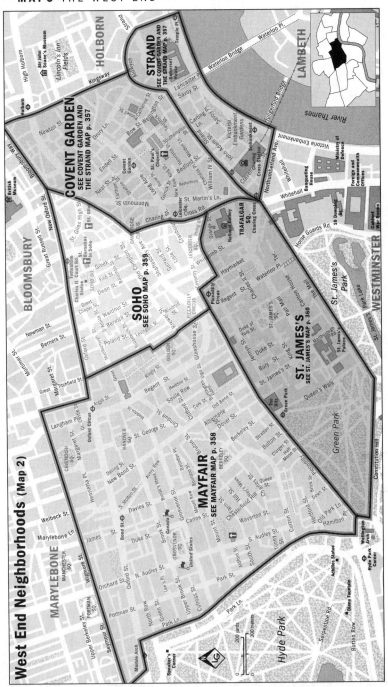

West End Neighborhoods (Map 2)

HOLBORN

STRAND
SEE COVENT GARDEN AND
THE STRAND MAP p. 357

LAMBETH

River Thames

Sir John
Soane's Museum
Lincoln's Inn
Fields

COVENT GARDEN
SEE COVENT GARDEN AND
THE STRAND MAP p. 357

BLOOMSBURY

British
Museum

SOHO
SEE SOHO MAP p. 359

TRAFALGAR
SQ.

ST. JAMES'S
SEE ST. JAMES'S MAP p. 360

WESTMINSTER

St. James's
Park

MARYLEBONE

MAYFAIR
SEE MAYFAIR MAP p. 358

Green Park

Hyde Park

Speaker's
Corner

Marble Arch

200 yards
200 meters

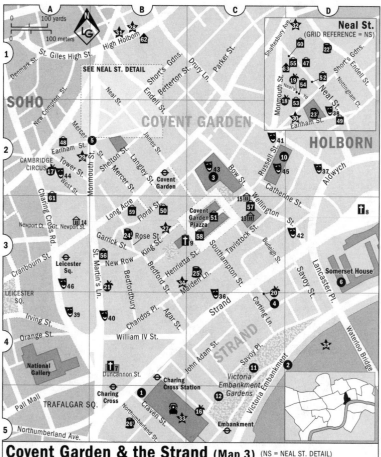

Covent Garden & the Strand (Map 3) (NS = NEAL ST. DETAIL)

SIGHTS

Charing Cross, **1**	B5
Cleopatra's Needle, **2**	D4
Royal Opera House, **3**	C2
The Savoy, **4**	C4
Seven Dials, **5**	B2
Somerset House, **6**	D3
St. Martin-in-the-Fields, **7**	B4
St. Mary-le-Strand, **8**	D3
St. Paul's Church, **9**	C3
Theatre Royal, Drury Lane, **10**	C2
Victoria Embankment Gardens, **11**	C4
York Watergate, **12**	C5

MUSEUMS

London's Transport Museum, **13**	C3
The Photographers' Gallery, **14**	A3
Theatre Museum, **15**	C3

FOOD

Gordon's Wine Bar, **16**	C5
The Ivy, **17**	A2
Monmouth Coffee Company, **18**	NS
Neal's Yard Bakery, Salad Bar & Tearoom, **19**	NS

The Savoy, **20**	C4
St. Martin's Lane Hotel, **21**	B3

PUBS

The Cross Keys, **22**	NS
Freedom Brewing Co., **23**	NS
Lamb and Flag, **24**	B3
Maple Leaf, **25**	C3
The Sherlock Holmes, **26**	B5

NIGHTLIFE

Africa Centre, **27**	B3
AKA, **28**	B1
The Box, **29**	A2
Detroit, **30**	NS
The End, **31**	B1
Freud, **32**	NS
Heaven, **33**	B5
The Spot, **34**	B3
T.S. Queen Mary, **35**	D4

ENTERTAINMENT

The Adelphi, **36**	C4
Aldwych Theatre, **37**	D2
Donmar Warehouse, **38**	NS
Duke of York's Theatre, **39**	A4
English National Opera, **40**	B4

Fortune Theatre, **41**	C2
Lyceum, **42**	D3
Royal Opera House, **43**	C2
St. Martin's Theatre, **44**	A2
Theatre Royal, Drury Lane, **45**	C2
Wyndham's Theatre, **46**	A3

SHOPPING

Apple Tree, **47**	NS
Cyberdog, **48**	A2
Diesel, **49**	NS
Diesel StyleLab, **50**	B3
Jubilee Market Hall, **51**	C3
Miss Sixty, **52**	NS
Neal's Yard Dairy, **53**	NS
Neal's Yard Remedies, **54**	NS
Office, **55**	NS
Office Sale Shop, **56**	B3
Penhaligon's, **57**	C3
Savage London, **58**	C3
Stanfords, **59**	B3
Swear, **60**	NS
Zwemmer, **61**	A3

ACCOMMODATIONS

High Holborn Residence, **62**	B1
Seven Dials Hotel, **63**	NS

Mayfair (Map 4)

● SIGHTS	
Burlington Arcade, 1	D3
Burlington House, 2	D3
Carnaby Street, 3	D2
Grosvenor Square, 4	B3
Marble Arch, 5	A2
Royal Arcade, 6	D3
Savile Row, 7	D3
Shepherd Market, 8	C4

🏛 MUSEUMS	
Annely Juda Fine Art, 9	C2
Gagosian Gallery, 10	D3
Marlborough Fine Arts, 11	D3
Robert Sandelson, 12	D3
Royal Academy of Art, 13	D3
Sotheby's, 14	D2

● FOOD	
Brown's, 15	D3
Carluccio's, 16	B1
La Madeleine, 17	D3
L'Autre, 18	C4
Mô, 19	D2
Tamarind, 20	C4

🛏 PUBS	
The Duke of York, 21	C2
The Sheperds Tavern, 22	C4

★ NIGHTLIFE	
Strawberry Moons, 23	D3
The Social, 24	D1

🎭 ENTERTAINMENT	
London Palladium, 25	D2

🛍 SHOPPING	
Browns Labels for Less, 26	C2
Butler & Wilson, 27	C2
Cinch, 28	E2
FCUK, 29	B2
Hamley's, 30	D2
John Lewis, 31	C1
Karen Millen, 32	D2
Liberty, 33	D2
Mango, 34	D2
Marks & Spencer, 35	B2
Niketown, 36	D1
Oscar Milo, 37	C2
Paul Smith Sale Shop, 38	C2
Selfridges, 39	B2
Shellys, 40	D1
Sotheran's of Sackville Street, 41	E3
Ted Baker, 42	D2
Therapy, 43	C1
Topshop/Topman/ Miss Selfridge, 44	D1
Tower Records, 45	E3
Zara, 46	D2

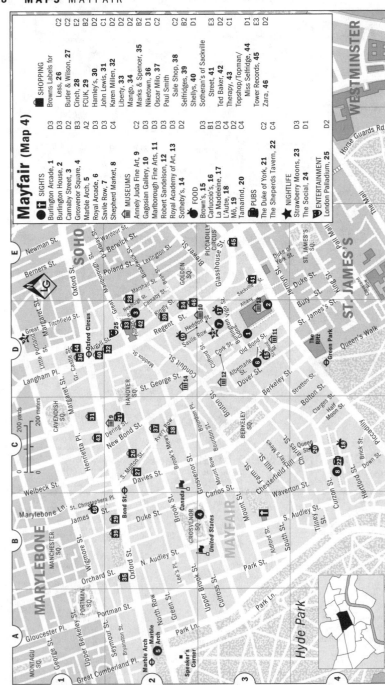

Soho (Map 5)

SIGHTS

Chinatown, **1**	C3
French Protestant Church, **2**	C1
Leicester Square, **3**	D4
Piccadilly Circus, **4**	B4
Soho Square, **5**	C1
St. Anne's, **6**	C3
St. Patrick's Catholic Church, **7**	C1
Statue of Eros, **8**	B4
Swiss Centre, **9**	C3

FOOD

Bar Italia, **10**	C2
Blue Room Café, **11**	C2
busaba eathai, **12**	B2
Café Emm, **13**	C2
Harbour City, **14**	C3
Itsu, **15**	B2
Masala Zone, **16**	A2
Mr. Kong, **17**	C3
Nusa Dua, **18**	B2
Ophim, **19**	B2
Pâtisserie Valerie, **20**	C2
Soba Noodle Bar, **21**	A2
Tomato, **22**	C2
Yo!Sushi, **23**	A2

PUBS

Admiral Duncan, **24**	C2
Comptons of Soho, **25**	C3
Dog and Duck, **26**	C2
The Toucan, **27**	C1

NIGHTLIFE

Bar Rumba, **28**	B3
BarCode, **29**	B3
G-A-Y, **30**	C1
Ku Bar, **31**	D3
Madame Jojo's, **32**	B2
Point 101, **33**	D1
Propaganda, **34**	B1
Rouge, **36**	C1
Sound, **35**	C3
Vespa Lounge, **37**	D1
Yo!Below, **38**	A2

ENTERTAINMENT

100 Club, **39**	B1
Borderline, **40**	C1
Comedy Store, **41**	C4
Criterion, **42**	B4
Curzon Soho, **43**	C2
Cycle Rickshaws, **44**	C2
London Astoria (LA1), **45**	D1
Palace Theatre, **46**	D2
Phoenix Theatre, **47**	D2
Pizza Express Jazz Club, **48**	B1
Prince Charles Cinema, **49**	C3
Prince Edward Theatre, **50**	C2
Prince of Wales, **51**	C4
Ronnie Scott's, **52**	C2
Soho Theatre, **53**	C2
tkts, **54**	C4

SHOPPING

Black Market, **55**	B2
Blackwell's, **56**	D2
Foyles, **57**	C2
Gerry's, **58**	C2
HMV, **59**	A1
Music Zone, **60**	B1
Proibito Sale Shop, **61**	A1
Sister Ray, **62**	B2
Turnkey, **63**	D2
Uptown Records, **64**	B1
Virgin Megastore, **65**	C1

ACCOMMODATIONS

Accommodation Outlet, **66**	C2
YHA Oxford St., **67**	B2

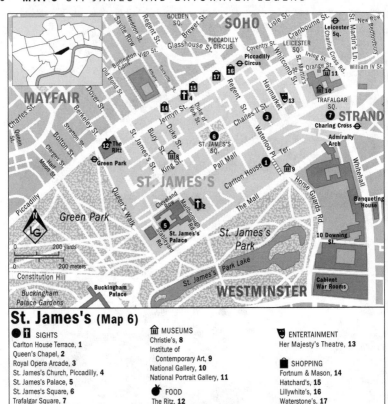

St. James's (Map 6)

● 🛈 SIGHTS
Carlton House Terrace, **1**
Queen's Chapel, **2**
Royal Opera Arcade, **3**
St. James's Church, Piccadilly, **4**
St. James's Palace, **5**
St. James's Square, **6**
Trafalgar Square, **7**

🏛 MUSEUMS
Christie's, **8**
Institute of
  Contemporary Art, **9**
National Gallery, **10**
National Portrait Gallery, **11**

● FOOD
The Ritz, **12**

♕ ENTERTAINMENT
Her Majesty's Theatre, **13**

🛍 SHOPPING
Fortnum & Mason, **14**
Hatchard's, **15**
Lillywhite's, **16**
Waterstone's, **17**

Bayswater & Notting Hill (Map 7)   SEE MAP, p. XXX

🏛 MUSEUMS
Serpentine Gallery, **1**   G4

● FOOD
Alounak Kebab, **2**   D2
Aphrodite Taverna, **3**   D2
Books for Cooks, **4**   B2
Durbar Tandoori, **5**   D2
Fluid, **6**   B2
George's Portobello
  Fish Bar, **7**   A1
The Grain Shop, **8**   B2
La Bottega del Gelato, **9**   D3
Lazy Daisy Café, **10**   C3
Le Piaf, **11**   C4
Lisboa Patisserie, **12**   A1
Manzara, **13**   C3
Royal China, **14**   E3
Tiger Lil's, **15**   E2
Tom's Delicatessan, **16**   B2

🍺 PUBS
Mitre, **17**   F3
Portobello Gold, **18**   B3
Prince Albert Pub, **19**   C4

★ NIGHTLIFE
192, **20**   B2
The Market, **21**   B2
Notting Hill Arts Club, **22**   C4
Pharmacy, **23**   B4

♕ ENTERTAINMENT
Electric Cinema, **24**   B2
Firstbowl, **25**   E3
The Gate, **26**   C3
Gate Cinema, **27**   C4
London's Skate Centre, **28**   E3

🛍 SHOPPING
Dolly Diamond, **29**   C3
Honest Jon's, **30**   A1
Intoxica!, **31**   B2
Nothing, **32**   B2

One of a Kind, **33**   B2
Rough Trade, **34**   B2
The Tea and Coffee
  Plant, **35**   B2
Teaze, **36**   C3
The Travel Bookshop, **37**   B2
Whiteleys Shopping Centre, **38**   D2
Willma, **39**   A1

🏠 ACCOMMODATIONS
Admiral Hotel, **40**   G2
Balmoral House Hotel, **41**   G2
Cardiff Hotel, **42**   G2
Garden Court Hotel, **43**   D2
Hyde Park Court Hotel, **44**   G2
Hyde Park Hostel, **45**   E3
Kensington Gardens Hotel, **46**   D3
Leinster Inn, **47**   D2
Palace Hotel, **48**   D3
Quest Hotel, **49**   E3
Vancover Studios, **50**   D3

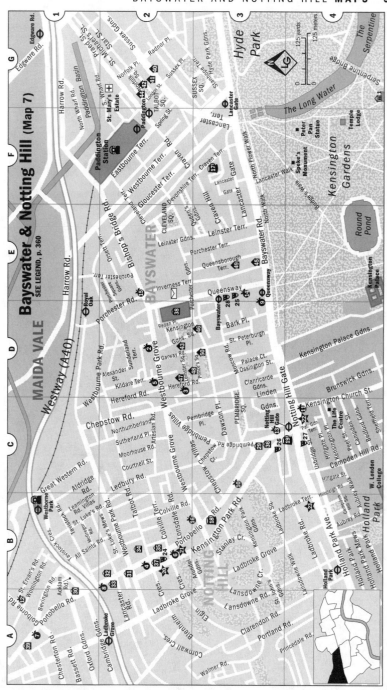

Bayswater & Notting Hill (Map 7)

SEE LEGEND, p. 360

Bloomsbury (Map 8)

● 🛈 SIGHTS

All Souls Langham Place, **1**	A4
Bedford Square, **2**	C4
British Library, **3**	C1
Coram's Fields, **4**	D2
Senate House, **5**	C3
St. George's Bloomsbury, **6**	C4
St. Pancras Station, **7**	C1
Thomas Coram Foundation, **8**	D2
University College London, **9**	B2

🏛 MUSEUMS

British Library Galleries, **10**	C1
The British Museum, **11**	C4
Brunei Gallery, **12**	C3
Percival David Foundation, **13**	C2
Pollock's Toy Museum, **14**	B3

🍖 FOOD

Da Beppe, **15**	B3
Diwana Bhel Poori House, **16**	B2
ICCo, **17**	B4
Navarro's Tapas Bar, **18**	B3
Pescatori, **19**	B4
Rasa Express, **20**	A2
Vats, **21**	D3
Wagamama, **22**	C4

🍺 PUBS

The Jeremy Bentham, **23**	B3
The Lamb, **24**	D3
The Museum Tavern, **25**	C4
The Queen's Larder, **26**	C3

🎭 ENTERTAINMENT

The Place, **27**	C2
RADA, **28**	B3
Renoir, **29**	C3
The Water Rats, **30**	D1

🛍 SHOPPING

Delta of Venus, **31**	B2
Gay's the Word, **32**	C2
James Smith & Sons, **33**	C4
L. Cornelissen & Son, **34**	C4
Paperchase, **35**	B3
Purves & Purves, **36**	B4
Unsworths, **37**	C4
Waterstone's, **38**	B3

🏠 ACCOMMODATIONS

Ashlee House, **39**	D1
Carr-Saunders Hall, **40**	A3
Commonwealth Hall, **41**	C2
Crescent Hotel, **42**	C2
The Generator, **43**	C2
George Hotel, **44**	C2
Indian YMCA, **45**	A3
Jenkins Hotel, **46**	C2
The Langland Hotel, **47**	B3
Mentone Hotel, **48**	C2
Passfield Hall, **49**	B2
Pickwick Hall International Backpackers, **50**	C3
Royal National Hotel, **51**	C3
Thanet Hotel, **52**	C3
YHA St. Pancras International, **53**	C1

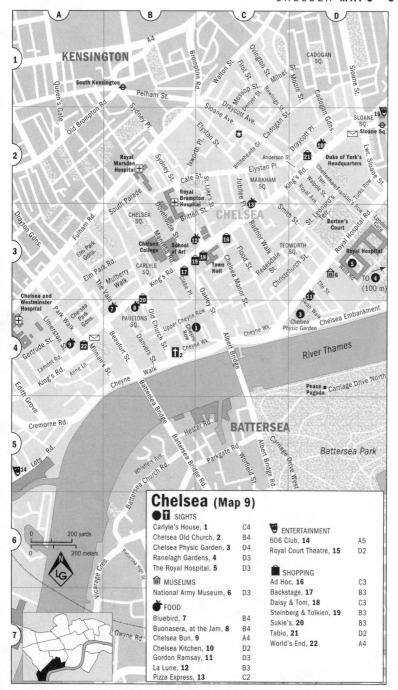

Chelsea (Map 9)

⬤ ⓘ SIGHTS

Carlyle's House, **1** C4
Chelsea Old Church, **2** B4
Chelsea Physic Garden, **3** D4
Ranelagh Gardens, **4** D3
The Royal Hospital, **5** D3

🏛 MUSEUMS

National Army Museum, **6** D3

🍴 FOOD

Bluebird, **7** B4
Buonasera, at the Jam, **8** B4
Chelsea Bun, **9** A4
Chelsea Kitchen, **10** D2
Gordon Ramsay, **11** D3
La Lune, **12** B3
Pizza Express, **13** C2

🎭 ENTERTAINMENT

606 Club, **14** A5
Royal Court Theatre, **15** D2

🛍 SHOPPING

Ad Hoc, **16** C3
Backstage, **17** B3
Daisy & Tom, **18** C3
Steinberg & Tolkien, **19** B3
Sukie's, **20** B3
Tabio, **21** D2
World's End, **22** A4

The City of London (Map 10)

● 🏛 SIGHTS

All Hallows-By-The-Tower, **1**	D5
Bank of England, **2**	C4
Barbican Centre, **3**	B2
Guildhall, **4**	B3
Lloyd's of London, **5**	D4
Lower Thames St., **6**	C5
Mansion House, **7**	C4
Monument, **8**	C4
Old Bailey, **9**	A3
Royal Exchange, **10**	C4
St. Dunstan-in-the-East, **11**	D5
St. Giles Cripplegate, **12**	B3
St. Magnus-the-Martyr, **13**	C5
St. Margaret Lothbury, **14**	C3
St. Mary-le-Bow, **15**	B4

St. Mary Woolnoth, **16**	C4
St. Paul's Cathedral, **17**	A4
St. Stephen Walbrook, **18**	C4
Stock Exchange, **19**	C4
Temple of Mithras, **20**	B4
Tower of London, **21**	D5

🏛 MUSEUMS

The Clockmakers' Museum & Guildhall Library, **22**	B3
Bank of England Museum, **23**	C4
Guildhall Art Gallery, **24**	B3
Museum of London, **25**	B3

🍴 FOOD

Café Spice Namaste, **26**	D4
Futures, **27**	C5
Leadenhall Market, **28**	C4
The Place Below , **29**	B4

🍺 PUBS

The Black Friar, **30**	A4
The Hung Drawn and Quartered, **31**	D5
The Samuel Pepys, **32**	B5
Simpson's, **33**	C4

🎭 ENTERTAINMENT

Barbican Centre, **34**	B2

Holborn & Clerkenwell (Map 11)

● ℹ **SIGHTS**

The Charterhouse, **1**	D3
Clerkenwell Green, **2**	C2
Clerkenwell Visitor Centre, **3**	C2
Elm Court, **4**	B5
Ely Place, **5**	C3
Fleet Street, **6**	C4
Gray's Inn, **7**	B3
Lincoln's Inn, **8**	A4
Marx Memorial Library, **9**	C2
Middle Temple Garden, **10**	B5
Middle Temple Hall, **11**	B5
Priory of St. John, **12**	C2
Royal Courts of Justice, **13**	B4
Smithfield Market, **14**	C3
St. Bartholomew The Great, **15**	D3
St. Bride's, **16**	C5
St. Clement Danes, **17**	B5
St. Dunstan-in-the-West, **18**	B4
St. Etheldreda's, **19**	C3
St. John's Gate, **20**	C2
The Temple, **21**	B5
Temple Church, **22**	B5

🏛 **MUSEUMS**

Courtauld Institute Galleries, **23**	A5
Gilbert Collection, **24**	A5
Hermitage Rooms, **25**	A5
The Hunterian Museum, **26**	A4
Museum of St. Bartholomew's Hospital, **27**	D4
Sir John Soane's Museum, **28**	A4
Somerset House, **29**	A5

🍴 **FOOD**

Al's Café/Bar, **30**	B2
Bleeding Heart Tavern, **31**	C3
St. John, **32**	C3
Woolley's, **33**	A3

🍺 **PUBS**

Cittie of York, **34**	B3
The Eagle, **35**	B2
Fox & Anchor, **36**	D3
The Jerusalem Tavern, **37**	C2

The Old Bank of England, **38**	B4
The Punch Tavern, **39**	C4
The Three Kings, **40**	C2
Ye Olde Cheshire Cheese, **41**	C4
Ye Olde Mitre Tavern, **42**	C3

⭐ **NIGHTLIFE**

Cafe Kick, **43**	B1
Fabric, **44**	C3
Fluid, **45**	C3
Match EC1, **46**	C2
Na Zdrowie, **47**	A4
Turnmills, **48**	C2

🎭 **ENTERTAINMENT**

Chuckle Club, **49**	A5
Peacock Theatre, **50**	A4
Sadler's Wells, **51**	B1

🛍 **SHOPPING**

Twining's, **52**	B5

🏠 **ACCOMMODATIONS**

City University Finsbury Residences, **53**	D2
Rosebery Hall, **54**	C1

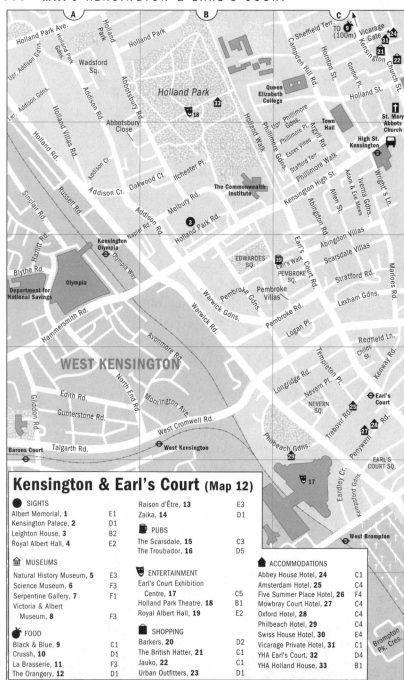

Kensington & Earl's Court (Map 12)

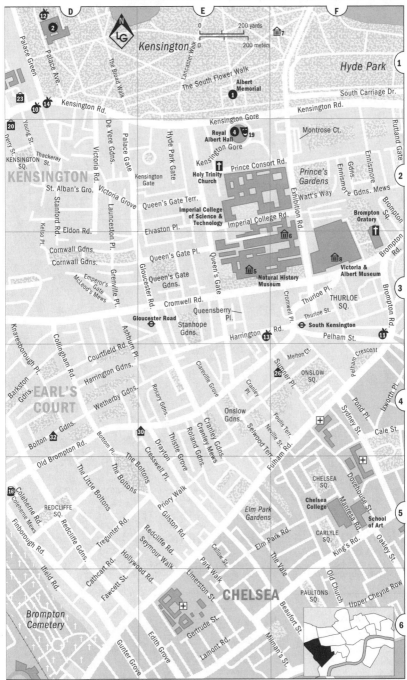

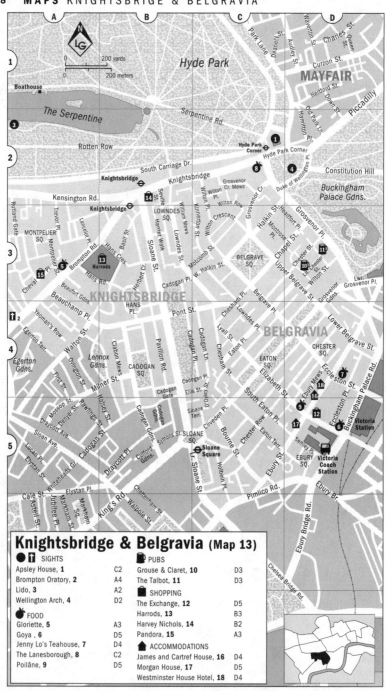

Knightsbridge & Belgravia (Map 13)

● 🛈 SIGHTS

Apsley House, **1**	C2
Brompton Oratory, **2**	A4
Lido, **3**	A2
Wellington Arch, **4**	D2

🍴 FOOD

Gloriette, **5**	A3
Goya , **6**	D5
Jenny Lo's Teahouse, **7**	D4
The Lanesborough, **8**	C2
Poilâne, **9**	D5

🍺 PUBS

Grouse & Claret, **10**	D3
The Talbot, **11**	D3

🛍 SHOPPING

The Exchange, **12**	D5
Harrods, **13**	B3
Harvey Nichols, **14**	B2
Pandora, **15**	A3

⚓ ACCOMMODATIONS

James and Cartref House, **16**	D4
Morgan House, **17**	D5
Westminster House Hotel, **18**	D4

Marylebone & Regent's Park (Map 14)

● 🛈 SIGHTS

Baker Street, **1**	C4
Edgware Road, **2**	B5
The London Planetarium, **3**	C3
London Zoo, **4**	C1
Madame Tussaud's, **5**	C3
Portland Place, **6**	D3
Queen Mary's Gardens, **7**	C2
Regent's Park, **8**	C1
St. John's Lodge, **9**	C2

🏛 MUSEUMS

The Wallace Collection, **10**	C4

🍖 FOOD

Giraffe, **11**	C4
Mandalay, **12**	A3
Patogh, **13**	A4
Ranoush Juice, **14**	B5
Royal China, **15**	C4
Spighetta, **16**	C4

🎭 ENTERTAINMENT

Open-Air Theatre, **17**	C2
Wigmore Hall, **18**	D5

🏠 ACCOMMODATIONS

Edward Lear Hotel, **19**	B5
Hadleigh Hotel, **20**	B5
International Student House, **21**	D3

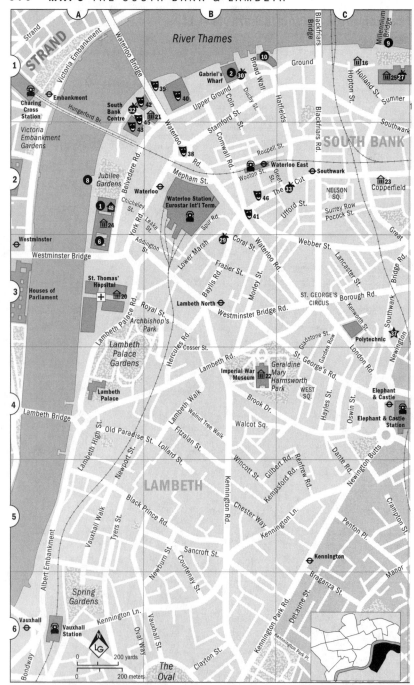

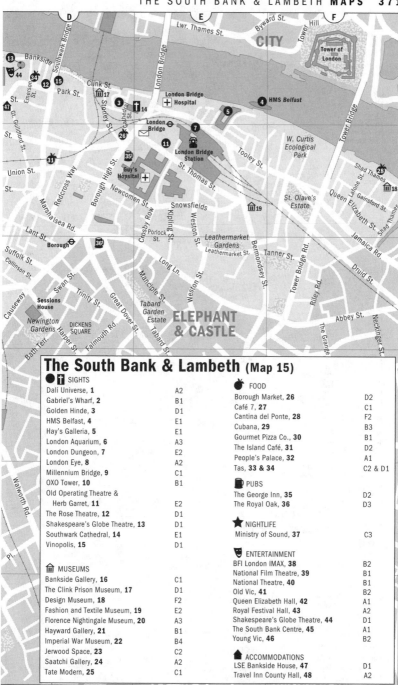

The South Bank & Lambeth (Map 15)

● 🛈 SIGHTS

Dalí Universe, **1**	A2
Gabriel's Wharf, **2**	B1
Golden Hinde, **3**	D1
HMS Belfast, **4**	E1
Hay's Galleria, **5**	E1
London Aquarium, **6**	A3
London Dungeon, **7**	E2
London Eye, **8**	A2
Millennium Bridge, **9**	C1
OXO Tower, **10**	B1
Old Operating Theatre & Herb Garret, **11**	E2
The Rose Theatre, **12**	D1
Shakespeare's Globe Theatre, **13**	D1
Southwark Cathedral, **14**	E1
Vinopolis, **15**	D1

🏛 MUSEUMS

Bankside Gallery, **16**	C1
The Clink Prison Museum, **17**	D1
Design Museum, **18**	F2
Fashion and Textile Museum, **19**	E2
Florence Nightingale Museum, **20**	A3
Hayward Gallery, **21**	B1
Imperial War Museum, **22**	B4
Jerwood Space, **23**	C2
Saatchi Gallery, **24**	A2
Tate Modern, **25**	C1

🍎 FOOD

Borough Market, **26**	D2
Café 7, **27**	C1
Cantina del Ponte, **28**	F2
Cubana, **29**	B3
Gourmet Pizza Co., **30**	B1
The Island Café, **31**	D2
People's Palace, **32**	A1
Tas, **33 & 34**	C2 & D1

🍺 PUBS

The George Inn, **35**	D2
The Royal Oak, **36**	D3

★ NIGHTLIFE

Ministry of Sound, **37**	C3

🎭 ENTERTAINMENT

BFI London IMAX, **38**	B2
National Film Theatre, **39**	B1
National Theatre, **40**	B1
Old Vic, **41**	B2
Queen Elizabeth Hall, **42**	A1
Royal Festival Hall, **43**	A2
Shakespeare's Globe Theatre, **44**	D1
The South Bank Centre, **45**	A1
Young Vic, **46**	B2

🏠 ACCOMMODATIONS

LSE Bankside House, **47**	D1
Travel Inn County Hall, **48**	A2

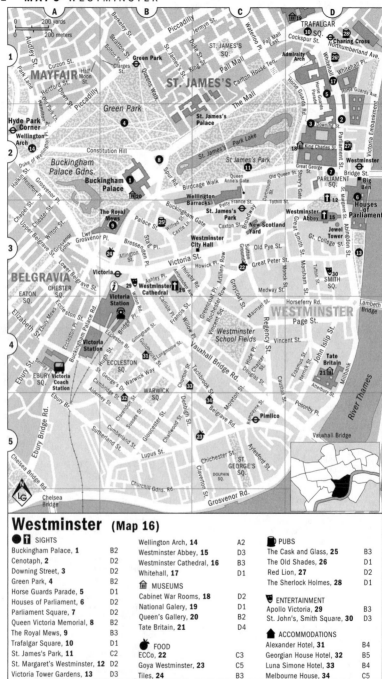

Westminster (Map 16)

● ⓘ SIGHTS

Buckingham Palace, **1**	B2
Cenotaph, **2**	D2
Downing Street, **3**	D2
Green Park, **4**	B2
Horse Guards Parade, **5**	D1
Houses of Parliament, **6**	D2
Parliament Square, **7**	D2
Queen Victoria Memorial, **8**	B2
The Royal Mews, **9**	B3
Trafalgar Square, **10**	D1
St. James's Park, **11**	C2
St. Margaret's Westminster, **12**	D2
Victoria Tower Gardens, **13**	D3
Wellington Arch, **14**	A2
Westminster Abbey, **15**	D3
Westminster Cathedral, **16**	B3
Whitehall, **17**	D1

🏛 MUSEUMS

Cabinet War Rooms, **18**	D2
National Galery, **19**	D1
Queen's Gallery, **20**	B2
Tate Britain, **21**	D4

🍴 FOOD

ECCo, **22**	C3
Goya Westminster, **23**	C5
Tiles, **24**	B3

🍺 PUBS

The Cask and Glass, **25**	B3
The Old Shades, **26**	D1
Red Lion, **27**	D2
The Sherlock Holmes, **28**	D1

🎭 ENTERTAINMENT

Apollo Victoria, **29**	B3
St. John's, Smith Square, **30**	D3

🏠 ACCOMMODATIONS

Alexander Hotel, **31**	B4
Georgian House Hotel, **32**	B5
Luna Simone Hotel, **33**	B4
Melbourne House, **34**	C5

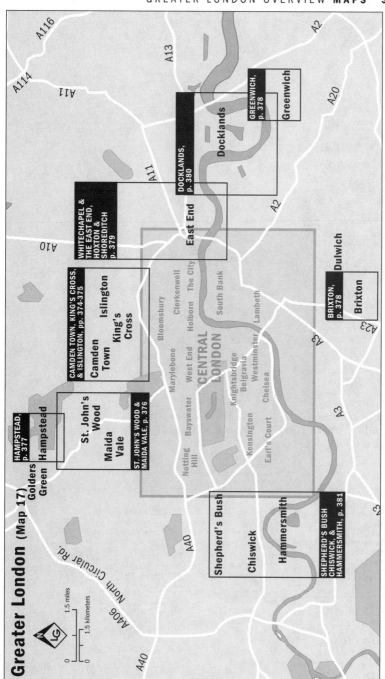

Greater London (Map 17)

GREENWICH, p. 378
Greenwich

DOCKLANDS, p. 380
Docklands

WHITECHAPEL &
THE EAST END,
HOXTON &
SHOREDITCH
p. 379

East End

BRIXTON,
p. 378
Brixton

Dulwich

CAMDEN TOWN, KING'S CROSS,
& ISLINGTON, pp. 374–375

Camden
Town   Islington
King's
Cross

HAMPSTEAD,
p. 377
Hampstead

Golders
Green

St. John's
Wood

Maida
Vale

ST. JOHN'S WOOD &
MAIDA VALE, p. 376

Bloomsbury
Clerkenwell
The City
Holborn
South Bank
West End
Marylebone
Lambeth
Knightsbridge
Belgravia
Westminster
Bayswater
Kensington
Chelsea
Notting
Hill
Earl's Court

**CENTRAL
LONDON**

Shepherd's Bush

Chiswick

Hammersmith

SHEPHERD'S BUSH,
CHISWICK, &
HAMMERSMITH, p. 381

North Circular Rd.

1.5 miles
1.5 kilometers
0

A116
A114
A11
A13
A2
A10
A11
A20
A2
A2
A23
A3
A3
A40
A40
A06

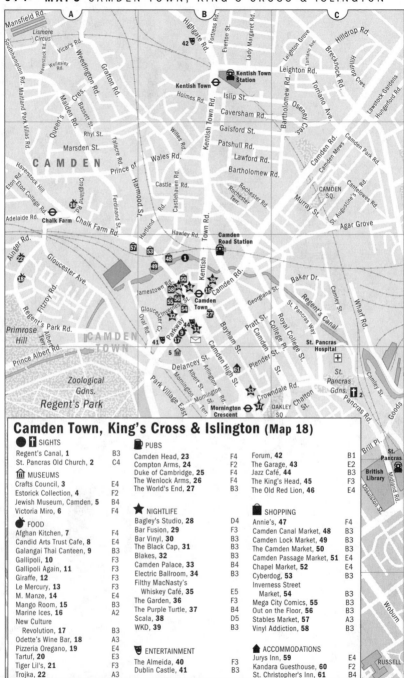

Camden Town, King's Cross & Islington (Map 18)

⬤ 🛈 SIGHTS

Regent's Canal, **1**	B3
St. Pancras Old Church, **2**	C4

🏛 MUSEUMS

Crafts Council, **3**	E4
Estorick Collection, **4**	F2
Jewish Museum, Camden, **5**	B4
Victoria Miro, **6**	F4

🍎 FOOD

Afghan Kitchen, **7**	F4
Candid Arts Trust Cafe, **8**	E4
Galangai Thai Canteen, **9**	B3
Gallipoli, **10**	F3
Gallipoli Again, **11**	F3
Giraffe, **12**	F3
Le Mercury, **13**	F3
M. Manze, **14**	E4
Mango Room, **15**	B3
Marine Ices, **16**	A2
New Culture Revolution, **17**	B3
Odette's Wine Bar, **18**	A3
Pizzeria Oregano, **19**	E4
Tartuf, **20**	E3
Tiger Lil's, **21**	F3
Trojka, **22**	A3

🍺 PUBS

Camden Head, **23**	F4
Compton Arms, **24**	F2
Duke of Cambridge, **25**	F4
The Wenlock Arms, **26**	F4
The World's End, **27**	B3

★ NIGHTLIFE

Bagley's Studio, **28**	D4
Bar Fusion, **29**	F3
Bar Vinyl, **30**	B3
The Black Cap, **31**	B3
Blakes, **32**	B3
Camden Palace, **33**	B4
Electric Ballroom, **34**	B3
Filthy MacNasty's Whiskey Café, **35**	E5
The Garden, **36**	F3
The Purple Turtle, **37**	B3
Scala, **38**	D5
WKD, **39**	B3

📺 ENTERTAINMENT

The Almeida, **40**	F3
Dublin Castle, **41**	B3

Forum, **42**	B1
The Garage, **43**	E2
Jazz Café, **44**	B3
The King's Head, **45**	F3
The Old Red Lion, **46**	E4

🛍 SHOPPING

Annie's, **47**	F4
Camden Canal Market, **48**	B3
Camden Lock Market, **49**	B3
The Camden Market, **50**	B3
Camden Passage Market, **51**	E4
Chapel Market, **52**	E4
Cyberdog, **53**	B3
Inverness Street Market, **54**	B3
Mega City Comics, **55**	B3
Out on the Floor, **56**	B3
Stables Market, **57**	A3
Vinyl Addiction, **58**	B3

🏠 ACCOMMODATIONS

Jurys Inn, **59**	E4
Kandara Guesthouse, **60**	F2
St. Christopher's Inn, **61**	B4

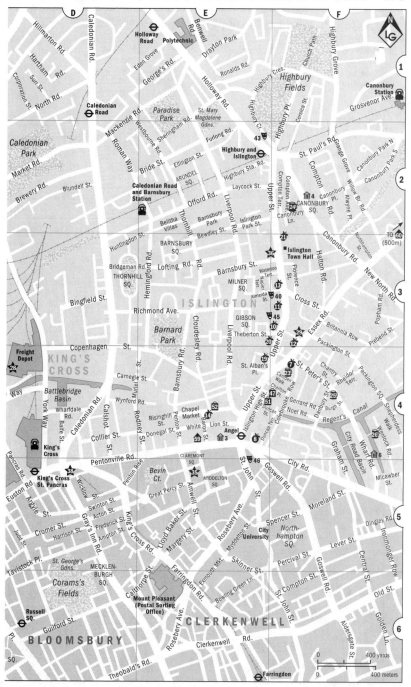

St. John's Wood & Maida Vale (Map 19)

● SIGHTS
Abbey Rd. Crossing, **5**
Abbey Rd. Studios, **4**
Lord's Cricket Ground, **6**

🏛 MUSEUMS
Freud Museum, **1**

🎭 ENTERTAINMENT
Canal Cafe Theatre, **8**
Hampstead Theatre, **3**
Puppet Theatre Barge, **7**
Tricycle / Tricycle Cinema, **2**

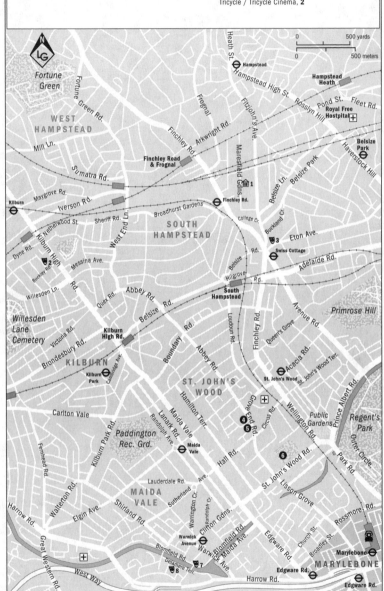

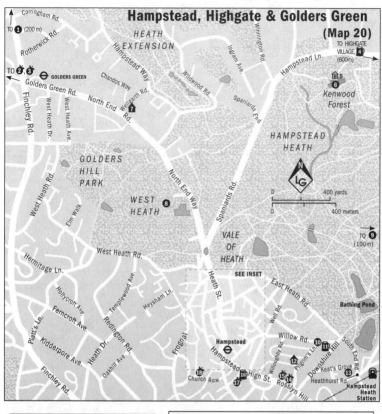

Hampstead, Highgate & Golders Green (Map 20)

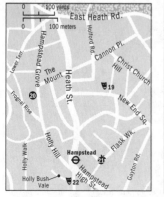

● SIGHTS
Fenton House, **20**
Golders Green Crematorium, **1**
Hill Garden, **8**
Keats House, **13**
Kenwood House, **6**
Parliament Hill, **9**
Two Willow Road, **10**

🏛 MUSEUMS
The Iveagh Bequest, **5**

🍅 FOOD
Al Casbah, **21**
Bar Room Bar, **15**
Bloom's, **3**
Carmelli Bakery, **2**
Le Cellier du Midi, **18**
Le Crêperie de Hampstead, **17**
Giraffe, **14**

🍺 PUBS
The Flask, **4**
Freemason's Arms, **11**
King William IV, **16**

🎭 ENTERTAINMENT
Everyman Cinema, **22**
New End Theatre, **19**

🏠 ACCOMMODATIONS
Hampstead Village
  Guest House, **12**
YHA Hampstead Heath, **7**

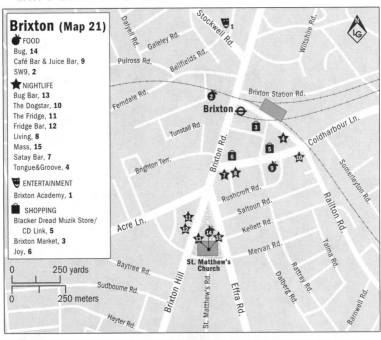

Brixton (Map 21)

🍴 FOOD
Bug, **14**
Café Bar & Juice Bar, **9**
SW9, **2**

⭐ NIGHTLIFE
Bug Bar, **13**
The Dogstar, **10**
The Fridge, **11**
Fridge Bar, **12**
Living, **8**
Mass, **15**
Satay Bar, **7**
Tongue&Groove, **4**

🎭 ENTERTAINMENT
Brixton Academy, **1**

🛍 SHOPPING
Blacker Dread Muzik Store/
CD Link, **5**
Brixton Market, **3**
Joy, **6**

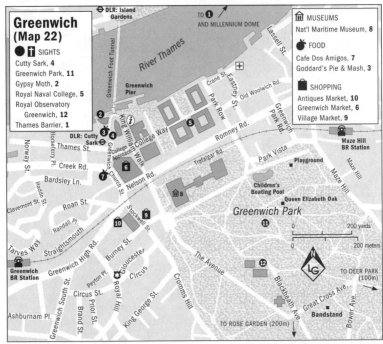

Greenwich (Map 22)

⬤ 🛈 SIGHTS
Cutty Sark, **4**
Greenwich Park, **11**
Gypsy Moth, **2**
Royal Naval College, **5**
Royal Observatory
Greenwich, **12**
Thames Barrier, **1**

🏛 MUSEUMS
Nat'l Maritime Museum, **8**

🍴 FOOD
Cafe Dos Amigos, **7**
Goddard's Pie & Mash, **3**

🛍 SHOPPING
Antiques Market, **10**
Greenwich Market, **6**
Village Market, **9**

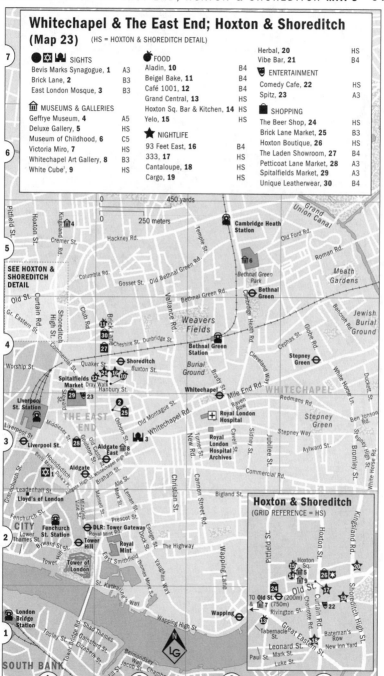

Whitechapel & The East End; Hoxton & Shoreditch
(Map 23) (HS = HOXTON & SHOREDITCH DETAIL)

● ✡ 🕌 SIGHTS
Bevis Marks Synagogue, **1** — A3
Brick Lane, **2** — B3
East London Mosque, **3** — B3

🏛 MUSEUMS & GALLERIES
Geffrye Museum, **4** — A5
Deluxe Gallery, **5** — HS
Museum of Childhood, **6** — C5
Victoria Miro, **7** — HS
Whitechapel Art Gallery, **8** — B3
White Cube², **9** — HS

🍴 FOOD
Aladin, **10** — B4
Beigel Bake, **11** — B4
Café 1001, **12** — B4
Grand Central, **13** — HS
Hoxton Sq. Bar & Kitchen, **14** — HS
Yelo, **15** — HS

⭐ NIGHTLIFE
93 Feet East, **16** — B4
333, **17** — HS
Cantaloupe, **18** — HS
Cargo, **19** — HS

Herbal, **20** — HS
Vibe Bar, **21** — B4

🎭 ENTERTAINMENT
Comedy Cafe, **22** — HS
Spitz, **23** — A3

🛍 SHOPPING
The Beer Shop, **24** — HS
Brick Lane Market, **25** — B3
Hoxton Boutique, **26** — HS
The Laden Showroom, **27** — B4
Petticoat Lane Market, **28** — A3
Spitalfields Market, **29** — A3
Unique Leatherwear, **30** — B4

450 yards
250 meters

Grand Union Canal

Pitfield St.
Hoxton St.
Kingsland Rd.

🏛 **4**

Cremer St.

Cambridge Heath Station

Old Ford Rd.

Hackney Rd.

Temple St.

5

SEE HOXTON & SHOREDITCH DETAIL

Columbia Rd.

Gosset St. Old Bethnal Green Rd.

🏛 **6**

Bethnal Green Park

Meath Gardens

Roman Rd.

Old St.
Gr. Eastern Rd.
Curtain Rd.
Shoreditch High St.
Club Rd.

Bethnal Green Rd.

Bethnal Green ⊖

Jewish Burial Ground

Bann00 Rd.

4

Brick Lane

Cheshire St. Dunbridge St.

Weavers Fields

Valance Rd.

Cambridge Heath Rd.

Globe Rd.

Worship St.
Quaker St.
Shoreditch ⊖
Buxton St.

30
27

Cephas St.

Stepney Green ⊖

White Horse Ln.
Duckett St.

21 24
12 Dray Walk **10**
Spitalfields Market
Hanbury St.

Bethnal Green Station

Burial Ground

Brady St.

Whitechapel ⊖

Cleveland Way

29 23
Liverpool St. Station

Whitechapel Rd.
Raven Row
Mile End Rd.
WHITECHAPEL
Redmans Rd.

Stepney Green

Ben Jonson Rd.
Stepney High St.
Bromley St.

3
Liverpool St. ⊖
Middlesex St.

THE EAST END

2
25

Old Montague St.

Royal London Hospital ✚

Stepney Way

Aylward St.

White Horse Rd.

Liverpool St.

Osborn St.

🏛 **3**

Whitechapel Rd.
New Rd.

Royal London Hospital Archives

Cavell St.
Sidney St.
Jubilee St.

Commercial Rd.

Houndsditch
Bevis Marks
8
Aldgate East ⊖
Braham St.

3
Liverpool St. ⊖

Leadenhall St.
Lloyd's of London

✡ **1**
Aldgate ⊖

Aldgate High St. Whitechapel High St.
Alie St.
Leman St.

Christian St.

Cannon Street Rd.

Bigland St.

Fenchurch St.
Gracechurch St.
Minories
Prescot St.

CITY
Fenchurch St. Station ⊖
Lower Thames St.

⊖ **DLR: Tower Gateway**
Royal Mint St.
Tower Hill ⊖

Royal Mint

The Highway

Wapping Lane

Hoxton & Shoreditch
(GRID REFERENCE = HS)

Byward St.
Tower

Tower of London

St. Katharine's Way

East Smithfield
Vaughan Way

Wapping High St.

Wapping ⊖

Pitfield St.
Hoxton Sq.
Hoxton St.
Kingsland Rd.

15
🏛 **5**
14
🏛 **9**
26 ✡
20

24
Old St.
17

TO Old St. (200m)
& 🏛 **7** (750m)
Rivington St.
22
19
Shoreditch High St.
Charlotte Rd.
Curtain Rd.

London Bridge Station ⊖

Tooley St.
Shad Thames
Gainsford St.
Queen Elizabeth St.

13
Tabernacle St.
Leonard St.
Paul St.
Mark St.
Luke St.
Great Eastern St.
18
New Inn Yard
Bateman's Row

Wapping High St.

Barmondsey Wall
Mill St.
Jacob St.
Chambers St.

SOUTH BANK

A   B   C   D

Docklands
(Map 25)

● SIGHTS
Canary Wharf, **4**
Mudchute Park, **6**

🍺 PUBS
Cat and Canary, **2**
Prospect of Whitby, **1**

🎭 ENTERTAINMENT
London Arena, **5**

🛍 SHOPPING
Cabot & Canada Place, **3**

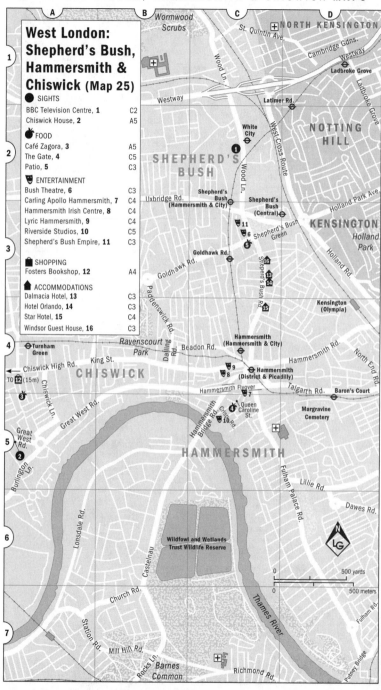

West London: Shepherd's Bush, Hammersmith & Chiswick (Map 25)

● SIGHTS
BBC Television Centre, **1** — C2
Chiswick House, **2** — A5

🍎 FOOD
Café Zagora, **3** — A5
The Gate, **4** — C5
Patio, **5** — C3

🎭 ENTERTAINMENT
Bush Theatre, **6** — C3
Carling Apollo Hammersmith, **7** — C4
Hammersmith Irish Centre, **8** — C4
Lyric Hammersmith, **9** — C4
Riverside Studios, **10** — C5
Shepherd's Bush Empire, **11** — C3

🛍 SHOPPING
Fosters Bookshop, **12** — A4

🏠 ACCOMMODATIONS
Dalmacia Hotel, **13** — C3
Hotel Orlando, **14** — C3
Star Hotel, **15** — C4
Windsor Guest House, **16** — C3

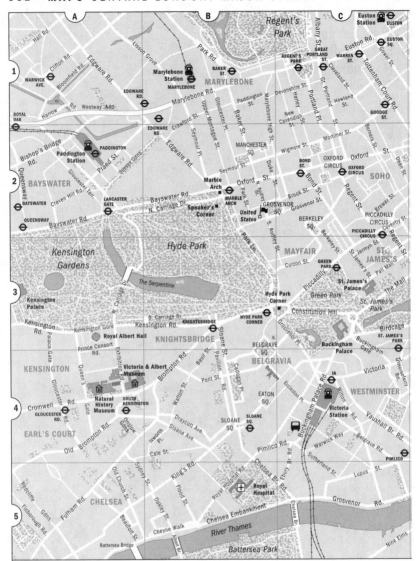

Central London: Major Street Finder (Map 26)

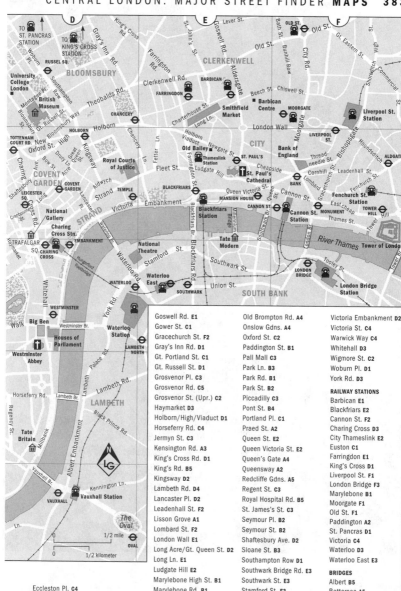